THIRD EDITION

MODERN ADVANCED

ACCOUNTING *in* CANADA

MURRAY W. HILTON

University of Manitoba

McGraw-Hill
Ryerson

Toronto   Montreal   Boston   Burr Ridge IL   Dubuque IA   Madison WI   New York
San Francisco   St Louis   Bangkok   Bogatá   Caracas   Kuala Lumpur   Lisbon   London
Madrid   Mexico City   Milan   New Delhi   Santiago   Seoul   Singapore   Sydney   Taipei

McGraw-Hill
Ryerson Limited

A Subsidiary of The **McGraw·Hill** *Companies*

MODERN ADVANCED ACCOUNTING IN CANADA
Third Edition

ISBN: 0-07-089396-9

1 2 3 4 5 6 7 8 9 10 TRI 0 9 8 7 6 5 4 3

Printed and bound in Canada

VICE PRESIDENT AND EDITORIAL DIRECTOR: Pat Ferrier
EXECUTIVE SPONSORING EDITOR: Nicole Lukach
DEVELOPMENTAL EDITOR: Hope Miller
SENIOR MARKETING MANAGER: Jeff MacLean
SUPERVISING EDITOR: Carrie Withers
COPY EDITOR: Nick Gamble
PRODUCTION COORDINATOR: Paula Brown
COMPOSITION: Lynda Powell
INTERIOR DESIGN: Lynda Powell
COVER DESIGN: Liz Harasymczuk
ART DIRECTOR: Dianna Little
PRINTER: Tri-Graphic Printing

Canadian Cataloguing in Publication Data

Hilton, Murray. W.
    Modern advanced accounting in Canada

3rd ed.
Includes bibliographical references and index.
ISBN 0-07-089396-9

Accounting—Canada. I. Title.

HF5635.H486 2002   657'.046   C2002-900129-3

To
Carole, Kerry, Kevin, Kayleigh, and Sean

Murray W. Hilton, FCA

Murray Hilton teaches graduate and undergraduate courses in financial accounting at the Asper School of Business, University of Manitoba. A Chartered Accountant with business degrees from the University of Saskatchewan and Oregon State University, he is the author of four advanced accounting textbooks. In addition, he has been active in university and faculty administration, having previously served as Head of the Department of Accounting and Finance, and Director of the Master of Accounting Program. He is currently the Director of the Asper School's Centre for Accounting Research and Education. Murray has also been involved with the accounting profession, teaching CA and CMA courses for many years, and serving on numerous national and provincial committees of both accounting bodies. He has on two separate occasions been a member of the National Examination Board of the Society of Management Accountants of Canada. In 1991, he received the FCA designation from the Institute of Chartered Accountants of Manitoba, and in 1994, he was made an honourary member of the Society of Management Accountants of Manitoba. For relaxation, he enjoys golfing and fishing.

Contents

Preface

Welcome to the third edition of *Modern Advanced Accounting in Canada*. This new edition covers topics usually taught in advanced accounting courses. They include business combinations, portfolio and significant influence investments, consolidated financial statements, investments in joint ventures, foreign currency transactions, translation and consolidation of foreign subsidiaries, international accounting, segmented disclosures, push-down accounting, comprehensive revaluations, bankruptcy and receivership, and not-for-profit accounting. The previous editions' emphasis on the direct (non–working paper) approach of preparing consolidated financial statements has been maintained and strengthened. Some illustrations of working papers are still provided in earlier chapters, while in later chapters they appear in appendices. The material on the preparation of statements is accompanied by the "building block" development of the basics of consolidations.

This is the most current, technically accurate, and concise advanced accounting text in Canada. It reflects today's standards as laid out in the *CICA Handbook*; consequently, its reputation for being the most up-to-date book on the market is well earned. Not only are the requirements of Canadian accounting standards thoroughly illustrated and explained, but also the applicable *Handbook* sections are reproduced to encourage students to independently read and interpret accounting standards. This feature is important because of the emphasis that self-directed learning will have on students' future accounting careers.

Moreover, this edition begins with a unique chapter that surveys international accounting practices. Latest developments at the International Accounting Standards Board are presented and emphasized upfront in Chapter 1, and emphasis is given to the international perspective throughout the book.

New Features

- All *CICA Handbook* changes up to January 1, 2002, have been fully incorporated, making this text the most current on the market. They include:
  - The elimination of the pooling of interests method.
  - New guidelines requiring the allocation of a larger portion of the acquisition cost to intangible assets other than goodwill.
  - The removal of the goodwill amortization requirement and its replacement with yearly tests for impairment. All examples and end-of-chapter problems now refer to impairment losses rather than to periods of amortization. The special treatment required to apply goodwill impairment tests to significant influence investments is also covered.
  - The removal of the requirement to defer and amortize foreign currency gains/losses from noncurrent monetary positions. All examples incorporate this change.

- Financial statements from real organizations have been added to further illustrate proper financial reporting.
- "Items of interest" containing real-world news items have been included where applicable, to enhance the reader's interest in the topics discussed.
- Additional examples and explanations have been added to make the book even more user-friendly.
- The number of multiple-choice questions has been increased by about 50 percent.
- While most of the previous case material has been maintained, 15 new cases have been added. They include real-life cases covering such topics as international accounting, business combinations, reverse takeovers, and the allocation of the acquisition cost to intangible assets other than goodwill. Further cases are available on the Online Learning Centre.
- In order to fit this book more comfortably into a normal three-credit hour framework, the previous edition's chapter on accounting for partnerships has been deleted. The content of this chapter, including all end-of-chapter materials, is available on the Online Learning Centre.

Organization

Chapter 1 is a survey of international accounting practices, and has been updated to include the latest reorganizations relating to the International Accounting Standards Board. Selected portions of the financial statements of public companies located in Switzerland, Germany, Japan, and Great Britain have been reproduced, and the Online Learning Centre contains the financial statements of a public company located in Mexico.

Chapter 2 commences with an overview of the CICA pronouncements and Emerging Issues Abstracts that make up the "big picture." Readers are encouraged to revisit this big picture many times as consolidation topics are developed in later chapters, so that they do not lose sight of the "forest" as they examine the myriad details that make up the "trees." The chapter continues with a comprehensive examination of temporary, portfolio, and significant influence investments and concludes with a self-study problem. (Coverage of the topics in this chapter could be postponed until after Chapter 8 without breaking continuity, or could be omitted altogether if it is felt that students have covered these topics adequately in previous intermediate accounting courses.)

Chapter 3 discusses the various methods that have been proposed or used to account for business combinations in past years. The reasons for abandoning the pooling of interests method in the United States and Canada are fully discussed. The acquisition of assets and the acquisition of voting shares are used to illustrate the purchase method of accounting for a business combination, while an appendix provides illustrations of the pooling method.

Chapter 4 examines the preparation of consolidated financial statements as at the date a parent obtains control over a subsidiary. The direct and working paper methods are both illustrated for 100 percent owned subsidiaries, as well as for subsidiaries that are less than 100 percent owned. Consolidation theory is introduced. Reverse takeovers are covered in an appendix.

Chapters 5 and 6 cover what is essentially one topic: the preparation of consolidated financial statements subsequent to the date of acquisition. Chapter 5 illustrates the procedures followed when the parent has used the equity method. The new requirements for accounting for goodwill and other intangibles are covered. Chapter 6 uses the same examples, but assumes that the cost method has been used. Both the direct and working paper approaches are shown. Each chapter concludes with a self-study problem and a solution prepared using the direct approach. Ten basic steps in the preparation of consolidated statements are introduced, which form the foundation for the consolidation topics in the chapters that follow.

Chapter 7 deals with the elimination of intercompany revenues and expenses, as well as intercompany unrealized profits in inventory and land. The income tax matching associated with the holdback and realization of intercompany profits forms an integral part of the discussion and illustrations. Consolidation theories are explained as they apply to intercompany profits. An additional feature is the introduction of the two new topics: acquisition dates other than at year-end, and discontinued operations and extraordinary items. The chapter concludes with a comprehensive self-study problem using the direct approach.

Chapter 8 highlights the elimination of intercompany profits in depreciable assets, the recognition of gains or losses resulting from the elimination of intercompany bondholdings, and the related income tax adjustments that are required. Two self-study problems are presented, with solutions using the direct approach.

Chapter 9 explains the preparation of the consolidated cash flow statement and such ownership issues as subsidiaries with preferred shares, step purchases, reduction of parent's interest, and indirect holdings. In all situations the direct approach is used.

Chapter 10 examines other consolidation reporting issues, including the proportionate consolidation of joint ventures, future income taxes and business combinations, and segment disclosures.

Chapter 11 discusses comprehensive revaluations of assets and liabilities, and bankruptcy and receivership. Push-down accounting for 100 percent owned subsidiaries, and for those less than 100 percent owned, is thoroughly illustrated. So is the preparation of the resulting consolidated financial statements. A comprehensive revaluation resulting from a bankruptcy type of reorganization is also illustrated. The chapter concludes with a discussion of some of the legal and practical concerns of bankruptcy and receivership.

Chapter 12 introduces the topic of foreign currency. Foreign currency transactions are discussed, as is the hedging of monetary positions with forward contracts. The handling of foreign currency gains and losses from both current and noncurrent monetary positions under the new *Handbook* provisions are also illustrated.

Chapter 13 concludes the foreign currency portion of the text by examining and illustrating the translation and subsequent consolidation of integrated and self-sustaining foreign operations. All examples are based on the January 1, 2002, revisions to the *Handbook*, which eliminate the requirements for deferral and amortization.

Chapter 14 examines in-depth the seven new not-for-profit sections in the *Handbook*. Much of the material has been rewritten and additional illustrations have been added. The chapter concludes with a comprehensive illustration of the required journal entries and the preparation of financial statements, using both the deferred contribution method and the restricted fund method. Seven new cases have been added and an appendix reproduces the financial statements of the Winnipeg Foundation, providing a real-life example of the deferred contribution method.

Technology

Online Learning Centre

The Online Learning Centre (http://www.mcgrawhill.ca/college/hilton) serves as an extension of the text, providing supplements, additional content, and regularly updated material for students and instructors. The Information Centre includes such material as the text preface, table of contents, and a sample chapter. The Student Centre contains an interactive student component with additional multiple-choice questions, true/false questions, and fill-in-the-blank questions, as well as bonus appendix material and Ready Notes to assist in lecture preparation. The Instructor Centre includes appendix material, additional cases and solutions, and download-able supplements.

Primis Online

Modern Advanced Accounting in Canada is available, at the instructor's discretion, through the eBook Bookstore. The text is downloaded to the student's computer in PDF-formatted files, and is printed or viewed on-screen. Ask your instructor about the eBook version of this text.

PageOut

PageOut is a McGraw-Hill online tool that enables instructors to easily create and post class-specific web pages. No knowledge of HTML is required.

WebCT/Blackboard

This textbook is available in two of the most popular delivery platforms, WebCT and Blackboard. These platforms provide instructors with more user-friendly, flexible teaching tools.

Supplements

The following instructor supplements are available for *Modern Advanced Accounting in Canada*:

- The Solutions Manual (ISBN 007-089378-0), containing thorough up-to-date solutions to the book's end-of-chapter material.
- PowerPoint slides to support and organize lectures. (The PowerPoint slides are also included as Ready Notes in the Online Learning Centre's Student Centre.)
- Online Learning Centre (see the previous page for detailed description).

Acknowledgements

The development and enhancement of this text were aided by the extensive feedback and suggestions that arose from our market research, which included surveys and reviews. Thank you to the following colleagues for their invaluable advice: Peter Secord of St. Mary's University (thanks for all of his fine case contributions too); Valorie Leonard of Laurentian University; Darrell Herauf of Carleton University; Wendy Doyle of Mount Saint Vincent University; Elenor Wardrop of CGA-Canada; David Carter of the University of Waterloo; Stuart Jones of the University of Calgary; Bill Salatka of Wilfrid Laurier University; and Scott Sinclair of BCIT.

Thanks also to the Canadian Institute of Chartered Accountants for granting permission to reproduce material from the *CICA Handbook*, as well as questions from UFE examinations; to the Certified General Accountants of Canada for its permission to reproduce questions adapted from past examinations; to CMA Canada for its permission to reproduce questions from past examinations and to the Winnipeg Foundation for permission to reproduce their financial statements.

I am very grateful to Nicole Lukach and Hope Miller, my editors at McGraw-Hill Ryerson, who applied pressure in a gentle but persistent manner when I strayed from the project's schedule; and to supervising editor Carrie Withers, copy editor Nick Gamble, and formatter Lynda Powell, whose work carried the project to its end.

And finally, I am again grateful to my wife Carole, for all of her support and encouragement.

Murray Hilton
Asper School of Business
University of Manitoba

McGraw-Hill Ryerson
Online Learning Centre

McGraw-Hill Ryerson offers you an online resource that combines the best content with the flexibility and power of the Internet. Organized by chapter, the HILTON Online Learning Centre (OLC) offers the following features to enhance your learning and understanding of Modern Advanced Accounting:

- Additional Cases
- Online Quizzes
- Chapter Web links
- Microsoft® PowerPoint® Presentations

By connecting to the "real world" through the OLC, you will enjoy a dynamic and rich source of current information that will help you get more from your course and improve your chances for success, both in accounting and in the future.

For the Instructor

Downloadable Supplements

All key supplements are available, password-protected for instant access!

PageOut

Create your own course Web page for free, quickly and easily. Your professionally designed Web site links directly to OLC material, allows you to post a class syllabus, offers an online gradebook, and much more! Visit www.pageout.net

Primis Online

Primis Online gives you access to our resources in the best medium for your students: printed textbooks or electronic ebooks. There are over 350,000 pages of content available from which you can create customized learning tools from our online database at www.mhhe.com/primis

Knowledge Gateway

Knowledge Gateway is a website-based service and resource for instructors teaching online. It provides instructional design services, and information and technical support for course management systems. It is located at http://mhhe.eduprise.com/

For the Student

Online Quizzes

Do you understand the material? You'll know after taking an Online Quiz! Try the Multiple Choice, True/False and Fill-in-the-Blank questions for each chapter. They're auto-graded with feedback and the option to send results directly to faculty. Also, don't forget the Internet Exercises for select chapters that will provide you with additional online practice.

Web Links

This section references various helpful accounting websites.

Microsoft® PowerPoint® Presentations

View and download presentations created for each chapter. Great for pre-class preparation and post-class review.

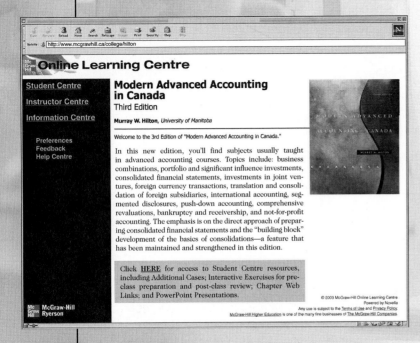

Your Internet companion to the most exciting educational tools on the Web!

The Online Learning Centre can be found at:

www.mcgrawhill.ca/college/hilton

CHAPTER 1

A Survey of International Accounting

CHAPTER OUTLINE

Introduction

A Survey of International Accounting

    Factors That Can Influence a Country's Accounting Standards

    Accounting in Other Countries

    Toward an Accounting Harmonization

Summary

Review and Multiple-choice Questions, Cases, and Problems

LEARNING OBJECTIVES

After studying this chapter, you should be able to do the following:

- Identify factors that can influence a country's accounting standards.
- Describe areas where Canada's accounting standards differ from those used in other countries.
- Identify the role the IASB plays in establishing global accounting standards.

Introduction

This book covers a number of topics that are often presented in the final course of the financial accounting sequence. The topics are presented and illustrated in accordance with the generally accepted accounting principles (GAAP) that exist today in Canada. Until a few years ago, the study of accounting principles as set out in the *CICA Handbook* was all that was necessary as preparation for students intending to pursue professional accounting as a career in Canada. But rapid changes have been taking place throughout the world, and even more drastic changes are likely to come. Canadian companies now view the entire world as their marketplace; not only are they exporting their products to more countries than ever before, but they are also establishing factories and offices in foreign locations. Companies used to raise capital resources strictly in their home countries; now they are finding that capital markets are available to them around the world. Because their shares trade on foreign stock exchanges, they are often required to prepare financial reports using foreign accounting principles. Many accounting firms have offices throughout the world, and there are abundant opportunities for their Canadian staff members to transfer to these offices. With all these changes taking place, an accounting education that takes a narrow, parochial view is clearly inadequate. Canadian students of accounting need to be fully aware of what is happening in other countries, and it is imperative that the textbooks of today address this topic.

A large portion of this book covers the preparation of consolidated financial statements and other directly related topics. Before we begin considering this very broad topic, we first survey the accounting principles and practices used in other countries. Where appropriate, later chapters will contain sections that compare the Canadian standards just discussed with those applied in other countries. It is hoped that this exposure to international accounting will inspire readers to continue studying this interesting and fast-growing area.

A Survey of International Accounting

Generally accepted accounting principles vary from country to country around the world. If a detailed study were made of the accounting practices used by every country in the world, it would probably conclude that no two countries use exactly the same standards for external financial reporting purposes. Some comparisons would yield minor differences; others would show substantial ones. Differences exist in style of presentation, as well as in methods of measurement and disclosure.

Differences in measurement range from departures from historical cost to varying standards within the historical cost model. A variety of methods exist worldwide for measuring and reporting inventories, research and development costs, fixed assets, leases, computer software, and deferred income taxes. Income-smoothing devices vary from country to country. In Canada and the U.S., GAAP allows little opportunity to smooth income, while in other countries income-smoothing devices are allowed under GAAP or are encouraged by government regulation. This is often accomplished by setting up reserves, which are special equity accounts, and using them to transfer amounts to and from the income statement as needed. Inadequate disclosures often mask the real effect on yearly income measurements.

Asset revaluations are acceptable in many countries. These circumstances range from price level–adjusted historical costs, used to counteract distortions resulting from very high inflation rates, to the regular or periodic adjustment of asset measurements to current replacement costs. Even under historical costs, great variations exist in yearly measurements. The accounting for the asset of goodwill, which arises as a result of one company buying another, is a prime example. Practices include the immediate write-off of purchased goodwill to equity; capitalization with amortization over greatly varying periods; capitalization without amortization (thus leaving it on the balance sheet forever); and capitalization and write-off to income only when there is evidence of impairment.

Not only are there differences in measurement, but there are often also differences in the presentation and description of elements in financial statements. For example, in many countries, long-term assets are presented before current assets on the balance sheet and shareholders' equity appears before liabilities. In addition, as we shall see later in this chapter, terms such as "stocks" and "turnover" may be used in some countries in ways that are confusing to a person more familiar with Canadian financial statements.

Examples of areas where disclosure differences lie are segment reporting, reporting financial forecasts, shareholder and environmental disclosures, and value added reporting. While many foreign multinational companies disclose the lines of business they are in and the geographic area in which they operate, there is inconsistency in the level of detail provided. While the provision of financial forecasts is not common in North America, some companies in Europe do provide this information. Foreign companies often provide voluminous disclosures about their shares, shareholders' rights, and changes in shareholders' equity. Finally, while not required by accounting standards, multinational companies are increasingly providing information about environmental safety and protection issues, and the ways in which they have added value to society by their distributions to owners, creditors, employees, and governments.

Exhibit 1.1 is the balance sheet of Heineken N.V. which, according to the notes to the financial statements, has been prepared under "the provisions of Title 9, book 2 of the Netherlands Civil Code." Note that the presentation is in the reverse order from that used in Canada and that there are some unfamiliar items and descriptions such as stocks, investment facilities equalization account, and provisions. If we could interpret these items from a Canadian context, we might conclude that this statement could easily be compared with that of a Canadian company in the same industry. However, such a comparison may not be easy, because the notes also disclose that the fixed assets are valued yearly at replacement cost, which is in accordance with Dutch accounting principles.

Differences in accounting standards have always existed, but they have been receiving greater attention in recent years because of the many changes taking place in the world economy. The Soviet empire has been dismantled, and accompanying this has been a major shift in the Communist Bloc from controlled to market-driven economies. Meanwhile, 15 nations have joined together to form the European Union. Also, the North American Free Trade Agreement has been signed by Canada, the United States, and Mexico, and this agreement may soon be expanded to include some countries in South America.

In the midst of all this, there have been major advances in computer and communication technology that are dramatically improving the global flow of information and changing how business activities are conducted. As a result, foreign currencies now trade 24 hours a day in the world's financial centres. Accompanying this

Exhibit 1.1

HEINEKEN N.V.
CONSOLIDATED BALANCE SHEET
After appropriation of profit — in millions of euros

	31 December 2000		31 December 1999	
Assets				
Fixed assets				
Tangible fixed assets	3,276		2,995	
Financial fixed assets	615		422	
		3,891		3,417
Current assets				
Stocks	550		490	
Accounts receivable	1,024		903	
Securities	23		42	
Cash at bank and in hand	801		1,165	
		2,398		2,600
		6,289		6,017
Liabilities				
Group funds				
Shareholders' equity	2,396		2,618	
Minority interests	124		248	
		2,520		2,866
Investment facilities equalization account		26		31
Provisions		976		770
Debts				
Long-term debts	875		490	
Current liabilities	1,892		1,860	
		2,767		2,350
		6,289		6,017

shift toward a global marketplace has been substantial growth in the size and number of multinational corporations. This growth has been achieved to a great extent by takeovers and mergers, often financed through the capital markets of *many* countries. Not only has there been a shift to a global marketplace for goods and services, but there has also been a shift toward a global capital market. Many of the world's stock exchanges now list foreign companies.

With such a global capital market comes the need to provide the suppliers of capital with useful accounting information. Fragmented accounting principles seriously compromise comparability, which is one of the key concepts associated with usefulness. To counter this, securities regulators in foreign countries often require foreign companies listed on their stock exchanges either to prepare financial statements in accordance with their domestic accounting standards, or to prepare reconciliations from foreign to domestic standards. For example, Canadian companies listed on U.S. stock exchanges are required by the Securities and Exchange Commission (SEC) to prepare reconciliations of net income measured in accordance with Canadian GAAP to net income in accordance with U.S. GAAP. These requirements substantially increase a company's costs of preparing financial statements. Investment analysts and other users then incur further additional costs when interpreting financial statements prepared under different standards. Because of these problems, the world's securities regulators have been increasing their demands for some sort of accounting harmonization. It is not yet known which particular country's accounting standards will form the basis of some new world standard. As we will see, this is a highly vexing problem that has not yet been solved. In order to fully understand the issues and how changes may occur in the future, we must first examine the major causes of differences in GAAP.

Factors That Can Influence a Country's Accounting Standards

Many factors can influence a country's accounting standards. Usually none of them is dominant. The following five factors can affect standards.

The Role of Taxation In some countries, income tax has a minimal effect on how net income is measured for financial reporting. Example: In Canada and the United States, companies often report net incomes on their operating statements that are substantially different from the taxable incomes they report on their tax returns. This has led to the GAAP concept of interperiod tax allocation, although in some countries where such differences exist, differences between net income and taxable income have not always resulted in tax allocation being used.

In other countries, taxation has a profound effect on how accounting income is measured. Accounting income will not differ much from taxable income if a country's tax statutes state that expenses must be recorded on the income statement if they are to be allowed as a deduction on the tax return. In countries where this is the case, the result is often the use of extreme conservatism in accounting measurements on the part of companies trying to keep their incomes as low as possible within the law. Germany and Japan are examples of countries whose tax laws strongly influence GAAP. In the United States, while taxable income and accounting income are different numbers, one area where consistency is required is the costing of inventory. If LIFO is to be used for tax purposes, it also must be used for financial reporting.

The Level of Development of Capital Markets In countries where publicly traded debt and equity securities play a substantial role in the financing of business activities, accounting and disclosure standards tend to be much more extensive than in countries where this is not the case. This is because highly developed public capital markets tend to have fairly sophisticated investors who demand current and useful information from those who have received their capital. Canada, the United Kingdom, and the United States all have highly developed capital markets and strong accounting and disclosure standards. In countries where business financing tends to be private rather than public, there is less reliance on extensive accounting standards, because the private suppliers of capital can demand and receive the information they need directly from the "consumers" of such capital. Japan is a prime example; there, corporate capital needs have been supplied by very large private suppliers such as banks. However, it should be noted that when Japan's economy took a severe dive in the 1990s, many of Japan's major banks incurred massive loan losses that nearly bankrupted them; this was cited as a major contributor to the Japanese recession. Germany and Switzerland also have very large banks that satisfy most of the capital needs of business. Historically, a large number of businesses in Mexico were state owned, but in the 1990s a change to private ownership resulted in a shift to financing through private and public capital markets.

Differing Legal Systems Two different kinds of legal system are in existence today: code law systems and common law systems. Code law systems, which originated with the Roman Empire, contain very detailed statutes that govern a wide range of human activities. In general they specify what individuals and corporations *can* do. Common law systems have less detailed statutes, and rely on the court system to interpret statutes and thus establish precedents through case law. In general, they specify what individuals and corporations *cannot* do (that is, what is illegal).

In many common law countries, governments tend to take a hands-off approach to the setting of accounting standards. While there may be statutes requiring that companies make information available to the providers of capital, the *type* of information required is left to the private sector. In the United States the SEC, which administers securities legislation, has given the right to develop accounting standards to a private group, the Financial Accounting Standards Board (FASB). In Canada, the *CICA Handbook* pronouncements constitute the accounting standards required by the various companies acts and the Ontario Securities Commission. The United Kingdom also uses a private standard-setting body.

In code law countries such as Germany, France, and Japan, the private sector is involved only in an advisory capacity, and accounting standards are reflected in legal statutes, often as protection for creditors and other capital suppliers. It should not be surprising to note that tax law also heavily influences accounting standards in these countries.

Ties Between Countries Political and economic ties between countries have historically had some effect on accounting standards. Example: The accounting standards and professional accounting organizations of countries that were once colonies are often patterned after those of the "home" country. There are strong similarities between the standards of India, South Africa, Australia, New Zealand, and Malaysia and those of Great Britain. During their early development, Canadian accounting standards were influenced by Great Britain's, but in later years this influence shifted away from Britain to the United States due to the very strong economic ties that developed between those two countries. The formation of the European Union has had some effect on the accounting standards of its member countries.

Inflation Levels The historical cost model, which implicitly assumes a relatively stable unit of measure, is used by many countries. However, the model is not useful when inflation rates are very high. Countries that have experienced high inflation rates often make financial reporting adjustments to counteract the effects of inflation. These adjustments involve price level–adjusted statements, or a shift from historical costs to current-value accounting, or both. Many countries in South America that have experienced inflation rates of 1,000 percent or more per annum have adopted inflation-based accounting.[1] Mexico uses price level accounting because of high inflation rates. Canada, the United States, and the United Kingdom all experimented with the supplemental reporting of price level and current value information in the 1970s when the inflation rate approached 20 percent. The experiment was not successful because of the high cost of providing such information and the general lack of comprehension on the part of financial statement users. All three countries abandoned the experiment when inflation declined.

---

[1] For example, Brazil's inflation rate was 2,500 percent in 1993.

Countries that have not had problems with inflation have usually stayed with the historical cost model, but there have been some exceptions. In the Netherlands, companies may choose to use current values instead of historical costs. This is not because of high inflation but rather because accounting education in that country has a strong economic component. Some major Dutch companies show current values in their financial statements. The balance sheet of Heineken N.V. (Exhibit 1.1) provides an example of this practice.

Accounting in Other Countries

The previous section outlined some of the factors that can influence a particular country's accounting standards, and suggested why those standards can vary. We now turn our attention to a small sample of countries and the different accounting standards used in each.

Germany   Germany has a well-established accounting profession whose major role in financial reporting is to audit financial statements and advise government on accounting standards. The standards themselves are set by Germany's parliament and result in income measurements that closely parallel taxable income. Because the standards are set by statute, changes occur very slowly (the most recent was a 1985 change made in accordance with the requirements of the European Union). The direct relationship between taxable and accounting income, and the fact that German companies pay higher rates of tax on that portion of earnings that is not distributed in dividends in a year, results in conservative earnings measurements. In strong earnings years, many companies make substantial charges against income for such items as major repairs that are expected to be carried out in future years. They do so by debiting an expense and crediting a provision account, the balance of which appears under liabilities on the balance sheet. In years of weaker earnings the provisions are reduced. This form of income smoothing is a quite acceptable business practice in Germany.

Under the law, companies present annually only a balance sheet and an income statement; a cash flow statement is not required, but is often presented. In format, these statements differ quite sharply from Canadian ones. Long-term assets appear first, with current assets following. On the other side, shareholders' equity appears first, with liabilities appearing next. No distinction is made between current and noncurrent liabilities, but due dates of liabilities are contained in footnotes. The income statement often shows details of total manufacturing cost incurred during the year, along with an item called "variation in inventory of work in process and finished goods," which appears in revenue and which is used to adjust the costs to those of inventory used and items sold. In terms of accounting measurements, LIFO and FIFO can be used only if these methods reflect the actual physical flow of goods. Depreciation can be either straight-line or reducing balance, at rates prescribed in the income tax statutes. Deferred income tax accounting is hardly ever used.

Exhibit 1.2 presents the December 31, 2000, balance sheet of Volkswagen. The financial statement notes indicate that "the consolidated financial statements of the Volkswagen Group have been prepared in accordance with the provisions of the German Commercial Code, with due regard to the provisions of the Corporation Act." They further state that the consolidated statements comprise all companies in which Volkswagen has a direct or indirect interest of over 50 percent, including 31

Exhibit 1.2

BALANCE SHEET OF THE VOLKSWAGEN GROUP AT DEC. 31, 2000
in millions of DM

	Note	Dec. 31, 2000	Dec. 31, 1999
Assets			
Fixed assets	(1)		
Intangible assets		1,888	903
Tangible assets		31,016	28,888
Financial assets		11,640	7,592
Leasing and rental assets		24,764	17,715
		69,308	55,098
Current assets			
Inventories	(2)	16,408	15,124
Receivables and other assets	(3)	61,256	51,502
Securities	(4)	7,967	3,500
Cash on hand, deposits at German Federal Bank and cash in banks		4,204	5,877
		89,835	76,003
Prepaid and deferred charges	(5)	439	170
Balance-sheet total		159,582	131,271
Stockholders' Equity and Liabilities			
Stockholders' equity			
Subscribed capital of Volkswagen AG	(6)	2,094	2,089
Ordinary shares	1,567		
Non-voting preferred shares	527		
Potential capital	363		
Capital reserve	(7)	8,402	8,361
Revenue reserves	(8)	10,482	7,708
Net earnings available for distribution		994	646
Minority interests		66	385
		22,038	19,189
Special items	(9)	496	513
Provisions	(10)	44,728	42,184
Liabilities	(11)	89,203	65,578
Deferred income	(12)	3,117	3,807
Balance-sheet total		159,582	131,271

German companies and 112 foreign companies. However, another note indicates that 48 German and 74 foreign subsidiaries are not consolidated, and have been omitted under "the provisions of Section 296 subsection 1, no. 2, and subsection 2 of the German Commercial Code." From a Canadian perspective all subsidiaries must be consolidated, and one would have to know the provisions of the German Commercial Code to ascertain why some have been excluded and the effect that the exclusion would have on the financial statements.

The reserves appearing in the stockholders' equity section and the provisions shown in liabilities may be used to smooth income — an acceptable practice in Germany.

German companies now have a choice between reporting under German GAAP or the IASB standards, and in the financial communications section of Volkswagen's annual report, it was revealed that the company's 2001 financial statements will be prepared using international accounting standards.

Japan   Japan is another country whose accounting principles are established by statute. The measurement of accounting income is heavily influenced by tax law. Many of Japan's accounting standards are the result of pronouncements by the Business Accounting Deliberation Council. Its members are drawn from the accounting profession, industry, government, and academe, but they are appointed by the Finance Ministry, and this gives the government full control over accounting standards.

Much like in Germany, income measurement in Japan tends to be conservative and involves smoothing and income minimization procedures. Because tax law requires that expenses deducted on the tax return also appear on the income statement, Japanese companies tend to maximize expenses as allowed in the tax statutes. For example, estimates for expenses such as bad debts, sales returns, and warranties do not have to bear a relationship with historical data or current economic conditions. Depreciation tends to be accelerated, using rates that reflect relatively short asset lives. Provisions are made for expected future maintenance costs. Because these types of deductions are allowed under tax laws, companies tend to take full advantage of them in order to minimize taxable (and thus accounting) income. In certain instances a special tax deduction is allowed if a company transfers a portion of retained earnings to a reserve. In later years, this reserve is transferred back to retained earnings and taxable income is increased.

Corporate and securities law requires reporting by means of a balance sheet and an income statement. A cash flow statement is not required. The format and terminology are very similar to what is used by Canadian companies. This stems from the influence the United States has had on Japan's economy since the end of the Second World War. However, there are differences in measurement that must be taken into account. We have already discussed methods used for smoothing income. Some other differences are discussed next.

Liabilities are recorded at face values, not at present values as is the case in many countries. Both lessees and lessors use the operating lease method. Because of the strong relationship between accounting and taxable income, there is little call for any form of deferred income tax accounting. Five years is the maximum amortization period allowed for items such as organizational, preoperational, and research and development costs. Pension liabilities reflect only 40 percent of the actuarial liability, because that is all that is allowed as a deduction for tax purposes. A legal reserve account appears as a component of shareholders' equity. The amount is determined by transferring an amount equal to 10 percent of yearly cash dividends from retained earnings to the reserve until such time as the balance in the reserve account is equal to 25 percent of the capital stock account. This effectively reduces a company's dividend-paying ability — presumably for the protection of creditors.

Along with accounting standards, business and cultural factors have a marked influence on the proper interpretation of Japanese financial statements. Japanese culture emphasizes group activities. Employees have a sense of belonging with their employers and are often connected with one company for life. And the companies themselves form strategic alliances with other companies in diverse industries. Companies within the group have equity interests in each other, loan money to each other, conduct business with each other, have interlocking directorates, and provide each other with financial and managerial assistance. It has been reported that six such corporate "families" consist of more than 12,000 companies in total. The major Japanese banks are an integral part of the families and provide much of the debt and equity financing for the member companies. From a Canadian perspective, what is missing is any kind of parent or holding company, in that the group is held together by co-operation rather than control. These cultural factors, along with Japan's unique accounting standards, result in performance indicators very different from those used by Canadian companies. Given the propensity to finance more with debt than with equity, debt ratios are much higher in Japan, even though lease liabilities are not reflected, and many companies in the group are not consolidated (this concept will be discussed in greater detail in a later chapter). Due to secret reserves and the expense maximization, profits are not as high, and as a result there is a general propensity to think in the long term as opposed to focusing on short-term profits. Return on investment ratios are relatively low, while price earnings ratios are high. Obviously, analysts need to consider many factors when trying to compare companies in countries like Japan with Canadian companies.

Exhibit 1.3 shows the 2001 consolidated balance sheet of the Honda Motor Company. The income statement is not reproduced here but looks surprisingly similar to that of a typical Canadian company. The 2001 net income was ¥232,241 million (US$1.874 billion). Large Japanese companies (like many European companies)

Exhibit 1.3

HONDA MOTOR CO., LTD. AND SUBSIDIARIES
CONSOLIDATED BALANCE SHEET
March 31, 2000 and 2001

	Yen (millions)		U.S. dollars (thousands) (note 2)
Assets	2000	2001	2001
Current assets:			
Cash and cash equivalents	¥ 430,587	¥ 417,519	$ 3,369,806
Trade accounts and notes receivable, net of allowance for doubtful accounts of ¥7,077 million in 2000 and ¥7,899 million ($63,753,000) in 2001	390,659	440,802	3,557,724
Finance subsidiaries–receivables, net (note 3)	731,580	762,368	6,153,091
Inventories (note 4)	567,705	620,754	5,010,121
Deferred income taxes (note 9)	154,277	151,722	1,224,552
Other current assets (note 7)	180,903	205,771	1,660,783
Total current assets	2,455,711	2,598,936	20,976,077
Finance subsidiaries — receivables, net (note 3)	878,242	1,304,994	10,532,639
Investments and advances:			
Investments in and advances to affiliates (note 5)	175,389	200,625	1,619,250
Other, including marketable equity securities (note 6)	213,705	175,562	1,416,965
Total investments and advances	389,094	376,187	3,036,215
Property, plant and equipment, at cost (note 7):			
Land	296,591	299,984	2,421,178
Buildings	783,055	831,868	6,714,027
Machinery and equipment	1,731,589	1,887,630	15,235,109
Construction in progress	63,408	99,552	803,487
	2,874,643	3,119,034	25,173,801
Less accumulated depreciation	1,753,603	1,864,411	15,047,707
Net property, plant and equipment	1,121,040	1,254,623	10,126,094
Other assets (notes 7 and 9)	54,341	132,669	1,070,775
Total assets	¥4,898,428	¥5,667,409	$45,741,800

continued

Exhibit 1.3   *continued*

Liabilities and Stockholders' Equity	Yen (millions) 2000	2001	U.S. dollars (thousands) (note 2) 2001
Current liabilities:			
Short-term debt (note 7)	¥ 495,953	¥ 910,417	$ 7,347,998
Current portion of long-term debt (note 7)	343,576	274,481	2,215,343
Trade payables:			
Notes	19,332	24,372	196,707
Accounts	677,544	795,882	6,423,584
Accrued expenses	483,917	539,348	4,353,091
Income taxes payable (note 9)	53,319	38,633	311,808
Other current liabilities (notes 7 and 9)	128,670	178,124	1,437,643
Total current liabilities	2,202,311	2,761,257	22,286,174
Long-term debt (note 7)	574,566	368,173	2,971,533
Other liabilities (notes 7, 8, 9	191,178	307,688	2,483,358
Total liabilities	2,968,055	3,437,118	27,741,065
Stockholders' equity:			
Common stock, authorized 3,600,000,000 shares, par value ¥50 ($0.40); issued 974,414,215 shares at March 31, 2000 and 2001	86,067	86,067	694,649
Capital surplus	172,529	172,529	1,392,486
Legal reserves (note 10)	27,545	27,929	225,416
Retained earnings (note 10)	2,218,848	2,428,293	19,598,814
Accumulated other comprehensive income (loss) (notes 6, 9, 11 and 13)	(574,616)	(484,527)	(3,910,630)
Total stockholders' equity	1,930,373	2,230,291	18,000,735
Commitments and contingent liabilities (notes 16 and 17)			
Total liabilities and stockholders' equity	¥4,898,428	¥5,667,409	$45,741,800

often provide English versions of their annual reports, and often translate the amounts into U.S. dollars. The rates used are the spot rates on the date of the balance sheet, and because all elements are translated at the same rate, no foreign currency gains and losses result from such translation. As we will see in Chapter 13, this would not be the case if the statements were translated in accordance with GAAP in Canada or the U.S. While the description and presentation of assets and liabilities seems to be similar to Canadian practice, the stockholders' equity section has some classifications that seem to have no counterpart in Canada. The reserves shown are required to be established under the Japanese Commercial Code. While it is presumed that the Japanese language financial statements would be prepared using Japanese accounting principles, these particular financial statements were prepared using U.S. GAAP. You should note that, in comparison with Canadian companies, the current ratio seems quite low, the return on assets is also fairly low, and the debt–equity ratio seems high. Because the statements reflect U.S. accounting principles, these abnormalities would appear to occur because of differences in culture and business practice rather than because of vastly different measurement standards.

United Kingdom   The U.K. is a prime example of a country whose capital markets are well respected and well established, and whose accounting standards are set by a private organization over which the government has minimal influence. Before the early 1990s, the Accounting Standards Committee, whose members came from the professional accountancy bodies, issued Statements of Standard Accounting Practices (SSAPs). A new standard-setting body, the Financial Reporting Council, made up of representatives from both the accounting profession and industry, now issues Financial Reporting Standards (FRSs). The Companies Act requires financial reporting that gives a "true and fair view" of a company's financial position and operations, but it does not specify how this is to be achieved. Accounting income and taxable income are not the same. This leads to interperiod income tax allocation, which is calculated in accordance with a modified version of the liability method. Timing differences are accounted for only to the extent that the differences are expected to reverse in the foreseeable future; footnote disclosure is required for any other timing differences that are not reflected in the financial statements.

Companies are required to present audited annual financial statements consisting of a balance sheet, income statement, cash flow statement, and accompanying footnote disclosures. There are striking differences from Canadian practice with respect to format and terminology, as the 2000 income statement and balance sheet of Cadbury Schweppes illustrate (see Exhibits 1.4 and 1.5). The following differences from Canadian financial statements are noted:

- The income statement is called the profit and loss account and contains, as a last item, a deduction for dividends.
- Group means consolidated.
- Assets are presented with low liquidity assets first and higher liquidity assets next. A number for total assets is not shown.
- Current liabilities are shown next, and a number for working capital is presented, described as net current (liabilities)/assets.
- Long-term liabilities are deducted next to arrive at a number for net assets. The resulting equation is net assets = shareholders equity.
- The balance sheet shows consolidated amounts and parent-only amounts.

There are a number of terminology differences:

- Turnover means sales.
- Stocks depict inventory.
- Debtors is the same as accounts receivable while accounts payable and other accrued liabilities are called creditors.
- The profit and loss classification in owner's equity is the same as the Canadian description of retained earnings.
- The revaluation reserve results from the periodic adjustments of fixed assets to current values.

From a measurement and disclosure standpoint, the following are some of the differences from Canadian practice. British companies can choose between valuing their assets at historical cost, and revaluing all or some of them at current values, with the revaluation adjustment appearing in a reserve account in shareholders' equity. The only exception is goodwill, which cannot be revalued; however, brand names, trademarks, and other intangibles often associated with goodwill can be revalued. Depreciation and amortization charges are based on current values of any

Exhibit 1.4

FINANCIAL STATEMENTS: CADBURY SCHWEPPES
Group Profit and Loss Account for the 52 weeks
ended 31 December 2000 (Note 1)

Notes		2000 £m	1999 £m	1998 £m
	Turnover			
	Continuing operations	**4,575**	4,234	3,999
2	Discontinued operations	**–**	67	107
		4,575	4,301	4,106
3	**Operating costs**			
	Trading expenses	**(3,813)**	(3,603)	(3,464)
	Major restructuring costs	**(49)**	(64)	(23)
	Exceptional items	**–**	–	(68)
		(3,862)	(3,667)	(3,555)
	Trading Profit			
	Continuing operations	**713**	618	525
2	Discontinued operations	**–**	16	26
	Group Operating Profit	**713**	634	551
12	Share of operating profit in associates	**65**	35	38
	Total Operating Profit including associates	**778**	669	589
2	Profit on sale of subsidiaries and investments	**27**	350	38
	Profit on Ordinary Activities before Interest	**805**	1,019	627
6	Net interest	**(49)**	(61)	(57)
	Profit on Ordinary Activities before Taxation	**756**	958	570
7	Taxation			
	– On operating profit, associates and interest	**(224)**	(181)	(172)
	– On profit on sale of subsidiaries and investments	**–**	(34)	(9)
		(224)	(215)	(181)
	Profit on Ordinary Activities after Taxation	**532**	743	389
22	Equity minority interests	**(12)**	(79)	(20)
22	Non-equity minority interests	**(24)**	(22)	(21)
	Profit for the Financial Year	**496**	642	348
8	Dividends paid and proposed to ordinary shareholders	**(209)**	(202)	(194)
	Profit Retained for the Financial Year	**287**	440	154
9	**Earnings per Ordinary Share of 12.5p**			
	Basic	**24.8**	31.7p	17.1p
	Diluted	**24.5**	31.3p	16.9p
	Underlying	**24.1**	19.5p	19.3p
	Underlying pre-restructuring	**25.8**	22.5p	20.4p

assets revalued, and a portion of the reserve is transferred to retained earnings based on the amount depreciated. Prior to 1998, British accounting standards allowed the choice of either capitalizing purchased goodwill or writing it off directly to retained earnings. At present, capitalization is required with amortization over a maximum of 20 years in most cases. However, if companies can justify the "durability" of goodwill, amortization is not required and it can be carried indefinitely on the balance sheet.

Exhibit 1.5

FINANCIAL STATEMENTS: CADBURY SCHWEPPES
Balance Sheets at 31 December 2000 (Note 1)

Notes		Group		Company	
		2000 £m	1999 £m	2000 £m	1999 £m
	Fixed Assets				
10	Intangible assets and goodwill	**3,163**	1,725	–	–
11	Tangible assets	**1,106**	1,091	**25**	19
12	Investments in associates	**300**	296	**11**	11
12	Investments	**156**	89	**4,842**	3,838
		4,725	3,201	**4,878**	3,868
	Current Assets				
13	Stocks	**458**	404	–	–
14	Debtors				
	– Due within one year	**845**	769	**43**	75
	– Due after one year	**78**	29	**6**	5
19	Investments	**334**	410	–	–
19	Cash at bank and in hand	**174**	151	–	–
		1,889	1,763	**49**	80
	Current Liabilities				
	Creditors: amounts falling due within one year				
19	– Borrowings	**(1,320)**	(432)	**(2,342)**	(1,435)
15	– Other	**(1,617)**	(1,283)	**(238)**	(304)
	Net Current (Liabilities)/Assets	**(1,048)**	48	**(2,531)**	(1,659)
	Total Assets less Current Liabilities	**3,677**	3,249	**2,347**	2,209
	Non-Current Liabilities				
	Creditors: amounts falling due after more than one year				
19	– Borrowings	**(417)**	(311)	**(972)**	(736)
15	– Other	**(72)**	(51)	–	–
16	Provisions for liabilities and charges	**(261)**	(263)	**(1)**	(1)
		(750)	(625)	**(973)**	(737)
	Net Assets	**2,927**	2,624	**1,374**	1,472
	Capital and Reserves				
21	Called up share capital	**255**	253	**255**	253
21	Share premium account	**991**	942	**991**	942
21	Capital redemption reserve	**90**	90	**90**	90
21	Revaluation reserve	**62**	61	**1**	1
21	Profit and loss account	**1,235**	894	**37**	186
	Shareholders' Funds	**2,633**	2,240	**1,374**	1,472
	Minority Interests				
22	Equity minority interests	**28**	139	–	–
22	Non-equity minority interests	**266**	245	–	–
		294	384	–	–
	Total Capital Employed	**2,927**	2,624	**1,374**	1,472

On behalf of the Board
Directors: D C Bonham, D J Kappler

23 February 2001

The United States   Financial reporting in the United States is very similar to that in Canada. The terminology is virtually the same, and so is the financial statement presentation. Canada's accounting standards for measurement and disclosures are probably closer to those of the United States than to any other country. In general, U.S. pronouncements tend to be more detailed; Canada's are broader and rely more on professional judgment in their application. In comparing the two countries' standards, we find many cases where the wording differs only slightly and the substance of the standards is the same.[2] But in other areas, there are accounting differences that can create substantial differences in results. These differences are great enough that Canadian textbooks are required in university and college accounting courses. Some of the differences arise in areas where Canadian practice is to defer and amortize while U.S. practice is to expense immediately: research and development expenditures are an example.

Canadian companies whose shares trade on U.S. stock exchanges are required to present reconciliations from Canadian GAAP to U.S. GAAP in the footnotes to their financial statements. These reconciliations often show substantial differences in net income. For example, in its 2000 Annual Report, Inco showed Canadian GAAP net income of $400 million and U.S. GAAP net income of $292 million. Both amounts are in U.S. dollars because Inco reports using the U.S. dollar as its measuring unit. Adjustments for pension costs and accounting for investments were the primary cause of the difference, which amounted to 27 percent of Canadian net income. It must be remembered that these differences will eventually reverse themselves. Accounting principles themselves do not affect cash flows unless taxable income is also affected.

Toward an Accounting Harmonization

A truly global economy will require some sort of harmonized accounting standards if it is to function properly. How this will be achieved is the big question. Two organizations that may play some role in formulating these standards are discussed next.

The European Union   In 1957, six European countries signed the Treaty of Rome, thereby establishing a common market for goods and services and common institutions for economic development. Originally called the European Economic Community, the agreement is now called the European Union (EU) and has 15 members.[3] Its major goal is the promotion of the free flow of goods, labour, and capital among member countries. In 1998, 12 of the countries[4] agreed to establish a European central bank, which took over monetary policy in 1999, and which issued a common currency called the euro. The currencies of the participating nations will gradually be phased out; the conversion will be completed in 2002. As part of these major steps toward a common capital market, the EU has attempted to harmonize the accounting principles used by its member countries by issuing "directives." In order to minimize conflict with the legal reporting

---

[2] *Handbook*, Section 1701, on segment reporting, was issued in 1997, and resulted from the joint efforts of the Accounting Standards Board of CICA and FASB in United States.

[3] The members are Austria, Belgium, Denmark, Finland, France, Germany, Greece, Ireland, Italy, Luxembourg, the Netherlands, the United Kingdom, Spain, Sweden, and Portugal.

[4] The countries that will not adopt a common currency on this date are the United Kingdom, Denmark, Sweden, and Greece.

requirements of certain of its member nations, these directives allow many alternative reporting practices. This is particularly true with respect to the first accounting directive. The second directive, issued in 1983, requiring the presentation of consolidated financial statements, has had a major impact on the accounting of many countries where consolidation was not previously a common practice. While flexibility appears to be contrary to the concept of harmonization, the adoption of the directives has nevertheless caused major changes to the accounting practices of some of its members. In addition, former Soviet Bloc counties, including Hungary and Poland, have established new accounting principles based on the EU directives, in anticipation of some day being admitted to the union. Even though progress has been made in harmonizing European accounting practices, there are still many accounting issues that are dealt with in Canadian GAAP but are not yet covered by the EU directives. A step in the right direction has been made, but harmonization is still a long way off.

The International Accounting Standards Board (IASB) This board became operational in 2001 as a result of a major restructuring of its former organization, which was called the International Accounting Standards Committee (IASC). This committee, based in London, was formed in 1973 by an agreement between the professional accounting bodies of 10 countries with the purpose of establishing worldwide accounting principles. The founding members came from Australia, Canada, France, Germany, Japan, Mexico, the Netherlands, the United Kingdom, Ireland, and the United States. Over the years the membership grew so that it represented more than 140 accounting organizations from over 100 countries. The IASC's operating costs of approximately £2 million a year were met by contributions from professional accounting bodies, accounting firms, and other organizations, and by the sale of IASC publications. It was governed by a board made up of representatives from 13 countries and 4 organizations. The committee met two or three times a year to release exposures of proposed standards, to examine public comments that resulted from them, and to issue International Accounting Standards. Initially, many of the standards issued by the IASC were characterized by the number of acceptable alternatives that were permitted; but in the early 1990s efforts were made to eliminate as many of these alternatives as possible. This initiative has been partially successful, but a number of standards still allow alternative treatments. Given that some of the board members came from countries whose accounting standards are reflected in legal statutes, it is understandable that the removal of alternatives can be a tricky political process requiring compromise. Notwithstanding this difficulty, achieving worldwide accounting uniformity will depend greatly on eliminating alternative accounting practices. To date, 41 standards have been issued and 34 are still in force. Exhibit 1.6 following provides a listing of the standards that were in force in October 2001. Where a standard has been superseded by a subsequent standard it is not included in the list.

The number of countries using IASB standards has been gradually increasing over the years. Most of the increase has been from countries that had not yet developed any semblance of accounting principles. Ten countries have fully adopted the IASB standards; an additional fourteen countries have adopted most of them, while allowing modifications to satisfy local circumstances. China, which has made great strides in moving toward a market economy, has enacted legislation requiring its companies to prepare their financial statements in accordance with IASB standards.

Exhibit 1.6

LIST OF CURRENT IASB STANDARDS
IN FORCE IN OCTOBER 2001

IAS 1   Presentation of Financial Statements

IAS 2   Inventories

IAS 7   Cash Flow Statements

IAS 8   Net Profit or Loss for the Period, Fundamental Errors and Changes in Accounting Policies

IAS 10   Events After the Balance Sheet Date

IAS 11   Construction Contracts

IAS 12   Income Taxes

IAS 14   Segment Reporting

IAS 15   Information Reflecting the Effects of Changing Prices

IAS 16   Property, Plant and Equipment

IAS 17   Leases

IAS 18   Revenue

IAS 19   Employee Benefits

IAS 20   Accounting for Government Grants and Disclosure of Government Assistance

IAS 21   The Effects of Changes in Foreign Exchange Rates

IAS 22   Business Combinations

IAS 23   Borrowing Costs

IAS 24   Related Party Disclosures

IAS 26   Accounting and Reporting by Retirement Benefit Plans

IAS 27   Consolidated Financial Statements

IAS 28   Investments in Associates

IAS 29   Financial Reporting in Hyperinflationary Economies

IAS 30   Disclosures in the Financial Statements of Banks and Similar Financial Institutions

IAS 31   Financial Reporting of Interests in Joint Ventures

IAS 32   Financial Instruments Disclosure and Presentation

IAS 33   Earnings per Share

IAS 34   Interim Financial Reporting

IAS 35   Discontinuing Operations

IAS 36   Impairment of Assets

IAS 37   Provisions, Contingent Liabilities and Contingent Assets

IAS 38   Intangible Assets

IAS 39   Financial Instruments Recognition and Measurement

IAS 40   Investment Property

IAS 41   Agriculture

Source: IASB website, October 2001 (http:www.iasb.org.uk). Copyright: International Accounting Standards Board, 166 Fleet Street, London EC4A 2DY, U.K. Copies of IASB publications are available direct from IASB, telephone: +44 (171) 427-5927.

In some countries, such as Switzerland and Germany, companies are allowed the choice of reporting using either their own country's standards or international standards. One of the major roadblocks to achieving some sort of harmonization is that no enforcement mechanisms exist to ensure that IASB standards are followed.

While its members agree to promote the acceptance of the IASB's standards in their home countries, it should be obvious from our previous discussions that often these efforts have not borne fruit. Canada, a founding member, is a case in point. The *CICA Handbook* contains a four-paragraph section on International Accounting Standards. None of the paragraphs is italicized; the entire section is made up of suggestions rather than recommendations. This section states that the Accounting Standards Board of the CICA supports the harmonization objectives of the IASB; it goes on to say:

> It may be desirable for Canadian entities, particularly those reporting in an international environment, to disclose whether their financial statements conform to International Accounting Standards. Cases in which adherence to the Handbook fails to satisfy or results in a deviation from an International Accounting Standard should be considered in terms of their significance; when significant, disclosure of the relevant facts is desirable. [1501.03]

A fairly lengthy appendix to Section 1501 summarizes significant differences between International Accounting Standards and the *Handbook* pronouncements. It is clear from this appendix that the differences between the two sets of standards are extensive. A recent publication[5] that compared the accounting principles of Canada, the United States, Mexico, Chile, and the IASC yields similar conclusions.

In 1997, the CICA established a task force to examine the standard-setting process in Canada. This task force was guided by the following principles:

- Canada endorses the principle of the internationalization of standard setting.
- Canada must continue to play a significant role in setting world accounting standards.
- Canada needs to work toward the elimination of the differences that exist not only in North America but also in the rest of the world.

A report issued by the task force indicated that there was no consensus as to whether harmonization should be achieved by adopting FASB standards or those of the IASC. The report recommended the short-term approach of working with both groups in trying to achieve harmonization.

Since the release of the report, the CICA has issued standards in conjunction with the FASB, and also in conjunction with both the FASB and the IASB. When the financial instrument standard is released in the future by the CICA, it will be the result of working jointly with the FASB, the IASB, and seven other national standard setters. It will be interesting to see if all of the bodies involved issue similar standards on this topic.

In March 2001, a major restructuring of the IASB was completed. A new entity, the IASC Foundation, was formed as a non-profit entity situated in the United States. Nineteen trustees run the Foundation and were chosen in the following manner:

- Six from North America.
- Six from Europe.
- Four from Asia-Pacific.
- Three from other areas, to achieve some semblance of geographical balance.

---

[5] "Significant Differences in GAAP in Canada, Chile, Mexico, and the United States," CICA, 2000.

Some trustees were nominated by various accounting organizations, and others were chosen strictly for their accounting expertise.

The objectives of the organization are:

- to develop high quality global accounting standards that are understandable and enforceable.
- to promote the use of these standards.
- to bring a harmonization of national standards and International Accounting Standards (IAS).

The role of the trustees is to assume responsibility for fundraising, and to appoint members to the following:

- The International Accounting Standards Board (IASB), the entity which will issue all future International Accounting Standards.
- The Standing Interpretations Committee, which will interpret and provide guidance on the implementation of International Accounting Standards.
- The Standards Advisory Council, which will provide guidance to the Board and establish priorities for future projects.

The International Accounting Standards Board is located in London, England, and has 14 members, 12 of whom are full time and 2 of whom are part time. The members are chosen more for their expertise than for geographical representation. However, seven of the members are expected to have formal liaison responsibilities with major national standard-setting bodies, but must not be actual members of such national bodies. These seven standard-setting bodies are located in Germany, France, the United States, Canada, Great Britain, Japan, and Australia–New Zealand. Presumably such a liaison will be instrumental in harmonizing the national standards of a very important group of countries with those of the IASB.

The Board will issue new standards in areas where no international standards exist. Existing standards will probably be modified to reduce the alternatives that are present in many of them. It is these alternative treatments that have presented major stumbling blocks on the road to worldwide harmonization. FASB in particular has been reluctant to endorse international standards for precisely this reason. It also seems clear that the FASB has to be on side if there is to be any future uniformity in worldwide accounting standards. The size of the United States' capital markets in relation to the rest of the world's capital markets makes this imperative.

As we have indicated, the rapid changes taking place in the world are demanding a move toward harmonization of the accounting standards used by multinational corporations. Whether the end result will be a single set of world standards or a significant reduction in the diversity that exists today remains to be seen. Canadian standards will have to change. It also remains to be seen whether these new standards will be applicable to all companies in Canada, or only to those whose shares trade on major world stock exchanges. The only thing that seems certain is that changes will occur.

The Real Nature of Accounting Harmonization

We are inundated with new exposure drafts and pronouncements from the CICA and the International Accounting Standards Committee (IASC). During 1996 and 1997 alone, these included such diverse matters as Financial Instruments, Pensions, Income Taxes, Foreign Currency, and Employees' Future Benefits from the CICA alone. The IASC has had a myriad of new exposure drafts and standards as well, with two new standards and five exposure drafts arising from the July meeting in Beijing (see www.iasc.org.uk for details). Other countries have similar commotion in standard setting.

Why the flurry of activity? Although several items have involved movement of Canadian standards closer to those of the United States, the movement is not all in one direction, with, for example, the Canadian position on Earnings Per Share becoming the basis for new IASC and FASB pronouncements. The reason is the search for accounting harmonization, because with harmony in accounting practices, difficulty in the interpretation of "foreign" accounting practices is reduced, leading to a general alleviation of risk and a measurable overall reduction in the cost of capital to business enterprises.

Harmonization is far removed from standardization. Uniform accounting practices worldwide is not the goal: a harmony of practices is. As the term harmony (a combination of sounds considered pleasing to the ear) is perhaps most widely used in music, a musical analogy may be helpful in reaching an understanding of at least one aspect of the harmonization debate, the nature of harmonization. This analogy follows:

> Imagine you were a musician, and were to join with a friend to play music. You will play the piano; your friend is to play the violin. With some discussion, you decide on the music you will play together. What would you play?

> On the same musical scale? Definitely …
> The same composition? Of course, perhaps after some discussion and compromise …
> Exactly the same notes? Not necessarily …

> The notes to be played would be complementary, not equivalent. They would blend to create harmony. The harmony will be recognizable as a part of the same framework, on the same scale, the same production. How close must the notes be? There are clearly degrees, yet harmony in music does not require standardization; the notes would not be identical; they would be in balance, in equilibrium, complementary. They work together, and, together, they are music. Variations would be limited to those readily understood and appreciated, in accordance with an accepted framework. Exceptions are tolerated: music is an art. The audience would decide if the music is pleasing. Perfect harmony would provide a happy audience. The greater the *lack* of harmony, the less enjoyment would be realized.

Accounting is the music of business. Accounting, too, can be an art. Accounting systems around the world play on different scales, however, and presently in a somewhat discordant manner. Harmonization of accounting is much the same as in music. If we are to play together, we must play on the same scale, within the same framework of rules or concepts. Then we play the same tune, using the same arrangement (of accounting reports). The fine details (the notes, i.e., the specifics of disclosure and measurement practices) do not have to be the same, but complementary. Even major exceptions can be justified, if adequately disclosed, explained or reconciled. With cooperation, the ensemble can grow to become an orchestra. Would everyone play the same notes? No … The same tune? …

Instruments whereby the musicians can play together, through amendments to the legal and regulatory framework and other provisions which will facilitate the learning process and limit the differences, can be provided and are actively on the agenda of such organizations as the IASC and the International Organization of Securities Commissions (see www.IOSCO.org), and within the majority of member countries. Not only must the composers and conductors work together: we must all make an investment in the resolution of accounting diversity to make beautiful music together.

Reprinted from *The Leading Edge*, Fall 1997.
Submitted by Peter Secord, Saint Mary's University

Note: An additional set of financial statements for Grupo Continental, S. A., is available on our website, www.mcgrawhill.ca/college/hilton.

SUMMARY

The diversity among the accounting principles in use throughout the world is seen as a major stumbling block toward achieving a truly global capital market. The IASB is attempting to narrow this diversity by issuing a set of international standards, with the hope that they will be adopted worldwide. While a great deal of progress has been made, the goal of global harmonization has not yet been reached and it is not clear at this time whether the ultimate solution will be the global adoption of the IASB standards.

REVIEW QUESTIONS

1. Why is it important to supplement studies of Canadian accounting principles with studies of the accounting practices used in other countries?
2. In what manner has there been a shift toward a global capital market in recent years?
3. List the factors that can influence the accounting standards used in a particular country.
4. The accounting standards of some countries tend to minimize the use of interperiod income tax allocation. Explain why.
5. What role does the stage of development of a country's capital markets have on the direction taken by the country's accounting standards?
6. In what way does the level of inflation influence the accounting standards of a particular country?
7. In which two countries mentioned in the chapter have accounting standards been set by statute?

8. Accounting standards determined by legislated authority often result in an income measurement of a certain type. Explain.

9. In what manner does the balance sheet format used by companies in the United Kingdom differ from the format used by Canadian companies?

10. Canadian companies whose shares trade on U.S. stock exchanges are required to reconcile Canadian GAAP income to U.S. GAAP income. What are some of the causes of differences?

11. What countries make up the European Union, and what is the EU's purpose?

12. What is the goal of the IASB?

13. It is often asserted that the future will see drastic changes being made to GAAP in Canada. Explain fully.

14. Compare and contrast a balance sheet produced by a British company with one produced by a company in Germany, with respect to presentation and measurement.

MULTIPLE CHOICE

1. Which of the following is not a reason for establishing international accounting standards?
   a. Some countries do not have the resources to develop accounting standards on their own.
   b. Comparability is needed between companies operating in different areas of the world.
   c. Some of the accounting principles allowed in various countries report markedly different results for similar transactions.
   d. Demand in Canada is heavy for an alternative to the principles found in the *CICA Handbook*.

2. The IASC was formed by representatives of several different
   a. Government agencies.
   b. Accounting bodies.
   c. Legislative organizations.
   d. Academic organizations.

3. According to critics, what is the major problem with the original standards produced by the IASC?
   a. Too many popular methods have been eliminated.
   b. Too many optional methods have remained.
   c. The IASB has failed to examine and report on key accounting issues.
   d. The pronouncements have tended to be too similar to Canadian GAAP.

4. In Great Britain, a balance sheet
   a. Begins with fixed assets and then reports current assets less current liabilities.
   b. Is not required except for companies of a specific size.
   c. Begins with stockholders' equity.
   d. Is similar to a balance sheet that would be produced by a Canadian company.

5. Accounting and other types of technology are imported and exported, and countries have similar accounting for this reason. Which one of the following reasons has been most significant in increasing the influence that the United States has had on accounting in Canada?

    a. Canadian companies routinely sell shares of stock or borrow money in the United States.

    b. The countries have similar political systems.

    c. Both countries are involved in the European Community.

    d. The countries are close geographically.

6. Which one of the following has been least affected by the accounting diversity that exists throughout the world?

    a. Managers of multinational corporations.

    b. Global investors.

    c. Accounting regulators.

    d. Managers of domestic corporations.

7. Why do some accountants question the desirability of an organized accounting harmonization effort?

    a. They believe that there is little interest in international harmonization efforts.

    b. They are concerned that international harmonization will result in decreased jobs for accountants and will therefore hurt the profession.

    c. They believe that accounting harmonization will occur through free market forces.

    d. They believe that most countries will eventually follow U.S. standards since the U.S. is an economic leader.

8. Which of the following is true with respect to international accounting?

    a. Accounting and disclosure standards tend to be more extensive in countries with more highly developed public capital markets.

    b. Government and regulatory bodies always have a very limited role in the development of accounting standards in foreign countries.

    c. The CICA supports efforts of the International Accounting Standards Board to harmonize accounting standards used in different countries.

    d. a. and b.

    e. a. and c.

    f. b. and c.

    g. All of the above.

9. Why would some German companies probably prefer to follow the accounting standards of the IASB?

    a. German accounting standards are complicated, so proper financial statements are very difficult to produce.

    b. Germany tends to follow U.S. GAAP rather than a set of standards of its own.

    c. Germany has virtually no accounting principles, so comparisons between companies is difficult.

    d. The use of IASB standards allows companies in Germany to be more easily compared with companies in other countries.

10. What is the goal of the IASB?

    a. To formulate accounting standards that can be used throughout the world.

    b. To promote adequate disclosure practices so that countries throughout the world can continue to use their unique reporting standards.

    c. To require that world standards be the same as those in the United States, in recognition of its position in the world's capital markets.

    d. a. and b.

    e. a. and c.

    f. b. and c.

    g. All of the above.

11. How would you describe accounting principles in Japan?
    a. They are issued by a professional accounting body.
    b. They are the same as IASB standards.
    c. They are determined by government.
    d. They are quite liberal in nature.

12. In British financial statements, what does the term "turnover" refer to?
    a. The age of the inventory.
    b. The time needed to collect the receivables.
    c. Sales.
    d. Net profit as percentage on assets.

CASES

Case 1* Megan Moody had watched the Teleglobe International acquisition of Excel Communications with great interest, from initial announcement and through every press release and filing. The investment she administered — 10,000 shares of Teleglobe — had done well during the 18 months Megan had followed the stock. Purchased in several small lots in late 1997, at an average price of $16.00, the share had soared to over $40.00 and was presently (spring 1999) trading at about $30.00.

As the treasurer and investment advisor for several affiliated Canadian not-for-profit organizations, Megan was responsible for making investment recommendations to a board of directors, which considered the investment policies of the organizational endowment funds only infrequently. Megan, as a result, was particularly interested in the long-run returns associated with this investment. A quarterly review of the investment portfolio was due, and the wide fluctuations in price and trading volume led her to believe that the Teleglobe investment would be a hot topic for debate.

Megan faced a practical difficulty. Teleglobe had reported for the most recent fiscal year under both U.S. and Canadian GAAP, and had reported widely differing results under these two different regimes. Further, the acquisition had been made only shortly after Teleglobe, which had been largely a domestic Canadian operation, had gone public. The Excel merger had changed many of the basic parameters of the firm, and compounded with the release of two parallel sets of financial statements prepared under different rules, analysis was anything but an easy task. Teleglobe was listed in both Toronto and New York, but the information most readily available in those markets differed.

Megan began to sketch out a summary of the information included in the annual reports for the most recent year, and her initial notes included the following summary, in millions of dollars (except per share):

	U.S. GAAP (U.S. Dollars)	Canadian GAAP (Canadian Dollars)
Extracts from the income statement for the year ending December 31, 1998		
Total revenue	$3,388.9	$2,611.9
Operating income	89.1	329.1
Income before extraordinary items	14.9	199.4
Net income	14.9	(66.2)
Earnings per share	$ 0.04	$ (0.50)

* Case prepared by Peter Secord, St. Mary's University.

	U.S. GAAP (U.S. Dollars)	Canadian GAAP (Canadian Dollars)
Extracts from the balance sheet at December 31, 1998		
Total current assets	$ 862.1	$1,360.7
Investments	233.1	59.2
Property, plant & equipment, net	889.9	1,866.5
Deferred income taxes	50.3	47.6
Intangibles, net	1,016.4	5,473.0
Total assets	$3,142.6	$9,072.1

The difficulty that faced Megan was now more clear — the differences between the statements could now be isolated. She began to write her report on the investment for the board of directors, and knew she would have to include in this report comments on the meaning of the differences between the two sets of financial statements. She would also have to close with a recommendation as to the advisability of retaining the investment.

Required:

(a) As Megan Moody, make a list of the items associated with accounting policies that you would need to complete the report on the investment in Teleglobe during spring 1999.

(b) Making reasonable assumptions, prepare the first draft of the report to the Board of Directors.

Case 2* Emera Inc. is a Canadian company headquartered in Halifax. The head office accounting staff were gathering information on the October 10, 2001, acquisition of all of the common shares of the Bangor Hydro Electric Company (BHEC) for US$26.806 per share in cash. The purchase increases Emera's customer base by 25 percent and broadens the company's presence in the expanding northeastern energy market. David Mann, President and CEO of Emera, had announced that Bangor Hydro was to play an important role. He said, "It complements our other energy businesses, and places us on the ground in the region we've targeted for further growth."

BHEC is a regulated electricity transmission and distribution company serving 110,000 customers in central and eastern Maine. It is a member of the New England Power Pool, and is interconnected with the other New England utilities to the south and with New Brunswick Power to the north. Emera also owns Nova Scotia Power, a fully integrated electric utility that supplies substantially all of the generation, transmission, and distribution of electricity in Nova Scotia, as well as Emera Fuels, a distribution company; and has an interest in the Maritimes & Northeast Pipeline, which transports Sable natural gas through Maine to Boston. With the latest acquisition, the organizational structure of Emera was reshaped as shown below.

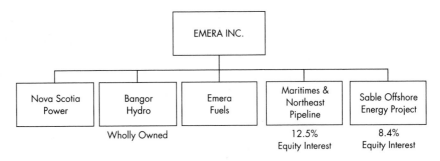

---

* Case prepared by Peter Secord, St. Mary's University.

By this time, the senior financial staff at Emera were already exploring the compatibility of the accounting systems and policies of the two companies. The new subsidiary not only operated in a regulated industry and was to some extent limited in the choice of accounting policies by debt covenants, but was also headquartered in a different country and subject to the financial reporting framework of the Financial Accounting Standards Board and the Securities and Exchange Commission of the United States. Pricing and other aspects of operation were subject to regulation by the Maine Public Utilities Commission and the United States Department of Energy.

Required:

It was clear that, under Canadian GAAP, BHEC would be reported as a consolidated subsidiary. However, there are distinct differences in the financial reporting environment faced by Emera and that faced by the new subsidiary. What procedures should be followed by Emera in the preparation for consolidation of BHEC? Comment on the difficulties that might arise in the preparation of combined or consolidated financial statements, and on how these difficulties should be addressed by Emera staff.

PROBLEMS

Problem 1   Listed below are some financial ratios used by analysts:
- Liquidity — current ratio; operating cash flow to current liabilities.
- Solvency — debt to equity; debt to assets.
- Profitability — return on assets; return on equity.

Assume that you are comparing the financial ratios of companies from each of the countries discussed in this chapter with those of Canadian companies.

Required:

(a) Discuss how accounting practices in the United Kingdom might affect your comparison for each of the six ratios in the list.
(b) Discuss how accounting practices in Germany might affect your comparison for each of the six ratios in the list.
(c) Discuss how accounting practices in Japan might affect your comparison for each of the six ratios in the list.
(d) Discuss how accounting practices in the United States might affect your comparison for each of the six ratios in the list.

Problem 2   The following balance sheet has been presented to you by a friend of yours:

	£(000)
Fixed assets	
Tangible assets	2,218
Investments	149
	2,367
Current assets and liabilities	
Stocks	113
Debtors	165
Cash in bank and on hand	290
	568
Creditors — due within one year	544
Net current assets	24
Total assets less current liabilities	2,391

Creditors — amounts due after one year	
Loan capital	302
Provisions for liabilities and charges	26
	328
	2,063
Capital and reserves	
Called up share capital	117
Share premium account	100
Revaluation reserve	755
Profit and loss account	1,091
Shareholders' funds	2,063

Your friend has taken an introductory course in Canadian financial accounting but is having trouble interpreting this balance sheet. She says that she forgot to bring the income statement, but remembers that the first item on the statement was called "Turnover from continuing operations."

Required:

(a) What country is this company located in?
(b) Compare the terminology used in the two statements with what would be used by a Canadian company.
(c) Prepare a balance sheet using the format and terminology followed in Canada.

Problem 3 The following websites contain financial statements for companies located in other countries:

- www.heinekencorp.com
- www.volkswagen-ir.de/english/
- www.world.honda.com
- www.cadburyschweppes.com
- www.gibsa.com/bimboenglish/index.html
- www.novartis.com
- www.rolls-royce.com
- www.renault.com

Required:

Download any three companies' financial statements. For each, identify five major differences in the company's financial statements, compared with those of a typical Canadian corporation.

Problem 4 The following reconciliation was included in the notes to the 2000 financial statements of Cadbury Schweppes.

Effect on profit of differences between UK and US generally accepted accounting principles (in millions of pounds)

Profit for the Financial Year from continuing operations, net of tax (per U.K. GAAP)	496
U.S. GAAP adjustments	
Amortization of goodwill and trademarks	(102)
Restructuring costs	9
Depreciation of capitalized interest	3
Pension costs	7
Exceptional item/disposal gain adjustment	(22)
Timing of recognition of foreign currency hedges	2
SAYE/LTIP	(9)
Other items	(5)
Deferred taxation	4
Profit for the Financial Year from continuing operations, net of tax, adjusted for U.S. GAAP	383

Required:

(a) Which country's accounting principles appear to be the most conservative? Why?

(b) Explain why you think the following adjustments were made:
  (i)   Goodwill and trade marks.
  (ii) Interest capitalization.
  (iii) Disposal gain.

(c) Download the financial statements from the company's website (www. cadburyschweppes.com) and see if you can further determine the differences between U.K. and U.S. GAAP. Outline any differences that you find.

CHAPTER 2

Temporary, Portfolio, and Significant Influence Investments

CHAPTER OUTLINE

LEARNING OBJECTIVES

After studying this chapter, you should be able to do the following:

- Describe the broad relationship between all the relevant sections of the *CICA Handbook* that comprise the "big picture."
- Distinguish between temporary, portfolio, and significant influence investments.
- Apply the basic concepts behind the cost and equity methods.
- Prepare equity method entries to amortize the purchase discrepancy.
- Prepare equity method journal entries to reflect unrealized profits on asset transfers.

Share Capital Investments — The Big Picture

This is the first of 10 chapters that make up a single accounting topic. This topic is described by the following question: How should a Canadian company report, in its financial statements, an investment in the share capital of another company? There are five types of investment in shares:

- Temporary.
- Portfolio.
- Significant influence.
- Control.
- Joint venture.

While it sounds simple, this is a complex topic, and you will have to read carefully and manipulate numbers extensively if you are to achieve a thorough understanding of the concepts and issues involved.

A major subset of this large topic is the preparation of consolidated financial statements, which in itself is fraught with complexity. There is always a danger that, in attempting to absorb a large amount of new material, you will concentrate on the details to the point of losing sight of the big picture. It is important that you don't lose sight of the forest when you study the trees.

Before proceeding with our examination of the "trees," it would be useful to look at this "forest." The question posed above provides a path into the forest. The accounting principles involved with this question are contained in numerous sections of the *CICA Handbook* and in the statements issued by the Emerging Issues Committee (EIC) of the CICA.

We will use a summarized balance sheet to illustrate the question, and then outline the possible answers that are contained in the *Handbook* sections.

Shown below is the balance sheet of J Company Ltd.:

J COMPANY LTD.
BALANCE SHEET

Miscellaneous assets	$ XXX	Liabilities	$ XXX
Investment in shares		Shareholders' equity	
of K Corporation	**XXX**	Capital stock	XXX
		Retained earnings	XXX
	$ XXX		$ XXX

Dollar amounts have been omitted from the table because our focus is on the amount that should be shown for "Investment in shares of K Corporation."

Four *Handbook* sections are directly related to providing an answer to this question; a further seven sections and numerous Emerging Issues Abstracts must also be considered. A brief summary of the provisions contained in the first four sections is presented next.

Directly Related *Handbook* Sections

1. Section 1590: "Subsidiaries"

If J Company controls K Corporation, then J Company is called a parent company and K Corporation is called a subsidiary, and GAAP requires the preparation of consolidated financial statements by J Company. This involves removing the investment in K Corporation from J Company's balance sheet and replacing it with the assets and liabilities from the balance sheet of K Corporation. This process is illustrated at the end of Chapter 3 and in the chapters that follow it.

Control exists if J Company has the continuing power to determine the strategic operating, investing, and financing policies of K Corporation without the co-operation of others.[1] Control would generally be presumed if J Company's investment consists of a majority of the voting shares of K Corporation; but as we will see in later discussions,[2] control can exist with smaller holdings and does not necessarily exist with majority holdings.

If the investment is not one that produces control, then *CICA Handbook*, sections 3010, 3050, and 3055 must be examined to determine the required financial reporting.

2. Section 3010: "Temporary Investments"

These are transitional investments in marketable debt and equity securities that have been made to obtain a temporary return on surplus cash. Investments of this type are shown in the current assets section of the balance sheet, often described as "marketable securities." They are initially recorded at cost and subsequently are valued at the lower of cost or market. Interest accruing on debt securities and dividends received from investments in equity securities are reported as revenue. This topic is covered in more detail later in this chapter.

3. Section 3050: "Long-term Investments"

This section describes the financial reporting required for two other types of investments: significant influence and portfolio.

Significant Influence   This refers to an investment that does not convey control and is not an investment in a joint venture, but that does allow the investor to exercise significant influence over the strategic operating, investing, and financing policies of the investee. The *Handbook* indicates that an investment of 20 percent or more of the voting shares of K Corporation, without control being present, would be presumed to be a significant influence investment, unless there is evidence to the contrary. Such evidence is discussed later.

If J Company's investment is one of significant influence, it must be reported by the equity method. Thus the investment is initially recorded at cost and then adjusted thereafter to include J Company's pro rata share of the earnings or losses of K Corporation adjusted for the purchase discrepancy[3] and the elimination and subsequent recognition of all intercompany profits that occur as a result of transactions between the two companies. Dividends received from K Corporation are recorded as a reduction of the investment.

Portfolio   A portfolio investment is a long-term investment that is not an investment in a joint venture or partnership and that does not give significant influence or control. It is presumed that an investment of less than 20 percent of the voting shares of K Corporation is a portfolio investment unless there is evidence that clearly indicates the presence of significant influence.

---

[1] *CICA Handbook*, paragraph 1590.03.

[2] The concept of control is discussed in greater detail in Chapter 4.

[3] The concept of a purchase discrepancy is discussed later.

A portfolio investment is reported by the cost method, whereby only dividends received are reported as revenue.

The accounting for portfolio and significant influence investments will be illustrated later.

4. Section 3055: "Investments in Joint Ventures"

If the investment is not one of the four just described, it may possibly be a joint venture investment if the following general provisions of this section are satisfied.

For a joint venture to exist, the owners (the venturers) must have made a contractual arrangement that establishes joint control over the venture. Under such joint control, each venturer shares in some manner the power to determine strategic operating, financing, and investing policies, and no single venturer is able to unilaterally control the venture.

Under this section, J Company Ltd. (the "venturer") reports its investment in K Corporation Ltd. (the "venture") by consolidating K Corporation using the proportionate consolidation method. This method involves applying the proprietary theory of consolidation and is illustrated in Chapter 10.

Other Related *Handbook* Sections

The remaining seven important *Handbook* sections are directly related to the four sections that were just outlined and are discussed briefly below.

5. Section 1581: "Business Combinations"

A business combination is an economic event whereby one company acquires net assets that constitute a business or equity interests of another company and, as a result, obtains control over that company.

J Company Ltd. obtains *control* over the net assets of K Corporation by either:

(a) investing in the voting shares of K Corporation (a parent–subsidiary relationship), or

(b) purchasing the net assets of K Corporation (not a parent–subsidiary relationship).

Prior to June 2001, there were two distinct methods of accounting for business combinations. Depending on the particular circumstances, a business combination was accounted for in accordance with the *purchase method* or the *pooling of interests method*. When the purchase method was used, any resulting goodwill had to be amortized over a maximum period of 40 years. On June 30, 2001, major changes were made to business combination accounting. Pooling of interests was banned, leaving only the purchase method as a means of accounting for a business combination. In addition, the periodic amortization of purchased goodwill was discontinued in favour of the regular testing of goodwill for impairment. Business combination accounting is explained in Chapter 3.

It should be noted that the term "control" is also used in Section 1590. On the date that a parent–subsidiary relationship is established, a business combination has occurred.

6. Section 1600: "Consolidated Financial Statements"

This section details the accounting principles to be followed in preparing consolidated financial statements. The pronouncements of this section will receive extensive attention in the chapters that follow.

7. Section 1625: "Comprehensive Revaluation of Assets and Liabilities"

A comprehensive revaluation of the assets and liabilities of an enterprise can take place under the provisions of this section when:

(a) there has been a change in control because all or virtually all of the equity interests of the enterprise have been acquired by another enterprise, *or*

(b) the enterprise has been subject to a financial reorganization, and as a result the previous owners have lost control.

A revaluation under the first condition is permitted but not required, and is the application of "push-down" accounting. Under the second condition, which arises when the entity is in serious financial distress, a revaluation is mandatory. The accounting involved for comprehensive revaluations will be discussed in Chapter 11.

8. Section 1650: "Foreign Currency Translation"

This section deals with the translation of the financial statements of foreign investees, subsidiaries, and joint ventures, and with the translation of transactions denominated in foreign currencies.

Provisions of this section would apply if:

(a) K Corporation was located in a foreign country and/or prepared its financial statements in a foreign currency, or

(b) J Company Ltd. had borrowings or lendings and/or export/import activities denominated in foreign currencies.

Chapters 12 and 13 examine the accounting concepts involved here.

9. Section 1701: "Segment Disclosures"

Consolidated financial statements may result in the aggregating of the statements of companies in diverse businesses located in countries throughout the world. Disaggregation into operating segments and disclosures about products, geographic areas, and major customers is required by this section in order to improve the information content of the consolidated statements. Segment disclosures are discussed in Chapter 10.

10. Section 3465: "Income Taxes"

This new section adds some complications to the asset valuations associated with business combinations and consolidated financial statements. These provisions, which became effective on January 1, 2000, are discussed in Chapter 10.

11. Section 3475: "Discontinued Operations"

This section discusses the reporting requirements when a business segment, such as a subsidiary or joint venture, has been sold.

This topic is well covered in most intermediate accounting texts.

Related EIC Abstracts

In 1988, the CICA formed its Emerging Issues Committee (EIC) to recommend the appropriate accounting for emerging accounting issues. These are issues that either have not been covered by existing *Handbook* sections or for which additional guidance is required regarding the appropriate accounting method. While the pronouncements of this committee do not carry the same degree of authority as the *Handbook* sections, they are considered to be within the broad domain of generally accepted accounting principles in Canada.[4] A number of the abstracts issued by the EIC are related to the *Handbook* sections outlined in this introduction. The appendix at the end of this chapter lists these particular abstracts and the *Handbook* sections to which they relate.

The big picture, the details of which are contained in a number of later chapters in this book, has been outlined in this overview. You will find it useful to refer to this overview and the "forest" described as you study the material that follows. We will now begin our examination of the "trees."

This chapter examines situations where a share investment does not constitute control or joint control. Section 3010, "Temporary Investments," and Section 3050, "Long-term Investments," cover these situations.

Temporary Investments

Section 3010, "Temporary Investments," deals with investments in equity or debt instruments that can be promptly liquidated, and where the intent of management is to invest surplus cash in the short term. Investments of this type are reported in the current assets section of the balance sheet, often right after (or occasionally combined with) cash assets. Because of its nature, this type of investment would normally contain highly liquid debt instruments rather than the common share investments that are our main focus in this chapter. These investments are measured at acquisition cost except when the market price has declined below cost. When this is the case, the investments are written down to market, and the resultant loss is reflected in income. When market is above cost, the market price is disclosed in the financial statements but no write-up is permitted.[5]

While the *Handbook* is silent on the details of application, it is considered acceptable to apply these concepts either to individual securities or, alternatively, on a portfolio basis. The individual basis is more conservative; it requires that individual investments be written down if their market prices have declined below cost, but ignores other investments whose market price is greater than cost. The portfolio basis compares the total cost with the total market price for all the different investments and adjusts the portfolio total to market by means a valuation allowance. This allowance has to be adjusted each year as the composition of the portfolio changes.

Income from temporary investments is reflected in the income statement and consists of interest earned, dividends received or receivable, and realized gains and losses from the sale of investments. The income statement also reflects any unrealized losses resulting from write-downs to market.

Long-term Investments

Section 3050, "Long-term Investments," covers two types of share investments and describes two methods of accounting for them. Here management's intent is to hold the investments for the long term, and for that reason they are reported as noncurrent assets on the balance sheet. The two types are portfolio investments and significant influence investments; the two distinct accounting methods are the cost method and the equity method.

---

[4] *CICA Handbook*, paragraph 1000.60.

[5] This may change when a new standard on financial instruments is released by CICA.

Portfolio Investments

The *Handbook* defines a portfolio investment by describing what it is not rather than what it is. Basically, the *Handbook* says that portfolio investments are not control or joint venture investments and, furthermore, that they do not allow the reporting enterprise to exercise significant influence over the investee corporation. They are also not temporary investments because they are long term in nature. The *Handbook* provides quantitative guidelines, which suggest that a holding of less than 20 percent of the voting shares indicates a portfolio investment. A block of shares of this size probably would not allow the investor to elect any members to the board of directors of the investee corporation; because of this, it probably cannot exert any influence on the decision-making processes of that company. However, 20 percent is only a guideline, and an examination of the facts may suggest some other type of investment. For example, if the investee's shares are widely distributed, and all the other shareholders hold very small blocks of shares and display indifference as to the make-up of the board of directors, an investment of less than 20 percent may be considered a significant influence investment. This certainly could be the case if some of the remaining shareholders gave the investor proxies to vote their shares. Another situation where an investment consisting of 15 percent in the voting shares of an investee would not be a portfolio investment (or significant influence) would occur when the investee was a joint venture.

Portfolio investments are reported using the cost method. Under this method the amount in the investment account remains at the original acquisition cost, and the investor's share of the dividends received is reported as revenue. There are only two exceptions to this:

1. Any dividends received that are greater than the total of the net incomes earned since acquisition are treated by the investor as a reduction in the investment account. Dividends are a company's method of distributing earnings to its owners; it follows that a company cannot distribute as income more than it has earned. When it does so it is really returning to its owners a portion of the capital that they have contributed (a liquidating dividend).

2. If the market price drops permanently below the original acquisition cost, the investment must be written down to market and the loss reflected in income. If the market subsequently recovers, a write-up is not permitted. Note that the market decline must be permanent for this treatment to be applicable, whereas a temporary investment must be reported at the lower of cost or market.

Illustration   On January 1, Year 1, Jenstar Corp. purchased 10 percent of the outstanding common shares of Safebuy Company at a cost of $95,000. Safebuy reported net incomes and paid dividends at the end of each year as follows:

	Net income	Dividends
December 31, Year 1	$100,000	$75,000
December 31, Year 2	65,000	75,000
December 31, Year 3	30,000	75,000

Utilizing the cost method to account for its investment, Jenstar would make the following journal entries:

Jan. 1, Year 1

Investment in Safebuy	95,000	
Cash		95,000

To record the acquisition of 10% of Safebuy's shares

Dec. 31, Year 1
Cash	7,500	
Dividend revenue		7,500
Receipt of dividend from Safebuy		

Dec. 31, Year 2
Cash	7,500	
Dividend revenue		7,500
Receipt of dividend from Safebuy		

Dec. 31, Year 3
Cash	7,500	
Dividend revenue		4,500
Investment in Safebuy		3,000
Receipt of dividend from Safebuy		

The entries in years 2 and 3 need further clarification. The dividends paid in Year 2 were greater than the net income for that year, and from Jenstar's perspective it is possible that a portion of the dividend received should be recorded as a reduction in the investment account. However, total net income earned since acquisition is greater than total dividends paid since that date, so the dividends received are considered revenue in both years. In Year 3 the dividends paid were greater than the net income earned, and so we again have to compare total net income earned with total dividends paid. Total income since acquisition date amounts to $195,000, while dividends in the same period are $225,000. Therefore, $30,000 of these dividends are really liquidating dividends from the point of view of Jenstar. Because no liquidating dividends have yet been recorded, $3,000 (10 percent × $30,000) is recorded as a reduction to the investment account in Year 3, and the remaining $4,500 is dividend revenue.

Significant Influence

A significant influence investment is an investment in the voting shares of a corporation that permits the investor to exercise significant influence over the strategic operating, financing, and investing policies of the investee; at the same time, however, it does not establish control or joint control over that investee. Note that the *Handbook*'s criteria for this type of investment require only the *ability* to exercise significant influence; there is no requirement to show that such influence is actually being exercised in a particular situation.

The following conditions are possible indicators that significant influence is present:

- The ability to elect members to the board of directors.
- The right to participate in the policymaking process.
- Significant intercompany transactions between the two companies.
- The size of ownership of the other shareholders of the investee.
- Exchanges of management and technology between the two companies.

Section 3050 suggests that a holding between 20 percent and 50 percent may indicate the presence of significant influence, but it also states that a holding of this size does not necessarily mean that such influence exists. The following scenarios will illustrate this.

Given that A Company owns 60 percent of the voting shares of C Company (probably a control investment), does B Company's holding of 30 percent of C Company's shares indicate that B Company has a significant influence investment? Not necessarily. If B Company is unable to obtain membership on the board of directors of C Company or participate in its strategic policymaking because of A Company's control, it would be difficult to justify calling B Company's holding a significant influence investment. In such a situation B Company's holding would be considered a portfolio investment. Would this situation be different if B Company were allowed membership on C Company's board of directors? Perhaps, based on the following:

> A substantial or majority ownership by another investor would not necessarily preclude an investor from exercising significant influence. [3050.04]

In other words, another company's control investment in C Company does not mean that B Company's 30 percent investment in C Company can never be considered to be significant influence. Determination of significant influence depends on the particular circumstances.

Furthermore, in the previous discussion on portfolio investments, an example was presented where an investment of less than 20 percent might qualify as a significant influence investment. From all these discussions and examples, it should be obvious that considerable professional judgment is required in distinguishing between portfolio and significant influence investments. In later chapters, when we discuss the criteria used to determine whether a particular investment establishes control over an investee, we will also conclude that professional judgment is required.

The *CICA Handbook* requires that significant influence investments be reported by the equity method. The basic concept behind the equity method is that the investor records its proportionate share of the investee's income as its own income and reduces the investment account by its share of investee dividends received.

Illustration of Equity Method Basics

We return to the example of the Jenstar and Safebuy companies. All the facts remain the same, including the 10 percent ownership, except that we assume this is a significant influence investment. Using the equity method, Jenstar's journal entries would be as follows:

Jan. 1, Year 1

Investment in Safebuy	95,000	
Cash		95,000
To record the acquisition of 10% of Safebuy's shares		

Dec. 31, Year 1

Investment in Safebuy	10,000	
Investment income		10,000
10% of Safebuy's Year 1 net income		
Cash	7,500	
Investment in Safebuy		7,500
Receipt of dividend from Safebuy		

Dec. 31, Year 2

Investment in Safebuy	6,500	
Investment income		6,500
10% of Safebuy's Year 2 net income		
Cash	7,500	
Investment in Safebuy		7,500
Receipt of dividend from Safebuy		

Dec. 31, Year 3

Investment in Safebuy	3,000	
Investment income		3,000
10% of Safebuy's Year 3 net income		
Cash	7,500	
Investment in Safebuy		7,500
Receipt of dividend from Safebuy		

Under the equity method, the investor's investment account changes in direct relation to the changes taking place in the investee's equity accounts. The accounting objective is to reflect in the investor's financial statements the financial results arising from the close relationship between the companies. The equity method is effective at achieving this. Because the investor is able to influence the investee's dividend policy, dividends could end up being paid in periods during which the investee was suffering considerable losses. The cost method of reporting would reflect investment income, whereas the equity method would report investment losses during these periods.

The equity method reflects the accrual method of income measurement; the cost method does not. Even so, there have been some arguments made against the use of equity method reporting. In order to permanently finance growth, some companies retain some of their earnings by paying dividends in amounts that are less than yearly income. Other companies do not pay dividends at all for long periods of time. So while the accrual method of revenue recognition generally reflects cash flows that have already occurred, or are expected to occur soon, a portion (or all) of equity method income may never result in a cash inflow to the investor. This is because a portion of the investee's income has been allocated to permanent capital by management decision, or alternatively, will result in a cash flow only at some time in the distant future. The Canadian standard setters seem to have dismissed these arguments:

> In those situations in which the investor has the ability to exercise significant influence, shareholders ought to be informed of the results of operations of the investee, and it is appropriate to include in the results of operations of the investor its share of income or losses of the investee. The equity method of accounting for the investment provides this information. [3050.11]

Additional Features Associated with the CICA Equity Method

The previous example illustrated the basic concepts of the equity method. Besides these fundamentals, three other major features referred to in the *Handbook* must be considered. These are the accounting for nonoperating income, intercompany profits, and considerations related to the investor's acquisition cost.

Investee Income from Nonoperating Sources   The following extract outlines the accounting treatment in this situation:

> In accounting for an investment by the equity method, the investor's proportionate share of the investee's discontinued operations, extraordinary items, changes in accounting policy, corrections of errors relating to prior period financial statements and capital transactions should be disclosed in the investor's financial statements in accordance with their nature. [3050.09]

Companies report certain items separately on their income statements so that financial statement users can distinguish between the portion of net income that comes from continuing operations and the portion that comes from other sources, such as discontinued operations and extraordinary items. Retroactive restatements of prior period results and capital transactions are shown as separate components of retained earnings, or are disclosed in the footnotes. What the above paragraph is telling us is that because the equity method reflects the investor's share of changes in equity of the investee, the reader of the investor's statements should be provided with information to distinguish changes that came from the investee's continuing operations, from all other changes that occurred.

Example A Company owns 30 percent of B Company. The income statement of B Company for the current year is as follows:

B COMPANY
INCOME STATEMENT — CURRENT YEAR

Sales	$500,000
Operating expenses	200,000
Operating income before income tax	300,000
Income tax	120,000
Income from operations	180,000
Loss from discontinued operations (net of tax)	40,000
Income before extraordinary items	140,000
Extraordinary gain (net of tax)	10,000
Net income	$150,000

Upon receiving this income statement, A Company makes the following journal entry to apply the equity method:

Investment in B Company (30% × 150,000)	45,000	
Investment loss, discontinued operations*	12,000	
Investment gain, extraordinary item**		3,000
Investment income (30% × 180,000)		54,000

*   30% × 40,000
**   30% × 10,000

All three investment income items, which total $45,000, will appear on A Company's income statement. The investment loss from discontinued operations and the investment gain from extraordinary items require the same presentation as would be made if A Company had discontinued operations or extraordinary items of its own. Full footnote disclosure is required to indicate that these particular items arise from a significant influence investment accounted for by the equity method. Materiality has to be considered because these items do not require special treatment in A Company's income statement if they are not material from A Company's point of view, even though they *are* material from B Company's perspective.

Two other major features of equity method reporting as envisioned in the *Handbook* are captured in the following paragraphs:

Investment income as calculated by the equity method should be that necessary to increase or decrease the investor's income to that which would have been recognized if the results of the investee's operations had been consolidated with those of the investor. [3050.08]

Accounting for an investment under the equity method generally results in the net income of the investor being the same as the consolidated net income would have been if the financial statements of the investee had been consolidated with those of the investor. Depreciation and amortization of investee assets are based on the assigned costs of such assets at the date(s) of acquisition. The portion of the difference between the investor's cost and the amount of its underlying equity in the net assets of the investee that is similar to goodwill (equity method goodwill) is not amortized. No part of an impairment writedown of an investment accounted for by the equity method is presented in the income statement as a goodwill impairment loss (see Goodwill and Other Intangible Assets, Section 3062). Unrealized intercompany gain or loss and any gain or loss that would arise in accounting for intercompany bond holdings are eliminated. [3050.12]

Taken by themselves, these two paragraphs are difficult to interpret at this stage because of the reference made to the consolidation process. This material, which is covered in Section 1600, will be the main focus of the remaining chapters of this book. Discussed next are two major features of the consolidation process that have applications to the equity method of accounting for significant influence investments.

Acquisition Costs Greater Than Book Values   In the previous examples we recorded Jenstar's investment at its cost, but we did not consider the implications of this cost with regard to Safebuy's book value at the time. We now add a new feature to equity method reporting by indeed paying attention to the book value of an investee's net assets.

Companies' shares often trade at prices that are different from their book values. There are many reasons for this, such as current economic conditions, anticipation of future profits, and the perceived worth of the company as a whole. It is this last reason that we will now focus on. Because it uses historical costs, a balance sheet does not reflect the worth of a company's assets. The asset values that do appear are often less than current values, and some assets do not appear at all. Stock market prices often reflect some of these differences. When an investor purchases an equity position in an investee that results in significant influence (or control or joint control), the cost to the investor has to be reflected when the investor's returns from the investment are measured. The logic behind this process can be captured in the following scenario.

An investor corporation that acquires all the revenue-earning assets of an investee will allocate the total acquisition cost to the assets purchased. In order to measure the returns from these assets, it will amortize their cost against the revenues they generate as part of the matching process. Suppose that instead of buying all of the assets, the investor buys all the common shares of the investee. Logic should direct us to the conclusion that if the price is identical, the net return should be identical.[6] The investor's return is its share (100 percent in this scenario) of the investee's yearly reported income. However, the investee's earnings are based on historical cost amortizations and allocations, which do not reflect the investor's acquisition cost. To properly measure the return from its common share investment, the investor has to adjust its share of the investee's yearly net income to take this acquisition cost into account. When the investment is less than 100 percent, as in the case of significant influence, the reasoning is similar.

---

[6] This assumes that the income tax effects of either scenario would be identical.

This process of properly measuring the investor's return from investment requires that we calculate, allocate, and amortize an item we call "the purchase discrepancy." This purchase discrepancy is calculated as the difference between the investor's cost and the investor's percentage of the book value of the investee's "identifiable" net assets. The investor allocates this discrepancy to specific assets[7] of the investee, and then amortizes the allocated components to reduce its income from the investment. The allocation is based on the investor's share of the difference between current fair values and carrying values as at the date of acquisition. The amortization is based on the estimated remaining lives of the specific assets.

Prior to June 30, 2001, any goodwill resulting from the allocation of the purchase discrepancy had to be amortized over its estimated useful life, which could not exceed 40 years. On this date the *Handbook*'s requirements were changed so that goodwill that is implicit from an investment accounted for by the equity method is no longer amortized, nor is it reviewed for impairment in the same manner as goodwill from a business combination. Instead, impairment of goodwill would be deemed to have happened if the market price of the shares had permanently declined below the investor's carrying value. The write-down of the investment would reduce the unamortized purchase discrepancy and would first be allocated to write down the goodwill until it was zero. After goodwill had been removed, any further write-down would be allocated to reduce the remaining unamortized purchase discrepancy.

Note that paragraph 3050.12, which was reproduced earlier, stated that impairment write-downs of significant influence investments are not presented separately on the income statement of the investor. Rather, they would be deducted to reduce the amount of the investment income from the investee that the investor company would otherwise report.

These new requirements will probably produce substantial differences in the amount of equity method income reported by an investor. While a significant influence investment allows an investor to have some say in the activities of the investee, it does not necessarily allow unlimited access to the investee's accounting records. Because the fair values of an investee's identifiable net assets are difficult for the investor to determine, a large portion of the purchase discrepancy is usually allocated to goodwill. Before the requirements were changed, the goodwill had to be amortized on a yearly basis, which reduced the amount reported by the investor as income from the investment. The new requirements do not require this yearly charge; thus, earnings from investment will be higher, and will only be reduced in years when an impairment loss occurs.

The following example will illustrate the allocation and amortization of the purchase discrepancy.

Example   Hartley Inc. paid $40,000 to acquire 30 percent of the outstanding voting shares of Ivan Company. Ivan's net assets had a book value of $90,000 at the time, and specific plant assets were undervalued by $22,000 relative to current fair values. Hartley will determine the purchase discrepancy and its allocation by the following calculation:

---

[7] The purchase discrepancy can also be allocated to liabilities. This concept will be examined in a later chapter.

Cost of 30% investment		$40,000
Book value of Ivan's net assets[8]	90,000	
Hartley's %	30%	27,000
Purchase discrepancy		13,000
Allocated:		
Undervalued plant assets 22,000 × 30%		6,600
Unallocated — goodwill		$ 6,400

The amount of the purchase discrepancy that cannot be allocated to specific identifiable assets of the investee is considered to be the intangible asset goodwill. In some situations this amount can be negative, but we will leave all discussions of this to later chapters. Hartley's journal entry to record its 30 percent investment is:

Investment in Ivan Company	40,000	
Cash		40,000

One year later, when Ivan reports a net income of $20,000, Hartley will make the following journal entry to take up its share of this income:

Investment in Ivan Company	6,000	
Investment income		6,000

In measuring this investment income on the basis of its acquisition cost, Hartley determines that the specific undervalued plant assets of Ivan have a remaining useful life of 6 years and decides that there has been no permanent decline in the market value of Ivan's shares.

The amortization of the purchase discrepancy is accomplished by the following journal entry:

Investment income	1,100	
Investment in Ivan Company		1,100

Amortization of the purchase discrepancy as follows:

Plant assets 6,600 ÷ 6 years	=	$1,100
Goodwill	=	0
Total amortization		$1,100

Hartley's acquisition cost is now properly reflected in the $4,900 investment income, which appears as a separate item on its income statement.

Unrealized Profits   As we will see in later chapters, consolidated financial statements are what you get when you combine the financial statement of a parent company with the financial statements of its subsidiaries. The end result is the financial reporting of a single economic entity, made up of a number of separate legal entities. One of the major tasks in this process is to eliminate all intercompany transactions — especially intercompany "profits" — so that the consolidated statements reflect only transactions with outsiders. The basic premise behind the elimination is that from the point of view of this single accounting entity, "you can't make a profit selling to yourself." Any such "unrealized profits" from intercompany transfers of inventory (or other assets) must be held back until the specific assets involved are sold to outside entities.

---

[8] Net assets are equal to total assets less total liabilities. Shareholders' equity also equals net assets. In making this type of calculation, it is often easier to use the amount for shareholder's equity rather than compute the amount for net assets.

In the case of a significant influence investment, any transactions between the investor and investee (they are related parties) must be scrutinized so that incomes are not overstated through the back-and-forth transfer of assets. From an accounting perspective, any transfer is acceptable provided that both parties record the transfer at the value that it is being carried at in the records of the selling company. However, if the transfer involves a profit, that profit must be held back on an after-tax basis in the investor's equity method journal entries. When the asset in question is sold outside or consumed by the purchaser, the after-tax profit is realized through an equity method journal entry, again made by the investor. The amount of before-tax profit being held back is the difference between cost and selling price, which in the case of inventory is the gross profit. The selling company pays tax on the profit, which means that it is the after-tax gross profit that is considered unrealized until it is confirmed by a sale to an outside entity. The final dollar amount used in the journal entry depends on whether the sale was "downstream" or "upstream." The following diagram illustrates the two streams:

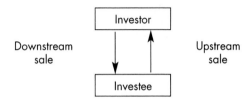

In the two examples that follow we will illustrate the differences in the handling of the two streams of sales.

Example Harrison Corp. owns 35 percent of Gunn Inc. and uses the equity method to account for this significant influence investment. During Year 1, Harrison sold inventory to Gunn and recorded a 60 percent gross profit on the transaction. At the end of Year 1, the inventory of Gunn contained items purchased from Harrison for $75,000. Harrison pays income tax at a rate of 40 percent. The items of inventory in question were sold by Gunn to outsiders in Year 2. Note that the total amount of inventory sales that Harrison made to Gunn in Year 1 is not mentioned. This amount is not an issue in this particular context, although there will have to be full disclosure about such sales in the footnotes to Harrison's financial statements.[9] What is an issue is the amount of profit that is unrealized because it has not been sold to outsiders. The calculations required are as follows:

Items in Gunn's inventory	$75,000
Gross profit percentage	60%
Unrealized before-tax profit	45,000
Income tax (40%)	18,000
Unrealized after-tax profit	$27,000

Harrison's equity method journal entry to hold back the unrealized profit from this downstream sale at the end of Year 1 is:

Investment income	27,000	
Investment in Gunn Inc.		27,000

To hold back the after-tax unrealized profit on the sale of inventory to Gunn

---

[9] *CICA Handbook*, paragraph 3840.43.

The investment income that is being reduced here is Harrison's share of Gunn's Year 1 net income. This deferral remains in force until the inventory is sold outside, at which time the entry is reversed. In this case the inventory was sold in Year 2, so the entry that Harrison will make at that time to realize the profit is:

Investment in Gunn Inc.	27,000	
Investment income		27,000
To realize the after-tax profit that was held back in Year 1		

Another Example   The previous example illustrated the handling of unrealized profits from downstream sales. In the present example, all of the facts (gross profit, tax rates, etc.) remain the same except that we assume an upstream sale in which Gunn sold the inventory to Harrison. The calculation changes slightly in this situation.

Items in Harrison's inventory	$75,000
Gross profit percentage	60%
Unrealized before-tax profit	45,000
Income tax (40%)	18,000
Unrealized after-tax profit	27,000
Harrison's ownership of Gunn	35%
Amount held back	$ 9,450

The amount of unrealized profit held back on an upstream sale is the investor's share of the profit that was recorded during the year by the investee. The investor takes up its share of the investee's net income for the year as a normal application of equity accounting, and then accounts for the fact that not all of this income was realized, because of an upstream sale of inventory.

Harrison's journal entry to hold back this unrealized profit at the end of Year 1 would be:

Investment income	9,450	
Investment in Gunn Inc.		9,450
To hold back the after-tax unrealized profit on Gunn's sale of inventory to Harrison		

At the end of Year 2, Harrison would make the following entry to realize the profit:

Investment in Gunn Inc.	9,450	
Investment income		9,450
To realize the after-tax profit that was held back in Year 1		

In the above illustrations of the holdback and realization of intercompany profits, the asset involved was inventory. The same basic concepts apply when assets other than inventory are sold in a similar manner. This topic will be discussed thoroughly in the consolidation chapters that follow.

Miscellaneous Considerations

The equity method as described in Section 3050 involves the investor recording its proportionate share of investee earnings from continuing operations adjusted for both the amortization of the purchase discrepancy and the holdback and realization of intercompany after-tax profits. Earnings from sources other than continuing operations are recorded separately. The following are some additional items that must also be considered.

Changes to and from the Equity Method The classification of long-term investments will change as the particular facts change. An investment may initially be portfolio and subsequently change to one of significant influence. This could transpire if additional shares were acquired. Once significant influence has been achieved, a switch from cost to equity methods is made on a prospective basis.[10] If there was more than one acquisition of shares, and it was the last one that gave significant influence, the investment cost used at the commencement of the equity method is the sum of the costs of the individual acquisitions. If circumstances change, significant influence may also be achieved without additional shares being acquired, in which case the equity method would commence. For example, the holdings of a large block of investee shares by another company could prevent an investor from exercising significant influence. But if that other company sells its block on the market, the investor's previous portfolio investment may now amount to significant influence.

When an investment changes from significant influence to portfolio, the equity method ceases to be appropriate and the cost method takes its place, also on a prospective basis. At this point the investment's carrying value, which was arrived at through the appropriate use of the equity method, becomes the new cost basis. The *Handbook* is unclear as to what to do with previously unrealized profits that were held back because of the related party status of the investor and investee. Logic would suggest that because the investor and investee are no longer related parties,[11] the investment account should be increased by the amounts that were previously held back.

When an investment changes from significant influence to control, the preparation of consolidated statements commences, again on a prospective basis. The concepts relating to this particular situation will be discussed at length in later chapters.

Loss in Value of Investment As previously mentioned, the carrying amount of a significant influence investment is reduced to market value if the decline is considered to be permanent. Evidence to support such permanence might include a prolonged period during which market was below carrying value, continued losses of the investee, suspension of trading in the investee, and serious going concern problems.

Losses Exceeding the Balance in the Investment Account A question arises as to the appropriate accounting when an investor's share of investee losses exceeds the carrying amount of the investment. There are two possible ways to treat this. The investor could reduce the investment account to zero and commence the use of the equity method when its share of investee earnings exceeds its share of losses. Alternatively, the investor could continue to accrue losses even though they result in a negative balance in the investment account. Section 3050 is silent on this issue, but the Emerging Issues Committee saw fit to address it with EIC-8. Their conclusion was that if the investor considers itself finished with the investee, it should not record losses past a zero balance in the investment account. However, if the investor has guaranteed the investee's obligations, or is committed to providing additional financial support, it would be appropriate to continue recording losses such that the balance in the investment account becomes negative. It is also appropriate to continue

---

[10] *Handbook*, Section 1506, "Accounting Changes," suggests that a switch from cost to equity is not considered a change in an accounting policy that would require retroactive accounting treatment (paragraph 1506.04).

[11] Paragraph 3840.03(g).

accruing investee losses if it appears that the investee is going to turn things around and become profitable at some future time. No mention is made of where to present this credit balance in the investor's balance sheet, but logically it should be shown under liabilities, and there should be full disclosure of the investor's commitments to the investee.

Gains and Losses on Sale of Investments   When all the shares that make up a long-term investment are sold, the gain (loss) is shown on the income statement and is calculated as the difference between the sale proceeds and the carrying value of the investment. When only some of the shares are sold, the gain is calculated using the average carrying value of the investment. Cost flows such as FIFO or LIFO or specific identification are not permitted. If a portion of a significant influence or a control investment is sold, a re-evaluation must be made to determine whether the previous classification is still valid.

An International Perspective

The concept of accounting for a significant influence investment using the equity method is fairly common. Many countries, including the United States, the United Kingdom, France, Germany, Spain, and Australia, use the quantitative ownership guideline of 20 percent, and so does the IASB. Some countries, including Mexico, Chile, and Brazil, use a 10 percent guideline. All of the above countries as well as the IASC require the use of the equity method. China requires the cost method for this type of investment, while Switzerland and India allow either method. Presumably, countries would apply the equity method in the same manner that Canada does — by amortizing the purchase discrepancy and deferring unrealized intercompany profits — but differences in approach may exist. For example, U.S. accounting standards require that only the investor's share of downstream unrealized profits be eliminated, while GAAP in Canada requires the elimination of all of this profit. Canada and the United States appear to be the only countries that have abandoned the amortization of goodwill, replacing it with periodic write-downs based on impairment.

Many countries have the equivalent of Canada's "temporary" and "portfolio" investments, although terms such as *minority* and *passive* seem more common than the term *portfolio*. It is in the area of valuation that we begin to see some significant differences. China values all investments (other than control) at historical cost. Investments classified as current assets are valued at the lower of cost or market in the United Kingdom, France, Germany, Australia, and Chile. Mexico reports such investments at market, with unrealized gains (losses) reflected in income. The United States also values at market, but treats gains (losses) differently in accordance with their nature: those arising from securities trading are taken into income, while those from "available for sale" securities are reflected in a separate component of shareholders' equity. The IASB allows valuation either at the lower of cost or market, or at market, and allows the unrealized gains (losses) to be reflected either in income or as a separate component of shareholders' equity.

The accounting for investments classified as long term also shows some variation. The concept of historical cost, adjusted for permanent market declines, is followed in Germany and Japan. The lower of cost or market is used in Spain, Denmark, Chile, and India; while New Zealand, Australia, France, Switzerland, and the United Kingdom allow the use of either cost or current market value. The United

States, Mexico, and Denmark require valuation at market. There is variation among these countries as to the location (income statement or equity) of adjustments to market. Predictably, the IASB allows choices regarding which valuation method is used and how the resulting unrealized gains (losses) are presented.

SUMMARY

Three types of share investments were discussed in this chapter. Temporary investments are shown in current assets because the intention is to invest surplus cash in the short term. Income from this type of investment is recognized as dividends are received, which is basically the cost method. The main focus of the chapter was on two types of long-term investments.

Portfolio investments do not allow the investor any influence over the affairs of the investee and are accounted for using the cost method. If, however, the investment enables the investor to influence the operations of the investee, it is called a significant influence investment and must be accounted for using the equity method, as described in Section 3050 of the *Handbook*. This requires the investor to record its share of all increases in the shareholders' equity of the investee, adjusted for the amortization of the purchase discrepancy and the holdback and realization of upstream and downstream profits from the sale of assets.

SELF-STUDY PROBLEM

Part A On January 1, 2002, High Inc. purchased 10% of the outstanding common shares of Lowe Corp. for $75,000. Lowe's shareholders' equity had a book value of $700,000 on this date. From High's perspective, Lowe was a long-term investment; however, it did not give High significant influence.

On January 1, 2003, High purchased an additional 25% of Lowe's shares for $300,000. This second purchase allowed High to exert significant influence over Lowe. As of this date the plant and equipment of Lowe, which had an estimated remaining life of 5 years, were undervalued by $90,000, and its patents, which had an estimated remaining life of 7 years, were undervalued by $30,000.

During the two years, Lowe reported the following:

	Net income	Dividends
2002	$200,000	$120,000
2003	270,000	130,000

Additional Information
- During 2002, High transferred assets to Lowe and recorded a profit of $35,000 on the transaction.
- During 2003, Lowe sold inventory to High at a gross profit rate of 40%. At the end of 2003, High's inventory contained purchases made from Lowe amounting to $75,000. High sold this inventory to its unrelated customers in 2004.
- Assume tax rates of 40% for both companies for all of the years involved in this question.
- On December 31, 2004, a $6,000 permanent decline in the market value of the investment was recognized.

Required:

With respect to this investment, prepare High's journal entries for both 2002 and 2003.

Part B The following are summarized income statements for the two companies for 2004:

	High Inc.	Lowe Corp.
Revenues	$900,000	$600,000
Expenses (including income tax)	450,000	400,000
Income before extraordinary items	450,000	200,000
Extraordinary loss (net of tax)	—	20,000
Net income	*$450,000	$180,000

* The net income of High does not include any investment income from its investment in Lowe Corp.

Lowe paid no dividends in 2004.

Required:

(a) Prepare the journal entries that High should make at the end of 2004 with respect to its investment in Lowe.
(b) Prepare the income statement of High, taking into consideration the journal entries in part (a).

Solution to Self-study Problem

Part A The 10% purchase is a portfolio investment in 2002, accounted for under the cost method. Because of this, the intercompany asset transfer that occurs in 2002 is considered to be between unrelated parties, which means that there are no unrealized profits as a result of the transaction. High's journal entries during 2002 are:

Investment in Lowe	75,000	
Cash		75,000
Purchase of 10% of shares of Lowe		

Cash	12,000	
Dividend revenue		12,000
10% × 120,000		

The 25% purchase in 2003 changes the investment to one of significant influence, which is accounted for prospectively. The following calculation is made as of this date:

Cost of 10%		$ 75,000
Cost of 25%		300,000
Total cost of significant influence investment		375,000
Book value of Lowe:		
On Jan. 1, 2002	700,000	
Net income 2002	200,000	
Dividends	(120,000)	
	780,000	
	35%	273,000
Purchase discrepancy		102,000
Allocated:		
Plant and equipment — 90,000 × 35%	31,500	
Patents — 30,000 × 35%	10,500	42,000
Balance — goodwill		$ 60,000

The yearly purchase discrepancy amortization during the next five years will be:

Plant and equipment	31,500 ÷ 5 years =	$ 6,300
Patents	10,500 ÷ 7 years =	1,500
		$ 7,800

Because this is now a significant influence investment, 2003 intercompany up-stream sales are between related parties, and any unrealized profits at the end of the year must be deferred. The calculation is as follows:

Items in High's inventory	$75,000
Gross profit percentage	40%
Unrealized before-tax profit	30,000
Income tax (40%)	12,000
Unrealized after-tax profit	18,000
High's ownership of Lowe	35%
Amount held back	$ 6,300

The journal entries that High makes in 2003 are as follows:

Investment in Lowe	300,000	
Cash		300,000
Purchase of 25% of shares of Lowe		
Investment in Lowe	94,500	
Investment income		94,500
35% × 270,000 net income		
Cash	45,500	
Investment in Lowe		45,500
35% × 130,000 dividends		
Investment income	7,800	
Investment in Lowe		7,800
Amortization of purchase discrepancy		
Investment income	6,300	
Investment in Lowe		6,300
To hold back unrealized profit on upstream sale of inventory		

Part B (a) Applying the CICA equity method, High makes the following journal entries in 2004:

Investment in Lowe*	63,000	
Investment loss extraordinary**	7,000	
Investment income***		70,000

```
*     35% × 180,000
**    35% × 20,000
***   35% × 200,000
```

Investment income	7,800	
Investment in Lowe		7,800
Amortization of purchase discrepancy		
Investment in Lowe	6,300	
Investment income		6,300
To realize profit on upstream sale of inventory held back in 2003		
Investment income	6,000	
Investment in Lowe		6,000
To recognize a goodwill impairment loss		

(b) Investment income — 2004

Share of ordinary net income	$70,000
Realization of profit on upstream sales	6,300
Purchase discrepancy amortization & goodwill impairment loss	(13,800)
	$62,500

HIGH INC.
INCOME STATEMENT
(year ended December 31, 2004)

Operating revenue	$900,000
Expenses (incl. income tax)	450,000
Income from operations	450,000
Investment income*	62,500
Income before extraordinary items	512,500
Investment loss — extraordinary (net of tax)*	7,000
Net income	$505,500

* A footnote would disclose that these items came from a 35% investment in Lowe, accounted for using the equity method.

APPENDIX

A Listing of Emerging Issue Abstracts

Number	Topic	Related Handbook Section
EIC–3	Mid-term Hedging of a Long-term Foreign Currency Denominated Monetary Item	1650
EIC–8	Recognition of an Equity Accounted Investee's Losses in Excess of the Investment	3050
EIC–10	Reverse Takeover Accounting	1581
EIC–11	Changes in Reporting Currency	1650
EIC–12	Capitalization of Interest Costs on Investments in Potential Takeover Targets	1581
EIC–14	Adjustments to the Purchase Equation Subsequent to the Acquisition Date	1581, 1600
EIC–16	Short-term Foreign Currency Obligations Under Long-term Debt Facilities	1650
EIC–17	Deferral and Amortization of Foreign Exchange Gains and Losses on Debt with Contractual Terms That Differ from the Intended Repayment Period	1650
EIC–26	Reductions in the Net Investment of Self-sustaining Foreign Operations	1650
EIC–35	Accounting for Discontinued Operations Subsequently Retained	3475
EIC–38	Accounting for Newly Formed Joint Ventures	3055
EIC–42	Costs Incurred in Business Combinations	1581
EIC–45	Discontinued Operations	3475
EIC–55	Identifiable Assets Acquired in a Business Combination	1581
EIC–62	Measurement of Cost of a Business Acquisition Effected by Issuing Shares	1581
EIC–63	Income Statement Presentation of Results of a Portion of a Business Segment Held for Disposal	3475
EIC–64	Goodwill Disclosures	1600, 3062

EIC–66	Transfer of a Business Between Entities Under Common Control	1581
EIC–73	Buy-out Transactions	1581
EIC–75	Scope of CICA 3860 — Interests in Subsidiaries Presented in Non-consolidated Financial Statements	3050
EIC–81	Non-monetary Transactions in Which the Transferor Receives an Equity Interest in the Transferee	1590, 3050, 3055
EIC–89	Exchanges of Ownership Interests Between Entities Under Common Control — Wholly and Partially-Owned Subsidiaries	1581, 1600
EIC–90	Future Income Tax Assets and Liabilities of an Integrated Foreign Operation — Accounting for Unrealized Translation Gains and Losses	1650, 3465
EIC–92	Arms-Length Buy-Out of a Business Followed by an Amalgamation	1581, 1600
EIC–99	Future Income Taxes in Business Combinations That Do Not Involve the Recognition of Goodwill as an Intangible Asset Presented Separately on the Balance Sheet	1581, 3465, 3062
EIC–106	Application of CICA 3465 to Investments Accounted for by the Equity Method	3050
EIC–110	Accounting for Acquired Future Tax Benefits in Certain Purchase Transactions	1581
EIC–115	Segment Disclosure — Application of the Aggregation Criteria in CICA 1701	1701
EIC–119	The Date of Acquisition of a Business Combination	1581, 1590, 1600
EIC–120	CICA 3465 — Future Income Taxes Related to Intangible Assets Acquired in a Business Combination	1581, 3062

REVIEW QUESTIONS

1. Business combinations and the preparation of consolidated financial statements are really only a subset of a "big picture." In one sentence, describe the big picture.

2. How is the concept of a business combination related to the concept of a parent–subsidiary relationship?

3. What is the purpose of the Emerging Issues Committee? Are the abstracts issued by this committee considered to be GAAP in Canada?

4. Distinguish between the financial reporting for portfolio investments and that for significant influence investments.

5. What is the difference between a "control" investment and a "joint control" investment?

6. What event is necessary before a Canadian company is permitted to revalue all its assets and liabilities?

7. What is the purpose of the *Handbook* section on segment disclosures?

8. What criteria would be used to determine whether the equity method should be used to account for a particular investment?

9. The equity method records dividends as a reduction in the investment account. Explain why.

10. What factors would be used as evidence that an investor had obtained significant influence over an investee?

11. The Ralston Company owns 35% of the outstanding voting shares of Purina Inc. Under what circumstances would Ralston determine that it is inappropriate to report this investment in its financial statements using the equity method?

12. Even though the equity method is considered to be part of GAAP, some theoretical arguments have been made against it. Explain what they are.

13. An investor uses the equity method to report its investment in an investee. During the current year the investee reports an extraordinary gain on its income statement. How should this item be reflected in the investor's financial statements?

14. Ashton Inc. acquired a 40% interest in Villa Corp. at a bargain price that was substantially below book value, because Villa had suffered significant losses in past years. Ashton's cost was $200,000. In the first year after acquisition, Villa reported a loss of $700,000. Using the equity method, how should Ashton account for this loss?

15. Under the equity method, a portion of an investor's purchase price is assigned either to specific assets of the investee or to goodwill. How is this done? Why is it done?

16. Able Company holds a 40% interest in Baker Corp. During the year, Able sold a portion of this investment. How should this investment be reported after the sale?

17. What differentiates a downstream sale from an upstream sale? Are the equity method journal entries the same for each?

MULTIPLE CHOICE

1. Which one of the following accounting methods is recommended by *Handbook* Section 3010 for reporting temporary investments?
   a. Portfolio method.
   b. Lower of cost or market method.
   c. Equity method.
   d. Consolidation.

2. Which one of the following would not be a factor to consider when determining whether an investment results in significant influence?
   a. Whether the investor held a position on the investee's board of directors.
   b. Whether the investor purchased a significant amount of the investee's production output.
   c. Whether the investor and the investee operated in the same country.
   d. Whether the investor and the investee exchanged technical expertise.

3. Perez Inc. owns 25% of Senior Ltd. During 2002, Perez sold goods with a 40% gross profit to Senior. Senior sold all of these goods in 2002. How should Perez report the effect of the intercompany sale on its 2002 income statement?
   a. Sales and cost of goods sold should be reduced by the amount of the intercompany sales.
   b. Sales and cost of goods sold should be reduced by 25% of the amount of the intercompany sales.
   c. Investment income should be reduced by 25% of the gross profit on the intercompany sales.
   d. No adjustment is necessary.

4. When an investor uses the equity method to account for investments in common stock, how should cash dividends received by the investor from the investee be recorded?
   a. As a deduction from the investor's share of investee profits.
   b. As dividend income.
   c. As a deduction from the shareholders' equity account dividend to shareholders.
   d. As a deduction from the investment account.

5. Which of the following is not an indication that an investor company has the ability to significantly influence an investee?
   a. Material intercompany transactions.
   b. The investor company owns 30% of the investee company but another owner holds the remaining 70%.
   c. Interchange of personnel.
   d. Technological dependency.

6. On January 1, 2000, X Company acquired 20% of Y Company for $4,000,000. On the acquisition date Y Company had common shares of $5,000,000 and retained earnings of $10,000,000. The only purchase price discrepancy adjustment is the annual amortization of the purchase discrepancy of $100,000 (X's portion). From January 1, 2000, to December 31, 2002, Y Company earned net income of $3,000,000 and paid dividends of $1,000,000. What would be the balance in the Investment in Y Company account in the accounting records of X Company on December 31, 2002?
   a. Assuming X Company uses the cost method, $4,100,000.
   b. Assuming X Company uses the cost method, $4,300,000.
   c. Assuming X Company uses the equity method, $4,100,000.
   d. Assuming X Company uses the equity method, $4,400,000.

   (CGA *adapted*)

7. How should an investment be accounted for where the investor exercises significant influence over the investee?
   a. At cost plus the parent's share of the subsidiary's change in retained earnings since the date of acquisition.
   b. At cost plus the parent's share of the subsidiary's net income, adjusted annually through retained earnings.
   c. At market value with changes in market value adjusted through income.
   d. At market value with changes in market value adjusted through retained earnings.

   (CGA *adapted*)

Use the following data for Questions 8 and 9.

AB Company purchased 25% of the shares of KC Corporation on July 1, 2002, for $100,000, which allows it to exercise significant influence. Both companies had December 31, 2002 year-ends. During 2002, KC had a net income of $120,000 ($10,000/month) and paid dividends of $80,000 ($20,000 every 3 months, on the last day of each fiscal quarter).

8. As at December 31, 2002, how much would AB's investment in KC be on AB's balance sheet?
   a. $100,000
   b. $105,000
   c. $110,000
   d. $120,000

9. Assuming that AB's 25% investment in KC did not allow it to exercise signifi-
    cant influence, how much income would AB report from its investment in
    KC for the year ended December 31, 2002?
    a. $10,000
    b. $20,000
    c. $30,000
    d. $40,000

10. RU Ltd. has invested in several domestic manufacturing corporations. Which
    of the following investments would most likely be accounted for under the
    equity method on the consolidated financial statements of RU?
    a. A holding of 2,000 of the 50,000 outstanding common shares of SU.
    b. A holding of 3,000 of the 10,000 outstanding preferred shares of TU.
    c. A holding of 15,000 of the 60,000 outstanding common shares of XU.
    d. A holding of 20,000 of the 25,000 outstanding common shares of VU.

    (CGA adapted)

11. On January 1, 2002, Top Company purchased a 10% interest in the common
    shares of Bottom Ltd. for $50,000. Bottom reported net incomes and paid
    dividends as follows:

    2002 — net income $60,000; dividends paid $80,000.

    2003 — net income $105,000; dividends paid $80,000.

    Assume that Top uses the cost method to account for its investment in
    Bottom. Which of the following is the amount that a balance sheet for Top
    would report as "Investment in Bottom" at December 31, 2003?
    a. $48,000
    b. $49,500
    c. $50,000
    d. $50,500
    e. none of the above.

12. Pipe Ltd. acquired a 30% interest in the common shares of Tobacco Ltd. on
    January 1, 2002. The purchase difference of $10,000 was identified and allo-
    cated entirely to patents, which were estimated to have a 10-year useful life.
    During 2002, Tobacco sold merchandise to Pipe at 50% gross profit. At
    December 31, 2002, Pipe's inventory includes merchandise from Tobacco pur-
    chased by Pipe for $4,800. For 2002, Tobacco reported net income of $70,000
    and paid dividends of $20,000. Both companies are subject to 40% tax rates.

    If Pipe uses the equity method to account for its investment in Tobacco,
    how much investment income will it report in 2002?
    a. $18,560
    b. $19,568
    c. $20,000
    d. $21,000

Use the following data for Questions 13 and 14.

On January 1, 2002, Xanadu Co. purchased a 20% interest in Zap Inc. for
$4,000,000. In 2002, Zap reported net income from operations of $525,000 and
an extraordinary gain of $83,000 (net of tax). Zap declared and paid dividends of
$90,000 on December 31, 2002.

13. Assume the above is a portfolio investment. Which of the following is the amount
    that would be reported on Xanadu's 2002 income statement relating to Zap?

    a. Investment income of $116,600.
    b. Dividend revenue of $90,000.
    c. Investment income of $105,000 and investment gain extraordinary item of $16,600.
    d. Dividend revenue of $18,000.

14. Assume the above is a significantly influenced investment. Which of the following is the amount that would be reported on Xanadu's 2002 income statement relating to Zap?
    a. Investment income of $121,600 and investment gain extraordinary item of $16,600.
    b. Investment income of $121,600.
    c. Investment income of $105,000 and investment gain extraordinary item of $16,600.
    d. Dividend revenue of $18,000.

Use the following data for Questions 15 to 17.

On January 1, 2002, Bean Co. purchased a 30% interest in Dod Co. for $250,000. On this date, Dod's shareholders' equity was $500,000. The carrying value of Dod's identifiable net assets was equal to book values, except for equipment, which was undervalued by $50,000. This equipment had an estimated remaining useful life of 10 years. Dod reported net income of $100,000 for 2002 and paid dividends of $20,000. Bean correctly reports this significant influence investment using the equity method. Both companies have a December 31 year-end.

During 2003, Dod sold merchandise it had purchased for $60,000 to Bean for $100,000. At the end of 2003, Bean held 50% of this merchandise in its inventory. Both companies are taxed at 40%. For the year ended December 31, 2003, Dod reported net income of $150,000 and paid dividends of $40,000. On December 31, 2003, Bean recorded a permanent decline in the market value of its investment amounting to $4,250.

15. Which of the following is the amount that Bean would report as its investment in Dod at December 31, 2002?
    a. $275,500
    b. $272,500
    c. $274,000
    d. $278,750

16. Which of the following is the amount that represents the adjustment required to the investment income in 2003 for unrealized profit (after tax)?
    a. $3,600
    b. $6,000
    c. $8,000
    d. $12,000

17. Which of the following is the amount that would be reported for investment income on Bean's 2003 financial statements?
    a. $45,000
    b. $35,650
    c. $41,400
    d. $27,600

18. INV owns 10% of the shares of PLA Inc. For five years now, PLA has been paying a regular dividend at the end of its fiscal year. PLA's year-end is December 31, while INV's is September 30. When should the dividend be recognized as revenue in INV's books?
    a. On September 30, since there is reasonable certainty that it will be paid.
    b. On the day on which INV receives the cheque.
    c. On the day on which PLA's board of directors adopts a resolution declaring a dividend.
    d. On the day that PL mails the cheque, the postmark providing proof.

(CGA adapted)

19. Price Co. has gradually been acquiring shares of Berry Co. and now owns 37% of the outstanding voting common shares. The remaining 63% of the shares are held by members of the family of the company founder. To date, the family has elected all members of the board of directors, and Price Co. has not been able to obtain a seat on the board. Price is hoping eventually to buy a block of shares from an elderly family member and thus one day own 60%.

    How should the investment in Berry Co. be reported in the financial statements of Price Co.?
    a. Consolidation.
    b. Cost method.
    c. Equity method.
    d. Market value.

(CGA adapted)

20. PCI is a distributor of maintenance equipment. Early in 2002, PCI acquired 165,000 voting shares of Duracom (a 25% voting interest) for a total consideration of $165,000. PCI is one of Duracom's major customers. PCI invested in Duracom to ensure a degree of stability in the price and quality of its supplies. In 2002 and 2003, Duracom earned a net income of $60,000 and $80,000 respectively, and declared annual dividends of $40,000 to holders of voting shares. On December 31, 2003, the fair market value of Duracom's shares was $0.90 per share. On March 15, 2004, when PCI's financial statements were finalized, Duracom shares were trading at $1.10.

    How should PCI record its investment in Duracom in its balance sheet as at December 31, 2003?
    a. At $148,500, with the $165,000 cost of the purchase presented as additional information.
    b. At $165,000, with the fair market value of the shares presented as additional information.
    c. At $180,000, with no additional information presented about fair market value.
    d. At $181,500, with the $165,000 cost of the purchase presented as additional information.

(CGA adapted)

CASES

Case 1   Floyd's Specialty Foods Inc. (FSFI) operates over 60 shops throughout Ontario. The company was founded by George Floyd when he opened a single shop in the city of Cornwall. This store sold prepared dinners and directed its products at customers who were too busy to prepare meals after a long day at work. The concept proved to be very successful and more stores were opened in Cornwall. Recently new stores were opened in five other Ontario cities. Up to the current year, the shares of FSFI have been owned entirely by Floyd. However during this year, the company suffered severe cash flow problems, due to too-rapid expansion exacerbated by a major decline in economic activity. Profitability suffered and creditors threatened to take legal action for long-overdue accounts. To avoid bankruptcy, Floyd sought additional financing from his old friend James Connelly, who is a majority shareholder of Cornwall Autobody Inc. (CAI). Subsequently, CAI paid $950,000 cash to FSFI to acquire enough newly issued shares of common stock for a one-third interest.

At the end of this year, CAI's accountants are discussing how they should properly report this investment in the company's financial statements.

One argues for maintaining the asset at original cost, saying, "What we have done is to advance money to bail out these stores. Floyd will continue to run the organization with little or no attention to us, so in effect we have loaned him money. After all, what does anyone in our company know about the specialty food business? My guess is that as soon as the stores become solvent, Floyd will want to buy back our shares."

Another accountant disagrees, stating that the equity method is appropriate. "I realize that our company is not capable of running a specialty food company. But the rules state that ownership of over 20% is evidence of significant influence."

A third accountant supports equity method reporting for a different reason. "If the investment gives us the ability to exert significant influence, that is all that is required. We don't have to actually exert it. One-third of the common shares certainly gives us that ability."

Required:

How should Cornwall Autobody Inc. account for its investment? Your answer should include a discussion of all three accountants' positions.

Case 2 Magno Industries Ltd. is a major supplier to the automotive replacement parts market, selling parts to nearly every segment of the industry. Magno has a September 30 year-end.

During January 2002, Magno acquired a 13% interest in the common stock of Grille-to-Bumper Automotive Stores and in June 2002 it acquired an additional 15 percent. Grille-to-Bumper is a retail chain of company-owned automotive replacement part stores operating in most Canadian provinces. Its shares trade on the Canadian Venture Exchange. Grille-to-Bumper has a December 31 year-end and, despite being profitable each year for the last 10 years, has never paid a dividend. While Magno occasionally makes sales to Grille-to-Bumper, it has never been one of its major suppliers.

After the second acquisition of Grille-to-Bumper's shares, Magno Industries contacted Grille-to-Bumper to obtain certain financial information and to discuss mutual timing problems with respect to financial reporting. In the initial contact, Magno found Grille-to-Bumper to be unco-operative. In addition, Grille-to-Bumper accused Magno of attempting to take it over. Magno replied that it had no intention of attempting to gain control, but rather was only interested in making a sound long-term investment. Grille-to-Bumper was not impressed with this explanation and refused to have any further discussions regarding future information exchanges and the problems created by a difference in year-ends.

At the year-end of September 30, 2002, Magno's management expressed a desire to use the equity method to account for its investment. On that date, the market value of its investment in Grille-to-Bumper common stock had declined by 8.5% over its acquisition cost.

Required:

1. What method of accounting would you recommend Magno Industries use for its investment in Grille-to-Bumper Automotive common stock? As part of your answer, discuss the alternatives available.
2. Why would the management of Magno want to use the equity method to account for the investment, as compared to other alternatives that you have discussed?
3. Are there any circumstances under which the method you have recommended might have to be changed? If so, how would Magno Industries account for such a change?

PROBLEMS

Problem 1 On January 1, 2002, Anderson Corporation paid $750,000 for 20% of the outstanding shares of Carter Inc. The investment was considered to be significant influence. The balance sheet of Carter showed net assets of $3,000,000 on this date. Any purchase discrepancy was allocated to equipment with a remaining life of 10 years. In 2002, Carter reported earnings of $95,000; in 2003 its earnings were $105,000. Dividends paid were $50,000 in each of the two years.

Required:

Calculate the balance in Anderson's investment account as at December 31, 2003.

Problem 2 Baskin's purchased 40% of Robbin's on January 1, 2002, at a cost of $550,000. This was considered to be significant influence. Robbin's balance sheet reported assets of $1,500,000 and liabilities of $600,000 on that date. A building with an estimated remaining life of 8 years is undervalued by $160,000 on Robbin's balance sheet. At the end of 2002, Robbin's reported a net income of $85,000 and declared dividends of $32,000. Baskin's wrote down its investment by $6,300 on December 31, 2002.

Required:

Calculate the balance in Baskin's investment account as at December 31, 2002.

Problem 3 Pender Corp. owns 30% of Saltspring Inc. On the last day of the current year, Saltspring buys inventory at a cost of $75,000 and sells it to Pender for $100,000 cash. Pender is still holding this inventory. Assume a 40% tax rate.

Required:

Prepare the journal entry relating to this transaction that Pender should make at the end of the current year, assuming that this is:
(a) a portfolio investment.
(b) a significant influence investment.

Problem 4 On January 1, 2002, Warner Corporation purchased 30% of the outstanding common shares of Rexdale Limited for $1,250,000. On that date the net assets of Rexdale had a book value of $4,000,000, and all of the individual assets of Rexdale had fair values that were equal to their book values except for:

	Fair value	Book value
Buildings (remaining life 10 years)	$890,000	$820,000

The following relates to Rexdale since the acquisition date:

Year	Net income	Dividends paid
2002	$ 35,000	$50,000
2003	100,000	50,000

Required:

(a) Assume that the number of shares held by Warner is enough to give it significant influence over Rexdale. Prepare all the journal entries that Warner should make regarding this investment in 2002 and 2003.

(b) Assume that Warner does *not* have significant influence. Prepare all the journal entries that Warner should make regarding this investment in 2002 and 2003.

Problem 5 Poole Corp. owns 45% of Campbell Company, which enables it to exercise significant influence over that company. During the current year the companies sold merchandise to each other. At the end of the current year a portion of this merchandise remained in the inventory of both companies.

Required:

(a) How is the amount of unrealized profit calculated?

(b) What is the distinction between an upstream transfer and a downstream transfer?

(c) Does the direction (upstream or downstream) affect the amount of profit held back?

(d) Explain how Poole would calculate the amount of investment income to recognize this year.

(e) Explain how Poole would calculate the amount of investment income next year.

(f) Suppose that none of the merchandise transferred between the two companies remained in inventory at the end of the current year, but each company recorded a substantial profit in its sales to the other company. Would the fact that these transfers were made during the year affect how the equity method was applied?

(g) How would these intercompany transfers affect the financial reporting in the current year by Campbell?

Problem 6 On January 1, Year 1, Investor Ltd. made an open market purchase representing 25% of the outstanding shares of Investee Corp. The cost of the investment was $195,000, and the shareholders' equity of Investee amounted to $510,000 on this date. Investor plans to treat any difference between the investment's cost and the proportionate share of the shareholders' equity of Investee as equipment to be amortized on a straight-line basis over 5 years.

Investee has a December 31 year-end. Its income statements for the next two years showed the following:

	Year 1	Year 2
Net income (loss) before extraordinary items	$300,000	$(50,000)
Extraordinary gain (net of tax)	45,000	—
Net income (loss)	$345,000	$(50,000)

On December 31 in each of years 1 and 2, Investee paid dividends of $90,000.

Required:

(a) Prepare Investor's journal entries in each of the two years, assuming that this is a significant influence investment.

(b) Prepare Investor's journal entries in each of the two years, assuming that this is a portfolio investment.

Problem 7   On January 1, 2002, Donatello Inc. acquired 30% of the outstanding voting shares of Nestell Corp. for $400,000. The balance sheet of Nestell and the fair market value of its assets and liabilities on this date were as follows:

		Fair value
Accounts receivable	$ 200,000	$200,000
Inventory	300,000	300,000
Plant assets (net)	800,000	860,000
	$1,300,000	
Liabilities	$ 100,000	100,000
Common shares	700,000	
Retained earnings	500,000	
	$1,300,000	

Nestell's plant assets had a remaining life of 10 years on this date.

The following are the income statements of the two companies as at December 31, 2002.

	Donatello	Nestell
Sales	$900,000	$700,000
Operating expenses (including tax)	600,000	500,000
Net income from continuing operations	300,000	200,000
Extraordinary gain (loss)(net of tax)	25,000	(80,000)
Net income	$325,000	$120,000

On December 31, 2002, Donatello received a dividend from Nestell amounting to $50,000. Because the company's accountant was not certain how to properly record it, an account called "suspense" was credited with $50,000. A permanent decline in the market value of the investment of $1,100 was also recorded.

Required:

PART A

Assume that this is a significant influence investment requiring the equity method of accounting.

(a) Prepare all the journal entries with regard to this investment that Donatello Inc. would be required to make in 2002.

(b) Prepare a summarized income statement for Donatello, taking into account the journal entries in (a) above.

PART B

Assume that this is a portfolio investment requiring the cost method of accounting.

(a) Prepare all the journal entries with regard to this investment that Donatello would be required to make in 2002.

(b) Prepare a summarized income statement for Donatello taking into account the journal entries in (a) above.

Problem 8   Crown Inc. owns 35% of the shares of Jewel Corp. and has the ability to significantly influence the operations and decision making of that company. On January 1, 2002, the balance in the investment in Jewel account was $340,000. Amortization associated with the investment was $12,000 per year. On December 31, 2002, Jewel reported earnings of $85,000 and declared dividends of $20,000. In 2001, Jewel had sold inventory costing $24,000 to Crown for $40,000. This merchandise was still on hand in Crown's inventory at December 31, 2001, and was finally sold to Crown's outside customers in 2002. During 2002, Crown sold inventory to Jewel and recorded a profit of $50,000 on the transaction. On December 31, 2002, 30% of this inventory was still on hand. Assume a 40% tax rate.

The following summarized income statement was prepared by the accountant for Crown Inc. before any equity method journal entries were prepared with respect to the investment in Jewel.

CROWN INC.
INCOME STATEMENT — 2002

Sales	$997,000
Operating expenses (including income tax)	625,000
Net income	$372,000

Required:

(a) Prepare a summarized income statement for Crown after the investment in Jewel has been accounted for in accordance with GAAP.
(b) What is the balance in the investment account at the end of 2002?

Problem 9   On January 1, Year 1, Parkade Company purchased, for $89,000, 35% of the outstanding voting shares of Summit Company. The following is Summit's balance sheet at that date:

	Book value
Cash	$ 20,000
Accounts receivable	30,000
Equipment (net)	80,000
	$130,000
Accounts payable	$ 10,000
Common stock	20,000
Retained earnings	100,000
	$130,000

Book values were equal to fair values except for equipment, which had a net fair value of $100,000. Summit is depreciating the equipment on a straight-line basis, and the remaining life is 7 years. The original salvage value was $10,000. Summit reported profits and paid dividends as follows:

	Profits	Dividends
Year 1	$10,000	$ 5,000
Year 2	15,000	15,000
Year 3	20,000	30,000

Required:

(a) Calculate the amount of goodwill at the date of acquisition of this investment.
(b) Calculate the balance in Parkade Company's investment account at the end of Year 3 if the equity method is used.
(c) Calculate the balance in this account if the cost method is used.

(*CGA adapted*)

CHAPTER 3
Business Combinations

CHAPTER OUTLINE

LEARNING OBJECTIVES

After studying this chapter, you should be able to do the following:

- Define a business combination, and describe the two basic forms for achieving a business combination.
- Describe the current acceptable method of accounting for a business combination.
- Compare and contrast the purchase and pooling methods.
- Prepare a balance sheet immediately after a purchase of net assets business combination, using the purchase method.
- Prepare a balance sheet immediately after a purchase of shares business combination, using the purchase method.

Introduction

In Chapter 2 we examined the accounting for two types of long-term intercorporate investments: portfolio and significant influence. The next seven chapters are largely devoted to the accounting for a third type — long-term investments that enable the investor to control the investee. Before we explore this topic, we must examine the accounting for a business combination. The definition of a business combination also uses the term *control*; it follows that there is a direct relationship between a business combination and the subsequent accounting for a long-term investment that grants control.

"Business combination" is an accounting term that describes a

transaction whereby one economic unit unites with or obtains control over another economic unit regardless of the legal avenue by which such control is obtained and regardless of the form of economic unit emerging from the transaction. A *conglomerate business combination* involves economic units operating in widely different industries. A *horizontal business combination* involves economic units whose products are similar. A *vertical business combination* involves economic units where the output from one can be used as input for another.[1]

Other terms that are often used synonymously with the term business combination are takeover, amalgamation, acquisition, and merger. The *CICA Handbook* defines and outlines the concept of a business combination in the following paragraphs:

A business combination occurs when an enterprise acquires net assets that constitute a business, or acquires equity interests of one or more other enterprises and obtains control over that enterprise or enterprises. [1581.06]

(Control in this section has the same meaning as the term that is defined and explained in Section 1590.)

A business combination might involve either incorporated or unincorporated enterprises. This Section applies equally to a business combination in which one or more enterprises are merged or become subsidiaries; one enterprise transfers net assets or its owners transfer their equity interests to another; or all enterprises transfer net assets or the owners of those enterprises transfer their equity interests to a newly formed enterprise (some of which are referred to as roll-up or put-together transactions). All such transactions are business combinations regardless of whether the form of consideration given is cash, other assets, a business or a subsidiary of the enterprise, debt, common or preferred shares, or other equity interests, or a combination of those forms, and regardless of whether the former owners of one of the combining enterprises as a group retain or receive a majority of the voting rights of the combined enterprise. An exchange of a business for a business also is a business combination. [1581.07]

This Section does not apply to the formation of a joint venture. However, this Section applies when a joint venture enters into a transaction meeting the definition of a business combination. [1581.04]

A business combination does not include the purchase of a single asset or a group of assets that does not constitute a business. [1581.08]

For a business combination to exist, one economic unit must control substantially all of the net assets of another economic unit. The purchase of some but not

---

[1] *Terminology for Accountants*, 4th edition, Toronto: CICA, 1992, p. 35.

all of an entity's assets is not considered a business combination. While the units involved are usually incorporated, this is not a requirement for a business combination. Also, the units involved cannot have been under common control immediately before the combination. The transfer of assets or the exchange of shares between two subsidiaries of the same parent, or between a parent and its subsidiary, would not be considered a business combination.[2]

Item of Interest   For example, in July 1998 the Bank of Nova Scotia announced that it was combining its two in-house investment management companies into a single company, to be called Scotia Cassels Investment Counsel Ltd. The companies involved were Scotia Investment Management Limited and Cassels Blaikie Investment Management. The announcement described this as a $13 billion merger, but because both of the combining companies were subsidiaries of the Bank of Nova Scotia, this amalgamation did not meet the accounting definition of a business combination.[3]

Business combinations are frequent events in Canada and the United States and throughout the world. Hardly a week passes without some reference in the press to actual or proposed takeovers and mergers. Attention often focuses on the key players and the strategies involved. The attempted leveraged buyout of the American company RJR Nabisco generated such interest that it was the subject of several books, as well as a movie, *Barbarians at the Gate*.

Business combinations can be described as either friendly or hostile. Often a merger is initiated by one company submitting a formal tender offer to the shareholders of another company. In a friendly combination, the top management and the board of directors of the companies involved negotiate the terms of the combination and then submit the proposal to the shareholders of both companies along with a recommendation for approval.

Sometimes one company will put up for sale a portion of its business that it no longer wishes to operate. A friendly combination occurs when another company either agrees to buy these assets at the requested selling price or submits a bid for them.

Item of Interest   In June 2001, Bristol-Myers Squibb Co. announced that it was buying the drug business of EI du Pont de Nemours & Co. in a US$7.8 billion cash deal. The purpose of the acquisition was to give Bristol-Myers a larger inventory of AIDS drugs. Dupont, the number one chemical company in the United States, announced that it would use some of the proceeds to buy back a portion of its outstanding shares.

Item of Interest   In 2000, Unilever Corp. paid $20.3 billion for Bestfoods Inc., which included 19 bakery plants in the state of New York with annual sales of $1.7 billion. To address antitrust concerns, Unilever put its bakery assets up for sale in 2001 and received bids from Sara Lee Corp, Grupo Bimbo de Mexico, and the eventually winner of the bidding process, George Weston Ltd. of Canada.

An unfriendly combination occurs when the board of directors of the target company recommends that its shareholders reject the tender offer.

---

[2] *CICA Handbook*, paragraph 1581.03.

[3] However, note that the accounting involved in the merger of these two companies into one would have been exactly the same as that which is described for a pooling of interests business combination (see Appendix B).

Item of Interest An example that dominated the news in the early part of 2001 was the Trilogy Retail Enterprises LP takeover offer for Chapters Inc. Trilogy, owned by Gerald Schwartz and Heather Reisman, wanted to merge Chapters with Indigo Books, owned by Reisman. The management of Chapters resisted the takeover and persuaded Future Shop Ltd. to come to its rescue with a competing offer. Eventually Trilogy won the battle and Chapters was merged with Indigo. Later in the year, Future Shop itself received a takeover offer from Best Buy Co. Inc., which is head-quartered in Minneapolis. The directors of Future Shop recommended acceptance of the offer.

The management of the target company will often employ defences to resist the takeover. They include:

- *Poison pill.* This occurs when a company issues rights to its existing shareholders, exercisable only in the event of a potential takeover, to purchase additional shares at prices below market. Chapters attempted to use such a plan to squash Trilogy's takeover, but on appeal by Trilogy, the Ontario Securities Commission disallowed the poison pill.

- *Pac-man defence.* This involves the target company making an unfriendly countervailing takeover offer to the shareholders of the company that is attempting to take it over.

- *White knight.* In this case, the target company searches out another company that will come to its rescue with a more appealing offer for its shares. Example: In February 2001, it was reported that Anadarko Petroleum Corp. had agreed to buy Berkley Petroleum Corp. for $1.7 billion in cash in a friendly deal that out-bid a hostile bid made by Hunt Oil Corp. Hunt had made an offer in December 2000, and Berkley's management scrambled to find a white knight after rejecting the offer and refusing to take it to their shareholders for approval.

- *Selling the crown jewels.* This involves selling certain desirable assets to other companies so the would-be acquirer loses interest.

Business combinations have always been a part of business life, but in the past decade or so they have been increasing dramatically, both in number and in sheer size. Each new combination that we hear about seems to be larger than any that preceded it.

Item of Interest The $180-billion AOL acquisition of Time Warner was the largest ever, and when it was announced analysts estimated that $158 billion of the acquisition price would be reflected as goodwill.

The media coverage of these mergers has been extensive; in addition, many government agencies have been scrutinizing them closely to ascertain whether antitrust or similar laws are being breached.

A major cause of this increased merger activity has been the emergence of the global corporation. In order to access markets in other countries, companies have been searching for takeover targets in these countries. In the high-tech area, companies have always looked for new innovative products, and often have determined that it is more suitable to buy them than to develop them on their own. While the ultimate aim is to increase future profitability, one writer has indicated that approximately two-thirds of all mergers result in a loss in value to the acquiring company.[4] Chrysler-Daimler Benz, ATT-NCR, and Nortel Networks are examples of well-known companies whose merger activities have been less than successful.

Item of Interest   In May 2001, Nortel Networks Corp. announced that it had closed the doors on Promatory Communications Inc. of Freemont, California. Nortel acquired Promatory in January 2000 for US$778 million in shares.

At least two companies are involved in a business combination, and the initial thrust to combine will usually come from one of the companies involved; thus, we can visualize one company (the acquirer) initiating the takeover of another company (the acquiree). The accounting for the combination involves looking at the event in a similar fashion. In some situations, the company that initiated the combination is accounted for as if it were the acquiree. Such a situation is described as a reverse takeover. The accounting for reverse takeovers is discussed in Chapter 4.

In the next section of this chapter we discuss the two basic forms of business combinations. The discussion then proceeds to the accounting for business combinations and the acceptable methods that have been used. We will then focus on current GAAP in Canada.

Forms of Business Combinations

Essentially, there are only two forms of business combinations. One company can obtain control over the net assets of another company by (a) purchasing its net assets, or (b) acquiring enough of its voting shares to control the use of its net assets. In examining these two forms of combination, one must also consider closely the method of payment used. Payment can be cash, or promises to pay cash in the future, or the issuance of shares, or some combination of these. As we will see later, the method of payment has a direct bearing on the determination of which company is the acquirer.

Purchase of Assets   An obvious way to obtain control over another company's assets is to purchase them outright. The selling company is left only with the cash or other consideration received as payment from the purchaser, and the liabilities present before the sale. Alternatively, the acquirer can purchase all of the assets of the acquiree and assume all its liabilities. In either case, the shareholders of the selling company have to approve the sale, as well as decide whether their company should be wound up or should continue operations.

Purchase of Shares   An alternative to the purchase of assets is for the acquirer to purchase enough voting shares from the shareholders of the acquiree that it can determine the acquiree's strategic operating, investing, and financing policies without the co-operation of others. This is the most common form of combination, and it is often achieved through a tender offer made by the management of the acquirer to the shareholders of the acquiree. These shareholders are invited to exchange their shares for cash or for shares of the acquirer company.

The share purchase form of combination is usually the least costly to the acquirer because control can be achieved by purchasing less than 100 percent of the outstanding voting shares. In addition, in Canada there can be important tax advantages to the vendor if shares rather than assets are purchased.

---

[4] See *CA magazine*, May 2001, p. 5.

Because the transaction is between the acquirer and the acquiree's shareholders, the acquiree's accounting for its assets and liabilities is not affected,[5] and this company carries on as a subsidiary of the acquirer. The acquirer becomes a parent company and therefore must consolidate its subsidiary when it prepares its financial statements.

Both forms of business combination result in the assets and liabilities of the acquiree being combined with those of the acquirer. If control is achieved by purchasing net assets, the combining takes place in the accounting records of the acquirer. If control is achieved by purchasing shares, the combining takes place when the consolidated financial statements are prepared.

Variations   One variation from the two basic forms of business combination occurs when the companies involved agree to create a new company, which either purchases the net assets of the combining companies, or purchases enough shares from the shareholders of the combining companies to achieve control of these companies. While this may appear to be a third form of combination, the substance of the transaction indicates otherwise.

Another variation that can occur is a *statutory amalgamation*, whereby under the provisions of federal or provincial law, two or more companies incorporated under the same companies act can combine and continue as a single entity. The shareholders of the combining companies become shareholders of the surviving company, and the nonsurviving companies are wound up. The substance of a statutory amalgamation indicates that it is simply a variation of one of the basic forms. If only one of the companies survives, it is essentially a purchase of assets, with the method of payment being shares of the surviving company.

Methods of Accounting for Business Combinations

There are three methods that have either been used in practice or discussed in theory over the years. These methods will be outlined below under the assumption that two companies are party to a business combination.

If one of the combining companies can be identified as the acquirer, the *purchase method* is used to account for the combination. Under this method, the acquiring company records the net assets of the acquired company at the price that it paid. This price includes any cash payment, the fair market value of any shares issued, and the present value of any promises to pay cash in the future. Any excess of the price paid over the fair market value of the acquired company's net assets is recorded as goodwill. The fair values of the net assets acquired are systematically charged against earnings in the normal manner of expense matching. In addition, any goodwill is regularly reviewed for impairment and any impairment loss is reflected as a charge against earnings. As a result, the price paid for the acquired company is reflected as a deduction from the revenues generated from that company over time. This method of accounting is consistent with the accounting of any assets acquired by a company. Such assets are initially recorded at the price paid for them, and subsequently their cost is charged against earnings over their useful lives.

The *pooling of interests method* has been used to account for those business combinations where an acquirer cannot be identified. Under this method, there is no concept of an acquired company, and so the book values of the combining companies

---

[5] An exception to this occurs when the acquiree applies "push-down accounting." This topic is discussed in Chapter 11.

are simply added together. The method is applied retroactively, so that prior years' financial statements of the companies involved are restated as if they have always been combined. If, under the terms of the combination, a cash payment is made by one of the combining companies, that company is identified as the acquirer and the purchase method must be used. Therefore, the pooling of interests method is possible only when there is a share exchange between the combining companies.

Under pooling, the price paid (the fair market value of the shares issued) is not reflected in the financial statements. Because the price paid is ignored, fair values are not used and no goodwill is recognized. Future earnings will be higher with pooling than they would be under the purchase method, because expenses measured after the combination are not based on fair values at the date of the combination and no goodwill impairment losses will be reflected in subsequent years. The idea behind pooling comes from the concept of "a merger of equals," where the shareholders of both companies agree to combine their companies. It is argued that because they are simply carrying on the business of two former entities as one company, with no major disruptions in operations or key personnel, there is no need to revalue the assets of either entity. A major problem arises in determining what the term "equals" means, and how to decide if two companies are really equal.

A third method, the *new entity method*, has been proposed in the past as an alternative to the pooling of interests. It has been suggested that a new entity has been created when two companies combine by the joining together of two ownership groups. As a result, the assets and liabilities contributed by the two combining companies should be recorded by this new entity at their fair values. This method has received virtually no support because of the revaluation difficulties and additional costs of implementation that would result. Furthermore, it has been argued that if the owners are simply combining their interests, there is no new invested capital and therefore no new entity has been created.

History of the Use of the Purchase and Pooling Methods

Prior to July 1, 2001, both the purchase and pooling methods were used in Canada — though not as alternatives. The purchase method was required when an acquirer could be identified, and the pooling of interests method was required when it was impossible to identify an acquirer. Based on the guidelines to be considered in identifying an acquirer, the vast majority of business combinations were accounted for as purchases, and a pooling rarely occurred in Canada. In the United States, which used quite different guidelines, there were far more poolings than in Canada; even so, the purchase method was still predominant.

Item of Interest   To illustrate how the different guidelines of the two countries produced different results, consider the facts behind the Exxon–Mobil merger that occurred in the United States. A new corporation was formed that issued shares to the shareholders of both companies. After the merger, former Mobil shareholders held 30 percent of the new company while former Exxon shareholders held 70 percent. Under FASB's rules this was accounted for as a pooling. Under Canadian rules it would have been a purchase, because if one shareholder group holds more than 50 percent of the shares of the combined company, that company (in this case Exxon) is identified as the acquirer.

During the years when both methods were in use, stories circulated suggesting that managements often attempted to structure mergers so they would satisfy the guidelines for pooling and therefore allow the new company to report higher future earnings. This was more difficult to accomplish in Canada because of its more stringent rules, and during the period 1973 to 1990 only two or three poolings in total were reported by the CICA publication *Financial Reporting in Canada*. Between 1991 and 1999, the publication reported 10 more poolings. Based on the differences in the lengths of the two time periods, this was a fairly substantial increase. Some of the more recent well-known poolings were Abitibi-Price–Stone-Consolidated, TransCanada PipeLines–Nova Corp., BC Telecom–Telus, and Barrick Gold–Homestake Mining. Two proposed bank mergers, CIBC–TD Bank and Royal Bank–Bank of Montreal — neither of which saw the light of day because of federal government vetoes — were also to be accounted for as poolings. In examining the information provided at the time of the announcements of these combinations, it was often difficult to conclude that they were truly "mergers of equals." One could surmise that, in some instances, the companies involved were structuring the terms of the merger agreement in order to qualify as a pooling.

Item of Interest   The 1998 Teleglobe–Excel Communications merger announcement stated that the share exchange between the two companies would be accounted for as a pooling of interests. The subsequent annual report issued by Teleglobe contained two sets of financial statements. One set, using U.S. GAAP, accounted for the merger as a pooling. The other set, prepared using Canadian GAAP, accounted for the mergers as a purchase.

Pooling No Longer Allowed

On July 1, 2001, both the CICA in Canada and the FASB in the United States issued revised standards that allow only one method of accounting for a business combination. This method is the purchase method. The CICA worked closely with the FASB on this project with the objective of harmonizing the accounting standards in this area. The two standards boards concluded that pooling is no longer acceptable on the basis of the following:

- Pooling does not reflect the values exchanged in the transaction because the fair value of the shares issued is ignored.
- Pooling information is less complete because the method does not reflect a record at all for any acquired assets or liabilities that were not previously recorded. The purchase method would record such assets at fair value.
- Pooling results in users of financial statements being unable to properly track the performance of the investment over the years. Subsequent rate-of-return measurements are inflated artificially under this method because the numerator (earnings) is higher and the denominator (assets) is lower.
- When two different methods are allowed to account for what is essentially the same economic event, investors have a difficult time comparing the results of companies that have used different methods.
- While future earnings will be different for many years, future cash flows will be the same under both methods.
- The purchase method is consistent with how the acquisition of individual assets is recorded, and the method of recording the acquisition of an individual asset is the same regardless of the nature of the consideration paid (cash or shares).

- "True mergers" do not exist and it is possible to identify an acquirer in all, or virtually all, business combinations.

- Pooling is not allowed, or is severely restricted, in most countries in the world.

Even though pooling of interests is no longer accepted as a method of accounting for business combinations, its effects on the financial statements of many large corporations in Canada and the United States will be felt for many years to come. Assets acquired in a combination often have lives ranging up to 20 or 30 years. Differences between the two methods in yearly reported earnings will continue for this amount of time because fair value amortizations have to take place under the purchase method. A large portion of the acquisition price of a purchase business combination is typically allocated to goodwill and, eventually, earnings will reflect goodwill write-offs due to impairment. Under pooling this did not take place. Even though pooling is no longer acceptable, financial statement analysts will need to understand its accounting and its affects on financial statements well into the future. Appendix B, on page 85, provides illustrations of pooling of interests accounting.

Current *Handbook* Provisions

The following *Handbook* sections outline the accounting requirements for business combinations:

> Accounting for a business combination by the purchase method follows the concepts normally applicable to the initial recognition and measurement of assets acquired, liabilities assumed or incurred, and equity instruments issued, as well as to the subsequent accounting for those items. The acquirer's interest in assets acquired and liabilities assumed is accounted for in accordance with this Section. Non-controlling interests are accounted for in accordance with CONSOLIDATED FINANCIAL STATEMENTS, Section 1600. [1581.10]
>
> The acquirer in a business combination should recognize the assets acquired and liabilities assumed from the date of acquisition, including any assets and liabilities that may not have been recognized on the balance sheet of the acquired enterprise. [1581.11]
>
> The financial statements of the acquirer for the period in which a business combination occurs should include the earnings and cash flows of the acquired enterprise from the date of acquisition only. [1581.12]

Section 1581 outlines the requirements for identifying the company that is the acquirer in the business combination. This is important because it is the net assets of the acquiree that are accounted for at fair values. Considerations in determining which company is the acquirer are as follows:

- If the means of payment is cash or a promise to pay cash in the future, the acquirer has been identified as the company making the payment.

- If shares are issued as a means of payment, a key element would be the relative holdings of the voting shares of the combined company by shareholders as a group of the combining companies. In a combination involving two companies, if one shareholder group holds more than 50 percent of the voting shares of the combined company, that company is the acquirer. If more than two companies are involved, the shareholder group that holds the largest number of voting shares identifies the company that is the acquirer.

- When an acquirer cannot seem to be determined by examining voting rights, because each group of shareholders owns the same percentage, then the makeup of the board of directors and senior management is examined to see which company is dominant.
- When there has been a share exchange, the acquirer is often (but not always) the company that issues shares.
- The acquirer is often (but not always) the larger company.
- Section 1581 makes it imperative that an acquirer be identified if the accounting requirements of the purchase method are to be applied.

After an acquirer has been identified, the acquisition cost has to be allocated to the assets and liabilities acquired.

Acquisition Cost   The acquisition cost is made up of:
- any cash paid, and/or
- the present value of any promises to pay cash in the future, and/or
- the fair market value of any shares issued.

The value of shares is based on the market price of the shares over a reasonable period of time before and after the date of the combination.

- If the fair market value of the shares cannot be determined, the fair value of the net assets acquired is used to determine the acquisition cost.
- Included in the acquisition cost are any direct expenses incurred in the combination. Examples would be the fees of consultants, accountants, and lawyers.
- Costs incurred in issuing shares are not considered part of the acquisition cost, but rather are deducted from the amount recorded for the share issue. Alternatively, share issue costs can be shown as a direct charge on the statement of retained earnings.
- Also included in the acquisition cost is contingent consideration. Contingent consideration is discussed in a later chapter.

Allocation of the Acquisition Cost   The acquisition cost is allocated to the acquirer's interest[6] in the fair value of the identifiable assets and liabilities of the acquired company. An identifiable asset is not necessarily one that is presently recorded in the records of the acquiree company. For example, the acquiree company may have patent rights that have a definite market value but are not shown on the balance sheet because they have been developed internally. Or the acquiree's balance sheet may show a pension asset, though an up-to-date actuarial valuation may make it necessary to report a net pension obligation.

The section of the *CICA Handbook* dealing with the new standard directs the management of the acquirer to make a strong effort to recognize and measure unrecorded intangible assets of the acquired company. A list of possible intangibles is reproduced in Appendix A. It has been implied in the past that a large portion of the acquisition cost in a business combination ends up as goodwill. This is because the amount recorded as goodwill is often made up of a mixture of goodwill itself plus intangible assets that were not identified and measured. Management is encouraged to be more diligent in identifying and measuring all intangibles when it allocates the acquisition cost.

---

[6] This reference to the acquirer's interest applies only to the consolidation of a subsidiary that is less than 100 percent owned.

Not all assets and liabilities on the balance sheet of the acquired entity are considered identifiable. Future income tax assets and liabilities are not fair valued and carried forward. Instead, new amounts for future tax assets and liabilities become part of the allocation of the acquisition cost. Because of the added complexity that this brings, discussion and illustration of this topic is saved until a later chapter.

Because goodwill is a residual and not considered to be an identifiable asset, any goodwill existing on the balance sheet of the acquired company on the date of the business combination is not carried forward.

If the acquisition cost is greater than the acquirer's interest in the identifiable assets and liabilities acquired, the excess is recorded in the acquirer's financial statements as goodwill. In theory, goodwill represents the amount paid for excess earning power; in practice, it represents the premium paid to achieve control.

If the acquisition cost is less than the fair value of the identifiable net assets acquired, we have what is sometimes described as a "negative goodwill" situation. The *Handbook* describes the accounting for such negative goodwill as follows:

> When the net of the amounts assigned to assets acquired and liabilities assumed exceeds the cost of the purchase ("excess" — sometimes referred to as negative goodwill):
>
> (a) that excess should be allocated as a pro rata reduction of the amounts that otherwise would be assigned to all of the acquired assets except:
>   (i)   financial assets other than investments accounted for by the equity method;
>   (ii) assets to be disposed of by sale;
>   (iii) future income tax assets;
>   (iv) prepaid assets relating to employee future benefit plans; and
>   (v)   any other current assets, to the extent the excess is eliminated; and
>
> (b) any remaining excess should be presented as an extraordinary gain. [1581.50]

> The remaining excess is presented and disclosed as an extraordinary gain, in accordance with the requirements of EXTRAORDINARY ITEMS, Section 3480 even though it does not satisfy the criteria in that Section for identifying extraordinary items. The gain is recognized in the period in which the business combination is completed, unless the business combination involves contingent consideration that, if paid or issued, would be recognized as an additional element of cost of the purchase (see paragraph 1581.52). When a gain is recognized before the purchase price allocation is complete, any subsequent adjustments to that gain as a result of finalizing the purchase price allocation are recognized in the period the contingency is resolved. [1581.51]

The accounting for negative goodwill is illustrated in Chapter 4.

Financial Reporting After the Combination   The net income generated by the net assets of the acquired company is reported in the financial statements of the acquirer commencing with the date of acquisition. The expenses used to arrive at this income must be based on the amortizations of the fair values used and any goodwill losses due to impairment. Prior years' comparative financial statements are not retroactively changed to reflect the combination.

Illustrations of Business Combination Accounting

To illustrate the accounting involved using the purchase method, we will use the summarized balance sheets of two companies. Summarized statements are used here so that we can focus completely on the broad accounting concepts. In later examples, detailed statements will be used. Exhibit 3.1 presents the December 31, Year 1, balance sheets of the two companies that are party to a business combination.

Because the identification of an acquirer requires the analysis of shareholdings after the combination, notes 1 and 2 are presented in the exhibit to identify the shareholders of each company as belonging to two distinct groups.

A Company Ltd. will initiate the takeover of B Corporation. The first two illustrations will involve the purchase of net assets with cash and the issuance of shares as the means of payment. Later illustrations will have A Company purchasing enough shares of B Corporation to obtain control over that company's net assets, and will introduce the preparation of consolidated statements.

Exhibit 3.1

A COMPANY LTD.
BALANCE SHEET
December 31, Year 1

Assets	$300,000
Liabilities	$120,000
Shareholders' equity	
Common stock (5,000 shares) (Note 1)	100,000
Retained earnings	80,000
	$300,000

Note 1
The shareholders of the 5,000 common shares issued and outstanding are identified as Group X.

B CORPORATION
BALANCE SHEET
December 31, Year 1

Assets	$ 88,000
Liabilities	$ 30,000
Shareholders' equity	
Common stock (———— shares) (Note 2)	25,000
Retained earnings	33,000
	$ 88,000

The fair market values of B Corporation's assets and liabilities are as follows as at December 31, Year 1:

Fair market value of assets	$109,000
Fair market value of liabilities	29,000
Fair market value of net assets	$ 80,000

Note 2
The shareholders of the common shares of B Corporation are identified as Group Y. The actual number of shares issued and outstanding has been purposely omitted because this number would have no bearing on the analysis required later.

Purchase of Assets

In the following illustrations, A Company offers to buy all assets and to assume all liabilities of B Corporation. The shareholders of B Corporation accept the offer.

Illustration 1 Assume that on January 1, Year 2, A Company pays $95,000 in cash to B Corporation for all of the net assets of that company, and that no direct expenses are involved. Because cash is the means of payment, A Company is the acquirer. The acquisition cost is allocated in the following manner:

Purchase price	$ 95,000
Fair market value of net assets acquired	80,000
Difference — goodwill	$ 15,000

A Company would make the following journal entry to record the acquisition of B Corporation's net assets:

Assets (in detail)	109,000	
Goodwill	15,000	
Liabilities (in detail)		29,000
Cash		95,000

A Company's balance sheet after the business combination would be as shown at the bottom of this page.

Using the purchase method to account for the business combination, the identifiable net assets acquired were recorded at fair market values, with the purchase price difference recorded as goodwill. The balance sheet of A Company is not a consolidated balance sheet. But note that if A Company had paid $95,000 cash for 100 percent of the common shares of B Corporation, the consolidated balance prepared immediately after the business combination would be identical to the one shown below. (See Exhibit 3.3.)

A COMPANY LTD.
BALANCE SHEET
January 1, Year 2

Assets (300,000 – 95,000* + 109,000)	$314,000
Goodwill	15,000
	$329,000
Liabilities (120,000 + 29,000)	$149,000
Shareholders' equity	
Common stock	100,000
Retained earnings	80,000
	$329,000

* $95,000 cash paid by A Company to B Corporation

While this illustration focuses on the balance sheet of A Company immediately after the business combination, it is also useful to look at B Corporation in order to see the effect of this economic event on that company. The balance sheet of B Corporation immediately after the sale of all of its net assets is shown below:

B CORPORATION LTD.
BALANCE SHEET
January 1, Year 2

Cash	$ 95,000
Shareholders' equity	
Common stock	$ 25,000
Retained earnings (33,000 + 37,000*)	70,000
	$ 95,000

* *The gain on sale of the net assets amounts to $37,000 ($95,000 – $58,000).*

The shareholders of B Corporation must now decide the future of their company. They could decide to invest the company's cash in productive assets and carry on in some other line of business. Alternatively, they could decide to wind up the company and distribute the sole asset (cash) to themselves on a pro rata basis.

Illustration 2 Assume that on January 1, Year 2, A Company issues 4,000 common shares, with a market value of $23.75 per share, to B Corporation as payment for the company's net assets. B Corporation will be wound up after the sale of its net assets. Because the method of payment is shares, the following analysis is made to determine which company is the acquirer.

	Shares of A Company
Group X now holds	5,000
Group Y will hold (when B Corporation is wound up)	4,000
	9,000

Group X will hold 5/9 (56 percent) of the total shares of A Company after the combination, and Group Y will hold 4/9 (44 percent) of this total after the dissolution of B Corporation. Because one shareholder group holds more than 50 percent of the voting shares, an acquirer has been identified. The purchase price is allocated in the following manner:

Purchase price (4,000 shares @ $23.75)	$ 95,000
Fair market value of net assets acquired	80,000
Difference — goodwill	$ 15,000

A Company would make the following journal entry to record the acquisition of B Corporation's net assets and the issuance of 4,000 common shares at fair market value on January 1, Year 2:

Assets (in detail)	109,000	
Goodwill	15,000	
Liabilities (in detail)		29,000
Common stock		95,000

A Company's balance sheet after the business combination would be as follows:

A COMPANY LTD.
BALANCE SHEET
January 1, Year 1

Assets (300,000 + 109,000)	$409,000
Goodwill	15,000
	$424,000
Liabilities (120,000 + 29,000)	$149,000
Shareholders' equity	
Common stock (100,000 + 95,000)	195,000
Retained earnings	80,000
	$424,000

This balance sheet was prepared by combining the book values of A Company's assets and liabilities with the fair values of those of B Corporation.

B Corporation's balance sheet immediately following the sale of its net assets is reproduced below:

B CORPORATION
BALANCE SHEET
January 1, Year 2

Investment in shares of A Company	$ 95,000
Shareholders' equity	
Common stock	$ 25,000
Retained earnings (33,000 + 37,000)	70,000
	$ 95,000

B Corporation is wound up and distributes the investment, consisting of 4,000 shares of A Company, to its shareholders (Group Y). The reason for winding up B Corporation should be intuitively obvious. B Corporation's sole asset is 4,000 of the issued shares of A Company. This single block represents a voting threat to A Company's shareholders (Group X). A Company will insist that B Corporation be wound up and distribute these 4,000 shares to its shareholders (Group Y), who presumably will not get together to determine how to vote them.

Introduction to Consolidated Financial Statements

When a parent–subsidiary relationship is the result of a business combination, the two (or more) companies involved continue as separate legal entities, with each maintaining separate accounting records and producing separate financial statements. GAAP ignores this separate-company legal status and views the substance of the relationship as one that has created a single economic entity that should report as such.

The requirement for, and rationale behind, the preparation of consolidated financial statements is stated in Section 1590 of the *CICA Handbook* as follows:

An enterprise should consolidate all of its subsidiaries. [1590.16]

Consolidated financial statements recognize that, even though the parent and its subsidiaries may be separate legal entities, together they constitute a single economic unit. Such financial statements provide the most appropriate basis for informing users of the parent's financial statements about the resources and results of operations of the parent and its subsidiaries as a group. This presentation, supplemented by segment information prepared in accordance with segment disclosures, Section 1701, and any other information necessary for fair presentation, is more informative to the shareholders than separate financial statements of the parent and each of its subsidiaries. [1590.17]

Before Section 1590 was issued in 1991, the requirements for consolidation were contained in Section 3050, "Long-term Investments." While this section required consolidation in most situations, it described as well situations where some subsidiaries could be excluded from consolidation. When the requirement for the presentation of consolidated statements was transferred from Section 3050 to Section 1590, and a new definition of control was introduced, these exclusions were removed. Basically, Section 1590 says that if control exists, consolidated statements must be prepared; when control ceases to exist, consolidation should also cease.

The previous illustrations examined the accounting for a business combination when net assets were purchased. We will now turn our attention to the most common form of combination, the purchase of shares. We will continue to use the financial statements of the two companies in Exhibit 3.1.

In the next two illustrations, A Company issues a tender offer to the shareholders of B Corporation (Group Y) for all of their shareholdings. Group Y accepts the offer.

Illustration 3   Assume that on January 1, Year 2, A Company pays $95,000 in cash to the shareholders of B Corporation for all of their shares, and that no expenses are involved. Because cash was the means of payment, A Company is the acquirer.

A Company's journal entry to record the acquisition of 100 percent of B Corporation's shares on January 1, Year 2, is as follows:

Investment in B Corporation	95,000	
Cash		95,000

The financial statements of B Corporation have not been affected by this transaction. A Company is now a parent company and must prepare consolidated financial statements for external reporting purposes. We will now illustrate the preparation of the consolidated balance sheet as at January 1, Year 2, using a working paper approach.

Before preparing the working paper, it is useful to calculate and allocate the purchase discrepancy. The purchase discrepancy is defined as "the difference between the amount paid by an acquiring company for shares and its proportionate interest in the net book value of the assets of the acquired limited company, at the date of acquisition."[7] This concept was introduced in Chapter 2.

The required calculation and allocation is shown in Exhibit 3.2.

---

[7] *Terminology for Accountants*, 4th edition, Toronto: CICA, 1992, p. 168.

Exhibit 3.2

CALCULATION AND ALLOCATION
OF THE PURCHASE DISCREPANCY

Cost of A Company's investment			$95,000
Net book value of B Company			
Common stock		25,000	
Retained earnings		33,000	
		58,000	
A Company's proportionate interest		100%	58,000
Purchase discrepancy			37,000

Allocated as follows:

	Fair value − Book value × Ownership percentage						
Assets	109,000	−	88,000	×	100%	= 21,000	
Liabilities	29,000	−	30,000	×	100%	= (1,000)	22,000
Balance — goodwill							$15,000

Section 1600 of the *Handbook*, "Consolidated Financial Statements," does not mention an item called the purchase discrepancy; instead, it describes the calculation of goodwill with the following statement:

> Where the cost of an investment exceeds the parent's portion of the costs assigned to the subsidiary's identifiable assets acquired and liabilities assumed, such an excess is a payment for an unidentifiable asset and should be accounted for in consolidated financial statements as goodwill. [1600.16]

The costs assigned to the subsidiary's net assets mentioned in this paragraph are fair market values on the date of acquisition. If we calculate goodwill in accordance with the *Handbook*'s description, we get the same amount for goodwill, as the following demonstrates:

Cost of A Company's investment			$95,000
Fair value of B Corporation's net assets			
Assets		109,000	
Liabilities		29,000	
		80,000	
A Company's proportionate interest		100%	80,000
Balance — goodwill			$15,000

Because consolidated working papers use the financial statements of the parent and its subsidiary, which do not contain fair values, the calculation and allocation of the purchase discrepancy is necessary because it provides the amounts needed to make the working paper eliminations and adjustments.

The working papers for the preparation of the consolidated balance sheet on the date of acquisition are shown in Exhibit 3.3.

The following points should be noted regarding the preparation of this working paper:

1. A Company's asset "Investment in B Corporation" and B Corporation's common shares and retained earnings do not appear on the consolidated balance

Exhibit 3.3

A COMPANY LTD.
CONSOLIDATED BALANCE SHEET WORKING PAPER
January 1, Year 2

	A Company	B Corp.	Adjustments and Eliminations Dr.		Cr.		Consolidated balance sheet
Assets	$205,000	$88,000	(2) $ 21,000				$314,000
Investment in B Corporation	95,000			(1)	95,000		
Purchase discrepancy			(1) 37,000	(2)	37,000		
Goodwill			(2) 15,000				15,000
	$300,000	$88,000					$329,000
Liabilities	$120,000	$30,000	(2) 1,000				$149,000
Common stock	100,000						100,000
Retained earnings	80,000						80,000
Common stock		25,000	(1) 25,000				
Retained earnings		33,000	(1) 33,000				
	$300,000	$88,000	$132,000		$132,000		$329,000

sheet. These items are eliminated by a working paper elimination entry because they are reciprocal in nature. The entry labelled (1) eliminates the parent's ownership percentage of the shareholders' equity of the subsidiary against the parent's investment account. These shareholders' equity accounts are separately shown in the working paper to facilitate this. The purchase discrepancy that results is the portion of the investment account not eliminated.

2. The purchase discrepancy does not appear on the consolidated balance sheet. With reference to the calculations of Exhibit 3.2, the purchase discrepancy is allocated to revalue the net assets of B Corporation for consolidation purposes. This is accomplished by the entry labelled (2).

3. When we add the book value of the net assets of B Corporation to 100 percent of the difference between their fair value and book value, the resulting amount used for the consolidation is the fair value of each individual asset and liability of B Corporation. This is only true for a 100 percent owned subsidiary. As we will see in the next chapter, it is not true when we have a subsidiary that is less than 100 percent owned.

4. The elimination entries are made on the working paper only. They are not entered in the accounting records of the parent or the subsidiary.

5. The consolidated balance sheet is prepared from the amounts shown in the last column of the working paper.

6. Under the purchase method of accounting, consolidated shareholders' equity on acquisition date is that of the parent.

Illustration 4   Assume that on January 1, Year 2, A Company issues 4,000 common shares, with a market value of $23.75 per share, to the shareholders of B Corporation

(Group Y) for all of their shares, and that there are no expenses involved. The analysis made in Illustration 2 indicates that A Company is the acquirer.

A Company's January 1, Year 2, journal entry to record the issuance of 4,000 shares at market value in payment for the acquisition of 100 percent of B Corporation's shares is:

Investment in B Corporation (4,000 × $23.75)	95,000	
Common stock		95,000

The calculation and allocation of the purchase discrepancy is identical to the one used in the last illustration (see Exhibit 3.2). The working papers for the preparation of the consolidated balance sheet as at January 1, Year 2, are shown in Exhibit 3.4.

Exhibit 3.4

A COMPANY LTD.
CONSOLIDATED BALANCE SHEET WORKING PAPER
January 1, Year 2

	A Company	B Corp.	Adjustments and Eliminations Dr.		Adjustments and Eliminations Cr.		Consolidated balance sheet
Assets	$300,000	$88,000	(2)	$ 21,000			$409,000
Investment in B Corporation	95,000				(1)	95,000	
Purchase discrepancy			(1)	37,000	(2)	37,000	
Goodwill			(2)	15,000			15,000
	$395,000	$88,000					$424,000
Liabilities	$120,000	$30,000	(2)	1,000			$149,000
Common stock	195,000						195,000
Retained earnings	80,000						80,000
Common stock		25,000	(1)	25,000			
Retained earnings		33,000	(1)	33,000			
	$395,000	$88,000		$132,000		$132,000	$424,000

The accounting for a business combination has been examined in four illustrations. The first two involved the acquisition of net assets, and the last two the acquisition of 100 percent of shareholdings. Because the amount paid was the same in each of these paired illustrations, the balance sheets prepared immediately after the combination are identical for each pair.

Financial Statement Disclosure

Section 1581 of the *CICA Handbook* sets forth detailed disclosure requirements with respect to business combinations completed during the year. One paragraph requires details of the assets and liabilities of an acquired entity to be presented in condensed form.

The following is an example of how a business combination might be disclosed in the footnotes of the acquiring company in the year of the combination:

Example During the year the company acquired all of the outstanding shares of XYZ Ltd. for cash of $4,100,000. This acquisition was accounted for as a purchase, with the results of operations included in the consolidated financial statements from the date of acquisition. The purchase price was allocated as follows:

Net assets acquired (in thousands of dollars)	
Cash	$ 200
Other current assets	1,800
Capital assets	2,100
Goodwill	1,500
Current liabilities	(600)
Long-term debt	(900)
Purchase price	$4,100

An International Perspective

The restrictions on pooling of interests and the treatment of goodwill in a purchase business combination are two major sites of variance in international accounting practices. With the elimination of pooling of interests in 2001 by United States, the number of poolings declined substantially because it was used in the U.S. far more than in any other country in the world. Great Britain, Germany, Japan, and Korea still allow its use in certain situations, as does the IASB. Many other countries, including Australia, New Zealand, France, Mexico, and now Canada, do not allow its use.

Even though most business combinations are accounted for using the purchase method, the subsequent accounting for goodwill varies so greatly among countries that financial statement readers need to fully educate themselves before they can assess the potential impact. Canada and the United States are the only countries that require periodic write-downs due to impairment losses instead of regular amortization over some maximum life. Some countries allow the choice of amortization or a direct write-off to equity on the date of acquisition. Germany is among such countries and Great Britain allowed this practice until 1998. The maximum allowable write-off period varies among different countries, and some countries also require periodic impairment reviews. Japan, Korea, and Germany allow a 5-year maximum period, while Chile and Spain allow 10 years and Mexico, Australia, and New Zealand allow 20 years. France requires amortization, but does not specify a maximum period. The IASB suggests that the maximum period should not exceed 5 years, unless a longer period (not to exceed 20 years) can be justified. Generally speaking, when accounting standards allow maximum amortization periods, many companies adopt this maximum because of the favourable effect on earnings. Furthermore, if standards permit it, many companies will choose the direct write-off of goodwill to equity because doing so produces earnings numbers that are closer to those that would be achieved under a pooling of interests.

The treatment of negative goodwill also varies widely. In Canada, the United States, Australia, and New Zealand, negative goodwill is allocated to reduce assets in some manner. Any unallocated balance is shown as an extraordinary item in both Canada and the U.S. The IASB presents negative goodwill on the balance sheet as deferred income and then amortizes it over a maximum of 5 years. Hong Kong writes it off immediately to a reserve in shareholders' equity. France, Mexico, and Chile show it on the balance sheet and then amortize it to earnings over varying periods. Spain recommends amortizing it only to reduce any losses incurred by the acquired company.

Purchased in-process research and development is another area that produces diversity in accounting practices, particularly between Canada and the United States. In-process research and development is often a valuable asset purchased in a takeover. The FASB requires that the amount of the acquisition price allocated to this asset be written off immediately, which is consistent with its requirements for internally generated research and development. Canada would allow the development component to be capitalized and amortized over its estimated useful life.

SUMMARY

A business combination takes place when one company gains control over the net assets of another company. Control can be achieved by the purchase of the net assets or by the purchase of enough voting shares to gain control over the use of the net assets. In the latter situation a parent–subsidiary relationship is created that requires the preparation of consolidated financial statements.

Prior to 2001, both the purchase method and the pooling of interests method were acceptable methods to account for a business combination. Pooling could be used only if there was a share exchange and even then only in exceptional circumstances. On July 1, 2001, pooling was disallowed in both Canada and the United States, leaving the purchase method as the only acceptable method to account for a business combination.

With the pooling of interests method, the assets, liabilities, and equities of the companies involved are combined at book values. With the purchase method, the assets and liabilities acquired are recorded at fair values, with the acquisition cost excess recorded as goodwill.

APPENDIX A

Examples of Identifiable Intangible Assets

This appendix contains examples, reproduced from Section 1581 of the *CICA Handbook*, of identifiable intangible assets that may be acquired in a business combination. As stated in paragraph 1580.38(e), identifiable intangible assets that can be separately identified and reliably measured should be separately recorded in the financial statements of the acquiring entity at their fair value. Each intangible asset listed below is not necessarily reliably measurable. That determination would be based on individual facts and circumstances. Those intangible assets that are identifiable but not reliably measurable, are included in goodwill.

The following are illustrative examples of intangible assets acquired in a business combination that meet the criteria for recognition as an asset apart from goodwill.

Examples of marketing-related intangible assets include:

(a) trademarks, trade names;
(b) service marks, collective marks, certification marks;
(c) trade dress (unique color, shape or package design);
(d) newspaper mastheads;
(e) Internet domain names; and
(f) non-competition agreements.

Marketing-related intangible assets are those assets that are primarily used in the marketing or promotion of products or services. Trademarks are words, names, symbols, or other devices used in trade to indicate the source of the product and to distinguish it from the products of others. A service mark identifies and distinguishes the source of a service rather than a product. Collective marks are used to identify the goods or services of members of a group and certification marks are used to certify the geographic origin or other characteristics of a good or service. Trademarks, service marks, collective marks, and certification marks may be protected legally through registration with government agencies, by continuous use in commerce, or by other means. When registered, or otherwise provided legal protection, a trademark or other mark is an intangible asset that meets the criterion for recognition apart from goodwill in paragraph 1581.48(a). Otherwise a trademark or other mark is recognized apart from goodwill only when the criterion in paragraph 1581.48(b) is met, which is normally the case.

The terms "brand" and "brand name" often are used as synonyms for trademarks and trade names. However, the former are general marketing terms that are typically used to refer to a group of complementary assets such as the trademark (or service mark) and its related trade name, formulae, recipes and technological expertise (which may or may not be patented). An enterprise may recognize, as a single asset apart from goodwill, a group of complementary intangible assets commonly referred to as a brand when the assets making up that group have similar useful lives.

An Internet domain name is a unique alpha-numeric name that is used to identify a particular numeric Internet address. Registration of a domain name associates the name with a designated computer on the Internet for the period the registration is in effect. Registered domain names are recognized as intangible assets apart from goodwill because they meet the criterion in paragraph 1581.48(a).

Examples of customer-related intangible assets include:

(a) customer lists;

(b) order or production backlog;

(c) customer contracts and the related customer relationships; and

(d) non-contractual customer relationships.

A customer list consists of information about customers such as their name and contact information. A customer list also may be in the form of a database that includes other information about the customers such as their order history and demographic information. A customer list does not arise from contractual or other legal rights. However, customer lists are valuable and are frequently leased or exchanged. Therefore, an acquired customer list meets the criterion in paragraph 1581.48(b) for recognition apart from goodwill. However, an acquired customer list does not meet that criterion when the terms of confidentiality or other agreements prohibit an enterprise from selling, leasing, or otherwise exchanging information about its customers.

When an acquired order or production backlog arises from contracts such as purchase or sales orders, it meets the criterion in paragraph 1581.48(a) for recognition apart from goodwill (even when the purchase or sales orders are cancellable).

When an enterprise establishes relationships with its customers such that the enterprise has information about the customer and has regular contact with the customer, and the customer has the ability to make direct contact with the enterprise, through contracts, those customer relationships arise from contractual rights. Therefore, customer contracts and the related customer relationships are intangible assets that meet the criterion in paragraph 1581.48(a) for recognition apart from goodwill, even when confidentiality or other contractual terms prohibit the sale or transfer of the contract separately from the acquired enterprise.

When a customer relationship does not arise from a contract, and it meets the criterion in paragraph 1581.48(b), the relationship is recognized as an intangible asset apart from goodwill. Exchange transactions for the same asset or a similar type of asset provide evidence of separability of a non-contractual customer relationship and might also provide information about exchange prices to be considered when estimating its fair value. For example, relationships with depositors may be exchanged with the related deposits and, thus, meet the criteria for recognition as an intangible asset apart from goodwill.

An acquired customer base is an intangible asset. However, that asset generally does not meet the criteria for recognition apart from goodwill. A customer base does not arise from contractual or other legal rights nor can it generally be bought and sold separately from the acquired enterprise.

Examples of artistic-related intangible assets include:

(a) plays, operas, ballets;

(b) books, magazines, newspapers, other literary works;

(c) musical works such as compositions, song lyrics, advertising jingles;

(d) pictures, photographs; and

(e) video and audio-visual material, including motion pictures, music videos, and television programs.

Artistic-related intangible assets meet the criteria for recognition apart from goodwill when the assets arise from contractual rights or legal rights, such as those provided by copyright. Copyrights can often be transferred either in whole through assignments or in part through licensing agreements. In determining the fair value of a copyright intangible asset, consideration is given to the existence of any assignments or licenses of the acquired copyright. An acquirer may recognize a copyright intangible asset and any related assignments or license agreements as a single intangible asset for financial reporting purposes when their useful lives are similar.

Examples of contract-based intangible assets include:

(a) licensing, royalty, standstill agreements;

(b) advertising, construction, management, service or supply contracts;

(c) lease agreements;

(d) construction permits;

(e) franchise agreements;

(f) operating and broadcast rights;

(g) use rights such as drilling, water, air, mineral, timber cutting, and route authorities;

(h) servicing contracts such as mortgage servicing contracts; and

(i) employment contracts.

Contract-based intangible assets represent the value of rights that arise from contractual arrangements. Customer contracts (see paragraph 1581.A26) are one particular type of contract-based intangible asset. While servicing is inherent in all financial assets, it becomes a distinct asset or liability only when contractually separated from the underlying financial assets by sale or securitization of the assets with servicing retained or through the separate purchase and assumption of the servicing. When mortgage loans, credit card receivables, or other financial assets are acquired in a business combination with servicing retained, this Section does not require recognition of the inherent servicing rights as an intangible asset. The fair value of the servicing intangible asset is considered in the measurement of the fair value of the acquired financial asset. However, a contract representing an acquired servicing asset is an intangible asset that is recognized apart from goodwill.

When the terms of a contract give rise to a liability or commitment (which might be the case when the terms of an operating lease or customer contract are unfavourable relative to market prices), that liability or commitment is recognized as required by paragraph 1581.43(j).

Examples of technology-based intangible assets include:

(a) patented technology;

(b) compute software;

(c) non-patented technology;

(d) databases; and

(e) trade secrets, such as secret formulae, processes, recipes.

Technology-based intangible assets relate to innovations or technological advances. As discussed in paragraphs 1581.A36–A38, the future economic benefits of those assets are often protected through contractual or other legal rights. Thus, many technology-based intangible assets meet the criterion in paragraph 1581.48(a) for recognition apart from goodwill.

When computer software and program formats are protected legally, such as by patent or copyright, they meet the criterion in paragraph 1581.48(a) for recognition apart from goodwill.

Databases are collections of information, often stored in electronic form (such as on computer disks or files). An acquired database that includes original works of authorship is entitled to copyright protection and, when so protected, meets the criterion in paragraph 1581.48(a) for recognition apart from goodwill. However, a database often includes information created as a consequence of an enterprise's normal operations, such as a customer list, or specialized information such as scientific data and credit information. Databases that are not protected by copyright can be (and often are) exchanged in their entirety or in part. Alternatively, they can be (and often are) licensed or leased to others. Thus, even when the future economic benefit of a database does not arise from legal rights, it meets the criterion in paragraph 1581.48(b) for recognition as an asset apart from goodwill.

A trade secret is information, including a formula, pattern, compilation, program, device, method, technique, or process, that derives independent economic value, actual or potential, from not being generally known, and is the subject of efforts that are reasonable under the circumstances to maintain its secrecy. When laws or regulations legally protect the future economic benefit of an acquired trade secret, that asset meets the criteria for recognition apart from goodwill in paragraph 1581.48(a). Otherwise, a trade secret is recognized apart from goodwill only when the criterion in paragraph 1581.48(b) is met, which is likely to be the case.

APPENDIX B

Pooling of Interests Illustrations

In this chapter, we presented four illustrations of business combinations accounted for using the purchase method. In two of them the method of payment was cash, while in the other two a share issue was the consideration. A cash payment could never result in a pooling; only a share issue could. We will now present the share issue illustrations using the pooling of interests method.

Illustration 5   In Illustration 2, on page 75, A Company issued 4,000 common shares with a total value of $95,000 to purchase all of B Corporations's assets and liabilities. The accounting in that particular illustration used the purchase method. We will use the same facts and present the accounting that would result if the pooling of interests method had been used.

Under pooling, the net assets acquired are recorded by A Company at the book values carried on the balance sheet of B Corporation, and no goodwill is recorded. A Company prepares a journal entry to record the acquisition of all the net assets of B Corporation and the issue of 4,000 common shares as payment on January 1, Year 2, as follows:

Assets (in detail)	88,000	
Liabilities (in detail)		30,000
Retained earnings		33,000
Common stock		25,000

A Company's balance sheet immediately after the business combination (a purchase of assets) would appear as follows:

A COMPANY LTD.
BALANCE SHEET
January 1, Year 2

Assets (300,000 + 88,000)	$388,000
Liabilities (120,000 + 30,000)	$150,000
Shareholders' equity	
Common stock (100,000 + 25,000)	125,000
Retained earnings (80,000 + 33,000)	113,000
	$388,000

Notice that this balance sheet has been prepared by adding all of the balance sheet components of the two companies. Fair market values are not used, and the 4,000 common shares issued are recorded at the $25,000 book value of the common shares of B Corporation, whereas under the purchase method they would be issued at their $95,000 fair market value. Note also that by purchasing assets, A company increased its retained earnings and its future legal dividend paying ability.

The balance sheet of B Corporation immediately after the sale of its assets and liabilities follows:

B CORPORATION
BALANCE SHEET
January 1, Year 2

Investment in shares of A Company	$95,000
Shareholders' equity	
Common stock	$25,000
Retained earnings (33,000 + 37,000)	70,000
	$95,000

When B Corporation is wound up, its shareholders (Group Y) surrender their shares and receive 4,000 shares of A Company, distributed on a pro rata basis.

Illustration 6 Assume that on January 1, Year 2, A Company issues 4,000 common shares to the shareholders of B Corporation (Group Y) for all of their shares. The fair market value of A Company's shares on this date is $95,000.

Notice that the facts are the same as Illustration 4 (page 79), which used the purchase method. Here we will present the accounting using the pooling of interests method. A purchase discrepancy calculation is made only when the parent–subsidiary relationship stems from a purchase business combination; therefore, we do not make this calculation in a pooling situation such as this one.

A Company would make the following journal entry for the acquisition on January 1, Year 2:

Investment in B Corporation	25,000	
Common stock		25,000

We are assuming that corporate legislation would allow A Company to record the 4,000 shares at the book value of B Corporation's share capital.

Exhibit 3.5 shows the preparation of the consolidated balance sheet working paper. The only working paper entry required is the one that eliminates the parent's ownership percentage of the common stock of the subsidiary against the investment account.

Exhibit 3.5

A COMPANY LTD.
CONSOLIDATED BALANCE SHEET WORKING PAPER
January 1, Year 1

	A Company	B Corp.	Adjustments and Eliminations Dr.	Cr.	Consolidated balance sheet
Assets	$300,000	$88,000			$388,000
Investment in					
B Corporation	25,000			(1) $25,000	
	$325,000	$88,000			$388,000
Liabilities	$120,000	$30,000			$150,000
Common stock	125,000				125,000
Retained earnings	80,000	33,000			113,000
Common stock		25,000	(1) $25,000		
	$325,000	$88,000	$25,000	$25,000	$388,000

Exhibit 3.6 compares A Company's consolidated balance sheet under the two methods.

By noting the differences in net asset values, it becomes obvious why pooling will result in higher future earnings. Some other differences, noted below, produce some interesting results in the financial statements.

If the combination takes place late in the fiscal year of the combined company, pooling leads to "instant earnings" because the net incomes of the companies are combined from the beginning of the year. Under the purchase method they are combined only from the date of the combination.

Exhibit 3.6		

A COMPANY
CONSOLIDATED BALANCE SHEET

	Purchase Method	Pooling Method
Assets	$409,000	$388,000
Goodwill	15,000	—
	$424,000	$388,000
Liabilities	$149,000	$150,000
Common stock	195,000	125,000
Retained earnings	80,000	113,000
	$424,000	$388,000

Pooling of interests requires that prior years' financial statements be restated as if the two companies had been combined for all of their historical lives. This means that prior years' financial statements that are presented for comparative purposes, and such items as 10-year summaries (which are often presented in annual reports), must be redone to reflect amounts as if the companies had been combined during those earlier periods. Under purchase accounting, prior years' results are not restated.

With pooling, additional profits can result in later years if assets of the former acquiree are sold. For example, an asset with a fair value of $150,000 and a book value of $90,000 might be sold shortly after the business combination. If pooling were used, a gain of $60,000 would be reported; if the purchase method were used, there would not be a gain.

REVIEW QUESTIONS

1. What key element must be present in a business combination?
2. "The form of a business combination determines the method used to account for the combination." Discuss this statement.
3. Can a statutory amalgamation be considered a form of business combination?
4. What is the basic condition that in the past determined whether purchase or pooling accounting could be used? Explain.
5. Explain how an acquirer is determined in a business combination.
6. Outline the accounting involved with the purchase method.
7. Outline the accounting involved with the pooling of interests method.
8. Briefly describe the accounting involved with the new entity method.
9. If one company issued shares as payment for the net assets of another company, it would probably insist that the other company be wound up after the sale. Explain why this condition would be part of the asset purchase agreement.
10. What is a purchase discrepancy, and where does it appear on the consolidated balance sheet?
11. The pooling of interests method can by its very nature lead to substantially different results than the purchase method. One such difference arises when assets originally belonging to the acquiree are sold after the date of the combination. Explain why a substantial difference might occur in this situation.

MULTIPLE CHOICE

1. Which of the following describes how to consolidate net assets using the pooling of interests method?
    a. Add together the companies' book values.
    b. Add together the companies' fair values.
    c. Add together the fair value of the acquired company and the book value of the acquiring company.
    d. Add together the book value of the acquired company and the fair value of the acquiring company.

2. When a parent uses the purchase method to consolidate a wholly owned subsidiary, what amount will appear as "common shares" in the equity section of the consolidated balance sheet?
    a. The book value of the parent's common shares plus the book value of the subsidiary's common shares.
    b. The book value of the parent's common shares plus the fair value of the subsidiary's common shares.
    c. The fair value of the parent's common shares on the date of the purchase of the subsidiary.
    d. The book value of the parent's common shares at the date of consolidation.

3. P Company acquires 100% of the common shares of S Company by issuing non-voting preferred shares. For both P Company and S Company, the fair value of all assets is equal to or greater than recorded book values. Which of the following approaches to consolidation will show the highest total asset value on the consolidated balance sheet on the date of acquisition?
    a. Pooling of interest.
    b. Purchase.
    c. New entity.
    d. Cannot be determined based on the information provided.

4. Which of the following characteristics is not associated with a business combination in Canada today?
    a. A clearly identified acquisition cost is evident for the transaction.
    b. Two subsidiaries of a single parent merge together as one.
    c. Cash or debt or shares can be used as payment for the acquired company.
    d. One company can always be identified as the acquirer.

The following data should be used for Questions 5 and 6.

Hampton Corp. has only three assets:

	Book value	Fair value
Inventory	$110,000	$150,000
Land	700,000	600,000
Buildings	700,000	900,000

Masters Inc. purchases Hampton's assets by issuing 100,000 common shares with a market value of $20 per share.

5. At what amount will the inventory, land, and buildings respectively appear on Masters' balance sheet?
    a. $110,000, $600,000, $900,000
    b. $110,000, $700,000, $700,000
    c. $150,000, $600,000, $900,000
    d. $150,000, $700,000, $900,000

6. What is the amount of goodwill from this business combination?
   a. $350,000
   b. Negative $350,000
   c. $490,000
   d. Nil

The following data should be used for Questions 7 and 8.

On January 1, 2002, Planet Company acquired 100% of the outstanding common shares of Sun Inc. by issuing 10,000 common shares. The book values and the fair values of both companies immediately before the acquisition were as follows:

	Planet Company		Sun Inc.	
	Book values	Fair values	Book values	Fair values
Assets	1,450,000	1,600,000	600,000	695,000
Liabilities	770,000	755,000	250,000	270,000
Common shares*	300,000		65,000	
Retained earnings	380,000		285,000	
	1,450,000		600,000	

*Immediately before the acquisition transaction, Planet Company had 20,000 common shares outstanding and Sun Inc. had 6,500 common shares outstanding. Planet's shares were actively trading at $50.00 on the date of the acquisition.

7. What amount would Planet Company report on its consolidated financial statements immediately after the acquisition transaction for "assets"?
   a. $2,050,000
   b. $2,145,000
   c. $2,220,000
   d. $2,295,000

8. What amount would Planet Company report on its consolidated financial statements immediately after the acquisition transaction for "common shares"?
   a. $300,000
   b. $365,000
   c. $800,000
   d. $865,000

CASES

Case 1   Z Ltd. is a public company with factories and distribution centres located throughout Canada. It has 100,000 common shares outstanding. In past years it has reported high earnings, but in 2002 its earnings declined substantially due in part to a loss of markets as a result of the North American Free Trade Agreement. In 2003 it closed a large number of its manufacturing and distribution facilities and reported a substantial loss for the year.

Prior to 2003, 70,000 of Z Ltd.'s shares were held by C Ltd., with the remaining shares being widely distributed in the hands of individual investors in Canada and the United States. During 2003, C Ltd. sold 40,000 of its shares in Z Ltd. to W Corporation.

W Corporation is a joint venture that was formed in 2003 by A Ltd. and B Inc. Each company owns 50 percent of the common shares of W Corporation, and they have agreed in writing that all major decisions will be made jointly. W Corporation's sole asset is its holding of 40,000 shares of Z Ltd.

Required:

(a) How should C Ltd. report its investment in Z Ltd., both before the sale of 40,000 shares and after the sale?

(b) How should W Corporation report its investment in Z Ltd.?

(c) How should A Ltd. and B Inc. report their investments in W Corporation?

Explain fully, and include in your answers a reference to Z Ltd.'s 2003 loss.

Case 2 Arden Corporation has made a market purchase of common shares of Borden Ltd. The accountant of Arden is taking his accounting education at night school, and while he has studied some of the accounting procedures related to this area, he is uncertain how to apply them when he attempts to prepare the company's yearly financial statements.

You have been asked to "clue him in." While you would like more information about this investment, it is not available at this time. With the *CICA Handbook* in hand, you proceed with your task.

Required:

Outline what you will say to the accountant of Arden Corporation.

Case 3* Manitoba Peat Moss (MPM) was the first Canadian company to provide a reliable supply of high-quality peat moss to be used for greenhouse operations. Owned by Paul Parker, the company's founder and president, MPM began operations in the late 1970s, when demand for peat moss was high. It has shown consistently high profits and stable growth for over 20 years. Parker holds all of the 50,000 outstanding common shares in MPM.

Prairie Greenhouses (PG), a publicly traded company that purchases over 70 percent of MPM's output, provides tree seedlings to various government agencies and logging companies for reforestation projects. In 2002 PG approached MPM with an offer to buy all of the company's outstanding shares in exchange for a part ownership in PG, with a view to vertically integrating. Parker was very interested in the offer, since he hoped to soon retire. PG currently has 100,000 shares outstanding and widely distributed. It would issue 100,000 new common shares in a two-for-one exchange for all of MPM's shares. PG's shares are currently trading on the TSE at $60 per share.

The board of directors of PG is uncertain as to the accounting implications of the proposed share exchange. They believe that since they are purchasing all of the outstanding common shares of MPM, it is similar to buying the company outright; as a result they want to report all of MPM's assets on PG's consolidated financial statements at fair market value. This will be very advantageous to PG, because the land carried on MPM's books was purchased in 1977 and has appreciated substantially in value over the years.

The board has asked you, as its accounting adviser, to prepare a report explaining how PG's purchase of shares should be reported. They are particularly interested in how the increase in the value of the land will be shown on the consolidated statements.

The condensed balance sheets of the two companies at the time of the offer are shown below:

---

* Case prepared by and © 1995 J.C. (Jan) Thatcher and Margaret Forbes, Faculty of Business Administration, Lakehead University.

	PG	MPM
Current assets	$ 870,000	$ 450,000
Fixed assets	8,210,000	2,050,000
	$9,080,000	$2,500,000
Current liabilities	$ 525,000	$ 200,000
Long-term debt	2,325,000	1,300,000
Common stock	4,000,000	500,000
Retained earnings	2,230,000	500,000
	$9,080,000	$2,500,000

Note: Land held by MPM at a book value of $1,000,000 has a fair market value of $6,000,000. All other assets of both companies have book values approximately equal to their fair market values.

Required:

Prepare the report to the board of directors.

Case 4   John Williams is the sole owner of Northern Flight Services, a small airline company with 12 float planes servicing remote communities in northern Manitoba and Ontario. He wants to expand, and approaches Billy Johnston, owner of Bearcat Airlines, which operates 15 planes providing freight and passenger services in the same area.

Scenario One   Williams suggests that they join together and form one company. "We can probably save money on maintenance and overhead, and we can benefit from the discounts that suppliers will give us when we issue larger orders. Instead of each of us owning a small company, we will be co-owners of a larger airline operating 27 planes in the same area. Our company will be more profitable if we combine. I currently own all of the 3,000 outstanding shares of Northern Flight Services, and I will issue shares to you in exchange for all of the shares of Bearcat Airlines."

Scenario Two   Williams approaches Johnston with a proposal, saying: "I will buy you out. I will pay cash for all of your assets or, if you prefer, for all of your shares. The amount will be based on our agreement as to the fair value of your company. You can continue to work for me or you can retire. I think it will be beneficial to have one company owning 27 planes."

Required:

What is the basic difference between Scenario One and Scenario Two? Explain how each scenario would be accounted for.

Case 5*   Effective May 31, 1999, Bruncor Inc. (Bruncor), Island Telecom Inc. (Island), Maritime Telegraph and Telephone Company Limited (MTT), and NewTel Enterprises Limited (NEL) combined their businesses to form Aliant Inc. This business combination was accounted for in the consolidated financial statements by the pooling of interests method.

Each of the predecessor companies operated the principal telecommunications companies in the provinces of New Brunswick (Bruncor), Prince Edward Island (Island), Nova Scotia (MTT), and Newfoundland (NEL). The shareholders of the predecessor companies exchanged all their shares for shares of Aliant Inc. as follows:

- Each Bruncor common share exchanged for 1.011 Aliant common shares;
- Each Island common share exchanged for 1.000 Aliant common share (other than those shares held by Maritime Holdings, a wholly owned subsidiary of MTT);
- Each MTT common share exchanged for 1.667 Aliant common shares;

---

* Case prepared by Peter Secord, St. Mary's University.

- Each MTT 7.00% preference share exchanged for 0.605 Aliant common shares; and
- Each NEL common share exchanged for 1.567 Aliant common shares.

The share exchange resulted in a total of 126,437,484 Aliant common shares being issued, with the shareholders of the predecessor companies holding the following shares:

Shareholder group	Number of Aliant common shares	% of shares outstanding
Bruncor former shareholders	44,151,541	34.9%
Island former shareholders (other than Maritime Holdings)	3,533,469	2.8%
MTT former shareholders	49,889,477	39.5%
NEL former shareholders	28,862,997	22.8%
	26,437,484	100.0%

The annual report of the new company for 1999 included a full set of consolidated financial statements. These statements included the consolidated statement of retained earnings shown below:

CONSOLIDATED STATEMENTS OF RETAINED EARNINGS
(Thousands of dollars)
For the years ended December 31

	1999	1998
Balance, beginning of year	$312,030	$235,537
Net income	148,230	171,709
	460,260	407,246
Merger costs	(8,888)	—
Dividends on common shares	(106,305)	(95,216)
Balance, end of year	$345,067	$312,030

Required:

The pooling of interest method was rarely applied in Canadian practice before it was disallowed in 2001, and the Aliant merger was thought of in some circles as "the exception that proves the rule." In this context:

(a) Explain how the characteristics of this situation make the pooling of interest method an appropriate choice in the case of this business combination.
(b) Explain the mechanics of the pooling of interest method as applied to this business combination. Reference may be made to the annual reports of the company which may be accessed at www.Aliant.ca or through www.Sedar.com.
(c) Should the pooling of interest approach be permitted in Canadian practice? Why or why not?
(d) Based on the *Handbook* changes that occurred on July 1, 2001, explain the mechanics of the accounting that would have to be applied to this business combination if it were to occur today.

PROBLEMS

Problem 1   G Company is considering the takeover of K Company, whereby it will issue 6,000 common shares for all of the outstanding shares of K Company. K Company will become a wholly owned subsidiary of G Company. The following information has been assembled:

	G Company		K Company	
	Book value	Fair value	Book value	Fair value
Current assets	$ 40,000	$47,500	$10,000	$ 9,200
Plant assets	60,000	70,000	20,000	25,000
	$100,000		$30,000	
Current liabilities	$ 20,000	20,000	$ 5,000	$ 5,000
Long-term debt	15,000	19,000	2,500	3,200
Common stock	30,000		10,000	
Retained earnings	35,000		12,500	
	$100,000		$30,000	

Required:

Prepare G Company's balance sheet immediately after the combination using:

(a) the pooling of interests method,

(b) the new entity method, and

(c) the purchase method.

(Assume that G Company's shares are trading at $4.90 on the date of the takeover.)

Problem 2 Three companies, A, L, and M, whose December 31, 2002, balance sheets appear below, have agreed to combine as at January 1, 2003.

Each of the companies has a very small proportion of an intensely competitive market dominated by four much larger companies. In order to survive, they have decided to merge into one company. The merger agreement states that Company A will buy the assets and liabilities of each of the other two companies by issuing 27,000 common shares to Company L and 25,000 common shares to Company M, after which the two companies will be wound up.

Company A's shares are currently trading at $5 per share.

Company A will incur the following expenses:

Costs of issuing shares	$ 8,000
Other costs	20,000
	$28,000

The following information has been assembled regarding the three companies:

COMPANY A

	Book value	Fair value
Current assets	$ 99,900	$102,000
Plant and equipment	147,600	160,000
	$247,500	
Liabilities	$ 80,000	$ 75,000
Common stock (50,000 NPV shares)	75,000	
Retained earnings	92,500	
	$247,500	

COMPANY L

	Book value	Fair value
Current assets	$ 60,000	$ 65,000
Plant and equipment	93,000	98,000
	$153,000	
Liabilities	$ 35,000	$ 36,000
Common stock (24,000 NPV shares)	48,000	
Retained earnings	70,000	
	$153,000	

COMPANY M

	Book value	Fair value
Current assets	$ 52,000	$ 68,000
Plant and equipment	115,000	120,000
	$167,000	
Liabilities	$ 72,000	$ 70,000
Common stock (33,000 NPV shares)	60,000	
Retained earnings	35,000	
	$167,000	

Required:

Prepare the balance sheet of Company A on January 2, 2003.

Problem 3   The balance sheet of Wigmore Corporation as at July 31, Year 3, is shown below:

WIGMORE CORPORATION
BALANCE SHEET
July 31, Year 3

	Book value	Fair value
Current assets	$ 350,000	$390,000
Plant and equipment	700,000	810,000
Patents	—	60,000
	$1,050,000	
Current liabilities	$ 210,000	$210,000
Long-term debt	300,000	320,000
Common stock	140,000	
Retained earnings	400,000	
	$1,050,000	

On August 1, Year 3, the directors of Wigmore were considering a takeover offer from Hall Inc. whereby the corporation would sell all of its assets and liabilities. Hall's costs of investigation and drawing up the merger agreement would amount to $15,000.

Required:

PART A
Assume that Hall made an $800,000 cash payment to Wigmore for its net assets. Prepare the journal entries in the accounting records of Hall to record the business combination.

PART B
Assume that Hall issued 100,000 common shares, with market value of $8 per share, to Wigmore for its net assets. Legal fees associated with issuing these shares amounted to $5,000 and were paid in cash. Hall had 150,000 shares outstanding prior to the takeover.
(a) Prepare the journal entries in the records of Hall to record the business combination.
(b) Prepare the balance sheet of Wigmore immediately after the sale.

Problem 4   The shareholders of Prong Company and Horn Company agreed to a statutory amalgamation under which a share exchange took place. On September 1, Year 5, Prong Company issued 50,000 common shares for all of the common shares of Horn Company, after which Horn Company was dissolved. The common shares of Prong Company traded at $7.00 per share on this date.

After the amalgamation, Prong Company changed its name to Pronghorn Corporation.

The balance sheets of the two companies on August 31, Year 5, were as follows:

	Prong Company	Horn Company
Current assets	$135,000	$170,000
Plant and equipment (net)	430,000	300,000
Other assets	41,000	20,000
	$606,000	$490,000
Current liabilities	$ 96,000	$ 30,000
Long-term debt	180,000	160,000
Common stock (note 1)	70,000	100,000
Retained earnings	260,000	200,000
	$606,000	$490,000
Note 1		
Common shares outstanding	70,000 sh.	25,000 sh.

The book values of the net assets of both companies were equal to fair values except for plant and equipment. The fair values of plant and equipment were:

Prong Company	$ 500,000
Horn Company	280,000

Required:

Prepare the balance sheet of Pronghorn Corporation immediately after the statutory amalgamation.

Problem 5   The balance sheet of Ajax Enterprises as at December 31, 2002, is as follows:

Assets

Cash	$ 90,000
Accounts receivable	130,000
Inventory	174,000
Land	120,000
Plant and equipment (net)	600,000
	$1,114,000

Liabilities and Equity

Current liabilities	$ 220,000
Bonds payable	320,000
Common stock	200,000
Retained earnings	374,000
	$1,114,000

Effective January 1, 2003, Ajax proposes to issue 75,000 common shares (currently trading at $20 per share) for all of the assets and liabilities of Borex Industries. Costs of the acquisition are expected to be:

Costs of issuing shares	$40,000
Other costs	35,000
	$75,000

The balance sheet of Borex Industries as at December 31, 2002, is as follows:

	Book value	Fair value
Cash	$ 50,000	$ 50,000
Accounts receivable	250,000	255,000
Inventory	170,000	162,000
Land	90,000	115,000
Plant and equipment (net)	700,000	810,000
	$1,260,000	
Current liabilities	$ 125,000	$125,000
Liability for warranties	90,000	118,000
Common stock	600,000	
Retained earnings	445,000	
	$1,260,000	

Borex Industries is to be wound up after the sale.

Required:

Assume that Ajax's offer is accepted by the shareholders of Borex on the proposed date. Prepare Ajax's January 2, 2003, balance sheet.

Problem 6 D Ltd. and H Corporation are both engaged in the manufacture of computers. On July 1, Year 5, they agree to a merger whereby D will issue 300,000 shares with current market value of $7.80 each for the net assets of H.

Summarized balance sheets of the two companies prior to the merger are presented below:

BALANCE SHEET
June 30, Year 5

	D Ltd. Book value	H Corporation Book value	H Corporation Fair value
Current assets	$ 450,000	$ 500,000	$ 510,000
Fixed assets (net)	4,950,000	3,200,000	3,500,000
	$5,400,000	$3,700,000	
Current liabilities	$ 600,000	$ 800,000	$ 800,000
Long-term debt	1,100,000	900,000	920,000
Common stock	2,500,000	500,000	
Retained earnings	$1,200,000	$1,500,000	
	$5,400,000	$3,700,000	

Required:

Prepare the July 1, Year 5, balance sheet of D, assuming that the merger would be considered:
(a) a purchase combination, and
(b) a pooling of interests combination.

Problem 7   The July 31, Year 3, balance sheets of two companies that are parties to a business combination as follows:

	Hill Corp. Book value	McGraw Inc. Book value	Fair value
Current assets	$ 500,000	$ 350,000	$390,000
Plant and equipment	900,000	700,000	810,000
Patents	—	—	60,000
	$1,400,000	$1,050,000	
Current liabilities	$ 300,000	$ 210,000	$210,000
Long-term debt	400,000	300,000	320,000
Common stock	600,000	140,000	
Retained earnings	100,000	400,000	
	$1,400,000	$1,050,000	

Effective on August 1, Year 3, the shareholders of McGraw accepted an offer from Hill Corporation to purchase all of their common shares. Hill's costs for investigating and drawing up the share purchase agreement amounted to $15,000.

Required:

PART A

Assume that Hill made an $800,000 cash payment to the shareholders of McGraw for 100% of their shares.

(a) Prepare the journal entry in the records of Hill to record the share acquisition.

(b) Prepare the consolidated balance sheet of Hill as at August 1, Year 3.

PART B

Assume that Hill issued 100,000 common shares, with market value of $8 per share, to the shareholders of McGraw for 100% of their shares. Legal fees associated with issuing these shares amounted to $5,000 and were paid in cash. Hill is identified as the acquirer.

(a) Prepare the journal entries in the records of Hill to record the share acquisition.

(b) Prepare the consolidated balance sheet of Hill as at August 1, Year 3.

PART C

Would the assumption in Part A result in higher future earnings to Hill than those resulting from the assumption in Part B? Explain.

Problem 8   The following are summarized balance sheets of three companies as at December 31, Year 3:

	Company X	Company Y	Company Z
Assets	$400,000	$300,000	$250,000
Liabilities	$232,500	$182,000	$155,000
Common stock (note 1)	75,000	48,000	60,000
Retained earnings	92,500	70,000	35,000
	$400,000	$300,000	$250,000
Note 1			
Shares outstanding	50,000 sh.	12,000 sh.	16,500 sh.

The fair values of the assets and liabilities of the three companies as at December 31, Year 3, were as follows:

	Company X	Company Y	Company Z
Assets	$420,000	$350,000	$265,000
Liabilities	233,000	180,000	162,000

On January 2, Year 4, Company X will purchase the assets and assume the liabilities of Company Y and Company Z. It has been agreed that Company X will issue common shares to each of the two companies as payment for their net assets as follows:

to Company Y — 13,500 shares
to Company Z — 12,000 shares

The shares of Company X traded at $14.00 on December 31, Year 3.
Company X will incur the following expenses associated with this acquisition:

Costs of registering and issuing shares	$12,000
Other expenses associated with the takeover	30,000
	$42,000

Company Y and Company Z will wind up after the sale.

Required:

(a) Prepare a summarized pro forma balance sheet of Company X as at January 2, Year 4.
(b) Prepare the pro forma balance sheets of Company Y and Company Z as at January 2, Year 4.

Problem 9 Myers Company Ltd. was formed ten years ago by the issuance of 22,000 common shares to three shareholders. Four years later the company went public and issued an additional 30,000 common shares.

The management of Myers is considering a takeover in which Myers would purchase all of the assets and assume all of the liabilities of Norris Inc. Other costs associated with the takeover would be as follows:

Legal, appraisal, and finders' fees	$ 5,000
Costs of issuing shares	7,000
	$12,000

Two alternative proposals are being considered:

PROPOSAL 1
Myers would offer to pay $300,000 cash for the Norris net assets, to be financed by a $300,000 loan due in five years.

PROPOSAL 2
Myers would issue 50,000 shares currently trading at $8.00 each for the Norris net assets. Norris shareholders would be offered five seats on the ten-member board of directors of Myers, and the management of Norris would be absorbed into the surviving company.

Balance sheet data for the two companies prior to the combination are as follows:

	Myers Book value	Norris Book value	Fair value
Cash	$ 140,000	$ 52,500	$ 52,500
Accounts receivable	167,200	61,450	56,200
Inventory	374,120	110,110	134,220
Land	425,000	75,000	210,000
Buildings (net)	250,505	21,020	24,020
Equipment (net)	78,945	17,705	15,945
	$1,435,770	$337,785	
Current liabilities	$ 133,335	$ 41,115	$ 41,115
Noncurrent liabilities	—	150,000	155,000
Common stock	500,000	100,000	
Retained earnings	802,435	46,670	
	$1,435,770	$337,785	

Required:

(a) Prepare the journal entries of Myers for each of the two proposals being considered.
(b) Prepare the balance sheet of Myers after the takeover for each of the proposals being considered.

Problem 10 Refer to Problem 9. All of the facts and data are the same except that in the proposed takeover, Myers Company will purchase all of the outstanding common shares of Norris Inc.

Required:

(a) Prepare the journal entries of Myers for each of the two proposals being considered.
(b) Prepare the balance sheet of Myers after the takeover for each of the proposals being considered.

CHAPTER 4

Consolidated Statements on Date of Acquisition

CHAPTER OUTLINE

LEARNING OBJECTIVES

After studying this chapter, you should be able to do the following:

- Understand how control is determined.
- Calculate and allocate the purchase discrepancy, including the further allocation necessary when negative goodwill exists.
- Prepare a consolidated balance sheet on acquisition date, using both the working paper and direct approaches when the parent owns 100 percent and less than 100 percent of the subsidiary.
- Explain the differences between the three consolidation theories, and apply these theories by preparing a consolidated balance sheet on acquisition date.
- Account for contingent consideration based on earnings and share prices.
- Explain and illustrate the concepts behind a reverse takeover.

Control and Consolidated Statements

This is the first of seven chapters covering the preparation of consolidated financial statements. The requirements for consolidation can be found in the *CICA Handbook*, as follows:

An enterprise should consolidate all of its subsidiaries. [1590.16]

The following definitions have been adopted for purposes of this section:

(a) A *subsidiary* is an enterprise controlled by another enterprise (the parent) that has the right and ability to obtain future economic benefits from the resources of the enterprise and is exposed to the related risks.
(b) *Control* of an enterprise is the continuing power to determine its strategic operating, investing and financing policies without the co-operation of others. [1590.03]

When a parent company has control over one or more subsidiaries, it has the right to benefit economically from the subsidiaries' resources and at the same time is exposed to the related risks involved. Consolidated financial statements reflect a group of economic resources that are under the common control of the parent company even though these resources are owned separately by the parent and the subsidiary companies. Notice that the key concept is *common control*. This concept is reinforced in Section 1000 of the *Handbook*, where the definition of an asset focuses on control rather than ownership.[1] When control over a subsidiary is present, the parent is required to consolidate its subsidiaries for external reporting purposes; this results in a set of financial statements for a fictitious single entity. If the companies that make up this entity conduct business with each other, all intercompany transactions are eliminated in the preparation of the consolidated statements. As a result, these statements reflect only transactions of this single entity with those outside the entity. (The process required to eliminate these intercompany transactions will be discussed thoroughly in later chapters.)

Consolidated statements are considered more useful to financial statement users than would be the separate financial statements of all of the companies that make up the group. Present and prospective shareholders of the parent company are interested in future profitability and cash flows. Creditors of the parent company have interests and information needs similar to those of the shareholders. The profitability and financial health of the parent is directly related to that of the companies it controls.

While consolidated statements are considered the best vehicle to satisfy user needs, they also have limitations. A poor performance by certain subsidiaries can be hidden as a result of the aggregation process. In addition, many parent companies have subsidiaries in different industries in various countries throughout the world, and this can be hidden in a single set of statements. Footnote disclosures that present details about the companies' operating segments help to alleviate this problem. Finally, the information needs of minority shareholders and creditors of the subsidiary companies are not served by consolidated statements. This sector relies on the separate statements to determine the operating results and financial position of these companies.

---

[1] *CICA Handbook*, paragraph 1000.29.

How Is Control Determined?   As we have seen from the *Handbook* definition, control is the continuing power of one company to determine the strategic operating, investing, and financing policies of another company without the co-operation of others. The ability to exercise this power is all that is required; it is not necessary to actually exercise it. Because the board of directors establishes the strategic policies of a corporation, the ability to elect a majority of the members of the board would generally be evidence of control. Therefore, control is presumed to exist if the parent owns directly or indirectly enough voting shares to elect the majority of the board of directors of a subsidiary. Indirect control would exist if, for example, B Company controls C Company and C Company controls D Company. B Company has direct control over C Company and indirectly controls D Company. Consolidation when control is achieved through indirect holdings is discussed in Chapter 7.

In most situations, more than 50 percent of the voting shares are required to elect the majority of the board, and so control is presumed to exist if the percentage owned is over 50 percent. However, we have to look at all factors and at the same time keep in mind the phrase "without the co-operation of others."

For example, if A Company owns 60 percent of the voting shares of B Company and C Company owns the other 40 percent, then we can presume that A Company controls B Company. But if C Company owns convertible bonds of B Company or options or warrants to purchase B Company shares, which if converted or exercised would give C Company 62 percent of the outstanding shares of B Company, then A Company needs the co-operation of C Company not to convert or exercise. A Company does not have the continuing power to control without the co-operation of others.

There is also a presumption that a holding of less than 50 percent of the voting shares does not constitute control. This presumption can be overcome if other factors clearly indicate control. For example, an irrevocable agreement with other shareholders to convey voting rights to the parent would constitute control, even when the parent owned less than 50 percent of the voting shares. A parent may also have control despite owning less than 50 percent of the voting shares if its holdings of rights, warrants, convertible debt, or convertible preferred shares would give it enough voting power to control the board of directors of the subsidiary. Exercise or conversion would not be necessary, only the right to exercise or convert.

In another example, X Company owns 40 percent of Y Company, which is the largest single block of shares of that company outstanding. The other 60 percent is very widely held and only a very small proportion of the holders appear at the annual meeting of Y Company. As a result, X Company has had no trouble electing the majority of the board of directors. While this appears to be control, it would not be considered so because the cooperation of the other 60 percent to not vote is needed by X Company.

If control is present, a parent must consolidate a subsidiary; if control ceases, consolidation is discontinued. The seizure of the company's assets by a trustee in a receivership or bankruptcy situation would be evidence that control has probably ceased, as would the imposition of governmental restrictions over a foreign subsidiary's ability to pay dividends to its parent.

While numerical guidelines are the starting point in determining whether or not control exists, professional judgment plays a major role because of all the relevant factors that must be taken into account.

The Consolidated Balance Sheet on Acquisition Date

The Canadian accounting principles involved in the preparation of consolidated financial statements are found in Section 1600 of the *Handbook*. In the material that follows in this and later chapters, the preparation of consolidated statements will follow this section's requirements unless the contrary is indicated. Consolidated statements consist of a balance sheet, an income statement, a retained earnings statement, and a cash flow statement and the accompanying footnotes. In this chapter we will illustrate the preparation of the consolidated balance sheet on the date that control is obtained by the parent company. Consolidation of other financial statements will be illustrated in later chapters.

In Chapter 3, we introduced the preparation of a consolidated balance sheet immediately after a business combination, using the purchase and pooling of interests methods. Summarized financial statements were used to focus on the basic concepts involved. In this chapter we elaborate on these concepts and use more detailed financial statements. Because pooling of interests combinations are no longer allowed in Canada, all future illustrations of the preparation of consolidated financial statements will assume the purchase method of accounting. The following example will form the basis of many of the illustrations that will be used in this chapter.

We will call the two companies to be consolidated P Ltd. and S Ltd. Both companies have a June 30 fiscal year-end. The balance sheets of the two companies on June 29, Year 1, are shown in Exhibit 4.1.

On June 30, Year 1, P Ltd. obtains control over S Ltd. by purchasing a portion of that company's outstanding common shares from the shareholders of S Ltd. The total cost of the shares includes the direct expenses involved in the business combination and is paid in cash by P Ltd. on this date. No additional transactions take place on this date. Immediately after the share acquisition, P Ltd. prepares a consolidated balance sheet.

Exhibit 4.1

BALANCE SHEET
June 29, Year 1

	P Ltd. Book value	S Ltd. Book value	S Ltd. Fair value
Cash	$100,000	$ 12,000	$12,000
Accounts receivable	90,000	7,000	7,000
Inventory	130,000	20,000	22,000
Plant	280,000	50,000	59,000
Patent	—	11,000	10,000
	$600,000	$100,000	
Current liabilities	$ 60,000	$ 8,000	$ 8,000
Long-term debt	180,000	22,000	25,000
Common stock	200,000	40,000	
Retained earnings	160,000	30,000	
	$600,000	$100,000	

100 Percent Ownership

Illustration 1   Assume that on June 30, Year 1, P Ltd. purchases 100 percent of S Ltd. for a total cost of $81,000. P Ltd.'s journal entry to record the acquisition is as follows:

Investment in S Ltd.	81,000	
Cash		81,000

P Ltd.'s year-end is June 30, and the only consolidated statement prepared at this time would be the balance sheet. The income statement, retained earnings statement, and cash flow statement presented with the consolidated balance sheet would not be consolidated statements.

The calculation and allocation of the purchase discrepancy is a useful first step in the preparation of the consolidated balance sheet. The information provided in this calculation forms the basis of the elimination and adjusting entries required. This calculation is shown in Exhibit 4.2.

The preparation of the consolidated balance sheet using a working paper is illustrated in Exhibit 4.3.

Note that the parent's cash has been reduced by the cost of the acquisition. Two elimination entries are used in the working paper. Entry #1 eliminates the parent's share of the shareholders' equity accounts of the subsidiary and the parent's investment account, with the difference established as the purchase discrepancy. Entry #2 allocates the purchase discrepancy to the identifiable assets and liabilities of the subsidiary, and establishes the goodwill resulting from the business combination. (It should be obvious that only one entry needs to be used if the purchase discrepancy is not established.) The amounts shown in the consolidated

Exhibit 4.2

CALCULATION AND ALLOCATION OF PURCHASE DISCREPANCY
(100 percent owned subsidiary)

Cost of investment in S Ltd.			$81,000
Shareholders' equity of S Ltd.			
Common stock		40,000	
Retained earnings		30,000	
		70,000	
P Ltd.'s ownership		100%	70,000
Purchase discrepancy			$11,000
Allocated:	*(FV – BV) × 100%		
Inventory	+ 2,000		
Plant	+ 9,000		
Patent	– 1,000		
	10,000		
Long-term debt	+ 3,000		7,000
Balance — goodwill			$ 4,000

* FV fair value
  BV book value

Exhibit 4.3

P LTD.
CONSOLIDATED BALANCE SHEET WORKING PAPER
June 30, Year 1

	P Ltd.	S Ltd.	Adjustments and Eliminations Dr.		Adjustments and Eliminations Cr.		Consolidated balance sheet
Cash	$ 19,000	$ 12,000					$ 31,000
Accounts receivable	90,000	7,000					97,000
Inventory	130,000	20,000	(2)	2,000			152,000
Plant	280,000	50,000	(2)	9,000			339,000
Patent		11,000			(2)	1,000	10,000
Investment in S Ltd.	81,000				(1)	81,000	
Purchase discrepancy			(1)	11,000	(2)	11,000	
Goodwill			(2)	4,000			4,000
	$600,000	$100,000					$633,000
Current liabilities	$ 60,000	$ 8,000					$ 68,000
Long-term debt	180,000	22,000			(2)	3,000	205,000
Common stock	200,000						200,000
Retained earnings	160,000						160,000
Common stock		40,000	(1)	40,000			
Retained earnings		30,000	(1)	30,000			
	$600,000	$100,000	$96,000		$96,000		$633,000

balance sheet column are used to prepare the consolidated balance sheet. The two working paper entries are summarized next:

#1	Common stock — S Ltd.	40,000	
	Retained earnings — S Ltd.	30,000	
	Purchase discrepancy	11,000	
	Investment in S Ltd.		81,000
#2	Inventory — S Ltd.	2,000	
	Plant — S Ltd.	9,000	
	Goodwill	4,000	
	Patent — S Ltd.		1,000
	Long-term debt — S Ltd.		3,000
	Purchase discrepancy		11,000

It must be emphasized that these entries[2] are made only in the working paper; they are *not* entered in the accounting records of either P Ltd. or S Ltd.

The Direct Approach An alternative approach to the preparation of consolidated financial statements is to prepare the statements directly without the use of a working paper. It should be obvious from examining the working paper that the investment account, the purchase discrepancy, and the shareholders' equity accounts of the

---

[2] In later chapters, the working paper eliminations will be illustrated without the intermediate step of setting up the purchase discrepancy.

subsidiary do *not* appear on the consolidated balance sheet. The calculation of the purchase discrepancy in a sense eliminates the investment and shareholders' equity accounts. The allocation of the purchase discrepancy provides the amounts used to revalue the net assets of the subsidiary. Having made the necessary calculations, the preparer ignores these accounts (i.e., eliminates them) and prepares the consolidated balance sheet. This is done by combining, on an item-by-item basis, the balance sheets of the parent and the subsidiary while at the same time revaluing for consolidation purposes the balance sheet items of the subsidiary. The basic process involved in the direct approach is as follows:

$$
\begin{array}{ccccccc}
\text{Book value} & & \text{Book value} & & \text{Purchase} & & \text{Consolidated} \\
\text{(parent)} & + & \text{(subsidiary)} & +(-) & \text{discrepancy} & = & \text{amounts}
\end{array}
$$

The preparation of the consolidated balance sheet using the direct approach is shown in Exhibit 4.4. The amounts shown in brackets come from the balance sheets of P Ltd. and S Ltd. and from the allocation of the purchase discrepancy. It should be noted that under the purchase method of accounting for a business combination, consolidated shareholders' equity on acquisition date is always that of the parent company.[3]

Income Statement in Year of Acquisition When a business combination is accounted for using the purchase method, only the net income earned by the subsidiary after the date of acquisition is included in consolidated net income. For example, if the acquisition occurred halfway through the fiscal year, consolidated net income would consist of the net income of the parent for the full year plus the half-year net income earned by the subsidiary after the acquisition date.[4] In the example used here, both

---

Exhibit 4.4

Illustration of the Direct Approach

P LTD.
CONSOLIDATED BALANCE SHEET
June 30, Year 1

Cash (100,000 – 81,000* + 12,000)	$ 31,000
Accounts receivable (90,000 + 7,000)	97,000
Inventory (130,000 + 20,000 + 2,000)	152,000
Plant (280,000 + 50,000 + 9,000)	339,000
Patent (11,000 – 1,000)	10,000
Goodwill	4,000
	$633,000
Current liabilities (60,000 + 8,000)	$ 68,000
Long-term debt (180,000 + 22,000 + 3,000)	205,000
Common stock	200,000
Retained earnings	160,000
	$633,000

* Cash paid by P Ltd. to acquire S Ltd.

---

[3] Under a pooling of interests, consolidated shareholders' equity would be the parent's plus the subsidiary's. (See Chapter 3, Appendix B.)

[4] The net income of the subsidiary earned after the acquisition date would be reduced by the amortization of the purchase discrepancy because the asset values in the accounting records of the subsidiary are not the values used for consolidation. This concept will be discussed in Chapter 5.

P Ltd. and S Ltd. have a June 30 year-end. P Ltd.'s financial statements for the year ended June 30, Year 1, would consist of a consolidated balance sheet and nonconsolidated statements of net income, retained earnings, and changes in financial position. These nonconsolidated statements would be those of P Ltd. alone. Footnotes to the financial statements should disclose revenues, net income, and earnings per share as though the acquisition had occurred at the beginning of the fiscal period.[5]

Push-down Accounting   Under push-down accounting, on the date of acquisition the subsidiary revalues its assets and liabilities based on the parent's acquisition cost. The allocation of the purchase discrepancy is "pushed down" to the actual accounting records of the subsidiary. This practice became permissible under GAAP in 1992 with the issuance of Section 1625, "Comprehensive Revaluation of Assets and Liabilities." Push-down accounting is allowed only when the subsidiary is at least 90 percent owned. The preparation of the consolidated balance sheet of P Ltd. would have been considerably simplified if S Ltd. had applied push-down accounting on June 30, Year 1. However, when the subsidiary is not 100 percent owned, push-down accounting is not simpler. Comprehensive revaluations are discussed fully in Chapter 11.

Subsidiary Formed by Parent   In some situations a subsidiary is not acquired through a share purchase, but rather by the parent company forming the subsidiary company. The parent company receives all of the initial share issue after the subsidiary is incorporated.[6] At this time, the book values and fair values of the subsidiary's net assets are obviously equal, and there is no goodwill. It should also be obvious that the subsidiary has no retained earnings at this time. The preparation of the consolidated balance sheet on the date of formation of the subsidiary is simplified, requiring only the elimination of the parent's investment account against the subsidiary's share capital.

Illustration 2 — Negative Goodwill   Assume that on June 30, Year 1, P Ltd. purchased 100 percent of the outstanding shares of S Ltd. at a total cost of $75,000. P Ltd.'s journal entry to record the acquisition is as follows:

Investment in S Ltd.	75,000	
Cash		75,000

The calculation and allocation of the purchase discrepancy on this date is shown in Exhibit 4.5.

The calculations for the purchase discrepancy and for its initial allocation are similar to what is shown in Exhibit 4.2. However, in this situation the goodwill is negative because the acquisition cost is lower than in the previous illustration. A business combination that results in negative goodwill is often described as a

---

[5] *CICA Handbook*, paragraph 1600.72.

[6] It is also possible for a parent to form a less than 100 percent owned subsidiary, or for a 100 percent owned subsidiary to later issue shares that are not purchased by the parent. In either case, the observations made in this paragraph are basically the same.

Exhibit 4.5	

CALCULATION AND AMORTIZATION OF PURCHASE DISCREPANCY
(negative goodwill)

Cost of investment in S Ltd.			$75,000
Shareholders' equity of S Ltd.			
Common stock		40,000	
Retained earnings		30,000	
		70,000	
P Ltd.'s ownership		100%	70,000
Purchase discrepancy			5,000
Allocated	(FV – BV) × 100%		
Inventory	+ 2,000		
Plant	+ 9,000		
Patent	– 1,000		
	10,000		
Long-term debt	+ 3,000		7,000
Balance — "negative goodwill"			$–2,000
Allocated to noncurrent assets			
Plant	59/69 × –2,000 =	1,710	
Patent	10/69 × –2,000 =	290	–2,000
Balance			0

SUMMARY OF ALLOCATION OF PURCHASE DISCREPANCY

Inventory	+ 2,000	+ 2,000
Plant	+ 9,000 – 1,710	+ 7,290
Patent	– 1,000 – 290	– 1,290
Allocated to assets		+ 8,000
Long-term debt		+ 3,000
Purchase discrepancy		$ 5,000

"bargain purchase." This means that the parent gained control over the subsidiary's assets and liabilities at a price that was less than the fair values assigned to those assets and liabilities. This can occur when share prices are depressed or the subsidiary has a recent history of operating losses. Regardless of the cause, the *Handbook* requires that negative goodwill be allocated to reduce the values assigned to certain assets of the subsidiary. The specific paragraph was reproduced on page 72.

Its requirements can be summarized as follows:

- Allocate the purchase discrepancy in the normal fashion.

- Any negative goodwill that results is allocated to reduce all of the amounts assigned to revalue the assets of the subsidiary, *except* for the following items:
  - Financial assets (cash, receivables, equity instruments of other entities) other than investments accounted for using the equity method.
  - Future tax assets (the allocation of the purchase discrepancy to create future tax assets and liabilities is discussed in a later chapter and will not be considered here).
  - Assets to be disposed of by sale.
  - Prepaid assets relating to future benefit plans.

- Any other current assets.
  (By examining all of these exceptions, we can interpret the direction as saying that the negative goodwill ends up being allocated basically to noncurrent assets but not to long-term investments accounted for using the equity method.)
- The allocation is based on relative fair market values.
- Any negative goodwill still remaining would be taken into consolidated income and shown as an extraordinary gain (even though it does not satisfy the requirements for such a gain).

The fair values of the noncurrent assets of S Ltd. are as follows:

Plant	$59,000
Patent	10,000
	$69,000

The allocation of the $2,000 negative goodwill in Exhibit 4.5 is based on these relative fair values. The working paper to prepare the consolidated balance sheet is shown in Exhibit 4.6.

Entry #1 eliminates the parent's share of the subsidiary's shareholders' equity accounts, and the parent's investment account, and establishes the difference as the purchase discrepancy. Entry #2 allocates the purchase discrepancy to revalue the net assets of the subsidiary, as shown in the summary at the bottom of Exhibit 4.5.

Exhibit 4.6

P LTD.
CONSOLIDATED BALANCE SHEET WORKING PAPER
June 30, Year 1

	P Ltd.	S Ltd.	Adjustments and Eliminations Dr.		Adjustments and Eliminations Cr.		Consolidated balance sheet
Cash	$ 25,000	$ 12,000					$ 37,000
Accounts receivable	90,000	7,000					97,000
Inventory	130,000	20,000	(2)	2,000			152,000
Plant	280,000	50,000	(2)	7,290			337,290
Patent		11,000			(2)	1,290	9,710
Investment in S Ltd.	75,000				(1)	75,000	
Purchase discrepancy			(1)	5,000	(2)	5,000	
	$600,000	$100,000					$633,000
Current liabilities	$ 60,000	$ 8,000					$ 68,000
Long-term debt	180,000	22,000			(2)	3,000	205,000
Common stock	200,000						200,000
Retained earnings	160,000						160,000
Common stock		40,000	(1)	40,000			
Retained earnings		30,000	(1)	30,000			
	$600,000	$100,000		$84,290		$84,290	$633,000

The two working paper elimination entries are shown next:

#1	Common stock — S Ltd.	40,000	
	Retained earnings — S Ltd.	30,000	
	Purchase discrepancy	5,000	
	Investment in S Ltd.		75,000

#2	Inventory — S Ltd.	2,000	
	Plant — S Ltd.	7,290	
	Patent — S Ltd.		1,290
	Long-term debt — S Ltd.		3,000
	Purchase discrepancy		5,000

It must be emphasized again that entries such as these are made only in the working paper; they are *not* entered in the accounting records of either P Ltd. or S Ltd.

The Direct Approach   Exhibit 4.7 shows the preparation of the consolidated balance sheet on June 30, Year 1, using the direct approach. The summary of the allocation of the purchase discrepancy (Exhibit 4.5) provides all the information needed to avoid having to use a working paper.

Negative Purchase Discrepancy   It is possible for a purchase discrepancy to be negative. In this situation the parent's interest in the book values of the subsidiary's net assets exceeds the acquisition cost. A negative purchase discrepancy is not the same as negative goodwill, nor does it necessarily imply that there will be negative goodwill. If the fair values of the subsidiary's net assets are less than their book values, the amounts used to revalue the specific identifiable net assets of the subsidiary downward could be greater than the negative purchase discrepancy, resulting in positive goodwill.

Exhibit 4.7

Illustration of the Direct Approach
(negative goodwill)

P LTD.
CONSOLIDATED BALANCE SHEET
June 30, Year 1

Cash (100,000 – 75,000* + 12,000)	$ 37,000
Accounts receivable (90,000 + 7,000)	97,000
Inventory (130,000 + 20,000 + 2,000)	152,000
Plant (280,000 + 50,000 + 7,290)	337,290
Patent (11,000 – 1,290)	9,710
	$633,000
Current liabilities (60,000 + 8,000)	$ 68,000
Long-term debt (180,000 + 22,000 + 3,000)	205,000
Common stock	200,000
Retained earnings	160,000
	$633,000

---

* Cash paid by P Ltd. to acquire S Ltd.

Illustration 3 — Subsidiary with Goodwill   The goodwill appearing on the balance sheet of a subsidiary on the date of a business combination is not carried forward when the consolidated balance sheet is prepared. At some date in the past the subsidiary was the acquirer in a business combination and recorded the goodwill as the difference between the acquisition cost and the fair value of the net identifiable assets acquired. Now this company has itself become an acquiree. From the perspective of its new parent, the goodwill is not considered to be an identifiable asset at the time of the business combination. The purchase discrepancy is calculated as if the goodwill had been written off by the subsidiary, even though in fact this is not the case. The following illustration will examine the consolidation process when the subsidiary has existing goodwill.

Assume that on June 30, Year 1, P Ltd. purchased 100 percent of the outstanding shares of S Ltd. for a total cost of $75,000, paid in cash. Exhibit 4.8 shows the balance sheets of the two companies at this time.

Notice that the goodwill (highlighted in boldface), in the amount of $11,000, was called a patent in Exhibit 4.1. Notice also that the acquisition cost is the same as in Illustration 2, where the result turned out to be negative goodwill. When we calculate and allocate the purchase discrepancy in this illustration, the result is positive goodwill of $8,000, as shown in Exhibit 4.9.

The working papers for the preparation of the June 30, Year 1, consolidated balance sheet are presented in Exhibit 4.10.

Three working paper entries are required. Entry #1 writes off the previous goodwill (labelled "old" goodwill in the working paper) to S Ltd.'s retained earnings for purposes of consolidation. Entry #2 eliminates the parent's share of the subsidiary's common stock and adjusted retained earnings and the parent's investment account, and establishes the difference as the purchase discrepancy. Entry #3 allocates the purchase discrepancy to revalue the net assets of the subsidiary and establishes the new goodwill from the business combination.

Exhibit 4.8

BALANCE SHEET
June 29, Year 1

	P Ltd. Book value	S Ltd. Book value	S Ltd. Fair value
Cash	$100,000	$ 12,000	$ 12,000
Accounts receivable	90,000	7,000	7,000
Inventory	130,000	20,000	22,000
Plant	280,000	50,000	59,000
Goodwill	—	11,000	
	$600,000	$100,000	
Current liabilities	$ 60,000	$ 8,000	$ 8,000
Long-term debt	180,000	22,000	25,000
Common stock	200,000	40,000	
Retained earnings	160,000	30,000	
	$600,000	$100,000	

Exhibit 4.9

CALCULATION AND ALLOCATION OF PURCHASE DISCREPANCY
(subsidiary with goodwill)

Cost of investment in S Ltd.			$75,000
Shareholders' equity of S Ltd.			
Common stock		40,000	
Retained earnings		30,000	
		70,000	
Deduct goodwill of S Ltd.		11,000	
Adjusted shareholders' equity		59,000	
P Ltd.'s ownership		100%	59,000
Purchase discrepancy			16,000
Allocated	(FV – BV) × 100%		
Inventory	+ 2,000		
Plant	+ 9,000		
	11,000		
Long-term debt	+ 3,000		8,000
Balance — goodwill			$ 8,000

Exhibit 4.10

P LTD.
CONSOLIDATED BALANCE SHEET WORKING PAPER
June 30, Year 1

	P Ltd.	S Ltd.	Adjustments and Eliminations Dr.		Adjustments and Eliminations Cr.		Consolidated balance sheet
Cash	$ 25,000	$ 12,000					$ 37,000
Accounts receivable	90,000	7,000					97,000
Inventory	130,000	20,000	(3)	2,000			152,000
Plant	280,000	50,000	(3)	9,000			339,000
Goodwill — old		11,000			(1)	11,000	
Investment in S Ltd.	75,000				(2)	75,000	
Purchase discrepancy			(2)	16,000	(3)	16,000	
Goodwill			(3)	8,000			8,000
	$600,000	$100,000					$633,000
Current liabilities	$ 60,000	$ 8,000					$ 68,000
Long-term debt	180,000	22,000			(3)	3,000	205,000
Common stock	200,000						200,000
Retained earnings	160,000						160,000
Common stock		40,000	(2)	40,000			
Retained earnings		30,000	(1)	11,000			
			(2)	19,000			
	$600,000	$100,000		$105,000		$105,000	$633,000

The three working paper elimination entries are shown below:

#1	Retained earnings — S Ltd.	11,000	
	Goodwill — old — S Ltd.		11,000
#2	Common stock — S Ltd.	40,000	
	Retained earnings — S Ltd.	19,000	
	Purchase discrepancy	16,000	
	Investment in S Ltd.		75,000
#3	Inventory — S Ltd.	2,000	
	Plant — S Ltd.	9,000	
	Goodwill	8,000	
	Long-term debt — S Ltd.		3,000
	Purchase discrepancy		16,000

Entry #1 was only a working paper entry and was not recorded in the records of S Ltd. If P Ltd. directs S Ltd. to actually write off its $11,000 goodwill as at June 30, Year 1, no further working paper entries will be required for this item in future years. However, if S Ltd. does not write off its recorded goodwill, the preparation of consolidated statements in Year 2 and all future years will require working paper entries, to write off any goodwill that still exists in S Ltd.'s records and to reverse any goodwill impairment that has been recorded.

The Direct Approach   Using the calculations shown in Exhibit 4.9, the consolidated balance sheet can easily be prepared without the use of a working paper, as Exhibit 4.11 shows.

Exhibit 4.11

Illustration of the Direct Approach
(subsidiary with goodwill)

P LTD.
CONSOLIDATED BALANCE SHEET
June 30, Year 1

Cash (100,000 – 75,000* + 12,000)	$ 37,000
Accounts receivable (90,000 + 7,000)	97,000
Inventory (130,000 + 20,000 + 2,000)	152,000
Plant (280,000 + 50,000 + 9,000)	339,000
Goodwill	8,000
	$633,000
Current liabilities (60,000 + 8,000)	$ 68,000
Long-term debt (180,000 + 22,000 + 3,000)	205,000
Common stock	200,000
Retained earnings	160,000
	$633,000

* Cash paid by P Ltd. to acquire S Ltd.

Less Than 100 Percent Ownership

Illustration 4 The first three illustrations were those of a 100 percent owned subsidiary. In such a situation the combining of the individual assets and liabilities of the subsidiary with the allocated purchase discrepancy results in the assets and liabilities of the subsidiary being recorded at fair values[7] in the consolidated balance sheet. When we have a less than 100 percent owned subsidiary, this is *not* the case. This illustration examines the consolidation of a less than 100 percent owned subsidiary.

Assume that on June 30, Year 1, P Ltd. purchased 80 percent of S Ltd. at a total cost of $64,800. P Ltd.'s journal entry to record this purchase is as follows:

Investment in S Ltd.	64,800	
Cash		64,800

When the consolidated balance sheet is prepared, the net assets of P Ltd. are combined with 100 percent of the net assets of S Ltd. even though P Ltd. owns only 80 percent of the outstanding shares of S Ltd. This factor introduces a new component of consolidated statements called the noncontrolling (or minority) interest. This component, representing the 20 percent not owned by the parent, requires a separate calculation. Section 1600 of the *Handbook* indicates that since the business combination did not involve the noncontrolling interest in the net assets of the subsidiary, the amount reflected in the consolidated balance sheet for this noncontrolling interest should be based on the book value of the subsidiary's net assets.[8] Before the consolidated balance sheet working paper is prepared at June 30, Year 1, calculations are made for the purchase discrepancy *and* for the noncontrolling interest. Both calculations are shown in Exhibit 4.12.

The working paper used to prepare the consolidated balance sheet is shown in Exhibit 4.13.

Three working paper entries are used. Entry #1 eliminates the parent's share of the subsidiary's shareholders' equity accounts and the parent's investment account, with the difference established as the purchase discrepancy. Entry #2 eliminates the noncontrolling interest's share of the subsidiary's shareholders' equity accounts and establishes the noncontrolling interest on the consolidated balance sheet. Entry #3 allocates the purchase discrepancy to revalue the net assets of the subsidiary and establishes the resulting goodwill.

The three working paper elimination entries are:

#1	Common stock — S Ltd.	32,000	
	Retained earnings — S Ltd.	24,000	
	Purchase discrepancy	8,800	
	Investment in S Ltd.		64,800
#2	Common stock — S Ltd.	8,000	
	Retained earnings — S Ltd.	6,000	
	Noncontrolling interest		14,000

---

[7] Book value + 100% x (FV − BV) = Fair value.

[8] *CICA Handbook*, paragraphs 1600.14–.15.

Exhibit 4.12

CALCULATION OF PURCHASE DISCREPANCY
AND NONCONTROLLING INTEREST
(less than 100 percent owned subsidiary)

Cost of investment in S Ltd.				$64,800
Shareholders' equity of S Ltd.				
Common stock			40,000	
Retained earnings			30,000	
			70,000	
P Ltd.'s ownership			80%	56,000
Purchase discrepancy				8,800
Allocated:	(FV – BV) × 80%			
Inventory	+ 2,000 × 80% =	+ 1,600		
Plant	+ 9,000 × 80% =	+ 7,200		
Patent	– 1,000 × 80% =	– 800		
		8,000		
Long-term debt	+ 3,000 × 80% =	+ 2,400		5,600
Balance — Goodwill				$ 3,200

CALCULATION OF NONCONTROLLING INTEREST

Shareholders' equity of S Ltd. (above)	$70,000
Noncontrolling ownership	20%
	$14,000

Exhibit 4.13

P LTD.
CONSOLIDATED BALANCE SHEET WORKING PAPER
June 30, Year 1

	P Ltd.	S Ltd.	Adjustments and Eliminations Dr.		Adjustments and Eliminations Cr.		Consolidated balance sheet
Cash	$ 35,200	$ 12,000					$ 47,200
Accounts receivable	90,000	7,000					97,000
Inventory	130,000	20,000	(3)	1,600			151,600
Plant	280,000	50,000	(3)	7,200			337,200
Patent		11,000			(3)	800	10,200
Investment in S Ltd.	64,800				(1)	64,800	
Purchase discrepancy			(1)	8,800	(3)	8,800	
Goodwill			(3)	3,200			3,200
	$600,000	$100,000					$646,400
Current liabilities	$ 60,000	$ 8,000					$ 68,000
Long-term debt	180,000	22,000			(3)	2,400	204,400
Common stock	200,000						200,000
Retained earnings	160,000						160,000
Common stock		40,000	(1)	32,000			
			(2)	8,000			
Retained earnings		30,000	(1)	24,000			
			(2)	6,000			
Noncontrolling interest					(2)	14,000	14,000
	$600,000	$100,000		$90,800		$90,800	$646,400

#3	Inventory — S Ltd.	1,600	
	Plant — S Ltd.	7,200	
	Goodwill	3,200	
	Patent — S Ltd.		800
	Long-term debt — S Ltd.		2,400
	Purchase discrepancy		8,800

The Direct Approach Using the calculations provided in Exhibit 4.12, the consolidated balance sheet can be prepared easily without a working paper. The investment account is eliminated against the parent's share of the shareholders' equity of the subsidiary. By calculating the noncontrolling interest, the remaining portion of the shareholders' equity of the subsidiary is eliminated. The consolidated balance sheet is prepared by (a) combining the balance sheet of the parent with that of the subsidiary adjusted for the allocation of the purchase discrepancy, then (b) including the amount for noncontrolling interest on the balance sheet. Shareholders' equity is the parent's shareholders' equity. Exhibit 4.14 illustrates the direct approach.

Exhibit 4.14

Illustration of the Direct Approach
(less than 100 percent owned subsidiary)

P LTD.
CONSOLIDATED BALANCE SHEET
June 30, Year 1

Cash (100,000 – 64,800* + 12,000)	$ 47,200
Accounts receivable (90,000 + 7,000)	97,000
Inventory (130,000 + 20,000 + 1,600)	151,600
Plant (280,000 + 50,000 + 7,200)	337,200
Patent (11,000 – 800)	10,200
Goodwill	3,200
	$646,400
Current liabilities (60,000 + 8,000)	$ 68,000
Long-term debt (180,000 + 22,000 + 2,400)	204,400
Total liabilities	272,400
Noncontrolling interest	14,000
Shareholders' equity	
Common stock	200,000
Retained earnings	160,000 360,000
	$646,400

Cash paid by P Ltd. to acquire S Ltd.

Illustrations 1 and 4 examined the preparation of the consolidated balance sheet when P Ltd. acquired 100 percent and 80 percent of S Ltd. A comparison of the calculation and allocation of the purchase discrepancies in both situations is shown in Exhibit 4.15. It should be noted that because the investment cost is proportional, the purchase discrepancy and the amounts allocated are also proportional. Goodwill for 80 percent ownership is 80 percent of the goodwill for 100 percent ownership. In other words, only the parent's share of the subsidiary's goodwill is recorded under current accounting standards.

Exhibit 4.15

P LTD.
COMPARISON OF PURCHASE DISCREPANCY CALCULATIONS
(100 percent owned vs. 80 percent owned)

	100% owned	*80% owned*
Cost of investment in S Ltd.	81,000	64,800
Shareholders' equity, S Ltd.	$70,000	$70,000
Parent's ownership	100%	80%
	70,000	56,000
Purchase discrepancy	$11,000	$ 8,800
Allocation		
Inventory	$ 2,000	$ 1,600
Plant	9,000	7,200
Patent	−1,000	−800
Goodwill	4,000	3,200
To assets	14,000	11,200
Long-term debt	3,000	2,400
Total allocated	$11,000	$ 8,800
Noncontrolling interest	N/A	$14,000

The Nature of Noncontrolling Interest   Consolidation theories have conflicting views as to whether noncontrolling interest should be presented as a liability or equity, or whether it should even appear in the consolidated statements. Section 1600 of the *Handbook* does not directly resolve the issue in that it refers to the basis of the calculation[9] of noncontrolling interest and concludes by stating that it should be presented separately from shareholders' equity[10] in the consolidated balance sheet. Many Canadian companies show noncontrolling interest between liabilities and shareholders' equity, while others present it in liabilities. From a student's perspective it is useful to view the noncontrolling interest as "another ownership interest" that is distinct and separate from the equity of the controlling shareholders. In this book, generally, noncontrolling interest will be presented between liabilities and shareholders' equity. It should be noted that some companies continue to present this item using the old and well-understood term "minority interest."

Introduction to Consolidation Theories

The approach to the preparation of consolidated statements discussed so far has focused on the accounting standards currently set out in the *CICA Handbook*. But accounting standards often change to meet new needs, and so it is useful at this time to pause in our examination of current practice and have a look at other possible ways of preparing consolidated statements.

There are three theories that could form the basis of consolidated financial statement preparation. These theories differ from one another only in situations where a subsidiary is less than 100 percent owned by a parent, because their basic concern is with the valuation of noncontrolling interest in the consolidated statements. Two

---

[9] *CICA Handbook*, paragraph 1600.15.
[10] *CICA Handbook*, paragraph 1600.69.

theories — proprietary and entity — can be viewed as falling at opposite ends of a continuum; the third theory — parent company — falls somewhere between. We will look at the two opposite theories first, then examine the theory in the middle.

Our discussions and illustrations will focus on our previous example of P Ltd. and S Ltd (see Exhibit 4.1).

We assume that on June 30, Year 1, P Ltd. acquired 80 percent of S Ltd. for $64,800. (Note that these are the same facts as were used in Illustration 4.)

Proprietary Theory

Proprietary theory views the consolidated entity from the standpoint of the shareholders of the parent company. It follows that the consolidated statements do not acknowledge or show the equity of the noncontrolling shareholders. The consolidated balance sheet on the date of acquisition reflects only the parent's share of the assets and liabilities of the subsidiary, based on their fair values, and the resultant goodwill from the combination. Using the information provided in Exhibit 4.1, goodwill would be determined as follows:

Cost of 80 percent acquisition of S Ltd.			$64,800
Fair value of S Ltd.'s net assets			
Cash		12,000	
Accounts receivable		7,000	
Inventory		22,000	
Plant		59,000	
Patent		10,000	
Current liabilities		(8,000)	
Long-term debt		(25,000)	
		77,000	
P Ltd.'s ownership		80%	61,600
Goodwill			$ 3,200

Using the direct approach, the consolidated balance sheet is prepared by combining, on an item-by-item basis, the book values of the parent with *the parent's share* of the fair values of the subsidiary. Goodwill is established based on the parent's acquisition cost. This process is shown in Exhibit 4.16.

Proprietary theory is not used in practice to consolidate a parent and its subsidiaries. However, its use is required by the *Handbook* as the means of reporting an investment in a joint venture, and the consolidation process is described as "proportionate consolidation." This topic will be fully covered in Chapter 10.

Entity Theory

Entity theory views the consolidated entity as having two distinct groups of shareholders — the controlling shareholders and the noncontrolling shareholders. This theory was described in an American Accounting Association publication, "The Entity Theory of Consolidated Statements," by Maurice Moonitz. Under this theory the consolidated balance sheet reflects the full fair values of the subsidiary's net assets and an amount for goodwill determined as if the parent had acquired 100 percent of the subsidiary's outstanding shares, instead of the less than 100 percent actually acquired. Noncontrolling interest is presented in consolidated shareholders' equity. The amount is based on the fair value of the subsidiary's net assets and the goodwill shown on the consolidated balance sheet. The calculation of the goodwill and the noncontrolling interest is shown in Exhibit 4.17.

Exhibit 4.16

Illustration of the Direct Approach
(proprietary theory)

P LTD.
CONSOLIDATED BALANCE SHEET
June 30, Year 1

Cash (100,000 – 64,800* + 80% × 12,000)	$ 44,800
Accounts receivable (90,000 + 80% × 7,000)	95,600
Inventory (130,000 + 80% × 22,000)	147,600
Plant (280,000 + 80% × 59,000)	327,200
Patent (80% × 10,000)	8,000
Goodwill	3,200
	$626,400
Current liabilities (60,000 + 80% × 8,000)	$ 66,400
Long-term debt (180,000 + 80% × 25,000)	200,000
Total liabilities	266,400
Shareholders' equity	
Common stock	200,000
Retained earnings	160,000 360,000
	$626,400

* Cash paid by P Ltd. to acquire S Ltd.

Exhibit 4.17

CALCULATION OF GOODWILL AND NONCONTROLLING INTEREST
(entity theory)

Cost of 80 percent acquisition of S Ltd.		$64,800
Implied cost of 100 percent of S Ltd.		$81,000
(64,800 ÷ 80%)		
Fair value of S Ltd.'s net assets		
Cash	12,000	
Accounts receivable	7,000	
Inventory	22,000	
Plant	59,000	
Patent	10,000	
Current liabilities	(8,000)	
Long-term debt	(25,000)	77,000
Goodwill		$ 4,000
Noncontrolling interest		
Fair value of net assets of S Ltd.		$77,000
Goodwill		4,000
Fair value of net assets including goodwill		81,000
Noncontrolling interest's share		20%
		$16,200

It should be noted that entity theory requires an inference as to what the cost of 100 percent would be when the parent has acquired less than 100 percent of the subsidiary's shares. In this particular situation it might be valid to assume that if P Ltd. paid $64,800 for 80 percent of the shares of S Ltd., the cost of 100 percent would have been approximately $81,000. However, in situations where the parent's owner-ship percentage is much smaller — say, for example, 55 percent — this approach loses much of its validity. It also loses validity in situations where the parent's own-ership percentage rises through a series of small purchases and control is eventually achieved after more than 50 percent of the subsidiary's shares have been acquired. This is probably the major reason why entity theory is not in accordance with GAAP in Canada.

Using the direct approach, the consolidated balance sheet is prepared by com-bining on an item-by-item basis the book values of P Ltd. with the fair values of S Ltd. The calculated goodwill is inserted on the asset side, and the calculated non-controlling interest is shown in shareholders' equity. Exhibit 4.18 illustrates the preparation of the consolidated balance sheet.

Exhibit 4.18	**Illustration of the Direct Approach**

Illustration of the Direct Approach
(entity theory)

P LTD.
CONSOLIDATED BALANCE SHEET
June 30, Year 1

Cash (100,000 – 64,800* + 12,000)		$ 47,200
Accounts receivable (90,000 + 7,000)		97,000
Inventory (130,000 + 22,000)		152,000
Plant (280,000 + 59,000)		339,000
Patent		10,000
Goodwill		4,000
		$649,200
Current liabilities (60,000 + 8,000)		$ 68,000
Long-term debt (180,000 + 25,000)		205,000
Total liabilities		273,000
Shareholders' equity		
Controlling interest		
Capital stock	200,000	
Retained earnings	160,000	
	360,000	
Noncontrolling interest	16,200	376,200
		$649,200

* Cash paid by P Ltd. to acquire S Ltd.

Parent Company Theory

Parent company theory is similar to proprietary theory in that the focus of the con-solidated statements is directed toward the shareholders of the parent company. However, noncontrolling interest is recognized and reflected as a liability in the con-solidated balance sheet; its amount is based on the book values of the net assets of the subsidiary. The consolidated balance sheet is prepared by combining, on an item-by-item basis, the book value of the parent with the book value of the sub-sidiary *plus* the parent's share of the fair value minus book value differences. This concept should sound familiar, because this was the method used in Illustration 4. The only difference is that in Illustration 4, noncontrolling interest was presented between liabilities and shareholders' equity (see Exhibit 4.14), while parent company theory would require it to be shown as a liability. Exhibit 4.19 shows the preparation of the consolidated balance sheet under parent company theory.

Accounting standards in Canada, as reflected in the *Handbook*, are very close to parent company theory. The major difference is that the *Handbook*'s requirements for the elimination of intercompany profits follow entity theory. This concept is revisited in Chapter 7.

Exhibit 4.19

Illustration of the Direct Approach
(parent company theory)

P LTD.
CONSOLIDATED BALANCE SHEET
June 30, Year 1

Cash (100,000 – 64,800* + 12,000)	$ 47,200
Accounts receivable (90,000 + 7,000)	97,000
Inventory (130,000 + 20,000 + 1,600)	151,600
Plant (280,000 + 50,000 + 7,200)	337,200
Patent (11,000 – 800)	10,200
Goodwill	3,200
	$646,400
Current liabilities (60,000 + 8,000)	$ 68,000
Long-term debt (180,000 + 22,000 + 2,400)	204,400
Noncontrolling interest	14,000
Total liabilities	286,400

Shareholders' equity		
Capital stock	200,000	
Retained earnings	160,000	360,000
		$646,400

* Cash paid by P Ltd. to acquire S Ltd.

Contingent Consideration

The terms of a business combination may require an additional cash payment, or an additional share issue contingent on some specified future event. The accounting for contingent consideration is contained in Section 1581 of the *Handbook*; the material that follows illustrates the concepts involved.[11]

If the amount of contingent consideration can be estimated on the date of the business combination, and the outcome is considered reasonably certain to occur, the estimated amount is recorded and is considered part of the purchase cost.

If the amount cannot be estimated, or the outcome is uncertain on the date of the combination, no recording takes place. The amount will be recorded at some future date if, and when, the contingency becomes payable, and it may be considered an additional cost of the purchase at that time depending on the circumstances. Disclosure of the contingency is made in the financial statements until it is resolved. If the contingency is based on earnings, it is considered an additional

---

[11] *CICA Handbook*, paragraphs 1581.29–.38.

cost of the purchase. If the contingency is based on share prices, the original cost is not affected and the payment of the contingency is treated as a capital transaction.

The following discussions illustrate the two types of contingent consideration discussed above.

Contingency Based on Earnings If the contingency is based on future earnings, any consideration issued at some future date is recorded at fair market value and is considered an additional cost of the purchase. The following example will illustrate this situation.

Able Corporation issues 500,000 no-par-value common shares for all of the outstanding common shares of Baker Company on January 1, Year 1. The shares issued have a fair value of $10 at that time. Able's journal entry on January 1, Year 1, is:

Investment in Baker Company	5,000,000	
Common shares		5,000,000

The business combination agreement states that if the earnings of Baker Company exceed an average of $1.75 per share over the next two years, Able Corporation will make an additional cash payment of $600,000 to the former shareholders of Baker Company. The amount of the possible future payment is known, but because there is no assurance that it will have to be paid, no provision is made for this contingency on January 1, Year 1.

Because Able's fiscal year end falls on December 31, Year 1, the consolidated financial statements are prepared using the $5,000,000 purchase price. This amount is allocated to the identifiable net assets of Baker Company in the usual manner and may result in goodwill, or "negative goodwill," which would require further allocation to reduce the noncurrent asset values used in the consolidation. If at the end of the two-year period it is determined that Baker's earnings exceeded the average of $1.75 per share, the required cash payment will be recorded by Able on December 31, Year 2, as follows:

Investment in Baker Corporation	$600,000	
Cash		$600,000

The total acquisition price has turned out to be $5,600,000, but the previous year's consolidated financial statements were prepared using the original $5,000,000 amount. The question thus arises as to how to account for this $600,000 addition to the acquisition price. The *Handbook* gives no direction in this regard, but the most logical treatment would be to allocate the amount to goodwill on the consolidated balance sheet. Disclosure of the amount paid and its disposition in the financial statements would be made in the footnotes to the Year 2 financial statements.

When EIC-14 was issued in June 1990, it appeared that its provisions might apply in a situation such as this. This possible interpretation was conveyed to the EIC, which responded in February 1992 with the following amendment to EIC-14:

> This Abstract does not alter the accounting for contingent consideration as discussed in CICA 1580. In accordance with CICA 1580, where contingent consideration is subsequently paid, adjustments to the cost of the purchase may be required and any such adjustments should be accounted for prospectively.[12]

---

[12] This EIC was issued when Section 1580 was part of the *Handbook*. Although Section 1580 has been replaced with Section 1581, the contingent consideration provisions remain unchanged.

In this case the $600,000 would be added to the balance of the consolidated goodwill and would be subject to yearly impairment tests.

A problem arises if the original allocation resulted in "negative" goodwill that was allocated to noncurrent assets; however, the same basic concepts discussed above would seem to apply. The allocation to noncurrent assets would be applied prospectively in the preparation of the Year 2 consolidated statements.

A further problem arises if the original allocation resulted in negative goodwill which, after further allocation to noncurrent assets, still left a balance unallocated. In this case the *Handbook* states that the unallocated balance should be presented on the consolidated balance sheet as a deferred credit until the contingency is resolved. Once the contingency is resolved, any unallocated balance still remaining is reflected as an extraordinary item.

Contingency Based on Share Prices   If the contingency is based on future share prices, any consideration issued at some future date will be recorded at fair market value but will not be considered an additional cost of the purchase. Instead, the consideration issued will be treated as a reduction in the amount recorded for the original share issue. The following example illustrates this.

Alpha Corporation issues 500,000 no-par-value common shares for all the outstanding common shares of Beta Company on July 1, Year 1. If the shares issued have a fair market value of $5.00, Alpha's journal entry is:

Investment in Beta Company	2,500,000	
Common shares		2,500,000

The combination agreement states that if the market price of Alpha's shares is below $5.00 one year from the date of the agreement, Alpha will make a cash payment to the former shareholders of Beta in an amount that will compensate them for their loss in value. On July 1, Year 2, the market price of Alpha's shares is $4.50. In accordance with the agreement, Alpha Corporation makes a cash payment of $250,000 (500,000 shares x $.50) and records the transaction as follows:

Common shares	250,000	
Cash		250,000

Footnote disclosure in the Year 2 statements will be made for the amount of the payment, providing the reasons therefor and the accounting treatment used.

Financial Statement Disclosure

Most Canadian companies disclose their policies with regard to long-term investments in accordance with the requirements of Section 1505, "Disclosure of Accounting Policies." The following footnote is taken from the financial statements of Moore Corporation Limited and is fairly typical in content:

> **Principles of consolidation** The financial statements of entities which are controlled by the Corporation, referred to as subsidiaries, are consolidated; entities which are jointly controlled are proportionately consolidated; entities which are not controlled and which the Corporation has the ability to exercise significant influence over are accounted for using the equity method; and investments in other entities are accounted for using the cost method.

The following two paragraphs contain the major disclosures requirements of Section 1590:

When a reporting enterprise does not own, directly or indirectly through subsidiaries, an equity interest carrying the right to elect the majority of the members of the board of directors of a subsidiary, the reporting enterprise should disclose (i) the basis for the determination that a parent-subsidiary relationship exists, (ii) the name of the subsidiary, and (iii) the percentage of ownership (if any). [1590.22]

When a reporting enterprise owns, directly or indirectly through subsidiaries, an equity interest carrying the right to elect the majority of the members of the board of directors of an investee that is not a subsidiary, the reporting enterprise should disclose (i) the basis for determination that a parent-subsidiary relationship does not exist, (ii) the name of the investee, (iii) the percentage ownership, and (iv) either separate financial statements of the investee, combined financial statements of similar investees or, provided all information significant to the consolidated financial statements is disclosed, condensed financial statements (including notes) of the investee. [1590.23]

Earlier in this chapter, we discussed the general presumptions regarding the factors that establish a control investment and noted that these presumptions could be overcome in certain situations. The above two disclosure paragraphs require a company to give full details when the normal quantitative guidelines of 50 percent ownership of voting shares are not used by an investor. Note that the last two words of paragraph 22 seem to indicate that it is possible for an investor to have a control investment without owning any shares of an investee.

An International Perspective

It is fairly standard practice throughout the world to report investments in controlled companies by means of consolidated financial statements. Control is often defined as greater than 50 percent of the voting shares, although some countries (Brazil and Italy for example) seem to follow Canada's method, which is to define control without mentioning a quantitative number. In the United States, consolidation can occur only if the parent owns, directly or indirectly, over 50 percent of the voting shares. This requirement is currently being reviewed by the FASB, and it is quite possible that control will eventually be defined in a manner similar to Canadian practices.

A number of countries require that all subsidiaries be consolidated, but allow for exclusions (1) if control is temporary, or (2) if the subsidiary is nonhomogeneous when compared with the other companies in the group so that consolidation would produce misleading results, or (3) if the subsidiary is immaterial in size, or (4) if the subsidiary is under reorganization or is bankrupt. Germany, Japan, Spain, New Zealand, and France fall into this group. The nonhomogeneous exclusion was used in the past in both Canada and the United States, where companies such as General Motors and Ford did not consolidate their finance subsidiaries, supposedly because the finance business is so different from automobile manufacturing that consolidation would have misled financial statement readers. Companies such as these were in both types of business, and as a result, when Canada and the United States removed these exclusions, a very substantial portion of debt was added to these companies' balance sheets.

The IASB requires that all subsidiaries be consolidated, except where control is temporary, or where there are long-term restrictions that impair the subsidiary's ability to transfer funds to its parent. The IASB describes control as the power to govern the financial and operating policies of an enterprise so as to benefit from its activities.

The South Korean government has recently begun requiring the consolidation of majority-owned subsidiaries, but enforcement has been weak and implementation slow. This is understandable when one considers that South Korea's economy is dominated by 30 large, diversified conglomerates held together (so it seems) by cross-guarantees and by cross-holdings of shares. The relationships thereby created are more brother–sister in nature than parent–subsidiary.

Brazil follows the general requirements of consolidation except that all subsidiaries' statements must first undergo price level restatement before consolidation can proceed. This is understandable, considering the history of hyperinflation in that country.

Germany requires consolidation except that an exemption is allowed when the parent is itself a subsidiary of a non-German parent. Sweden and Chile require both consolidated and parent-only financial statements, while India permits consolidation but does not require it.

SUMMARY

Consolidated financial statements present the financial position and operating results of a group of companies under common control as if they constitute a single entity. When one company gains control over another company, it becomes a parent company and GAAP requires it to present consolidated statements for external reporting purposes. The preparation involves eliminating the parent's investment account and the parent's share of the subsidiary's shareholders' equity accounts; revaluing the net assets of the subsidiary; and establishing the noncontrolling interest in the book value of the subsidiary's net assets. If the subsidiary applies push-down accounting, the revaluations used to consolidate are recorded in the records of the subsidiary; this simplifies the consolidation process. A working paper can be used to prepare the consolidated statements, and is necessary if there are a large number of subsidiaries to consolidate. A computerized spreadsheet is particularly useful in this situation. When there are only one or two subsidiaries, the direct approach is by far the fastest way to arrive at the desired results.

APPENDIX

Reverse Takeovers

Section 1581 of the *Handbook* describes a reverse takeover in the following paragraph:

Occasionally, an enterprise obtains ownership of the shares of another enterprise but, as part of the transaction, issues enough voting shares as consideration that control of the combined enterprise passes to the shareholders of the acquired enterprise (commonly referred to as a "reverse takeover"). Although legally the enterprise that issues the shares is regarded as the parent or continuing enterprise, the enterprise whose former shareholders now control the combined enterprise is treated as the acquirer. As a result, the issuing enterprise is deemed to be a continuation of the acquirer and the acquirer is deemed to have acquired control of the assets and business of the issuing enterprise in consideration for the issue of capital. [1581.17]

While not a common event, this form of business combination is often used by active nonpublic companies as a means to obtain a stock exchange listing without having to go through the listing procedures established by the exchange. A takeover of a dormant company that has a stock exchange listing is arranged in such a way that the dormant company emerges as the parent company.

While paragraph 1581.17 describes how a reverse takeover can occur, it does not adequately explain how to account for it. There must have been a need for guidance in this matter, because in 1990 the Emerging Issues Committee issued an abstract to deal with the accounting involved. The following example illustrates the required accounting as outlined in EIC-10, "Reverse Takeover Accounting."

Reverse Takeover Illustration The balance sheets of Reverse Ltd. and Takeover Co. on the date of a reverse takeover business combination are shown in Exhibit 4.20.

Reverse is a dormant company (not currently engaged in any business activity) with a listing on a major stock exchange. Takeover is an active company not listed on any exchange. A business combination is initiated by Takeover whereby Reverse issues 240 shares to the shareholders of Takeover for 100 percent of their shareholdings. By structuring the combination in this manner, Reverse becomes the legal parent and Takeover the legal subsidiary.

An examination of the shares held by the two shareholder groups in the following manner clearly indicates that Takeover is identified as the acquirer:

	Shares of Reverse Ltd.	%
Shareholders of Reverse Ltd.	160	40%
Shareholders of Takeover Co.	240	60%
	400	100%

Exhibit 4.20

BALANCE SHEETS

	Reverse Ltd. Book value	Reverse Ltd. Fair value	Takeover Co. Book value
Current assets	$ 560	$ 700	$1,560
Fixed assets	1,600	1,650	5,100
	$2,160		$6,660
Liabilities	$ 720	720	$3,060
Common stock (160 shares)	500		
Retained earnings	940		
Common stock (96 shares)*			1,080
Retained earnings			2,520
	$2,160		$6,660

* The shares of Takeover Co. have a current market value of $30 per share.

Under the purchase method of accounting for a business combination, the fair value of the net assets of the acquiree is combined with the book value of the net assets of the acquirer. Because Takeover is the acquirer, the acquisition cost is determined *as if* Takeover had issued shares to the shareholders of Reverse. A calculation has to be made to determine the number of shares that Takeover would have issued to achieve the same result (i.e., so that its shareholders would end up holding 60 percent of Takeover's outstanding shares). The number of shares can be determined as follows:

1. Before the combination the shareholders of Takeover hold 96 shares in that company.

2. Takeover would have to issue X additional shares, such that the 96 shares will represent 60 percent of the total shares outstanding.

3. After the share issue, the total shares outstanding will be 96 + X shares.

4. $96 = 0.6 (96 + X)$. Therefore, $X = 64$ shares.

If Takeover had issued 64 shares, the holdings of the two groups of shareholders would have been as follows:

	Shares of Takeover Co.	%
Shareholders of Takeover	96	40%
Shareholders of Reverse	64	60%
	160	100%

The acquisition cost is the number of shares that Takeover would have issued valued at their fair market value, and is allocated in the following manner:

Acquisition cost — 64 shares @ $30	$1,920
Fair value of net assets of Reverse Co.	1,630
Goodwill	$ 290

The balance sheet of the combined company immediately after the business combination is prepared by combining the fair value of the net assets of Reverse, including the goodwill from the combination, with the book value of the net assets of Takeover. It should be noted that Takeover's shareholders' equity becomes the shareholders' equity of the combined company. The amount shown for common stock is determined by summing the common stock of Takeover before the combination and the deemed issue of 64 shares at market value. However, the number of shares shown as issued are the outstanding shares of the legal parent Reverse. The consolidated balance sheet of Reverse immediately after the reverse takeover takes place is shown in Exhibit 4.21.

The financial statements of Reverse would contain the following footnote to describe this event:

During the year Reverse Ltd. entered into a share exchange agreement with the shareholders of Takeover Co. Under this agreement Reverse exchanged 240 common shares for 100% of the issued and outstanding shares of Takeover. As a result of the share exchange, Reverse obtained control over Takeover.

Legally Reverse is the parent of Takeover, however, as a result of the share exchange, control of the combined companies passed to the shareholders of

Exhibit 4.21

REVERSE LTD.
CONSOLIDATED BALANCE SHEET
(immediately after the reverse takeover)

Current assets (700 + 1,560)	$2,260
Fixed assets (1,650 + 5,100)	6,750
Goodwill	290
	$9,300
Liabilities (720 + 3,060)	$3,780
Common stock* (1,080 + 1,920)	3,000
Retained earnings	2,520
	$9,300

* The number of shares issued and outstanding would be shown as 400 shares (160 + 240).

Takeover, which for accounting purposes is deemed to be the acquirer. For financial reporting purposes, this share exchange is considered to be a reverse takeover and Reverse is considered to be a continuation of Takeover. The net assets of Takeover are included in the balance sheet at book values, and the deemed acquisition of Reverse is accounted for by the purchase method, with the net assets of Reverse recorded at fair market values. The fair market value of Reverse on the date of acquisition was as follows:

Current assets	$ 700
Fixed assets	1,650
Goodwill	290
Liabilities	(720)
	$1,920

In this example the acquisition cost was determined by multiplying the number of shares that the legal subsidiary would have had to issue by the market price of that company's shares. This market price is probably the most appropriate one to use, because if the legal parent is dormant, the market price of its shares may not be indicative of true value, or its shares may not be trading on the exchange. However, because the legal subsidiary is often a private company, the market value of its shares may have to be determined using business valuation concepts. If a market price cannot be determined for the shares of the legal subsidiary, the fair value of the net assets of the legal parent would be used to determine acquisition cost.

Comparative amounts presented in the consolidated financial statements of the legal parent are those of the legal subsidiary. In the year of the reverse takeover, consolidated net income is made up of the income of the legal subsidiary *before* the takeover and the income of the combined company *after* the takeover.

Because the outstanding shares shown on the consolidated balance sheet are those of the legal parent, the calculation of earnings per share is based on these shares; so is the calculation of the weighted average shares outstanding in the year of the takeover.

In the example of Reverse, assuming the combination date was July 31, the weighted average shares outstanding for the fiscal year December 31 is 307 shares, calculated as follows:

- 240 shares deemed outstanding for 7 months, *and*
- 400 shares outstanding for 5 months

This calculation is in contrast to the normal calculation of weighted average shares outstanding and requires further clarification. Remember that the consolidated statements of Reverse (the legal parent) are considered to be a continuation of those of Takeover (the legal subsidiary) and that the accounting assumes that the legal subsidiary acquired the legal parent. But the shares outstanding are those of the legal parent.

Consolidated net income for the year *does not* contain the income of Reverse prior to the takeover date because this income is considered to be preacquisition earnings. Reverse picked up the first seven months' income of Takeover with the issue of 240 shares. The last five months' income is that of Takeover and Reverse, during which time 400 shares (160 + 240) were outstanding.

The consolidated balance sheet of Reverse Ltd. (Exhibit 4.21) was prepared using a non–working paper (or direct) approach. We will now illustrate the preparation of the consolidated balance sheet using a working paper (Exhibit 4.22). On the date of the reverse takeover, Reverse (the legal parent) would make the following journal entry to record the acquisition of 100 percent of the outstanding shares of Takeover by the issuance of 240 common shares:

Investment in Takeover Co.	1,920	
Common shares (new)		1,920

These "new" shares are issued at the deemed acquisition cost and are shown separately on the working paper to simplify the consolidation process.

The calculation and allocation of the purchase discrepancy is as follows:

Acquisition cost of Takeover Co.			$1,920
Book value of Reverse Ltd.			
Common stock		500	
Retained earnings		940	1,440
Purchase discrepancy			480
Allocated	(FV – BV) × 100%		
Current assets	140		
Fixed assets	50		190
Goodwill			$ 290

Elimination entry #1 eliminates Reverse's investment in Takeover against *Reverse's precombination shareholders' equity,* with the purchase discrepancy the balancing amount.

Elimination #2 allocates the purchase discrepancy to revalue the net assets of Reverse.

The consolidated common stock is the common stock of Takeover (the legal subsidiary) before the takeover plus the new shares issued by Reverse, which are valued at Takeover's deemed acquisition cost of Reverse.

Exhibit 4.22

REVERSE LTD.
CONSOLIDATED BALANCE SHEET WORKING PAPER
(immediately after the reverse takeover)

	Reverse Ltd.	Takeover Co.		Adjustments and Eliminations Dr.		Cr.	Consolidated balance sheet
Current assets	$ 560	$1,560	(2)	140			$2,260
Fixed assets	1,600	5,100	(2)	50			6,750
Investment in Takeover Co.	1,920				(1)	1,920	
Purchase discrepancy			(1)	480	(2)	480	
Goodwill			(2)	290			290
	$4,080	$6,660					$9,300
Liabilities	$ 720	$3,060					$3,780
Common stock (old)	500		(1)	500			
Retained earnings	940		(1)	940			
Common stock		1,080					3,000
Common stock (new)	1,920						
Retained earnings		2,520					2,520
	$4,080	$6,660		$2,400		$2,400	$9,300

REVIEW QUESTIONS

Questions, cases, and problems that deal with the appendix material are denoted with an asterisk.

1. What criteria must be met for a subsidiary to be consolidated? Explain.

2. What part do irrevocable agreements, convertible securities, and warrants play in determining whether control exists? Explain.

3. Majority ownership of voting shares usually constitutes control. Can control exist without this? Explain.

4. In the preparation of a consolidated balance sheet, the parent's share of the fair value–book value differences is used. Would these differences be used if the subsidiary applied push-down accounting? Explain.

5. Is a negative purchase discrepancy the same as negative goodwill? Explain.

6. With respect to noncontrolling interest, what are the major differences between proprietary, parent, and entity theories?

7. Outline the calculation and amortization of the purchase discrepancy.

8. How is the goodwill appearing on the balance sheet of a subsidiary prior to a business combination treated in the subsequent preparation of consolidated statements? Explain.

9. Under the entity theory, consolidated goodwill is determined by inference. Describe how this is achieved and comment on its shortcomings.

10. What is noncontrolling interest, and how is it reported in the consolidated balance sheet if Canadian GAAP is applied?

11. Explain the accounting for contingent consideration in the year that the contingency is paid.

*12. What is a reverse takeover, and why is such a transaction entered into?

*13. Explain how the acquisition cost is determined for a reverse takeover.

MULTIPLE CHOICE

1. When one company controls another company, the *CICA Handbook* recommends that the parent report the subsidiary on a consolidated basis. Which of the following best describes the primary reason for this recommendation?
   a. To report the combined retained earnings of the two companies, allowing shareholders to better predict dividend payments.
   b. To allow for taxation of the combined entity.
   c. To report the total resources of the combined economic entity under the control of the parent's shareholders.
   d. To meet the requirements of federal and provincial securities commissions.

2. Which of the following best describes the accounting treatment acceptable under GAAP for negative goodwill?
   a. It should be disclosed as a long-term credit on the consolidated financial statements.
   b. It should reduce consolidated common shares.
   c. It should be disclosed as a separate line item in consolidated shareholders' equity.
   d. It should reduce the values assigned in the purchase transaction to non-current assets.

3. Which of the following does the proprietary theory require the parent to record when consolidating its subsidiary?
   a. The subsidiary's assets at 100% of book value plus the parent's share of fair value increments or decrements.
   b. The subsidiary's assets at the parent's share of fair values.
   c. The subsidiary's assets at the parent's share of book values.
   d. The subsidiary's assets at 100% of fair value.

The following data should be used for Questions 4 and 5.

On January 1, 2002, Poor Co. acquired 80% of the outstanding common shares of Standard Inc. by paying cash of $275,000. The book values and fair values of both companies immediately before the acquisition were as follows:

	Poor Co.		Standard Inc.	
	Book values	Fair values	Book values	Fair values
Current assets	$ 470,000	485,000	$100,000	120,000
Fixed assets	2,879,000	3,200,000	175,000	250,000
Intangibles	45,000	50,000	50,000	75,000
Total assets	$3,394,000		$325,000	
Current liabilities	$ 367,000	355,000	$125,000	125,000
Long-term debt	1,462,000	1,460,000	50,000	40,000
Common stock	1,000,000		60,000	
Retained earnings	565,000		90,000	
	$3,394,000		$325,000	

4. Assume that Standard's intangibles do not include goodwill. What amount would Poor Co. report on its consolidated financial statements immediately after the acquisition transaction for "intangibles" (including goodwill from the acquisition, if any)?
   a. $115,000
   b. $162,000
   c. $166,000
   d. $182,000

5. What amount would Poor Co. report on its consolidated financial statements immediately after the acquisition transaction for "fixed assets"?
   a. $3,129,000
   b. $3,114,000
   c. $3,079,000
   d. $3,054,000

*6. At December 31, 2002, Alpha Company has 20,000 common shares outstanding while Beta Inc. has 10,000 common shares outstanding. Alpha wishes to enter into a reverse takeover of Beta to gain its listing on the stock exchange. Which one of the following describes how many shares would have to be issued, and by which company, for this to occur?
   a. Alpha would have to issue more than 10,000 shares.
   b. Alpha would have to issue more than 20,000 shares.
   c. Beta would have to issue more than 10,000 shares.
   d. Beta would have to issue more than 20,000 shares.

*7. Refer to Question 6. Which company's name would appear on the financial statements of the combined company after the reverse takeover?
   a. Alpha Company.
   b. Beta Inc.
   c. Both names would appear on the statements, by law.
   d. A new name would have to be created to identify the new economic entity that has been created.

8. Which of the following is *not* a necessary condition for consolidating another enterprise in a reporting enterprise's financial statements?
   a. The reporting enterprise has control over the other enterprise.
   b. The reporting enterprise has the right and ability to obtain future economic benefits from the resources of the other enterprise.
   c. The reporting enterprise is exposed to the risks associated with the other enterprise.
   d. The reporting enterprise owns, either directly or indirectly, more than 50% of the other enterprise's voting shares.

(CICA adapted)

The following scenario applies to Questions 9 and 10, although each question should be considered independently.

(CICA adapted)

A parent company acquires 80% of the shares of a subsidiary for $400,000. The carrying value of the subsidiary's net assets is $350,000. The market value of the net assets of the subsidiary is $380,000.

9. Which of the following represents the amount of goodwill that should be recorded at the time of the acquisition?
   a. $16,000
   b. $20,000
   c. $96,000
   d. $120,000

10. Which of the following represents the noncontrolling shareholder's interest that should be recorded when the acquisition takes place?
   a. $70,000
   b. $76,000
   c. $80,000
   d. $100,000

11. When is the recognition of a deferred credit required in consolidating financial information?
   a. When negative goodwill exists.
   b. When any bargain purchase is created.
   c. When the negative goodwill is greater than the value of the noncurrent assets held by the acquired company.
   d. When the negative goodwill is greater than the value of the noncurrent assets held by the acquired company, and a contingency remains unresolved.

12. Which of the following is not an appropriate reason for leaving a subsidiary unconsolidated?
   a. The subsidiary is in bankruptcy.
   b. The subsidiary is in an industry that is significantly different from that of the parent.
   c. A foreign government threatens to take over the assets of the subsidiary.
   d. The subsidiary is to be sold in the near future.

CASES

Case 1   During 2002, XYZ Ltd. purchased all of the 100,000 outstanding Class B shares of Sub Limited. Each share carries one vote. The previous owner, Mr. Bill, retained all 80,000 outstanding Class A shares of Sub, each also carrying one vote. In order to avoid sudden changes, Mr. Bill stipulated in the sale agreement that he was to retain the right to veto management appointments for Sub and to approve any significant transactions of Sub.

Required:

Should XYZ consolidate the operations of Sub in its 2002 financial statements, which are to be issued in accordance with GAAP? If not, how should the investment be reported? Provide support for your recommendation.

(CICA adapted)

Case 2   *PART A*
On its year end date, Donna Ltd. purchased 80% of the outstanding shares of Gunn Ltd. Before the purchase, Gunn had a deferred loss on foreign currency exchange of $10.5 million on its balance sheet. (A loss of this nature occurs as a result of the translation into Canadian dollars of a monetary position denominated in a foreign currency. The loss is deferred in the year it occurs and is amortized by charges to income in future periods.)

Required:

What amount should be reported in Donna's consolidated statements, issued in accordance with GAAP, for Gunn's deferred loss on foreign exchange? Provide support for your recommendation.

PART B

CE Ltd. purchased 100% of the outstanding common shares of May Ltd. by issuing shares of CE to the shareholders of May. The former shareholders of May now own 65% of the outstanding common shares of CE. Before the purchase date, May had a deferred loss on foreign currency exchange of $10.5 million in its balance sheet.

Required:

What amount should be reported in CE's consolidated financial statements, issued in accordance with GAAP, for May's deferred loss on foreign currency exchange? Provide support for your recommendations.

(CICA adapted)

Case 3[a] Factory Optical Distributors (FOD) is a publicly held manufacturer and distributor of high-quality eyeglass lenses located in Burnaby, B.C. For the past 10 years, the company has sold its lenses on a wholesale basis to optical shops across Canada. Beginning in 1998, the company began to offer franchise opportunities to opticians wanting to sell only FOD lenses.

The franchise agreements contain the following stipulations:

- Each franchise must be a corporation. FOD (Burnaby) will purchase 35% of the corporation's outstanding common shares and the franchisee will hold the remaining 65%. No other equity instruments can be issued.
- Franchises can be established in new locations or in existing locations under the name Factory Optical Distributors. If a new building is required, FOD (Burnaby) will guarantee the mortgage to ensure that the best interest rates can be obtained. If an existing location is used, it must be renovated to meet company specifications, and again FOD (Burnaby) will guarantee any required financing.
- To qualify as a franchisee, an individual must be a licensed optician, and must commit to 40 hours a week in the franchise location, managing the day-to-day activities.
- Franchisees are to be paid a salary that does not exceed 1.5 times the industry average for opticians with equivalent experience.
- The franchise agreement specifies that only FOD lenses can be sold in franchise locations. FOD lenses can be purchased by franchisees at 5% below normal selling price for the first $500,000 of purchases, and at 10% below cost if purchases exceed $500,000.
- The agreement also requires that frames sold by the franchisee be purchased from designated suppliers, to ensure the best quality and fit to FOD lenses.
- All franchise advertising must be approved by FOD (Burnaby). Franchisees must allocate 1% of revenue to advertising each month.
- The franchisee is required to participate in special promotions and seasonal sales as determined by FOD (Burnaby).
- A franchise fee of 2% of sales is payable monthly to FOD (Burnaby).

---

[a] Case prepared by and © J.C. (Jan) Thatcher and Margaret Forbes, Faculty of Business Administration, Lakehead University.

During 2002, eight franchise agreements were signed in locations across Canada. At December 31, 2002, the company's year end, five of these locations were open for business.

It is now January 2003. You are the senior auditor on the FOD (Burnaby) account. The company's comptroller has come to you with the franchise agreement to discuss how FOD must report its share ownership in the five operating franchises. She has heard that recent changes to the *CICA Handbook* have expanded the definition of control to include some situations where 50% share ownership does not exist.

Required:

Examine the details of the franchise agreement. Do you think FOD controls the franchise operations? Would consolidation be required?

Case 4 The following are a number of scenarios that show variations in the nature of long-term intercorporate investments.

1. A Ltd. owns 45% of B Co. Typically, only about 70% of the outstanding shares are voted at the annual meetings of B Company. Because of this, A Ltd. always casts a majority of the votes on every ballot when it votes the shares it holds.

2. A Ltd. holds no shares of B Co.; however, it holds convertible bonds issued by B Co. which, if A Ltd. converted them, would result in the ownership of 51% of the outstanding shares of B Co.

3. A Ltd. owns 75% of B Co. Recently a receiver, acting on behalf of a bank, seized a portion of B Co.'s inventory when B Co. defaulted on a loan.

4. Last year B Co. was a wholly owned subsidiary of C Inc. At the beginning of this year, B Co. was put up for sale and A Ltd. purchased all of its 100,000 voting shares from C Inc. by making a cash payment of 40% of the purchase price and by issuing a promissory note for the balance owing, due in equal instalments over the next two years.

   B Co. has a bond issue outstanding that can be converted at the option of the holder into 150,000 voting common shares of that company. At the time of the sale, C Inc. held 80% of these bonds; and it has agreed to sell these bonds proportionately to A Ltd. as it receives the proceeds from the promissory note.

5. A Ltd. owns 100% of B Co., which is insolvent. All of its assets have been seized by a licensed trustee in bankruptcy.

6. B Co. is located in a foreign country. This country requires that a majority of the ownership of all businesses be held by its citizens. A Ltd. has the expertise and technical knowledge required to successfully operate B Co. In order to satisfy the country's foreign ownership requirements, B Co. has been structured as a partnership, with 50 partners each having a 2% equity interest. Forty-nine of the partners, who are all citizens of the foreign country, have signed an irrevocable agreement that establishes A Ltd. as the managing partner, with complete authority to determine the operating, financing, and investing policies of B Co.

Required:

For each scenario, discuss how A Ltd. should report its investment in B Co.

Case 5^b Uni-Invest Ltd. was traded on the Canadian Venture Exchange, under the symbol "UIL." The company holds commercial and residential real estate interests, located in Nova Scotia, New Brunswick, Prince Edward Island, Alberta, and British Columbia. On October 23, 2000, Basic Realty Investment Corporation acquired 100% of the outstanding common shares of Uni-Invest Ltd. in exchange for 32,584,051 common shares of Basic.

---

b Case prepared by Peter Secord, St. Mary's University.

At October 31, 1999, Basic had 3,333,320 common shares, and 6,000,001 Class C preferred shares issued and outstanding. Prior to the acquisition, the 6,000,001 Class C preferred shares were converted to common shares on a share-for-share basis. Then, on October 23, 2000, the 9,333,321 common shares were consolidated five for one to yield 1,866,664 common shares, with a book value of $746, to which a net value of $2,042,568 was attributed at the time of the intercorporate investment. Values involved are summarized as follows:

Capital stock issued	Number of shares	Amount
Balance at October 31, 1999 (Basic's previous fiscal year end)	1,866,664	$ 746
Issued to effect investment on October 23, 2000, net of costs of $84,177	32,584,051	33,236,248
Balance December 31, 2000	34,450,715	$33,236,994

Details of the assets acquired and liabilities assumed on the transaction are as follows:

Assets acquired	
Property and equipment	$4,632,398
Cash	28,517
Other assets	242,919
	$4,903,834
Liabilities acquired	
Long-term debt	$2,707,504
Other liabilities	143,000
	$2,850,504
Net assets acquired at fair market value	$2,053,330

The net assets acquired of $2,053,330 pertain to the increased value of the property and equipment over the net book value of Basic at the time of the acquisition.

Required:

Based on this information, how should this investment be accounted for? More specifically, which company is the parent? Which is the subsidiary? Why? What earnings, and for what period, are reported in the consolidated financial statements for the year ended December 31, 2000? Why?

PROBLEMS

Problem 1 The balance sheets of Pork Co. and Barrel Ltd. on December 31, Year 2, are shown next:

	Pork Co.	Barrel Ltd.
Cash	$ 4,000	$ 60,000
Accounts receivable	80,000	48,000
Inventory	120,000	102,000
Plant and equipment (net)	400,000	270,000
Investment in Barrel Ltd.	312,000	—
	$916,000	$480,000
Current liabilities	$216,000	$ 72,000
Long-term debt	240,000	108,000
Common stock	260,000	120,000
Retained earnings	200,000	180,000
	$916,000	$480,000

Pork acquired 70% of the outstanding shares of Barrel on December 30, Year 2, for $300,000. Direct expenses of the acquisition amounted to $12,000. The book values of the net assets of Barrel approximated fair values except for plant and equipment, which had a fair value of $320,000.

Required:

Prepare a consolidated balance sheet on December 31, Year 2.

Problem 2   The balance sheets of Par Ltd. and Sub Ltd. on December 31, Year 1, are as follows:

	Par Ltd.	Sub Ltd.
Cash	$100,000	$ 2,000
Accounts receivable	25,000	7,000
Inventory	30,000	21,000
Plant	175,000	51,000
Trademarks	—	7,000
	$330,000	$88,000
Current liabilities	$ 50,000	$10,000
Long-term debt	80,000	20,000
Common stock	110,000	30,000
Retained earnings	90,000	28,000
	$330,000	$88,000

The fair values of the identifiable net assets of Sub on December 31, Year 1, are:

Cash		$ 2,000
Accounts receivable		7,000
Inventory		26,000
Plant		60,000
Trademarks		14,000
		109,000
Current liabilities	10,000	
Long-term debt	19,000	29,000
Net assets		$ 80,000

Assume that the following took place on January 1, Year 2. (Par acquired the shares with a cash payment to the shareholders of Sub.)

Case 1. Par paid $95,000 to acquire all of the common shares of Sub.
Case 2. Par paid $76,000 to acquire 80% of the common shares of Sub.
Case 3. Par paid $80,000 to acquire all of the common shares of Sub.
Case 4. Par paid $70,000 to acquire all of the common shares of Sub.
Case 5. Par paid $63,000 to acquire 90% of the common shares of Sub.

Required:

For each of the five cases, prepare a consolidated balance sheet as at January 1, Year 2.

Problem 3   The balance sheets of P Co. and S Co. on June 29, Year 2, were as follows:

	P Co.	S Co.
Cash and receivables	$ 64,000	$ 13,000
Inventory	38,000	6,000
Plant assets (net)	152,000	47,000
Intangible assets	16,000	4,000
	$270,000	$ 70,000
Current liabilities	$ 42,000	20,000
Long-term debt	65,000	30,000
Common stock	102,000	31,000
Retained earnings (deficit)	61,000	(11,000)
	$270,000	$ 70,000

On June 30, Year 2, P purchased 90% of the outstanding shares of S for $24,600 cash. Legal fees involved with the acquisition were an additional $1,000. The book value of S's net assets was equal to fair value except for:

	Fair value
Inventory	7,000
Plant assets	54,000
Intangible assets	6,000
Long-term debt	26,000

Required:

Prepare the consolidated balance sheet of P Co. on June 30, Year 2. (Round all calculations to the nearest dollar.)

Problem 4   The balance sheets of Red Corp. and Sax Ltd. on December 31, Year 4, are shown below:

	Red Corp. book value	Sax Ltd. book value
Cash	$ 10,000	$ 5,000
Accounts receivable	100,000	35,000
Inventory	90,000	160,000
Land	70,000	40,000
Plant and equipment	360,000	290,000
Investment in Sax Ltd.	261,000	—
Goodwill	90,000	30,000
	$981,000	$560,000
Current liabilities	$120,000	$ 80,000
Long-term debt	320,000	220,000
Common stock	400,000	300,000
Retained earnings	141,000	(40,000)
	$981,000	$560,000

On December 30, Year 4, Red purchased all of the common shares of Sax for $261,000. On this date the inventory of Sax had a fair value of $165,000, its land had a fair value of $70,000, and its plant and equipment had a fair value of $280,000.

Required:

Prepare a consolidated balance sheet as at December 31, Year 4.

Problem 5   Following are the balance sheets of Blue Ltd. and Joy Corp. on December 31, Year 2.

	Blue Ltd. book value	Joy Corp. book value
Cash	$ 17,000	$ 5,000
Accounts receivable	78,000	35,000
Inventory	105,000	170,000
Plant and equipment	440,000	320,000
Investment in Joy Corp.	188,000	—
Goodwill	80,000	50,000
	$908,000	$580,000
Current liabilities	$168,000	$ 80,000
Long-term debt	250,000	240,000
Common stock	422,000	300,000
Retained earnings	68,000	(40,000)
	$908,000	$580,000

On December 30, Year 2, Blue purchased a percentage of the outstanding common shares of Joy. On this date all but two categories of Joy's assets and liabilities had fair values equal to book values.

Below is the consolidated balance sheet for Blue at December 31, Year 2.

BLUE LTD.
CONSOLIDATED BALANCE SHEET
(Year 2)

Cash	$ 22,000
Accounts receivable	113,000
Inventory	259,000
Plant and equipment	768,000
Goodwill	108,000
	$1,270,000
Current liabilities	$ 248,000
Long-term debt	490,000
Noncontrolling interest	42,000
Common stock	422,000
Retained earnings	68,000
	$1,270,000

Required:

(a) From the information presented in the separate entity financial statements, determine the percentage of Joy's common shares purchased by Blue on December 30, Year 2.

(b) Which of Joy's assets or liabilities had fair values that were not equal to their book values at acquisition? Calculate the fair value of each of these assets at December 30, Year 2.

Problem 6 The balance sheets of E Ltd. and J Ltd. on December 30, Year 6, were as follows:

	E Ltd.	J Ltd.
Cash and receivables	$ 96,000	$ 19,500
Inventory	57,000	9,000
Plant assets (net)	228,000	70,500
Intangible assets	24,000	6,000
	$405,000	$105,000
Current liabilities	$ 63,000	$ 30,000
Long-term debt	97,500	45,000
Common stock	153,000	46,500
Retained earnings (deficit)	91,500	(16,500)
	$405,000	$105,000

On December 31, Year 6, E issued 500 shares, with a fair value of $40 each, for all of the outstanding shares of J. Costs involved in the acquisition, paid in cash, were as follows:

Costs of arranging the acquisition	$2,500
Costs of issuing shares	1,600
	$4,100

The book values of J's net assets were equal to fair values on this date except for these:

	Fair value
Plant assets	$65,000
Long-term debt	40,000

E was identified as the acquirer in the combination.

Required:

Prepare the consolidated balance sheet of E Ltd. on December 31, Year 6. (Round all calculations to the nearest dollar.)

Problem 7 On December 31, Year 1, P Company purchased 80% of the outstanding shares of S Company for $6,960 cash.

The balance sheets of the two companies immediately after the acquisition transaction were as follows:

	P Company Book value	S Company Book value	Fair market value
Cash	$ 1,500	$ 1,050	$1,050
Accounts receivable	3,150	1,800	1,800
Inventory	5,160	3,750	3,900
Plant and equipment (net)	8,100	6,900	6,000
Investment in S Company	6,960	—	
	$24,870	$13,500	
Accounts payable	$ 600	$ 700	$ 700
Other current liabilities	1,200	1,800	1,800
Long-term liabilities	4,200	2,000	2,000
Common stock	10,500	3,000	
Retained earnings	8,370	6,000	
	$24,870	$13,500	

Required:

Prepare a consolidated balance sheet under each of the following:

(a) proprietary theory

(b) parent theory

(c) entity theory

Problem 8* The balance sheets of X Ltd. and Y Ltd. on December 30, Year 7, are as follows:

	X Ltd. Book value	X Ltd. Fair value	Y Ltd. Book value	Y Ltd. Fair value
Current assets	$ 300	$ 300	$1,000	$1,000
Fixed assets	1,500	1,700	2,700	2,800
	$1,800		$3,700	
Current liabilities	$ 400	$ 400	$ 900	$ 900
Long-term debt	300	300	800	800
Common shares — issued 100 sh.	400			
Common shares — issued 60 sh.			600	
Retained earnings	700		1,400	
	1,800		3,700	

On December 31, Year 7, X issued 150 common shares for all 60 outstanding common shares of Y. The fair value of each of Y's common shares was $40 on this date.

Required:

(a) Explain why this share issue most likely occurred.
(b) Prepare the consolidated balance sheet of X Ltd. on December 31, Year 7.

(CICA adapted)

Problem 9 On January 1, 2002, Black Corp. purchased 90% of the common shares of Whyte Inc. On this date the following differences were observed with regard to specific net assets of Whyte:

	Fair value–book value differences
Land	+50,000
Buildings (net)	+20,000
Equipment (net)	–10,000
Notes payable	+ 5,000

The unconsolidated and consolidated balance sheets of Black Corp. on January 1, 2002, are presented below. If this was a pooling of interests combination, consolidated retained earnings would be $911,000.

	Unconsolidated	Consolidated
Cash	$ 36,000	$ 52,000
Accounts receivable	116,000	168,000
Inventory	144,000	234,000
Investment in Whyte	295,000	—
Land	210,000	275,000
Buildings (net)	640,000	718,000
Equipment (net)	308,000	339,000
Goodwill	—	47,500
	$1,749,000	$1,833,500
Accounts payable	$ 88,000	$ 96,000
Notes payable	510,000	564,500
Noncontrolling interest	—	22,000
Common stock	380,000	380,000
Retained earnings	771,000	771,000
	$1,749,000	$1,833,500

Required:

Prepare the January 1, 2002, balance sheet of Whyte Inc.

CHAPTER 5

Consolidated Financial Statements Subsequent to Acquisition Date — Equity Method

CHAPTER OUTLINE

LEARNING OBJECTIVES

After studying this chapter, you should be able to do the following:
- Explain how goodwill impairment tests are performed.
- Explain the basic differences between the cost and equity methods of reporting investments.

- Describe the composition of yearly consolidated net income.
- Prepare consolidated financial statements in years subsequent to acquisition date when the parent has used the equity method to account for its investment.

In Chapters 3 and 4, we discussed and illustrated the preparation of a consolidated balance sheet immediately after a parent company gained control over a subsidiary. Other financial statements prepared at that time (i.e., an income statement, retained earnings statement, and cash flow statement) would be those of the parent only and would not be consolidated. We now consider the preparation of the consolidated income statement, retained earnings statement, and balance sheet at fiscal year ends after the date of acquisition. The consolidated cash flow statement will be discussed in a later chapter.

Before we illustrate the preparation of consolidated statements subsequent to the acquisition date, we must further examine the accounting for goodwill and other intangible assets resulting from a business combination.

Accounting for Goodwill and Other Intangibles

As was illustrated in Chapter 4, goodwill is measured as the excess of the cost of an acquired entity over the amount assigned to the identifiable assets acquired and liabilities assumed. In the past, the amount assigned to goodwill has often been a substantial proportion of the acquisition cost. (For an example, see the Nortel "Item of Interest" on page 146.) One of the reasons for this has been the inability of the management of the acquirer to properly identify and measure certain other intangible assets.

Not only was the amount of goodwill substantial in many cases but also, prior to July 1, 2001, any goodwill recognized as a result of a business combination had to be amortized over its estimated useful life provided that this life did not exceed 40 years. This resulted in substantial reductions to reported earnings due to yearly goodwill amortization. On July 1, 2001, Section 1581, "Business Combinations," and Section 3062, "Accounting For Goodwill and Other Intangible Assets," were introduced into the *Handbook*. These new sections provide more workable guidelines for the recognition and measurement of intangibles other than goodwill and, in addition, replace the annual amortization of goodwill with periodic reviews for impairment. In the material that follows, the requirements of these new sections are discussed.

Recognition of Acquired Identifiable Intangible Assets

The guidelines for separating certain intangibles from goodwill are contained in the following paragraph:

An intangible asset should be recognized apart from goodwill when:
(a) the asset results from contractual or other legal rights (regardless of whether those rights are transferable or separable from the acquired enterprise or from other rights and obligations); or
(b) the asset is capable of being separated or divided from the acquired enterprise and sold, transferred, licensed, rented, or exchanged (regardless of whether there is an intent to do so).

Otherwise it should be included in the amount recognized as goodwill. [1581.48]

Any intangible assets that do not meet the criteria for separation from goodwill as outlined above, or that do meet these criteria but cannot be reliably measured, are included in the amount assigned to goodwill. Appendix A, Chapter 3, provides a comprehensive list of the types of intangibles that could be acquired in a business combination. The objective of these lists and the *Handbook* guidelines is to aid management in the allocation of the acquisition cost so that more intangible assets are recognized separately from goodwill.

Intangible assets recognized in a business combination should be amortized over their useful lives unless their lives are considered to be indefinite. Intangible assets that are subject to amortization are periodically reviewed for impairment in accordance with Section 3061, "Property, Plant and Equipment." Intangible assets that are not subject to amortization are tested for impairment annually by comparing their fair value to their carrying amount, and any resultant losses are included in income. In addition to providing guidelines for testing the impairment of intangibles other than goodwill, the new sections also outline the special impairment tests required for goodwill.

Testing Goodwill for Impairment

Once recognized, goodwill is periodically tested for impairment, and if the fair value of the goodwill is less than its carrying amount, it is written down and a loss is reported in income. The process is described in the paragraphs that follow.

Impairment testing is carried out at the level of a reporting unit. A reporting unit is described in the *Handbook* as

> the level of reporting at which goodwill is tested for impairment and is either an operating segment (see SEGMENT DISCLOSURES, Section 1701), or one level below (referred to as a component). A component of an operating segment is a reporting unit when the component constitutes a business for which discrete financial information is available and segment management regularly reviews the operating results of that component. (Segment management consists of one or more segment managers, as that term is defined in SEGMENT DISCLOSURES, Section 1701.) However, two or more components of an operating segment are aggregated and deemed a single reporting unit when the components have similar economic characteristics. An operating segment is deemed to be a reporting unit when all of its components are similar, when none of its components is a reporting unit, or when it is comprised of only a single component. [3062.05(d)]

Often when a business combination occurs, the acquired company is itself a parent with many subsidiaries. While the initial allocation of the acquisition cost is carried out at the entity level, the resultant goodwill has to be allocated to the various subsidiaries or divisions (reporting units) in the acquirer's internal documents for the purpose of testing for impairment. The basic process is to allocate the acquisition cost to reporting units and compare this on an individual basis with the fair value of each reporting unit's identifiable net assets, with any excess being the goodwill of the particular reporting unit.

There are two steps involved in testing goodwill for impairment.

1. The fair value of each reporting unit is compared with its carrying amount, including goodwill. If the fair value exceeds the carrying amount, there is no goodwill impairment and step 2 is not performed.

2. If the carrying amount of the reporting unit exceeds its fair value, the fair value of the goodwill is compared with its carrying amount. The fair value of the goodwill is determined in the same fashion that the goodwill of a business combination is determined. This means that the fair value of the entity has to be allocated to the reporting units, as do the fair values of the entity's assets and liabilities. The difference between the fair value of a reporting unit and the sum of the fair values of the unit's net assets is the fair value of the goodwill of that unit. If the carrying amount of a reporting unit's goodwill exceeds its fair value, the difference is reported on the income statement as an impairment loss and the carrying amount of the entity's goodwill on the balance sheet is reduced by this amount.

The goodwill impairment test is performed annually unless there are clear indicators that no impairment has occurred, such as:

(a) There has been very little change in the make-up of the assets and liabilities of the reporting unit since the most recent fair value determination; *and*

(b) The most recent fair value determination yielded an amount that substantially exceeded the carrying amount of the reporting unit; *and*

(c) Based on the analysis of events since the most recent fair value determination, it is unlikely that a current fair value determination would be less than the carrying value of the reporting unit.

There may also be indicators that suggest that the impairment test should be performed more often than annually, such as when circumstances or events have occurred that make it more likely than not that fair values of the reporting unit are less than carrying amounts.

Impairment testing commenced on January 1, 2002, for all companies whose fiscal year end occurs on or after that date.

Item of Interest The December 31, 2000, balance sheet of Nortel Networks Corporation showed total assets amounting to $42.2 billion, of which $17.4 billion was unamortized goodwill. Nortel measures its financial statements in U.S. dollars and prepares them in accordance with both United States and Canadian GAAP. The numbers quoted above are in accordance with Canadian GAAP. During 2000, Nortel acquired 11 corporations for a total acquisition cost of $20.4 billion, of which $18.5 billion was allocated to goodwill. For these particular acquisitions, goodwill amounted to over 90 percent of the total acquisition cost. In June 2001, Nortel reported a second-quarter loss of $19.2 billion, which was the largest loss ever recorded by a Canadian company. Nortel also announced that it was streamlining its business and was discontinuing certain of its operations. As result of these changes, it announced that it was taking an $830 million restructuring charge and in addition it intended to write down intangible assets (mostly goodwill) in the amount of $12.3 billion. This is the type of write-down that would result from performing the goodwill impairment test outlined above.

Methods of Accounting for an Investment in a Subsidiary

There are two methods available to a parent company to account for an investment in a subsidiary in periods subsequent to the date of acquisition: the *cost method* and the *equity method*. The cost and equity methods of accounting were discussed in depth in Chapter 2 with regard to portfolio and significant influence investments.

While this chapter is concerned with control investments (requiring consolidation), the accounting concepts involved with the cost and equity methods are identical to those presented in Chapter 2. These concepts will be outlined again in this chapter and in the ones that follow. The key difference is that here they are discussed in relation to the preparation of consolidated financial statements, whereas before, the emphasis was on the presentation in an investor's unconsolidated financial statements.

The *Handbook* describes the *cost method* as

> a basis of accounting for long-term investments whereby the investment is initially recorded at cost; earnings from such investments are recognized only to the extent received or receivable. When the investment is in the form of shares, dividends received in excess of the investor's pro rata share of post acquisition income are recorded as a reduction of the amount of the investment.[1]

The cost method is the simplest of the two methods because the only entry made by the parent each year is to record, as revenue, its pro rata share of dividends declared by the subsidiary from net income earned subsequent to the acquisition date.

The *equity method* is described as

> a basis of accounting for long-term investments whereby the investment is initially recorded at cost and the carrying value adjusted thereafter to include the investor's pro-rata share of post acquisition retained earnings of the investee, computed by the consolidation method. The amount of the adjustment is included in the determination of net income by the investor and the investment account is also increased or decreased to reflect the investor's share of capital transactions and changes in accounting policies and corrections of errors relating to prior period financial statements applicable to post acquisition periods. Profit distributions received or receivable from an investee reduce the carrying amount of the investment.[2]

Under the equity method, the parent records its pro rata share of the subsidiary's post-acquisition net income as revenue and as an increase to the investment account, and reduces the investment account with its share of the dividends declared by the subsidiary. The phrase "computed by the consolidation method" refers to Section 1600, which describes the preparation of consolidated statements. This means that the investment revenue is reduced by the yearly amortization and write-offs associated with the purchase discrepancy because, although the subsidiary's net assets are being consolidated using fair values, these fair values are not reflected in the subsidiary's records, and therefore the subsidiary's expenses are incorrect for consolidated purposes.[3] In addition, any unrealized intercompany profits are not reflected in consolidated net income until they are realized through a sale to outsiders. From a single-entity point of view, "you cannot record a profit selling to yourself." An equity method journal entry is required to adjust for the effect of such unrealized profits.[4]

The parent company is free to choose which method it will use to account for the investment. The consolidated financial statements are the same regardless of which method the parent uses, but the approach used to prepare the statements is

---

[1] *CICA Handbook*, paragraph 3050.02.

[2] Ibid.

[3] We are assuming in all cases that subsidiary companies do not use push-down accounting. Consolidation when the subsidiary has used push-down accounting is discussed in Chapter 11.

[4] The accounting for unrealized profits is discussed in chapters 7 and 8.

specific to the method chosen. This chapter will discuss the preparation of the consolidated statements when the parent has used the equity method. Consolidation when the parent has used the cost method will be discussed in Chapter 6.

Consolidated Income and Retained Earnings Statements

Before examining the details for preparing consolidated income and retained earnings statements, it is useful to outline the overall consolidation process. Just as a consolidated balance sheet is prepared basically by combining, on an item-by-item basis, the assets and liabilities of the parent and the subsidiary, the consolidated income statement is prepared by combining, on an item-by-item basis, the revenues and expenses of the two companies. The parent's investment does not appear on the consolidated balance sheet, and some of the subsidiary's assets and liabilities are revalued to reflect the fair values used in the consolidation process. In a similar manner, the parent's investment revenue from its subsidiary does not appear on the consolidated income statement, and some of the expenses of the subsidiary are revalued to reflect the amortizations of the fair values being used in the consolidated balance sheet. But except for the eliminations and adjustments that are required, the whole consolidation process is basically one of combining the components of financial statements. No preparation is required for the consolidated retained earnings statement when the parent has used the equity method.[5]

We commence our discussion of the preparation of the consolidated income statement by describing the make-up of the bottom line: consolidated net income. Consolidated net income for any fiscal year is made up of the following:

	The net income of the parent from its own operations	
	(i.e., excluding any income resulting from its investment in the subsidiary)	$ XXX
plus:	**the parent's share of the net income of the subsidiary**	XXX
less:	**the amortization of the purchase discrepancy**	(XXX)
equals:	**consolidated net income**	$ XXX

Take, for example, a 100 percent owned subsidiary that was purchased at book value (i.e., no purchase discrepancy and no fair value–book value differences). Consolidated net income will be made up of the sum of the parent's and the subsidiary's net incomes. If the subsidiary was purchased at a price greater than book value, the subsidiary's net income will not be correct from a consolidated-single-entity point of view because the subsidiary's expenses have not been measured using amortizations of the fair values being used in the consolidated balance sheet. Therefore, the third component — the amortization of the purchase discrepancy — must be deducted in determining consolidated net income.

A purchase discrepancy is allocated to revalue the assets and liabilities of the subsidiary for consolidated purposes. Some of the allocations are to assets that are subject to periodic amortizations reflected on the income statement (examples are buildings, equipment, and patents). Inventory is not amortized, but is reflected on the income statement as cost of goods sold expense when it is sold. The amount allocated to land is not amortized and its cost is only reflected as a charge on the income statement when it is sold. Goodwill is also not amortized, but instead a loss is reflected on the income statement when a test indicates that it is impaired. All of

---

[5] This statement is not correct when the parent has used the cost method.

these charges against consolidated income will collectively be referred to as "the amortization of the purchase discrepancy," even though technically some of them are not really amortizations. In the same manner the balances not yet written off for consolidation purposes will be referred to as the "unamortized purchase discrepancy."

Consolidated retained earnings on the date of acquisition is the parent's retained earnings only, if the purchase method has been used to account for the combination. The changes in consolidated retained earnings subsequent to acquisition consist of the yearly consolidated net incomes, less the yearly dividends declared by the parent. When dividends are paid by a 100 percent owned subsidiary, the subsidiary's cash decreases and the parent's cash increases, but the single entity's cash remains unchanged, as does the shareholders' equity of the entity.

The following example will be used to illustrate the preparation of consolidated financial statements subsequent to the date of acquisition. The first illustrations assume that the subsidiary is 100 percent owned. Later illustrations will assume a less than 100 percent owned subsidiary.

Consolidation of a 100 Percent Owned Subsidiary

Company P purchased 100 percent of the outstanding common shares of Company S on January 1, Year 1, for $19,000. On that date Company S's common stock was $10,000 and its retained earnings balance was $6,000. The inventory of Company S had a fair market value that was $2,000 greater than book value, and the book values of all other assets and liabilities of Company S were equal to fair market values. Any goodwill will be tested yearly for impairment. Both companies have a December 31 year-end. The journal entry made by Company P to record the acquisition of 100 percent of Company S was as follows:

Investment in S	19,000	
Cash		19,000

There is no compelling reason for Company P to prepare a consolidated balance sheet on acquisition date; however, it is useful to illustrate its preparation as the starting point for the preparation of consolidated statements in subsequent years. The calculation and allocation of the purchase discrepancy is shown in Exhibit 5.1.

Exhibit 5.1

COMPANY P
CALCULATION OF PURCHASE DISCREPANCY
January 1, Year 1

Cost of 100 percent of Company S		$19,000
Book value of Company S:		
Common stock	10,000	
Retained earnings	6,000	
	16,000	
Parent's ownership	100%	16,000
Purchase discrepancy		3,000
Allocated:	FV – BV	
Inventory	2,000	2,000
Balance — goodwill		$ 1,000

Below are the individual balance sheets of Company P and Company S on January 1, Year 1, along with Company P's consolidated balance sheet prepared using the *direct approach*.

BALANCE SHEETS — January 1, Year 1

	Company P	Company S	Consolidated
Assets (miscellaneous)	$139,000	$17,000	$156,000
Inventory	22,000	10,000	34,000
Investment in S	19,000	—	—
Goodwill	—	—	1,000
	$180,000	$27,000	$191,000
Liabilities	$ 45,000	$11,000	$ 56,000
Shareholders' equity			
Common stock	50,000	10,000	50,000
Retained earnings	85,000	6,000	85,000
	$180,000	$27,000	$191,000

The consolidated balance sheet was prepared by eliminating the shareholders' equity of Company S ($16,000) against Company P's investment account ($19,000) and then allocating the resultant purchase discrepancy ($3,000) to the inventory of Company S ($2,000), with the unallocated balance recorded as goodwill ($1,000).

On December 31, Year 1, Company S reported a net income of $7,300 for the year and paid a cash dividend of $2,500. Company P's net income for the year was $18,300 at this time (not including income from its investment in Company S). Using the equity method to account for its investment, Company P will record the cash dividend received as a reduction to the investment account and increase the investment account with its share (100 percent) of Company S's net income. An additional entry is required to record the amortization of the purchase discrepancy. Company P prepares a purchase discrepancy amortization schedule to be used both for the equity method journal entries required and for the actual preparation of the consolidated financial statements. This amortization schedule is prepared as follows:

PURCHASE DISCREPANCY AMORTIZATION SCHEDULE

	Balance Jan. 1, Year 1	Amortization Year 1	Balance Dec. 31, Year 1
Inventory	$2,000	$2,000	—
Goodwill	1,000	50	950
	$3,000	$2,050	$950

The details of the Year 1 amortizations are explained as follows:

1. The inventory of Company S was revalued for consolidated purposes on January 1, Year 1, to reflect its fair value. It is safe to assume that this inventory was sold during Year 1, and if we further assume that Company S uses a FIFO cost flow, the cost of sales of Company S does not reflect the $2,000 additional cost.[6] Cost of sales on the Year 1 consolidated income statement will be increased by $2,000 to reflect all of this. If Company S uses LIFO, an examination of the inventory layers would have to be made to determine whether all or part of this $2,000 should be expensed.

---

[6] Because very few Canadian companies use LIFO, we will assume a FIFO cost flow in all examples.

2. An impairment test on goodwill conducted on December 31, Year 1, indicated that a $50 loss had occurred.

3. The $1,000 goodwill is not reflected in the financial statements of Company S, nor is the impairment loss. The consolidated income statement will have to reflect this loss, and at December 31, Year 1, the consolidated balance sheet will have to show the balance not written off.

Because the amortizations affect consolidated net income, they must also be reflected in the parent's December 31, Year 1, equity method journal entries. These entries are shown below:

Investment in S	7,300	
Investment income		7,300
100 percent of Company S Year 1 net income		
Cash	2,500	
Investment in S		2,500
Dividend received from Company S		
Investment income	2,050	
Investment in S		2,050
Purchase discrepancy amortization — Year 1		

After these journal entries are posted, the account for Investment in S and the investment income account in the records of P Company will show the following changes and balances:

	Investment in S	Investment income
January 1, Year 1	$19,000	nil
December 31, Year 1:		
Income from S	7,300	7,300
Dividends from S	(2,500)	—
Purchase discrepancy amort.	(2,050)	(2,050)
Balance, December 31, Year 1	$21,750	$5,250

Company P adds the investment income ($5,250) to its earnings from its own operations ($18,300) and reports a final net income of $23,550.

Consolidated Statements, End of Year 1, Direct Approach

The financial statements of Company P and Company S prepared on December 31, Year 1, are presented in Exhibit 5.2.

These financial statements and the purchase discrepancy amortization schedule become the basis for the preparation of Company P's consolidated financial statements. While a working paper can be used, the statements can also be prepared using the direct approach, as follows.

When the parent has used the equity method to account for its investment, the following true relationships exist:

- Parent's net income equals consolidated net income.
- Parent's retained earnings equal consolidated retained earnings.

Exhibit 5.2

YEAR 1 INCOME STATEMENTS

	Company P	Company S
Sales	$ 50,000	$30,000
Investment income	5,250	—
Total revenue	$ 55,250	$30,000
Cost of sales	$ 26,500	$14,700
Expenses (miscellaneous)	5,200	8,000
Total expenses	$ 31,700	$22,700
Net income	$ 23,550	$ 7,300

YEAR 1 RETAINED EARNINGS STATEMENTS

	Company P	Company S
Balance, January 1	$ 85,000	$ 6,000
Net income	23,550	7,300
	108,550	13,300
Dividends	6,000	2,500
Balance, December 31	$102,550	$10,800

BALANCE SHEETS — December 31, Year 1

	Company P	Company S
Assets (miscellaneous)	$147,800	$18,300
Inventory	30,000	14,000
Investment in S (equity method)	21,750	—
	$199,550	$32,300
Liabilities	$ 47,000	$11,500
Common stock	50,000	10,000
Retained earnings	102,550	10,800
	$199,550	$32,300

The preparation of the consolidated income statement will be discussed first. The revenue item of Company P "Investment income," which is determined using the equity method, does not appear in the consolidated income statement; it is replaced with the revenues and expenses from the income statement of Company S adjusted for the amortization of the purchase discrepancy. This replacement leaves the net income of Company P unchanged. The replacement that takes place is illustrated below:

Replace —

Investment income (from S)			$ 5,250

With —

	Company S statement	Amortization of purch. disc.	
Sales	30,000		30,000
Cost of sales	14,700	2,000	16,700
Expenses (misc.)	8,000	—	8,000
Goodwill impairment loss	—	50	50
Total expense	22,700	2,050	24,750
Revenues less adjusted expenses			$ 5,250

No preparation is required for the consolidated retained earnings statement when the parent has used the equity method of accounting. The consolidated retained earnings statement is identical, on a line-by-line basis, with that of the parent.

The consolidated balance sheet is prepared in much the same way as the consolidated income statement. When the parent has used the equity method, consolidated shareholders' equity is identical to that of the parent company. Company P's asset "Investment in S" does not appear in the consolidated balance sheet; it is replaced with the individual assets and liabilities from the balance sheet of Company S, revalued by the unamortized purchase discrepancy. This replacement is illustrated as follows:

Replace —

Investment in S			$21,750

With —

	Company S statement	Unamortized purch. disc.	
Assets (miscellaneous)	$18,300	—	$18,300
Inventory	14,000	—	14,000
Goodwill	—	950	950
	32,300	950	33,250
Liabilities	11,500	—	11,500
Net assets	$20,800	$950	$21,750

The preparation of the Year 1 consolidated financial statements is shown in Exhibit 5.3. The consolidated amounts were determined by adding the amounts shown in brackets. These amounts came from the financial statements of Company P and Company S and from the purchase discrepancy amortization schedule.

Note the bracketed amounts shown for goodwill impairment loss and for the goodwill on the balance sheet. The two zero amounts indicate that these items do not appear in the financial statements of Company P and Company S.

Consolidated Statements, End of Year 1, Working Paper Approach

Exhibit 5.4 shows the preparation of Company P's consolidated financial statements using a working paper. In Chapters 3 and 4 the working paper entries were described as "adjustments and eliminations." Here we have shortened the description to "eliminations." Before we explain the three elimination entries used, a few comments about the overall format would be useful.[7]

1. In observing the effect of the elimination entries, the reader must take into account the debit and credit balances of the financial statement items. Revenues, net income, retained earnings, liabilities, and share capital accounts have credit balances, while expenses, dividends, and assets have debit balances. The debit and credit elimination entries are either increasing or decreasing these financial statement items depending on their nature.

---

[7] It should be emphasized again that the elimination entries shown in the working paper are not recorded in the accounting records of either the parent or the subsidiary.

Exhibit 5.3	**Year 1 Consolidated Financial Statements**

(direct approach)

COMPANY P
CONSOLIDATED INCOME STATEMENT
for the Year Ended December 31, Year 1

Sales (50,000 + 30,000)	$80,000
Cost of sales (26,500 + 14,700 + 2,000)	43,200
Goodwill impairment loss (0 + 0 + 50)	50
Expenses (miscellaneous) (5,200 + 8,000)	13,200
	$56,450
Net income	$23,550

COMPANY P
CONSOLIDATED STATEMENT OF RETAINED EARNINGS
for the Year Ended December 31, Year 1

Balance, January 1	$ 85,000
Net income	23,550
	108,550
Dividends	6,000
Balance, December 31	$102,550

COMPANY P
CONSOLIDATED BALANCE SHEET
December 31, Year 1

Assets (miscellaneous) (147,800 + 18,300)		$166,100
Inventory (30,000 + 14,000)		44,000
Goodwill (0 + 0 + 950)		950
		$211,050
Liabilities (47,000 + 11,500)		$ 58,500
Shareholders' equity		
Common stock	$ 50,000	
Retained earnings	102,550	152,550
		211,050

2. Some elimination entries affect two or more of the financial statements, but the total debits and credits for each entry are equal.

3. The totals from the net income line from the income statement, including the totals of the elimination entries made there, are carried down to the net income line in the retained earnings statement. In a similar manner, the end-of-year retained earnings totals are carried down to the retained earnings on the balance sheet. Because the cumulative effect of the elimination entries from each statement has been carried down to the balance sheet, the total elimination debits and credits on that statement are equal.

The working paper elimination entries are reproduced below, with an explanation of each.

#1	Investment income — Company P	5,250	
	Dividends — Company S		2,500
	Investment in S — Company P		2,750

Exhibit 5.4

CONSOLIDATED FINANCIAL STATEMENT WORKING PAPER
December 31, Year 1 (equity method)

	P	S	Eliminations Dr.		Cr.		Consolidated
Sales	$ 50,000	$30,000					$ 80,000
Investment income	5,250		(1)	5,250			
	$ 55,250	$30,000					$ 80,000
Cost of sales	$ 26,500	$14,700	(3)	2,000			$ 43,200
Goodwill impair. loss			(3)	50			50
Miscellaneous exp.	5,200	8,000					13,200
	$ 31,700	$22,700					$ 56,450
Net income	$ 23,550	$ 7,300		$ 7,300			$ 23,550
Retained earnings, Jan. 1	$ 85,000	$ 6,000	(2)	6,000			$ 85,000
Net income	23,550	7,300		7,300			23,550
	108,550	13,300					108,550
Dividends	6,000	2,500			(1)	2,500	6,000
Retained earnings, Dec. 31	$102,550	$10,800		$13,300		$ 2,500	$102,550
Assets, misc.	$147,800	$18,300					$166,100
Inventory	30,000	14,000					44,000
Investment in S	21,750				(1)	2,750	
					(2)	19,000	
Purchase discrepancy			(2)	3,000	(3)	3,000	
Goodwill			(3)	950			950
	$199,550	$32,300					$211,050
Liabilities	$ 47,000	$11,500					$ 58,500
Common stock	50,000	10,000	(2)	10,000			50,000
Retained earnings	102,550	10,800		13,300		2,500	102,550
	$199,550	$32,300		$27,250		$27,250	$211,050

The parent's equity method investment income does not appear in the consolidated income statement, and the subsidiary's dividends do not appear in the consolidated retained earnings statement. Through an elimination of the investment income and the parent's share of the subsidiary's dividends against the investment account, this account has been adjusted to its start-of-year balance ($19,000).

#2	Retained earnings Jan. 1 — Company S	6,000	
	Common stock — Company S	10,000	
	Purchase discrepancy	3,000	
	Investment in S — Company P		19,000

This entry eliminates the parent's share of the start-of-year retained earnings and common stock of Company S, and the investment in S account of Company P, and establishes the purchase discrepancy at the beginning of the year. (In Year 1 this is the purchase discrepancy on acquisition date.)

#3 Cost of sales — Company S	2,000	
Goodwill impairment loss (expense)	50	
Goodwill	950	
Purchase discrepancy		3,000

This entry eliminates the purchase discrepancy established by entry #2 and allocates it in accordance with the purchase discrepancy amortization schedule by (a) adjusting the expenses of Company S and (b) reflecting the unamortized balance at the end of the year on the consolidated balance sheet.

At this point it is useful to discuss a further relationship that results from the use of the equity method of accounting. Please refer back to the financial statements of Company P and Company S on December 31, Year 1 (see Exhibit 5.2). The elimination of Company P's share of the shareholders' equity accounts of Company S against Company P's investment account leaves as a balance the total amount of the unamortized purchase discrepancy. The following illustrates this:

Investment in S (Dec. 31, Year 1)		$21,750
Shareholders' equity, Company S (Dec. 31, Year 1)		
Common stock	10,000	
Retained earnings	10,800	
	20,800	
Parent's ownership	100%	20,800
Unamortized purchase discrepancy		$ 950

We will now continue our example by illustrating the preparation of Company P's Year 2 consolidated statements.

On December 31, Year 2, Company S reported earnings of $10,000 for the year and paid a cash dividend of $3,000. Company P's net income for the year was $19,000 at this time (excluding any income from its investment in Company S). An impairment test conducted on December 31, Year 2, indicated that the goodwill had a fair value of $870. As a result a loss of $80 has occurred. Company P prepared the following purchase discrepancy amortization schedule at the end of Year 2:

PURCHASE DISCREPANCY AMORTIZATION SCHEDULE

	Balance Dec. 31, Year 1	Amortization Year 2	Balance Dec. 31, Year 2
Inventory	—	—	—
Goodwill	950	80	870
	$950	$80	$870

On December 31, Year 2, Company P makes the following equity method journal entries:

Investment in S	10,000	
Investment income		10,000
100 percent of Company S Year 2 net income		

Cash	3,000	
Investment in S		3,000
Dividend received from Company S		

Investment income	80
Investment in S	80
Purchase discrepancy amortization — Year 2	

After these journal entries are posted, the investment in S account and the investment income account in the records of Company P show the following changes and balances:

	Investment in S	Investment income
Balance, December 31, Year 1	$21,750	nil
December 31, Year 2:		
Income from S	10,000	10,000
Dividends from S	(3,000)	—
Purchase discrepancy amort.	(80)	(80)
Balance, December 31, Year 2	$28,670	$ 9,920

Company P combines its Year 2 investment income ($9,920) with the earnings from its own operations ($19,000) and reports a final net income of $28,920.

The financial statements of Company P and Company S on December 31, Year 2, are shown in Exhibit 5.5.

Exhibit 5.5

YEAR 2 INCOME STATEMENTS

	Company P	Company S
Sales	$ 60,000	$40,000
Investment income	9,920	—
Total revenue	$ 69,920	$40,000
Cost of sales	$ 32,000	$18,000
Expenses (miscellaneous)	9,000	12,000
Total expenses	$ 41,000	$30,000
Net income	$ 28,920	$10,000

YEAR 2 RETAINED EARNINGS STATEMENTS

	Company P	Company S
Balance, January 1	$102,550	$10,800
Net income	28,920	10,000
	131,470	20,800
Dividends	8,000	3,000
Balance December 31	$123,470	$17,800

BALANCE SHEETS — December 31, Year 2

	Company P	Company S
Assets (miscellaneous)	$131,800	$21,000
Inventory	35,000	16,000
Investment in S (equity method)	28,670	—
	$195,470	$37,000
Liabilities	$ 22,000	$ 9,200
Common stock	50,000	10,000
Retained earnings	123,470	17,800
	$195,470	$37,000

Consolidated Statements, End of Year 2, Direct Approach

The two replacements that are made in the consolidation process when the parent has used the equity method are shown below:

Replace —

Investment income (from S)		$ 9,920

With —

	Company S statement	Amortization of purch. disc.	
Sales	40,000		40,000
Cost of sales	18,000		18,000
Expenses (misc.)	12,000		12,000
Goodwill impairment loss	—	80	80
Total expense	30,000	80	30,080
Revenues less adjusted expenses			$ 9,920

Replace —

Investment in S		$28,670

With —

	Company S statement	Unamortized purch. disc.	
Assets (misc)	$21,000	—	$21,000
Inventory	16,000	—	16,000
Goodwill	—	870	870
	37,000	870	37,870
Liabilities	9,200	—	9,200
Net assets	$27,800	$870	$28,670

The consolidated financial statements for Year 2 are shown in Exhibit 5.6. The amounts shown in brackets came from the financial statements of the two companies and the purchase discrepancy amortization schedule. The consolidated retained earnings statement was prepared by reproducing, line by line, the retained earnings statement of Company P.

Consolidated Statements, End of Year 2, Working Paper Approach

Exhibit 5.7 illustrates the preparation of Company P's consolidated statements on December 31, Year 2, using a working paper.

The working paper elimination entries are reproduced below, with an explanation of each.

#1	Investment income — Company P	9,920	
	Dividends — Company S		3,000
	Investment in S — Company P		6,920

This entry eliminates Company P's investment income account and the dividend account of Company S against the investment in S account of Company P. This leaves the investment account with a December 31, Year 1, balance of $21,750.

Exhibit 5.6	

Year 2 Consolidated Financial Statements
(direct approach)

COMPANY P
CONSOLIDATED INCOME STATEMENT
for the Year Ended December 31, Year 2

Sales (60,000 + 40,000)	$100,000
Cost of sales (32,000 + 18,000)	$ 50,000
Goodwill impairment loss (0 + 0 + 80)	80
Expenses (miscellaneous) (9,000 + 12,000)	21,000
	$ 71,080
Net income	$ 28,920

COMPANY P
CONSOLIDATED STATEMENT OF RETAINED EARNINGS
for the Year Ended December 31, Year 2

Balance, January 1	$102,550
Net income	28,920
	131,470
Dividends	8,000
Balance, December 31	$123,470

COMPANY P
CONSOLIDATED BALANCE SHEET
December 31, Year 2

Assets (miscellaneous) (131,800 + 21,000)		$152,800
Inventory (35,000 + 16,000)		51,000
Goodwill (0 + 0 + 870)		870
		$204,670
Liabilities (22,000 + 9,200)		$ 31,200
Shareholders' equity		
Common stock	50,000	
Retained earnings	123,470	173,470
		$204,670

#2	Retained earnings Jan. 1 — Company S	10,800	
	Common stock — Company S	10,000	
	Purchase discrepancy	950	
	Investment in S		21,750

This entry eliminates the capital stock and retained earnings of Company S on December 31, Year 1, against the December 31, Year 1, balance of Company P's investment account; it also establishes the difference as the *unamortized* purchase discrepancy on that date. This relationship was illustrated on page 156.

#3	Goodwill impairment loss (expense)	80	
	Goodwill	870	
	Purchase discrepancy		950

This entry eliminates the unamortized purchase discrepancy at the end of Year 1 and allocates it in accordance with the Year 2 purchase discrepancy amortization schedule.

Exhibit 5.7

CONSOLIDATED FINANCIAL STATEMENT WORKING PAPER
December 31, Year 2 (equity method)

	P	S	Eliminations Dr.		Cr.		Consolidated
Sales	$ 60,000	$40,000					$100,000
Investment income	9,920		(1)	9,920			
	$ 69,920	$40,000					$100,000
Cost of sales	$ 32,000	$18,000					$ 50,000
Goodwill impair. loss			(3)	80			80
Miscellaneous exp.	9,000	12,000					21,000
	$ 41,000	$30,000					$ 71,080
Net income	$ 28,920	$10,000		$10,000			$ 28,920
Retained earnings, Jan. 1	$102,550	$10,800	(2)	10,800			$102,550
Net income	28,920	10,000		10,000			28,920
	131,470	20,800					131,470
Dividends	8,000	3,000			(1)	3,000	8,000
Retained earnings, Dec. 31	$123,470	$17,800		$20,800		$ 3,000	$123,470
Assets, misc.	$131,800	$21,000					$152,800
Inventory	35,000	16,000					51,000
Investment in S	28,670				(1)	6,920	
					(2)	21,750	
Purchase discrepancy			(2)	950	(3)	950	
Goodwill			(3)	870			870
	$195,470	$37,000					$204,670
Liabilities	$ 22,000	$ 9,200					$ 31,200
Common stock	50,000	10,000	(2)	10,000			50,000
Retained earnings	123,470	17,800		20,800		3,000	123,470
	$195,470	$37,000		$32,620		$32,620	$204,670

Consolidation of an 80 Percent Owned Subsidiary

The first example was used to illustrate the consolidation of Company P and its 100 percent owned subsidiary Company S over a two-year period. The next example will examine the consolidation of a less than 100 percent owned subsidiary using the same financial statements of Company P and Company S.

Assume that on January 1, Year 1, instead of purchasing 100 percent of Company S for $19,000, Company P purchased 80 percent for $15,200. All other facts about the two companies remain the same as in the previous example. The journal entry of Company P on January 1, Year 1, is:

Investment in S	15,200	
Cash		15,200

The calculation and allocation of the purchase discrepancy and the calculation of the noncontrolling interest on January 1, Year 1, are shown in Exhibit 5.8.

Exhibit 5.8

COMPANY P
CALCULATION OF PURCHASE DISCREPANCY
January 1, Year 1

Cost of 80% of Company S			$15,200
Book value of Company S, Jan. 1, Year 1:			
Common stock		10,000	
Retained earnings		6,000	
		16,000	
Parent's ownership		80%	12,800
Purchase discrepancy			2,400
Allocated:	FV – BV × 80%		
Inventory	2,000 × 80%		1,600
Balance — goodwill			$ 800

CALCULATION OF NONCONTROLLING INTEREST — January 1, Year 1

Shareholders' equity, Company S (above)	$16,000
Noncontrolling interest's ownership	20%
Noncontrolling interest	$ 3,200

The individual balance sheets of Company P and Company S, and Company P's consolidated balance sheet on January 1, Year 1, prepared using the direct approach, are shown below.

BALANCE SHEETS — January 1, Year 1

	Company P	Company S	Consolidated
Assets (miscellaneous)	$142,800	$ 17,000	$159,800
Inventory	22,000	10,000	33,600
Investment in S	15,200	—	—
Goodwill	—	—	800
	$180,000	$ 27,000	$194,200
Liabilities	$ 45,000	$ 11,000	$ 56,000
Noncontrolling interest	—	—	3,200
Shareholders' equity			
Common stock	50,000	10,000	50,000
Retained earnings	85,000	6,000	85,000
	$180,000	$ 27,000	$194,200

The consolidated balance sheet was prepared by eliminating Company P's share (80 percent) of the shareholders' equity of Company S ($12,800) against Company P's investment account ($15,200) and allocating the resultant purchase discrepancy ($2,400) to the inventory of Company S ($1,600), with the unallocated balance shown as goodwill ($800). The portion of the shareholders' equity of Company S not eliminated ($3,200) appears as noncontrolling interest on the consolidated balance sheet.

On December 31, Year 1, Company S reported a net income of $7,300 for the year and paid a cash dividend of $2,500. Company P's net income for the year was $18,300 at this time (not including income from its investment in Company S). An impairment test on goodwill conducted on December 31, Year 1, indicated that a $40 loss had occurred. To assist in the preparation of the Year 1 consolidated financial statements, and the equity method journal entries that will be made, Company P prepares the following schedule:

PURCHASE DISCREPANCY AMORTIZATION SCHEDULE

	Balance Jan. 1, Year 1	Amortization Year 1	Balance Dec. 31, Year 1
Inventory	$1,600	$1,600	—
Goodwill	800	40	760
	$2,400	$1,640	$760

Company P makes the following journal entries using the equity method to account for its investment:

Investment in S	5,840	
Investment income		5,840
80% of Company S Year 1 net income		
Cash	2,000	
Investment in S		2,000
80% of the dividend paid by Company S		
Investment income	1,640	
Investment in S		1,640
Purchase discrepancy amortization — Year 1		

After these journal entries are posted, the two related accounts in the records of Company P will show the following changes and balances:

	Investment in S	Investment income
January 1, Year 1	$15,200	nil
December 31, Year 1		
Income from S	5,840	5,840
Dividends from S	(2,000)	—
Purchase discrepancy amort.	(1,640)	(1,640)
Balance, December 31, Year 1	$17,400	$4,200

Company P increases its earnings from its own operations ($18,300) by the investment income ($4,200) and reports a final net income of $22,500 in Year 1.

The financial statements of Company P and Company S as at December 31, Year 1, are presented in Exhibit 5.9. These statements, along with the purchase discrepancy amortization schedule, are used to prepare the Year 1 consolidated statements.

Consolidated Statements, End of Year 1, Direct Approach

The approach used to prepare a consolidated income statement when the subsidiary is 80 percent owned is basically the same as the one used for 100 percent ownership. All of the revenues and expenses of Company S are used even though the consolidated net income contains only 80 percent of the net income of Company S. This introduces a new "expense" or deduction in the consolidated income statement that is described as noncontrolling interest. The amount is determined by multiplying the reported net income of Company S by the ownership percentage not owned by

Exhibit 5.9

YEAR 1 INCOME STATEMENTS

	Company P	Company S
Sales	$ 50,000	$30,000
Investment income	4,200	—
Total revenue	$ 54,200	$30,000
Cost of sales	$ 26,500	$14,700
Expenses (miscellaneous)	5,200	8,000
Total expenses	$ 31,700	$22,700
Net income	$ 22,500	$ 7,300

YEAR 1 RETAINED EARNINGS STATEMENTS

	Company P	Company S
Balance, January 1	$ 85,000	$ 6,000
Net income	22,500	7,300
	107,500	13,300
Dividends	6,000	2,500
Balance, December 31	$101,500	$10,800

BALANCE SHEETS — December 31, Year 1

	Company P	Company S
Assets (miscellaneous)	$151,100	$18,300
Inventory	30,000	14,000
Investment in S (equity method)	17,400	—
	$198,500	$32,300
Liabilities	$ 47,000	$11,500
Common stock	50,000	10,000
Retained earnings	101,500	10,800
	$198,500	$32,300

Company P. In Year 1, the noncontrolling interest on the consolidated income statement amounts to $1,460 (20% × $7,300 = $1,460). The replacement that takes place in the preparation of the consolidated income statement is shown below:

Replace —

Investment income (from S)			$ 4,200

With —

	Company S statement	Amortization of purch. disc.	
Sales	$30,000		$30,000
Cost of sales	$14,700	$1,600	$16,300
Expenses (misc.)	8,000	—	8,000
Goodwill impairment loss	—	40	40
Total expense	$22,700	$1,640	$24,340
Revenues less adjusted expenses			5,660
Less noncontrolling interest			1,460
			$ 4,200

Because Company P owns 80 percent of the common shares of Company S, the noncontrolling interest's share of the assets and liabilities of Company S must be shown in the consolidated balance sheet. The calculation of the amount shown for noncontrolling interest as at December 31, Year 1, is:

Common stock — Company S	$10,000
Retained earnings — Company S	10,800
	20,800
	20%
	$ 4,160

The following replacement takes place on the balance sheet:

Replace —

Investment in S	$17,400

With —

	Company S statement	Unamortized purch. disc.	
Assets (misc.)	$18,300	—	$18,300
Inventory	14,000	—	14,000
Goodwill	—	760	760
	32,300	760	33,060
Liabilities	11,500	—	11,500
Net assets	$20,800	$760	21,560
Noncontrolling interest			4,160
			$17,400

Exhibit 5.10 shows the Year 1 consolidated financial statements prepared using the direct approach.

The bracketed items come from the statements of Company P and Company S and the purchase discrepancy amortization schedule. A new item has been introduced in the consolidated income statement called "Net income — entity." This amount is the difference between consolidated revenues and expenses. There are two equities shown on a consolidated balance sheet: the equity of the controlling interest (the parent's shareholders' equity) and the noncontrolling interest equity. The income earned by this single consolidated entity is allocated to the two equity interests. The allocation of the net income to the controlling interest is readily seen in the consolidated retained earnings statement. Consolidated financial statements do not show the changes that have taken place in the noncontrolling interest because the statements are directed to the shareholders of the parent company. The changes in noncontrolling interest *could* be presented, in a statement similar to the retained earnings statement, as follows:

CHANGES IN NONCONTROLLING INTEREST

Balance, January 1	$3,200
Allocated income of entity	1,460
	$4,660
Dividends to noncontrolling shareholders	500*
Balance, December 31	$4,160

* $2,500 × 20% = $500.

Exhibit 5.10	**Year 1 Consolidated Financial Statements**

(direct approach)

COMPANY P
CONSOLIDATED INCOME STATEMENT
for the Year Ended December 31, Year 1

Sales (50,000 + 30,000)	$ 80,000
Cost of sales (26,500 + 14,700 + 1,600)	$ 42,800
Goodwill impairment loss (0 + 0 + 40)	40
Expenses (miscellaneous) (5,200 + 8,000)	13,200
	$ 56,040
Net income — entity	$ 23,960
Less noncontrolling interest	1,460
Net income	$ 22,500

COMPANY P
CONSOLIDATED STATEMENT OF RETAINED EARNINGS
for the Year Ended December 31, Year 1

Balance, January 1	$ 85,000
Net income	22,500
	107,500
Dividends	6,000
Balance, December 31	$101,500

COMPANY P
CONSOLIDATED BALANCE SHEET
December 31, Year 1

Assets (miscellaneous) (151,100 + 18,300)		$169,400
Inventory (30,000 + 14,000)		44,000
Goodwill (0 + 0 + 760)		760
		$214,160
Liabilities (47,000 + 11,500)		$ 58,500
Noncontrolling interest		4,160
Shareholders' equity		
Common stock	50,000	
Retained earnings	101,500	151,500
		$214,160

While this statement is not part of consolidated financial statements, it is often useful to prepare this reconciliation when preparing a solution to consolidation problems, because it helps show where the allocated income of this single entity and the dividends of the subsidiary end up in the consolidated financial statements. The consolidated retained earnings statement does not contain the dividends of the subsidiary. In this example, Company S paid $2,500 in dividends. Eighty percent of this amount ($2,000) was paid to Company P and therefore did not leave the consolidated entity. The other 20 percent ($500) was paid to the noncontrolling shareholders and reduced the equity of that group, as shown in the statement.

Consolidated Statements, End of Year 1, Working Paper Approach

Exhibit 5.11 illustrates the preparation of the consolidated financial statements as at December 31, Year 1. The only new items here are the entries required to establish the noncontrolling interest. The working paper entries are produced and explained below.

#1	Investment income — Company P	4,200	
	Dividends — Company S		2,000
	Investment in S — Company P		2,200

Exhibit 5.11

CONSOLIDATED FINANCIAL STATEMENT WORKING PAPER
December 31, Year 1 (equity method)

	P	S	Eliminations Dr.		Eliminations Cr.		Consolidated
Sales	$ 50,000	$30,000					$ 80,000
Investment income	4,200		(1)	4,200			
	$ 54,200	$30,000					$ 80,000
Cost of sales	$ 26,500	$14,700	(3)	1,600			$ 42,800
Goodwill impair. loss			(3)	40			40
Misc. expense	5,200	8,000					13,200
	$ 31,700	$22,700					$ 56,040
Net income — entity							$ 23,960
Noncontrolling interest			(4)	1,460			1,460
Net income	$ 22,500	$ 7,300		$ 7,300			$ 22,500
Retained earnings, Jan. 1	$ 85,000	$ 6,000	(2)	6,000			$ 85,000
Net income	22,500	7,300		7,300			22,500
	$107,500	$13,300					$107,500
Dividends	6,000	2,500			(1)	2,000	6,000
					(5)	500	
Retained earnings, Dec. 31	$101,500	$10,800		$13,300		$ 2,500	$101,500
Assets, misc.	$151,100	$18,300					$169,400
Equipment (net)	30,000	14,000					44,000
Investment in S	17,400				(1)	2,200	
					(2)	15,200	
Purchase discrepancy			(2)	2,400	(3)	2,400	
Goodwill			(3)	760			760
	$198,500	$32,300					$214,160
Liabilities	$ 47,000	$11,500					$ 58,500
Common stock	50,000	10,000	(2)	10,000			50,000
Retained earnings	101,500	10,800		13,300		2,500	101,500
Noncontrolling interest					(2)	3,200	
			(5)	500	(4)	1,460	4,160
	$198,500	$32,300		$26,960		$26,960	$214,160

This entry eliminates the investment income and Company P's share of the dividends of Company S against the investment account. The investment account has now been adjusted to the balance at the beginning of the year ($15,200).

#2	Retained earnings, Jan. 1 — Company S	6,000	
	Common stock — Company S	10,000	
	Purchase discrepancy	2,400	
	Investment in S — Company P		15,200
	Noncontrolling interest		3,200

This entry eliminates 100 percent of the start-of-year shareholders' equity of Company S and the investment account, and establishes the purchase discrepancy and the noncontrolling interest as at the beginning of the year.

#3	Cost of sales — Company S	1,600	
	Goodwill impairment loss	40	
	Goodwill	760	
	Purchase discrepancy		2,400

In accordance with the schedule, this entry reflects the purchase discrepancy amortization on the consolidated income statement and the unamortized balance of the purchase discrepancy on the consolidated balance sheet.

#4	Noncontrolling interest (income statement)	1,460	
	Noncontrolling interest (balance sheet)		1,460

This entry allocates the noncontrolling interest in the entity's income to the noncontrolling interest in the consolidated balance sheet.

#5	Noncontrolling interest (balance sheet)	500	
	Dividends — Company S		500

This final entry eliminates 20 percent of the dividends of Company S that were paid to the noncontrolling interest shareholders and reduces the equity of that group on the consolidated balance sheet.

As a final look at the consolidated process in Year 1, we again examine the relationship that exists when the equity method has been used.

Investment in S (Dec. 31, Year 1)			$17,400
Shareholders' equity, Company S (Dec. 31, Year 1)			
Common stock		10,000	
Retained earnings		10,800	
		20,800	
Parent's ownership		80%	16,640
Unamortized purchase discrepancy			$ 760
Noncontrolling interest (20% × 20,800)			$ 4,160

On December 31, Year 2, Company S reported earnings of $10,000 for the year and paid a cash dividend of $3,000. Company P's earnings for the year were $19,000 at this time (excluding any income from its investment in

Company S). An impairment test conducted on December 31, Year 2, indicated that the goodwill had a fair value of $696, and therefore a $64 impairment loss had occurred. Company P prepared the following purchase discrepancy amortization schedule:

PURCHASE DISCREPANCY AMORTIZATION SCHEDULE

	Balance Dec. 31, Year 1	Amortization Year 2	Balance Dec. 31, Year 2
Inventory	—	—	—
Goodwill	760	64	696
	$760	$64	$696

On December 31, Year 2, Company P makes the following equity method journal entries:

Investment in S	8,000	
Investment income		8,000
80% of Company S, Year 2, net income		

Cash	2,400	
Investment in S		2,400
Dividend received from Company S.		

Investment income	64	
Investment in S		64
Purchase discrepancy amortization — Year 2		

After these journal entries are posted, the investment in S account and the investment income account in the records of P Company will show the following changes and balances:

	Investment in S	Investment income
December 31, Year 1	$17,400	nil
December 31, Year 2		
Income from S	8,000	8,000
Dividends from S	(2,400)	
Purchase discrepancy amort.	(64)	(64)
Balance, December 31, Year 2	$22,936	$7,936

Company P combines its Year 2 investment income ($7,936) with the earnings from its own operations ($19,000) and reports a final net income of $26,936.

The financial statements of Company P and Company S on December 31, Year 2, are shown in Exhibit 5.12.

Exhibit 5.12

YEAR 2 INCOME STATEMENTS

	Company P	Company S
Sales	$ 60,000	$40,000
Investment income	7,936	—
Total revenue	$ 67,936	$40,000
Cost of sales	$ 32,000	$18,000
Expenses (miscellaneous)	9,000	12,000
Total expenses	$ 41,000	$30,000
Net income	$ 26,936	$10,000

YEAR 2 RETAINED EARNINGS STATEMENTS

	Company P	Company S
Balance, January 1	$101,500	$10,800
Net income	26,936	10,000
	128,436	20,800
Dividends	8,000	3,000
Balance, December 31	$120,436	$17,800

BALANCE SHEETS — December 31, Year 2

	Company P	Company S
Assets (miscellaneous)	$134,500	$21,000
Inventory	35,000	16,000
Investment in S (equity method)	22,936	—
	$192,436	$37,000
Liabilities	$ 22,000	$ 9,200
Common stock	50,000	10,000
Retained earnings	120,436	17,800
	$192,436	$37,000

Consolidated Statements, End of Year 2, Direct Approach

The two replacements that are made in the consolidation process when the parent has used the equity method are shown below:

Replace —

Investment income (from S)	$ 7,936

With —

	Company S statement	Amortization of purch. disc.	
Sales	40,000		$40,000
Cost of sales	18,000		$18,000
Expenses (misc.)	12,000		12,000
Goodwill impairment loss	—	64	64
Total expense	30,000	64	$30,064
Revenues less adjusted expenses			9,936
Less noncontrolling interest			
(20% × 10,000)			2,000
			$ 7,936

Replace —

Investment in S			$ 22,936

With —

	Company S statement	Unamortized purch. disc.	
Assets (misc.)	$21,000	—	$21,000
Inventory	16,000	—	16,000
Goodwill	—	696	696
	37,000	696	37,696
Liabilities	9,200	—	9,200
Net assets	$27,800	$696	28,496
Noncontrolling interest (20% × 27,800)			5,560
			$22,936

The consolidated financial statements for Year 2 are shown in Exhibit 5.13. The amounts shown in brackets came from the financial statements of the two companies and the purchase discrepancy amortization schedule. The consolidated retained earnings statement was prepared by reproducing, line by line, the retained earnings statement of Company P.

Consolidated Statements, End of Year 2, Working Paper Approach

Exhibit 5.14 illustrates the preparation of the Year 2 consolidated financial statements of Company P using a working paper. Each of the five elimination entries is reproduced and explained below.

#1	Investment income — Company P	7,936	
	Dividends — Company S		2,400
	Investment in S — Company P		5,536

This entry eliminates Company P's investment income account and 80 percent of the dividends of Company S against Company P's investment account. The investment account now has a December 31, Year 1, balance of $17,400. The remaining 20 percent of the dividends of Company S are eliminated in entry #5.

#2	Retained earnings, January 1 — Company S	10,800	
	Common stock — Company S	10,000	
	Purchase discrepancy	760	
	Investment in S — Company P		17,400
	Noncontrolling interest		4,160

This entry eliminates 100 percent of the start-of-year retained earnings and common stock accounts of Company S against the start-of-year balance in Company P's investment account, and establishes both the unamortized purchase discrepancy and the noncontrolling interest at the beginning of Year 2. The amount for noncontrolling interest ($4,160) is 20 percent of the start-of-year common stock and retained earnings accounts of Company S.

#3	Goodwill impairment loss	64	
	Goodwill	696	
	Purchase discrepancy		760

Exhibit 5.13		

Year 2 Consolidated Financial Statements
(direct approach)

COMPANY P
CONSOLIDATED INCOME STATEMENT
for the Year Ended December 31, Year 2

Sales (60,000 + 40,000)	$100,000
Cost of sales (32,000 + 18,000)	$ 50,000
Goodwill impairment loss (0 + 0 + 64)	64
Expenses (misc.) (9,000 + 12,000)	21,000
	$ 71,064
Net income — entity	$ 28,936
Less noncontrolling interest	2,000
Net income	$ 26,936

COMPANY P
CONSOLIDATED STATEMENT OF RETAINED EARNINGS
for the Year Ended December 31, Year 2

Balance, January 1	$101,500
Net income	26,936
	128,436
Dividends	8,000
Balance, December 31	$120,436

COMPANY P
CONSOLIDATED BALANCE SHEET
December 31, Year 2

Assets (misc.) (134,500 + 21,000)		$155,500
Inventory (35,000 + 16,000)		51,000
Goodwill (0 + 0 + 696)		696
		$207,196
Liabilities (22,000 + 9,200)		$ 31,200
Noncontrolling interest		5,560
Shareholders' equity		
Common stock	50,000	
Retained earnings	120,436	170,436
		$207,196

Entry #3 allocates the unamortized purchase discrepancy in accordance with the Year 2 amortization schedule.

#4	Noncontrolling interest (income statement)	2,000	
	Noncontrolling interest (balance sheet)		2,000

Entry #4 allocates the net income of the entity for Year 2 to the equity of the noncontrolling interest on the balance sheet.

#5	Noncontrolling interest (balance sheet)	600	
	Dividends — Company S		600

Exhibit 5.14

CONSOLIDATED FINANCIAL STATEMENT WORKING PAPER
December 31, Year 2 (equity method)

	P	S	Eliminations Dr.		Eliminations Cr.		Consolidated
Sales	$ 60,000	$40,000					$100,000
Investment income	7,936		(1)	7,936			
	$ 67,936	$40,000					$100,000
Cost of sales	$ 32,000	$18,000					$ 50,000
Goodwill impair. loss			(3)	64			64
Misc. expense	9,000	12,000					21,000
	$ 41,000	$30,000					$ 71,064
Net income — entity							$ 28,936
Noncontrolling interest			(4)	2,000			2,000
Net income	$ 26,936	$10,000		$10,000			$ 26,936
Retained earnings, Jan. 1	$101,500	$10,800	(2)	10,800			$101,500
Net income	26,936	10,000		10,000			26,936
	$128,436	$20,800					$128,436
Dividends	8,000	3,000			(1)	2,400	8,000
					(5)	600	
Retained earnings, Dec. 31	$120,436	$17,800		$20,800		$ 3,000	$120,436
Assets, misc.	$134,500	$21,000					$155,500
Inventory	35,000	16,000					51,000
Investment in S	22,936				(1)	5,536	
					(2)	17,400	
Purchase discrepancy			(2)	760	(3)	760	
Goodwill			(3)	696			696
	$192,436	$37,000					$207,196
Liabilities	$ 22,000	$ 9,200					$ 31,200
Common stock	50,000	10,000	(2)	10,000			50,000
Retained earnings	120,436	17,800		20,800		3,000	120,436
Noncontrolling interest			(2)	4,160			5,560
			(5)	600	(4)	2,000	
	$192,436	$37,000		$32,856		$32,856	$207,196

The final entry eliminates the remaining 20 percent of the dividends of Company S and reduces the equity of the noncontrolling interest on the balance sheet by this amount.

The preceding illustrations have presented the basics for preparing consolidated financial statements when the parent has used the equity method to account for its investment subsequent to the date of acquisition. Chapter 6 will examine the preparation of the consolidated statements in situations where the parent has used the cost method.

Intercompany Receivables and Payables

Consolidated financial statements are designed to reflect the results of transactions between the consolidated single entity and those outside the entity. All transactions between the parent and its subsidiaries, or between the subsidiaries of a parent, must be eliminated in the consolidation process to reflect this single-entity concept. While many of these intercompany eliminations are discussed in later chapters, we will introduce the topic now by discussing the elimination of intercompany receivables and payables. If the parent's accounts receivable contain a receivable of $5,000 from its subsidiary, then the accounts payable of the subsidiary must contain a $5,000 payable to the parent. If these intercompany receivables and payables were not eliminated in the consolidation process, both the accounts receivable and the accounts payable on the consolidated balance sheet would be overstated from a single-entity point of view. The working paper entry to eliminate these intercompany balances would be:

Accounts payable — subsidiary	5,000	
Accounts receivable — parent		5,000

Because the net assets (assets less liabilities) are unchanged after this elimination, the equities of the noncontrolling and controlling interests are not affected.

When Control Ceases

After control has been obtained, GAAP requires the parent to prepare consolidated statements for purposes of external reporting. When control ceases, the former parent ceases consolidation and determines which type of investment it now has.[8] If it is considered to be a portfolio investment, it is reported using the cost method. The balance in the investment account immediately after the loss of control is the balance obtained by using the equity method while control existed. The cost method is used from this point on, and prior years' statements are not adjusted retroactively.[9]

If the investment is considered to be significant influence, the former parent ceases to consolidate and subsequently reports using the equity method, without retroactive restatement of prior years' statements.

If a parent has decided to dispose of a subsidiary, it continues to consolidate until the date of disposal. During this interval, it applies the provisions of Section 3475, "Discontinued Operations," to segregate the operations of the subsidiary in the consolidated income statement.

---

[8] *CICA Handbook*, paragraph 1590.20.
[9] *CICA Handbook*, paragraph 3050.17.

SUMMARY

While a parent company can account for its investment by either the equity method or the cost method, the consolidated statements are the same regardless of the method used.

The preparation of consolidated statements when the parent has used the equity method was illustrated in this chapter. Two approaches were used: the direct approach and the working paper approach. The working paper approach allows the reader to see where all of the eliminations end up. However, as we proceed with some of the more difficult aspects of consolidated statement preparation, the number of elimination entries used becomes overwhelming. When a consolidation question appears on a professional accounting examination, it is most prudent to use the direct approach if the question is to be answered in the allotted time. Readers are encouraged to master the direct approach.

SELF-STUDY PROBLEM

On January 1, 1997, Allen Company acquired 70% of the outstanding common shares of Bell Company for $88,500 in cash. On that date Bell had common stock of $50,000 and retained earnings of $45,000. At acquisition, the identifiable assets and liabilities of Bell had fair values that were equal to book values except for plant assets, which had fair values $20,000 greater than book value; inventory, which had a fair value $8,000 less than book value; and bonds payable, which had fair values $10,000 greater than book value. The plant assets had a remaining useful life of 8 years on January 1, 1997, and the bonds payable mature on December 31, 2004. Both companies amortize on a straight-line basis.

Financial statements for the 2002 fiscal year are as follows:

	Allen	Bell
Income statements		
Sales	$400,000	$100,000
Rent revenue	15,000	—
Investment revenue	4,065	—
	$419,065	$100,000
Cost of sales	200,000	$ 45,000
Depreciation	55,000	20,000
Interest expense	32,000	7,700
Other expense	28,000	17,300
	315,000	$ 90,000
Net income	$104,065	$ 10,000
Retained earnings statements		
Balance, January 1	453,925	$135,000
Net income	104,065	10,000
	557,990	145,000
Dividends	30,000	5,000
Balance, December 31	$527,990	$140,000

	Allen	Bell
Balance sheets		
Cash	$ 11,500	$ 10,000
Accounts receivable	60,000	25,000
Inventory	200,000	40,000
Investment in Bell — equity	142,990	—
Plant and equipment	1,200,000	470,000
Accumulated depreciation	(300,000)	(220,000)
	$1,314,490	$325,000
Accounts payable	$ 86,500	$ 25,000
Bonds payable	400,000	110,000
Common stock	300,000	50,000
Retained earnings	527,990	140,000
	$1,314,490	$325,000

Additional Information

Prior to 2002, goodwill amortization amounted to $10,300. An impairment test conducted on December 31, 2002, indicated a loss of $2,060.

On December 31, 2002, Bell Company owes Allen Company $9,000.

Required:

1. Using the direct approach, prepare the following 2002 consolidated financial statements:
   (a) Income statement.
   (b) Retained earnings statement.
   (c) Balance sheet.
2. Prepare a schedule of the 2002 changes in noncontrolling interest.

Solution to Self-study Problem

Cost of 70% of Bell			$88,500
Book value of Bell			
Common stock		50,000	
Retained earnings		45,000	
		95,000	
Allen's ownership		70%	66,500
Purchase discrepancy — January 1, 1997			22,000
Allocated	FV – BV		
Plant assets	20,000 × 70% =	14,000	
Inventory	– 8,000 × 70% =	– 5,600	
		8,400	
Bonds payable	10,000 × 70% =	7,000	1,400
Goodwill			$20,600

PURCHASE DISCREPANCY AMORTIZATION SCHEDULE

	Balance Jan. 1/97	Amortization To end of 2001	Amortization 2002	Balance Dec. 31/02
Plant assets	14,000	8,750	1,750	3,500
Inventory	– 5,600	– 5,600	—	—
Goodwill	20,600	10,300	2,060	8,240
	29,000	13,450	3,810	11,740
Bonds payable	7,000	4,375	875	1,750
	$22,000	$ 9,075	$2,935	$ 9,990

1. (a)

ALLEN COMPANY
CONSOLIDATED INCOME STATEMENT
for the Year Ended December 31, 2002

Sales (400,000 + 100,000)	$500,000
Rent revenue	15,000
	$515,000
Cost of sales (200,000 + 45,000)	$245,000
Depreciation (55,000 + 20,000 + 1,750)	76,750
Interest expense (32,000 + 7,700 – 875)	38,825
Other expense (28,000 + 17,300)	45,300
Goodwill impairment loss	2,060
	$407,935
Net income — entity	$107,065
Less noncontrolling interest (30% x 10,000)	3,000
Net income	$104,065

(b)

ALLEN COMPANY
CONSOLIDATED RETAINED EARNINGS STATEMENT
for the Year Ended December 31, 2002

Balance, January 1	$453,925
Net income	104,065
	557,990
Dividends	30,000
Balance, December 31	$527,990

CALCULATION OF NONCONTROLLING INTEREST — December 31, 2002

Common stock — Bell	$ 50,000
Retained earnings — Bell	140,000
	190,000
	30%
	$ 57,000

(c)

ALLEN COMPANY
CONSOLIDATED BALANCE SHEET
December 31, 2002

Cash (11,500 + 10,000)	$ 21,500
Accounts receivable (60,000 + 25,000 – 9,000)	76,000
Inventory (200,000 + 40,000)	240,000
Plant and equipment (1,200,000 + 470,000 + 14,000)	1,684,000
Accumulated depreciation	
(300,000 + 220,000 + 8,750 + 1,750)	(530,500)
Goodwill	8,240
	$1,499,240
Accounts payable (86,500 + 25,000 – 9,000)	$ 102,500
Bonds payable (400,000 + 110,000 + 1,750)	511,750
	614,250
Noncontrolling interest	57,000
Shareholders' equity	
Common stock	300,000
Retained earnings	527,990

Common stock		300,000
Retained earnings	527,990	827,990
		$1,499,240

2.

2002 CHANGES IN NONCONTROLLING INTEREST

Balance, January 1 (30% × 185,000*)	$55,500
Allocation of entity net income	3,000
	58,500
Dividends (30% × 5,000)	1,500
Balance, December 31	$57,000

* Common stock	$ 50,000
Retained earnings, January 1	135,000
	$185,000

REVIEW QUESTIONS

1. When the parent has used the equity method, the parent's net income equals consolidated net income, and the parent's retained earnings equal consolidated retained earnings. However, the parent's financial statements are not the same as consolidated statements. On consolidated statements, which assets and income are replaced from the parent's statements, and what are they replaced with?

2. A parent company's 75% owned subsidiary declared and paid a dividend totalling $10,000. How would the parent company record this dividend under the equity method? And under the cost method?

3. By which method — cost or equity — does the *CICA Handbook* require a parent company to record its investment in a subsidiary? Why?

4. A consolidated retained earnings statement shows dividends declared during the year. Do these dividends consist of the parent's, or the subsidiary's, or both? Explain.

5. "A purchase discrepancy allocated to revalue the land of a subsidiary on acquisition date will always appear on subsequent consolidated balance sheets." Do you agree? Explain.

6. Describe the make-up of consolidated net income in any year subsequent to acquisition date.

7. How are dividends received in excess of the parent's share of post-acquisition earnings recorded by the parent company under the cost method?

8. "Under the equity method, the investment account is adjusted for the investor's share of post-acquisition earnings computed by the consolidation method." Explain this statement.

9. A 75% owned subsidiary paid dividends of $50,000 during the year. How would these dividends be reflected in the consolidated balance sheet prepared at the end of the year?

10. At the end of the year, the parent's investment account had an equity method balance of $125,000. At this time its 75% owned subsidiary had shareholders' equity totalling $125,000. How much was the unamortized purchase discrepancy at the end of the year?

11. On the consolidated balance sheet, what effect does the elimination of intercompany receivables and payables have on shareholders' equity and noncontrolling interest?

12. Explain how the parent reports its investment in the subsidiary after losing control of the subsidiary.

13. Briefly outline the process for determining if goodwill is impaired.

14. Is the impairment test for intangibles other than goodwill the same as the one used for goodwill? Briefly explain.

MULTIPLE CHOICE

1. When a company uses the equity method to record its investment in a subsidiary during the year, which of the following will be included in the journal entry to record the parent's share of the subsidiary's net income (assuming a positive net income)?
   a. Debit cash.
   b. Credit investment in subsidiary.
   c. Debit investment income.
   d. Credit investment income.

Use the following data for Questions 2 to 5.

The following information appeared on the balance sheets and income statements of Plunge Inc. and Sink Co. on December 31, 2002:

	Plunge	Sink
Common stock (1,200,000 shares)	$1,200,000	
Common stock (480,000 shares)		$480,000
Retained earnings at January 1, 2002	720,000	120,000
Net income from operations	320,000	100,000
Dividends declared	120,000	40,000

Plunge acquired an 80% interest in Sink on January 1, 2002, for $600,000. At the date of acquisition, it was determined that Sink's plant assets with a 10-year remaining useful life were undervalued by $50,000, and patents with a 5-year life were undervalued by $100,000.

2. What was the amount of goodwill that arose on the acquisition of Sink's shares by Plunge on January 1, 2002?
   a. Negative goodwill arose, which would be allocated to nonmonetary assets.
   b. $0
   c. $70,000
   d. $80,000

3. What is the amount that Plunge would report on the equity basis for "investment income" from Sink at December 31, 2002? Assume there were no intercompany transactions during the year.
   a. $60,000
   b. $61,000
   c. $64,000
   d. $80,000

4. What is the amount that Plunge would report as "noncontrolling interest" relating to its investment in Sink on its consolidated financial statements at December 31, 2002?
   a. $96,000
   b. $120,000
   c. $132,000
   d. $140,000

5. Under the working paper approach to consolidation, which of the following will be included in the elimination journal entry to remove investment income and Plunge's "investment in Sink" account at December 31, 2002?
   a. Debit dividends $32,000.
   b. Credit dividends $32,000.
   c. Debit dividends $40,000.
   d. Credit dividends $40,000.

6. Parent Inc. purchased all of the outstanding shares of Sub Ltd on January 1, Year 1, for $214,000. Annual amortization of the purchase discrepancy amounted to $16,000. Parent Inc. reported net income of $100,000 in Year 1 and $110,000 in Year 2, and paid $40,000 in dividends each year. Sub Ltd reported net income of $33,000 in Year 1 and $39,000 in Year 2, and paid $8,000 in dividends each year. What is the Investment in Sub Ltd. balance on Parent's books as at December 31, Year 2, if the equity method has been used?
   a. $238,000
   b. $246,000
   c. $278,000
   d. $286,000

7. Burns Ltd. purchased 100% of the outstanding shares of Simon Inc. on January 1, Year 1, at a price that was in excess of the subsidiary's fair market value. On that date, Burns' equipment (10-year life) had a book value of $300,000 and a fair market value of $400,000. Simon had equipment with a book value of $200,000 and a fair market value of $300,000. Burns uses the equity method to record its investment. On December 31, Year 3, Burns has equipment with a book value of $210,000 and a fair value of $330,000.

Simon has equipment with a book value of $140,000 and a fair value of $270,000. What is the balance for equipment on the consolidated balance sheet on December 31, Year 3?
   a. $600,000
   b. $490,000
   c. $480,000
   d. $420,000

8. Noncontrolling interest on a consolidated balance sheet prepared in accordance with GAAP represents which of the following?
   a. An equity interest in a subsidiary company that exists because the parent's interest in the subsidiary is less than 100%.
   b. A liability of the parent company.
   c. The net amount by which subsidiary assets and liabilities have been revalued following a business combination.
   d. a and b.
   e. b and c.
   f. None of the above.

9. OP Corporation acquired 60% of KD Corporation on March 31, 2002. Because OP controls KD, it uses the consolidation method for *reporting* its investment. OP should use which of the following for *recording* its investment in KD?
   a. The cost method must be used.
   b. The equity method must be used.
   c. The cost method or the equity method may be used.
   d. The consolidation method must be used.

(CGA adapted)

10. What would be the effect on the consolidated financial statements if an unconsolidated subsidiary is accounted for by the equity method but consolidated financial statements are prepared with other subsidiaries?
   a. Dividend revenue from the unconsolidated subsidiary will be reflected in consolidated net income.
   b. All of the unconsolidated subsidiary's accounts will be included individually in the consolidated financial statements.
   c. The consolidated retained earnings will not reflect the earnings of the unconsolidated subsidiary.
   d. The consolidated retained earnings will be the same as if the subsidiary had been included in the consolidation.

(CGA adapted)

11. Albany Ltd. purchased all of the outstanding shares of Gerrard Inc. on January 1, 2001, for $1,200,000. The price resulted in a $90,000 allocation to equipment and goodwill of $75,000. Because the subsidiary earned especially high profits, Albany was required to pay the previous owners of Gerrard an additional $200,000 on January 1, 2003. How should this extra amount be reported?
   a. The $200,000 additional payment is reflected as a reduction in consolidated retained earnings.
   b. A retroactive adjustment is made to record the $200,000 as an additional expense for 2001.
   c. Consolidated goodwill is increased by $200,000 as at January 1, 2003.
   d. The $200,000 is recorded as an expense in 2003.

12. Jonston Ltd owns 75% of the outstanding shares of Saxon Corp. Saxon currently owes Jonston $400,000 for inventory acquired during the last month. In preparing consolidated financial statements, what amount of this debt should be eliminated?
    a. $0
    b. $100,000
    c. $300,000
    d. $400,000

CASES

Case 1* In May 2001, Valero Energy Corp. and Ultramar Diamond Shamrock Corp. (UDS) jointly announced that the companies had reached an agreement for Valero to acquire UDS, which will make Valero the second-largest North American refiner of petroleum products. The new organization will have 23,000 employees in the United States and Canada, 13 refineries, and a total throughput capacity of just under 2 million barrels per day (BPD). Valero will also be one of the continent's largest retailers, with more than 5,000 retail outlets in the U.S. and Canada. With this acquisition, Valero will have annual revenues of US$32 billion and total assets of more than $10 billion. In terms of refining capacity, Valero will be second in North America only to ExxonMobil. The Canadian operations of the combined company will continue to operate under the Ultramar brand.

Valero is recognized throughout the industry as a leader in the production of premium, environmentally clean products. A Fortune 500 company based in San Antonio, Texas, Valero has approximately 3,100 employees and 2000 revenues of nearly $15 billion. Also based in San Antonio, UDS has about $17 billion in annual revenues and more than 20,000 employees.

Bill Greehey, Valero's Chairman and CEO, announced that "combining Valero's complex refining system and the extensive UDS refining, logistics and retail network gives us a superior asset portfolio that will allow us to effectively compete in this rapidly consolidating business. We will realize tremendous synergies and strategic benefits while enhancing earnings stability. And, we are fortunate to bring aboard such a high-quality management team and workforce that is among the best in the industry."

The total consideration was approximately $6 billion, made up of a mixture of assumed debt, cash, and Valero shares, and represented approximately a 30% premium over the market value of UDS in the weeks leading up to the acquisition. This premium was justified by the operating efficiencies and synergies to be gained from the increased scale and scope of operations. Savings were estimated at $200 million per year.

The retail assets included in the acquisition included included the brands Ultramar, Diamond Shamrock, Beacon, and Total. UDS has more than 2,500 company-owned sites in the U.S. and Canada, as well as supplying 2,500 dealer, truck stop, and cardlock sites. The company-owned stores have extensive brand support programs, such as proprietary consumer and fleet credit cards, radio and television brand support, and strong in-store marketing programs, to which Valero will be able to add its 350-store retail network in California. In addition, UDS operates one of the largest home heating oil businesses in North America, which sells heating oil to about 250,000 households.

Greehey also noted, "We are fortunate because UDS has created one of the best retail networks in the country with excellent leadership and strategic vision. And with the size and quality of their retail network, we will benefit from the earnings stability that can be achieved by having retail exposure without diluting the leverage we have to refining margins. So we will truly have the best of both worlds."

---

* Case prepared by Peter Secord, St. Mary's University.

The acquisition clearly included more than the physical assets of Ultramar Diamond Shamrock. A variety of unrecorded intangible assets were represented in the portfolio of assets held by UDS, and these are the matters which require your attention.

Required:

With reference to Section 1581 of the *CICA Handbook* (especially paragraph 1581.48 and Appendix A, "Implementation Guidance"), prepare a memorandum to the chief financial officer of Valero. In this memo:

- Discuss the valuation of the various intangible assets included in this acquisition.
- Indicate which items should be included in the amount assigned to goodwill in the acquisition.
- Indicate which items should be separately identified and valued as intangible assets.
- Discuss how you would assign values to the various items identified and what amortization policy (if any) is appropriate.

Case 2* The following paragraph was included in a press release issued jointly by Conoco Inc. and Gulf Canada Resources Limited:

> Houston, Texas, and Calgary, Alberta, Canada, (May 29, 2001) — Conoco Inc. (NYSE: COC.A) (NYSE: COC.B) and Gulf Canada Resources Limited (NYSE: GOU and TSE: GOU) today announced that their boards of directors have unanimously approved an acquisition agreement under which a wholly owned Canadian subsidiary of Conoco will acquire Gulf Canada for Cdn$12.40 (US$8.02) per ordinary share in cash, or approximately Cdn$6.7 (US$4.3) billion in total equity. Conoco also will assume approximately Cdn$3.1 (US$2.0) billion of Gulf Canada's net debt, preferred stock and minority interests. The transaction price represents a premium of 35 percent over Gulf Canada's closing stock price of Cdn$9.18 on Friday, May 25, 2001.

This business combination was to be accounted for as a purchase. Included in the assets of Gulf Canada Resources Limited (Gulf) that were to be acquired were proved reserves of over 1 billion barrels of oil equivalent (BOE). The acquired properties also included the potential to add 1.2 billion BOE from probable reserves already identified. Conoco Chairman and CEO Archie W. Dunham noted, "The management of Gulf Canada have greatly strengthened their operating portfolio and balance sheet during the last few years, and we consider the Gulf Canada management team and employees a major asset in this transaction." More details associated with the assets acquired are as follows:

- Conoco will add nearly 1.4 trillion cubic feet (TCF) of net proved gas reserves and an additional 2.9 net TCF of probable gas reserves in North America..
- Longer term, Gulf Canada's four million acres of undeveloped land in Western Canada and leading position in Canada's Mackenzie Delta will augment Conoco's ongoing North American natural gas development program.
- Conoco's Rocky Mountain and Mid-Continent refining capacity provides a ready market for Gulf's Western Canadian conventional and heavy crude oil production, resulting in increased value added and cost savings.
- Gulf subsidiaries included a 72% interest in Gulf Indonesia Resources Limited, including over 180 million BOE, and access to 1.5 TCF of probable gas reserves in the region.

---

* Case prepared by Peter Secord, St. Mary's University.

- Gulf has major long-term natural gas sales contracts in Southeast Asia for delivery of 3 TCF (net), with production exceeding 400 million cubic feet/day (net) in 2005.
- Gulf has had recent exploration successes on the island of Sumatra, in the Natuna Sea, and offshore Java, as well as having a 9 percent interest in Syncrude Canada Ltd., a joint venture that produces and upgrades heavy tar sands into light, sweet crude oil. Syncrude has unbooked resource potential of 5 billion barrels of oil (400 million barrels net).

Required:

(a) Many of the assets acquired in this business combination have considerable uncertainty as to their ultimate value to the business, and the assets detailed above may represent particular challenges. Provide guidance to the financial staff of the new Canadian subsidiary of Conoco as to how the aggregate purchase price is to be allocated among the various tangible and intangible assets and liabilities included in the portfolio of Gulf Canada Resources Limited that has been acquired. Explain your answer in terms of the provisions of the *CICA Handbook*.

(b) World oil prices are an important variable in the determination of the value to the business of oil and gas reserves, and in the months following this business combination wide fluctuations in oil prices were experienced. How would these fluctuations in oil prices affect the valuation of the purchase in subsequent financial statements of Conoco? Why?

PROBLEMS

Problem 1   Peach Ltd. acquired 70% of the common shares of Cherry Company on January 1, Year 4. On that date, Cherry had common stock of $600,000 and retained earnings of $300,000.

The following is a summary of the changes in Peach's investment account from January 1, Year 4, to December 31, Year 6:

INVESTMENT IN CHERRY

January 1, Year 4	Cost	$650,000
December 31, Year 4	Investment income	52,000
	Dividends	(28,000)
December 31, Year 5	Investment income	66,000
	Dividends	(35,000)
December 31, Year 6	Investment income	80,000
	Dividends	(42,000)
	Balance	$743,000

Other Information

- Dividends declared by Cherry each year were equal to 50% of Cherry's reported net income each year.
- On January 1, Year 4, the book values of the identifiable net assets of Cherry were equal to fair values.

Required:

Calculate the following:

(a) The amount of dividends declared by Cherry in Year 4.
(b) The reported net income of Cherry for Year 5.
(c) The amount for noncontrolling interest that would appear in the Year 6 consolidated income statement and balance sheet.
(d) The amount of goodwill that would appear on the December 31, Year 6, consolidated balance sheet.

Problem 2   Poplar Ltd. purchased 100% of Ash Company on January 1, Year 1, for $600,000, when the balance sheet of Ash showed common stock of $400,000 and retained earnings of $100,000. On that date, the inventory of Ash was undervalued by $40,000, and a patent with an estimated remaining life of 5 years was overvalued by $70,000.

Ash reported the following subsequent to January 1, Year 1:

	Net income	Dividends
Year 1	$ 80,000	$25,000
Year 2 (loss)	(35,000)	10,000
Year 3	100,000	40,000

A test for goodwill impairment by Poplar on December 31, Year 3, resulted in a loss of $19,300 being recorded.

Required:

PART A

Prepare the equity method journal entries of Poplar each year.

PART B

Compute the following on December 31, Year 3:
(a) Investment in Ash.
(b) Consolidated goodwill.
(c) The unamortized purchase discrepancy using the account "Investment in Ash Company" from section (a).

Problem 3   On June 30, 2002, the following financial statements were prepared. Peters Ltd. uses the equity method to account for its investment.

	Peters	Singer
INCOME STATEMENTS		
Sales	$ 90,000	$54,000
Investment income	10,728	—
Total revenue	$100,728	$54,000
Cost of sales	$ 46,700	$31,460
Expenses (miscellaneous)	10,360	9,400
Total expenses	$ 57,060	$40,860
Net income	$ 43,668	$13,140
RETAINED EARNINGS STATEMENTS		
Balance, July 1	$153,000	$10,800
Net income	43,668	13,140
	196,668	23,940
Dividends	10,800	4,500
Balance, June 30	$185,868	$19,440
BALANCE SHEETS — June 30, 2002		
Miscellaneous assets	$291,980	$42,940
Equipment (net)	34,000	15,200
Investment in Singer	34,488	—
	$360,468	$58,140
Liabilities	$ 84,600	$20,700
Common stock	90,000	18,000
Retained earnings	185,868	19,440
	$360,468	$58,140

Other Information

Peters purchased 80% of the common shares of Singer on July 1, 2001, for $27,360. On that date the equipment of Singer had a fair market value that was $7,200 less than book value, with an estimated remaining life of 8 years. All other assets and liabilities of Singer had book values equal to market values. A goodwill impairment test on June 30, 2002, indicated a loss of $504.

Required:

(a) Prepare the consolidated financial statements of Peters as at June 30, 2002.
(b) Prepare a schedule showing the changes in noncontrolling interest during the year.

Problem 4   Foster Corporation acquired a 90% interest in Spencer Ltd. on December 31, Year 1, for $700,000. On that date Spencer had common stock of $350,000 and retained earnings of $300,000. The purchase discrepancy was allocated $80,000 to inventory, with the balance to unrecorded patents being amortized over 10 years. Spencer reported a net income of $50,000 in Year 2 and $70,000 in Year 3. While no dividends were declared in Year 2, Spencer declared dividends amounting to $35,000 in Year 3.

Required:

(a) Prepare the equity method journal entries of Foster for Years 2 and 3.
(b) Calculate consolidated patents on December 31, Year 3.
(c) Prepare a statement that shows the changes in the noncontrolling interest in Year 3.

Problem 5   On July 1, 2001, A Ltd. purchased 80% of the voting shares of B Ltd. for $543,840. The balance sheet of B Ltd. on that date was as follows:

B LTD.
BALANCE SHEET
as at July 1, 2001

	Net book value	Fair market value
Cash	$ 96,000	$ 96,000
Accounts receivable	120,000	144,000
Inventory	180,000	228,000
Fixed assets (net)	540,000	450,000
	$936,000	
Current liabilities	$107,200	$107,200
Bonds payable	200,000	190,000
Common shares	120,000	
Retained earnings	508,800	
	$936,000	

The accounts receivable of B Ltd. were collected in October 2001, and the inventory was completely sold by May 2002. The fixed assets of B Ltd. had a remaining life of 15 years on July 1, 2001, and the bonds payable mature on June 30, 2005. After properly accounting for the fair-value differences, any remaining purchase discrepancy was allocated to unrecorded patents (10-year life) of B Ltd.

The financial statements for A Ltd. and B Ltd. at December 31, 2003, are as follows:

BALANCE SHEETS

	A Ltd.	B Ltd.
Cash	$ 120,000	$ 84,000
Accounts receivable	180,000	114,000
Inventory	300,000	276,000
Fixed assets (net)	720,000	540,000
Investment in B Ltd. (equity method)	520,960	—
Other investments	250,666	—
	$2,091,626	$1,014,000
Current liabilities	180,200	115,000
Bonds payable	315,000	220,800
Common shares	300,600	120,000
Retained earnings	1,219,026	554,800
Net income	126,800	8,400
Dividends	(50,000)	(5,000)
	$2,091,626	$1,014,000

INCOME STATEMENTS

	A Ltd.	B Ltd.
Sales	$1,261,000	$1,200,000
Investment income (equity method)	4,800	—
Income from other investments	25,000	—
	$1,290,800	$1,200,000
Cost of goods sold	$ 840,000	$1,020,000
Depreciation	60,000	54,000
Interest	37,000	26,400
Other	227,000	91,200
	$1,164,000	$1,191,600
Net income	$ 126,800	$ 8,400

Required:

Prepare the consolidated financial statements for the year ended December 31, 2003.

Problem 6   On January 1, Year 1, Parent Company acquired 90% of the common shares of Subsidiary Corporation at a total cost of $500,000. The following information was taken from the records of Subsidiary on January 1, Year 1:

	Carrying value	Fair value
Miscellaneous assets	$ 800,000	$ 800,000
Inventory (FIFO)	150,000	175,000
Land 110,000	110,000 ~~140,000~~	140,000
Equipment	225,000	240,000
	1,285,000	1,355,000
Miscellaneous liabilities	835,000	835,000
Net assets	$ 450,000	$ 520,000

Subsidiary records depreciation on its equipment using the reducing balance method at a 20% rate. A goodwill impairment loss of $2,400 occurred in Year 3. During the three-year period ending December 31, Year 3, Subsidiary's net income totalled

$84,000 and dividends totalling $45,000 were declared and paid. Parent uses the equity method to account for its investment.

Required:

(a) Prepare a purchase discrepancy amortization schedule for the three-year period ending December 31, Year 3.

(b) Compute the balance in the account "Investment in Subsidiary Corporation common stock" on December 31, Year 3.

(c) Verify the total unamortized purchase discrepancy on December 31, Year 3, by using the amounts computed in part (b).

(d) Compute the noncontrolling interest on December 31, Year 3.

Problem 7 The following financial statements were prepared by Peter Corp. on December 31, Year 6.

BALANCE SHEET

	Nonconsolidated	Consolidated
Cash	$ 300,000	$ 400,000
Accounts receivable	200,000	125,000
Inventory	2,000,000	2,420,000
Plant and equipment	3,000,000	6,090,000
Accumulated depreciation	(750,000)	(1,285,000)
Goodwill	—	210,000
Investment in Saint Company — at equity	2,335,000	—
	$7,085,000	$7,960,000
Liabilities	$ 900,000	$1,125,000
Noncontrolling interest	—	650,000
Capital stock	3,850,000	3,850,000
Retained earnings	2,335,000	2,335,000
	$7,085,000	$7,960,000

INCOME STATEMENT

Sales	$4,000,000	$5,000,000
Investment income	230,000	
Total revenue	$4,230,000	$5,000,000
Cost of sales	$2,500,000	$2,900,000
Miscellaneous expenses	320,000	390,000
Depreciation expense	80,000	140,000
Goodwill impairment loss	—	20,000
Noncontrolling interest	—	100,000
Income tax expense	250,000	370,000
Total	$3,150,000	$3,920,000
Net income	$1,080,000	$1,080,000

RETAINED EARNINGS STATEMENT

Balance, January 1	$1,755,000	$1,755,000
Net income	1,080,000	1,080,000
	2,835,000	2,835,000
Dividends	500,000	500,000
Balance, December 31	$2,335,000	$2,335,000

Other Information

Peter Corp. purchased 75% of the outstanding voting stock of Saint Company for $2,500,000 on July 1, Year 2, at which time Saint's common stock was $1,600,000 and its retained earnings were $400,000. The purchase discrepancy on this date was allocated as follows:

- 30% to undervalued inventory.
- 40% to equipment; remaining life 8 years.
- Balance to goodwill.

Saint owes Peter $75,000 on December 31, Year 6.

Saint's common share balance has remained constant, and its dividends for Year 6 were $200,000.

Goodwill impairment losses were recorded as follows:

- Year 4: $70,000.
- Year 6: $20,000.

Required:

Prepare the financial statements for Peter's subsidiary, Saint Company, as at December 31, Year 6.

Problem 8   Balance sheet and income statement data for two affiliated companies for the current year are given below:

BALANCE SHEET DATA
as of December 31, Year 4

	Able	Baker
Cash	$ 40,000	$ 21,000
Receivables	92,000	84,000
Inventories	56,000	45,000
Land 20,000	60,000	
Plant and equipment	200,000	700,000
Accumulated depreciation	(80,000)	(350,000)
Investment in Baker Company (equity)	344,240	—
Advances to Baker Company	100,000	—
	$772,240	$560,000
Accounts payable	$130,000	$ 96,500
Advances payable	—	100,000
Common stock	400,000	200,000
Beginning retained earnings	229,580	154,000
Net income for the year	34,660	17,500
Dividends	(22,000)	(8,000)
	$772,240	$560,000

INCOME STATEMENT DATA
Year Ended December 31, Year 4

Sales revenues	$600,000	$400,000
Interest income	6,700	—
Investment income	11,360	—
Total revenues	$618,060	$400,000
Cost of goods sold	$334,000	$225,000
Depreciation expense	20,000	70,000
Selling and administrative expense	207,000	74,000
Interest expense	1,700	6,000
Income taxes expense	20,700	7,500
Total expenses	$583,400	$382,500
Net income	$ 34,660	$ 17,500

Other Information

1. Able acquired an 80% interest in Baker on January 1, Year 1, for $272,000. On that date the following information was noted about specific net assets of Baker:

	Book value	Fair value
Inventory	$20,000	$50,000
Land	25,000	45,000
Equipment (estimated life 15 years)	60,000	78,000
Misc. intangibles (estimated life 20 years)	—	42,000

2. On January 1, Year 1, Baker had a retained earnings balance of $30,000.
3. Able carries its investment at equity.

Required:

Prepare the following:
(a) Consolidated income statement.
(b) Consolidated retained earnings statement.
(c) Consolidated balance sheet.

Problem 9   On January 2, Year 1, Shy Ltd. purchased 80% of the outstanding shares of Meek Ltd. for $4,120,000. On that date Meek's balance sheet and the fair market value of its identifiable assets and liabilities were as follows:

	Book value	Fair value
Cash	$ 500,000	$ 500,000
Accounts receivable	1,500,000	1,500,000
Inventory	2,000,000	2,200,000
Plant and equipment (net)	4,500,000	4,500,000
Patents (net)	1,000,000	1,500,000
	$9,500,000	
Accounts payable	$2,000,000	$2,000,000
10% bonds payable	3,000,000	3,300,000
Common stock	2,000,000	
Retained earnings	2,500,000	
	$9,500,000	

The patents had a remaining life of 10 years, and the bonds mature on December 31, Year 10. Goodwill impairment losses were recorded as follows:

- Year 1: $20,000.
- Year 3: $10,000.

On December 31, Year 3, the financial statements of the two companies are as follows:

	Shy	Meek
BALANCE SHEETS		
Cash	$ 400,000	$ 600,000
Accounts receivable	1,000,000	1,300,000
Inventory	4,600,000	1,900,000
Plant and equipment (net)	8,000,000	5,000,000
Patents (net)	—	700,000
Investment in Meek (equity)	4,362,000	—
	$18,362,000	$9,500,000
Accounts payable	$ 3,000,000	$1,400,000
Bonds payable	4,000,000	3,000,000
Common stock	5,000,000	2,000,000
Retained earnings	6,362,000	3,100,000
	$18,362,000	$9,500,000
INCOME STATEMENTS		
Sales	$10,000,000	$5,000,000
Investment revenue	134,000	—
	$10,134,000	$5,000,000
Cost of goods sold	$ 7,000,000	$3,000,000
Depreciation expense	900,000	400,000
Patent amortization expense	—	100,000
Interest expense	480,000	300,000
Other expense	680,000	850,000
Income taxes	600,000	150,000
	$ 9,660,000	$4,800,000
Net income	$ 474,000	$ 200,000
RETAINED EARNINGS		
Balance, January 1	$ 6,188,000	$3,000,000
Net income	474,000	200,000
	6,662,000	3,200,000
Dividends	300,000	100,000
Balance, December 31	$ 6,362,000	$3,100,000

Required:

Prepare consolidated financial statements as at December 31, Year 3.

CHAPTER 6

Consolidated Financial Statements Subsequent to Acquisition Date — Cost Method

CHAPTER OUTLINE

LEARNING OBJECTIVES

After studying this chapter, you should be able to do the following:
* Calculate yearly consolidated net income when the parent has used the cost method to account for its investment.
* Calculate consolidated retained earnings when the parent has used the cost method to account for its investment.
* Prepare consolidated financial statements in years subsequent to acquisition date when the parent has used the cost method to account for its investment.
* Explain how the approach required for the preparation of consolidated financial statements differs when the parent has used the equity rather than the cost method to account for the investment in the subsidiary.
* Describe the preparation of consolidated statements when the subsidiary is acquired on a date other than the fiscal year-end, or when the subsidiary has discontinued operations or extraordinary items.

In Chapter 5, we illustrated the preparation of consolidated financial statements subsequent to the date of acquisition when the parent has used the equity method to account for its investment in a subsidiary. In this chapter we will use the same examples of Company P and Company S, but here we will assume that Company P uses the cost method to account for its investment. Following the major focus of this text with respect to consolidations, all illustrations will use the direct method of preparing consolidated financial statements. In the appendix at the end of the chapter, the working paper approach for the same examples will be illustrated.

Consolidation of a 100 Percent Owned Subsidiary — Direct Approach

Company P purchased 100 percent of the outstanding common shares of Company S on January 1, Year 1, for $19,000. On that date the common stock and retained earnings of Company S totalled $16,000, and its inventory had a fair market value that was $2,000 greater than book value. The book values of all other assets and liabilities of Company S were equal to fair market values, and any goodwill will be tested yearly for impairment. Both companies have a December 31 year-end. The journal entry made by Company P to record the acquisition of 100 percent of Company S was as follows:

Investment in S	19,000	
Cash		19,000

The calculation and allocation of the purchase discrepancy is shown in Exhibit 6.1.

Exhibit 6.1

COMPANY P
CALCULATION OF PURCHASE DISCREPANCY
January 1, Year 1

Cost of 100 percent of Company S		$19,000
Book value of Company S		
Common stock	10,000	
Retained earnings	6,000	
	16,000	
Parent's ownership	100%	16,000
Purchase discrepancy		3,000
Allocated:	FV – BV	
Inventory	2,000	2,000
Balance — goodwill		$ 1,000

The following are the individual balance sheets of Company P and Company S on January 1, Year 1, and Company P's consolidated balance sheet prepared using the *direct approach*.

BALANCE SHEETS — January 1, Year 1

	Company P	Company S	Consolidated
Assets (misc.)	$139,000	$ 17,000	$156,000
Inventory	22,000	10,000	34,000
Investment in S	19,000	—	—
Goodwill	—	—	1,000
	$180,000	$ 27,000	$191,000
Liabilities	$ 45,000	$ 11,000	$ 56,000
Shareholders' equity			
Common stock	50,000	10,000	50,000
Retained earnings	85,000	6,000	85,000
	$180,000	$ 27,000	$191,000

The consolidated balance sheet was prepared by eliminating the shareholders' equity of Company S ($16,000) against Company P's investment account ($19,000) and allocating the resultant purchase discrepancy ($3,000) to the inventory of Company S ($2,000), with the unallocated balance recorded as goodwill ($1,000).

Consolidated Statements, End of Year 1

On December 31, Year 1, Company S reported a net income of $7,300 for the year and paid a cash dividend of $2,500. Company P's net income for the year was $18,300 at this time (not including income from its investment in Company S). Using the cost method to account for its investment, Company P makes a single entry to record the dividend received from Company S on December 31, Year 1, as follows:

Cash	2,500	
Dividend income		2,500
Dividend received from Company S		

Company P adds the dividend income ($2,500) to its earnings from its own operations ($18,300) and reports a final net income for Year 1 of $20,800. An impairment test on goodwill conducted on December 31, Year 1, indicated that a $50 loss had occurred.

The financial statements of Company P and Company S as at December 31, Year 1, are presented in Exhibit 6.2.

Before beginning to prepare the consolidated financial statements, Company P prepares the following schedule, which shows the amortization of the purchase discrepancy for Year 1:

PURCHASE DISCREPANCY AMORTIZATION SCHEDULE

	Balance Jan. 1, Year 1	Amortization Year 1	Balance Dec. 31, Year 1
Inventory	$2,000	$2,000	—
Goodwill	1,000	50	950
	$3,000	$2,050	$950

This schedule and the financial statements of the two companies shown in Exhibit 6.2 form the basis for the preparation of Company P's Year 1 consolidated statements.

In Chapter 5 it was shown that when the parent has used the equity method to account for its investment, the following relationship exists:

- Parent's net income equals consolidated net income, and
- Parent's retained earnings equal consolidated retained earnings.

When the parent has used the cost method, the equalities shown above do *not* exist and additional computations are required. Recall from Chapter 5 that the make-up of consolidated net income can be described as shown below:

	The net income of the parent from its own operations (i.e., excluding any income resulting from its investment in the subsidiary)	$XXX
Plus:	**the parent's share of the net income of the subsidiary**	XXX
Less:	**the amortization of the purchase discrepancy**	(XXX)
Equals:	**consolidated net income.**	$XXX

Exhibit 6.2

YEAR 1 INCOME STATEMENT

	Company P	Company S
Sales	$ 50,000	$ 30,000
Dividend income	2,500	—
Total revenue	$ 52,500	$ 30,000
Cost of sales	$ 26,500	$ 14,700
Expenses (miscellaneous)	5,200	8,000
Total expenses	$ 31,700	$ 22,700
Net income	$ 20,800	$ 7,300

YEAR 1 RETAINED EARNINGS STATEMENTS

	Company P	Company S
Balance, January 1	$ 85,000	$ 6,000
Net income	20,800	7,300
	105,800	13,300
Dividends	6,000	2,500
Balance, December 31	$ 99,800	$ 10,800

BALANCE SHEETS — December 31, Year 1

	Company P	Company S
Assets (misc.)	$147,800	$ 18,300
Inventory	30,000	14,000
Investment in S (cost method)	19,000	—
	$196,800	$ 32,300
Liabilities	$ 47,000	$ 11,500
Common stock	50,000	10,000
Retained earnings	99,800	10,800
	$196,800	$ 32,300

Using this approach, we make the following calculation:

CALCULATION OF CONSOLIDATED NET INCOME — Year 1

Company P net income — cost method		$20,800
Less dividend income from Company S		2,500
Company P net income, own operations		18,300
Company S net income	7,300	
Company P ownership	100%	
	7,300	
Less purchase discrepancy amortization	2,050	5,250
Company P net income — equity method, which is equal to consolidated net income		$23,550

This calculation restates Company P's reported net income (computed using the cost method) *to what it would have been* had Company P used the equity method; it also gives us a net income number to work toward in preparing the consolidated income statement. Note that dividend income from Company S is not included in consolidated net income. The consolidated income statement is prepared by excluding the dividend income and adding the revenues and expenses of the two companies, while adjusting the expenses of Company S with the purchase discrepancy amortization for the year (see Exhibit 6.3).

In Chapter 5 we indicated that no preparation is required for the consolidated retained earnings statement when the parent has used the equity method, because the parent's net income and retained earnings are always equal to consolidated net income and retained earnings. When the parent has used the cost method, this is not the case. If we are consolidating more than one year after acquisition, we have to calculate a number for consolidated retained earnings at the beginning of the year. If we are consolidating only one year after acquisition (as in this case), consolidated retained earnings and the parent's retained earnings on acquisition date are equal.[1] The Year 1 consolidated retained earnings statement is prepared using the January 1 retained earnings of Company P, consolidated net income, and Company P's dividends (see Exhibit 6.3).

The parent's investment account does not appear on the consolidated balance sheet. Consolidated shareholders' equity contains the capital stock accounts of the parent and retained earnings from the consolidated retained earnings statement. The net assets of the parent are combined with the net assets of the subsidiary revalued with the unamortized purchase discrepancy.

Exhibit 6.3 shows the preparation of Company P's Year 1 consolidated financial statements using the direct approach. The bracketed amounts are taken from the individual financial statements of the two companies and the purchase discrepancy amortization schedule.

Consolidated Statements, End of Year 2

On December 31, Year 2, Company S reported a net income of $10,000 for the year and paid a cash dividend of $3,000. Company P's net income for the year was $19,000 at this time (not including income from its investment in Company S). An

---

[1] This is true in situations where we have a purchase-type business combination. It would not be the case in a pooling of interests.

Exhibit 6.3

Year 1 Consolidated Financial Statements
(direct approach)

COMPANY P
CONSOLIDATED INCOME STATEMENT
for the Year Ended December 31, Year 1

Sales (50,000 + 30,000)	$ 80,000
Cost of sales (26,500 + 14,700 + 2,000)	$ 43,200
Goodwill impairment loss (0 + 0 + 50)	50
Expenses (misc.) (5,200 + 8,000)	13,200
	$ 56,450
Net income	$ 23,550

COMPANY P
CONSOLIDATED STATEMENT OF RETAINED EARNINGS
for the Year Ended December 31, Year 1

Balance, January 1	$ 85,000
Net income	23,550
	108,550
Dividends	6,000
Balance, December 31	$102,550

COMPANY P
CONSOLIDATED BALANCE SHEET
December 31, Year 1

Assets (misc.) (147,800 + 18,300)		$166,100
Inventory (30,000 + 14,000)		44,000
Goodwill (0 + 0 + 950)		950
		$211,050
Liabilities (47,000 + 11,500)		$ 58,500
Shareholders' equity		
Common stock	50,000	
Retained earnings	102,550	152,550
		$211,050

impairment test conducted on December 31, Year 2, indicated that the goodwill had a fair value of $870. As a result a loss of $80 has occurred.

On December 31, Year 2, Company P makes the following cost-method journal entry:

Cash	3,000	
Dividend income		3,000
Dividend received by Company S		

The dividend income ($3,000) combined with the previous operating earnings ($19,000) gives Company P a final net income for Year 2 of $22,000.

The financial statements of the two companies as at December 31, Year 2, are presented in Exhibit 6.4.

Exhibit 6.4

YEAR 2 INCOME STATEMENTS

	Company P	Company S
Sales	$ 60,000	$40,000
Dividend income	3,000	—
Total revenue	$ 63,000	$40,000
Cost of sales	$ 32,000	$18,000
Expenses (misc.)	9,000	12,000
Total expenses	$ 41,000	$30,000
Net income	$ 22,000	$10,000

YEAR 2 RETAINED EARNINGS STATEMENTS

	Company P	Company S
Balance, January 1	$ 99,800	$10,800
Net income	22,000	10,000
	121,800	$20,800
Dividends	8,000	3,000
Balance, December 31	$113,800	$17,800

BALANCE SHEETS — December 31, Year 2

	Company P	Company S
Assets (misc.)	$131,800	$21,000
Inventory	35,000	16,000
Investment in S (cost method)	19,000	—
	$185,800	$37,000
Liabilities	$ 22,000	$ 9,200
Common stock	50,000	10,000
Retained earnings	113,800	17,800
	$185,800	$37,000

Company P prepared the following purchase discrepancy amortization schedule at the end of Year 2:

PURCHASE DISCREPANCY AMORTIZATION SCHEDULE

	Balance Jan. 1, Year 1	Amort. to end of Year 1	Balance Dec. 31, Year 1	Amort. Year 2	Balance Dec. 31, Year 2
Inventory	$2,000	$2,000	—	—	—
Goodwill	1,000	50	950	80	870
	$3,000	$2,050	$950	$80	$870

Because Company P has used the cost method, it is necessary to make two preliminary calculations before preparing the consolidated income statement and retained earnings statement. We first calculate consolidated net income for Year 2, as follows:

Company P net income — cost method		$22,000
Less dividend income from Company S		3,000
Company P net income, own operations		19,000
Company S net income	10,000	
Company P ownership	100%	
	10,000	
Less purchase discrepancy amortization	80	9,920
Company P net income — equity method, which is equal to consolidated net income		$28,920

As discussed previously, this calculation is simply adjusting Company P's Year 2 net income under the cost method to what it would have been under the equity method; it gives us a net income number to work toward when we prepare the consolidated income statement.

Because we are consolidating more than one year after the date of acquisition, an additional calculation is required. Company P's retained earnings on January 1, Year 2, are not equal to consolidated retained earnings. A calculation must be made to adjust these retained earnings to the balance that would result if Company P had used the equity method.

The calculation of consolidated retained earnings as at January 1, Year 2, is as follows:

Company P retained earnings, Jan. 1, Year 2 (cost method)		$ 99,800
Company S retained earnings, Jan. 1, Year 2	10,800	
Company S retained earnings, acquisition date	6,000	
Increase since acquisition	4,800	
Company P's ownership	100%	
	4,800	
Less purchase discrepancy amortization to end of Year 1	2,050	2,750
Company P retained earnings — equity method, which is equal to consolidated retained earnings		$102,550

The points that follow are presented as further explanation of why a calculation of this nature adjusts a parent's retained earnings under the cost method to retained earnings under the equity method. These points require careful reading, because it is very important for you to understand fully why this particular process actually works.

1. Consolidated retained earnings at acquisition date consists only of the retained earnings of the parent company.

2. Consolidated net income in any single year since acquisition date consists of the net income of the parent company, plus the parent's share of the net income of the subsidiary, less the purchase discrepancy amortization for that year.

3. It should logically follow that the consolidated retained earnings balance at any time subsequent to the acquisition date must contain the parent's share of the subsidiary's net incomes earned since acquisition date less the total of the amortization of the purchase discrepancy to that date.

4. If the parent has used the equity method, the parent's retained earnings balance at any time subsequent to acquisition does contain, as required, the parent's

share of the subsidiary's net incomes less the total purchase discrepancy amortization to date.

5. If the parent has used the cost method, the parent's retained earnings contain only the parent's share of the dividends that the subsidiary has declared since acquisition date.

6. The sum of net incomes less the sum of dividends — both measured from the acquisition date — equals the change (increase or decrease) in retained earnings measured from the same date.

7. When we add the parent's share of the change in the retained earnings of the subsidiary to the retained earnings of the parent (which contain the parent's share of the subsidiary's dividends under the cost method), the resulting calculated amount now contains the parent's share of the subsidiary's net income earned since the date of acquisition. By deducting the total amortization of the purchase discrepancy to date from this amount, we arrive at a retained earnings number that represents the retained earnings of the parent under the equity method, which of course is equal to consolidated retained earnings.

The consolidated income statement is prepared — using the income statements of the two companies (Exhibit 6.4), the Year 2 purchase discrepancy amortization schedule, and the calculation of consolidated net income for Year 2 — by adding the revenues and expenses of the two companies, adjusting the expenses for the Year 2 amortization, excluding the dividend income, and verifying that the net income on the statement equals the calculated net income.

The consolidated retained earnings statement for Year 2 is prepared using the calculated amount for consolidated retained earnings for January 1, by adding consolidated net income and deducting the dividends of Company P.

The consolidated balance sheet is prepared in the usual manner except that the amount for retained earnings is taken from the consolidated retained earnings statement.

Exhibit 6.5 shows the preparation of the Year 2 consolidated financial statements using the direct approach.

Consolidation of an 80 Percent Owned Subsidiary — Direct Approach

We now illustrate the consolidation of Company P and its 80 percent owned subsidiary Company S over a two-year period when the cost method has been used to account for the investment.

Assume that on January 1, Year 1, instead of purchasing 100 percent of Company S for $19,000, Company P purchased 80 percent for $15,200. All other facts about the two companies are the same as in the previous example. The journal entry of Company P on January 1, Year 1, is as follows:

Investment in S	15,200	
Cash		15,200

The calculation and allocation of the purchase discrepancy and the calculation of the noncontrolling interest on January 1, Year 1, are shown in Exhibit 6.6.

Exhibit 6.5	

Year 2 Consolidated Financial Statements
(direct approach)

COMPANY P
CONSOLIDATED INCOME STATEMENT
for the Year Ended December 31, Year 2

Sales (60,000 + 40,000)	$100,000
Cost of sales (32,000 + 18,000)	$ 50,000
Goodwill impairment loss (0 + 0 + 80)	80
Expenses (misc.) (9,000 + 12,000)	21,000
	$ 71,080
Net income	$ 28,920

COMPANY P
CONSOLIDATED STATEMENT OF RETAINED EARNINGS
for the Year Ended December 31, Year 2

Balance, January 1	$102,550
Net income	28,920
	131,470
Dividends	8,000
Balance, December 31	$123,470

COMPANY P
CONSOLIDATED BALANCE SHEET
December 31, Year 2

Assets (misc.) (131,800 + 21,000)		$152,800
Inventory (35,000 + 16,000)		51,000
Goodwill (0 + 0 + 870)		870
		$204,670
Liabilities (22,000 + 9,200)		$ 31,200
Shareholders' equity		
Common stock	$ 50,000	
Retained earnings	123,470	173,470
		$204,670

The following are the individual balance sheets of Company P and Company S, as well as Company P's consolidated balance sheet on January 1, Year 1, prepared using the direct approach.

BALANCE SHEETS — January 1, Year 1

	Company P	Company S	Consolidated
Assets (misc.)	$142,800	$17,000	$159,800
Inventory	22,000	10,000	33,600
Investment in S	15,200	—	—
Goodwill	—	—	800
	$180,000	$27,000	$194,200
Liabilities	$ 45,000	$11,000	$ 56,000
Noncontrolling interest	—	—	3,200
Shareholders' equity			
Common stock	50,000	10,000	50,000
Retained earnings	85,000	6,000	85,000
	$180,000	$27,000	$194,200

Exhibit 6.6

COMPANY P
CALCULATION OF PURCHASE DISCREPANCY
January 1, Year 1

Cost of 80% of Company S		$15,200
Book value of Company S, Jan. 1, Year 1		
Common stock	10,000	
Retained earnings	6,000	
	16,000	
Parent's ownership	80%	12,800
Purchase discrepancy		2,400
Allocated:	(FV – BV) × 80%	
Inventory	2,000 × 80%	1,600
Balance — goodwill		$ 800

CALCULATION OF NONCONTROLLING INTEREST — January 1, Year 1

Shareholders' equity, Company S (above)	$16,000
Noncontrolling interest's ownership	20%
Noncontrolling interest	$ 3,200

The consolidated balance sheet was prepared by eliminating Company P's share (80 percent) of the shareholders' equity of Company S ($12,800) against Company P's investment account ($15,200) and then allocating the resulting purchase discrepancy ($2,400) to the inventory of Company S ($1,600), with the unallocated balance shown as goodwill ($800). The portion of the shareholders' equity of Company S not eliminated ($3,200) appears as noncontrolling interest on the consolidated balance sheet.

Consolidated Statements, End of Year 1

On December 31, Year 1, Company S reported a net income of $7,300 for the year and paid a cash dividend of $2,500. Company P's net income for the year was $18,300 at this time (not including income from its investment in Company S).

The cost method journal entry of Company P on December 31, Year 1 is:

Cash	2,000	
Dividend income		2,000
80% of the dividend paid by Company S		

Company P's net income for Year 1 is reported as $20,300 after the receipt of the dividend from Company S. An impairment test on goodwill conducted on December 31, Year 1, indicated that a $40 loss had occurred. The financial statements of Company P and Company S as at December 31, Year 1, are shown in Exhibit 6.7.

Exhibit 6.7

YEAR 1 INCOME STATEMENTS

	Company P	Company S
Sales	$ 50,000	$30,000
Dividend income	2,000	—
Total revenue	$ 52,000	$30,000
Cost of sales	$ 26,500	$14,700
Expenses (miscellaneous)	5,200	8,000
Total expenses	$ 31,700	$22,700
Net income	$ 20,300	$ 7,300

YEAR 1 RETAINED EARNINGS STATEMENTS

	Company P	Company S
Balance, January 1	$ 85,000	$ 6,000
Net income	20,300	7,300
	105,300	13,300
Dividends	6,000	2,500
Balance, December 31	$ 99,300	$10,800

BALANCE SHEETS — December 31, Year 1

	Company P	Company S
Assets (misc.)	$151,100	$18,300
Inventory	30,000	14,000
Investment in S (cost method)	15,200	—
	$196,300	$32,300
Liabilities	$ 47,000	$11,500
Common stock	50,000	10,000
Retained earnings	99,300	10,800
	$196,300	$32,300

The Year 1 amortizations and consolidated net income must be calculated before the consolidated financial statements can be prepared, as shown below.

PURCHASE DISCREPANCY AMORTIZATION SCHEDULE

	Balance Jan. 1, Year 1	Amortization Year 1	Balance Dec. 31, Year 1
Inventory	$1,600	$1,600	—
Goodwill	800	40	760
	$2,400	$1,640	$760

CALCULATION OF CONSOLIDATED NET INCOME — Year 1

Company P net income — cost method		$20,300
Less dividend income from Company S		2,000
Company P net income, own operations		18,300
Company S net income	7,300	
Company P ownership	80%	
	5,840	
Less purchase discrepancy amortization	1,640	4,200
Company P net income — equity method, which is equal to consolidated net income		$22,500
Noncontrolling interest in Company S net income (20% × 7,300)		$ 1,460

These calculations form the basis for preparing the Year 1 consolidated financial statements for both the direct and the working paper approaches (see Appendix).

Exhibit 6.8 shows the preparation of the consolidated financial statements when the direct approach is used.

The consolidated income statement is prepared by combining the revenues and expenses of the two companies, adjusted for the Year 1 amortization of the purchase discrepancy. Company P's dividend income is excluded, and the noncontrolling interest in the income of Company S is shown in the statement as an allocation of the income of the single entity.

Exhibit 6.8

Year 1 Consolidated Financial Statements
(direct approach)

COMPANY P
CONSOLIDATED INCOME STATEMENTS
for the Year Ended December 31, Year 1

Sales (50,000 + 30,000)	$ 80,000
Cost of sales (26,500 + 14,700 + 1,600)	$ 42,800
Goodwill impairment loss (0 + 0 + 40)	40
Expenses (miscellaneous) (5,200 + 8,000)	13,200
	$ 56,040
Net income — entity	$ 23,960
Less noncontrolling interest	1,460
Net income	$ 22,500

COMPANY P
CONSOLIDATED STATEMENT OF RETAINED EARNINGS
for the Year Ended December 31, Year 1

Balance, January 1	$ 85,000
Net income	22,500
	107,500
Dividends	6,000
Balance, December 31	$101,500

COMPANY P
CONSOLIDATED BALANCE SHEET
December 31, Year 1

Assets (miscellaneous) (151,100 + 18,300)		$169,400
Inventory (30,000 + 14,000)		44,000
Goodwill (0 + 0 + 760)		760
		$214,160
Liabilities (47,000 + 11,500)		$ 58,500
Noncontrolling interest		4,160
Shareholders' equity		
Common stock	50,000	
Retained earnings	101,500	151,500
		$214,160

The consolidated retained earnings statement contains the retained earnings of Company P at the beginning of the year, consolidated net income, and the dividends of Company P.

The consolidated balance sheet is prepared by combining the assets and liabilities of the two companies, adjusted for the unamortized purchase discrepancy. The parent's investment account is excluded, and the noncontrolling interest in the net assets of the subsidiary is shown between liabilities and shareholders' equity. This amount is 20 percent of the December 31 shareholders' equity of Company S.

Consolidated Statements, End of Year 2

On December 31, Year 2, Company S reported earnings of $10,000 for the year and paid a cash dividend of $3,000. Company P's earnings for the year were $19,000 at this time (excluding any income from its investment in Company S). Company P's journal entry to record the dividend received from Company S is:

Cash	2,400	
Dividend income		2,400
80% of the dividend paid by Company S		

Company P reports earnings of $21,400 in Year 2. That amount includes this dividend income. An impairment test conducted on December 31, Year 2, indicated that the goodwill had a fair value of $696, and therefore a $64 impairment loss had occurred. The financial statements of the two companies as at December 31, Year 2, are shown in Exhibit 6.9.

Regardless of the approach to be used (direct or working paper), the following four calculations must be made before the consolidated financial statements are prepared:

PURCHASE DISCREPANCY AMORTIZATION SCHEDULE

	Balance Jan. 1, Year 1	Amort. to end of Year 1	Balance Dec. 31, Year 1	Amort. Year 2	Balance Dec. 31, Year 2
Inventory	$1,600	$1,600	—	—	—
Goodwill	800	40	760	64	696
	$2,400	$1,640	$760	$64	$696

CALCULATION OF CONSOLIDATED NET INCOME — Year 2

Company P net income — cost method			$21,400
Less dividend income from Company S			2,400
Company P net income, own operations			19,000
Company S net income		10,000	
Company P ownership		80%	
		8,000	
Less purchase discrepancy amortization		64	7,936
Company P net income — equity method, which is			
equal to consolidated net income			$26,936
Noncontrolling interest — Year 2 net income			
(20% × 10,000)			$ 2,000

Exhibit 6.9

De 31, YR2

YEAR 2 INCOME STATEMENTS

	Company P	Company S
Sales	$ 60,000	$40,000
Dividend income	2,400	—
Total revenue	$ 62,400	$40,000
Cost of sales	$ 32,000	$18,000
Expenses (misc.)	9,000	12,000
Total expenses	$ 41,000	$30,000
Net income	$ 21,400	$10,000

YEAR 2 RETAINED EARNINGS STATEMENTS

	Company P	Company S
Balance, Jan. 1	$ 99,300	$10,800
Net income	21,400	10,000
	120,700	20,800
Dividends	8,000	3,000
Balance, Dec. 31	$112,700	$17,800

BALANCE SHEETS — December 31, Year 2

	Company P	Company S
Assets (misc.)	$134,500	$21,000
Inventory	35,000	16,000
Investment in S (cost method)	15,200	—
	$184,700	$37,000
Liabilities	$ 22,000	$ 9,200
Common stock	50,000	10,000
Retained earnings	112,700	17,800
	$184,700	$37,000

CALCULATION OF CONSOLIDATED RETAINED EARNINGS
as at January 1, Year 2

Company P retained earnings, Jan. 1, Year 2 (cost method)		$ 99,300
Company S retained earnings, Jan. 1, Year 2	10,800	
Company S retained earnings, acquisition date	6,000	
Increase since acquisition	4,800	
Company P's ownership	80%	
	3,840	
Less purchase discrepancy amortization to end of Year 1	1,640	2,200
Company P retained earnings — equity method, which is equal to consolidated retained earnings		$101,500

CALCULATION OF NONCONTROLLING INTEREST
December 31, Year 2

Shareholders' equity — Company S	
Common stock	$10,000
Retained earnings	17,800
	27,800
Noncontrolling interest's ownership	20%
	$ 5,560

These four calculations are the starting point for the preparation of the consolidated financial statements whether the direct or the working paper approach is used.

Exhibit 6.10 shows the consolidated financial statements prepared using the direct approach. The concepts involved are the same as were outlined earlier for a

---

Exhibit 6.10

Year 2 Consolidated Financial Statements
(direct approach)

COMPANY P
CONSOLIDATED INCOME STATEMENT
for the Year Ended December 31, Year 2

Sales (60,000 + 40,000)	$100,000
Cost of sales (32,000 + 18,000)	50,000
Goodwill impairment loss (0 + 0 + 64)	64
Expenses (misc.) (9,000 + 12,000)	21,000
	$ 71,064
Net income — entity	$ 28,936
Less noncontrolling interest	2,000
Net income	$ 26,936

COMPANY P
CONSOLIDATED STATEMENT OF RETAINED EARNINGS
for the Year Ended December 31, Year 2

Balance, January 1	$101,500
Net income	26,936
	128,436
Dividends	8,000
Balance, December 31	$120,436

COMPANY P
CONSOLIDATED BALANCE SHEET
December 31, Year 2

Assets (misc.) (134,500 + 21,000)		$155,500
Inventory (35,000 + 16,000)		51,000
Goodwill (0 + 0 + 696)		696
		$207,196
Liabilities (22,000 + 9,200)		$ 31,200
Noncontrolling interest		5,560
Shareholders' equity		
Common stock	50,000	
Retained earnings	120,436	170,436
		$207,196

100 percent owned subsidiary. The only difference here is that the noncontrolling interest is reflected in the consolidated income statement and balance sheet.

Additional Calculations The preparation of the consolidated financial statements of companies P and S for Year 2 has been illustrated. Because the parent, Company P, used the cost method, additional calculations had to be made to determine certain consolidated amounts. One more calculation can be made to verify the consolidated retained earnings shown on the balance sheet. This calculation is shown below.

CALCULATION OF CONSOLIDATED RETAINED EARNINGS
as at December 31, Year 2

Company P retained earnings, Dec. 31, Year 2 — cost method		$112,700
Company S retained earnings, Dec. 31, Year 2	17,800	
Company S retained earnings, acquisition date	6,000	
Increase since acquisition	11,800	
Company P's ownership	80%	
	9,440	
Less purchase discrepancy amortization to the end of Year 2		
(1,640 + 64)	1,704	7,736
Company P retained earnings — equity method, which is		
equal to consolidated retained earnings		$120,436

This concludes our basic illustrations of the preparation of consolidated financial statements subsequent to the date that a parent company purchased a subsidiary. Before we proceed to Chapter 7, there are two additional topics that need to be addressed.

Subsidiary Acquired on Date Other Than Year-end

In all of our examples to date, we have assumed that the parent acquired the subsidiary on the last day of the fiscal year. As a result, when we prepared the first consolidated income statement at the end of the next fiscal year it contained all of the subsidiary's revenue and expenses for that year. We will now describe the consolidation process if the acquisition took place *during* the year.

Assume that Parent Inc. (which has a December 31 year-end) acquired 80% of Subsidiary Ltd. on September 30, 2002. The 2002 operations of Subsidiary would impact the December 31, 2002, consolidated income statement in the following manner:

Revenues: Subsidiary's revenues Oct. 1 to Dec. 31

Expenses: Subsidiary's expenses Oct. 1 to Dec. 31

Noncontrolling interest: 20% x Subsidiary's net income for period Oct. 1 to Dec. 31

Net impact on consolidated net income: Increased by 80% of Subsidiary's net income for last three months.

This form of presentation makes subsequent-year comparisons difficult for readers. To solve this problem, a pro-forma consolidated income statement could be prepared as if the subsidiary had been acquired at the beginning of the fiscal year. This pro-forma consolidated income statement could be presented in summary form in the notes to the financial statements.

Subsidiary with Discontinued Operations and Extraordinary Items

The *Handbook* describes the presentation of items such as these as follows:

> In calculating consolidated net income, a deduction is made in the amount of any non-controlling interest's proportion of the subsidiary company's income or loss before discontinued operations and extraordinary items. ... The parent company's portion of discontinued operations and extraordinary items reported by a subsidiary are disclosed as such in the consolidated income statement if the items represent discontinued operations or are extraordinary to the parent. [1600.66]

In other words, the noncontrolling interest on a consolidated income statement is based on the subsidiary's after-tax operating income before extraordinary items and discontinued items. After arriving at consolidated net income (after taxes), a deduction (or addition) is made for the parent's share of the after-tax discontinued operations and extraordinary items of the subsidiary, to arrive at the final consolidated net income. However, if these items were not considered discontinued or extraordinary from the point of view of consolidated statements, this separate disclosure would not be necessary. It would also not be necessary if the amounts were immaterial when viewed from the amounts presented in the consolidated statements.

SUMMARY

This chapter has illustrated the preparation of consolidated financial statements covering a two-year period after the date of acquisition when the parent has used the cost method to account for its investment. The same examples that were used in Chapter 5, under the equity method, were used here. When the cost method has been used, additional calculations must be made for consolidated net income and consolidated retained earnings.

The basic steps in the consolidation process when the parent has used the equity and cost methods are outlined in Exhibit 6.11. It is important to have a good grasp of the procedures under both methods because chapters 5 and 6 are the foundation for the consolidation issues we will introduce in the chapters that follow.

Exhibit 6.11

PREPARATION OF CONSOLIDATED FINANCIAL STATEMENTS
Basic Steps

	Cost method	Equity method
1. Calculate and allocate the purchase discrepancy on the date of acquisition.	Yes	Yes
2. Prepare a purchase discrepancy amortization schedule (date of acquisition to present date).	Yes	Yes
3. Calculate consolidated net income—current year.	Yes	No*
4. Prepare the consolidated income statement.	Yes	Yes
5. Calculate the start-of-year balance of consolidated retained earnings.	Yes	No*
6. Prepare the consolidated retained earnings statement.	Yes	Yes
7. Calculate the end-of-year balance of consolidated retained earnings (optional).	Yes	No*
8. Calculate noncontrolling interest at the end of the year (for the consolidated balance sheet).	Yes	Yes
9. Prepare a statement of changes in noncontrolling interest (optional).	Yes	Yes
10. Prepare a consolidated balance sheet.	Yes	Yes

* If the parent company uses the equity method of accounting, the parent's net income equals consolidated net income, and the parent's retained earnings always equal consolidated retained earnings. Therefore, the calculations in steps 3, 5, and 7 are not necessary.

SELF-STUDY PROBLEM

On January 1, 1997, Allen Company acquired 70% of the outstanding common shares of Bell Company for $88,500 in cash. On that date Bell had common stock of $50,000 and retained earnings of $45,000. At acquisition the identifiable assets and liabilities of Bell had fair values that were equal to book values except for plant assets, which had a fair value $20,000 greater than book value; inventory, which had a fair value $8,000 less than book value; and bonds payable, which had a fair value $10,000 greater than book value. The plant assets had a remaining useful life of 8 years on January 1, 1997, and the bonds payable mature on December 31, 2004. Both companies amortize on a straight-line basis.

Financial statements for the 2002 fiscal year are as follows:

	Allen	Bell
Income statements		
Sales	$ 400,000	$100,000
Rent revenue	15,000	—
Dividend revenue	3,500	—
	$ 418,500	$100,000
Cost of sales	$ 200,000	$ 45,000
Depreciation	55,000	20,000
Interest expense	32,000	7,700
Other expense	28,000	17,300
	$ 315,000	$ 90,000
Net income	$ 103,500	$ 10,000

	Allen	*Bell*
Retained earnings statements		
Balance, January 1	$ 400,000	$135,000
Net income	103,500	10,000
	503,500	145,000
Dividends	30,000	5,000
Balance, December 31	$ 473,500	$140,000
Balance sheets		
Cash	$ 11,500	$ 10,000
Accounts receivable	60,000	25,000
Inventory	200,000	40,000
Investment in Bell — cost method	88,500	—
Plant and equipment	1,200,000	470,000
Accumulated depreciation	(300,000)	(220,000)
	$1,260,000	$325,000
Accounts payable	$ 86,500	$ 25,000
Bonds payable	400,000	110,000
Common stock	300,000	50,000
Retained earnings	473,500	140,000
	$1,260,000	$325,000

Other Information

Prior to December 31, 2001, goodwill amortization amounted to $10,300. On January 1, 2002, new standards requiring tests for impairment came into effect. An impairment test conducted on December 31, 2002, indicated a loss of $2,060.

On December 31, 2002, Bell Company owes Allen Company $9,000.

Required:

1. Using the direct approach, prepare the following 2002 consolidated financial statements:
   (a) Income statement.
   (b) Retained earnings statement.
   (c) Balance sheet.
2. Prepare a schedule of the 2002 changes in noncontrolling interest.

Solution to Self-study Problem

Cost of 70% of Bell			$88,500
Book value of Bell			
Common stock		50,000	
Retained earnings		45,000	
		95,000	
Allen's ownership		70%	66,500
Purchase discrepancy — January 1, 1997			22,000
Allocated	FV – BV		
Plant assets	20,000 × 70% =	14,000	
Inventory	– 8,000 × 70% =	– 5,600	
		8,400	
Bonds payable	10,000 × 70% =	7,000	1,400
Goodwill			$20,600

PURCHASE DISCREPANCY AMORTIZATION SCHEDULE

	Balance Jan. 1/97	Amortization To end of 2001	2002	Balance Dec. 31/02
Plant assets	$14,000	$ 8,750	$1,750	$ 3,500
Inventory	− 5,600	− 5,600	—	—
Goodwill	20,600	10,300	2,060	8,240
	29,000	13,450	3,810	11,740
Bonds payable	7,000	4,375	875	1,750
	$22,000	$ 9,075	$2,935	$ 9,990

CALCULATION OF CONSOLIDATED NET INCOME — 2002

Net income — Allen		$103,500
Less dividend from Bell		3,500
		100,000
Net income — Bell	10,000	
Allen's ownership	70%	
	7,000	
Less purchase discrepancy amort.	2,935	4,065
		$104,065

1.(a)

ALLEN COMPANY
CONSOLIDATED INCOME STATEMENT
for the Year Ended December 31, 2002

Sales (400,000 + 100,000)	$500,000
Rent revenue	15,000
	$515,000
Cost of sales (200,000 + 45,000)	$245,000
Depreciation (55,000 + 20,000 + 1,750)	76,750
Interest expense (32,000 + 7,700 − 875)	38,825
Other expense (28,000 + 17,300)	45,300
Goodwill impairment loss	2,060
	$407,935
Net income — entity	$107,065
Less noncontrolling interest (30% x 10,000)	3,000
Net income	$104,065

CALCULATION OF CONSOLIDATED RETAINED EARNINGS
January 1, 2002

Retained earnings — Allen		$400,000
Retained earnings — Bell	135,000	
Acquisition retained earnings	45,000	
Increase since acquisition	90,000	
Allen's ownership	70%	
	63,000	
Less purchase discrepancy amort.	9,075	53,925
		$453,925

(b)
ALLEN COMPANY
CONSOLIDATED RETAINED EARNINGS STATEMENT
for the Year Ended December 31, 2002

Balance, January 1	$453,925
Net income	104,065
	557,990
Dividends	30,000
Balance, December 31	$527,990

Proof:

CALCULATION OF CONSOLIDATED RETAINED EARNINGS
December 31, 2002

Retained earnings — Allen		$473,500
Retained earnings — Bell	140,000	
Acquisition	45,000	
Increase since acquisition	95,000	
Allen's ownership	70%	
	66,500	
Less purchase discrepancy amort. (9,075 + 2,935)	12,010	54,490
		$527,990

CALCULATION OF NONCONTROLLING INTEREST
December 31, 2002

Common stock — Bell	$ 50,000
Retained earnings — Bell	140,000
	190,000
	30%
	$ 57,000

(c)
ALLEN COMPANY
CONSOLIDATED BALANCE SHEET
December 31, 2002

Cash (11,500 + 10,000)		$ 21,500
Accounts receivable (60,000 + 25,000 – 9,000)		76,000
Inventory (200,000 + 40,000)		240,000
Plant and equipment (1,200,000 + 470,000 + 14,000)		1,684,000
Accumulated depreciation		
(300,000 + 220,000 + 8,750 + 1,750)		(530,500)
Goodwill		8,240
		$1,499,240
Accounts payable (86,500 + 25,000 – 9,000)		$ 102,500
Bonds payable (400,000 + 110,000 + 1,750)		511,750
		$ 614,250
Noncontrolling interest		57,000
Shareholders' equity		
Common stock	300,000	
Retained earnings	527,990	827,990
		$1,499,240

2.

2002 CHANGES IN NONCONTROLLING INTEREST

Balance, January 1 (30% × *185,000)	$55,500
Allocation of entity net income	3,000
	58,500
Dividends (30% × 5,000)	1,500
Balance, December 31	$57,000

*		
	Common stock	$ 50,000
	Retained earnings, January 1	135,000
		$185,000

APPENDIX

Preparing Consolidated Financial Statements Using the Working Paper Approach

In this chapter we have illustrated the direct approach for preparing consolidated financial statements when the parent has used the cost method to account for its investment. In the examples used, we first examined the situation where the subsidiary was 100% owned, and then the situation where the parent's ownership was 80%. We will now illustrate the working paper approach using the same examples.

Year 1 Consolidated Financial Statement Working Paper

A number of methods can be used to prepare consolidated financial statement working papers when the parent has used the cost method. All methods used must result in identical consolidated amounts. The approach that we will illustrate adjusts the parent's accounts on the working paper to what they would have been if the equity method had been used to account for the investment. This requires the same additional calculations used in the direct approach. After the accounts have been adjusted, the working paper eliminations illustrated in Chapter 5 under the equity method are repeated. Exhibit 6.12 shows the preparation of the consolidated financial statements for Year 1 using a working paper, assuming Company S is a 100 percent owned subsidiary of Company P. To compare it with the direct approach, see Exhibit 6.3.

Entry #a adjusts the accounts of Company P as at December 31, Year 1, to what they would have been under the equity method. The information for this entry is contained in the calculation of consolidated net income for Year 1.

#a	Dividend income — Company P	2,500	
	Investment in S — Company P	2,750	
	Investment income — Company P		5,250

All relevant items in the financial statements of Company P except the December 31, Year 1, retained earnings contain balances arrived at using the equity method.

The remaining working paper entries are the same equity method elimination entries used in Exhibit 5.4 and are reproduced next without further elaboration:

#1	Investment income — Company P	5,250	
	Dividends — Company S		2,500
	Investment in S — Company P		2,750

Exhibit 6.12

CONSOLIDATED FINANCIAL STATEMENT WORKING PAPER
December 31, Year 1 (cost method)

	P	S	Eliminations Dr.		Eliminations Cr.		Consolidated
Sales	$ 50,000	$30,000					$ 80,000
Dividend income	2,500		(a)	2,500			
Investment income			(1)	5,250	(a)	5,250	
	$ 52,500	$30,000					$ 80,000
Cost of sales	$ 26,500	$14,700	(3)	2,000			$ 43,200
Goodwill impair. loss			(3)	50			50
Misc. expense	5,200	8,000					13,200
	$ 31,700	$22,700					$ 56,450
Net income	$ 20,800	$ 7,300		$ 9,800		$ 5,250	$ 23,550
Retained earnings, Jan. 1	$ 85,000	$ 6,000	(2)	6,000			$ 85,000
Net income	20,800	7,300		9,800		5,250	23,550
	$105,800	$13,300					$108,550
Dividends	6,000	2,500			(1)	2,500	6,000
Retained earnings, Dec. 31	$ 99,800	$10,800		$15,800		$ 7,750	$102,550
Assets, misc.	$147,800	$18,300					$166,100
Inventory	30,000	14,000					44,000
Investment in S	19,000		(a)	2,750	(1)	2,750	
					(2)	19,000	
Purchase discrepancy			(2)	3,000	(3)	3,000	
Goodwill			(3)	950			950
	$196,800	$32,300					$211,050
Liabilities	$ 47,000	$11,500					$ 58,500
Common stock	50,000	10,000	(2)	10,000			50,000
Retained earnings	99,800	10,800		15,800		7,750	102,550
	$196,800	$32,300		$32,500		$32,500	$211,050

#2 Retained earnings, Jan. 1 — Company S		6,000	
Common stock — Company S		10,000	
Purchase discrepancy		3,000	
Investment in S — Company P			19,000
#3 Cost of sales — Company S		2,000	
Goodwill impairment loss (expense)		50	
Goodwill		950	
Purchase discrepancy			3,000

Year 2 Consolidated Financial Statement Working Paper

The working papers for the preparation of the Year 2 consolidated financial statements are presented in Exhibit 6.13. See Exhibit 6.5 to compare the direct approach.

Exhibit 6.13

CONSOLIDATED FINANCIAL STATEMENT WORKING PAPER
December 31, Year 2 (cost method)

	P	S	Eliminations Dr.		Eliminations Cr.		Consolidated
Sales	$ 60,000	$40,000					$100,000
Dividend income	3,000		(b)	3,000			
Investment income			(1)	9,920	(b)	9,920	
	$ 63,000	$40,000					$100,000
Cost of sales	$ 32,000	$18,000					$ 50,000
Goodwill impair. loss			(3)	80			80
Expense, misc.	9,000	12,000					21,000
	$ 41,000	$30,000					$ 71,080
Net income	$ 22,000	$10,000	$13,000		$ 9,920		$ 28,920
Retained earnings,							
Jan. 1	$ 99,800	$10,800	(2)	10,800	(a)	2,750	$102,550
Net income	22,000	10,000		13,000		9,920	28,920
	$121,800	$20,800					$131,470
Dividends	8,000	3,000			(1)	3,000	8,000
Retained earnings,							
Dec. 31	$113,800	$17,800	$23,800		$15,670		$123,470
Assets, misc.	$131,800	$21,000					$152,800
Inventory	35,000	16,000					51,000
Investment in S	19,000		(a)	2,750	(1)	6,920	
			(b)	6,920	(2)	21,750	
Purchase							
discrepancy			(2)	950	(3)	950	
Goodwill			(3)	870			870
	$185,800	$37,000					$204,670
Liabilities	$ 22,000	$ 9,200					$ 31,200
Common stock	50,000	10,000	(2)	10,000			50,000
Retained earnings	113,800	17,800		23,800		15,670	123,470
	$185,800	$37,000	$45,290		$45,290		$204,670

The elimination entries #a and #b adjust the accounts of Company P to equity method balances. These entries are reproduced below.

#a Investment in S — Company P   2,750
        Retained earnings, Jan. 1 — Company P   2,750

This entry adjusts the investment in S account and the January 1 retained earnings of Company P to the equity method balances at the beginning of the year. The amount used is readily apparent in the calculation of consolidated retained earnings as at January 1, Year 2.

#b Dividend income — Company P   3,000
      Investment in S — Company P   6,920
          Investment income — Company P   9,920

Entry #b adjusts the accounts of Company P to the equity method balances at the end of Year 2. The calculation of consolidated net income for Year 2 provides the amount for this entry.

After these entries have been made in the working paper, all of the accounts of Company P contain balances arrived at using the equity method. The remaining elimination entries recorded in the working paper, which are reproduced below, are identical to those that were discussed in Chapter 5 (see Exhibit 5.7).

#1	Investment income — Company P	9,920	
	Dividends — Company S		3,000
	Investment in S — Company P		6,920
#2	Retained earnings, Jan. 1 — Company S	10,800	
	Common stock — Company S	10,000	
	Purchase discrepancy	950	
	Investment in S — Company P		21,750
#3	Goodwill impairment loss (expense)	80	
	Goodwill	870	
	Purchase discrepancy		950

80 Percent Owned Subsidiary — Year 1

Exhibit 6.14 shows the preparation of the consolidated financial statements as at December 31, Year 1, using a working paper. See Exhibit 6.8 to compare the direct approach.

Working paper elimination entry #a adjusts the accounts of Company P as at December 31, Year 1, to what they would have been under the equity method. The information for this entry is contained in the calculation of consolidated net income for Year 1.

#a	Dividend income — Company P	2,000	
	Investment in S — Company P	2,200	
	Investment income — Company P		4,200

After this entry has been entered in the working paper, all relevant items in the financial statements of Company P, except retained earnings as of December 31, Year 1, contain balances arrived at under the equity method.

The remaining working paper entries are the same equity method elimination entries as were used in Exhibit 5.11. These entries are reproduced below, without further elaboration.

#1	Investment income — Company P	4,200	
	Dividends — Company S		2,000
	Investment in S — Company P		2,200
#2	Retained earnings, Jan. 1 — Company S	6,000	
	Common stock — Company S	10,000	
	Purchase discrepancy	2,400	
	Investment in S — Company P		15,200
	Noncontrolling interest		3,200
#3	Cost of sales — Company S	1,600	
	Goodwill impairment loss	40	
	Goodwill	760	
	Purchase discrepancy		2,400

Exhibit 6.14

CONSOLIDATED FINANCIAL STATEMENT WORKING PAPER
December 31, Year 1 (cost method)

	P	S	Eliminations Dr.		Eliminations Cr.		Consolidated
Sales	$ 50,000	$30,000					$ 80,000
Dividend income	2,000		(a)	2,000			
Investment income			(1)	4,200	(a)	4,200	
	$ 52,000	$30,000					$ 80,000
Cost of sales	$ 26,500	$14,700	(3)	1,600			$ 42,800
Goodwill impair. loss			(3)	40			40
Misc. expense	5,200	8,000					13,200
	$ 31,700	$22,700					$ 56,040
Net income — entity							$ 23,960
Noncontrolling interest			(4)	1,460			1,460
Net income	$ 20,300	$ 7,300		$ 9,300		$ 4,200	$ 22,500
Retained earnings, Jan. 1	$ 85,000	$ 6,000	(2)	6,000			$ 85,000
Net income	20,300	7,300		9,300		4,200	22,500
	$105,300	$13,300					$107,500
Dividends	6,000	2,500			(1)	2,000	6,000
					(5)	500	
Retained earnings, Dec. 31	$ 99,300	$10,800		$15,300		$ 6,700	$101,500
Assets, misc.	$151,100	$18,300					169,400
Equipment (net)	30,000	14,000					44,000
Investment in S	15,200		(a)	2,200	(1)	2,200	
					(2)	15,200	
Purchase discrepancy			(2)	2,400	(3)	2,400	
Goodwill			(3)	760			760
	$196,300	$32,300					$214,160
Liabilities	$ 47,000	$11,500					$ 58,500
Common stock	50,000	10,000	(2)	10,000			50,000
Retained earnings	99,300	10,800		15,300		6,700	101,500
Noncontrolling interest					(2)	3,200	
			(5)	500	(4)	1,460	4,160
	$196,300	$32,300		$31,160		$31,160	$214,160

		Dr.	Cr.
#4	Noncontrolling interest (income statement)	1,460	
	Noncontrolling interest (balance sheet)		1,460
#5	Noncontrolling interest (balance sheet)	500	
	Dividends — Company S		500

80 Percent Owned Subsidiary — Year 2

Exhibit 6.15 shows the working paper approach to the preparation of the Year 2 consolidated financial statements. See Exhibit 6.10 to compare the direct approach.

The elimination entries #a and #b adjust the accounts of Company P to equity method balances. These entries are reproduced below.

#a Investment in S — Company P	2,200	
Retained earnings, Jan. 1 — Company P		2,200

Exhibit 6.15

CONSOLIDATED FINANCIAL STATEMENT WORKING PAPER
December 31, Year 2 (cost method)

	P	S	Eliminations Dr.		Eliminations Cr.		Consolidated
Sales	$ 60,000	$40,000					$100,000
Dividend income	2,400		(b)	2,400			
Investment income			(1)	7,936	(b)	7,936	
	$ 62,400	$40,000					$100,000
Cost of sales	$ 32,000	$18,000					$ 50,000
Goodwill impair. loss			(3)	64			64
Expense, misc.	9,000	12,000					21,000
	$ 41,000	$30,000					$ 71,064
Net income — entity							$ 28,936
Noncontrolling interest			(4)	2,000			2,000
Net income	$ 21,400	$10,000		$12,400		$ 7,936	$ 26,936
Retained earnings, Jan. 1	$ 99,300	$10,800	(2)	10,800	(a)	2,200	$101,500
Net income	21,400	10,000		12,400		7,936	26,936
	$120,700	$20,800					$128,436
Dividends	8,000	3,000			(1)	2,400	8,000
					(5)	600	
Retained earnings, Dec. 31	$112,700	$17,800		$23,200		$13,136	$120,436
Assets, misc.	$134,500	$21,000					$155,500
Inventory	35,000	16,000					51,000
Investment in S	15,200		(a)	2,200	(1)	5,536	
			(b)	5,536	(2)	17,400	
Purchase discrepancy			(2)	760	(3)	760	
Goodwill			(3)	696			696
	$184,700	$37,000					$207,196
Liabilities	$ 22,000	$ 9,200					$ 31,200
Common stock	50,000	10,000	(2)	10,000			50,000
Retained earnings	112,700	17,800		23,200		13,136	120,436
Noncontrolling interest					(2)	4,160	5,560
			(5)	600	(4)	2,000	
	$184,700	$37,000		$42,992		$42,992	$207,196

This entry adjusts the investment account and the January 1 retained earnings of Company P to the equity method balances at the beginning of the year. The amount used is readily apparent in the calculation of consolidated retained earnings as at January 1, Year 2.

#b	Dividend income — Company P	2,400	
	Investment in S — Company P	5,536	
	Investment income — Company P		7,936

Entry #b adjusts the accounts of Company P to the equity method balances at the end of Year 2. The calculation of consolidated net income for Year 2 provides the amount for this entry.

After these entries have been made in the working paper, all of the accounts of Company P contain balances arrived at using the equity method. The remaining elimination entries recorded in the working paper, which are reproduced below, are identical to those that were discussed in Chapter 5 (see Exhibit 5.14).

#1	Investment income — Company P	7,936	
	Investment in S — Company P		5,536
	Dividends — Company S		2,400

#2	Retained earnings, January 1 — Company S	10,800	
	Common stock — Company S	10,000	
	Purchase discrepancy	760	
	Investment in S — Company P		17,400
	Noncontrolling interest		4,160

#3	Goodwill impairment loss	64	
	Goodwill	696	
	Purchase discrepancy		760

| #4 | Noncontrolling interest (income statement) | 2,000 | |
| | Noncontrolling interest (balance sheet) | | 2,000 |

| #5 | Noncontrolling interest (balance sheet) | 600 | |
| | Dividends — Company S | | 600 |

REVIEW QUESTIONS

1. Outline the calculation of the following when the parent company accounts for its investment using the cost method:
   (a) Consolidated net income.
   (b) Consolidated retained earnings.

2. What accounts in the financial statements of the parent company have balances that differ depending on whether the cost or equity method has been used?

3. A parent company uses the cost method. Is it always true that at the end of the first year after acquisition, the parent's opening retained earnings are equal to opening consolidated retained earnings?

4. Why does adding the parent's share of the increase in retained earnings of the subsidiary and the parent's retained earnings under the cost method result in consolidated retained earnings? Assume that there is no purchase discrepancy.

5. What are the initial entries on the working paper when the parent has used the cost method to account for its investment?

6. A subsidiary was acquired during the fiscal year end of the parent. Describe the preparation of the consolidated income statement for the year. What additional disclosures are required?

7. Describe how a subsidiary's discontinued operations and extraordinary items are presented in consolidated financial statements.

MULTIPLE CHOICE

1. When a company uses the cost method to record its investment in a subsidiary during the year, which of the following will be included in the journal entry to record the parent's share of the subsidiary's dividends when they are received?
   a. Debit dividend revenue.
   b. Credit investment income.
   c. Debit cash.
   d. Credit investment in subsidiary.

2. Which of the following best describes why a company would use the cost method to record its investment in a subsidiary rather than the equity method?
   a. It results in the same net income and retained earnings as consolidation.
   b. It is easy and inexpensive to use.
   c. It is required by the *CICA Handbook*.
   d. It is required by Revenue Canada for tax purposes.

Use the following data for Questions 3 to 9.

On January 1, 2001, Place Inc. acquired an 80% interest in Setting Co. for $800,000 cash. At that time, Setting's assets and liabilities had book values equal to fair market values, except for the following:

Inventory	Undervalued by $75,000	Turns over 6 times a year
Plant and equipment	Undervalued by $50,000	Remaining useful life: 10 years
Bonds	Overvalued by $40,000	Maturity Date: December 31, 2005

At January 1, 2001, Setting had 100,000 no-par-value common shares outstanding with a book value of $550,000 and retained earnings of $50,000.

The abbreviated financial statements of Place and Setting on December 31, 2003, are as follows:

BALANCE SHEETS

	Place	Setting
Current assets	$ 950,000	$ 800,000
Investment in Setting	800,000	—
Plant and equipment (net)	1,250,000	1,555,000
	$3,000,000	$2,355,000
Current liabilities	$ 500,000	$ 280,000
10% bonds payable	—	800,000
Common stock	1,000,000	550,000
Retained earnings	1,500,000	725,000
	$3,000,000	$2,355,000

COMBINED INCOME AND RETAINED EARNINGS STATEMENTS

Sales	$2,500,000	$900,000
Cost of goods sold	1,200,000	330,000
Expenses	400,000	220,000
	1,600,000	550,000
Net operating income	$ 900,000	$350,000
Dividends received from Setting	100,000	—
Net income	$1,000,000	$350,000
Retained earnings, Jan. 1, 2003	800,000	500,000
	$1,800,000	$850,000
Dividends declared and paid	300,000	125,000
Retained earnings, Dec. 31, 2003	$1,500,000	$725,000

3. Which of the following is the amount of the inventory fair value increment that will be recognized on Place's consolidated income statement for the year ended December 31, 2001?
   a. $0
   b. $56,250
   c. $60,000
   d. $75,000

4. Which of the following is the amount of the fair value increment relating to plant and equipment (net) that will be recognized as an increase to depreciation expense on Place's consolidated income statement for the year ended December 31, 2002?
   a. $4,000
   b. $5,000
   c. $8,000
   d. $32,000

5. Which of the following is the correct adjustment to interest expense for the amortization of the bond fair value increment on Place's consolidated income statement for the year ended December 31, 2001?
   a. $8,000 increase.
   b. $6,400 increase.
   c. $8,000 decrease.
   d. $6,400 decrease.

6. How many years' worth of fair value increment amortizations must be used to calculate consolidated beginning retained earnings at January 1, 2003, from Place's cost-basis accounting records?
   a. 0
   b. 1
   c. 2
   d. 3

7. Which of the following is the amount of the noncontrolling interest on Place's consolidated balance sheet at December 31, 2002?
   a. $110,000
   b. $120,000
   c. $210,000
   d. $255,000

8. At December 31, 2001, Place's consolidated balance sheet reported a noncontrolling interest of $180,000. Setting did not declare any dividends during 2001. What did Place's consolidated income statement for the year ended December 31, 2001, report as the noncontrolling interest's portion of consolidated income?

   a. $60,000
   b. $70,000
   c. $120,000
   d. $300,000

9. Which one of the following is the amount of consolidated retained earnings that will be reported on Place's consolidated balance sheet at December 31, 2003, if an impairment loss for goodwill of $56,400 has occurred?

   a. $1,500,000
   b. $1,892,400
   c. $1,930,800
   d. $2,027,400

10. On January 1, 2002, Company P paid $692,000 for 80% of the outstanding shares of Company S. On that date, Company S had net assets with a book value of $760,000 and equipment with a fair value that was $60,000 greater than its book value. If a goodwill impairment loss amounting to $7,200 was recorded in 2003, what is the consolidated goodwill balance on December 31, 2003?

    a. $20,800
    b. $28,800
    c. $34,200
    d. $67,200

11. On January 1, 2002, Donald Corp. reported net assets of $880,000 on its balance sheet, although a building (with a 10-year life) having a book value of $330,000 is now worth $400,000. Ober Ltd. paid $840,000 on that date for 80% of Donald's outstanding shares. The balance of the purchase discrepancy was allocated to intangible assets other than goodwill to be written of over 20 years. The December 31, 2004, income statement of Donald showed total expenses of $621,000, while the income statement of Ober showed total expenses of $714,000. What is the amount of total expenses on the 2004 consolidated income statement.

    a. $1,335,000
    b. $1,339,000
    c. $1,345,300
    d. $1,344,600

12. Company P acquired 70% of the voting shares of Company S several years ago. During 2003 Company S recorded a loss, before taxes, from discontinued operations of $1,000,000. Company S has an income tax rate of 40%. On the consolidated income statement, what would be the value of the loss from discontinued operations?

    a. $420,000
    b. $600,000
    c. $700,000
    d. $1,000,000

(CGA adapted)

PROBLEMS

Problem 1 When Pierce Ltd. acquired 95% of Sill Corporation on January 1, Year 1, for $240,000, the $60,000 purchase discrepancy was allocated entirely to goodwill. On December 31, Year 1, a goodwill loss of $1,500 was recognized. Pierce uses the cost method to account for its investment. Pierce reported a separate entity Year 1 net income of $25,000 and declared no dividends. Sill reported a separate entity net income of $40,000 and paid dividends of $9,000 in Year 1.

Required:

Compute the following:
(a) Consolidated net income for Year 1.
(b) Noncontrolling interest that would appear on the Year 1 consolidated income statement.
(c) Investment in Sill at December 31, Year 1 (equity method).

Problem 2 Panta Ltd. purchased 80% of Santos Company for $412,000 on January 1, Year 1, when the balance sheet of Santos showed common stock of $400,000 and retained earnings of $100,000. On that date the inventory of Santos was undervalued by $30,000, and a patent with an estimated remaining life of 5 years was overvalued by $65,000. To date, $8,000 in goodwill impairment losses have been reflected in the consolidated statements. On December 31, Year 4, Panta had separate entity retained earnings amounting to $90,000, while Santos had separate entity retained earnings of $225,000. Panta uses the cost method.

Required:

Compute the following on December 31, Year 4:
(a) Consolidated retained earnings.
(b) Noncontrolling interest.
(c) Investment in Santos — equity method.
(d) Consolidated goodwill.
(e) Proof of consolidated goodwill using the account "Investment in Santos — equity method" from part (c).

Problem 3 Summarized balance sheets of Corner Company and its subsidiary Brook Corporation on December 31, Year 4, are as follows:

	Corner	Brook	Consolidated
Current assets	$ 160,000	$ 700,000	$ 860,000
Investment in Brook (cost)	640,000	—	—
Other assets	600,000	900,000	1,500,000
	$1,400,000	$1,600,000	$2,360,000
Liabilities	$ 800,000	$ 200,000	$1,000,000
Noncontrolling interest	—	—	280,000
Common stock	900,000	600,000	900,000
Retained earnings	(300,000)	800,000	180,000
	$1,400,000	$1,600,000	$2,360,000

On the date that Corner acquired its interest in Brook, there was no purchase discrepancy and the book values of Brook's net assets were equal to fair market values. During Year 4, Corner reported a net loss of $60,000 while Brook reported a net income of $140,000.

No dividends were declared by either company during Year 4. Corner uses the cost method to account for its investment.

Required:

Compute the following:

(a) The percentage of Brook's shares owned by Corner.

(b) Consolidated net income for Year 4.

(c) Corner's December 31, Year 3, retained earnings if it had used the equity method to account for its investment.

(d) The retained earnings of Brook on the date that Corner acquired its interest in Brook.

Problem 4 Peony Ltd. acquired an 85% interest in Spirea Corp. on December 31, Year 1, for $650,000. On that date Spirea had common stock of $500,000 and retained earnings of $100,000. The purchase discrepancy was allocated $78,200 to inventory, with the balance to patents being amortized over 10 years. Spirea reported net income of $30,000 in Year 2 and $52,000 in Year 3. While no dividends were declared in Year 2, Spirea declared a dividend of $15,000 in Year 3.

Peony, which uses the cost method, reported a net income of $28,000 in Year 1 and a net *loss* of $45,000 in Year 3. Peony's retained earnings on December 31, Year 3, were $91,000.

Required:

Compute the following:

(a) Noncontrolling interest in net income for Year 2 and Year 3.

(b) Consolidated net income for Year 2 and Year 3.

(c) Consolidated retained earnings on December 31, Year 3.

(d) Noncontrolling interest on December 31, Year 3.

(e) Investment in Spirea on December 31, Year 3, if Peony had used the equity method.

(f) Consolidated patents on December 31, Year 3.

Problem 5 The following statements of income and retained earnings were prepared by Pierre Corporation and Savoy Company on December 31 of the current year:

	Pierre	Savoy
Sales	$900,000	$500,000
Dividend income	60,000	—
	$960,000	$500,000
Cost of sales	$600,000	$300,000
Operating expenses	200,000	80,000
	$800,000	$380,000
Net income	$160,000	$120,000
Retained earnings, January 1	301,000	584,000
	461,000	704,000
Dividends	150,000	80,000
Retained earnings, December 31	$311,000	$624,000

Pierre obtained its 75% interest in Savoy eight years ago when Savoy had retained earnings of $53,000. The $80,000 purchase discrepancy on acquisition date was allocated entirely to equipment with an estimated remaining life of 10 years. Pierre uses the cost method to account for its investment.

Required:

Prepare the following statements for the current year:
(a) Consolidated income statement.
(b) Consolidated retained earnings statement.

Problem 6   On June 30, 2003, the following financial statements were prepared. Pushkin uses the cost method to account for its investment.

INCOME STATEMENTS

	Pushkin	Soong
Sales	$ 270,000	$162,000
Investment income	10,800	—
	$ 280,000	$162,000
Cost of sales	$ 140,100	$ 94,380
Expenses (misc.)	31,080	28,200
	171,180	122,580
Net income	$ 109,620	$ 39,420

[handwritten note in left margin: R/E of Soong date of acquisition is $32,400]

RETAINED EARNINGS STATEMENTS

	Pushkin	Soong
Balance, July 1	$ 459,000	$ 32,400
Net income	109,620	39,420
	568,620	71,820
Dividends	32,400	13,500
Balance, June 30	$ 536,220	$ 58,320

BALANCE SHEETS — June 30, 2003

	Pushkin	Soong
Miscellaneous assets	$ 875,940	$128,820
Equipment (net)	102,000	45,600
Investment in Soong	82,080	—
	$1,060,020	$174,420
Liabilities	$ 253,800	$ 62,100
Common stock	270,000	54,000
Retained earnings	536,220	58,320
	$1,060,020	$174,420

Additional Information

On July 1, 2002, Pushkin purchased 80% of the outstanding common shares of Soong for $82,080 (net of related costs of arranging the acquisition). On that date Soong's equipment had a fair market value that was $21,600 less than book value. The equipment had an estimated remaining useful life of 8 years. All other assets and liabilities had book values equal to fair values. On ~~December 31~~, 2003, a $1,512 goodwill impairment loss was recognized. *[handwritten: JUNE 30]*

Required:

(a) Prepare the consolidated financial statements of Pushkin as at June 30, 2003.
(b) Prepare a schedule showing the changes in noncontrolling interest during the year.

Problem 7   On July 1, 2001, Aaron Co. purchased 80% of the voting shares of Bondi Ltd. for $543,840. The balance sheet of Bondi on that date was as follows:

BONDI LTD.
BALANCE SHEET
as at July 1, 2001

	Net book value	Fair market value
Cash	$ 96,000	$ 96,000
Accounts receivable	120,000	144,000
Inventory	180,000	228,000
Fixed assets (net)	540,000	450,000
	$936,000	
Current liabilities	$107,200	107,200
Bonds payable	200,000	190,000
Common shares	120,000	
Retained earnings	508,800	
	$936,000	

The accounts receivable of Bondi were collected in October 2001, and the inventory was completely sold by May 2002. Bondi's fixed assets had a remaining life of 15 years on July 1, 2001, and the bonds payable mature on June 30, 2005. After properly accounting for the fair-value differences, any remaining purchase discrepancy was allocated to unrecorded patents (10-year life) of Bondi Ltd.

The financial statements for Aaron and Bondi at December 31, 2003, are presented below. Aaron has used the cost method to account for its investment in Bondi.

BALANCE SHEETS

	Aaron	Bondi
Cash	$ 120,000	$ 84,000
Accounts receivable	180,000	114,000
Inventory	300,000	276,000
Fixed assets (net)	720,000	540,000
Investment in Bondi	543,840	—
Other investments	250,666	—
	$2,114,506	$1,014,000
Current liabilities	$ 180,200	$ 115,000
Bonds payable	315,000	220,800
Common shares	300,600	120,000
Retained earnings	1,242,706	554,800
Net income	126,000	8,400
Dividends	(50,000)	(5,000)
	$2,114,506	$1,014,000

INCOME STATEMENTS

Sales	$1,261,000	$1,200,000
Dividend income	4,000	—
Income from other investments	25,000	—
	$1,290,000	$1,200,000
Cost of goods sold	$ 840,000	$1,020,000
Depreciation	60,000	54,000
Interest	37,000	26,400
Other	227,000	91,200
	$1,164,000	$1,191,600
Net income	$ 126,000	$ 8,400

Required:

Prepare the consolidated financial statements for the year ended December 31, 2003.

Problem 8 The following financial statements were prepared on December 31, Year 6.

BALANCE SHEET

	Pearl	Silver
Cash	$ 300,000	$ 100,000
Accounts receivable	200,000	—
Inventory	2,000,000	420,000
Plant and equipment	3,000,000	2,690,000
Accumulated depreciation	(750,000)	(310,000)
Investment in Silver Company — at cost	2,500,000	—
	$7,250,000	$2,900,000
Liabilities	$ 900,000	$ 300,000
Capital stock	3,850,000	1,600,000
Retained earnings	2,500,000	1,000,000
	$7,250,000	$2,900,000

INCOME STATEMENT

Sales	$4,000,000	$1,000,000
Dividend income	150,000	—
	$4,150,000	$1,000,000
Cost of sales	$2,500,000	$ 400,000
Miscellaneous expenses	320,000	70,000
Depreciation expense	80,000	10,000
Income tax expense	250,000	120,000
	$3,150,000	$ 600,000
Net income	$1,000,000	$ 400,000

RETAINED EARNINGS STATEMENT

Balance, January 1	$2,000,000	$ 800,000
Net income	1,000,000	400,000
	3,000,000	1,200,000
Dividends	500,000	200,000
Balance, December 31	$2,500,000	$1,000,000

Other Information

Pearl purchased 75% of the outstanding voting shares of Silver for $2,500,000 on July 1, Year 2, at which time Silver's retained earnings were $400,000. The purchase discrepancy on this date was allocated as follows:

- 30% to undervalued inventory.
- 40% to equipment — remaining life 8 years.
- Balance to goodwill.

During Year 3, a goodwill impairment loss of $70,000 was recognized, and an impairment test conducted as at December 31, Year 6, indicated that a further loss of $20,000 had occurred.

Silver owes Pearl $75,000 on December 31, Year 6.

Required:

Prepare consolidated financial statements on December 31, Year 6.

Problem 9 Balance sheet and income statement data for two affiliated companies for the current year are as follows:

BALANCE SHEET DATA
as of December 31, Year 4

	Albeniz	Bach
Cash	$ 40,000	$ 21,000
Receivables	92,000	84,000
Inventories	56,000	45,000
Land	20,000	60,000
Plant and equipment	200,000	700,000
Accumulated depreciation	(80,000)	(350,000)
Investment in Bach Company (cost)	272,000	—
Advances to Bach Company	100,000	—
Total assets	$700,000	$560,000
Accounts payable	$130,000	$ 96,500
Advances payable	—	100,000
Common stock	400,000	200,000
Beginning retained earnings	162,300	154,000
Net income for the year	29,700	17,500
Dividends	(22,000)	(8,000)
Total liabilities and shareholders' equity	$700,000	$560,000

INCOME STATEMENT DATA
Year Ended December 31, Year 4

	Albeniz	Bach
Sales revenues	$600,000	$400,000
Interest income	6,700	—
Dividend income	6,400	—
Total revenues	$613,100	$400,000
Cost of goods sold	$334,000	$225,000
Depreciation expense	20,000	70,000
Selling and administrative expense	207,000	74,000
Interest expense	1,700	6,000
Income taxes expense	20,700	7,500
Total expenses	$583,400	$382,500
Net income	$ 29,700	$ 17,500

Other Information

- Albeniz acquired an 80% interest in Bach on January 1, Year 1, for $272,000. On that date the following information was noted about specific net assets of Bach:

	Book value	Fair value
Inventory	$20,000	$50,000
Land	25,000	45,000
Equipment (estimated life 15 years)	60,000	78,000
Misc. intangibles (estimated life 20 years)	—	42,000

- On January 1, Year 1, Bach had a retained earnings balance of $30,000.
- Albeniz carries its investment at cost.

Required:

Prepare the following:
(a) Consolidated income statement.
(b) Consolidated retained earnings statement.
(c) Consolidated balance sheet.

Problem 10 On January 2, Year 1, Brady Ltd. purchased 80% of the outstanding shares of Partridge Ltd. for $4,120,000. On that date Partridge's balance sheet and the fair market values of its identifiable assets and liabilities were as follows:

	Book value	Fair value
Cash	$ 500,000	500,000
Accounts receivable	1,500,000	1,500,000
Inventory	2,000,000	2,200,000
Plant and equipment (net)	4,500,000	4,500,000
Patents (net)	1,000,000	1,500,000
	$9,500,000	
Accounts payable	$2,000,000	2,000,000
10% bonds payable	3,000,000	3,300,000
Common stock	2,000,000	
Retained earnings	2,500,000	
	$9,500,000	

The patents had a remaining life of 10 years, and the bonds mature on December 31, Year 10. Goodwill impairment losses were recorded as follows:

- Year 1: $20,000.
- Year 3: $10,000.

On December 31, Year 3, the financial statements of the two companies are as follows:

These items are eliminated to stop the double-counting of revenues and expenses. This has no effect on the calculation of the noncontrolling interest in the net income of the subsidiary companies.

Intercompany Profits in Assets

When one affiliated company sells assets to another affiliated company, it is possible that the profit or loss recorded on the transaction has not been realized from the point of view of the consolidated entity. If the purchasing affiliate has sold these assets outside the group, all profits (losses) recorded are realized. If, however, all or a portion of these assets have not been sold outside the group, we must eliminate the remaining intercompany profit (loss) from the consolidated statements. The intercompany profit (loss) will be realized for consolidation purposes during the accounting period in which the particular asset is sold to outsiders. The sale to outsiders may also result in an additional profit (loss) that is not adjusted in the consolidation process. Three types of unrealized intercompany profits (losses) are eliminated:

- Profits in inventory.
- Profits in nondepreciable assets.
- Profits in depreciable assets.

The first two of these will be discussed in this chapter, the last one in Chapter 8.

Income Taxes on Intercompany Profits   Not only do we have to hold back an unrealized profit for consolidation purposes, but we must also make an adjustment for the income taxes relating to that profit. The company that recorded the profit also paid (or accrued) income taxes on it, and the income tax expense on its income statement reflects this. The matching of expenses with revenues is a basic accounting concept, and the adjustment made for income taxes on intercompany profits is a perfect example of this matching process. Section 1000 of the *Handbook* reinforces this concept as follows:

> Expenses that are linked to revenue generating activities in a cause and effect relationship are normally matched with revenue in the accounting period in which the revenue is recognized. [1000.51]

Section 1600 is more specific when, in discussing the holdback of unrealized intercompany profits, it says:

> Any income taxes paid or recovered by the transferor as a result of the transfer would be recognized as an asset or a liability in the consolidated financial statements until the gain or loss is recognized by the consolidated entity. [1600.27]

In December 1997 a new section on income taxes was introduced. Section 3465, "Income Taxes," moves from the income statement approach of accounting for timing differences required by Section 3470, to a balance sheet approach of accounting for temporary differences. The balance sheet approach requires an accounting for the differences between the carrying value and the tax basis of the assets and liabilities of an enterprise.[1] This new section took effect on January 1, 2000. Its provisions have not changed the accounting for taxes on intercompany profits required in Section 1600. Because Section 3465 refers to "future" income tax assets and liabilities, we will use that terminology in our discussions.

The examples that follow illustrate the holdback of unrealized intercompany profits in one accounting period and the realization of the profit in a subsequent period. The holdback and realization of intercompany losses will not be illustrated. Note, however, that the same principles apply.

As a means of illustrating the concepts involved in the elimination of intercompany profits, we will use as a simple example the financial statements of a parent and its 90 percent owned subsidiary one year after the acquisition date. We will prepare the consolidated financial statements as if there were no intercompany transactions between the two companies. We will then introduce the concept of unrealized profits that were "overlooked" when we prepared the consolidated statements, and redo the consolidation so that the effects and differences can be observed.

On January 1, Year 1, Parent Company acquired 90 percent of the common shares of Sub Incorporated for $11,250. On that date Sub had common stock of $8,000 and retained earnings of $4,500, and there were no differences between the fair values and the book values of its identifiable net assets. The purchase discrepancy was calculated as follows:

Cost of 90% of Sub		$11,250
Book value of Sub		
Common stock	8,000	
Retained earnings	4,500	
	12,500	
Parent's ownership	90%	11,250
Purchase discrepancy		–0–

On December 31, Year 1, Parent reported earnings from its own operations of $3,400 and declared dividends of $2,000. Sub reported a net income of $1,700 and did not declare dividends during the year. Parent accounts for its investment using the cost method, and because there were no dividends declared by Sub, no entry was made on December 31, Year 1.

The financial statements of Parent and Sub as at December 31, Year 1, are presented in Exhibit 7.1.

Because Parent has used the cost method, we calculate consolidated net income, and the noncontrolling interest's allocation of the entity's net income, before preparing the consolidated income statement.

---

[1] Section 3465 also adds some complications to the valuation of assets in a business combination that is accounted for as a purchase. The new section's requirements with respect to business combinations will be discussed in Chapter 10.

Exhibit 7.1

YEAR 1 INCOME STATEMENTS

	Parent	Sub
Sales	$20,000	$ 8,000
Cost of sales	$13,000	$ 4,300
Miscellaneous expense	1,400	900
Income tax expense	2,200	1,100
	$16,600	$ 6,300
Net income	$ 3,400	$ 1,700

YEAR 1 RETAINED EARNINGS STATEMENTS

	Parent	Sub
Balance, January 1	$12,000	$ 4,500
Net income	3,400	1,700
	15,400	6,200
Dividends	2,000	—
Balance, December 31	$13,400	$ 6,200

BALANCE SHEETS — December 31, Year 1

	Parent	Sub
Assets (misc.)	$21,650	$19,200
Inventory	7,500	4,000
Investment in Sub Inc.	11,250	—
	$40,400	$23,200
Liabilities	$12,000	$ 9,000
Common stock	15,000	8,000
Retained earnings	13,400	6,200
	$40,400	$23,200

CALCULATION OF CONSOLIDATED NET INCOME — Year 1

Net income — Parent Co.		$3,400
Net income — Sub Inc.	1,700	
Parent Co.'s share	90%	1,530
Consolidated net income		$4,930
Noncontrolling interest (10% × 1,700)		$ 170

The consolidated income statement is prepared by combining the revenues and expenses of the two companies and deducting the noncontrolling interest from the income of the entity (see Exhibit 7.2). In examining both the consolidated income statement (Exhibit 7.2) and the calculation of consolidated net income (shown above), the reader will note the following:

Net income — Parent Co.	$3,400
Plus net income — Sub Inc.	1,700
Equals net income — entity	$5,100

The consolidated retained earnings statement is made up of the following: the January 1 retained earnings of Parent, consolidated net income, and the dividends of Parent (see Exhibit 7.2).

Before the consolidated balance sheet is prepared, the following calculation is made:

CALCULATION OF NONCONTROLLING INTEREST
December 31, Year 1

Shareholders' equity — Sub Inc.	
Common stock	8,000
Retained earnings	6,200
	14,200
Noncontrolling interest's share	10%
	$ 1,420

Exhibit 7.2

Year 1 Consolidated Statements
(direct approach)

PARENT COMPANY
CONSOLIDATED INCOME STATEMENT
for the Year Ended December 31, Year 1

Sales (20,000 + 8,000)	$28,000
Cost of sales (13,000 + 4,300)	$17,300
Miscellaneous expense (1,400 + 900)	2,300
Income tax expense (2,200 + 1,100)	3,300
	$22,900
Net income — entity	$ 5,100
Less noncontrolling interest	170
Net income	$ 4,930

PARENT COMPANY
CONSOLIDATED RETAINED EARNINGS STATEMENT
for the Year Ended December 31, Year 1

Balance, January 1	$12,000
Net income	4,930
	16,930
Dividends	2,000
Balance, December 31	$14,930

PARENT COMPANY
CONSOLIDATED BALANCE SHEET
December 31, Year 1

Assets — miscellaneous (21,650 + 19,200)		$40,850
Inventory (7,500 + 4,000)		11,500
		$52,350
Liabilities (12,000 + 9,000)		$21,000
Noncontrolling interest		1,420
Shareholders' equity		
Common stock	15,000	
Retained earnings	14,930	29,930
		$52,350

The consolidated balance sheet is prepared by ignoring the parent's investment account and the shareholders' equity of the subsidiary, and combining the assets and liabilities of the two companies. Shareholders' equity is made up of the common stock of the parent and consolidated retained earnings. The calculated amount for noncontrolling interest is "inserted" between liabilities and shareholders' equity in the balance sheet (see Exhibit 7.2).

Intercompany Inventory Profits — Subsidiary Selling

We now assume that there were intercompany transactions during Year 1 that were overlooked when the consolidated statements were prepared. These transactions were as follows:

1. During Year 1, Sub made sales to Parent amounting to $5,000 at a gross profit rate of 30 percent.

2. At the end of Year 1, Parent's inventory contained items purchased from Sub for $2,000.

3. Sub paid (or accrued) income tax on its taxable income at a rate of 40 percent.

Holdback of Inventory Profits — Year 1 It should be noted that the subsidiary recorded a gross profit of $1,500 (30% × $5,000) on its sales to the parent during the year and paid income tax of $600 (40% × 1,500) on this profit. If the parent had sold all of its intercompany purchases to customers outside the entity, this $1,500 gross profit would be considered realized from the point of view of this consolidated single entity. But the parent's inventory contains items purchased from the subsidiary for $2,000. There is an unrealized intercompany profit of $600 (30% × $2,000) in this inventory, which must be held back from consolidated income in Year 1 and realized in the period in which it is sold to outsiders. In addition, the $240 tax expense relating to this profit must also be held back from the Year 1 consolidated income statement. When this $600 gross profit is realized on a future consolidated income statement, the income tax expense will be matched on that statement with the profit realized.

Using the direct approach, we will now prepare the Year 1 consolidated statements after adjusting for intercompany transactions. The intercompany transactions that require elimination are as follows:

Intercompany sales and purchases	$5,000
Intercompany inventory profits:	
Ending inventory — Sub Inc. selling	$ 600
Income tax (40%)	240
After-tax profit	$ 360

Before preparing the consolidated income statement, it is useful to calculate consolidated net income, as follows:

CALCULATION OF CONSOLIDATED NET INCOME — Year 1

Net income — Parent Co.		$3,400
Net income — Sub Inc.	1,700	
Less profit in ending inventory	360	
Adjusted net income — Sub Inc.	1,340	
Parent Co.'s share	90%	1,206
Consolidated net income		$4,606
Noncontrolling interest (10% × 1,340)		$ 134

Remember that the purpose of this calculation is to adjust the parent's cost-method net income to what it would have been under the equity method. Notice that the after-tax profit is deducted from the net income of Sub, because the subsidiary was the selling company and its net income contains this profit being held back for consolidation purposes. Note also that the noncontrolling interest's share of the Year 1 income is based on the *adjusted income* of Sub.

Exhibit 7.3 illustrates the preparation of the Year 1 consolidated financial statements.

The first two numbers in brackets are from the statements of Parent and Sub. Any additional numbers, which are in boldface and labelled, are adjustments made to eliminate the intercompany transactions. The eliminations made on the income statement require further elaboration:

1. The eliminations of intercompany sales and purchases are equal reductions of revenues and expenses that do not change the net income of the consolidated entity or the amount allocated to the noncontrolling and controlling equities. These eliminations are labelled (i).

2. To hold back the gross profit of $600 from the consolidated entity's net income, we increase cost of goods sold by $600. The elimination entry for the gross profit is labelled (ii). The reasoning is as follows:

   (a) Cost of goods sold is made up of opening inventory, plus purchases, less ending inventory.

   (b) The ending inventory contains the $600 gross profit.

   (c) If we subtract the $600 profit from the ending inventory, the resulting amount represents cost to the consolidated entity.

   (d) A reduction of $600 from ending inventory increases cost of goods sold by $600.

   (e) This increase of cost of goods sold reduces the before-tax net income earned by the entity by $600.

3. Because the entity's before-tax net income has been reduced by $600, it is necessary to reduce the income tax expense (the tax paid on the profit held back) by $240. The elimination entry for income tax is labelled (iii).

4. A reduction of income tax expense increases the net income of the consolidated entity.

5. A $600 increase in cost of goods sold, together with a $240 reduction in income tax expense, results in the after-tax profit of $360 being removed from the entity's net income.

Exhibit 7.3	

Year 1 Consolidated Statements
Elimination of Intercompany Profits in Inventory
(direct approach)

PARENT COMPANY
CONSOLIDATED INCOME STATEMENT
for the Year Ended December 31, Year 1

Sales (20,000 + 8,000 − **5,000**)(i)	$23,000
Cost of sales (13,000 + 4,300 − **5,000**(i) + **600**)(ii)	$12,900
Miscellaneous expense (1,400 + 900)	2,300
Income tax expense (2,200 + 1,100 − **240**)(iii)	3,060
	$18,260
Net income — entity	$ 4,740
Less noncontrolling interest	134
Net income	$ 4,606

PARENT COMPANY
CONSOLIDATED RETAINED EARNINGS STATEMENT
for the Year Ended December 31, Year 1

Balance, January 1	$12,000
Net income	4,606
	$16,606
Dividends	2,000
Balance, December 31	$14,606

PARENT COMPANY
CONSOLIDATED BALANCE SHEET
December 31, Year 1

Assets — miscellaneous (21,650 + 19,200)		$40,850
Inventory (7,500 + 4,000 − **600**)(ii)		10,900
Future income tax (0 + 0 + **240**)(iii)		240
		$51,990
Liabilities (12,000 + 9,000)		$21,000
Noncontrolling interest		1,384
Shareholders' equity		
Common stock	15,000	
Retained earnings	14,606	29,606
		$51,990

Again it is important to note the following components of the entity's net income:

Net Income — Parent Co.	$3,400
Adjusted net income — Sub Inc.	1,340
Net income — entity	$4,740

The consolidated retained earnings statement has been prepared in the normal manner. It should be noted that the net income carried forward to this statement has been reduced by $324, which is 90 percent of the after-tax unrealized inventory profit. The $360 after-tax reduction on the consolidated income statement was allocated to the two equities as follows:

To noncontrolling interest (10% × 360)	$ 36
To controlling interest (90% × 360)	324
Total after-tax reduction allocated	$360

Before preparing the consolidated balance sheet, we must prepare the following calculation:

CALCULATION OF NONCONTROLLING INTEREST
December 31, Year 1

Shareholders' equity — Sub Inc.	
Common stock	$ 8,000
Retained earnings	6,200
	14,200
Less profit in ending inventory	360
Adjusted shareholders' equity	13,840
Noncontrolling interest's share	10%
	$ 1,384

The only new concepts relating to the preparation of the consolidated balance sheet involve the adjustments made on the asset side (a) to eliminate the unrealized profit in inventory and (b) to set up the future income tax on this profit. These adjustments are shown in boldface in Exhibit 7.3 and are labelled to correspond with the adjustments made on the income statement. The reasons for these adjustments can be further explained as follows:

1. The holdback of the $600 gross profit on the consolidated income statement was accomplished by reducing the amount of ending inventory in calculating the cost of goods sold. (A reduction in ending inventory increases cost of goods sold.) The ending inventory in the cost of goods sold calculation is the asset inventory on the consolidated balance sheet. Removing the $600 gross profit from the asset results in the consolidated inventory being reflected at cost to the entity. This elimination is labelled (ii).

2. On the consolidated income statement, we reduced income tax expense by $240, representing the tax paid on the gross profit. As far as the consolidated entity is concerned, this $240 is an asset and will become an expense when the inventory is sold to outsiders. This future tax asset is "added into" the assets on the consolidated balance sheet by the elimination labelled (iii). (The illustration assumes that neither the parent nor the subsidiary had future income taxes on their individual balance sheets.)

3. A reduction of $600 from inventory and a $240 increase in future income taxes results in a net reduction to consolidated assets of $360, which equals the $360 reduction that has been made on the equity side.

Equity Method Journal Entries While our example has assumed that Parent uses the cost method to account for its investment, it is useful to see where the differences would lie if the equity method were used. If Parent was using the equity method, the following journal entries would be made on December 31, Year 1:

Investment in Sub Inc.	1,530	
Investment income		1,530
90% of the net income of Sub Inc.		
(90% × 1,700 = 1,530)		

Investment income	324	
Investment in Sub Inc.		324
To hold back 90% of the inventory profit recorded		
by Sub Inc. (90% × 360 = 324)		

After these entries were posted, the two related equity-method accounts of Parent would show the following changes and balances:

	Investment in Sub Inc.	Investment income
January 1, Year 1	$11,250	—
December 31, Year 1		
Income from Sub Inc.	1,530	1,530
Inventory profit (held back)	(324)	(324)
Balance, December 31, Year 1	$12,456	$1,206

The appendix at the end of this chapter illustrates the working paper approach to the preparation of the Year 1 consolidated financial statements when the equity and cost methods are used.

Realization of Inventory Profits — Year 2 The previous example illustrated the holdback of an unrealized intercompany inventory profit in Year 1. We will continue our example of Parent Company and Sub Inc. by looking at the events that transpired in Year 2. On December 31, Year 2, Parent reported earnings from its own operations of $4,050 and declared dividends of $2,500. Sub reported a net income of $3,100 and again did not declare a dividend. Using the cost method, Parent made no journal entries with respect to the operations of Sub. During Year 2 there were no intercompany transactions, and at year end the inventory of Parent contained no items purchased from Sub. In other words, the December 31, Year 1, inventory of Parent was sold during Year 2, and the unrealized profit that was held back for consolidated purposes in Year 1 will have to be realized in Year 2.

The financial statements of Parent and Sub are presented in Exhibit 7.4.

Before we prepare the Year 2 consolidated income statement, we must do the following calculations:

Intercompany inventory profits:	
Opening inventory — Sub Inc. selling	$600
Income tax (40%)	240
After-tax profit	$360

Exhibit 7.4

YEAR 2 INCOME STATEMENTS

	Parent	Sub
Sales	$25,000	$12,000
Cost of sales	$16,000	$ 5,500
Miscellaneous expense	2,350	1,400
Income tax expense	2,600	2,000
	$20,950	$ 8,900
Net income	$ 4,050	$ 3,100

YEAR 2 RETAINED EARNINGS STATEMENTS

	Parent	Sub
Balance, January 1	$13,400	$ 6,200
Net income	4,050	3,100
	17,450	9,300
Dividends	2,500	—
Balance, December 31	$14,950	$ 9,300

BALANCE SHEETS — December 31, Year 2

	Parent	Sub
Assets (misc.)	$22,800	$20,800
Inventory	9,900	7,500
Investment in Sub Inc.	11,250	—
	$43,950	$28,300
Liabilities	$14,000	$11,000
Common stock	15,000	8,000
Retained earnings	14,950	9,300
	$43,950	$28,300

CALCULATION OF CONSOLIDATED NET INCOME — Year 2

Net income — Parent Co.		$4,050
Net income — Sub Inc.	3,100	
Add profit in opening inventory	360	
Adjusted net income — Sub Inc.	3,460	
Parent Co.'s share	90%	3,114
Consolidated net income		$7,164
Noncontrolling interest (10% × 3,460)		$ 346

The after-tax inventory profit of $360 that was held back in Year 1 is being realized in Year 2 and is added to the net income of Sub, because the subsidiary was the company that originally recorded the profit. Note that the noncontrolling interest share of the Year 2 net income of Sub is based on the *adjusted net income* of that company.

Exhibit 7.5 illustrates the preparation of the Year 2 consolidated financial statements using the *direct* approach.

In preparing the Year 2 consolidated income statement, we make consolidation adjustments that bring the original before-tax profit into the income statement and increase income tax expense for the tax on this profit. The eliminations (i.e., adjustments) made are shown in boldface and are labelled. The elimination entries are explained as follows:

1. There were no intercompany sales or purchases in Year 2, and therefore no elimination is required on the income statement.

Exhibit 7.5	**Year 2 Consolidated Statements**
	(direct approach)

PARENT COMPANY
CONSOLIDATED INCOME STATEMENT
for the Year Ended December 31, Year 2

Sales (25,000 + 12,000)	$37,000
Cost of sales (16,000 + 5,500 **– 600**)(i)	$20,900
Miscellaneous expense (2,350 + 1,400)	3,750
Income tax expense (2,600 + 2,000 **+ 240**)(i)	4,840
	$29,490
Net income — entity	$ 7,510
Less noncontrolling interest	346
Net income	$ 7,164

PARENT COMPANY
CONSOLIDATED RETAINED EARNINGS STATEMENT
for the Year Ended December 31, Year 2

Balance, January 1	$14,606
Net income	7,164
	21,770
Dividends	2,500
Balance, December 31	$19,270

PARENT COMPANY
CONSOLIDATED BALANCE SHEET
December 31, Year 2

Assets — miscellaneous (22,800 + 20,800)		$43,600
Inventory (9,900 + 7,500)		17,400
		$61,000
Liabilities (14,000 + 11,000)		$25,000
Noncontrolling interest		1,730
Shareholders' equity		
Common stock	15,000	
Retained earnings	19,270	34,270
		$61,000

2. To realize the gross profit of $600 in Year 2, we decrease cost of goods sold by $600 by the elimination labelled (i). The reasoning behind this is as follows:

   (a) Cost of goods sold is made up of opening inventory, plus purchases, less ending inventory.

   (b) The opening inventory contains the $600 gross profit. After we reduce it by $600, the opening inventory is at cost to the entity.

   (c) A reduction of $600 from opening inventory decreases cost of goods sold by $600.

   (d) This decrease in cost of goods sold increases the before-tax net income earned by the entity by $600.

3. Using the concepts of matching, we increase income tax expense by $240 in order to match it with the $600 gross profit being realized. The increase in tax expense is accomplished by the elimination entry labelled (i). Note that the future tax asset on the December 31, Year 1, consolidated balance sheet (see Exhibit 7.3) becomes an expense on the Year 2 consolidated income statement, because the December 31, Year 1, inventory was sold in Year 2.

4. A $600 decrease in cost of goods sold, together with a $240 increase in income tax expense, results in the after-tax intercompany Year 1 profit of $360 being realized for consolidation purposes in Year 2.

In comparing the consolidated income statement (Exhibit 7.5) with the calculation of consolidated net income for Year 2, you will note that the entity's net income is made up of the following two components:

Net income — Parent Co.	$4,050
Adjusted net income — Sub Inc.	3,460
Net income — entity	$7,510

Because the parent has used the cost method, we must calculate consolidated retained earnings as at January 1, Year 2, before preparing the Year 2 consolidated retained earnings statement. This calculation is as follows:

CALCULATION OF CONSOLIDATED RETAINED EARNINGS
January 1, Year 2

Retained earnings — Parent Co.		$13,400
Retained earnings — Sub Inc.	6,200	
Acquisition retained earnings	4,500	
Increase since acquisition	1,700	
Less profit in opening inventory	360	
Adjusted increase since acquisition	1,340	
Parent Co.'s share	90%	1,206
Consolidated retained earnings		$14,606

Note that this calculation adjusts the retained earnings of the parent from cost method to an equity method balance.

The Year 2 consolidated retained earnings statement is prepared using the January 1 calculated balance, the net income from the consolidated income statement, and the dividends of the parent.

Before the consolidated balance sheet is prepared, the following calculation is made:

CALCULATION OF NONCONTROLLING INTEREST
December 31, Year 2

Capital stock — Sub Inc.	$ 8,000
Retained earnings — Sub Inc.	9,300
	$17,300
	10%
	$ 1,730

The preparation of the consolidated balance sheet on December 31, Year 2, is straightforward because no inventory profit eliminations are required. The inventory of Parent does not contain an unrealized profit, and there is no related future tax asset on the balance sheet. All previous unrealized inventory profits have now been realized for consolidation purposes.

When you view the adjustments that were made to prepare the Year 2 consolidated statements (see Exhibit 7.5) it may strike you that the adjustments made on the income statement have not been reflected in the rest of the consolidated statements, and that as a result the statements should not balance. But they *do* balance, so the $360 increase in the after-tax net income of the entity must have been offset by a $360 change in the retained earnings statement and balance sheet.

To see where this $360 difference ended up, it is useful to prepare a calculation that shows the changes in noncontrolling interest during Year 2. This calculation is shown below:

CHANGES IN NONCONTROLLING INTEREST — Year 2

Sub Inc.		
Capital stock	8,000	
Retained earnings — January 1	6,200	
	14,200	
Less unrealized inventory profit	360	
Adjusted	13,840	
	10%	
Noncontrolling interest, January 1		$1,384
Allocation of Year 2 entity net income		346
Noncontrolling interest, December 31		$1,730

In examining this calculation and the calculation of consolidated retained earnings on January 1 (see page 247), we see that the $360 increase in the entity's Year 2 consolidated net income was offset by a $360 *decrease* in the January 1 balances of noncontrolling interest and retained earnings, allocated as follows:

To noncontrolling interest (10% × 360)	$ 36
To controlling interest (90% × 360)	324
	$360

Equity Method Journal Entries If Parent had used the equity method, the following journal entries would have been made on December 31, Year 2:

Investment in Sub Inc.	2,790	
Investment income		2,790
To record 90% of the reported income of Sub Inc. (90% × 3,100)		

Investment in Sub Inc.	324	
Investment income		324
To realize in Year 2 the inventory profit held back in Year 1 (90% × 360)		

After these entries are posted, the two related equity-method accounts of Parent show the following changes and balances:

	Investment in Sub Inc.	Investment income
January 1, Year 2	$12,456	—
December 31, Year 2		
Income from Sub Inc.	2,790	2,790
Inventory profit (realized)	324	324
Balance, Dec. 31, Year 2	$15,570	$3,114

Note that the January 1 balance ($12,456) included the $324 holdback, and that this amount was realized during the year with a journal entry. It should be obvious that the December 31 balance ($15,570) does not contain any holdback.

The appendix at the end of this chapter illustrates the working paper approach to preparing the Year 2 consolidated financial statements when the equity and cost methods are used.

Intercompany Inventory Profits — Parent Selling

In our previous example, the subsidiary was the selling company in the intercompany profit transaction. This resulted in the $360 after-tax profit elimination being allocated to the controlling and noncontrolling equities. Recall that our example was based on the assumption that we had forgotten to take intercompany transactions into account when we originally prepared the consolidated statements. We then corrected the statements by eliminating the intercompany revenues and expenses and the unrealized inventory profit.

Suppose we had assumed that it was the parent company that sold the inventory to the subsidiary. The calculation of consolidated net income for each of the two years should indicate where the differences would lie.

CALCULATION OF CONSOLIDATED NET INCOME — Year 1

Net income — Parent Co.		$3,400
Less profit in ending inventory		360
Adjusted net income — Parent Co.		3,040
Net income — Sub Inc.	1,700	
Parent Co.'s share	90%	1,530
Consolidated net income		$4,570
Noncontrolling interest (10% × 1,700)		$ 170

Notice that the after-tax profit is deducted from the net income of Parent because it was the selling company, and that Parent's net income contains this profit being held back for consolidation purposes. Notice also that "Net income — entity" remains unchanged, as the following calculation indicates:

Adjusted net income — Parent Co.	$3,040
Net income — Sub Inc.	1,700
Net income — entity	$4,740

The eliminations on the consolidated income statement for intercompany sales and purchases and for unrealized profit in inventory, and the related adjustment to income tax expense, would not change. This means that consolidated revenues and expenses are identical to those in the previous example (see Exhibit 7.3). But consolidated net income is different, as the following partial consolidated income statement indicates:

PARENT COMPANY
PARTIAL CONSOLIDATED INCOME STATEMENT — Year 1

Net income — entity	$4,740
Less noncontrolling interest	170
Net income	$4,570

Because Parent was the selling company, all of the $360 holdback was allocated to net income and none was allocated to the noncontrolling interest.

On the December 31, Year 1, consolidated balance sheet, the elimination entries to adjust inventory and future income taxes would be the same as before. However, the noncontrolling interest on the consolidated balance sheet is based on the December 31, Year 1, balances of the common stock and retained earnings of Sub. The after-tax inventory holdback is *not* allocated to noncontrolling interest; because Parent was the selling company, it has been allocated entirely to consolidated retained earnings.

Year 2 consolidated net income would be calculated as follows:

Net income — Parent Co.		$4,050
Add profit in opening inventory		360
Adjusted net income — Parent Co.		4,410
Net income — Sub Inc.	3,100	
Parent Co.'s share	90%	2,790
Consolidated net income		$7,200
Noncontrolling interest (10% × 3,100)		$ 310

"Net income — entity" for Year 2 has not changed and is made up of:

Adjusted net income — Parent Co.	$4,410
Net income — Sub Inc.	3,100
Net income — entity	$7,510

The elimination entries on the Year 2 consolidated income statement would be the same as in the previous illustration (see Exhibit 7.5), but because the amount for noncontrolling interest is $310, the consolidated net income is a higher amount, as the following partial consolidated income statement indicates:

PARENT COMPANY
PARTIAL CONSOLIDATED INCOME STATEMENT — Year 2

Net income — entity	$7,510
Less noncontrolling interest	310
Net income	$7,200

To summarize, the holdback and subsequent realization of intercompany profits in assets is allocated to the noncontrolling and controlling equities *only if* the subsidiary was the original seller in the intercompany transaction. If the parent was the original seller, the allocation is entirely to the controlling equity.

Equity Method Journal Entries   If Parent used the equity method to account for its investment, it would make the following entries as at December 31, Year 1:

Investment in Sub Inc.	1,530	
Investment income		1,530
To record 90% of the reported Year 1 net income of Sub Inc. (90% × 1,700)		
Investment income	360	
Investment in Sub Inc.		360
To hold back the inventory profit recorded by Parent Co. in Year 1		

An astute reader will notice that because the parent was the selling company, the second entry is removing the profit from accounts that did not contain it in the first place. This of course is quite true. However, it is the investment income account that establishes the equality between Parent's net income (under the equity method) and consolidated net income. In the same manner, the investment in Sub on the balance sheet of Parent establishes the equality between Parent's retained earnings (under the equity method) and consolidated retained earnings. This means that all adjustments that affect consolidated net income are reflected in these two accounts.

On December 31, Year 2, Parent would make the following journal entries if it used the equity method:

Investment in Sub Inc.	2,790	
Investment income		2,790
To record 90% of the reported net income of Sub Inc.		
Investment in Sub Inc.	360	
Investment income		360
To realize in Year 2 the inventory profit held back in Year 1		

Intercompany Land Profit Holdback

The holdback and realization of an intercompany profit in land is accomplished in a more straightforward manner on the consolidated income statement. Suppose that in Year 1 there was an intercompany sale of land on which a before-tax profit of $600 was recorded, that $240 tax was accrued, and that on December 31, Year 1, the land was still held by the purchasing company. (We are assuming that this was not a capital gain for tax purposes.)

The selling company would make the following entry to record the intercompany transaction:

Cash	2,600	
Land		2,000
Gain on sale of land		600

The purchasing company would record the intercompany transaction as follows:

Land	2,600	
Cash		2,600

When consolidated financial statements are prepared, the profit elimination and the related income-tax adjustment will take place as follows:

PARENT COMPANY
CONSOLIDATED INCOME STATEMENT
Year 1

Gain on sale of land (600 – 600)	$ 0
Income tax expense (P + S – 240)	XXX
Net income — entity	XXX
Less noncontrolling interest	XXX
Net income	$XXX

It should be obvious that the holdback of the gain, along with the reduction of the income tax expense, has reduced the entity's net income by $360. If the subsidiary is the selling company, the $360 after-tax profit held back will be used to calculate noncontrolling interest in the consolidated income statement; in this manner it will be allocated to the two equities. If the parent is the selling company, noncontrolling interest will not be affected and the entire profit holdback will be allocated to the controlling entity.

The following shows the eliminations required in the preparation of the Year 1 balance sheet:

PARENT COMPANY
CONSOLIDATED BALANCE SHEET
December 31, Year 1

Assets	
Land (2,600 – 600)	$2,000
Future income tax (+ 240)	240
Total assets	$ XXX

The balance sheet eliminations for a land profit are very similar to those for an inventory profit. The before-tax profit is deducted from land rather than inventory. The addition of future income tax into the consolidated balance sheet is the same for both types of profit.

The equity side of the balance sheet is not presented. If the subsidiary is the selling company, the calculation of noncontrolling interest on December 31, Year 1, will have to reflect this fact. If the parent is the selling company, the entire $360 profit holdback is automatically reflected in the retained earnings shown in the balance sheet.

Realization of Intercompany Land Profits

An unrealized intercompany inventory profit held back for consolidated purposes in Year 1 is considered realized in Year 2. It is assumed that the FIFO method of inventory costing is being used and that any inventory on hand at the beginning of a year has been sold by the end of that year. This is usually true.

When are intercompany land profits considered realized for consolidation purposes? The answer is this: when the land is sold to outsiders, which may be many years later. At the end of each successive year prior to the sale to outsiders, the preparation of the consolidated balance sheet requires the same adjustments as those of Year 1. Consolidated income statements require no adjustment until the year of the sale outside because, in each year prior to that event, the income statements of both affiliates will not contain any transactions with regard to the land.

However, assuming that Parent Company uses the cost method, the calculation of beginning consolidated retained earnings each year will have to include an adjustment to hold back the $360 unrealized land profit. The calculation would be identical to that shown on page 247 except that it would be described as land profit rather than profit in opening inventory. (This particular calculation is based on the assumption that Sub Inc. was the selling company.) Each successive year would require the same adjustment until the land is sold to outsiders.

In this case, let us assume that the land was sold outside during Year 8 at a profit of $1,300. The company making the sale in Year 8 would record the following journal entry:

Cash	3,900	
Land		2,600
Gain on sale of land		1,300

While the selling company recorded a gain of $1,300, the gain to the entity is $1,900 (1,300 + 600). On the Year 8 consolidated income statement, the gain held back in Year 1 is realized and the income tax expense adjusted as follows:

PARENT COMPANY
CONSOLIDATED INCOME STATEMENT
Year 8

Gain on sale of land (1,300 + 600)	$1,900
Income tax expense (P + S + 240)	XXX
Net income — entity	XXX
Less noncontrolling interest	XXX
Net income	$ XXX

The entity's net income is increased by $360 (600 – 240). If the subsidiary was the original selling company, the net income of the noncontrolling interest is affected in Year 8; the entire $360 is allocated to the controlling interest if the parent was the original seller.

Equity Method Journal Entries   Parent Co.'s equity journal entries for the land gain in years 1 and 8 would be identical to the entries illustrated previously for inventory in years 1 and 2, depending of course on which company was the original seller in the intercompany profit transaction.

Intercompany Transfer Pricing

In our coin example at the beginning of this chapter, we saw a loonie sold for a gross profit of $40, which was allocated to the four related companies as follows:

Parent	$ 9
Sub 1	5
Sub 2	10
Sub 3	16
Total	$40

From a financial reporting point of view we are not concerned with the amount of profit earned by each company; but only with eliminating intercompany transactions and profits that are unrealized because they have not been sold outside the consolidated "single entity." From a taxation point of view, the consolidated entity is not subject to tax; rather each company pays tax on its taxable income. It should seem obvious that the management of the parent company would be interested in maximizing the after-tax profit of this single entity if possible. If all of the companies are in one taxation jurisdiction, there is nothing that management can do to increase the after-tax profit. However, if some of the companies are in jurisdictions with low rates of corporate income tax while others are in high tax rate jurisdictions, management may try to structure each company's transfer price so that the majority (or all) of the $40 profit is earned in low tax rate jurisdictions. This will often bring companies into conflict with the governments of the high tax rate jurisdictions, as the following item of interest illustrates.

Item of Interest   In July 2001, the Canada Customs and Revenue Agency announced that it was commencing court action against Canadian subsidiaries of multinational drug companies for overpaying by as much as 40 times the going rate for chemical ingredients. These items were manufactured by affiliated companies in other countries, whose corporate tax rates are much lower than those in Canada. By overpaying their foreign affiliates, the Canadian arms of the GlaxoSmithKline, and Hoffman-La Roche groups were able to claim less taxable profit in Canada.

Consolidation Theories and Intercompany Profits

In Chapter 4 we discussed three theories of consolidation and concluded that the pronouncements of the *CICA Handbook* seemed to follow parent theory, particularly with respect to asset valuations on acquisition date. It was also indicated that this was not the case with regard to the elimination of intercompany profits. We will now return to the three theories and examine what they have to say regarding the elimination of intercompany profits.

There are two types of intercompany profits to consider:

- Those resulting from downstream sales (i.e., where the parent sells to its subsidiaries).
- Those resulting from upstream[2] sales (i.e., where a subsidiary sells to the parent).

Regardless of the type, theoretical considerations come into play only when the subsidiary is less than 100 percent owned.

Proprietary theory views the entity from the perspective of the shareholders of the parent company and does not acknowledge the existence of a noncontrolling interest in the consolidated financial statements.

Because the noncontrolling interest is considered to be an outside group under proprietary theory, profits resulting from sales to or purchases from this group are considered to be partially realized. Therefore, only the parent company's share of the intercompany profits from upstream and downstream transactions is eliminated when consolidated statements are being prepared. This is known as the "fractional elimination" of intercompany profits. We will see more of this in a later chapter, when we discuss the proportionate consolidation of a joint venture.

Parent theory also views the entity from the perspective of the shareholders of the parent company; however, it *does* acknowledge the existence of a noncontrolling interest by showing it as a liability.

Since this noncontrolling interest is considered to be an outside group, the fractional elimination of intercompany profits resulting from upstream and downstream transactions is seen as appropriate.

Entity theory views the consolidated entity as having two distinct groups of shareholders: the controlling shareholders and the noncontrolling interest. The shareholders' equity section of the consolidated balance sheet would include the equities of both groups; the consolidated income statement would allocate the entity's income to both groups.

All intercompany profits (downstream and upstream) are eliminated, following the broad concept that "you cannot make a profit by selling to yourself." The profit eliminated as a result of an upstream transaction is allocated to both the controlling and the noncontrolling interests.

Section 1600 of the *CICA Handbook* considered the argument that a portion of an intercompany transaction may be viewed as being at arm's length to the extent of the noncontrolling interest, and therefore could be considered as realized in the consolidated statements. This view was rejected because the existence of control indicates that a parent and a subsidiary are not dealing at arm's length with each other. The relevant statements regarding the elimination of intercompany profits (losses) are reproduced below.[3]

> Unrealized intercompany gains and losses arising subsequent to the date of an acquisition on assets remaining within the consolidated group should be

---

[2] There are also "lateral" sales, where a subsidiary sells to another subsidiary. The accounting problems here are identical to those involved with upstream sales, so our discussions will treat the two as if they were the same.

[3] The existence of an intercompany loss may be an indication of a permanent decline in the value of the asset sold. In this situation, *CICA Handbook*, paragraph 1600.27, suggests that this loss should be allowed to stand and should not be eliminated when consolidated statements are being prepared.

eliminated. The amount of elimination from assets should not be affected by the existence of a non-controlling interest. [1600.30]

Where there is an unrealized intercompany gain or loss recognized by a subsidiary company in which there is a non-controlling interest, such gain or loss should be eliminated proportionately between the parent and non-controlling interest in that company's income. [1600.32]

These requirements regarding the elimination of unrealized intercompany profits follow the dictates of entity theory. We can conclude from this discussion that the Canadian standard setters chose parts from each theory in establishing desirable practice.

An International Perspective

The elimination of unrealized intercompany profits is such an integral part of the consolidation process, that one must assume that countries requiring the preparation of consolidated statements also require the elimination of these profits. It is quite possible that some countries use the fractional elimination method, which produces somewhat different results (net income remains the same but the amount reported for noncontrolling interest is affected). The IASB requires that unrealized profits be completely eliminated and also follows the balance sheet approach to interperiod income tax allocation, as does FASB #109 in the United States. It is interesting that both the IASB and the FASB have retained the term "deferred" with respect to income tax allocation, whereas Canada's new standard uses the term "future income taxes."

SUMMARY

To ensure that consolidated financial statements reflect only transactions between the single entity and those outside the entity, all intercompany transactions are eliminated. The elimination of intercompany revenues and expenses does not affect the net income of this entity; therefore, it cannot affect the amounts allocated to the two equities in the balance sheet.

Intercompany profits in assets are not recognized in the consolidated financial statements until the assets have been sold outside the group or consumed. (The concept of realization as a result of consumption is discussed in the next chapter.)

The elimination of unrealized intercompany profits in assets reduces the net income of the entity. Also, it will affect the amount allocated to noncontrolling interest only if the subsidiary was the selling company. The income tax recorded on the unrealized profit is also removed from the consolidated income statement, and is shown as a future tax asset until a sale to outsiders takes place.

When the assets that contain the intercompany profit are sold outside (or consumed), the profit is considered realized and is reflected in the consolidated income statement. The appropriate income tax is removed from the consolidated balance sheet and reflected as an expense in the income statement.

SELF-STUDY PROBLEM

The following are the 2002 financial statements of Peter Corporation and its subsidiary, Salt Company:

	Peter	Salt
2002 income statements		
Sales	$900,000	$250,000
Management fees	25,000	—
Interest	—	3,600
Gain on land sale	—	20,000
Dividends	12,000	—
	$937,000	$273,600
Cost of sales	$540,000	$162,000
Interest expense	3,600	—
Other expense	196,400	71,600
Income tax expense	80,000	16,000
	$820,000	$249,600
Net income	$117,000	$ 24,000
2002 retained earnings statements		
Balance, January 1	$153,000	$ 72,000
Net income	117,000	24,000
	270,000	96,000
Dividends	50,000	15,000
Balance, December 31	$220,000	$ 81,000
Balance sheets — December 31, 2002		
Cash	$ 12,000	$ 8,000
Accounts receivable	70,000	10,000
Notes receivable	—	60,000
Inventory	32,000	27,000
Land 175,000	19,000	
Plant and equipment (net)	238,000	47,000
Investment in Salt Co.	65,000	—
	$592,000	$171,000
Notes payable	$ 60,000	—
Other liabilities	212,000	40,000
Common stock	100,000	50,000
Retained earnings	220,000	81,000
	$592,000	$171,000

Other Information

1. On January 1, 2000, Peter purchased 80% of the common shares of Salt for $65,000. On that date, Salt had retained earnings of $10,000 and the book values of its net assets were equal to fair values.

2. The companies sell merchandise to each other. Peter sells to Salt at a gross profit rate of 35%; Salt earns a gross profit of 40% from its sales to Peter.

3. The December 31, 2001, inventory of Peter contained purchases made from Salt amounting to $7,000. There were no intercompany purchases in the inventory of Salt on this date.

4. During 2002 the following intercompany transactions took place:

(a) Salt made a $25,000 payment to Peter for management fees, which was recorded as "other expense."

(b) Salt made sales of $75,000 to Peter. The December 31, 2002, inventory of Peter contained merchandise purchased from Salt amounting to $16,500.

(c) Peter made sales of $100,000 to Salt. The December 31, 2002, inventory of Salt contained merchandise purchased from Peter amounting to $15,000.

(d) On July 1, 2002, Peter borrowed $60,000 from Salt and signed a note bearing interest at 12% per annum. Interest on this note was paid on December 31, 2002.

(e) In 2002, Salt sold land to Peter, recording a gain of $20,000. This land is being held by Peter on December 31, 2002.

5. Goodwill impairment tests have been conducted yearly since the date of acquisition. Losses due to impairment were as follows: 2000, $2,600; 2001, $800; 2002, $1,700.

6. Peter accounts for its investment using the cost method.

7. Both companies pay income tax at a rate of 40%.

Required:

1. Prepare the 2002 consolidated financial statements.
2. Prepare the following:
   (a) A calculation of consolidated retained earnings as at December 31, 2002.
   (b) A statement of changes in noncontrolling interest for 2002.
   (c) A statement of changes in future income taxes for 2002.
3. Assume that Peter uses the equity method.
   (a) Calculate the balance in the investment account as at December 31, 2001.
   (b) Prepare Peter's equity-method journal entries for 2002.

Solution to Self-study Problem

1.

CALCULATION AND AMORTIZATION OF THE PURCHASE DISCREPANCY

Cost of 80% of Salt, Jan. 1, 2000		$ 65,000
Book value of Salt, Jan. 1, 2000		
Common stock	50,000	
Retained earnings	10,000	
	60,000	
	80%	48,000
Purchase discrepancy		17,000
Allocated to revalue the net assets of Salt		–0–
Goodwill, Jan. 1, 2000		17,000
Amortized (impairment losses):		
2000–2001	3,400	
2002	1,700	5,100
Goodwill, Dec. 31, 2002		$ 11,900

INTERCOMPANY ITEMS

Notes receivable and payable	$ 60,000
Management fee revenue and expense	$ 25,000
Sales and purchases (100,000 + 75,000)	$175,000
Interest revenue and expense (12% × 60,000 × 1/2 yr.)	$ 3,600
Dividend from Salt (80% × 15,000)	$ 12,000

UNREALIZED PROFITS

	Before tax	40% tax	After tax
Inventory			
Opening (7,000 × 40%) — Salt selling	$ 2,800	$ 1,120	$ 1,680
Ending			
Salt selling (16,500 × 40%)	$ 6,600	$ 2,640	$ 3,960
Peter selling (15,000 × 35%)	5,250	2,100	3,150
	$11,850	$ 4,740	$ 7,110
Land — Salt selling	$20,000	$ 8,000	$ 12,000

CALCULATION OF CONSOLIDATED NET INCOME — 2002

Income of Peter			$117,000
Less: Dividends from Salt		12,000	
Amortization of purchase discrepancy*		1,700	
Ending inventory profit		3,150	16,850
Adjusted net income			100,150
Income of Salt		24,000	
Less: Ending inventory profit	3,960		
Land gain	12,000	15,960	
		8,040	
Add opening inventory profit		1,680	
Adjusted net income		9,720	
		80%	7,776
Consolidated net income			$107,926
Noncontrolling interest (20% × 9,720)		$ 1,944	

* In Chapter 4 we deducted this amortization from the parent's share of the subsidiary's net income. When we relocate this deduction as shown, the adjusted net incomes of the two companies equal the amount "Net income — entity" on the consolidated income statement.

PETER CORPORATION
CONSOLIDATED INCOME STATEMENT — 2002

Sales (900,000 + 250,000 − 175,000)	$975,000*
Cost of sales (540,000 + 162,000 − 175,000 − 2,800 + 11,850)	$536,050**
Other expense (196,400 + 71,600 − 25,000)	243,000
Goodwill impairment loss	1,700
Income tax (80,000 + 16,000 − 8,000 + 1,120 − 4,740)	84,380
Total expense	$865,130
Net income — entity	$109,870
Less noncontrolling interest	1,944
Net income	$107,926

* Revenue items completely eliminated from statement:	
Management fees	$25,000
Interest	3,600
Land gain	20,000
Dividends	12,000
** Expense items completely eliminated from statement:	
Interest	$ 3,600

CALCULATION OF CONSOLIDATED RETAINED EARNINGS
January 1, 2002

Retained earnings — Peter		$153,000
Less purchase discrepancy amortization 2000–01		3,400
Adjusted		149,600
Retained earnings — Salt	72,000	
Acquisition	10,000	
Increase	62,000	
Less opening inventory profit	1,680	
Adjusted increase	60,320	
	80%	48,256
Consolidated retained earnings, Jan. 1, 2002		$197,856

PETER CORPORATION
CONSOLIDATED RETAINED EARNINGS STATEMENT — 2002

Balance, January 1	$197,856
Net income	107,926
	305,782
Dividends	50,000
Balance, Dec. 31	$255,782

CALCULATION OF FUTURE INCOME TAX — December 31, 2002

Ending inventory	$ 4,740
Land	8,000
	$12,740

CALCULATION OF NONCONTROLLING INTEREST — December 31, 2002

Common stock — Salt		$ 50,000
Retained earnings — Salt		81,000
		131,000
Less: Ending inventory profit	3,960	
Land gain	12,000	15,960
Adjusted		115,040
		20%
		$ 23,008

PETER CORPORATION
CONSOLIDATED BALANCE SHEET — December 31, 2002

Cash (12,000 + 8,000)		$ 20,000
Accounts receivable (70,000 + 10,000)		80,000
Inventory (32,000 + 27,000 – 11,850)		47,150
Land (175,000 + 19,000 – 20,000)		174,000
Plant and equipment (net) (238,000 + 47,000)		285,000
Goodwill		11,900
Future income tax		12,740
		$630,790
Other liabilities (212,000 + 40,000)		$252,000
Noncontrolling interest		23,008
Shareholders' equity		
Common stock	100,000	
Retained earnings	255,782	355,782
		$630,790

2. (a)

CALCULATION OF CONSOLIDATED RETAINED EARNINGS,
December 31, 2002

Retained earnings, Dec. 31, 2002 — Peter		$220,000
Less: Purchase discrepancy amortization	5,100	
Ending inventory profit	3,150	8,250
Adjusted		211,750
Retained earnings, Dec. 31, 2002 — Salt	81,000	
Acquisition	10,000	
Increase	71,000	
Less: Ending inventory profit	3,960	
Land gain	12,000	15,960
Adjusted increase		55,040
		80%
		44,032
Consolidated retained earnings, December 31, 2002		$255,782

(b)

CHANGES IN NONCONTROLLING INTEREST — 2002

Common stock — Salt	$ 50,000
Retained earnings, Jan. 1, 2002 — Salt	72,000
	122,000
Less profit in inventory	1,680
	120,320
	20%
Noncontrolling interest, Jan. 1, 2002	24,064
Allocation of entity income, 2002	1,944
	26,008
Dividends (20% × 15,000)	3,000
Noncontrolling interest, December 31, 2002	$ 23,008

(c)

CHANGES IN FUTURE INCOME TAXES — 2002

Balance, Jan. 1, 2002 (inventory)		$ 1,120
Taxes paid in 2002 but deferred		
Inventory	4,740	
Land	8,000	12,740
		13,860
Expensed 2002		1,120
Balance, Dec. 31, 2002		$12,740

3. (a)

Investment in Salt, Dec. 31, 2001 (cost method)		$ 65,000
Retained earnings, Dec. 31, 2001 — Salt	72,000	
Acquisition	10,000	
Increase	62,000	
Less inventory profit	1,680	
Adjusted increase	60,320	
	80%	48,256
		113,256
Less purchase discrepancy amort. to date		3,400
Investment in Salt, December 31, 2001 (equity method)		$109,856

3. (b)   *2002 Equity Method Journal Entries*
(see calculation of consolidated net income)

Investment in Salt Co.	7,776	
Investment income		7,776
80% of adjusted net income of Salt Co.		
Cash	12,000	
Investment in Salt Co.		12,000
Dividends from Salt Co.		
Investment income	1,700	
Investment in Salt Co.		1,700
2002 purchase discrepancy amortization		
Investment income	3,150	
Investment in Salt Co.		3,150
Ending inventory profit — Peter selling		

APPENDIX

Preparing Consolidated Financial Statements Using the Working Paper Approach

In this chapter we have illustrated the direct approach for preparing the consolidated financial statements of Parent Company over a two-year period. In the example used, an inventory profit recorded by Sub Inc. was held back for consolidated purposes in Year 1, and realized in the consolidated statements in Year 2. The example assumed that Parent had used the cost method, but the journal entries that would have been made if Parent had used the equity method were also illustrated.

We will now illustrate the preparation of the consolidated financial statements for years 1 and 2 using the working paper approach. For each year, we will present the working paper under the equity method, followed by the working paper under the cost method. The reason for proceeding in this particular order is that when the cost method has been used, the first working paper entries adjust the accounts of the parent to equity method balances. The working paper elimination entries are then made that are appropriate for the equity method.

Year 1 Working Paper (equity method)   Exhibit 7.6 illustrates the working paper for the preparation of the Year 1 consolidated financial statements when Parent Co. has used the equity method.

The elimination entries used were as follows:

#1 Investment income — Parent Co.	1,206	
Investment in Sub Inc. — Parent Co.		1,206

This entry eliminates the investment income from the income statement and restates the investment account to the balance at the beginning of the year.

#2 Retained earnings, January 1 — Sub Inc.	450	
Common stock — Sub Inc.	800	
Noncontrolling interest (balance sheet)		1,250

Exhibit 7.6

CONSOLIDATED FINANCIAL STATEMENT WORKING PAPER
Equity Method
ELIMINATION OF INVENTORY PROFIT — December 31, Year 1

	Parent	Sub	Dr.		Cr.		Consolidated
				Eliminations			
Sales	$20,000	$ 8,000	(i)	5,000			$23,000
Investment income	1,206		(1)	1,206			
	$21,206	$ 8,000					$23,000
Cost of sales	$13,000	$ 4,300	(ii)	600	(i)	5,000	$12,900
Misc. expense	1,400	900					2,300
Income tax exp.	2,200	1,100			(iii)	240	3,060
	$16,600	$ 6,300					$18,260
Net income — entity							$ 4,740
Noncontrolling interest			(4)	134			134
Net income	$ 4,606	$ 1,700		$ 6,940		$ 5,240	$ 4,606
Retained earnings, Jan. 1	$12,000	$ 4,500	(2)	450			$12,000
			(3)	4,050			
Net income	4,606	1,700		6,940		5,240	4,606
	16,606	6,200					16,606
Dividends	2,000	—					2,000
Retained earnings, Dec. 31	$14,606	$ 6,200		$11,440		$ 5,240	$14,606
Assets, misc.	$21,650	$19,200					$40,850
Inventory	7,500	4,000			(ii)	600	10,900
Future income tax			(iii)	240			240
Investment in Sub	12,456				(3)	11,250	
					(1)	1,206	
	$41,606	$23,200					$51,990
Liabilities	$12,000	$ 9,000					$21,000
Common stock	15,000	8,000	(2)	800			15,000
			(3)	7,200			
Retained earnings	14,606	6,200		11,440		5,240	14,606
Noncontrolling interest			(2)			1,250	
			(4)			134	1,384
	$41,606	$23,200		$19,680		$19,680	$51,990

This entry eliminates 10 percent of the shareholders' equity of Sub Inc. at the beginning of the year and establishes the noncontrolling interest as at that date.

#3 Retained earnings, January 1 — Sub Inc.	4,050	
Common stock — Sub Inc.	7,200	
Investment in Sub Inc. — Parent Co.		11,250

This entry eliminates the parent's share of the shareholders' equity of the subsidiary at the beginning of the year against the parent's investment account. Usually the difference represents the unamortized purchase discrepancy on that date, but in this particular example there is no purchase discrepancy.

| #4 | Noncontrolling interest (income statement) | 134 | |
| | Noncontrolling interest (balance sheet) | | 134 |

This entry allocates the applicable portion of the net income of the entity to the noncontrolling interest. The amount requires a separate calculation, as follows:

Net income — Sub Inc.	$1,700
Less profit in ending inventory	360
Adjusted net income — Sub Inc.	1,340
	10%
Noncontrolling interest	$ 134

The remaining working paper entries eliminate the intercompany transactions for Year 1.

| #i | Sales | 5,000 | |
| | Cost of sales | | 5,000 |

To eliminate intercompany sales and purchases.

| #ii | Cost of sales | 600 | |
| | Inventory | | 600 |

To hold back the before-tax profit, on the consolidated income statement and (from inventory) on the consolidated balance sheet.

| #iii | Future income tax | 240 | |
| | Income tax expense | | 240 |

The income tax effect of the inventory profit held back in #(ii).

Year 1 Working Paper (cost method) Exhibit 7.7 illustrates the working paper for the preparation of the Year 1 consolidated financial statements, assuming that Parent has used the cost method to account for its investment.

Entry #a adjusts Parent's accounts from the cost to the equity method. The numbers used are obtained from the calculation of consolidated net income for Year 1 (see page 241).

| #a | Investment in Sub Inc. — Parent Co. | 1,206 | |
| | Investment income — Parent Co. | | 1,206 |

Now that Parent's accounts have been adjusted to the equity method, the remaining working paper entries are identical to those presented in Exhibit 7.6.

Year 2 Working Paper (equity method) The working paper for the preparation of the Year 2 consolidated financial statements when the parent has used the equity method are shown in Exhibit 7.8. The inventory profit held back in Year 1 is

Exhibit 7.7

CONSOLIDATED FINANCIAL STATEMENT WORKING PAPER
Cost Method
ELIMINATION OF INVENTORY PROFIT — December 31, Year 1

	Parent	Sub		Dr.		Cr.	Consolidated
				Eliminations			
Sales	$20,000	$ 8,000	(i)	5,000			$23,000
Investment income			(1)	1,206	(a)	1,206	
	$20,000	$ 8,000					$23,000
Cost of sales	$13,000	$ 4,300	(ii)	600	(i)	5,000	$12,900
Misc. expense	1,400	900					2,300
Income tax exp.	2,200	1,100			(iii)	240	3,060
	$16,600	$ 6,300					$18,260
Net income — entity							$ 4,740
Noncontrolling interest			(4)	134			134
Net income	$ 3,400	$ 1,700		$ 6,940		$ 6,446	$ 4,606
Retained earnings, Jan. 1	$12,000	$ 4,500	(2)	450			$12,000
			(3)	4,050			
Net income	3,400	1,700		6,940		6,446	4,606
	15,400	6,200					16,606
Dividends	2,000	—					2,000
Retained earnings, Dec. 31	$13,400	$ 6,200		$11,440		$ 6,446	$14,606
Assets, misc.	$21,650	$19,200					$40,850
Inventory	7,500	4,000			(ii)	600	10,900
Future income tax			(iii)	240			240
Investment in Sub	11,250				(3)	11,250	
			(a)	1,206	(1)	1,206	
	$40,400	$23,000					$51,990
Liabilities	$12,000	$ 9,000					$21,000
Common stock	15,000	8,000	(2)	800			15,000
			(3)	7,200			
Retained earnings	13,400	6,200		11,440		6,446	14,606
Noncontrolling interest			(2)			1,250	
			(4)			134	1,384
	$40,400	$23,200		$20,886		$20,886	$51,990

realized in Year 2; because the subsidiary was the original selling company, the resulting increase in after-tax income is allocated to the controlling and noncontrolling equities.

The working paper entries are reproduced below, with brief explanations:

#1 Investment income — Parent Co.   3,114
        Investment in Sub Inc. — Parent Co.   3,114

The investment income account is eliminated against the investment account, which establishes the start-of-year balance in this account.

#2	Retained earnings, January 1 — Sub Inc.	620	
	Common stock — Sub Inc.	800	
	Noncontrolling interest (balance sheet)		1,420

This entry eliminates 10 percent of the shareholders' equity of Sub Inc. as at the beginning of the year, with the amount used to establish the noncontrolling interest as at January 1, Year 2. Note that this opening balance is not the same as the closing

Exhibit 7.8

CONSOLIDATED FINANCIAL STATEMENT WORKING PAPER
Equity Method Realization of Inventory Profit
December 31, Year 2

	Parent	Sub	Eliminations Dr.		Eliminations Cr.		Consolidated
Sales	$25,000	$12,000					$37,000
Investment income	3,114		(1)	3,114			
	$28,114	$12,000					$37,000
Cost of sales	$16,000	$ 5,500			(i)	600	$20,900
Misc. expense	2,350	1,400					3,750
Income tax exp.	2,600	2,000	(i)	240			4,840
	$20,950	$ 8,900					$29,490
Net income — entity							$ 7,510
Noncontrolling interest			(4)	346			346
Net income	$ 7,164	$ 3,100		$ 3,700	$	600	$ 7,164
Retained earnings, Jan. 1	$14,606	$ 6,200	(2)	620			$14,606
			(3)	5,580			
Net income	7,164	3,100		3,700		600	7,164
	21,770	9,300					21,770
Dividends	2,500						2,500
Retained earnings, Dec. 31	$19,270	$ 9,300		$ 9,900	$	600	$19,270
Assets, misc.	$22,800	$20,800					$43,600
Inventory	9,900	7,500					17,400
Investment in Sub	15,570		(i)	324	(1)	3,114	
					(3)	12,780	
	$48,270	$28,300					$61,000
Liabilities	$14,000	$11,000					$25,000
Common stock	15,000	8,000	(2)	800			15,000
			(3)	7,200			
Retained earnings	19,270	9,300		9,900		600	19,270
Noncontrolling interest			(i)	36	(2)	1,420	1,730
					(4)	346	
	$48,270	$28,300		$18,260		$18,260	$61,000

balance at the end of Year 1, because it does not contain a portion of the inventory profit being held back at that time. This difference is adjusted in entry #i as follows:

#i Income tax expense	240	
Investment in Sub Inc. — Parent Co.	324	
Noncontrolling interest (balance sheet)	36	
Cost of sales		600

There are two parts to this entry. The credit to cost of sales is made in order to realize in the Year 2 consolidated income statement the inventory profit that was held back in Year 1. The debit to income tax expense matches the expense to the profit realized. (Remember that the Year 1 consolidated balance sheet contained a future tax asset of this amount.) These two entries increase the after-tax income of the consolidated entity by $360. The debit of $36 (10% × 360) establishes the correct opening balance in noncontrolling interest. The debit of $324 (90% × 360) establishes the investment account with a balance of $12,780 as at the beginning of the year. Before this entry, the investment account had a correct equity-method balance of $12,456, which included the holdback of 90 percent of the unrealized inventory profit at the end of Year 1. This entry reverses the holdback so that the next entry can be made.

#3 Retained earnings, January 1 — Sub Inc.	5,580	
Common stock — Sub Inc.	7,200	
Investment in Sub Inc. — Parent Co.		12,780

The parent's share (90 percent) of the shareholders' equity of the subsidiary at the beginning of the year is eliminated against the parent's investment account.

#4 Noncontrolling interest (income statement)	346	
Noncontrolling interest (balance sheet)		346

This final entry allocates the applicable portion of the entity's Year 2 net income to the noncontrolling interest, based on the adjusted income of the subsidiary, calculated as follows:

Net income — Sub Inc.	$3,100
Add profit in opening inventory	360
Adjusted net income — Sub Inc.	3,460
	10%
	$ 346

Year 2 Working Paper (cost method)   Exhibit 7.9 contains the Year 2 working paper based on the assumption that the parent has used the cost method.

Entry #a adjusts the investment account of the parent to the equity method balance at the beginning of Year 2. The source of the amounts used can be found in the calculation of consolidated retained earnings as at January 1, Year 2, presented on page 247.

Entry #b adjusts the investment account to the equity method balance as at December 31, Year 2. (See the calculation of Year 2 consolidated net income on page 245.)

Once the parent's accounts have been adjusted to reflect the equity method, the remaining entries are identical to those shown in Exhibit 7.8.

Exhibit 7.9

CONSOLIDATED FINANCIAL STATEMENT WORKING PAPER
Cost Method
REALIZATION OF INVENTORY PROFIT
December 31, Year 2

	Parent	Sub	Eliminations Dr.		Cr.		Consolidated
Sales	$25,000	$12,000					$37,000
Investment income			(1)	3,114	(b)	3,114	
	$25,000	$12,000					$37,000
Cost of sales	$16,000	$ 5,500			(i)	600	$20,900
Misc. expense	2,350	1,400					3,750
Income tax exp.	2,600	2,000	(i)	240			4,840
	$20,950	$ 8,900					$29,490
Net income — entity							$ 7,510
Noncontrolling interest			(4)	346			346
Net income	$ 4,050	$ 3,100		$ 3,700		$ 3,714	$ 7,164
Retained earnings, Jan. 1	$13,400	$ 6,200	(2)	620	(a)	1,206	$14,606
			(3)	5,580			
Net income	4,050	3,100		3,700		3,714	7,164
	17,450	9,300					21,770
Dividends	2,500	—					2,500
Retained earnings, Dec. 31	$14,950	$ 9,300		$ 9,900		$ 4,920	$19,270
Assets — miscellaneous	$22,800	$20,800					$43,600
Inventory	9,900	7,500					17,400
Investment in Sub	11,250		(b)	3,114			
			(i)	324	(1)	3,114	
			(a)	1,206	(3)	12,780	
	$43,950	$28,300					$61,000
Liabilities	$14,000	$11,000					$25,000
Common stock	15,000	8,000	(2)	800			15,000
			(3)	7,200			
Retained earnings	14,950	9,300		9,900		4,920	19,270
Noncontrolling interest			(i)	36	(2)	1,420	1,730
					(4)	346	
	$43,950	$28,300		$22,580		$22,580	$61,000

REVIEW QUESTIONS

1. In what way are an individual's pants with four pockets similar to a parent company with three subsidiaries? Explain, with reference to intercompany revenues and expenses.

2. List the types of intercompany revenue and expenses that are eliminated in the preparation of a consolidated income statement, and indicate the effect that each elimination has on the amount of noncontrolling interest in net income.

3. "From a single-entity point of view, intercompany revenue and expenses and intercompany borrowings do nothing more than transfer cash from one bank account to another." Explain.

4. If an intercompany profit is recorded on the sale of an asset to an affiliate within the consolidated entity in period 1, when should this profit be considered realized? Explain.

5. "The reduction of a $1,000 intercompany gross profit from ending inventory should be accompanied by a $400 increase to future income taxes in consolidated assets." Do you agree? Explain.

6. A parent company rents a sales office to its wholly owned subsidiary under an operating lease requiring rent of $2,000 a month. What adjustments to income tax expense should accompany the elimination of the parent's $24,000 rent revenue and the subsidiary's $24,000 rent expense when a consolidated income statement is being prepared? Explain.

7. "Intercompany losses recorded on the sale of assets to an affiliate within the consolidated entity should always be eliminated when consolidated financial statements are prepared." Do you agree with this statement? Explain.

8. Describe the effects that the elimination of intercompany sales and intercompany profits in ending inventory will have on the various elements of the consolidated financial statements.

9. An intercompany gain on the sale of land is eliminated in the preparation of the consolidated statements in the year that the gain was recorded. Will this gain be eliminated in the preparation of subsequent consolidated statements? Explain.

10. What is fractional elimination of intercompany profits? Which consolidation theories would advocate this type of elimination? Why?

11. "The *CICA Handbook* seems to have chosen parts of all three consolidation theories in determining current GAAP." Discuss this statement.

MULTIPLE CHOICE

Use the following data for Questions 1 to 10.

On January 1, 1998, Post Company purchased 70% of the outstanding voting shares of Stamp Company for $850,000 in cash. On that date, Stamp had retained earnings of $400,000 and common stock of $500,000. On the acquisition date, the identifiable assets and liabilities of Stamp had fair values that were equal to their carrying values except for the following:

	Fair value	Carrying value
Equipment	$ 800,000	$ 600,000
Long-term liabilities	1,200,000	1,100,000

The equipment had a remaining useful life of 10 years on January 1, 1998, and the long-term liabilities mature on December 31, 2007. Both companies use the straight-line method to calculate all depreciation and amortization.

The financial statements of Post Company and Stamp Company on December 31, 2002, were as follows:

BALANCE SHEETS

	Post	Stamp
Assets		
Cash	$ 50,000	$ 10,000
Current receivables	250,000	100,000
Inventories	3,000,000	520,000
Equipment (net)	6,150,000	2,500,000
Buildings (net)	2,600,000	500,000
Investment in Stamp (at cost)	850,000	—
	$12,900,000	$3,630,000
Liabilities and shareholders' equity		
Current liabilities	$ 300,000	$ 170,000
Long-term liabilities	4,000,000	1,100,000
No-par common stock	3,000,000	500,000
Retained earnings	5,600,000	1,860,000
	$12,900,000	$3,630,000

STATEMENTS OF INCOME AND RETAINED EARNINGS

	Post	Stamp
Sales revenue	$ 3,500,000	$ 900,000
Other revenues	300,000	30,000
	3,800,000	930,000
Cost of goods sold	1,700,000	330,000
Depreciation expense	300,000	100,000
Other expenses	200,000	150,000
Income tax expense	300,000	70,000
	2,500,000	650,000
Net Income	1,300,000	280,000
Retained earnings, beginning balance	4,500,000	1,600,000
	5,800,000	1,880,000
Dividends declared	200,000	20,000
Retained earnings, ending balance	$ 5,600,000	$1,860,000

Additional Information

- Post carries its investment in Stamp on its books by the cost method.
- During 2001, Post sold Stamp $100,000 worth of merchandise, of which $60,000 was resold by Stamp in the year. During 2002, Post had sales of $200,000 to Stamp, of which 40% was resold by Stamp. Intercompany sales are priced to provide Post with a gross profit of 30% of the sales price.
- On December 31, 2001, Post had in its inventories $150,000 of merchandise purchased from Stamp during 2001. On December 31, 2002, Post had in its ending inventories $100,000 of merchandise that had resulted from purchases of $250,000 from Stamp during 2002. Intercompany sales are priced to provide Stamp with a gross profit of 60% of the sale price.

- At December 31, 2001, a goodwill impairment test indicated that a loss of $5,000 had occurred.
- Both companies are taxed at 25%.

1. What amount of sales revenue would appear on Post's consolidated income statement for the year ended December 31, 2002?
   a. $4,400,000
   b. $4,200,000
   c. $4,150,000
   d. $3,950,000

2. What amount of other revenue would appear on Post's consolidated income statement for the year ended December 31, 2002?
   a. $300,000
   b. $310,000
   c. $316,000
   d. $330,000

3. To calculate Post's consolidated cost of goods sold, the first step is to add together the unadjusted totals from Post's and Stamp's separate entity financial statements. What is the amount of adjustment necessary to this figure for unrealized profits in beginning inventory for the year ended December 31, 2002?
   a. –$102,000
   b. –$96,000
   c. –$76,500
   d. –$6,000

4. Refer to Question #3. What is the total amount of adjustment necessary to consolidated cost of goods sold for intercompany sales for 2002 and unrealized profits in ending inventory at December 31, 2002?
   a. –$348,000
   b. –$354,000
   c. –$378,000
   d. –$456,000

5. To calculate Post's consolidated depreciation, the first step is to add together the unadjusted totals from Post's and Stamp's separate entity financial statements. What is the amount of adjustment necessary to this figure for the amortization of the purchase discrepancy for the year ended December 31, 2002?
   a. $70,000
   b. $56,000
   c. $20,000
   d. $14,000

6. To calculate Post's consolidated other expenses (which include interest expense but not goodwill impairment loss), the first step is to add together the unadjusted totals from Post's and Stamp's separate entity financial statements. What is the amount of adjustment necessary to this figure for the amortization of the purchase discrepancy for the year ended December 31, 2002?
   a. –$7,000
   b. $0
   c. $7,000
   d. $28,000

7. What amount of goodwill impairment loss would appear on Post's consolidated income statement for the year ended December 31, 2002?
    a. $0
    b. $333
    c. $3,333
    d. $5,000

8. To calculate Post's consolidated income tax expense, first add together the unadjusted totals from Post's and Stamp's separate entity financial statements. What amount of adjustment is necessary to this figure for the unrealized profit in beginning inventory for the year ended December 31, 2002?
    a. $22,500
    b. $24,000
    c. $25,500
    d. $28,000

9. Which of the following would appear on Post's consolidated income statement for the year ended December 31, 2002, for noncontrolling interest?
    a. $77,250
    b. $84,000
    c. $90,750
    d. $99,000

10. Which of the following would appear on Post's consolidated balance sheet for the year ended December 31, 2002, for noncontrolling interest?
    a. $694,500
    b. $708,000
    c. $714,750
    d. $721,500

11. If unrealized inventory profits have occurred, what is the impact on consolidated financial statements between upstream and downstream transfers?
    a. Downstream transfers may be ignored since they are made by the parent company.
    b. Downstream transfers affect the computation on the noncontrolling interest's share of the subsidiary's net income but upstream transfers do not.
    c. No difference exists in consolidated financial statements between upstream and downstream transfers.
    d. Upstream transfers affect the computation on the noncontrolling interest's share of the subsidiary's net income but downstream transfers do not.

12. Castle Corp. owns 75% of the outstanding shares of Moat Ltd. During 2002, Moat sold merchandise to Castle for $200,000. At December 31, 2002, 50% of this merchandise remains in Castle's inventory. For 2002, gross profit percentages were 30% for Castle and 40% for Moat. How much unrealized profit should be eliminated from ending inventory in the consolidation process at December 31, 2002?
    a. $80,000
    b. $40,000
    c. $32,000
    d. $30,000

13. Bell Co. owns 90% of Tower Inc. During 2001 Tower sold inventory costing $75,000 to Bell for $100,000. A total of 16 percent of this inventory was not sold to outsiders until 2002. During 2002, Bell sold inventory which cost

$96,000 to Tower for $120,000. Thirty-five percent of this inventory was not sold to outsiders until 2003. Bell reported cost of goods sold of $380,000 in 2002, while Tower reported an amount of $210,000. What amount should be reported as cost of goods sold on the 2002 consolidated income statement?
   a. $465,600
   b. $473,440
   c. $474,400
   d. $522,400

14. Hardwood Inc. owns 90% of the outstanding shares of Softwood Corp. During 2001, Softwood sold inventory which cost $77,000 to Hardwood for $110,000. A total of $40,000 of this inventory was still on hand on December 31, 2001, and was sold in 2002. During 2002, Softwood sold inventory costing $72,000 to Hardwood for $120,000. On December 31, 2002, $50,000 of this inventory was still on hand. In 2002 Hardwood reported a net income of $150,000 while Softwood reported $90,000. Assuming a 40% tax rate, what is the amount of the noncontrolling interest that would be reported on the 2002 consolidated income statement?
   a. $8,200
   b. $8,520
   c. $9,000
   d. $9,800

PROBLEMS

Problem 1 The consolidated balance sheet of Pearl Company and its 85% owned subsidiary Shand Company showed future income taxes of $31,600 at December 31, Year 5, arrived at as follows:

	Intercompany profit	Income tax 40%
Inventory	$10,000	$ 4,000
Land	14,000	5,600
Trademark	55,000	22,000
		$31,600

During Year 6, one-quarter of the land was sold to outsiders. On December 31, Year 6, the inventories of Pearl contained items purchased from Shand for $35,000, and the inventories of Shand contained purchases made from Pearl for $50,000. Both companies record gross profits at the rate of 35% on their intercompany sales. Income tax rates remained unchanged during the year. The trademark, which was purchased from Shand in Year 2, is considered to have an unlimited life.

Required:

(a) Calculate the total change (increase or decrease) that will be made to income tax expense on the Year 6 consolidated income statement.
(b) Calculate the amount of future income taxes that will appear on the December 31, Year 6, consolidated balance sheet.

Problem 2 Narn Corporation acquired a 90% interest in the common stock of Mary Corporation at the beginning of Year 1. The $40,000 purchase discrepancy on that date was allocated 30% to inventory, with the remainder to goodwill. Goodwill impairment losses occurred as follows: Year, $4,000; Year 2, $1,600; Year 3, $2,800. The retained earnings of Mary Corporation at date of acquisition were $18,000, and Narn has carried its investment under the cost method. Both companies have a 40% income tax rate.

The information below, extracted from the accounting records of the two companies, relates to operations during Year 3.

	Narn	Mary
Net income (including dividend revenues)	$125,000	$66,000
Dividends paid during Year 3	60,000	30,000
Retained earnings, end of Year 3 (after books have been closed)	375,000	95,000
Intercompany profits on sales made by Mary Corporation to Narn Corporation, included in Narn's inventory		
Beginning of Year 3	15,000	
End of Year 3	12,000	

Required:

(a) Prepare a statement of consolidated retained earnings for Year 3, including supporting schedules showing how all figures were derived.

(b) Prepare a schedule showing the change in the noncontrolling interest in the retained earnings of Mary Corporation during Year 3.

Problem 3 The following consolidated income statement of a parent and its 90% owned subsidiary was prepared by an accounting student before reading this chapter:

CONSOLIDATED INCOME STATEMENT

Sales	$500,000
Rental revenue	24,000
Interest revenue	50,000
Total revenue	$574,000
Cost of goods sold	$350,000
Rental expense	24,000
Interest expense	35,000
Miscellaneous administration expense	45,000
Noncontrolling interest in net income	9,000
Income tax expense	42,000
Total costs and expenses	$505,000
Net income	$ 69,000

The following items were overlooked when the statement was prepared:
- The opening inventory of the parent contained an intercompany profit of $5,000.
- During the year, intercompany sales were made at a 30% gross profit rate, as follows:

By the parent	$100,000
By the subsidiary	80,000

- At the end of the year, half of the items purchased from the parent remained in the inventory of the subsidiary.
- All of the rental revenue and 70% of the interest revenue was intercompany and appeared on the income statement of the parent.
- Assume a 40% rate for income tax.

Required:

Prepare a correct consolidated income statement.

Problem 4   Brown Company purchased a 70% interest in Green Company several years ago in order to obtain retail outlets for its major products. Since that time Brown has sold to Green a substantial portion of its merchandise requirements. At the beginning of the current year, Green's inventory of $690,000 was composed 80% of goods purchased from Brown at markups averaging 30% on Brown's cost. Sales from Brown to Green during the current year were $5,600,000. The estimated intercompany profit in Green's ending inventory was $194,000.

Brown owns buildings and land used in Green's retail operations and rented to Green. Rentals paid by Green to Brown during the current year amounted to $743,000. At the end of the current year, Brown sold to Green for $250,000 land to be used in the development of a shopping centre that had cost Brown $203,500. The gain was included in Brown's net income for the current year. Brown also holds a one-year, 6% note of Green on which it has accrued interest revenues of $22,500 during the current year.

During the current year, Brown reported net income of $568,100 and Green reported net income of $248,670. Brown uses the cost method to account for its investment.

Required:

Calculate the current year's consolidated net income (assume a 40% tax rate).

Problem 5   L Company owns a controlling interest in M Company and Q Company. L Co. purchased an 80% interest in M Co. at a time when M Co. reported retained earnings of $500,000. L Co. purchased a 70% interest in Q Co. at a time when Q Co. reported retained earnings of $50,000.

An analysis of the changes in retained earnings of the three companies during the current year appears below:

	L Co.	M Co.	Q Co.
Retained earnings balance, beginning of current year	$ 976,000	$ 843,000	$ 682,000
Net income	580,000	360,000	240,000
Dividends paid or declared	(250,000)	(200,000)	(150,000)
Retained earnings balance, end of current year	$1,306,000	$1,003,000	$ 772,000

Q Co. sells parts to L Co., which after further processing and assembly are sold by L Co. to M Co., where they become a part of the finished product sold by M Co. Intercompany profits included in inventories at the beginning and end of the current year are estimated as follows:

	Beginning inventory	Ending inventory
Intercompany profit in inventory		
On sales from Q to L	$90,000	$ 35,000
On sales from L to M	52,000	118,000

L Co. uses the cost method to account for its investments, and income tax allocation at a 40% rate when it prepares consolidated financial statements.

Required:

(a) Calculate consolidated net income for the current year.
(b) Prepare a statement of consolidated retained earnings for the current year.

Problem 6 X Company acquired 75% of Y Company on January 1, Year 1, when Y Co. had common stock of $100,000 and retained earnings of $70,000. The purchase discrepancy was allocated as follows on this date:

Inventory	$ 60,000
Equipment (15-year life)	45,000
Total purchase discrepancy	$105,000

Since this date the following events have transpired:

Year 1

- Y Co. reported a net income of $130,000 and paid dividends of $25,000.
- On July 1, X Co. sold land to Y Co. for $102,000. This land was carried in the records of X Co. at $75,000.
- On December 31, Year 1, the inventory of X Co. contained an intercompany profit of $30,000.
- X Co. reported a net income of $400,000 from its own operations.

Year 2

- Y Co. reported a net loss $15,000 and paid dividends of $5,000.
- Y Co. sold the land that it purchased from X Co. to an unrelated company for $130,000.
- On December 31, Year 2, the inventory of Y Co. contained an intercompany profit of $12,000.
- X Co. reported a net income from its own operations of $72,000.

Required:

Assume a 40% tax rate.
(a) Prepare X Co's equity method journal entries for each of years 1 and 2.
(b) Calculate consolidated net income for each of years 1 and 2.
(c) Prepare a statement showing the changes in noncontrolling interest in each of years 1 and 2.
(d) Calculate the balance in X Co's account "Investment in Y Co. (equity method)" as at December 31, Year 2.

Problem 7 H Company has controlling interests in three subsidiaries, as shown in the data below:

	H Co.	L Co.	J Co.	K Co.
			Subsidiaries	
Retained earnings at acquisition		$30,000	$40,000	$25,000
Percent of ownership		95%	90%	85%
Retained earnings, Jan. 1, Year 5	12,000	50,000	43,000	30,000
Net income (loss), Year 5		20,000	(5,000)	30,000
Dividends paid, Year 5	10,000	5,000	3,000	15,000
Intercompany sales		50,000	70,000	

K Co. had items in its inventory on January 1, Year 5, on which L Co. had made a profit of $5,000.

J Co. had items in its inventory on December 31, Year 5, on which K Co. had made a profit of $10,000.

J Co. rents premises from L Co. at an annual rental of $8,500.

The parent company has no income (other than from its investments) and no expenses. It uses the equity method of recording its investments but has made no entries during Year 5. Assume a 40% tax rate.

Required:

Prepare the following:
(a) Entries that H Co. would make in Year 5.
(b) A calculation of consolidated net income for Year 5.
(c) A statement of consolidated retained earnings for Year 5.

Problem 8   On January 2, Year 1, Big Ltd. acquired 70% of the outstanding voting shares of Mak Ltd. The purchase discrepancy of $280,000 on that date was allocated in the following manner:

Inventory	$100,000	
Land	50,000	
Plant and equipment	60,000	estimated life 5 years
Patent	40,000	estimated life 8 years
Goodwill	30,000	
	$280,000	

The Year 5 income statements and retained earnings statements for the two companies were as follows:

	Big	Mak
Sales	$4,000,000	$2,100,000
Intercompany investment income	204,700	—
Rental revenue	—	70,000
Total revenue	$4,204,700	$2,170,000
Cost of goods sold	$2,000,000	$ 800,000
Selling and administrative expense	550,000	480,000
Interest expense	250,000	140,000
Depreciation	450,000	225,000
Patent amortization	—	25,000
Rental expense	35,000	—
Income tax	300,000	200,000
Total expenses	$3,585,000	$1,870,000
Net income	$ 619,700	$ 300,000
Retained earnings, January 1	$2,000,000	$ 900,000
Add net income	619,700	300,000
	2,619,700	1,200,000
Less dividends	100,000	50,000
Retained earnings, December 31	$2,519,700	$1,150,000

Additional Information

- Mak regularly sells merchandise to Big. Intercompany sales in Year 5 totalled $400,000.
- Intercompany profits in the inventories of Big were as follows:

January 1, Year 5	$75,000
December 31, Year 5	40,000

- Big's entire rental expense relates to equipment rented from Mak.
- A goodwill impairment loss of $3,000 occurred in Year 5.

- Big uses the equity method to account for its investment, and uses income tax allocation at the rate of 40% when it prepares consolidated statements.

Required:

Prepare the following consolidated financial statements for Year 5:
(a) Income statement.
(b) Retained earnings statement.

Problem 9 The combined income and retained earnings statements of Par Company and its subsidiaries, Subone Company and Subtwo Company, were prepared as at December 31, Year 6, and are shown below:

	Par	Subone	Subtwo
Revenues			
Sales	$450,000	$270,000	$190,000
Dividends	43,750	—	—
Rent	—	130,000	—
Interest	10,000	—	—
	$503,750	$400,000	190,000
Expenses			
Cost of sales	$300,000	$163,000	$145,000
General and administrative	50,000	20,000	15,000
Interest	—	10,000	—
Depreciation	18,000	28,000	—
Rent	25,000	—	14,000
Income tax	27,000	75,000	7,000
	$420,000	$296,000	$181,000
Net Income	$ 83,750	$104,000	$ 9,000
Retained earnings, Jan. 1, Year 6	700,000	92,000	75,000
	783,750	196,000	84,000
Dividends	80,000	50,000	5,000
Retained earnings, Dec. 31, Year 6	$703,750	$146,000	$ 79,000

Additional Information

- Par purchased its 80% interest in Subone on January 1, Year 1. On this date, Subone had a retained earnings balance of $40,000 and the purchase discrepancy amounting to $15,000 was allocated entirely to plant and equipment with an estimated remaining life of 8 years.
- Par purchased its 75% interest in Subtwo on December 31, Year 3. On this date, Subtwo had a retained earnings balance of $80,000. The purchase discrepancy amounting to $19,000 was allocated to goodwill; however, because Subtwo had failed to report adequate profits, the goodwill was entirely written off for consolidated purposes by the end of Year 5.
- Par has established a policy that any intercompany sales will be made at a gross profit rate of 30%.
- On January 1, Year 6, the inventory of Par contained goods purchased from Subone for $15,000.
- During Year 6 the following intercompany sales took place:

Par to Subone	$ 90,000
Subone to Subtwo	120,000
Subtwo to Par	150,000

- On December 31, Year 6, the inventories of each of the three companies contained items purchased on an intercompany basis in the following amounts:

  Inventory of:
Par	$90,000
Subone	22,000
Subtwo	40,000

- In addition to its merchandising activities, Subone is in the office equipment rental business. Both Par and Subtwo rent office equipment from Subone, and the rental expense on their Year 6 income statements is entirely from this type of transaction.
- During Year 6, Subone paid $10,000 interest to Par for intercompany advances.
- Par Company uses the cost method to account for investments, and uses tax allocation at a rate of 40% when it prepares consolidated financial statements.

Required:

Prepare a combined consolidated income and retained earnings statement for Year 6.

Problem 10 The income statements of Evans Company and Falcon Company for the current year are shown below:

	Evans	Falcon
Sales revenues	$450,000	$600,000
Dividend revenues	32,000	—
Rental revenues	33,600	—
Interest revenues	—	18,000
	$515,600	$618,000
Cost of goods sold	$288,000	$353,000
Operating expenses	104,000	146,000
Interest expense	30,000	—
Income taxes	31,700	43,500
	$453,700	$542,500
Net income	$ 61,900	$ 75,500
Beginning retained earnings	632,000	348,000
Dividends	(30,000)	(40,000)
Ending retained earnings	$663,900	$383,500

Evans owns 80% of the outstanding common stock of Falcon, purchased at the time the latter company was organized.

Evans sells parts to Falcon at a price that is 25% above cost. Total sales from Evans to Falcon during the year were $85,000. Included in Falcon's inventories were parts purchased from Evans amounting to $21,250 in beginning inventories and $28,750 in the ending inventory.

Falcon sells back to Evans certain finished goods, at a price that gives Falcon an average gross profit of 30% on these intercompany sales. Total sales from Falcon to Evans during the year were $177,000. Included in the inventories of Evans were parts acquired from Falcon amounting to $11,000 in beginning inventories and $3,000 in ending inventories.

Falcon rents an office building from Evans, and pays $2,800 per month in rent. Evans has borrowed $600,000 through a series of 5% notes, of which Falcon holds $360,000 as notes receivable. Use income tax allocation at a 40% rate.

Required:

(a) Prepare a consolidated income statement.
(b) Prepare a consolidated statement of retained earnings.

Problem 11   The partial trial balance of P Co. and S Co. at December 31, Year 5, was:

	P Co. Dr.	P Co. Cr.	S Co. Dr.	S Co. Cr.
Investment in S. Co.	90,000			
Common stock		150,000		60,000
Retained earnings (charged with dividends, no other changes during the year)		101,000		34,000

Additional Information

- The investment in the shares of S Co. (a 90% interest) was acquired January 2, Year 1, for $90,000. At this time, the shareholders' equity of this company was as follows: capital stock, $60,000; retained earnings, $20,000.
- Net incomes of the two companies for the year were:

P Co.	$60,000
S Co.	48,000

- During Year 5, sales of P Co. to S Co. were $10,000, and sales of S Co. to P Co. were $50,000. Rates of gross profit on intercompany sales in Year 4 and Year 5 were 40% of sales.
- On December 31, Year 4, the inventory of P Co. included $7,000 of merchandise purchased from S Co., and the inventory of S Co. included $3,000 of merchandise purchased from P Co. On December 31, Year 5, the inventory of P Co. included $20,000 of merchandise purchased from S Co. and inventory of S Co. included $5,000 of merchandise purchased from P Co.
- During the year ended December 31, Year 5, P Co. paid dividends of $12,000 and S Co. paid dividends of $10,000.
- At the time that P Co. purchased the stock of S Co., the purchase discrepancy was allocated to patents of S Co. These patents are being amortized for consolidation purposes over a period of five years.
- In Year 3, land that originally cost $45,000 was sold by S Co. to P Co. for $50,000. The land is still owned by P Co.
- Assume a corporate tax rate of 40%.

Required:

Prepare the following:

(a) A statement of consolidated retained earnings for the year ended December 31, Year 5.

(b) Your calculations of the amount of noncontrolling interest that would appear in the consolidated balance sheet at December 31, Year 5.

Problem 12 The balance sheets at the end of the current year, and the income statements for the current year, for the Purvis and Slater Companies are given below:

BALANCE SHEETS

	Purvis	Slater
Cash	$ 13,000	$ 47,000
Receivables	31,000	106,000
Inventories	80,000	62,000
Investment in Slater	257,340	—
Other assets	91,000	157,000
Total assets	$472,340	$372,000
Current liabilities	$160,000	$ 83,000
Capital stock	200,000	150,000
Beginning retained earnings	101,260	126,000
Net income	36,080	63,000
Dividends	(25,000)	(50,000)
Total liabilities & capital	$472,340	$372,000

INCOME STATEMENT DATA

Sales revenues	$340,000	$820,000
Intercompany investment income	40,080	—
Interest revenues	—	1,250
Gain on sale of land	13,000	—
Total revenues	$393,080	$821,250
Beginning inventory	$ 44,000	$ 93,600
Purchases	237,000	583,400
Ending inventory	(80,000)	(62,000)
Cost of goods sold	$201,000	$615,000
Operating expenses	135,600	100,450
Interest expense	6,500	—
Income taxes	13,900	42,800
Total expenses	$357,000	$758,250
Net income	$ 36,080	$ 63,000

Purvis owns 90% of the shares of Slater, purchased for $225,000 six years ago when Slater's retained earnings were $56,000. Since that date Purvis has amortized 60% of the excess of the cost of the investment over the carrying value of the underlying net assets of Slater. The management of Purvis regarded this excess payment as the cost of copyrights, and authorized amortization over a period of 10 years.

Purvis owes Slater $25,000 on a three-year 5% note. During the current year Purvis sold to Slater land at a price $13,000 in excess of Purvis's cost. This was not a capital gain for tax purposes.

Purvis buys all its merchandise from Slater and has done so for several years. The average gross profit realized by Slater on these sales is approximately the same as on sales to outsiders and has remained stable for the last two years. Purvis has used the equity method, and uses income tax allocation for consolidated statement preparation at a rate of 40%.

Required:

Prepare consolidated financial statements for the current year.

Problem 13   On January 1, Year 3, the Plenty Company purchased 80% of the outstanding voting shares of the Sparse Company for $1.6 million in cash. On that date, Sparse's balance sheet and the fair values of its identifiable assets and liabilities were as follows:

	Carrying	Fair
Cash	$ 25,000	$ 25,000
Accounts receivable	310,000	290,000
Inventories	650,000	600,000
Plant and equipment (net)	2,015,000	2,050,000
Total assets	$3,000,000	
Current liabilities	$ 300,000	$ 300,000
Long-term liabilities	1,200,000	1,100,000
Common stock	500,000	
Retained earnings	1,000,000	
Total liabilities and shareholders' equity	$3,000,000	

On January 1, Year 3, Sparse's plant and equipment had a remaining useful life of eight years. Its long-term liabilities mature on January 1, Year 7. Goodwill, if any, is to be tested yearly for impairment.

The balance sheets as at December 31, Year 9, and the retained earnings statements for the year ending December 31, Year 9, for the two companies are as follows:

BALANCE SHEETS
December 31, Year 9

	Plenty	Sparse
Cash	$ 500,000	$ 40,000
Accounts receivables	1,700,000	500,000
Inventories	2,300,000	1,200,000
Plant and equipment (net)	8,200,000	4,000,000
Investment in Sparse (at cost)	1,600,000	—
Land	700,000	260,000
Total assets	$15,000,000	$6,000,000
Current liabilities	$ 600,000	$ 200,000
Long-term liabilities	3,000,000	3,000,000
Common stock	1,000,000	500,000
Retained earnings	10,400,000	2,300,000
Total liabilities and shareholders' equity	$15,000,000	$6,000,000

RETAINED EARNINGS — Year 9

	Plenty	Sparse
Balance, January 1, Year 9	$ 9,750,000	$2,000,000
Net income, Year 9	1,000,000	400,000
	10,750,000	2,400,000
Dividends, Year 9	350,000	100,000
Balance, December 31, Year 9	$10,400,000	$2,300,000

Additional Information

- The inventories of both companies have a maximum turnover period of one year. Receivables have a maximum turnover period of 62 days.
- On July 1, Year 7, Plenty sold a parcel of land to Sparse for $100,000. Plenty had purchased this land in Year 4 for $150,000. On September 30, Year 9, Sparse sold the property to another company for $190,000.
- During Year 9, $2 million of Plenty's sales were to Sparse. Of these sales, $500,000 remain in the December 31, Year 9, inventories of Sparse. The December 31, Year 8, inventories of Sparse contained $312,500 of merchandise purchased from Plenty. Plenty's sales to Sparse are priced to provide it with a gross profit of 20%.
- During Year 9, $1.5 million of Sparse's sales were to Plenty. Of these sales, $714,280 remain in the December 31, Year 9, inventories of Plenty. The December 31, Year 8, inventories of Plenty contained $857,140 of merchandise purchased from Sparse. Sparse's sales to Plenty are priced to provide it with a gross profit of 25%.
- Dividends declared on December 31, Year 9, were:

Plenty	$350,000
Sparse	100,000

- Goodwill impairment tests resulted in losses of $52,500 in Year 4, and $8,700 in Year 9.
- Assume a 40% tax rate for both companies.

Required:

(a) Prepare the consolidated retained earnings statement.
(b) Prepare the consolidated balance sheet.

Problem 14 The following are the financial statements of Post Corporation and its subsidiary Sage Company as at 31 December, Year 3:

BALANCE SHEETS
December 31, Year 3

	Post Corp.	Sage Co.
Cash	$ 12,200	$ 12,900
Accounts receivable	17,200	9,100
Notes receivable	—	55,000
Inventory	32,000	27,000
Land	175,000	19,000
Plant and equipment	520,000	65,000
Accumulated depreciation	(229,400)	(17,000)
Investment in Sage, at cost	65,000	—
	$592,000	$171,000
Accounts payable	$212,000	$ 40,000
Notes payable	55,000	—
Capital stock	100,000	50,000
Retained earnings, January 1	158,000	72,000
Net income	117,000	24,000
Dividends	(50,000)	(15,000)
	$592,000	$171,000

INCOME STATEMENTS — Year 3

	Post Corp.	Sage Co.
Sales	$900,000	$240,000
Management fee revenue	26,500	—
Interest revenue	—	6,800
Gain on sale of land	—	30,000
Dividend revenue	10,500	—
	$937,000	$276,800
Cost of goods sold	$540,000	$162,000
Interest expense	20,000	—
Other expense	180,000	74,800
Income tax expense	80,000	16,000
	$820,000	$252,800
Net income	$117,000	$ 24,000

Additional Information

- Post purchased 70% of the outstanding shares of Sage on January 1, Year 1, at a cost of $65,000, and has used the cost method to account for its investment. On that date Sage had retained earnings of $15,000, and fair values were equal to carrying values for all its net assets except inventory (overvalued by $12,000) and equipment (undervalued by $18,000). The equipment had an estimated remaining life of five years.
- The companies sell merchandise to each other at a gross profit rate of 25%.
- The December 31, Year 2, inventory of Post contained purchases made from Sage amounting to $14,000. There were no intercompany purchases in the inventory of Sage on this date.
- During Year 3 the following intercompany transactions took place:
  - Sage made a payment of $26,500 to Post for management fees, which was recorded under the category "other expenses."
  - Sage made sales of $90,000 to Post. The December 31, Year 3, inventory of Post contained merchandise purchased from Sage amounting to $28,000.
  - Post made sales of $125,000 to Sage. The December 31, Year 3, inventory of Sage contained merchandise purchased from Post amounting to $18,000.
  - On July 1, Year 3, Post borrowed $55,000 from Sage and signed a note bearing interest at 12% per annum. The interest on this note was paid on December 31, Year 3.
  - During the year Sage sold land to Post and recorded a gain of $30,000 on the transaction. This land is being held by Post on December 31, Year 3.
- Goodwill impairment losses occurred as follows: Year 1, $2,600; Year 2, $460; Year 3, $1,530.
- Both companies pay income tax at 40% on their taxable incomes.

Required:

Prepare the following consolidated financial statements for Year 3:
(a) Income statement.
(b) Retained earnings statement.
(c) Balance sheet.

Problem 15* On January 1, 2002, the Vine company purchased 60,000 of the 80,000 common shares of the Devine company for $80 per share. On that date, Devine had common stock of $3,500,000, and retained earnings of $2,100,000. When acquired, Devine had inventories with fair values $100,000 less than carrying value, a parcel of land with a fair value $200,000 greater than the carrying value, and equipment with a fair value $200,000 less than carrying value. There are also internally generated patents with an estimated market value of $400,000 and a five-year remaining life. A long-term liability had a market value $100,000 greater than book value; this liability was paid off December 31, 2005. All other identifiable assets and liabilities of Devine had fair values equal to their carrying values. At the acquisition date, the equipment had an expected remaining useful life of 12 years. Goodwill is to be treated in accordance with the provisions of the *CICA Handbook*, Section 3062. Both companies use the straight-line method for all depreciation and amortization calculations and the FIFO inventory cost flow assumption. Assume a 40% income tax rate on all applicable items.

On September 1, 2006, Devine sold a parcel of land to Vine, and recorded a total nonoperating gain of $400,000.

Sales from Vine to Devine totalled $1,000,000 in 2005 and $2,000,000 in 2006. These sales were priced to provide a gross profit margin on selling price of 33 $^1/_3$% to the Vine Company. Devine's December 31, 2005, inventory contained $300,000 of these sales; December 31, 2006, inventory contained $600,000.

Sales from Devine to Vine were $800,000 in 2005 and $1,200,000 in 2006. These sales were priced to provide a gross profit margin on selling price of 40% to the Devine Company. Vine's December 31, 2005, inventory contained $100,000 of these sales; the December 31, 2006, inventory contained $500,000.

Vine's investment in Devine's account is carried in accordance with the cost method, and includes advances to Devine of $200,000.

There are no intercompany amounts other than those noted, except for the dividends of $500,000 (total amount) declared and paid by Devine.

INCOME STATEMENTS
for Year Ending December 31, 2006
(in $000s)

	Vine	Devine
Sales	$11,600	$3,000
Dividends, investment income, and gains	400	1,000
Total revenues	$12,000	$4,000
Cost of goods sold	8,000	1,500
Other expenses	500	300
Income taxes	500	200
Total expenses	9,000	2,000
Net income	$ 3,000	$2,000

---

* Problem prepared by Peter Secord, St. Mary's University.

BALANCE SHEETS
December 31, 2006

	Vine	Devine
Cash and current receivables	$ 900	$ 300
Inventories	4,600	2,400
Investment in Devine (cost)	5,000	
Plant and equipment	13,000	6,800
Land	6,000	2,500
Total assets	$29,500	$12,000
Current liabilities	$ 700	$ 300
Long-term liabilities	6,600	1,100
Future income taxes	200	100
Common stock	10,000	3,500
Retained earnings	12,000	7,000
Total liabilities and equity	$29,500	$12,000

Required:

(a) Show the allocation of the purchase price at acquisition and the related amortization schedule. Show and label all calculations.

(b) Compute the investment income under the equity method that would be reported if Vine had been permitted to used the equity method, rather than consolidate, in 2006.

(c) Prepare a consolidated income statement for the Vine company and its subsidiary for the year ending December 31, 2006.

(d) Prepare a consolidated balance sheet for Vine company at December 31, 2006.

(e) Prepare a proof of consolidated retained earnings at December 31, 2006.

CHAPTER 8

(A) Intercompany Profits in Depreciable Assets
(B) Intercompany Bondholdings

CHAPTER OUTLINE

LEARNING OBJECTIVES

After studying this chapter, you should be able to do the following:

- Prepare consolidated financial statements that reflect the elimination of upstream and downstream intercompany profits in depreciable assets.
- Prepare consolidated financial statements that reflect the realization of upstream and downstream intercompany profits in depreciable assets.
- Calculate the gain or loss that results from the elimination of intercompany bondholdings and the allocation of such gain or loss to the equities of the controlling and noncontrolling interests.

- Prepare consolidated financial statements that reflect the gains or losses that are the result of an intercompany bond acquisition during the year.
- Prepare consolidated financial statements that account for intercompany bond gains or losses in years subsequent to the year of intercompany purchase.

In this chapter we complete our examination of intercompany profits in assets; we also examine the consolidation issues that arise from intercompany bondholdings. Because these transactions are so distinctly different in their impact on the consolidated statements, this chapter is divided into two parts.

Part (A) looks at the elimination and realization of intercompany profits (losses) in depreciable assets. The concepts involved in the holdback of profits (losses) are similar to those examined previously with regard to intercompany land profits (losses), but the realization concepts are different because they are based on consumption rather than a sale.

Part (B) examines the gains (losses) that are created in the consolidated financial statements when some types of intercompany bondholdings are eliminated.

(A) Intercompany Profits in Depreciable Assets

Holdback and Realization — Year 1

In Chapter 7, we illustrated the holdback of an intercompany profit in inventory and land. In both cases the before-tax profit of $600 and the corresponding income tax of $240 were held back in the year of the intercompany transaction and realized in the year that the asset was sold to outsiders. We will now examine the holdback and the realization in the consolidated statements of an intercompany profit in a depreciable asset.

We return to the Chapter 7 example of Parent Company and its 90 percent owned subsidiary, Sub Inc. The Year 1 financial statements of the two companies are shown in Exhibit 8.1. Parent has used the cost method to account for its investment.

Notice that although the net incomes and total assets of the two companies are unchanged, the details on each statement have been changed so that we can focus on the following intercompany transaction involving equipment that occurred during the year:

On July, 1 Year 1, Sub sold highly specialized equipment with a very short useful life to Parent and recorded a profit of $600 on the transaction. We are assuming that Sub purchased this equipment for $1,500 on this date with the intention of using it, but instead immediately sold it to Parent for $2,100. This intercompany transaction was recorded in the following manner by the two companies:

Parent Company			Sub Inc.		
Equipment	2,100		Cash	2,100	
Cash		2,100	Equipment		1,500
			Gain on sale of equipment		600

Exhibit 8.1

YEAR 1 INCOME STATEMENTS

	Parent	Sub
Sales	$20,000	$ 7,400
Gain on sale of equipment	—	600
	$20,000	$ 8,000
Depreciation expense	$ 700	—
Miscellaneous expense	13,700	5,200
Income tax expense	2,200	1,100
	$16,600	$ 6,300
Net income	$ 3,400	$ 1,700

YEAR 1 RETAINED EARNINGS STATEMENTS

	Parent	Sub
Balance, January 1	$12,000	$ 4,500
Net income	3,400	1,700
	15,400	6,200
Dividends	2,000	—
Balance, December 31	$13,400	$ 6,200

BALANCE SHEETS — December 31, Year 1

	Parent	Sub
Assets (misc.)	$27,750	$23,200
Equipment	2,100	—
Accumulated depreciation	(700)	—
Investment in Sub Inc.	11,250	—
	$40,400	$23,200
Liabilities	$12,000	$ 9,000
Common stock	15,000	8,000
Retained earnings	13,400	6,200
	$40,400	$23,200

It is also assumed that this transaction was not a capital gain for tax purposes, and that Sub's tax rate is 40 percent. This means that Sub paid $240 (40% × 600) income tax on this profit. We further assume that this is the only depreciable asset held by either company and that the equipment is expected to be obsolete in one-and-a-half years. On December 31, Year 1, Parent recorded depreciation expense on this equipment in the following manner:

Depreciation expense	700	
Accumulated depreciation		700

To record depreciation for half a year
$(2,100 \div 1^1/2 = 1,400 \times {}^1/2 = 700)$

It should be noted that if Sub had sold the equipment at cost, Parent's Year 1 depreciation expense would have been $500 ($1{,}500 \div 1^1/_2 \times {}^1/_2 = 500$). This is the amount of depreciation expense that should appear in the income statement of the entity (i.e., in the consolidated income statement) for Year 1, in that it represents depreciation based on the historical cost of the equipment to the entity.

When we examine the separate income statements of the two companies (Exhibit 8.1), it should be obvious that the $600 gain is not a gain from a single-entity point of view, and that the $700 depreciation expense does not represent historical cost depreciation to the entity. Two adjustments need to be made when the Year 1 consolidated income statement is prepared; these have opposite effects on the before-tax income of the entity. The first adjustment eliminates the gain on sale of equipment recorded on July 1, Year 1, because as of that date the gain is unrealized from the single-entity point of view. This adjustment reduces before-tax income by $600 and holds back this profit for consolidation purposes. A corresponding reduction of $240 should be made to income tax expense so that a net after-tax gain of $360 is held back. This concept is similar in all respects to the holdback of the land gain that was illustrated in Chapter 7.

The second adjustment reduces depreciation expense by $200 ($600 \div 1^1/_2 \times {}^1/_2$). The amount of the reduction represents the depreciation taken in Year 1 on this $600 gain, and results in a consolidated depreciation expense of $500 based on historical cost, as required. This reduction of depreciation expense increases the before-tax income of the entity by $200; in this way it realizes, for consolidation purposes, the portion of the original $600 gain that was held back. This concept bases the realization of the gain on the consumption (by depreciation) of the asset that contains the unrealized gain. A corresponding increase of $80 should be made to income tax expense to match the tax with the portion of the gain realized. The result will be a net after-tax realization of $120 for consolidation purposes.

The net effect of the two after-tax adjustments results in the entity's Year 1 net income being reduced by $240 ($360 - 120$). Because Sub was the selling company, this $240 reduction is allocated to the noncontrolling and controlling interests in the same manner as was illustrated in Chapter 7.

The preceding paragraphs have briefly outlined the concepts involved in the holdback and realization of an intercompany gain in a depreciable fixed asset. We will now apply these concepts by preparing the Year 1 consolidated financial statements of Parent using the direct approach. It is useful to start by preparing the following three calculations:

EQUIPMENT GAIN — SUB INC. SELLING

	Before tax	40% tax	After tax
Gain, July 1, Year 1	$600	$240	$360
Less realized by depreciation, Year 1	200	80	120
Balance, unrealized Dec. 31, Year 1	$400	$160	$240

CALCULATION OF CONSOLIDATED NET INCOME — Year 1

Net income — Parent Co.		$3,400
Net income — Sub Inc.	1,700	
Less gain on sale of equipment	360	
	1,340	
Add gain realized by depreciation	120	
Adjusted net income — Sub Inc.	1,460	
Parent Co.'s share	90%	1,314
Consolidated net income		$4,714
Noncontrolling interest (10% × 1,460)		$ 146

CALCULATION OF NONCONTROLLING INTEREST
December 31, Year 1

Shareholders' equity — Sub Inc.	
Common stock	$ 8,000
Retained earnings	6,200
	14,200
Less net unrealized equipment gain	240
Adjusted shareholders' equity	13,960
Noncontrolling interest's share	10%
	$ 1,396

It should be noted that the calculation of consolidated net income is made to adjust the net income of the parent from the cost method to the equity method. If the parent had used the equity method, we would still have to make the other two noncontrolling interest calculations.

Exhibit 8.2 illustrates the preparation of the consolidated financial statements using the direct approach.

The consolidated income statement was prepared by combining, line by line, the revenues and expenses of the two companies. The amount for noncontrolling interest is based on the *adjusted income* of Sub. The intercompany eliminations are shown in Exhibit 8.2 in boldface and are summarized as follows:

(i) Eliminates the $600 gain on the equipment and adjusts the income tax expense for the tax on this gain. The net effect is to reduce the after-tax income of the entity by $360.

(ii) Eliminates the portion of the gain that was depreciated in Year 1. Consolidated depreciation is now based on historical cost. Because this elimination results in a realization of $200 of the original gain held back, income tax expense is increased by $80 to match the tax with the gain realized. The net result is an after-tax realization of $120.

The two eliminations decreased the entity's net income by $240, which was allocated to the two equities as follows:

To noncontrolling interest (10% × 240)	$ 24
To controlling interest (90% × 240)	216
	$240

The consolidated retained earnings statement has been prepared in the normal manner. Because we are consolidating one year after acquisition, the parent's retained earnings at the beginning of the year are equal to consolidated retained earnings on that date.

Exhibit 8.2

Year 1 Consolidated Statements
Adjusted for Intercompany Equipment Profit
(direct approach)

PARENT COMPANY
CONSOLIDATED INCOME STATEMENT
for the Year Ended December 31, Year 1

Sales (20,000 + 7,400)	$27,400
Gain on sale of equipment (0 + 600 − **600**)(i)	–0–
	$27,400
Depreciation expense (700 + 0 − **200**)(ii)	$ 500
Miscellaneous expense (13,700 + 5,200)	18,900
Income tax expense (2,200 + 1,100 − **240**(i) + **80**)(ii)	3,140
	$22,540
Net income — entity	$ 4,860
Less noncontrolling interest	146
Net income	$ 4,714

PARENT COMPANY
CONSOLIDATED RETAINED EARNINGS STATEMENT
for the Year Ended December 31, Year 1

Balance, January 1	$12,000
Net income	4,714
	$16,714
Dividends	2,000
Balance, December 31	$14,714

PARENT COMPANY
CONSOLIDATED BALANCE SHEET
December 31, Year 1

Assets — miscellaneous (27,750 + 23,200)		$50,950
Equipment (2,100 + 0 − **600**)(i)		1,500
Accumulated depreciation (700 + 0 − **200**)(ii)		(500)
Future income tax (0 + 0 + **240**(i) − **80**)(ii)		160
		$52,110
Liabilities (12,000 + 9,000)		$21,000
Noncontrolling interest		1,396
Shareholders' equity		
Common stock	15,000	
Retained earnings	14,714	29,714
		$52,110

The consolidated balance sheet was prepared by combining the assets and liabilities of the two companies and making the following adjustments (shown in Exhibit 8.2 in boldface) for the equipment gain:

(i) When the before-tax gain of $600 is removed from the equipment, the resulting balance of $1,500 represents the original cost to the entity. The $240 increase to future income tax represents the tax on this gain and corresponds with the reduction of tax expense in the income statement.

(ii) Removes the amount of the gain contained in accumulated depreciation. The resulting amount ($500) is the accumulated depreciation on the original cost. The $80 decrease to future income tax corresponds with the increase in income tax expense made in the income statement.

Note that the $400 reduction of the net book value of the equipment ($600 − $200), together with an increase in future income taxes of $160 (40% × $400), results in total consolidated assets being reduced by $240, which corresponds to the reduction made to the entity's net income in the consolidated income statement. The fact that this reduction was allocated to the two equities was noted on page 291.

Equity Method Journal Entries Our example has assumed that Parent uses the cost method to account for its investment. If Parent was using the equity method, the following journal entries would be made on December 31, Year 1:

Investment in Sub Inc.	1,530	
Investment income		1,530
90% of the net income of Sub Inc. (90% × 1,700 = 1,530)		

Investment income	324	
Investment in Sub Inc.		324
To hold back 90% of the equipment profit recorded by Sub (90% × 360 = 324)		

Investment in Sub Inc.	108	
Investment income		108
To realize 90% of the profit realized by depreciation (90% × 120 = 108)		

After these entries are posted, the two related equity-method accounts of Parent will show the following changes and balances:

	Investment in Sub Inc.	Investment income
January 1, Year 1	$11,250	
December 31, Year 1		
Income from Sub Inc.	1,530	1,530
Equipment profit (held back)	(324)	(324)
Equipment profit realized	108	108
Balance, December 31, Year 1	$12,564	$1,314

Appendix A, at the end of this chapter, illustrates the working paper approach to the preparation of the Year 1 consolidated financial statements. Because the cost method approach first adjusts the parent's accounts to the equity method, cost method working papers are the only ones illustrated.

Realization of Remaining Gain — Year 2

The equipment sold to the parent on July 1, Year 1, had a remaining life of $1^1/2$ years on that date. When the Year 1 consolidated income statement was prepared, both the holdback of the total gain and the realization of one-third of the gain took place. When the Year 2 consolidated income statement is prepared, adjustments will be made to realize the remaining two-thirds of the gain. This intercompany gain will be fully realized for consolidation purposes at the end of Year 2, only because the equipment had an unusually short remaining life of $1^1/2$ years on the date of the intercompany sale.

The Year 2 financial statements for the two companies are shown in Exhibit 8.3.

Before the consolidated financial statements are prepared, we must make the following four calculations:

EQUIPMENT GAIN — SUB INC. SELLING

	Before tax	40% tax	After tax
Gain, July 1, Year 1	$600	240	360
Less realized by depreciation, Year 1	200	80	120
Balance unrealized, Dec. 31, Year 1	$400	160	240
Less realized by depreciation, Year 2	400	160	240
Balance unrealized, Dec. 31, Year 2	–0–	–0–	–0–

CALCULATION OF CONSOLIDATED NET INCOME — Year 2

Net income — Parent Co.		$4,050
Net Income — Sub Inc.	3,100	
Add equipment gain realized by depreciation	240	
Adjusted net income — Sub Inc.	3,340	
Parent Co.'s share	90%	3,006
Consolidated net income		$7,056
Noncontrolling interest (10% × 3,340)		$ 334

CALCULATION OF CONSOLIDATED RETAINED EARNINGS
January 1, Year 2

Retained earnings — Parent Co.		$13,400
Retained earnings — Sub Inc.	6,200	
Acquisition retained earnings	4,500	
Increase since acquisition	1,700	
Less unrealized equipment gain, Jan. 1	240	
Adjusted increase since acquisition	1,460	
Parent Co.'s share	90%	1,314
Consolidated retained earnings		$14,714

Exhibit 8.3

YEAR 2 INCOME STATEMENTS

	Parent	Sub
Sales	$25,000	$12,000
Depreciation expense	$ 1,400	—
Miscellaneous expense	16,950	6,900
Income tax expense	2,600	2,000
	$20,950	$ 8,900
Net income	$ 4,050	$ 3,100

YEAR 2 RETAINED EARNINGS STATEMENTS

	Parent	Sub
Balance, January 1	$13,400	$ 6,200
Net income	4,050	3,100
	17,450	9,300
Dividends	2,500	—
Balance, December 31	$14,950	$ 9,300

BALANCE SHEETS — December 31, Year 2

	Parent	Sub
Assets (misc.)	$32,700	$28,300
Equipment	2,100	—
Accumulated depreciation	(2,100)	—
Investment in Sub Inc.	11,250	—
	$43,950	$28,300
Liabilities	$14,000	$11,000
Common stock	15,000	8,000
Retained earnings	14,950	9,300
	$43,950	$28,300

CALCULATION OF NONCONTROLLING INTEREST
December 31, Year 2

Capital stock — Sub Inc.	$ 8,000
Retained earnings — Sub Inc.	9,300
	$17,300
	10%
	$ 1,730

The Year 2 consolidated financial statements prepared using the direct approach are shown in Exhibit 8.4. (Eliminations required for the intercompany equipment gain are shown in boldface.)

When the consolidated income statement is prepared, the depreciation expense is reduced by $400. The result is a consolidated depreciation expense of $1,000 based on the entity's cost. This adjustment realizes $400 of the equipment gain for consolidation purposes. Income tax expense is increased by $160 to match expense with the gain realized. The net effect of the two adjustments in the income statement is to increase the entity's net income by an after-tax realization amounting to $240.

The Year 2 consolidated retained earnings statement is prepared using the calculated January 1 balance, consolidated net income, and the dividends of Parent Company.

Exhibit 8.4

Year 2 Consolidated Statements
Adjusted for Intercompany Equipment Profit
(direct approach)

PARENT COMPANY
CONSOLIDATED INCOME STATEMENT
for the Year Ended December 31, Year 2

Sales (25,000 + 12,000)	$37,000
Depreciation expense (1,400 + 0 − **400**)(i)	$ 1,000
Miscellaneous expense (16,950 + 6,900)	23,850
Income tax expense (2,600 + 2,000 + **160**)(i)	4,760
	$29,610
Net income — entity	$ 7,390
Less noncontrolling interest	334
Net income	$ 7,056

PARENT COMPANY
CONSOLIDATED RETAINED EARNINGS STATEMENT
for the Year Ended December 31, Year 2

Balance, January 1	$14,714
Net income	7,056
	21,770
Dividends	2,500
Balance, December 31	$19,270

PARENT COMPANY
CONSOLIDATED BALANCE SHEET
December 31, Year 2

Assets — miscellaneous (32,700 + 28,300)		$61,000
Equipment (2,100 + 0 − **600**)(ii)		1,500
Accumulated depreciation (2,100 + 0 − **600**)(ii)		(1,500)
		$61,000
Liabilities (14,000 + 11,000)		$25,000
Noncontrolling interest		1,730
Shareholders' equity		
Common stock	15,000	
Retained earnings	19,270	34,270
		$61,000

Two adjustments are required in the preparation of the consolidated balance sheet. A reduction of $600 in equipment removes the gain and restates the equipment to the $1,500 historical cost to the entity. This equipment is fully depreciated on December 31, Year 2; therefore, the accumulated depreciation balance of $2,100 contains the $600 intercompany gain. When the accumulated depreciation is reduced by $600, the resulting balance ($1,500) is based on the entity's historical cost.

Note that when both the equipment and the accumulated depreciation are reduced by $600, total consolidated assets are not changed. The net gain held back on the Year 1 consolidated balance sheet has been realized as at the end of Year 2. If no unrealized gains are being held back, there will be no future income tax adjustments made in the consolidated balance sheet. The future income tax asset of $160 that appeared in the December 31, Year 1, consolidated balance sheet became an expense in the Year 2 consolidated income statement.

As discussed above, the adjustments made in the consolidated income statement increased the entity's net income by $240, while the adjustments made in the asset side of the consolidated balance sheet did not change total assets. In order for this to balance out, there must have been both an increase and a decrease of $240 on the liability side of the consolidated balance sheet. The $240 increase occurred in the income statement and was allocated to the two equities in the balance sheet. An examination of the calculation of the start-of-year balance of consolidated retained earnings (see page 294) shows a decrease of $216 (90% × 240 = 216). If we prepare a schedule showing the changes in noncontrolling interest for the year, it is obvious where the remaining $24 (10% × 240 = 24) decrease went.

CHANGES IN NONCONTROLLING INTEREST — Year 2

Sub Inc.:	
Common stock	$ 8,000
Retained earnings, Jan. 1	6,200
	14,200
Less equipment profit	240
Adjusted	$13,960
	10%
Noncontrolling interest Jan. 1	$ 1,396
Year 2 entity net income allocated	334
Noncontrolling interest, Dec. 31	$ 1,730

Equity Method Journal Entries   If Parent had been using the equity method, the following journal entries would have been made on December 31, Year 2:

Investment in Sub Inc.	2,790	
Investment income		2,790
90% of Sub Inc.'s Year 2 net income (90% × 3,100 = 2,790)		

Investment in Sub Inc.	216	
Investment income		216
90% of the portion of the equipment gain realized by depreciation in Year 2		
(90% × 240 = 216)		

After these entries are posted, the two related equity method accounts of Parent show the following changes and balances:

	Investment in Sub Inc.	Investment income
January 1, Year 2	$12,564	
December 31, Year 2		
Income from Sub Inc.	2,790	2,790
Equipment gain realized	216	216
Balance, December 31, Year 2	$15,570	$3,006

Appendix A of this chapter illustrates the working paper approach to the preparation of the Year 2 consolidated financial statements.

Comparison of Realization of Inventory and Equipment Profits over Two-year Period

In Chapter 7 the holdback and realization of an intercompany profit in inventory was illustrated. In this chapter we have illustrated the holdback and realization of an intercompany gain in equipment. In both cases the after-tax profit (gain) was $360 (60% × 600), and the subsidiary was the selling company. The following summarizes the effect on the entity's net income over a two-year period.

INTERCOMPANY INVENTORY PROFIT

	Year 1	Year 2	Total
Parent Co., net income	$3,400	$4,050	$ 7,450
Sub Inc., net income	1,700	3,100	4,800
	5,100	7,150	12,250
After-tax profit (held back) realized	(360)	360	–0–
Net income — consolidated entity	$4,740	$7,510	$12,250
Allocated to the two equities:			
Noncontrolling interest	$ 134	$ 346	$ 480
Consolidated retained earnings	4,606	7,164	11,770
	$4,740	$7,510	$12,250

INTERCOMPANY EQUIPMENT GAIN

	Year 1	Year 2	Total
Parent Co., net income	$3,400	$4,050	$ 7,450
Sub Inc., net income	1,700	3,100	4,800
	5,100	7,150	12,250
After-tax gain (held back) realized	(360)	240	–0–
	120		
Net income — consolidated entity	$4,860	$7,390	$12,250
Allocated as follows:			
Noncontrolling interest	$ 146	$ 334	$ 480
Consolidated retained earnings	4,714	7,056	11,770
	$4,860	$7,390	$12,250

The two-year summaries shown above help illustrate a number of significant points in relation to consolidated financial statements.

1. The consolidated entity's net income is measured at the end of time periods that are usually one year in length.

2. During this measurement process, the holdback and subsequent realization of profits (losses) resulting from intercompany transactions takes place.

3. The realization of previously held back profits (losses) occurs during the period in which the acquiring company either sells the asset containing the profit (loss) to outsiders, or depreciates the asset, therefore consuming the asset.

4. If we examine a time period longer than one year, and if, at the end of that period, the assets of the constituent companies do not contain intercompany profits, the following becomes evident:

   The consolidated entity's net income for this longer period consists of

   (a) the reported net income of the parent company, exclusive of intercompany investment or dividend income, *plus*

   (b) the reported net income of the subsidiary company (or companies), *minus*

   (c) the purchase discrepancy amortization.

   In the above illustration we assumed that the purchase discrepancy was zero.

5. The entity's net income measurement for this longer time period is not affected by the fact that assets were sold at intercompany profits (losses) during the period. (See the two-year total column.) The same is true of the allocation to the two equities.

6. When consolidated statements are prepared at the end of an intervening time period (for example Year 1, Year 2) we have to determine whether there were profits (losses) recorded by any of the constituent companies that were not realized by the end of the period, and whether there were profits (losses) from prior periods, or in the current period, that were realized during the period.

7. The profit holdbacks and realizations are used in the measurement of the entity's net income and are adjustments to the reported net income of the selling constituent in the allocation of that net income.

In Chapter 7 we also illustrated the holdback and realization of a $360 after-tax intercompany gain in land. In this case the realization process took place in Year 8; however, the overall concepts discussed above remain the same.

(B) Intercompany Bondholdings

Our discussions so far have focused on gains (losses) resulting from the intercompany sale of inventory, land, and depreciable assets. The treatment of these gains (losses) in the preparation of consolidated financial statements can be summarized as follows: gains (losses) resulting from the intercompany sale of assets are realized subsequent to the recording of the intercompany transaction by the selling affiliate.

Occasionally, one affiliate will purchase all or a portion of the bonds issued by another affiliate. When consolidated financial statements are being prepared, the elimination of the intercompany accounts (investment in bonds and bonds payable; interest revenue and interest expense) may result in a gain (loss) being reflected in those statements. The treatment of this type of gain (loss) can be summarized in the following manner: gains (losses) arising because of the elimination of intercompany bondholding accounts are realized prior to the recording of these gains (losses) by the affiliates. Before we examine how these gains and losses occur in the elimination of the intercompany accounts, let us look at intercompany bondholding situations that do not result in gains or losses.

Intercompany Bondholdings — No Gain or Loss

Not all intercompany bondholdings result in gains or losses being reflected in the consolidated statements. For example, let us assume that one affiliate issued $10,000 in bonds, and that another affiliate acquired the whole issue.

(The amounts used are unrealistically low for a bond issue, but are realistic in relation to the size of Parent Company and Sub Inc., the two companies that we have been using in our illustrations. In any case, the concepts are the same regardless of the amounts used.)

Immediately after the issue, the records of the two companies would show the following accounts:

Acquiring Affiliate's Records		*Issuing Affiliate's Records*	
Investment in bonds	10,000	Bonds payable	10,000

From the entity's point of view, the two accounts are similar to intercompany receivables and payables and would be eliminated by the following working paper entry when the consolidated balance sheet is being prepared:

Bonds payable	10,000	
Investment in bonds		10,000

It is important to note that the eliminations are equal, and because of this, there is no gain or loss resulting from the working paper elimination of these two intercompany accounts. At the end of each succeeding year, this working paper elimination is repeated until the bonds mature. After that date, the two accounts no longer exist in the affiliates' records and further working paper eliminations are not required.

The consolidated balance sheet is not the only statement requiring working paper eliminations. If we assume that the bonds pay interest at the rate of 10 percent, the income statement of the issuing affiliate will show interest expense of $1,000, while the income statement of the acquiring affiliate will show interest revenue of $1,000. These intercompany revenue and expense accounts are eliminated by the following working paper entry when the consolidated income statement is being prepared:

Interest revenue	1,000	
Interest expense		1,000

Again, it is important to note that amounts are equal, and that because of this there is no gain or loss resulting from this working paper elimination. The consolidated income statement working paper elimination is repeated each year until the bonds mature.

Our example has assumed that the bonds were issued at par. Suppose, now, that the bonds were issued to the purchasing affiliate at a premium or discount. Provided that both affiliates use the same methods to amortize the issue premium or discount, and the purchase premium or discount, the amounts in the intercompany accounts on all successive balance sheets and income statements will be equal. The important concept of equal eliminations on both statements would still be true.

In earlier chapters, we illustrated that the equal elimination of intercompany receivables and payables does not change the amounts of the two equities on the consolidated balance sheet. Furthermore, the equal elimination of intercompany revenues and expenses does not change the net income of the consolidated entity, and therefore can have no effect on the amount of net income that is allocated to the two equities. As a result, it does not matter which affiliate is the parent company and which is a subsidiary, or whether both affiliates are subsidiary companies — in all cases the working paper eliminations would be similar to those illustrated.

Intercompany Bondholdings — With Gain or Loss

When the market rate is different from the coupon rate on the date of a bond issue, the bonds will be issued at a price that is different from the par or face value. If the interest rates are higher (lower) than the coupon rate, the bonds will be issued at a discount (premium). Subsequent to the issue, bond market prices will rise (fall) if the market interest rate falls (rises). It is the market price differential on the date of an intercompany purchase, combined with any unamortized issue discount or premium, that causes the consolidated gains or losses that result from the elimination of intercompany bondholdings. Let us change our example slightly to illustrate this.

Parent Co. has a $10,000 bond issue outstanding that pays 10 percent interest annually on December 31. The bonds were originally issued at a premium, which is being amortized by the company on a straight-line basis. On December 31, Year 1, this unamortized issue premium amounts to $200. The bonds mature on December 31, Year 5.

On December 31, Year 1, Sub purchases all of the outstanding bonds of Parent on the open market at a cost of $9,600. Immediately after Sub acquires these bonds, the records of the two companies would show the following accounts.

Sub Inc.'s Records		*Parent Co.'s Records*	
Investment in bonds of		Bonds payable	$10,000
Parent Co.	$10,000	Add unamortized issue	
Less discount on purchase	400	premium	200
Net	$ 9,600	Net	$10,200

The net amounts reflect our assumption of how the asset and the liability would be presented on the respective balance sheets of the two companies on December 31, Year 1. The preparation of the consolidated balance sheet on this date would require the elimination of the two intercompany amounts by the following working paper entry:

(i)	Bonds Payable — Parent Co.	10,200	
	Investment in bonds of Parent Co. — Sub. Inc.		9,600
	Gain on bond retirement		600

To eliminate the intercompany bond accounts and to recognize the resulting gain on the retirement of bonds

The eliminations of the asset and liability would appear in the consolidated balance sheet working paper. The balancing amount of the elimination entry "Gain on bond retirement" appears in the consolidated income statement working paper. From the consolidated entity's point of view, the bonds of the entity have been purchased on the open market and retired. The retirement gain can be calculated in the following manner:

Carrying amount of the bond liability	$10,200
Cost of investment in bonds	9,600
Gain on bond retirement	$ 600

Note that if Parent had acquired and retired its own bonds in the same manner, it would have recorded a gain on bond retirement of the same amount. This gain would appear on Parent's income statement and would also appear on the consolidated income statement. The actual event was different (Sub purchased the bonds), but because the two companies are a single economic entity, the gain will still appear on the consolidated income statement. The only difference is that the gain on the consolidated income statement does not appear on the income statement of the parent. Instead, it appears on the consolidated income statement as a result of the unequal elimination of the intercompany asset and liability accounts in the preparation of the consolidated balance sheet.

An examination of the make-up of the asset and liability accounts (see page 301) will indicate why there is a gain of $600. If the bonds had originally been issued at par (face value), and if the bonds had been acquired on the open market at a price equal to par, there would be no gain on retirement. It is the unamortized issue premium and the discount on the bond purchase that cause the gain. This premium and discount will be amortized by the two companies in Years 2 to 5, and thus will be reflected in the individual income statements of the two companies in those future periods. This will become clearer when we examine the consolidation procedures in Year 2. The important point to note at this stage is that the constituent companies will pay tax on this gain in future periods when the actual recording of the gain takes place. The consolidated entity is realizing the gain in Year 1; therefore, this timing difference requires income tax allocation if a proper matching is to take place. Assuming a 40 percent tax rate, the following additional working paper elimination entry is required:

(ii) Income tax expense   240
          Future income tax   240
      To record the future income liability and expense on the Year 1
      intercompany bond gain (40% × 600 = 240)

The effect of eliminations (i) and (ii) on the Year 1 consolidated income is to increase the net income of the equity by $360 (600 − 240 = 360). The entity's net income consists of the net income of the parent, plus the net income of the subsidiary; therefore, the after-tax increase must affect one or the other, or perhaps both.

There are four possible approaches that could be taken:

1. Allocate the gain to the issuing company, because the company purchasing the bonds is acting as an agent for the issuing company.

2. Allocate the gain to the purchasing company, because its investment led to the retirement of the bonds for consolidation purposes.

3. Allocate the gain to the parent company, because its management controls the actions of all the affiliated companies in the group. This would only be a separate alternative if both parties to the transaction were subsidiaries of that parent.

4. Allocate the gain between the issuing and purchasing companies, because each will record its portion of the gain in future periods.

An allocation of the gain would not be required in the case of 100 percent owned subsidiaries because there would be no noncontrolling interest in the consolidated financial statements. The approach adopted is very important when the subsidiaries are less than 100 percent owned, because approaches 1, 2, and 4 could result in all or a portion of the gain being allocated to the subsidiary company, and this would affect noncontrolling interest. The *CICA Handbook* is silent regarding the approach to be taken. However, an exposure draft issued prior to the release of Section 1600 indicated a preference for alternative 4. When Section 1600 was released, the preference indicated in the exposure draft had been deleted. In the illustrations that follow, any gains (losses) from the elimination of intercompany bondholding will be allocated to the purchasing and issuing affiliates (approach 4), because it reflects how each company will actually record the transaction in future years. The agency approach is briefly discussed on page 316.

Calculation of the Portion of the Gain Allocated to the Affiliates

From the point of view of the purchasing affiliate, the cost of the acquisition is compared with the par value of the bonds acquired, the difference being a gain or loss. From the point of view of the issuing affiliate, it cost an amount equal to the par value of bonds to retire the carrying value of the liability, with the difference also resulting in a gain or loss.

The gain and its allocation can be calculated in the following manner:

Par (face) value of bond liability	$10,000
Cost of investment in bonds	9,600
Gain allocated to purchasing affiliate — before tax	$ 400
Carrying amount of bond liability	$10,200
Par (face) value of bond liability	10,000
Gain allocated to issuing affiliate — before tax	$ 200

Notice that the gain to the entity of $600 is made up of the two gains allocated to the affiliates (400 + 200 = 600). Both the entity's gain and the amounts allocated are expressed in before-tax dollars. The following chart is useful in calculating the after-tax amounts required when the entity's after-tax net income is being allocated to the two equities.

	Entity			Parent Co.			Sub Inc.		
	Before tax	40% tax	After tax	Before tax	40% tax	After tax	Before tax	40% tax	After tax
Gain on bond retirement — Dec. 31, Year 1	$600	$240	$360	$200	$80	$120	$400	$160	$240

The Year 1 financial statements of the two companies are shown in Exhibit 8.5. Parent Co. has used the cost method to account for its investment.

The net incomes and total assets of the two companies are unchanged from previous examples. However, the details on each statement have been changed to reflect the intercompany bond transaction that occurred on December 31, Year 1. Remember that the intercompany bond purchase occurred on that date, and that the interest expense of Parent for Year 1 was paid to bondholders outside the consolidated entity. The amount of expense ($950) is made up of the $1,000 interest paid less the $50 amortization of the issue premium.

Exhibit 8.5

YEAR 1 INCOME STATEMENTS

	Parent	Sub
Sales	$20,000	$ 8,000
Interest expense	$ 950	—
Miscellaneous expense	13,450	5,200
Income tax expense	2,200	1,100
	$16,600	$ 6,300
Net income	$ 3,400	$ 1,700

YEAR 1 RETAINED EARNINGS STATEMENTS

	Parent	Sub
Balance, January 1	$12,000	$ 4,500
Net income	3,400	1,700
	15,400	6,200
Dividends	2,000	—
Balance, December 31	$13,400	$ 6,200

BALANCE SHEETS — December 31, Year 1

	Parent	Sub
Assets (misc.)	$29,150	$13,600
Investment in Parent Co. bonds	—	9,600
Investment in Sub Inc.	11,250	—
	$40,400	$23,200
Miscellaneous liabilities	$ 1,800	$ 9,000
Bonds payable	10,200	—
Common stock	15,000	8,000
Retained earnings	13,400	6,200
	$40,400	$23,200

Before the Year 1 consolidated financial statements are prepared, the following two calculations are made:

CALCULATION OF CONSOLIDATED NET INCOME — Year 1

Net income — Parent Co.		$3,400
Add bond gain allocated		120
Adjusted		3,520
Net income — Sub Inc.	1,700	
Add bond gain allocated	240	
Adjusted	1,940	
Parent Co. ownership	90%	1,746
Consolidated net income		$5,266
Noncontrolling interest (10% × 1,940)		$ 194

CALCULATION OF NONCONTROLLING INTEREST
December 31, Year 1

Sub Inc.		
Common stock		$ 8,000
Retained earnings		6,200
		14,200
Add bond gain allocated		240
Adjusted		14,440
		10%
		$ 1,444

Exhibit 8.6 illustrates the direct approach to the preparation of the Year 1 consolidated financial statements.

Elimination entries (i) and (ii) were described earlier. At this stage it is useful to prepare the following proof of the retained earnings amount shown in the consolidated balance sheet:

CALCULATION OF CONSOLIDATED RETAINED EARNINGS
December 31, Year 1

Retained earnings — Parent Co.		$13,400
Add bond gain allocated		120
Adjusted		13,520
Retained earnings — Sub Inc.	6,200	
Acquisition	4,500	
Increase since acquisition	1,700	
Add bond gain allocated	240	
Adjusted	1,940	
	90%	1,746
		$15,266

The chart prepared to allocate the gain in both before-tax and after-tax dollars (page 303) was used in preparing the consolidated income statement and in calculating consolidated net income and retained earnings, as follows:

1. The entity column reflects the amounts used in preparing the consolidated income statement. Note that the after-tax column is not used.

Exhibit 8.6	

Year 1 Consolidated Statements
Adjusted for Intercompany Bondholdings
(direct approach)

PARENT COMPANY
CONSOLIDATED INCOME STATEMENT
for the Year Ended December 31, Year 1

Sales (20,000 + 8,000)	$28,000
Gain on bond retirement (0 + 0 + **600**)(i)	600
	$28,600
Interest expense (950 + 0)	$ 950
Miscellaneous expense (13,450 + 5,200)	18,650
Income tax expense (2,200 + 1,100 + **240**)(ii)	3,540
	$23,140
Net income — entity	$ 5,460
Less noncontrolling interest	194
Net income	$ 5,266

PARENT COMPANY
CONSOLIDATED RETAINED EARNINGS STATEMENT
for the Year Ended December 31, Year 1

Balance, January 1	$12,000
Net income	5,266
	17,266
Dividends	2,000
Balance, December 31	$15,266

PARENT COMPANY
CONSOLIDATED BALANCE SHEET
December 31, Year 1

Assets — miscellaneous (29,150 + 13,600)		$42,750
Investment in Parent Co. bonds (0 + 9,600 – **9600**)(i)		–0–
		$42,750
Miscellaneous liabilities (1,800 + 9,000)		$10,800
Bonds payable (10,200 + 0 – **10,200**)(i)		–0–
Future income tax (0 + 0 + **240**)(ii)		240
Total liabilities		11,040
Noncontrolling interest		1,444
Shareholders' equity		
Common stock	15,000	
Retained earnings	15,266	30,266
		$42,750

2. Both of the allocation columns (Parent Co. and Sub Inc.) were used to calculate consolidated net income and noncontrolling interest for the year, and to calculate noncontrolling interest and consolidated retained earnings at the end of the year, but only in after-tax amounts. This is because they are used to adjust the after-tax net incomes and equities of the two companies. The before-tax and tax columns are presented only to show that the columns cross-add.

In summary, the eliminations made for the intercompany bondholdings had the following effect on the consolidated statements:

1. The elimination of $9,600 in assets and $10,200 in liabilities resulted in a $600 before-tax gain, which was reflected in the income statement.

2. An increase of $240 (40% x 600) to income tax expense and to a future tax liability reflected the tax effects of the gain.

3. The two adjustments in the income statement increased the net income of the entity by $360; this was allocated to the two equities in the balance sheet, as follows:

	Total	Noncontrolling interest	Controlling interest
Gain allocated to Parent Co.	$120	—	$120
Gain allocated to Sub Inc.	240	24	216
	$360	$24	$336

4. The adjustments made in preparing the consolidated balance sheet can be summarized conceptually as follows:

Asset side:
Investment in bonds — 9,600

Liability side:
Bonds payable	– 10,200
Future income tax	+ 240
Noncontrolling interest	+ 24
Consolidated retained earnings	+ 336
	– 9,600

Equity Method Journal Entries If Parent has used the equity method, the following entries are made on December 31, Year 1:

Investment in Sub Inc.	1,530	
Investment income		1,530
90% of the Year 1 net income of Sub Inc.		
(90% x 1,700 = 1,530)		

Investment in Sub Inc.	120	
Investment income		120
Bond gain allocated to Parent Co.		

Investment in Sub Inc.	216	
Investment income		216
90% of bond gain allocated to Sub Inc.		
(90% x 240 = 216)		

The related equity-method accounts of Parent will show the following changes and balances in Year 1:

	Investment in Sub Inc.	Investment income
January 1, Year 1	$11,250	
December 31, Year 1		
Income from Sub Inc.	1,530	1,530
Bond gain to parent	120	120
90 percent of bond gain to subsidiary	216	216
Balance, December 31, Year 1	$13,116	$1,866

Appendix B of this chapter illustrates the working paper approach to the preparation of the Year 1 consolidated financial statements.

Accounting for Gain in Subsequent Years

We will now focus on Year 2 so that we can illustrate the consolidation eliminations that must be made in years subsequent to the original intercompany bond purchase.

At the end of Year 2, the two companies prepared the financial statements shown in Exhibit 8.7.

Focus initially on the items "interest revenue" and "interest expense," which each company recorded in the following manner:

Parent Company

Interest expense	1,000	
Cash		1,000
To record payment of Year 2 interest		

Bonds payable	50	
Interest expense		50
To amortize issue premium $(200 \div 4 = 50)$		

Sub Inc.

Cash	1,000	
Interest revenue		1,000
To record receipt of Year 2 interest		

Investment in bonds of Parent Co.	100	
Interest revenue		100
To amortize discount on the purchase of bonds $(400 \div 4 = 100)$		

Notice that the entry recording the amortization of the issue premium and the purchase discount increased the respective net incomes of the two companies. Thus, in Year 2, Parent recorded one-quarter of the original gain allocated to it in Year 1 $(200 \times 1/4 = 50)$; in the same manner, Sub also recorded one-quarter of the original gain allocated to it in Year 1 $(400 \times 1/4 = 100)$. Because the bonds mature four years after the date of the intercompany purchase, and because the original gain on bond retirement was created because of the existence of the unamortized issue premium and the discount on the intercompany purchase of bonds $(200 + 400 = 600)$, the concept that the gain is realized on the consolidated financial statements before it is recorded by the constituent companies becomes evident.

Both Sub's interest revenue of $1,100 $(1,000 + 100)$ and Parent's interest expense of $950 $(1,000 - 50)$ represent intercompany revenues and expenses that are eliminated on the Year 2 consolidated income statement with the following incomplete working paper entry:

Exhibit 8.7

YEAR 2 INCOME STATEMENTS

	Parent	Sub
Sales	$25,000	$10,900
Interest revenue	—	1,100
	$25,000	$12,000
Interest expense	$ 950	—
Miscellaneous expense	17,400	6,900
Income tax expense	2,600	2,000
	$20,950	$ 8,900
Net income	$ 4,050	$ 3,100

YEAR 2 RETAINED EARNINGS STATEMENTS

	Parent	Sub
Balance, January 1	$13,400	$ 6,200
Net income	4,050	3,100
	17,450	9,300
Dividends	2,500	—
Balance, December 31	$14,950	$ 9,300

BALANCE SHEETS — December 31, Year 2

	Parent	Sub
Assets (misc.)	$32,700	$18,600
Investment in Parent Co. bonds	—	9,700
Investment in Sub Inc.	11,250	—
	$43,950	$28,300
Miscellaneous liabilities	$ 3,850	$11,000
Bonds payable	10,150	—
Common stock	15,000	8,000
Retained earnings	14,950	9,300
	$43,950	$28,300

Interest revenue	1,100	
Interest expense		950

To eliminate Year 2 intercompany interest revenue and expense

In past examples, the elimination of intercompany revenues and expenses (sales and purchases, rental revenue and expense, etc.) had no effect on the net income of the entity, because the amounts eliminated were always equal. Referring back to the journal entries made by both companies, you will see that this equal component is still present. We are still eliminating $1,000 interest revenue and expense in the working paper elimination. However, we are also eliminating the portions of the gain on bond retirement that were recorded by both companies as a result of the amortization of the premium and discount in Year 2. Failure to do this would result in the gain on bond retirement being recorded twice over the life of the bonds. It is because we do not allow this portion of the gain to be reflected in the Year 2 consolidated income statement that we have an unequal elimination of intercompany revenue and expense on the working paper elimination entry. The elimination of $1,100 intercompany interest revenue and $950 intercompany interest expense decreases the before-tax net income of the entity by $150. We will describe this reduction of the entity's before-tax net income as the "interest elimination loss."

The realization of a gain on bond retirement on the consolidated income statement in the year of acquisition of intercompany bonds will always result in an "interest elimination loss" affecting the entity's before-tax net income in all subsequent consolidated income statements until the bonds mature. This "interest elimination loss" does not appear as such in the consolidated income statement, because it results from eliminating an amount of intercompany interest revenue that is larger than the amount of intercompany interest expense eliminated. Conversely, the realization of a loss on bond retirement in the year of acquisition of intercompany bonds will always result in an "interest elimination gain" in all subsequent consolidated income statements, because the amount of interest expense eliminated will always be larger than the amount of interest revenue eliminated.

As stated previously, the entity's Year 2 before-tax net income has been decreased by $150. This results from eliminating the portion of the gain on bond retirement recorded by the constituent companies in Year 2. Recall that the entire before-tax gain was realized for consolidated purposes in Year 1; and also, that to satisfy the matching process an income tax expense was recorded and a future tax liability was set up on the consolidated balance sheet. Both companies paid (or accrued) income tax on a portion of this gain in Year 2 — a total of $60 (150 × 40%). These companies also recorded the income tax paid (or accrued) as an expense, but from a consolidated point of view, the payment was a reduction of the future tax liability previously set up. We must therefore decrease income tax expense when preparing the consolidated income statement[1] because it is not a consolidated expense. The complete income statement working paper elimination entry is as follows:

(i)	Interest revenue	1,100	
	Interest expense		950
	Income tax expense		60

To eliminate Year 2 intercompany interest revenue and expense and to adjust for the income tax effect of the elimination

The addition of the income tax expense entry still leaves us with an unequal elimination on the consolidated income statement. However, this "interest elimination loss" is now in after-tax dollars and amounts to $90 (1,100 – 950 – 60). A reconstruction of the intercompany bond chart for the life of the bonds will illustrate how this loss is allocated to the two constituents each year.

---

[1] We must also reduce the amount of the future tax liability that was set up in Year 1 by $60.

	Entity			Parent Co.			Sub Inc.		
	Before tax	40% tax	After tax	Before tax	40% tax	After tax	Before tax	40% tax	After tax
Gain on bond, Dec. 31, Year 1	$600	$240	$360	$200	$80	$120	$400	$160	$240
Interest elimination loss — Year 2	150	60	90	50	20	30	100	40	60
Balance — gain — Dec. 31, Year 2	450	180	270	150	60	90	300	120	180
Interest elimination loss — Year 3	150	60	90	50	20	30	100	40	60
Balance — gain — Dec. 31, Year 3	300	120	180	100	40	60	200	80	120
Interest elimination loss — Year 4	150	60	90	50	20	30	100	40	60
Balance — gain — Dec. 31, Year 4	150	60	90	50	20	30	100	40	60
Interest elimination loss — Year 5	150	60	90	50	20	30	100	40	60
Balance, Dec. 31, Year 5	-0-	-0-	-0-	-0-	-0-	-0-	-0-	-0-	-0-

To further illustrate this, examine the interest accounts of the two companies from the date of the intercompany purchase to the date of maturity of the bonds.

Year ended Dec. 31	Parent's interest expense	Sub's interest revenue	Difference
Year 2	$ 950	$1,100	$150
Year 3	950	1,100	150
Year 4	950	1,100	150
Year 5	950	1,100	150
	$3,800	$4,400	$600

The preparation of a bond chart would be the first step in the preparation of the Year 2 consolidated statements. This chart would have the same format as the one shown above, but would be comprised of only the first three lines from that particular chart. The next step would be a calculation of consolidated net income for Year 2, as follows:

Net income — Parent Co.		$4,050
Less interest elimination loss allocated		30
Adjusted		4,020
Net income — Sub Inc.	3,100	
Less interest elimination loss allocated	60	
Adjusted	3,040	
Parent Co. ownership	90%	2,736
Consolidated net income		$6,756
Noncontrolling interest (10% × 3,040)		$ 304

The Year 2 consolidated financial statements prepared using the direct approach are shown in Exhibit 8.8.

Exhibit 8.8

Year 2 Consolidated Statements
Adjusted for Intercompany Bondholdings
(direct approach)

PARENT COMPANY
CONSOLIDATED INCOME STATEMENT
for the Year Ended December 31, Year 2

Sales (25,000 + 10,900)	$35,900
Interest revenue (0 + 1,100 − **1,100**)(i)	–0–
	$35,900
Interest expense (950 + 0 − **950**)(i)	–0–
Miscellaneous expense (17,400 + 6,900)	24,300
Income tax expense (2,600 + 2,000 − **60**)(i)	4,540
	$28,840
Net income — entity	$ 7,060
Less noncontrolling interest	304
Net income	$ 6,756

PARENT COMPANY
CONSOLIDATED RETAINED EARNINGS STATEMENT
for the Year Ended December 31, Year 2

Balance, January 1	$15,266
Net income	6,756
	22,022
Dividends	2,500
Balance, December 31	$19,522

PARENT COMPANY
CONSOLIDATED BALANCE SHEET
December 31, Year 2

Assets — miscellaneous (32,700 + 18,600)		$51,300
Investment in Parent Co. bonds (0 + 9,700 − **9,700**)(ii)		–0–
		$51,300
Miscellaneous liabilities (3,850 + 11,000)		$14,850
Bonds payable (10,150 + 0 − **10,150**)(ii)		–0–
Future income tax (0 + 0 + **180**)(ii)		180
Total liabilities		15,030
Noncontrolling interest		1,748
Shareholders' equity		
Common stock	15,000	
Retained earnings	19,522	34,522
		$51,300

The unequal elimination of the intercompany interest revenue and expense, and the income tax adjustment made in the preparation of the consolidated income statement, were explained on page 310. This created the "hidden" after-tax interest elimination loss of $90, in this statement. This loss is depicted and allocated in the bond chart on page 311.

Before the consolidated retained earnings statement is prepared, the calculation shown below is made.

Using this calculation, consolidated net income, and the dividends of Parent, we can now prepare the Year 2 consolidated retained earnings as shown.

Before preparing the Year 2 consolidated balance sheet, we must first calculate noncontrolling interest. This calculation is shown below.

CALCULATION OF CONSOLIDATED RETAINED EARNINGS
January 1, Year 2

Retained earnings — Parent Co.		$13,400
Add bond gain allocated (Dec. 31, Year 1)		120
Adjusted		13,520
Retained earnings — Sub Inc.	6,200	
Acquisition retained earnings	4,500	
Increase since acquisition	1,700	
Add bond gain allocated (Dec. 31, Year 1)	240	
Adjusted	1,940	
Parent Co. ownership	90%	1,746
Consolidated retained earnings		$15,266

CALCULATION OF NONCONTROLLING INTEREST
December 31, Year 2

Sub Inc.	
Common stock	$ 8,000
Retained earnings	9,300
	17,300
Add bond gain allocated as at Dec. 31, Year 2	180
Adjusted shareholders' equity	17,480
	10%
	$ 1,748

The eliminations made in the preparation of the Year 2 consolidated balance sheet require elaboration. The item "Investment in Parent Co. bonds" in the balance sheet of Sub has a balance of $9,700 after the Year 2 amortization of the discount on purchase (9,600 + 100). Bonds payable in the balance sheet of Parent Co. has a balance of $10,150 after the Year 2 amortization on the issue premium (10,200 – 50). When the consolidated balance sheet is being prepared, these two intercompany accounts are eliminated by the following *incomplete* entry:

Bonds payable	10,150	
Investment in Parent Co. bonds		9,700
To eliminate the intercompany bonds on December 31, Year 2		

This entry is somewhat similar to the entry made on December 31, Year 1 (see page 301), except that the before-tax amount needed to balance at this time is a gain of $450 instead of the $600 gain that was required a year ago. Furthermore, the $450 gain does not appear as such in the consolidated income statement in Year 2. Recall that the $600 gain appeared on the Year 1 consolidated income statement. A gain on bond retirement appears as such only once in the year of the intercompany purchase. Recall also that a portion of the gain was recorded in Year 2 by Parent and Sub, was eliminated in preparing the Year 2 consolidated income statement, and is not reflected again. The $450 needed to balance is a before-tax gain as at December 31, Year 2. A referral to the bond chart (page 311) indicates that the entity's future income tax liability with respect to this gain is $180 as at this date. We can now complete the working paper entry by including the future tax component as follows:

Bonds payable	10,150	
Investment in Parent Co. bonds		9,700
Future income tax		180

To eliminate the intercompany bond accounts and set up the future tax liability as at December 31, Year 2

The after-tax gain needed to balance is now $270. The bond chart shows this gain as allocated $90 to Parent and $180 to Sub.

To summarize, the Year 2 elimination entries made for the intercompany bond-holdings had the following effect on the consolidated statements.

1. The adjustments made in the income statement created an after-tax interest elimination loss of $90, which decreased the entity's net income and was allocated to the two equities as follows:

	Total	Noncontrolling interest	Controlling interest
Loss allocated to Parent Co.	$30	—	$30
Loss allocated to Sub Inc.	60	6	54
	$90	$6	$84

2. The elimination of $9,700 in assets and $10,150 in bond liabilities, together with the adjustment to reflect the $180 future tax liability, resulted in an after-tax increase of $270 in the equity side of the balance sheet. This was allocated to the two equities, at December 31, Year 2, as follows:

	Total	Noncontrolling interest	Controlling interest
Loss allocated to Parent Co.	$ 90	—	$ 90
Loss allocated to Sub Inc.	180	18	162
	$270	$18	$252

Remember that the original $600 gain in Year 1 was allocated to the two equities in the consolidated balance sheet as at December 31, Year 1 (see page 303).

3. The adjustments made in the preparation of both the December 31, Year 2, balance sheet and the Year 2 income statement can be summarized conceptually with respect to their effect on the consolidated balance sheet as follows:

Asset side: Investment in bonds				– $ 9,700
Liability side:				
Bonds payable				– $10,150
Future income tax				+ 180
Noncontrolling interest				
Balance, Dec. 31, Year 1	+	24		
Year 2 entity net income	–	6	+	18
Consolidated retained earnings				
Balance, Dec. 31, Year 1	+	336		
Year 2 entity net income	–	84	+	252
				– $ 9,700

The $252 increase in consolidated retained earnings is automatically reflected when the consolidated income and retained earnings statements are prepared. The $18 increase in noncontrolling interest is captured in the calculation of the amount of this equity (see page 313).

Equity Method Journal Entries   If Parent has used the equity method, the following entries will be made on December 31, Year 2:

Investment in Sub Inc.	2,790	
Investment income		2,790
90% of the Year 2 net income of Sub Inc. (90% × 3,100 = 2,790)		
Investment income	30	
Investment in Sub Inc.		30
Interest elimination loss allocated to Parent Co.		
Investment income	54	
Investment in Sub Inc.		54
90% of interest elimination loss allocated to Sub Inc. (90% × 60 = 54)		

The related equity-method accounts of Parent will show the following changes and balances in Year 2:

	Investment in Sub Inc.	Investment income
December 31, Year 1	$13,116	
December 31, Year 2		
Income from Sub Inc.	2,790	2,790
Interest loss to parent	(30)	(30)
90% of interest loss to subsidiary	(54)	(54)
Balance, December 31, Year 2	$15,822	$2,706

Appendix B, later in this chapter, illustrates the working paper approach to preparing the Year 2 consolidated financial statements.

Less Than 100 Percent Purchase of Affiliate's Bonds

Our example assumed that Sub purchased 100 percent of Parent's bonds for $9,600 on December 31, Year 1. Suppose we changed the assumption so that only 40 percent of Parent's bonds were purchased, for $3,840. The elimination needed to prepare the Year 1 consolidated statements would be:

Bonds payable (40% × 10,200)	4,080	
Investment in bonds of Parent Co.		3,840
Gain on bond retirement		240

If only 40 percent of the bond liability has been eliminated, the consolidated balance sheet will show bonds payable amounting to $6,120, representing the 60 percent that is not intercompany and is payable to bondholders outside the entity.

When consolidated income statements are later prepared, only 40 percent of the interest expense will be eliminated; the remaining 60 percent will be left as consolidated interest expense.

Intercompany Purchases During the Fiscal Year

Our previous example also assumed that the intercompany purchase of bonds took place on the last day of the fiscal year. If the purchase took place *during* the fiscal year, the Year 1 consolidated income statement contains both the gain on bond retirement and the hidden loss resulting from the elimination of intercompany interest revenue earned and expense incurred for the period subsequent to the acquisition.

Gains (losses) Not Allocated to the Two Equities

On page 302 the four approaches that can be taken to allocate bond gains (losses) were outlined. The illustrations used approach 4; the calculations for this approach are more complicated than for approaches 1 to 3. Because the *CICA Handbook* is silent in this matter, any of these approaches may be used. Under approaches 1 to 3, the gain or loss is allocated to only one of the companies, and the bond chart (page 311) is much simpler, as it needs only the entity columns.

The "agency" method (#1) may well have the greatest merit: because only a company that has issued bonds can logically retire them, allocating the gain or loss to the issuing company puts the emphasis on the economic substance of the transaction rather than on its actual form. In the example used, the entire $600 gain would be allocated to Parent Co. If the example used was changed so that the bonds were originally issued by Sub. Inc., and the agency method was followed, the $600 gain would at first be allocated to the subsidiary; however, because Parent owns 90 percent of Sub, noncontrolling interest would reflect 10 percent of this gain.

Gains (losses) Allocated to Two Equities — Loss to One, Gain to the Other

Suppose that the issuing affiliate had $10,000 in bonds outstanding with a carrying value of $10,700, and the purchasing affiliate paid $10,100 to acquire all of the issue on the open market. From the entity point of view there is a before-tax gain on bond retirement of $600, calculated as follows:

Carrying amount of bonds	$10,700
Cost of investment in bonds	10,100
Gain on bond retirement	$ 600

If we allocate the gain to the two affiliates (approach 4), we see that the issuing affiliate is allocated a gain of $700, while the purchasing affiliate is allocated a loss of $100. This can be verified by the following calculation:

Carrying amount of bond liability	$10,700
Par value of bond liability	10,000
Gain to issuing affiliate	$ 700

Cost of investment in bonds	$10,100
Par value of bond liability	10,000
Loss to purchasing affiliate	$ 100

In subsequent years the entity's "interest elimination loss" will be allocated as a *loss* to the issuing affiliate and a *gain* to the purchasing affiliate.

Effective Yield Method of Amortization

Our previous examples have assumed that both companies use the straight-line method to amortize the premiums and discounts. This method leads to fairly easy calculations because the yearly amortizations are equal. If one or both companies use the effective yield method of amortization, the calculations become more complex, but the concepts remain the same. Remember that it is the reversal of the affiliates' amortization of premiums or discounts that causes the interest elimination losses or gains in years subsequent to the date of the intercompany purchase.

SUMMARY

This chapter completed the illustrations of the holdback and realization of intercompany profits and gains in assets, by examining the consolidation procedures involved when the profit is in an asset subject to amortization. When the assets are inventory or land, profit realization is based on the sale of the asset outside the entity. Profit realization on assets subject to amortization takes place as the assets are consumed by the amortization process. Because there are differences between the periods in which the tax is paid and the periods in which the gains are realized in the consolidated statements, income tax must be allocated. While all illustrations used in this chapter were gains, the same basic concepts apply to intercompany losses.

The second part of the chapter examined the gains and losses that are created in the consolidated statements by the elimination of intercompany bondholdings. These gains and losses can occur only if there were premiums or discounts involved in the issue or purchase of these bonds. In the case of intercompany bondholdings, the gains or losses are recognized in the consolidated statements before they are recorded by the affiliated companies; whereas intercompany asset gains are recorded by the affiliated companies before they are recognized in the consolidated statements.

Our initial examination of consolidations in earlier chapters focused first on the working paper approach and then on the direct approach. As the concepts became more complex we concentrated on the direct approach, and working papers were shifted to end-of-chapter appendices. This change of focus was intentional. Examination problems often contain complex purchase discrepancy allocations as well as intercompany asset and bond transactions. Readers who have mastered the direct approach will probably find that they can answer exam questions more quickly with it.

SELF-STUDY PROBLEM 1

The following are the 2002 financial statements of Penn Company and its subsidiary Sill Corp.

	Penn	Sill
2002 income statements		
Miscellaneous revenues	$500,000	$300,000
Investment income	9,194	—
Gain on sale of equipment	14,000	—
Gain on sale of patent	—	7,500
	$523,194	$307,500
Miscellaneous expenses	$309,600	$186,500
Depreciation expense	120,000	80,000
Patent amortization expense	800	—
Income tax expense	33,000	16,000
	$463,400	$282,500
Net income	$ 59,794	$ 25,000
2002 retained earnings statements		
Balance, January 1	$162,000	$154,000
Net income	59,794	25,000
	221,794	179,000
Dividends	25,000	8,000
Balance, December 31	$196,794	$171,000
Balance sheets, December 31, 2002		
Miscellaneous assets	$271,600	$131,000
Land and buildings	200,000	656,000
Equipment	—	44,000*
Accumulated depreciation	(80,000)	(250,000)
Patent (net)	19,200	—
Investment in Sill Corp.	285,994	—
	$696,794	$581,000
Miscellaneous liabilities	$100,000	$210,000
Common stock	400,000	200,000
Retained earnings	196,794	171,000
	$696,794	$581,000

* For illustrative purposes, we are assuming that this is the only equipment owned by either company.

Other Information

Penn owns 80% of Sill and has used the equity method to account for its investment. The purchase discrepancy on acquisition date has been fully amortized for consolidation purposes prior to 2002, and there were no unrealized intercompany profits or losses in the assets of the companies on December 31, 2001. During 2002, the following intercompany transactions took place:

1. On January 1, 2002, Penn sold used equipment to Sill and recorded a $14,000 gain on the transaction as follows:

Selling price of equipment		$44,000
Book value of equipment sold		
Cost	60,000	
Accumulated depreciation — Dec. 31, 2001	30,000	30,000
Gain on sale of equipment		$14,000

This equipment had an estimated remaining life of 8 years on this date.

2. On January 1, 1992, Sill developed a patent at a cost of $34,000. It has been amortizing this patent over the maximum legal life of 17 years. On October 1, 2002, Sill sold the patent to Penn and recorded a $7,500 gain, calculated as follows:

Selling price of patent			$20,000
Book value of patent sold			
Cost	34,000		
Amortization:			
To December 31, 2001 (10 × 2,000)	20,000		
2002 ($3/4$ × 2,000)	1,500	21,500	12,500
Gain on sale of patent			$ 7,500

Penn is amortizing this patent over its remaining legal life of $6^1/4$ years.

3. Both gains were assessed income tax at a rate of 40%.

Required:

(a) Using the reported net incomes of both companies, prepare a calculation that shows that Penn's net income is equal to consolidated net income.
(b) Using Penn's investment account, prepare a calculation that shows that the purchase discrepancy is fully amortized.
(c) Prepare the following 2002 consolidated financial statements:
  (i) Income statement.
  (ii) Retained earnings statement.
  (iii) Balance sheet.

Solution to Self-study Problem 1

UNREALIZED PROFITS

	Before tax	40% tax	After tax
Equipment (Penn selling):			
Gain recorded, Jan. 1, 2002	$14,000	$5,600	$8,400
Depreciation, 2002 (14,000 ÷ 8)	1,750	700	1,050
Balance unrealized, Dec. 31, 2002	$12,250	$4,900	$7,350
Patent (Sill selling):			
Gain recorded, Oct. 1, 2002	$ 7,500	$3,000	$4,500
Amortization, 2002 (7,500 ÷ $6^1/4$ × $1/4$)	300	120	180
Balance unrealized Dec. 31, 2002	$ 7,200	$2,880	$4,320
Future income taxes — December 31, 2002:			
Equipment profit		$4,900	
Patent profit		2,880	
		$7,780	

(a)

Net income, Penn Co.		$59,794
Less investment income		9,194
Net income, Penn Co. — own operations		50,600
Less January 1 equipment gain		8,400
		42,200
Add equipment gain realized in 2002		1,050
Adjusted net income		43,250
Net income, Sill Corp.	25,000	
Less October 1 patent gain	4,500	
	20,500	
Add patent gain realized in 2002	180	
Adjusted net income	20,680	
Penn's ownership	80%	16,544
Consolidated net income		$59,794

Penn Company — investment income:		
Adjusted net income, Sill Corp (above)		$20,680
		80%
		16,544
Less unrealized equipment gain, Dec. 31, 2002 (8,400 − 1,050)		7,350
		$ 9,194

(b)

Investment in Sill Corp. (equity method):		
Balance, Dec. 31, 2002		$285,994
Add unrealized equipment gain, Dec. 31, 2002		7,350
		293,344
Sill Corp., Dec. 31, 2002:		
Common stock	200,000	
Retained earnings	171,000	
	371,000	
Less unrealized patent gain, Dec. 31, 2002	4,320	
Adjusted shareholders' equity	366,680	
Penn's ownership	80%	293,344
Unamortized purchase discrepancy		–0–

(c) (i)

2002 CONSOLIDATED INCOME STATEMENT

Miscellaneous revenues (500,000 + 300,000)	$800,000
Miscellaneous expenses (309,600 + 186,500)	$496,100
Depreciation expense (120,000 + 80,000 − **1,750**)	198,250
Patent amortization expense (800 − **300**)	500
Income tax expense (33,000 + 16,000 − **7,780**)	41,220
	$736,070
Net income — entity	$ 63,930
Less noncontrolling interest	4,136*
Net income	$ 59,794

* 20,680 × 20% = 4,136 *(see part a)*

(ii)

2002 CONSOLIDATED RETAINED EARNINGS STATEMENT

Balance, January 1	$162,000
Net income	59,794
	221,794
Dividends	25,000
Balance, December 31	$196,794

(iii)

CONSOLIDATED BALANCE SHEET — December 31, 2002

Miscellaneous assets (271,600 + 131,000)	$402,600
Land and buildings (200,000 + 656,000)	856,000
Equipment (44,000 − **14,000** + **30,000***)	60,000
Accumulated depreciation (80,000 + 250,000 − **1,750** + **30,000***)	(358,250)
Patent (19,200 − **7,200**)	12,000
Future income tax (0 + 0 + 7,780)	7,780
	$980,130
Miscellaneous liabilities (100,000 + 210,000)	$310,000
Noncontrolling interest**	73,336
Common stock	400,000
Retained earnings	196,794
	$980,130

* It is necessary to increase equipment and accumulated depreciation by $30,000 in order to re-establish the original historical cost of the equipment and the accumulated depreciation as at the date of the intercompany sale.

** Sill Corp. —

Adjusted shareholders' equity (see part (b))	$366,680
	20%
Noncontrolling interest	$ 73,336

SELF-STUDY PROBLEM 2

The following are the financial statements of Parson Corp. and Sloan Inc. prepared on December 31, 2002:

2002 INCOME STATEMENTS

	Parson	Sloan
Miscellaneous revenues	$650,000	$200,000
Interest revenue	5,625	—
Dividend revenue	7,500	—
	$663,125	$200,000
Miscellaneous expense	$432,000	$129,600
Interest expense	—	9,700
Income tax expense	92,000	24,000
	$524,000	$163,300
Net income	$139,125	$ 36,700

2002 RETAINED EARNINGS STATEMENTS

Balance, January 1	$245,000	$ 90,000
Net income	139,125	36,700
	384,125	126,700
Dividends	70,000	10,000
Balance, December 31	$314,125	$116,700

BALANCE SHEETS — December 31, 2002

Miscellaneous assets	$605,000	$372,600
Investment in Sloan shares	98,000	—
Investment in Sloan bonds	61,125	—
	$764,125	$372,600
Miscellaneous liabilities	$300,000	$ 75,000
Bonds payable	—	100,000
Premium on bonds	—	900
Common stock	150,000	80,000
Retained earnings	314,125	116,700
	$764,125	$372,600

Other Information

1. Parson acquired 75% of Sloan on January 1, 1998, at a cost of $98,000. On this date Sloan's retained earnings amounted to $40,000, and the purchase discrepancy was allocated entirely to goodwill. Impairment tests conducted yearly since acquisition yielded a loss of $3,200 in 1999 and a further loss of $800 in 2002. Parson uses the cost method to account for the investment.

2. Sloan has a 10%, $100,000 bond issue outstanding. These bonds were originally issued at a premium and mature on December 31, 2005. On January 1, 2002, the unamortized issue premium amounted to $1,200. Sloan uses the straight-line method to amortize the premium.

3. On January 1, 2002, Parson acquired $60,000 face value of Sloan's bonds at a cost of $61,500. The purchase premium is being amortized by Parson using the straight-line method.

4. Both companies pay income tax at a rate of 40%.

5. Gains and losses from intercompany bondholdings are to be allocated to the two companies when consolidated statements are prepared.

Required:

(a) Prepare the following 2002 consolidated financial statements:
   (i) Income statement.
   (ii) Retained earnings statement.
   (iii) Balance sheet.
(b) Prepare a calculation of consolidated retained earnings on December 31, 2002.
(c) Prepare the 2002 journal entries that would be made by Parson if the equity method was used to account for the investment in Sloan's shares.
(d) Calculate the balance in the "Investment in Sloan shares" account as at December 31, 2002, if Parson had used the equity method.

Solution to Self-study Problem 2

Cost of 75% of Sloan		$98,000
Book value of Sloan, January 1, 1998		
Common stock	80,000	
Retained earnings	40,000	
	120,000	
Parson's ownership	75%	90,000
Purchase discrepancy — January 1, 1998		8,000
Allocated to revalue Sloan's net assets		–0–
Balance — goodwill		8,000
Impairment losses		
1998 to 2001	3,200	
2002	800	4,000
Balance — goodwill, December 31, 2002		$ 4,000

INTERCOMPANY TRANSACTIONS
2002 BEFORE-TAX BOND LOSS

Cost of 60% of Sloan's bonds acquired Jan. 1, 2002		$61,500
Carrying amount of liability		
Bonds payable	100,000	
Bond premium	1,200	
	101,200	
Amount acquired by Parson	60%	60,720
Bond loss to be reflected in the 2002 income statement		$ 780
Allocated as follows:		
Cost of bonds		$61,500
Face value of bonds (intercompany portion)		60,000
Before-tax loss — Parson		$ 1,500
Face value of bonds		$60,000
Carrying amount of bonds (intercompany portion)		60,720
Before-tax gain — Sloan		$ 720

INTERCOMPANY INTEREST REVENUE AND EXPENSE

Interest expense		
10% × 100,000	10,000	
Premium amortization (1,200 ÷ 4)	300	
Total expense	9,700	
Intercompany portion	60%	$5,820
Interest revenue		
10% × 60,000	6,000	
Premium amortization (1,500 ÷ 4)	375	5,625
Before tax interest elimination gain to entity		$ 195
Allocated:		
Before tax loss to Sloan (300 × 60%)		$ 180
Before tax gain to Parson		375
Total gain allocated (before-tax dollars)		$ 195

SUMMARY

	Entity			Parson Co.			Sloan Inc.		
	Before tax	40% tax	After tax	Before tax	40% tax	After tax	Before tax	40% tax	After tax
Jan. 1/02 bond loss (gain)	$780	$312	$468	$1,500	$600	$900	$(720)	$(288)	$(432)
Int. elim. gain (loss) 2002	195	78	117	375	150	225	(180)	(72)	(108)
Dec. 31/02 balance loss (gain)	$585	$234	$351	$1,125	$450	$675	$(540)	$(216)	$(324)

(a) (i)

CALCULATION OF CONSOLIDATED NET INCOME, 2002

Net income — Parson		$139,125
Less: Dividend from Sloan	7,500	
Purchase discrepancy amortization	800	
January 1 bond loss allocated	900	9,200
		129,925
Add 2002 interest elimination gain allocated		225
Adjusted net income		130,150
Net income — Sloan	36,700	
Less 2002 interest elimination loss allocated	108	
	36,592	
Add January 1 bond gain allocated	432	
Adjusted net income	37,024	
Parson's ownership	75%	27,768
Consolidated net income		$157,918
Noncontrolling interest (25% × 37,024)		$ 9,256

2002 CONSOLIDATED INCOME STATEMENT

Miscellaneous revenues (650,000 + 200,000)	$850,000
Miscellaneous expense (432,000 + 129,600)	$561,600
Loss on bond retirement	780
Interest expense (9,700 – 5,820)	3,880
Goodwill impairment loss	800
Income tax expense (92,000 + 24,000 – 234)	115,766
	$682,826
Net income, entity	$167,174
Less noncontrolling interest	9,256
Net income	$157,918

(ii)

CALCULATION OF CONSOLIDATED RETAINED EARNINGS
January 1, 2002

Retained earnings — Parson		$245,000
Less goodwill impairment loss		3,200
Adjusted retained earnings		241,800
Retained earnings — Sloan	90,000	
Acquisition	40,000	
Increase since acquisition	50,000	
Parson's ownership	75%	37,500
Consolidated retained earnings, Jan. 1, 2002		$279,300

2002 CONSOLIDATED RETAINED EARNINGS STATEMENT

Balance, January 1	$279,300
Net income	157,918
	437,218
Dividends	70,000
Balance, December 31	$367,218

(iii)
CALCULATION OF NONCONTROLLING INTEREST
December 31, 2002

Shareholders' equity — Sloan		
Common stock		$ 80,000
Retained earnings		116,700
		196,700
Add net 2002 bond gain allocated		324
Adjusted shareholders' equity		197,024
		25%
		$ 49,256

CONSOLIDATED BALANCE SHEET — December 31, 2002

Miscellaneous assets (605,000 + 372,600)		$977,600
Future income tax		234
Goodwill		4,000
		$981,834
Miscellaneous liabilities (300,000 + 75,000)		$375,000
Bonds payable (100,000 – 60,000)		40,000
Premium on bonds (900 – 540)		360
Total liabilities		415,360
Noncontrolling interest		49,256
Shareholders' equity		
Common stock	150,000	
Retained earnings	367,218	517,218
		$981,834

(b)
PROOF — CONSOLIDATED RETAINED EARNINGS
December 31, 2002

Retained earnings — Parson		$314,125
Less goodwill impairment losses (3,200 + 800)	4,000	
Net 2002 bond loss allocated	675	4,675
Adjusted retained earnings		309,450
Retained earnings — Sloan	116,700	
Acquisition	40,000	
Increase since acquisition	76,700	
Add net 2002 bond gain allocated	324	
Adjusted increase	77,024	
Parsons' ownership	75%	57,768
Consolidated retained earnings		$367,218

(c)
EQUITY METHOD JOURNAL ENTRIES

Investment in Sloan	27,525	
Investment income		27,525
75% of Sloan's 2002 net income (75% × 36,700)		
Investment in Sloan	243	
Investment income		243
75% of the net 2002 bond gain allocated to Sloan (75% × 324)		

Cash	7,500	
Investment in Sloan		7,500
Dividends received from Sloan		
Investment income	800	
Investment in Sloan		800
2002 goodwill impairment loss		
Investment income	675	
Investment in Sloan		675
2002 net bond loss allocated to Parson		

(d)

	Investment in Sloan shares
Balance, December 31, 2001 — cost method	$ 98,000
Increase in retained earnings to Jan. 1, 2002 (50,000 × 75%)	37,500
Purchase discrepancy amortization to 2001	(3,200)
Balance, December 31, 2001 — equity method	132,300
Investment income, 2002 (see equity method journal entries)	26,293
Dividends from Sloan	(7,500)
Balance, December 31, 2002 — equity method	$151,093

APPENDIX A

Working Papers for Intercompany Profits in Depreciable Fixed Assets

Exhibit 8.9 illustrates the working paper for the preparation of Year 1 consolidated financial statements when Parent Company has used the cost method to account for its investment.

The following working paper entries were made to arrive at the consolidated amounts:

#a	Investment in Sub Inc. — Parent Co.	1,314	
	Investment income — Parent Co.		1,314
	To adjust the financial statements of Parent to the equity method (see the calculation of consolidated net income on page 291)		
#1	Investment income — Parent Co.	1,314	
	Investment in Sub Inc. — Parent Co.		1,314
	To restate the investment account to the balance at the beginning of the year		
#2	Retained earnings, January 1 — Sub Inc.	450	
	Common stock — Sub Inc.	800	
	Noncontrolling interest (balance sheet)		1,250
	To eliminate 10% of the shareholders' equity of the subsidiary as at the beginning of the year and establish the noncontrolling interest at that date		
#3	Retained earnings, January 1 — Sub Inc.	4,050	
	Common stock — Sub Inc.	7,200	
	Investment in Sub Inc. — Parent Co.		11,250
	To eliminate the parent's share of the shareholders' equity of the subsidiary at the beginning of the year against the parent's investment account		

Exhibit 8.9

**CONSOLIDATED FINANCIAL STATEMENT WORKING PAPER —
COST METHOD
ELIMINATION OF EQUIPMENT PROFIT** — December 31, Year 1

	Parent	Sub	Eliminations Dr.		Eliminations Cr.		Consolidated
Sales	$20,000	$ 7,400					$ 27,400
Gain on sale of equipment		600	(i)	600			
Investment income			(1)	1,314	(a)	1,314	
	$20,000	$ 8,000					$ 27,400
Depreciation exp.	$ 700				(ii)	200	$ 500
Misc. expense	13,700	5,200					18,900
Income tax exp.	2,200	1,100			(iii)	160	3,140
	$16,600	$ 6,300					$ 22,540
Net income, entity							$ 4,860
Noncontrolling interest			(4)	146			146
Net income	$ 3,400	$ 1,700		$ 2,060		$ 1,674	$ 4,714
Retained earnings, Jan. 1	$12,000	$ 4,500	(2)	450			$ 12,000
			(3)	4,050			
Net income	3,400	1,700		2,060		1,674	4,714
	15,400	6,200					16,714
Dividends	2,000						2,000
Retained earnings, Dec. 31	$13,400	$ 6,200		$ 6,560		$ 1,674	$ 14,714
Assets, misc.	$27,750	$23,200					$ 50,950
Equipment	2,100				(i)	600	1,500
Accumulated depreciation	(700)		(ii)	200			(500)
Future income tax			(iii)	160			160
Investment in Sub	11,250		(a)	1,314	(1)	1,314	
					(3)	11,250	
	$40,400	$23,200					$ 52,110
Liabilities	$12,000	$ 9,000					$ 21,000
Common stock	15,000	8,000	(2)	800			15,000
			(3)	7,200			
Retained earnings	13,400	6,200		6,560		1,674	14,714
Noncontrolling interest					(2)	1,250	1,396
					(4)	146	
	$40,400	$23,200		$16,234		$16,234	$ 52,110

#4 Noncontrolling interest (income statement)   146
       Noncontrolling interest (balance sheet)   146
    To allocate the applicable portion of the net income of the entity to the
    noncontrolling interest (see the calculation of consolidated net income on
    page 291)

#i	Gain on sale of equipment — Sub Inc.	600	
	Equipment — Parent Co.		600
	To eliminate the unrealized gain on the income statement and balance sheet		

#ii	Accumulated depreciation — Parent Co.	200	
	Depreciation expense — Parent Co.		200
	To adjust for the intercompany gain contained in each account		

#iii	Future income tax	160	
	Income tax expense		160
	To recognize the tax effect of the unrealized gain being held back		

Exhibit 8.10 contains the Year 2 consolidated financial statement working papers.

The following working paper entries were used:

#a	Investment in Sub Inc. — Parent Co.	4,320	
	Investment income — Parent Co.		3,006
	Retained earnings, Jan. 1 — Parent Co.		1,314
	To adjust the statements of Parent to the equity method (see calculation of consolidated net income and calculation of consolidated retained earnings, page 294)		

#1	Investment income — Parent Co.	3,006	
	Investment in Sub Inc. — Parent Co.		3,006
	To adjust investment account to start-of-year balance		

#2	Retained earnings, Jan. 1 — Sub Inc.	620	
	Common stock — Sub Inc.	800	
	Noncontrolling interest (balance sheet)		1,420
	To eliminate 10% of the shareholders' equity of Sub Inc. at the beginning of the year		

#i	Investment In Sub Inc. — Parent Co.	216	
	Noncontrolling interest (balance sheet)	24	
	Income tax expense	160	
	Depreciation expense		400
	The Year 2 realization of the after-tax equipment profit of $240, and the holdback of the profit from start-of-year noncontrolling interest, and the reversal of the holdback from the start-of-year balance in the investment account		

#ii	Accumulated depreciation	600	
	Equipment		600
	To establish the two accounts to cost		

#3	Retained earnings, Jan. 1 — Sub Inc.	5,580	
	Common stock — Sub Inc.	7,200	
	Investment in Sub Inc. — Parent Co.		12,780
	To eliminate parent's share of start-of-year shareholders' equity of subsidiary against the investment account		

#4	Noncontrolling interest (income statement)	334	
	Noncontrolling interest (balance sheet)		334
	Allocation of entity's Year 2 net income (see calculation of consolidated net income, page 294)		

Exhibit 8.10

CONSOLIDATED FINANCIAL STATEMENT WORKING PAPER — COST METHOD
REALIZATION OF EQUIPMENT PROFIT — December 31, Year 2

	Parent	Sub	Eliminations Dr.		Eliminations Cr.		Consolidated
Sales	$25,000	$12,000					$37,000
Investment income			(1)	3,006	(a)	3,006	
	$25,000	$12,000					$37,000
Depreciation expense	$ 1,400				(i)	400	$ 1,000
Miscellaneous expense	16,950	6,900					23,850
Income tax expense	2,600	2,000	(i)	160			4,760
	$20,950	$ 8,900					$29,610
Net income — entity							$ 7,390
Noncontrolling interest			(4)	334			334
Net income	$ 4,050	$ 3,100		$ 3,500		$ 3,406	$ 7,056
Retained earnings, Jan. 1	$13,400	$ 6,200	(2)	620	(a)	1,314	$14,714
			(3)	5,580			
Net income	4,050	3,100		3,500		3,406	7,056
	17,450	9,300					21,770
Dividends	2,500						2,500
Retained earnings, Dec. 31	$14,950	$ 9,300		$ 9,700		$ 4,720	$19,270
Assets — miscellaneous	$32,700	$28,300					$61,000
Equipment	2,100				(ii)	600	1,500
Accumulated depreciation	(2,100)		(ii)	600			(1,500)
Investment in Sub Inc.	11,250		(a)	4,320	(1)	3,006	
			(i)	216	(3)	12,780	
	$43,950	$28,300					$61,000
Liabilities	$14,000	$11,000					$25,000
Common stock	15,000	8,000	(2)	800			15,000
			(3)	7,200			
Retained earnings	14,950	9,300		9,700		4,720	19,270
Noncontrolling interest			(i)	24	(2)	1,420	1,730
					(4)	334	
	$43,950	$28,300		$22,860		$22,860	$61,000

APPENDIX B

Working Papers for Intercompany Bondholdings

Exhibit 8.11 illustrates the working paper for the preparation of the Year 1 consolidated financial statements when Parent Company has used the cost method to account for its investment.

The following working paper entries were used:

#a	Investment in Sub Inc. — Parent Co.	1,866	
	Investment income — Parent Co.		1,866

To adjust the financial statements of Parent to the equity method as follows:

Adjusted net income — Sub Inc. (see page 305)	$1,940	
	90%	
	$1,746	
Add bond gain allocated to Parent Co.	120	
	$1,866	

#1	Investment income — Parent Co.	1,866	
	Investment in Sub Inc. — Parent Co.		1,866

To restate the investment account to the balance at the beginning of the year

#2	Retained earnings, January 1 — Sub Inc.	4,500	
	Common stock — Sub Inc.	8,000	
	Investment in Sub Inc. — Parent Co.		11,250
	Noncontrolling interest (balance sheet)		1,250

To eliminate the investment account and the shareholders' equity of the subsidiary, and establish the noncontrolling interest; all as at the beginning of the year

#3	Noncontrolling interest (income statement)	194	
	Noncontrolling interest (balance sheet)		194

To allocate entity net income to noncontrolling interest (see calculation of consolidated net income, page 305)

#i	Bonds payable — Parent Co.	10,200	
	Investment in Parent Co. bonds (Sub Inc.)		9,600
	Gain on bond retirement		600

To eliminate the intercompany bonds and record the resultant gain as at December 31, Year 1

#ii	Income tax expense (income statement)	240	
	Future income tax (balance sheet)		240

To record the income tax on the bond gain recorded

Exhibit 8.12, on page 333, contains the working papers for the preparation of the Year 2 consolidated financial statements.

The working paper entries are as follows:

#a	Investment in Sub Inc. — Parent Co.	4,572	
	Investment income — Parent Co.		2,706
	Retained earnings, Jan. 1 — Parent Co.		1,866

To adjust the statements of Parent Co. to the equity method (see calculations of consolidated net income, page 311, and consolidated retained earnings, page 313)

Exhibit 8.11

**CONSOLIDATED FINANCIAL STATEMENT WORKING PAPER —
COST METHOD
ELIMINATION OF INTERCOMPANY BONDHOLDINGS**
December 31, Year 1

	Parent	Sub	Eliminations Dr.		Eliminations Cr.		Consolidated
Sales	$20,000	$ 8,000					$28,000
Gain on bond retirement					(i)	600	600
Investment income			(1)	1,866	(a)	1,866	
	$20,000	$ 8,000					$28,600
Interest expense	$ 950						$ 950
Miscellaneous expense	13,450	5,200					18,650
Income tax expense	2,200	1,100	(ii)	240			3,540
	$16,600	$ 6,300					$23,140
Net income — entity							$ 5,460
Noncontrolling interest			(3)	194			194
Net income	$ 3,400	$ 1,700		$ 2,300		$ 2,466	$ 5,266
Retained earnings, Jan. 1	$12,000	$ 4,500	(2)	4,500			$12,000
Net income	3,400	1,700		2,300		2,466	5,266
	15,400	6,200					17,266
Dividends	2,000						2,000
Retained earnings, Dec. 31	$13,400	$ 6,200		$ 6,800		$ 2,466	$15,266
Assets — miscellaneous	$29,150	$13,600					$42,750
Investment in Parent bonds		9,600			(i)	9,600	
Investment in Sub Inc.	11,250		(a)	1,866	(1)	1,866	
					(2)	11,250	
	$40,400	$23,200					$42,750
Miscellaneous liabilities	$ 1,800	$ 9,000					$10,800
Bonds payable	10,200		(i)	10,200			
Future income tax					(ii)	240	240
Common stock	15,000	8,000	(2)	8,000			15,000
Retained earnings	13,400	6,200		6,800		2,466	15,266
Noncontrolling interest					(2)	1,250	1,444
					(3)	194	
	$40,400	$23,200		$26,866		$26,866	$42,750

#1	Investment income — Parent Co.	2,706	
	Investment in Sub Inc. — Parent Co.		2,706
	To adjust the investment account to start-of-year balance		

#2	Retained earnings, Jan. 1 — Sub Inc.	6,200	
	Common stock — Sub Inc.	8,000	
	Noncontrolling interest (balance sheet)		1,420
	Investment in Sub Inc. — Parent Co.		12,780
	To eliminate the shareholders' equity of the subsidiary at the beginning of the year, of which 10% is allocated to the noncontrolling interest, and 90% to reduce the investment account as at the beginning of the year		

#i	Interest revenue	1,100	
	Bonds payable	10,150	
	Interest expense		950
	Income tax expense		60
	Investment in Parent Co. bonds		9,700
	Future income tax		180
	Investment in Sub Inc. — Parent Co.		336
	Noncontrolling interest (balance sheet)		24

This involved elimination entry is explained in the following manner. The elimination of interest revenue (1,100) and interest expense (950), and the adjustment to income tax (60), made on the income statement reduces the entity's after-tax net income by $90. We have described this previously as the "interest elimination loss" for the year. These income statement entries reverse the bond gain recorded by the constituent companies in Year 2.

The elimination of bonds payable (10,150) and investment in bonds (9,700), and the related adjustment to future income tax (180), made on the balance sheet, increases the equity side of the balance sheet by $270, and thus establishes the bond gain as at December 31, Year 2.

The two remaining balancing entries reverse from the investment account the bond gain allocated to Parent at the end of Year 1. They also allocate the Year 1 bond gain to noncontrolling interest. Noncontrolling interest now contains the correct balance as at December 31, Year 1.

#3	Noncontrolling interest (income statement)	304	
	Noncontrolling interest (balance sheet)		304
	To allocate entity Year 2 net income to noncontrolling interest (see calculation of consolidated net income, page 311)		

REVIEW QUESTIONS

1. Explain how an intercompany gain of $2,700 on the sale of a depreciable asset is held back on the consolidated income statement in the year of sale and realized on subsequent consolidated income statements. What income tax adjustments should be made in each instance?

2. "The realization of intercompany inventory and depreciable asset profits is really an adjustment made in the preparation of consolidated income statements to arrive at historical cost numbers." Explain.

Exhibit 8.12

CONSOLIDATED FINANCIAL STATEMENT WORKING PAPER
COST METHOD
ELIMINATION OF INTERCOMPANY BONDHOLDINGS
December 31, Year 2

	Parent	Sub	Eliminations Dr.		Eliminations Cr.		Consolidated
Sales	$25,000	$10,900					$35,900
Interest revenue		1,100	(i)	1,100			
Investment income			(1)	2,706	(a)	2,706	
	$25,000	$12,000					$35,900
Interest expense	950				(i)	950	
Miscellaneous expense	17,400	6,900					24,300
Income tax expense	2,600	2,000			(i)	60	4,540
	$20,950	$ 8,900					$28,840
Net income — entity							$ 7,060
Noncontrolling interest			(3)	304			304
Net income	$ 4,050	$ 3,100		$ 4,110		$ 3,716	$ 6,756
Retained earnings, Jan. 1	$13,400	$ 6,200	(2)	6,200	(a)	1,866	$15,266
Net income	4,050	3,100		4,110		3,716	6,756
	17,450	9,300					22,022
Dividends	2,500						2,500
Retained earnings, Dec. 31	$14,950	$ 9,300		$10,310		$ 5,582	$19,522
Assets — miscellaneous	$32,700	$18,600					$51,300
Invest. in bonds of Parent		9,700			(i)	9,700	
Investment in Sub Inc.	11,250		(a)	4,572	(1)	2,706	
					(2)	12,780	
					(i)	336	
	$43,950	$28,300					$51,300
Liabilities	$ 3,850	$11,000					$14,850
Bonds payable	10,150		(i)	10,150			
Future income tax					(i)	180	180
Common stock	15,000	8,000	(2)	8,000			15,000
Retained earnings	14,950	9,300		10,310		5,582	19,522
Noncontrolling interest					(i)	24	1,748
					(2)	1,420	
					(3)	304	
	$43,950	$28,300		$33,032		$33,032	$51,300

3. An intercompany inventory profit is realized when the inventory is sold outside the entity. Is this also the case with respect to an intercompany profit in a depreciable asset? Explain.

4. An intercompany gain on a depreciable asset resulting from a sale by the parent company is subsequently realized by an adjustment to the subsidiary's depreciation expense in the preparation of consolidated income statements. Should this adjustment be taken into account in the calculation of noncontrolling interest in net income? Explain.

5. Consolidated income statements report the earnings of a single economic entity. Will the total reported earnings of this entity, measured at the end of a period of time greater than one year, be affected by the fact that intercompany sales of assets at a profit occurred during this period of time? Explain.

6. Four approaches could be used to allocate gains (losses) on the elimination of intercompany bondholdings in the preparation of consolidated financial statements. Outline these four approaches. Which approach is conceptually superior? Explain.

7. "An 'interest elimination gain (loss)' does not appear as a distinguishable item on a consolidated income statement." Explain.

8. The adjustment for the holdback of an intercompany gain in assets requires a corresponding adjustment to a consolidated future tax asset. The adjustment for a gain from intercompany bondholdings requires a corresponding adjustment to a consolidated future tax liability. In both cases the tax adjustment is made because of a gain. Why is the tax adjustment different? Explain.

9. "Some intercompany gains (losses) are realized for consolidation purposes subsequent to their actual recording by the affiliates, while others are recorded by the affiliates subsequent to their realization for consolidation purposes." Explain, referring to the type of gains (losses) that apply in each case.

MULTIPLE CHOICE

Use the following data to answer Questions 1 to 10.

On January 1, 1998, Present Inc. purchased 80% of the outstanding voting shares of Sunrise Co. for $3,000,000. On that date, Sunrise's shareholders' equity consisted of retained earnings of $2,000,000 and common stock of $1,000,000. Sunrise's identifiable assets and liabilities had fair values that were equal to their carrying values on January 1, 1998, except for the following:

	Fair value	Carrying value
Inventory	$250,000	$350,000

The balance sheets of Present Inc. and Sunrise Co. on December 31, 2002, were as follows:

BALANCE SHEETS

	Present	Sunrise
Assets		
Cash and current receivables	$ 900,000	$ 400,000
Temporary investments	—	1,100,000
Inventories	400,000	200,000
Property, plant, and equipment (net)	2,100,000	3,500,000
Investment in Sunrise (at cost)	3,000,000	—
	$6,400,000	$5,200,000
Liabilities and shareholders' equity		
Current liabilities	$ 600,000	$ 100,000
Long-term liabilities	1,200,000	800,000
Future income taxes	500,000	300,000
Common stock	1,500,000	1,000,000
Retained earnings	2,600,000	3,000,000
	$6,400,000	$5,200,000

Additional Information

- Present carries its investment in Sunrise on its books by the cost method.

- At the beginning of 2001, Sunrise sold Present a machine for its fair market value of $700,000. Sunrise had purchased the machine in 1998. The book value at the time of the sale to Present was $490,000. The machine had an estimated remaining useful life of 7 years on the date of the intercorporate sale.

- At December 31, 2001, Present had goods in its inventories that had been purchased from Sunrise at $60,000 profit to Sunrise. During 2002, Present purchased goods for $2,000,000 from Sunrise, and on December 31, 2002, 30% of these goods remained in Present's inventories.

- At December 31, 2001, Sunrise had goods in its inventories that had been purchased from Present at $80,000 profit to Present. During 2002, Sunrise purchased goods for $1,400,000 from Present, and all of these goods had been sold externally by December 31, 2002.

- Intercompany sales are priced to provide both companies with a gross profit of 50% of the sale price.

- Any goodwill arising from the business combination is to be tested annually for impairment. In 2000, an impairment loss of $85,000 was recorded.

- Both companies use the straight-line method for all depreciation and amortization.

- Both companies are taxed at 40%.

1. What was the amount of goodwill that arose from Present's acquisition of Sunrise?
   a. Negative goodwill arose, which would be allocated to nonmonetary assets.
   b. $80,000
   c. $520,000
   d. $680,000

2. Which of the following is the adjustment that is necessary as a result of the intercompany sale of machinery to calculate depreciation expense on Present's consolidated income statement for the year ended December 31, 2002?
   a. $100,000
   b. $30,000
   c. $24,000
   d. $18,000

3. What is the amount that would appear on Present's consolidated balance sheet at December 31, 2002, for property, plant, and equipment?
   a. $5,450,000
   b. $5,510,000
   c. $5,600,000
   d. $5,750,000

4. Which of the following is the increase that is necessary as a result of profits in beginning inventory to calculate cost of goods sold on Present's consolidated income statement at December 31, 2002?
   a. $84,000
   b. $124,000
   c. $140,000
   d. $280,000

5. Which of the following is the adjustment that is necessary as a result of inter-company sales during the year and profits in ending inventory to calculate cost of goods sold on Present's consolidated income statement at December 31, 2002?
   a. Decrease by $3,400,000 and increase by $300,000.
   b. Decrease by $3,400,000 and decrease by $300,000.
   c. Decrease by $3,400,000 and increase by $180,000.
   d. Decrease by $3,400,000 and increase by $1,000,000.

6. Which of the following would be the balance of inventories on Present's consolidated balance sheet at December 31, 2002?
   a. $300,000
   b. $420,000
   c. $600,000
   d. $740,000

7. Which of the following is the decrease that is necessary to calculate income tax expense on Present's consolidated income statement for the year ended December 31, 2002?
   a. $52,000
   b. $64,000
   c. $76,000
   d. $188,000

8. Which of the following would be the balance of future income taxes on Present's consolidated balance sheet at December 31, 2002?
   a. $980,000
   b. $800,000
   c. $680,000
   d. $620,000

9. Which of the following would be the balance of noncontrolling interest on Present's consolidated balance sheet at December 31, 2002?
   a. $710,000
   b. $746,000
   c. $764,000
   d. $800,000

10. Assume that Present wanted to prepare separate entity financial statements using the equity method. Which of the following would be the balance of the investment in Sunrise account on Present's balance sheet at December 31, 2002?
    a. $3,795,000
    b. $3,584,000
    c. $3,579,000
    d. $3,419,000

11. Black Ltd. owns all of the outstanding shares of White Inc. On January 1, 2002, White sold equipment to Black and recorded a before-tax profit of $10,000 on the transaction. (White's tax rate is 40%.) Black is depreciating this equipment over 5 years, using the straight-line method. The net adjustments to calculate the 2002 and 2003 consolidated net income would be an increase (decrease) of how much?

	2002	*2003*
a.	($8,000)	$2,000
b.	($10,000)	0
c.	($4,800)	$1,200
d.	($10,000)	$2,000

12. A parent company has bonds outstanding that were originally issued at a premium. At the beginning of the current year, a subsidiary purchased all of the parent's bonds on the open market at a discount. Which of the following statements is true?
    a. The interest income and expense will agree in amount and should be offset when the consolidated income statement is prepared.
    b. Whether the balances agree or not, both the bond interest income and expense should be reported in the consolidated income statement.
    c. In computing noncontrolling interest, the interest expense should be included but the interest income should not.
    d. Whether the balances agree or not, both the bond interest income and expense should be eliminated when preparing the consolidated income statement.

13. A subsidiary issues bonds directly to its parent at a discount. Both use the same amortization method. Which of the following statements is true?
    a. Because of the discount, the bond interest accounts on the two sets of financial statements will not agree.
    b. Since the bond was issued by the subsidiary, the amount of noncontrolling interest will be affected.
    c. Bond interest income and expense will be equal in amount and must be eliminated when preparing the consolidated income statement.
    d. Elimination is not necessary for consolidation purposes because the bond was acquired directly from the subsidiary.

14. A bond that had been issued by a subsidiary at a premium was acquired several years ago by its parent on the market at a discount. The bond issue is still outstanding. Which of the following statements is true?

    a. The bond issue has no impact on the preparation of current consolidated financial statements because the bond acquisition was made in the past.

    b. The original gain would be reported in the current year's consolidated income statement.

    c. The interest income and interest expense balances exactly offset so that no adjustment to retained earnings or to income is necessary.

    d. For consolidated purposes, retained earnings must be increased at the beginning of the current year, but by an amount that is smaller than the original gain.

PROBLEMS

Problem 1 X Company owns 80% of Y Company and uses the equity method to account for its investment. On January 1, Year 2, the investment in Y Company account had a balance of $86,900, and Y Company's capital stock and retained earnings totalled $100,000. The unamortized purchase discrepancy had an estimated remaining life of 6 years at this time. The following intercompany asset transfers took place in Years 2 and 3: January 1, Year 2, sale of asset to X at a profit of $45,000; April 30, Year 3, sale of asset to Y at a profit of $60,000. Both assets purchased are being depreciated over 5 years. In Year 2, Y reported a net income of $125,000 and dividends paid of $70,000, while in Year 3 its net income and dividends were $104,000 and $70,000 respectively.

Required:

Calculate the December 31, Year 3, balance in the account "Investment in Y." (Assume a 40% tax rate.)

Problem 2 Peggy Company owns 75% of Sally Inc. and uses the cost method to account for its investment. The following data were taken from the Year 4 income statements of the two companies:

	Peggy	Sally
Gross profit	$580,000	$270,000
Miscellaneous expenses	110,000	85,000
Depreciation expense	162,000	97,000
Income tax expense	123,000	35,000
Total expense	$395,000	$217,000
Net income	$185,000	$ 53,000

    In Year 2, Sally sold equipment to Peggy at a profit of $15,000. Peggy has been depreciating this equipment over a 5-year period. Use income tax allocation at a rate of 40%.

Required:

Using only the information supplied above:

(a) Calculate consolidated net income for Year 4.

(b) Prepare a consolidated income statement for Year 4.

(c) Calculate the amount of the asset "future income tax" that would appear on the Year 4 consolidated balance sheet.

Problem 3   The comparative consolidated income statements of a parent and its 75% owned sub-sidiary were prepared incorrectly as at December 31. The following items were over-looked when the statements were prepared:

- The Year 5 gain on sale of assets resulted from the subsidiary selling equipment to the parent on September 30. The parent immediately leased the equipment back to the subsidiary at an annual rental of $12,000. This was the only intercompany rent transaction that occurred each year. The equipment had a remaining life of 5 years on the date of sale.
- The Year 6 gain on sale of assets resulted from the January 1 sale of a building, with a remaining life of 7 years, by the subsidiary to the parent.
- Both gains were taxed at a rate of 40%.

CONSOLIDATED INCOME STATEMENTS

	Year 5	Year 6
Miscellaneous revenues	$750,000	$825,000
Gain on sale of assets	8,000	42,000
Rental revenue	3,000	12,000
	$761,000	$879,000
Miscellaneous expense	$399,800	$492,340
Rental expense	52,700	64,300
Depreciation expense	75,000	80,700
Income tax expense	81,000	94,500
Noncontrolling interest	32,500	5,160
	$641,000	$737,000
Net income	$120,000	$142,000

Required:

Prepare correct consolidated income statements for years 5 and 6.

Problem 4   Parent Company purchased 80% of Subsidiary Company on January 1, Year 1, when Subsidiary had a retained earnings balance of $10,000. The resulting purchase discrep-ancy of $48,000 is being amortized over a 40-year life. Parent uses the cost method to account for its investment. An analysis of the retained earnings account for Year 7 appears below:

	Parent	Subsidiary
Balance, Jan. 1	$ 6,000	$20,000
Net income (loss)	4,000	(1,000)
	10,000	19,000
Dividends		8,000
Balance, Dec. 31	$10,000	$11,000

Other Information

On July 1, Year 3, Parent sold equipment to Subsidiary at a profit of $19,000. This equipment had a remaining estimated life of 5 years on this date.

Parent has purchased a substantial portion of its merchandise requirements from Subsidiary since control was acquired. Unrealized profits in Parent's inventory are as follows:

Beginning inventory	$16,500
Ending inventory	9,500

Required:

Prepare a statement of consolidated retained earnings for Year 7. Assume a corporate tax rate of 40%.

Problem 5 Financial statements of Burks Ltd. and its 80% owned subsidiary Falls Ltd. as at December 31, Year 5, are presented below:

BALANCE SHEETS — December 31, Year 5

	Burks	Falls
Cash	$ 18,100	$ 20,600
Accounts receivable	60,000	55,000
Inventories	35,000	46,000
Investment in Falls — at cost	129,200	—
Land, building, and equipment	198,000	104,000
Accumulated depreciation	(86,000)	(30,000)
	$354,300	$195,600
Accounts payable	$ 56,000	$ 70,100
Dividends payable	5,000	5,500
Capital stock	225,000	50,000
Retained earnings, January 1	45,500	68,000
Net income	42,800	13,000
Dividends	(20,000)	(11,000)
	$354,300	$195,600

INCOME STATEMENTS — Year Ended December 31, Year 5

	Burks	Falls
Sales	$535,400	$270,000
Dividend and miscellaneous income	9,900	—
	545,300	270,000
Cost of sales	$364,000	$206,000
Selling expense	78,400	24,100
Administrative expense (including depreciation)	46,300	20,700
Income taxes	13,800	6,200
	$502,500	$257,000
Net income	$ 42,800	$ 13,000

Other Information

- Burks acquired its 80% interest in Falls on January 1, Year 1. The retained earnings of Falls were $12,000 on that date, and there have been no subsequent changes in the capital stock accounts. On January 1, Year 1, fair values were equal to carrying values except for the following:

	Carrying value	Fair value
Inventory	$50,000	$32,000
Patent	–0–	14,000

- The patent of Falls had remaining legal life of 8 years on January 1, Year 1, and any goodwill was to be tested annually for impairment. As a result impairment losses occurred as follows: Year 2, $20,000; Year 4, $13,120; Year 5, $8,280.

- On January 1, Year 5, the inventories of Burks contained items purchased from Falls on which Falls had made a profit of $1,900. During Year 5 Falls sold goods to Burks for $92,000, of which $21,000 remained unpaid at the end of the year. Falls made a profit of $3,300 on goods remaining in Burks's inventory at December 31, Year 5.
- On January 1, Year 3, Falls sold equipment to Burks at a price that was $10,500 in excess of its book value. The equipment had an estimated remaining life of 6 years on that date.
- Burks sold a tract of land to Falls in Year 2 at a profit of $7,000. This land is still held by Falls at the end of Year 5.
- Assume a corporate tax rate of 40%.

Required:

Prepare the following consolidated financial statements:
(a) Income statement.
(b) Retained earnings statement.
(c) Balance sheet.

 Income statements of M Co. and K Co. for the year ended December 31, Year 6, are presented below:

	M Co.	K Co.
Sales	$600,000	$350,000
Rent revenue	—	50,000
Interest revenue	6,700	—
Income from subsidiary	30,070	—
Gain on land sale	—	8,000
	$636,770	$408,000
Cost of goods sold	$334,000	$225,000
Depreciation expense	20,000	70,000
Administrative expense	207,000	74,000
Interest expense	1,700	6,000
Income tax expense	20,700	7,500
	$583,400	$382,500
Net income	$ 53,370	$ 25,500

Additional Information

- M Co. uses the equity method to account for its investment in K Co.
- M Co. acquired its 80% interest in K Co. on January 1, Year 1. On that date the purchase discrepancy of $25,000 was allocated entirely to buildings; it is being amortized over a 20-year period.
- M Co. made an advance of $100,000 to K Co. on July 1, Year 6. This loan is due on call and requires the payment of interest at 12% per year.
- M Co. rents marine equipment from K Co. During Year 6, $50,000 rent was paid and was charged to administrative expense.
- In Year 4, M Co. sold land to K Co. and recorded a profit of $10,000 on the sale. K Co. held the land until October, Year 6, when it was sold to an unrelated company.
- During Year 6, K Co. made sales to M Co. totalling $90,000. The December 31, Year 6, inventories of M Co. contain an unrealized profit of $5,000. The January 1, Year 6, inventories of M Co. contained an unrealized profit of $12,000.
- On January 1, Year 4, M Co. sold machinery to K Co. and recorded a profit of $13,000. The remaining useful life on that date was 5 years. Assume straight-line depreciation.

✓• Tax allocation is to be used, and you are to assume a 40% average corporate tax rate for this purpose.

Required:

Prepare a consolidated income statement for Year 6.

The financial statements of Para and Medic as at December 31, Year 3, are shown below:

BALANCE SHEETS
December 31, Year 3

	Para	Medic
Assets		
Cash	$ 14,000	$ 16,800
Receivables	25,000	21,000
Inventories	45,000	50,000
Property, plant, and equipment	195,000	260,000
Accumulated depreciation	(35,000)	(40,000)
Other assets	79,600	—
Investment in Medic stock	150,000	—
	$473,600	$307,800
Liabilities and shareholders' equity		
Current liabilities	$ 36,400	$ 37,800
Long-term liabilities	—	102,500
Common stock	350,000	125,000
Retained earnings, January 1	77,600	25,000
Net income	34,600	29,500
Dividends	(25,000)	(12,000)
	$473,600	$307,800

INCOME STATEMENTS
Year 3

	Para	Medic
Sales revenues	$460,200	$270,000
Dividend income	10,200	—
Interest revenues	2,200	—
	$472,600	$270,000
Cost of goods sold	$350,000	$173,000
Depreciation expense	18,000	28,000
General and administrative expenses	57,000	19,000
Interest expense	—	9,500
Income taxes	13,000	11,000
	$438,000	$240,500
Net income	$ 34,600	$ 29,500

Additional Information

✓• Para acquired 85% of Medic's common stock on January 1 of Year 1 for $150,000. At the date of acquisition, Medic reported a retained earnings balance of $20,000, and its net assets were believed to be carried on its records at reasonable valuations with the exception of inventory, which was undervalued in the amount of $15,000, and land, which was undervalued in the amount of $8,000. Yearly impairment tests of goodwill resulted in losses of $1,000 in Year 1, $440 in Year 2, and $720 in Year 3.

- Para accounts for its investment in Medic by the cost method.
- Interest revenues are 100% intercompany.
- Medic's sales during Year 3 include $60,000 of sales to Para. Goods purchased from Medic and included in Para's inventories were $20,000 at the beginning of Year 3 and $30,000 at the end of Year 3 (Medic's cost on sales to Para averages 70% of selling price.) At the end of Year 3, Para owed Medic $9,100 on open account.
- At the beginning of Year 2, Para sold equipment to Medic for $70,000. The book value of the equipment on Para's records at date of sale was $55,000. Medic has depreciated the equipment on a straight-line basis at the rate of 20% per year.
- Para uses tax allocation for consolidation purposes. Assume a 40% corporate tax rate.

Required:

Prepare in good form the following:
(a) Consolidated income statement.
(b) Consolidated retained earnings statement.
(c) Consolidated balance sheet.

Problem 8 On December 31, Year 1, the Pridmore Company purchased 80% of the outstanding voting shares of the Stubbin Company for $964,000 in cash. The balance sheet of Stubbin on that date and the fair values of its tangible assets and liabilities were as follows:

	Book value	Fair value
Cash and accounts receivable	$ 200,000	$175,000
Inventories	300,000	300,000
Plant and equipment	600,000	700,000
Accumulated depreciation	(100,000)	
	$1,000,000	
Current liabilities	$ 100,000	$100,000
Long-term liabilities	200,000	150,000
No-par common stock	500,000	
Retained earnings	200,000	
	$1,000,000	

The difference between the fair value and book value of cash and accounts receivable of the subsidiary at December 31, Year 1, was adjusted by Stubbin in Year 2. At the acquisition date, the plant and equipment had an estimated remaining useful life of 10 years with no net salvage value. The long-term liabilities mature on December 31, Year 6. Any goodwill arising from the business combination will be tested for impairment. Pridmore uses the cost method to account for its investment in Stubbin. Both Pridmore and Stubbin use the straight-line method to calculate all depreciation and amortization.

The statements of income and changes in retained earnings of the two companies for the year ending December 31, Year 5, were as follows:

	Pridmore	Stubbin
Sales of merchandise	$6,000,000	$1,000,000
Other revenues	200,000	20,000
Total revenues	$6,200,000	$1,020,000
Cost of goods sold	$2,500,000	$ 400,000
Depreciation expense	500,000	80,000
Interest expense	400,000	20,000
Other expenses (including income tax)	1,300,000	190,000
Total expenses	$4,700,000	$ 690,000
Net income	$1,500,000	$ 330,000
Retained earnings, 1/1/Year 5	4,200,000	300,000
Dividends	(200,000)	(50,000)
Retained earnings, 31/12/Year 5	$5,500,000	$ 580,000

Other Information

- Goodwill impairment losses were recorded as follows: Year 2, $3,600; Year 4, $30,000; Year 5, $11,200.
- On December 31, Year 4, Stubbin sold a warehouse to Pridmore for $63,000. It had been purchased on January 1, Year 3, for $100,000 and had an estimated 20-year life on that date with no salvage value.
- During Year 4, Stubbin sold merchandise that it had purchased for $120,000 to Pridmore for $250,000. None of this merchandise had been resold by Pridmore by December 31, Year 4. Both companies account for inventories on the first-in, first-out basis.
- Pridmore had sales of $200,000 to Stubbin during Year 4, which gave rise to a gross profit of $125,000. This inventory was resold by Stubbin during Year 4 for $225,000.
- During Year 5, Stubbin sold merchandise that had been purchased for $160,000 to Pridmore for $300,000. Since the sales occurred in December of Year 5, all of this merchandise remained in the December 31, Year 5, inventories of Pridmore and had not been paid for by Pridmore.
- During September of Year 5, Pridmore had sales of $280,000 to Stubbin, which increased Pridmore's gross profit by $160,000. By December 31, Year 5, one-half of this merchandise had been sold to the public by Stubbin.
- On January 1, Year 5, Pridmore sold to Stubbin for $28,000 a machine that had cost $40,000. On January 1, Year 5, it had been depreciated for 6 years of its estimated 8-year life. This sale was not considered an extraordinary transaction by Pridmore.
- During Year 5, Pridmore charged Stubbin $25,000 for management fees.
- Assume a 40% corporate tax rate.

Required:

(a) Prepare a consolidated income statement for Pridmore and its subsidiary, Stubbin, for the year ending December 31, Year 5, in accordance with the recommendations of the *CICA Handbook*.

(b) Prepare a consolidated statement of retained earnings for Pridmore and its subsidiary, Stubbin, for the year ending December 31, Year 5.

(SMA adapted)

Problem 9   On January 1, Year 1, Porter Inc. purchased 85% of the voting shares of Sloan Ltd. for $3,025,000 in cash. On this date, Sloan had no-par common stock outstanding in the amount of $2,200,000 and retained earnings of $1,100,000. The identifiable assets and liabilities of Sloan had fair values that were equal to their carrying values except for the following:

- Plant and equipment (net) had a fair value $200,000 greater than its carrying value. The remaining useful life on January 1, Year 1, was 20 years with no anticipated salvage value.
- Accounts receivable had a fair value $75,000 less than carrying value.
- Long-term liabilities had a fair value $62,500 less than carrying value. These liabilities mature on June 30, Year 9.

Other Information

- Between January 1, Year 1, and December 31, Year 3, Sloan earned $345,000 and paid dividends of $115,000.
- Goodwill impairment tests yielded losses as follows: Year 1, $30,300; Year 2, $6,075; Year 4, $12,125.
- On January 1, Year 2, Sloan sold a patent to Porter for $165,000. On this date, the patent had a carrying value on the books of Sloan of $185,000, and a remaining useful life of 5 years.
- On September 1, Year 3, Porter sold land to Sloan for $93,000. The land had a carrying value on the books of Porter of $72,000. Sloan still owned this land on December 31, Year 4.
- For the year ending December 31, Year 4, the statements of income revealed the following:

	Porter	Sloan
Total revenues	$2,576,000	$973,000
Cost of goods sold	$1,373,000	$467,000
Depreciation expense	483,000	176,000
Other expenses (including income tax)	352,000	153,000
Total expenses	$2,208,000	$796,000
Net income	$ 368,000	$177,000

Porter records its investment in Sloan using the cost method and includes dividend income from Sloan in its total revenues.

- Porter and Sloan paid dividends of $125,000 and $98,000 respectively in Year 4.
- Sloan issued no common stock subsequent to January 1, Year 1. Selected balance sheet accounts for the two companies as at December 31, Year 4, were:

	Porter	Sloan
Accounts receivable (net)	$ 987,000	$ 133,000
Inventories	1,436,000	787,000
Plant and equipment (net)	3,467,000	1,234,000
Patents (net)	263,000	–0–
Land	872,000	342,000
Long-term liabilities	1,876,000	745,000
Retained earnings	4,833,000	1,409,000

- During Year 4, Porter's merchandise sales to Sloan were $150,000. The unrealized profits in Sloan's inventory on January 1 and December 31, Year 4, were $14,000 and $10,000 respectively. At December 31, Year 4, Sloan still owed Porter $5,000 for merchandise purchases.

- During Year 4, Sloan's merchandise sales to Porter were $55,000. The unrealized profits in Porter's inventory on January 1 and December 31, Year 4, were $1,500 and $2,500 respectively. At December 31, Year 4, Porter still owed Sloan $2,000 for merchandise purchases.
- Use income tax allocation at a rate of 40%.

Required:

(a) Compute the balances that would appear in the consolidated balance sheet of Porter and Sloan as at December 31, Year 4, for the following:
   (i)   Patent (net).
   (ii) Goodwill.
   (iii) Noncontrolling interest.
   (iv) Retained earnings.
   (v)   Future income taxes.

(b) Porter has decided not to prepare consolidated financial statements and will report its investment in Sloan by the equity method. Calculate the total revenues, including investment income, that would be disclosed in the income statement drawn up by Porter for the year ended December 31, Year 4.

(SMA adapted)

Problem 10 Alpha Corporation owns 90% of the common stock of Beta Corporation and uses the equity method to account for its investment.

On January 1, Year 4, Alpha purchased $160,000 par of Beta's 10% bonds for $152,000. Beta's bond liability on this date consisted of $800,000 par 10% bonds due January 1, Year 8, and unamortized discount of $16,000. Interest payment dates are June 30 and December 31.

Both companies have a December 31 year-end. Alpha uses income tax allocation at 40% tax rate when it prepares consolidated financial statements.

Beta reported a net income of $114,000 in Year 4 and declared a dividend of $30,000 on December 31.

Required:

(a) Calculate the amount of the gain or loss that will appear as a separate item on the Year 4 consolidated income statement, as a result of the bond transaction that occurred during the year.

(b) Prepare the equity method journal entries that Alpha would make on December 31, Year 4.

(c) Calculate the amount of the bond liability that will appear on the December 31, Year 4, consolidated balance sheet.

Problem 11 Parent Co. owns 75% of Sub Co. and uses the cost method to account for its investment. The following are summarized income statements for the year ended December 31, Year 7. (Sub Co. did not declare or pay dividends in Year 7.)

INCOME STATEMENTS — Year 7

	Parent	Sub
Interest revenue	$ 8,750	—
Other misc. revenues	900,000	500,000
	$908,750	500,000
Interest expense	—	$ 44,000
Other misc. expense	600,000	350,000
Income tax expense	124,000	42,000
	$724,000	$436,000
Net income	$184,750	$ 64,000

Other Information

On July 1, Year 7, Parent purchased 40% of the outstanding bonds of Sub for $152,500. On that date Sub had $400,000 of 10% bonds payable outstanding, which mature in 5 years. The bond discount on the books of Sub on July 1, Year 7, amounted to $20,000. Interest is payable January 1 and July 1. Any gains (losses) are to be allocated to each company.

Required:

Prepare a consolidated income statement for Year 7 using a 40% tax rate.

Problem 12 Palmer Corporation owns 70% of the common stock of Scott Corporation and uses the equity method to account for its investment.

Scott purchased $80,000 par of Palmer's 10% bonds on October 1, Year 5, for $76,000. Palmer's bond liability on October 1, Year 5, consisted of $400,000 par of 10% bonds due on October 1, Year 9, with unamortized discount of $8,000. Interest payment dates are April 1 and October 1 of each year and straight-line amortization is used. Intercompany bond gains (losses) are to be allocated to each affiliate.

Both companies have a December 31 year-end. Scott's financial statements for Year 5 indicate that it earned a net income of $70,000 and that on December 31, Year 5, it declared a dividend of $15,000.

Required:

(a) Prepare the equity journal entries that Palmer would make in Year 5. (Assume a 40% tax rate.)
(b) Compute the amount of the bond liability that will appear on the December 31, Year 5, consolidated balance sheet.

Problem 13 Shown below are selected ledger accounts from the trial balance of a parent and its subsidiary as of December 31, Year 9.

	P Co.	S Co.
Investment in bonds of P	—	$ 39,000
Investment in stock of S (equity method)	$139,899	—
Sales	630,000	340,000
Interest income	—	1,850
Investment income	15,339	—
Gain on sale of land	7,000	—
Capital stock	300,000	100,000
Retained earnings	85,000	50,000
Bonds payable 8 percent	198,000	—
Cost of sales	485,000	300,000
Interest expense	17,000	—
Selling and administrative expense	50,000	20,000
Income tax expense	34,000	8,740
Dividends	10,000	8,000

Other Information

- P Company purchased its 90% interest in S Company in Year 1, on the date that S Company was incorporated, and has followed the equity method to account for its investment since that date.
- On April 1, Year 5, land that had originally cost $15,000 was sold by S Company to P Company for $21,000. P purchased the land with the intention of developing it; but in Year 9 it decided that the location was not suitable and the land was sold to a chain of drug stores.
- On January 1, Year 2, P Company issued $200,000 face value bonds due in 10 years. The proceeds from the bond issue amounted to $190,000.
- On July 1, Year 9, S Company purchased $40,000 of these bonds on the open market at a cost of $38,750. Intercompany bondholding gains (losses) are allocated between the two affiliates.
- S Company had $75,000 in sales to P Company during Year 9.
- Use income tax allocation at a 40% tax rate.

Required:

(a) Prepare a statement of consolidated net income for Year 9.
(b) Prepare a consolidated statement of retained earnings for Year 9.

Problem 14   The Preston Company purchased 70% of the capital stock of Silver Company on January 1, Year 6, for $480,000 when the latter company's capital stock and retained earnings were $500,000 and $40,000 respectively. On this date an appraisal of the assets of Silver disclosed the following differences:

	Carrying value	Fair value
Inventory	$120,000	$108,000
Land	150,000	200,000
Plant and equipment	700,000	770,000

The plant and equipment had an estimated life of 20 years on this date.
The balance sheets of Preston and Silver, prepared on December 31, Year 11, follow:

	Preston	Silver
Cash	$ 41,670	$ 57,500
Accounts receivable	215,350	170,000
Inventory	225,000	180,000
Investment in Silver Co. stock (equity method)	541,510	—
Investment in Silver Co. bonds	227,000	—
Land 100,000	150,000	
Plant and equipment	625,000	940,000
Less accumulated depreciation	(183,000)	(220,000)
Patent (net of amortization)	31,500	—
	$1,824,030	$1,277,500
Accounts payable	$ 56,030	$ 100,000
Bonds payable (due Year 20)	—	477,500
Capital stock	750,000	500,000
Retained earnings	1,018,000	200,000
	$1,824,030	$1,277,500

Other Information

- Goodwill impairment tests have resulted in losses totalling $19,800.
- On January 1, Year 1, Silver issued $500,000 of $8\,^1/_2\%$ bonds at 90, maturing in 20 years (on December 31, Year 20).
- On January 1, Year 11, Preston acquired $200,000 of Silver's bonds on the open market at a cost of $230,000.
- On July 1, Year 8, Silver sold a patent to Preston for $63,000. The patent had a carrying value on Silver's books of $42,000 on this date and an estimated remaining life of 7 years.
- Preston uses tax allocation (rate 40%) and allocates bond gains between affiliates when it consolidates Silver.
- Preston uses the equity method to account for its investment.

Required:

Prepare a consolidated balance sheet as at December 31, Year 11.

Problem 15 The balance sheets of Park Company and Savoy Company are presented below as at December 31, Year 8.

BALANCE SHEETS — December 31, Year 8

	Park	Savoy
Cash	$ 13,000	$ 48,800
Receivables	31,000	106,000
Inventories	80,000	62,000
Investment in stock of Savoy	201,900	—
Plant and equipment	740,000	460,000
Accumulated depreciation	(625,900)	(348,400)
Patents	—	4,500
Investment in bonds of Park	—	39,100
	$440,000	$372,000
Current liabilities	$ 55,500	$ 53,000
Dividends payable	6,000	30,000
Bonds payable 6%	98,500	—
Capital stock	200,000	150,000
Retained earnings, Jan. 1	64,000	126,000
Net income	41,000	63,000
Dividends	(25,000)	(50,000)
	$440,000	$372,000

Additional Information

- Park acquired 90% of Savoy for $201,900 on July 1, Year 1, and accounts for its investment under the cost method. At that time the shareholders' equity of Savoy amounted to $175,000, and the assets of Savoy were undervalued by the following amounts:

Inventory	$12,000	
Buildings	$20,000	remaining life 9 years
Patents	$15,000	remaining life 10 years

- During Years 2 to 7, goodwill impairment losses totalled $1,950. An impairment test conducted in Year 8 indicated a further loss of $150.

- Park sells goods to Savoy on a regular basis at a gross profit of 30%. During Year 8 these sales totalled $150,000. On January 1, Year 8, the inventory of Savoy contained goods purchased from Park amounting to $18,000, while the December 31, Year 8, inventory contained goods purchased from Park amounting to $22,000.
- On August 1, Year 6, Savoy sold land to Park at a profit of $16,000. During Year 8, Park sold one-quarter of the land to an unrelated company.
- Park had $100,000 of 6% bonds outstanding on January 1, Year 8. These will mature in 4 years. On that date Savoy acquired $40,000 of these bonds on the open market at a cost of $38,800.

     The Year 8 income statements of the two companies show the following with respect to bond interest.

	Park	Savoy
Interest expense	$6,500	
Interest revenue		$2,700

- Savoy owes Park $22,000 on open account on December 31, Year 8.
- Assume a 40% corporate tax rate and allocate bond gains (losses) between the two companies.

Required:

(a) Prepare the following statements:
   (i) Consolidated balance sheet.
   (ii) Consolidated retained earnings statement.
(b) Prepare the Year 8 journal entries that would be made on the books of Park if the equity method was used to account for the investment.

Problem 16   On January 2, Year 1, Jackson Ltd. purchased 80% of the outstanding shares of Brown Ltd. for $2,000,000. At that date Brown had common stock of $500,000 and retained earnings of $1,250,000. Jackson acquired the Brown stock to obtain control of copyrights held by Brown. These copyrights, with a remaining life of 8 years, had a fair value of $750,000 in excess of their carrying value. Except for the copyrights, the carrying values of the recorded assets and liabilities of Brown were equal to their fair values. On December 31, Year 4, the trial balances of the two companies are as follows:

	Jackson	Brown
Cash	$ 1,000,000	$ 500,000
Accounts receivable	2,000,000	356,000
Inventory	3,000,000	2,250,000
Plant and equipment	14,000,000	2,500,000
Copyrights (net)	—	400,000
Investment in Brown (cost)	2,000,000	—
Investment in Jackson bonds	—	244,000
Cost of goods sold	2,400,000	850,000
Other expenses	962,000	300,000
Interest expense	38,000	—
Income tax expense	600,000	350,000
Dividends	600,000	250,000
	$26,600,000	$8,000,000

	Jackson	Brown
Accounts payable	$ 2,492,000	$2,478,500
Accumulated depreciation: plant and equipment	4,000,000	1,000,000
Bonds payable	500,000	—
Premium on bonds payable	8,000	—
Common stock	4,500,000	500,000
Retained earnings, January 1	10,000,000	2,000,000
Sales	4,900,000	2,000,000
Dividend revenue	200,000	—
Interest revenue	—	21,500
	$26,600,000	$8,000,000

Additional Information

- The Year 4 net incomes of the two companies are as follows:

Jackson Ltd.	$1,100,000
Brown Ltd.	521,500

- On January 2, Year 2, Brown sold equipment to Jackson for $500,000. The equipment had a net book value of $400,000 at the time of the sale. The remaining useful life of the equipment was 5 years.
- The Year 4 opening inventories of Jackson contained $500,000 of merchandise purchased from Brown during Year 3. Brown had recorded a gross profit of $200,000 on this merchandise.
- During Year 4 Brown's sales to Jackson totalled $1,000,000. These sales were made at a gross profit rate of 40%.
- Jackson's ending inventory contains $300,000 of merchandise purchased from Brown.
- Other expenses include depreciation expense and copyright amortization expense.
- On January 2, Year 2, Jackson issued 8%, 7-year bonds with a face value of $500,000 for $514,000. Interest is paid annually on December 31. On January 2, Year 4, Brown purchased one-half of this issue in the open market at a cost of $242,500. Intercompany bond gains (losses) are to be allocated between the two affiliates.
- Tax allocation will be at a rate of 40%.

Required:

(a) Prepare the following consolidated financial statements:
   (i) Income statement.
   (ii) Retained earnings statement.
   (iii) Balance sheet.
(b) Calculate the December 31, Year 4, balance in the account "Investment in Brown" if Jackson had used the equity method to account for its investment.

CHAPTER 9

Consolidated Cash Flows: Ownership Issues

LEARNING OBJECTIVES

After studying this chapter, you should be able to do the following:

- Prepare a consolidated cash flow statement by applying concepts learned in prior courses and unique consolidation concepts discussed here.
- Prepare consolidated financial statements in situations where the parent's ownership has increased (step purchase) or decreased.
- Calculate noncontrolling interest when the subsidiary has preferred shares in its capital structure.
- Calculate consolidated net income and noncontrolling interest in situations where a parent has direct and indirect control over a number of subsidiary companies.

In this chapter we examine a variety of special problems associated with the preparation of consolidated financial statements. We commence with a discussion of certain factors that are unique to the overall consolidation process and that must be considered when the consolidated cash flow statement is prepared. We then turn our attention to three distinct issues associated with ownership: changes in a parent's ownership interest, subsidiaries with preferred shares, and indirect shareholdings.

Consolidated Cash Flow Statement

In the previous chapters we illustrated the direct approach to preparing the consolidated balance sheet and the consolidated income and retained earnings statements. In this approach, the individual statements of the parent and its subsidiaries are combined. We will now focus on the preparation of the final consolidated statement — the cash flow statement. While this statement could be prepared by combining the separate cash flow statements of the parent and its subsidiaries, this would involve eliminating all intercompany transactions, including intercompany transfers of cash. It is much easier to prepare the cash flow statement using comparative consolidated balance sheets and the consolidated income statement, because these statements do not contain any intercompany transactions. In all cases we assume that cash flows from operations are presented using the indirect method, whereby net income is adjusted for the effects of noncash items such as amortizations and changes in working capital items, and for gains and losses associated with investing and financing cash flows.

The preparation of the cash flow statement for a single unconsolidated company is well covered in introductory and intermediate accounting texts. The basic process used to determine the reasons for the change in cash or cash equivalents is one of analyzing the changes that have occurred in all noncash items on the balance sheet. The procedures used to carry out this analysis (a working paper or a series of T-accounts) will not be repeated here. Instead, we will describe items that are unique to consolidated statements and that must be taken into account in the analysis. The major items that require special attention are summarized below:

1. Acquisition-date fair value differences are amortized in the consolidated income statement. While some of the amortizations may be obvious from their descriptions in the income statement, others may be buried in some expense accounts. Because amortizations have no effect on cash flows, we must adjust the year's net income for them in order to arrive at cash flow from operations.

2. Noncontrolling interest in the consolidated income statement is an allocation of the entity's net income and does not affect cash flows. We must add it back to net income in the same manner as depreciation in order to arrive at the operating cash flow.

3. Dividends paid by subsidiaries to the parent company do not change the entity's cash. Dividends paid by the parent to its shareholders, and dividends paid by the subsidiaries to noncontrolling shareholders, reduce the cash of the consolidated entity. The *Handbook* requires separate disclosure of dividends paid to noncontrolling shareholders.[1]

---

[1] *CICA Handbook*, paragraph 1540.12(g).

4. A change in the parent's ownership percentage during the year requires a careful analysis to determine its effect on consolidated assets, liabilities, and equities. This will be illustrated in a later section of this chapter (on ownership changes).

5. In the year that a subsidiary is acquired, special disclosures are required in the cash flow statement. The following example illustrates this.

Showing the Acquisition of a Subsidiary in the Consolidated Cash Flow Statement

The consolidated balance sheet of Parent Company and its five subsidiaries as at December 31, Year 1, is shown below.

PARENT COMPANY
CONSOLIDATED BALANCE SHEET
December 31, Year 1

Cash	$ 500,000
Other assets	900,000
Goodwill	120,000
	$1,520,000
Liabilities	$ 500,000
Noncontrolling interest	100,000
Common shares	200,000
Retained earnings	720,000
	$1,520,000

On January 2, Year 2, Parent acquired 80 percent of the outstanding common shares of its sixth subsidiary, Sable Ltd., for a total cost of $140,000. The shareholders of Sable received cash of $90,000 and common shares of Parent with a market value of $50,000 in this transaction. The management of Parent determined that the other assets of Sable had a fair value of $205,000 on this date. The balance sheet of Sable on December 31, Year 1, is shown below:

SABLE LTD.
BALANCE SHEET
December 31, Year 1

Cash	$ 30,000
Other assets	200,000
	$230,000
Liabilities	$ 70,000
Common shares	100,000
Retained earnings	60,000
	$230,000

Parent's journal entry to record the acquisition of 80 percent of the common shares of Sable would be as follows on January 2, Year 2:

Investment in Sable Ltd.	140,000	
Common shares		50,000
Cash		90,000

We will now prepare the consolidated balance sheet of Parent on January 2, Year 2, incorporating the latest acquisition.

The calculation and allocation of the purchase discrepancy for the Sable investment is shown below:

Cost of investment in Sable		$140,000
Book value of Sable	160,000	
	80%	128,000
Purchase discrepancy		$ 12,000
Allocated:		
Other assets (5,000 × 80%)		4,000
Goodwill		$ 8,000
Noncontrolling interest (160,000 × 20%)		$ 32,000

The consolidated balance sheet appears below:

PARENT COMPANY
CONSOLIDATED BALANCE SHEET
January 2, Year 2

Cash (500,000 + 30,000 – 90,000)	$ 440,000
Other assets (900,000 + 200,000 + 4,000)	1,104,000
Goodwill (120,000 + 8,000)	128,000
	$1,672,000
Liabilities (500,000 + 70,000)	$ 570,000
Noncontrolling interest (100,000 + 32,000)	132,000
Common shares (200,000 + 50,000)	250,000
Retained earnings	720,000
	$1,672,000

Consolidated Cash Flow Statement

We can now prepare the consolidated cash flow statement for the two-day period that has elapsed by analyzing the changes in the two consolidated balance sheets. We know that the only transaction that has taken place is Parent's acquisition of 80 percent of Sable. The journal entry of Parent to record the acquisition was illustrated earlier. If we were preparing the cash flow statement of the parent company, we would use our knowledge of this entry in our analysis. But we are preparing the consolidated cash flow statement, and the account "Investment in Sable" does not appear in the consolidated balance sheet. In order to do the proper analysis we need to visualize the effect of this new acquisition on the consolidated balance sheet. We can depict this effect in the form of a "consolidating entry" in the following manner:

Cash	**30,000**	
Other assets (200,000 + 4,000)	**204,000**	
Goodwill	**8,000**	
Liabilities		**70,000**
Noncontrolling interest		**32,000**
Cash		90,000
Common shares		50,000

Notice that the portion of the entry shown in boldface is the amount of the account "Investment in Sable" that made up the parent's acquisition journal entry shown on page 354.

Using either the working paper or the T-account approach to analyze the changes that have taken place between the two consolidated balance sheets, we can now prepare the statement shown below.

PARENT COMPANY
STATEMENT OF CASH FLOWS
for the Two-day Period Ended January 2, Year 2

Operating cash flow:	$	nil
Investing cash flow:		
Acquisition of Sable, less cash acquired in acquisition $30,000 [note 1]		60,000
Financing cash flow:		nil
Net change in cash for the two-day period		(60,000)
Cash, December 31, Year 1		500,000
Cash, January 2, Year 2		$440,000

Note 1: Effective January 2, Year 2, the company acquired 80% of the common shares of Sable for a total consideration of $140,000. The acquisition, which was accounted for by the purchase method, is summarized as follows:

Net assets acquired:	
Other assets	$204,000
Goodwill	8,000
Liabilities	(70,000)
Noncontrolling interest	(32,000)
	$110,000
Consideration given:	
Common shares	$ 50,000
Cash	90,000
	140,000
Less cash acquired on acquisition	30,000
	$110,000

In our discussion of the consolidated cash flow statement, we have focused entirely on items unique to consolidated statements, on the assumption that the overall process for preparing such statements has been covered in earlier financial accounting courses. The next major topic in this chapter, *ownership change*, also presents items that require analysis as to their effects on consolidated cash flows. The cash flow effects will be discussed in the appropriate sections.

Ownership Changes

A parent's ownership interest will change if:

(a) the parent purchases additional holdings in its subsidiary (block acquisitions); *or*

(b) the parent sells some of its holdings in its subsidiary; *or*

(c) the subsidiary issues additional common shares to the public, and the parent does not maintain its previous ownership percentage.

When the parent's ownership changes, the percentage of subsidiary common stock held by the noncontrolling interest also changes. This percentage change in noncontrolling interest does not present any particular problems in the preparation of consolidated financial statements. The major consolidation problem involved with ownership change is the effect such changes have on the valuation of subsidiary net assets in the consolidated statements. When the parent's ownership percentage *increases*, there will be an additional purchase discrepancy that must be allocated to revalue the net assets of the subsidiary as at that date. When the parent's ownership *decreases*, a reduction of the unamortized purchase discrepancy occurs. We will use a simple example to examine the calculations involved in a reduction; we will then look at a situation where the parent's percentage increases through block purchases and then decreases as a result of its own actions or the actions of its subsidiary.

Effect on Purchase Discrepancy of Ownership Reduction

Assume that P Company purchased 60 percent of the outstanding common shares of S Company at a cost of $150,000. On this date S Company's shareholders' equity was as follows:

Common stock (10,000 shares)	$100,000
Retained earnings	90,000
	$190,000

The book values of all of S Company's net assets were equal to current fair values, except for specialized equipment, which was undervalued by $9,000, and unrecognized patents that had a fair value of $51,000. The calculation and allocation of the purchase discrepancy is as follows:

Cost of 60% of S		$150,000
Book value of S's net assets:		
Common stock	100,000	
Retained earnings	90,000	
Total shareholders' equity	190,000	
P's ownership interest	60%	114,000
Purchase discrepancy		36,000
Allocated:		
Equipment (9,000 × 60%)	5,400	
Patents (51,000 × 60%)	30,600	36,000
Balance		$ nil

Now let us assume that on the same day that P Company purchased these 6,000 shares in S Company, P sold 600 shares on the open market for $18,000. (This is not a very realistic assumption, but we use it to illustrate the effect that such a transaction will have on the purchase discrepancy.)

Note that after the sale, P Company's ownership percentage is 54 percent (5,400 ÷ 10,000). Note also that P Company has disposed of 10 percent of its investment in S Company (600 ÷ 6,000). Another way of calculating the percentage of investment disposed is as follows:

Ownership before sale	60%
Ownership after sale	54%
Change	6%

Percentage of investment sold: 6 ÷ 60 = 10%.

P Company would make the following journal entry to record the sale of 600 shares:

Cash	18,000	
Investment in S (10% × $150,000)		15,000
Gain on sale of shares		3,000

The $3,000 gain on sale would appear on P Company's current income statement and would also appear on the consolidated income statement. Now let us recalculate the purchase discrepancy immediately after the sale of 600 shares:

Investment in S (150,000 – 15,000)		$135,000
Shareholders' equity — S Company	$190,000	
P's ownership interest	54%	102,600
Purchase discrepancy		$ 32,400

The purchase discrepancy has been reduced by 10 percent of its original amount. The effect of this reduction on the amounts allocated to revalue S Company's net assets can be shown as follows:

	Purchase discrepancy prior to sale	Reduction due to sale of 10%	Purchase discrepancy after sale
Equipment	$ 5,400	$ 540	$ 4,860
Patents	30,600	3,060	27,540
	$36,000	$3,600	$32,400

This 10 percent reduction in the purchase discrepancy should cause no real surprise. Remember that the $36,000 original purchase discrepancy was "buried" in the investment in S Company amount of $150,000. When Parent's journal entry to record the sale removed 10 percent from the investment account, it also removed 10 percent of the purchase discrepancy.

The above example can be considered unrealistic because the sale took place on the same date that the parent purchased the subsidiary. However, the effect would be the same if the sale had occurred subsequent to the date of acquisition, except that the unamortized purchase discrepancy would be reduced by 10 percent rather than the original purchase discrepancy. This concept will be illustrated in a later example (see page 364).

Block Acquisitions of Subsidiary (step purchases)

The consolidation illustrations that we have used in previous chapters have assumed that the parent company achieved its control in a subsidiary by making a single purchase of the subsidiary's common shares. This is not always the case. In some instances a parent company will achieve its ownership interest through a series of block acquisitions (sometimes described as step purchases). The consolidation problems are basically the same whether control was achieved in the first purchase, with any additional purchase(s) simply increasing the parent's ownership interest, or whether control was not present after the first purchase but was achieved with subsequent purchases. For each purchase, a purchase discrepancy is calculated and allocated to revalue the net assets of the subsidiary, with the balance allocated to goodwill. We will illustrate this concept with an example.

Purchase of First Block of Shares On January 1, Year 1, Par Company purchases 60 percent of the outstanding common shares of Sub Company at a cost of $150,000. On this date Sub's shareholders' equity is as follows:

SUB COMPANY
SHAREHOLDERS' EQUITY
January 1, Year 1

Common stock (10,000 Shares)	$100,000
Retained earnings	90,000
	$190,000

The book values of Sub's net assets are equal to current fair values except for specialized equipment, which is undervalued by $9,000, and patents, which are undervalued by $51,000. The equipment has an estimated remaining life of 5 years and the patents are to be amortized over a 10-year period. The purchase discrepancy calculation and allocation is the same as that shown on page 357 because all amounts used in the two illustrations are identical. On December 31, Year 1, Sub reports a net income of $30,000 and pays dividends amounting to $8,000. Before Par's equity method journal entries are recorded for Year 1, the amortization of the purchase discrepancy is calculated as follows:

	Balance, January 1, Year 1	Amortization Year 1	Unamortized balance, December 31, Year 1
Equipment	$ 5,400	$1,080	$ 4,320
Patents	30,600	3,060	27,540
	$36,000	$4,140	$31,860

Par Company's December 31, Year 1, journal entries (equity method) are:

Investment in Sub	18,000	
Investment income		18,000
To record 60% of Sub's net income for Year 1 (30,000 × 60%)		

Cash	4,800	
Investment in Sub		4,800
To record dividends received from Sub in Year 1 (8,000 × 60%)		

Investment income	4,140	
Investment in Sub		4,140
To record the amortization of the purchase discrepancy for Year 1		

Consolidated financial statements for Year 1 would be prepared in the same manner as was illustrated in previous chapters.

Purchase of Second Block of Shares   On January 1, Year 2, Par Company purchases an additional 3,000 shares of Sub Company for $78,200. This represents 30 percent of Sub's outstanding shares, and Par's total ownership interest is now 90 percent. On this date the book values of Sub's net assets are equal to current fair values except for the specialized equipment, which is now undervalued by $12,000. This equipment now has an estimated life of four years. Any goodwill is to be tested yearly for impairment. The purchase discrepancy and its allocation for the second block is calculated below.

Cost of 30% of Sub		$78,200
Book value of Sub's net assets		
Common stock	100,000	
Retained earnings (90,000 + 30,000 − 8,000)	112,000	
Total shareholders' equity	212,000	
Par's ownership interest	30%	63,600
Purchase discrepancy		14,600
Allocated:		
Equipment (12,000 × 30%)		3,600
Balance — goodwill		$11,000

On December 31, Year 2, Sub reports a net income of $35,000 and pays dividends amounting to $10,000. A goodwill impairment test conducted on this date indicates a loss of $1,100. The purchase discrepancy amortization schedule for Year 2 is prepared in the manner shown below.

PURCHASE DISCREPANCY AMORTIZATION SCHEDULE

	First Purchase		Second Purchase		Total
	Equip.	Patents	Equip.	Goodwill	
Balance, December 31, Year 1	$4,320	$27,540	—	—	$31,860
Purchase, January 1, Year 2	—	—	3,600	11,000	14,600
	4,320	27,540	3,600	11,000	46,460
Amortization, Year 2	1,080	3,060	900	1,100	6,140
Balance, December 31, Year 2	$3,240	$24,480	$2,700	$ 9,900	$40,320

Par Company's equity method journal entries for Year 2 would be as follows:

Investment in Sub	31,500	
Investment income		31,500
To record 90% of Sub's net income for Year 2 (35,000 × 90%)		
Cash	9,000	
Investment in Sub		9,000
To record dividends received from Sub in Year 2 (10,000 × 90%)		
Investment income	6,140	
Investment in Sub		6,140
To record the amortization of the purchase discrepancy for Year 2		

On December 31, Year 2, the account "Investment in Sub" on Par's books would have a balance of $253,620, calculated as follows:

Cost of first purchase (60%), January 1, Year 1	$150,000
Year 1 equity method journal entries	
Sub net income (30,000 × 60%)	18,000
Sub dividends (8,000 × 60%)	(4,800)
Purchase discrepancy amortization	(4,140)
Balance, December 31, Year 1	159,060
Cost of second purchase (30%), January 1, Year 2	78,200
Year 2 equity method journal entries	
Sub net income (35,000 × 90%)	31,500
Sub dividends (10,000 × 90%)	(9,000)
Purchase discrepancy amortization	(6,140)
Balance, December 31, Year 2	$253,620

The preceding example has assumed that there were no intercompany transactions involving unrealized profits during the two-year period. When this is the case, the elimination of the parent's ownership interest in the shareholders' equity of the subsidiary against the investment in subsidiary account will always yield a balance equal to the unamortized purchase discrepancy. This can be illustrated as follows:

Investment in Sub, December 31, Year 2			$253,620
Shareholders' equity of Sub			
Common stock		100,000	
Retained earnings			
Balance, January 1, Year 1	90,000		
Net income, Years 1 and 2			
(30,000 + 35,000)	65,000		
Dividends, Years 1 and 2			
(8,000 + 10,000)	(18,000)	137,000	
Balance, December 31, Year 2		237,000	
Par's ownership interest		90%	213,300
Balance — unamortized purchase discrepancy			$ 40,320

The preparation of the Year 2 consolidated financial statements will not be shown because the procedures are basically the same as have been illustrated in previous chapters. A glance at the Year 2 purchase discrepancy amortization schedule on page 360 should make it obvious that in preparing the consolidated balance sheet, the equipment of Sub Company is revalued by a total of $5,940 (3,240 + 2,700), patents are revalued by $24,480, while consolidated goodwill is $9,900.

The amortization of the purchase discrepancies for Year 2 is reflected in the consolidated income statement, as follows:

Depreciation expense (1,080 + 900)	$1,980
Patent amortization	3,060
Goodwill impairment loss	1,100
	$6,140

Consolidated Cash Flow Analysis Par Company's second block purchase of shares (on January 1, Year 2) requires further analysis to determine the effect on the Year 2 consolidated balance sheet. Par's journal entry to record the second purchase was:

Investment in Sub	78,200	
Cash		78,200

This cash has left the consolidated entity, so the effect of the transaction must appear on the Year 2 consolidated cash flow statement. By examining the calculation of the purchase discrepancy for the second purchase (see page 360) and the calculation of the decrease in noncontrolling interest (shown below) we can depict the effect of this transaction on the consolidated balance sheet with the following entry:

Equipment	3,600	
Goodwill	11,000	
Noncontrolling interest*	63,600	
Cash		78,200

*CHANGES IN NONCONTROLLING INTEREST

Balance before second purchase (40% × 212,000)	$84,800
Balance after second purchase (10% × 212,000)	21,200
Decrease in noncontrolling interest	$63,600

The $78,200 cash outflow should appear and be described on the consolidated cash flow statement under the caption "Investing activities."

In summary, the only new consolidation concept involved with block acquisitions is the revaluation of the subsidiary's net assets at the time each block is acquired. Paragraph 1600.13 of the *Handbook* describes the process as follows:

> Where an investment in a subsidiary is acquired through two or more purchases, the parent company's interest in the subsidiary's identifiable assets and liabilities should be determined as follows:
>
> (a) the assignable costs of the subsidiary's identifiable assets and liabilities should be determined as at each date on which an investment was acquired;
>
> (b) the parent company's interest in the subsidiary's identifiable assets and liabilities acquired at each step in the purchase should be based on the assignable costs of all such assets and liabilities at that date.

The *Handbook* also suggests that this process should commence the first time that the equity method becomes appropriate and, in addition, that it would be practical to treat numerous small purchases, especially those made over short periods of time, as a single purchase. These concepts are discussed in the two sections that follow.

No Control from Initial Acquisition The previous example assumed that the parent first purchased 60 percent and later an additional 30 percent of the shares in its subsidiary. Suppose instead that the 90 percent ownership was achieved in the following manner:

	% purchased	Cost
Year 1	8%	$ 50,000
Year 3	27%	225,000
Year 4	55%	500,000

In this situation control was achieved after the third acquisition, and therefore the preparation of consolidated financial statements would only commence after this Year 4 purchase. We assume that the Year 1 acquisition was not large enough to convey even significant influence and so during the time that the 8 percent was held it was a portfolio investment to be accounted for using the cost method. A purchase discrepancy calculation is not necessary and the investor's revenue is simply 8 percent of the dividends paid by the investee.

After the 27 percent purchase made in Year 3, the total holdings become 35 percent, which we assume is sufficient for significant influence. If this is the case, the investment is accounted for using the equity method commencing from the date of the Year 3 purchase. The purchase discrepancy is calculated at that time by taking the total cost of 35 percent, which is $275,000 (50,000 + 225,000), and subtracting from it 35 percent of the shareholders' equity of the investee. This purchase discrepancy is allocated to 35 percent of the difference between fair value and book value of identifiable net assets, with the remainder allocated to goodwill. When the 55 percent is acquired, we have the second block acquisition, which would be accounted for in a manner similar to our last example.

An argument could be made that the 35 percent is made up of two acquisitions (8 percent and 27 percent) and that a purchase discrepancy calculation and allocation should be made for each. Furthermore, it could be argued that a retroactive adjustment to the equity method should be made in Year 3 for the 8 percent acquisition that was made in Year 1. This treatment would be required under American accounting standards. The *CICA Handbook* suggests that it is probably impractical to calculate a purchase discrepancy at times prior to the achievement of significant influence,[2] and also indicates that retroactive restatement to the equity method is not required.[3]

Numerous Small Purchases

Assume that a parent company owns 75 percent of a subsidiary and decides that it will attempt to increase this percentage by making daily open market purchases of the subsidiary's shares. At the end of two months it abandons the idea. During this period it has made 35 separate share purchases that in total represent 9 percent of the subsidiary's outstanding shares. Since it would be impractical to calculate 35 purchase discrepancies, the *Handbook* recommends taking the total cost of these purchases and treating it as a single block purchase of 9 percent.

Consolidated Retained Earnings — Cost Method

The examples used to illustrate block purchases have assumed that the parent company uses the equity method to account for its investment. When the parent has used the cost method, a calculation adjusting to the equity method is required when consolidated statements are prepared. This calculation has been extensively illustrated in earlier chapters and requires only slight modification when block acquisitions have been made. Using our most recent example, we can illustrate the basic idea behind the calculation of consolidated retained earnings at the end of Year 5 in the following manner:

---

[2] *CICA Handbook*, paragraph 1600.11.
[3] *CICA Handbook*, paragraph 3050.13.

CALCULATION OF CONSOLIDATED RETAINED EARNINGS
December 31, Year 5

Retained earnings of parent — cost method		$ xxx
Less: Purchase discrepancy amortizations		
Year 3 purchase	xxx	
Year 4 purchase	xxx	xxx
Adjusted		xxx
Retained earnings of subsidiary at the time of		
Year 4 purchase	xxx	
Retained earnings of subsidiary at the time of		
Year 3 purchase	xxx	
Increase since Year 3 purchase	xxx	
Parent's ownership percentage	35%	xxx
Retained earnings of subsidiary — Dec. 31, Year 5	xxx	
Retained earnings of subsidiary at the time		
of Year 4 purchase	xxx	
Increase since Year 4 purchase	xxx	
Parent's ownership percentage	90%	xxx
Consolidated retained earnings		$ xxx

Reduction in Parent's Interest in Subsidiary

The effect of a reduction in a parent's ownership interest on a single block purchase discrepancy was illustrated earlier in this chapter (page 358). We will now carry on our illustration of Par Company and its subsidiary Sub Company to examine the effects of a reduction of ownership interest on a multiple block purchase. We will examine two alternative ways that a reduction of ownership interest could occur: (1) the parent sells a portion of its holdings in its subsidiary, and (2) the subsidiary issues additional common shares to the public. In each alternative, we assume that the ownership change took place on January 1, Year 3.

Alternative #1: Parent Sells a Portion of Its Holdings
On January 1, Year 3, Par Company sold 900 shares of its holdings in Sub Company for $30,000. This represents 10 percent of its investment (900 ÷ 9,000) and as a result its ownership interest has declined from 90 percent to 81 percent (8,100 ÷ 10,000).

Par would make the following journal entry on January 1, Year 3, to record the sale of 900 shares:

Cash	30,000	
Investment in Sub (253,620 × 10%)		25,362
Gain on sale of investment		4,638
To record the sale of 900 shares of Sub		

We observed in our previous example that a 10 percent reduction in the investment account results in a 10 percent reduction in the unamortized purchase discrepancy. In this example there are two unamortized purchase discrepancies because there were two purchases of stock. Does the reduction affect the first, or the second, or both? The answer is that the reduction affects both, because paragraph 1600.42 of the *Handbook* requires that the reduction of the carrying amount of the investment should be based on the average carrying value. Therefore, because we have reduced the investment account by 10 percent, we have also reduced the two unamortized purchase discrepancies by 10 percent.

On December 31, Year 3, Sub reported a net income of $40,000 and paid dividends amounting to $15,000. A goodwill impairment test conducted on December 31, Year 3, indicated that a further loss of $1,000 had occurred. The following purchase discrepancy amortization schedule would be made on December 31, Year 3:

	First Purchase		Second Purchase		Total
	Equip.	*Patents*	*Equip.*	*Goodwill*	
Balance, December 31, Year 2	$3,240	$24,480	$2,700	$9,900	$40,320
10 percent disposal, January 1, Year 3	324	2,448	270	990	4,032
Balance after disposal	2,916	22,032	2,430	8,910	36,288
Amortization — Year 3	972	2,754	810	1,000	5,536
Balance, December 31, Year 3	$1,944	$19,278	$1,620	$7,910	$30,752

Note that the Year 3 amortization is based on the years of life remaining from the original estimates, which is three years for equipment and eight years for the patents. Alternatively, the amortization amounts could be calculated by taking 90 percent of the amortization amounts shown in the schedule on page 360. (If 10 percent of the investment has been sold, 90 percent of the original investment is left to amortize, and therefore, the subsequent amounts of amortization are 90 percent of the original amounts.)

Par's equity-method journal entries for Year 3 would be as follows:

```
Investment in Sub                                             32,400
    Investment income                                                    32,400
To record 81% of Sub's net income for Year 3 (40,000 × 81%)


Cash                                                          12,150
    Investment in Sub                                                    12,150
To record dividends received from Sub in Year 3 (15,000 × 81%)


Investment income                                              5,536
    Investment in Sub                                                     5,536
To record the amortization of the purchase discrepancy for Year 3
```

On December 31, Year 3, the account "Investment in Sub" would have a balance of $242,982, calculated as follows:

Balance, December 31, Year 2 (9,000 shares)	$253,620
Sale of 10% of investment (900) shares)	(25,362)
Year 3 equity method journal entries	
Sub net income (40,000 × 81%)	32,400
Sub dividends (15,000 × 81%)	(12,150)
Purchase discrepancy amortization	(5,536)
Balance, December 31, Year 3	$242,972

In the preparation of the consolidated balance sheet on December 31, Year 3, the elimination of Sub's shareholders' equity against the investment account will result in the unamortized purchase discrepancy, as follows:

Investment in Sub Company — December 31, Year 3		$242,972
Shareholders' equity of Sub		
Common stock	100,000	
Retained earnings		
(137,000 + 40,000 – 15,000)	162,000	
	262,000	
Par's ownership interest	81%	212,220
Balance — unamortized purchase discrepancy		$ 30,752

The schedule on page 365 indicates that this amount would be allocated to equipment $3,564 (1,944 + 1,620), patents $19,278, and goodwill $7,910 in the preparation of the consolidated balance sheet. Noncontrolling interest would appear in the amount of $49,780 (262,000 × 19%).

The following are the Year 3 income statements of Par and Sub:

	Par	Sub
Miscellaneous revenue	$200,000	$150,000
Gain on sale of investment	4,638	—
Investment income	26,874	—
	$231,512	$150,000
Miscellaneous expense	$130,000	$ 90,000
Equipment depreciation expense	—	20,000
	$130,000	$110,000
Net income	$101,512	$ 40,000

The gain on sale of investment is not eliminated and therefore appears on the consolidated income statement. Investment income is replaced with the revenues and expenses of Sub, the amortization of the purchase discrepancies, and the noncontrolling interest. The Year 3 consolidated income statement prepared using the direct approach appears below:

PAR COMPANY
CONSOLIDATED INCOME STATEMENT
Year Ended December 31, Year 3

Miscellaneous revenues (200,000 + 150,000)	$350,000
Gain on sale of investment (4,638 + 0)	4,638
	$354,638
Miscellaneous expenses (130,000 + 90,000)	$220,000
Equipment depreciation (0 + 20,000 + 972 + 810)	21,782
Patent amortization (0 + 0 + 2,754)	2,754
Goodwill impairment loss (0 + 0 + 1,000)	1,000
	$245,536
Net income — entity	$109,102
Less noncontrolling interest (19% × 40,000)	7,600
Net income	$101,502

Consolidated Cash Flow Analysis   Par's journal entry to record the sale of 900 shares is shown on page 364. We can see that this transaction increased the entity's cash by $30,000, and we know that the gain appears on the consolidated income statement. But "Investment in Sub" does not appear on the consolidated balance sheet. By examining the purchase discrepancy amortization schedule on page 365, as well as realizing that noncontrolling interest increased with the parent's sale of the shares, we can prepare the following entry, which shows the effect of the transaction on the consolidated financial statements:

Cash	30,000	
Equipment (324 + 270)		594
Patents		2,448
Goodwill		990
Noncontrolling interest*		21,330
Gain on sale of investment		4,638

*CHANGES IN NONCONTROLLING INTEREST

Balance after parent's sale (19% × 237,000)	$45,030
Balance before parent's sale (10% × 237,000)	23,700
Increase in noncontrolling interest	$21,330

The $30,000 increase in cash would appear as an investing activity in the Year 3 consolidated cash flow statement, and the $4,638 gain would be deducted from net income to arrive at cash flow from operating activities.

Alternative #2: Subsidiary Issues Additional Shares to Public

 Let us assume that alternative #1 did not take place, and that, instead, Sub Company issued an additional 2,500 shares for $83,000 on January 1, Year 3. Sub would record this transaction as follows:

Cash	83,000	
Common stock		83,000
To record the issuance of 2,500 shares		

Sub now has 12,500 common shares issued. Because Par did not buy any of the new issue, its holdings have remained constant (9,000 shares), but its ownership interest has declined to 72 percent (9,000 ÷ 12,500). This represents a 20 percent reduction in its investment, calculated as follows:

Ownership before share issue	90%
Ownership after share issue	72%
Change	18%
Percentage of investment reduced: 18 ÷ 90 = 20%	

The effect of this reduction on the unamortized purchase discrepancy is the same as if the parent had sold a portion of its holding in the subsidiary (*CICA Handbook*, paragraphs 1600.46–47). In this case 20 percent of the unamortized purchase discrepancy has been "disposed of" as a result of the share issue. However, at this point the only entry made to record the transaction is the entry made by Sub. Parent must also adjust its investment account to record the effect of this transaction on its investment. The following analysis indicates the amount of the adjustment:

Loss due to reduction of investment account — 20% × 253,620	$50,724
Gain due to ownership of new assets resulting from subsidiary	
share issue — 72% × 83,000	$59,760
Net gain to parent due to share issue	$ 9,036

In our previous example, we explained the reasoning for removing 20 percent from the investment account. The unamortized purchase discrepancy is included in the $253,620 amount, and if this discrepancy has been reduced by 20 percent, a logical extension is to remove 20 percent from the total investment balance. If the subsidiary had issued the 2,500 shares for no consideration, the investment account would have to be reduced by $50,724, and a loss equal to that amount would be recorded by Par. But Sub received $83,000 for its new share issue, and Par now controls 72 percent of the net assets of its subsidiary, including the additional cash received as a result of the new share issue. Par has gained by the 72 percent ownership interest in the assets received by Sub. It should be obvious that net gain or loss resulting from the transaction depends on the amount that the subsidiary received from its new share issue. Given the facts of this particular example, Par would make the following journal entry on January 1, Year 3:

Investment in Sub	9,036	
Gain from subsidiary share issue		9,036
To record the effect of subsidiary's issue of 2,500 shares on parent's investment		

As in our previous example, we assume that in Year 3, Sub reported a net income of $40,000 and paid $15,000 in dividends. The following purchase discrepancy amortization schedule would be prepared on December 31, Year 3:

	First Purchase		Second Purchase		Total
	Equip.	Patents	Equip.	Goodwill	
Balance, December 31, Year 2	$3,240	$24,480	$2,700	$9,900	$40,320
20% "disposed" January 1, Year 3	648	4,896	540	1,980	8,064
Balance after disposal	2,592	19,584	2,160	7,920	32,256
Amortization — Year 3	864	2,448	720	1,000	5,032
Balance, December 31, Year 3	$1,728	$17,136	$1,440	$6,920	$27,224

Par's equity method journal entries for Year 3 would be as follows:

Investment in Sub	28,800	
Investment income		28,800
To record 72% of Sub's net income for Year 3 (40,000 × 72%)		

Cash	10,800	
Investment in Sub		10,800
To record dividends received from Sub in Year 3 (15,000 × 72%)		

Investment income	5,032	
Investment in Sub		5,032
To record the amortization of the purchase discrepancy for Year 3		

In the same manner as previous examples, the elimination of the parent's interest in the subsidiary's shareholders' equity against the parent's investment account leaves a balance equal to the unamortized purchase discrepancy. This will now be illustrated.

Investment in Sub

Balance, December 31, Year 2	$253,620
Increase due to subsidiary share issue	9,036
Sub net income (40,000 × 72%)	28,800
Sub dividends (15,000 × 72%)	(10,800)
Purchase discrepancy amortization	(5,032)
Balance, December 31, Year 3	275,624

Shareholders' equity of Sub

Common stock — December 31, Year 2	100,000	
Share issue — Year 3	83,000	
Common stock, December 31, Year 3	183,000	
Retained earnings, December 31, Year 3		
(137,000 + 40,000 – 15,000)	162,000	
Total, December 31, Year 3	345,000	
Par's ownership interest	72%	248,400
Balance — unamortized purchase discrepancy		$ 27,224

The amortization schedule on page 368 shows how the unamortized purchase discrepancy would be allocated to equipment, patents, and goodwill in the preparation of the consolidated balance sheet on December 31, Year 3. Noncontrolling interest would appear in the amount of $96,600 (28% × 345,000).

The Year 3 income statements of Par and Sub are shown below, and are followed by the consolidated income statement.

	Par Company	Sub Company
Miscellaneous revenue	$200,000	$150,000
Gain from subsidiary share issue	9,036	—
Investment income	23,768	—
	$232,804	$150,000
Miscellaneous expense	$130,000	$ 90,000
Equipment depreciation expense	—	20,000
	$130,000	$110,000
Net income	$102,804	$ 40,000

PAR COMPANY
CONSOLIDATED INCOME STATEMENT
Year Ended December 31, Year 3

Miscellaneous revenues (200,000 + 150,000)	$350,000
Gain from subsidiary share issue	9,036
	$359,036
Miscellaneous expense (130,000 + 90,000)	$220,000
Equipment depreciation (0 + 20,000 + 864 + 720)	21,584
Patent amortization	2,448
Goodwill impairment loss (0 + 0 + 1,000)	1,000
	$245,032
Net income — entity	$114,004
Less noncontrolling interest (28% × 40,000)	11,200
Net income	$102,804

Consolidated Cash Flow Analysis   To recap, the issue of 2,500 shares on January 1, Year 3, was recorded by Sub Company with the following journal entry:

Cash	83,000	
Common stock		83,000

Also, in order to record the effect of the reduction on its investment, Par made the following journal entry on this date:

Investment in Sub	9,036	
Gain from subsidiary share issue		9,036

The effect of this transaction on the consolidated financial statements can be depicted as follows:

Cash	83,000	
Equipment (648 + 540)		1,188
Patents		4,896
Goodwill		1,980
Noncontrolling interest*		65,900
Gain from subsidiary share issue		9,036

*CHANGES IN NONCONTROLLING INTEREST

Balance after subsidiary share issue		
Shareholders' equity before issue	237,000	
New share issue	83,000	
	320,000	
	28%	89,600
Balance before subsidiary share issue (10% × 237,000)		23,700
Increase in noncontrolling interest		$65,900

The $83,000 increase in cash would appear as a financing activity in the Year 3 consolidated cash flow statement; the $9,036 gain would be deducted from net income to arrive at cash flow from operating activities.

Subsidiary with Preferred Shares Outstanding

All of the consolidation examples that we have used up to this point have assumed that the subsidiary companies have only one class of shares — common shares — in their capital structures. We now examine situations where the subsidiary also has preferred shares. The basic concepts of consolidation do not change, but when there is more than one class of shares outstanding, there is an additional problem involved in determining the amount of noncontrolling interest in the net assets and net income of the subsidiary. The following example will illustrate the approach that is used.

Illustration — Preferred Shareholdings

On December 31, Year 1, the shareholders' equity of Sonco Inc. was as follows:

Preferred shares, no par value, $10 dividend,	
cumulative, redeemable at $105 per share	
Issued and outstanding 1,000 shares	$100,000
Common shares, no par value	
Issued and outstanding 30,000 shares	360,000
Total contributed capital	460,000
Retained earnings (note 1)	140,000
	$600,000

Note 1: On December 31, Year 1, dividends on preferred shares are one year in arrears.

On January 1, Year 2, Parco Ltd. purchased 27,000 common shares of Sonco for $450,000. The purchase discrepancy was allocated entirely to franchise agreements, to be amortized over a 10-year period.

Because the parent company acquired control by purchasing 90 percent of the voting common shares, the noncontrolling interest consists of the shareholdings represented by 10 percent of the common shares and 100 percent of the preferred shares. In order to calculate any purchase discrepancy associated with the common share purchase, and the amount of the noncontrolling interest in both classes of shares, it is necessary to split the shareholders' equity of Sonco into its preferred and common share capital components in the following manner:

	Total	Preferred	Common
Preferred stock	$100,000	$100,000	—
Redemption premium on preferred	—	5,000	(5,000)
Common stock	360,000	—	360,000
Total contributed capital	460,000	105,000	355,000
Retained earnings	140,000	10,000	130,000
	$600,000	$115,000	$485,000

The $115,000 allocated to preferred share capital represents the total amount that the company would have to pay to the preferred shareholders if the preferred shares were redeemed on this date. It is made up of the redemption price on 1,000 shares ($105,000) and the one year's dividends in arrears ($10,000) on these shares.

By using the two components of shareholders' equity, both the purchase discrepancy and the noncontrolling interest on the date of acquisition can be calculated, as follows:

Cost of 90 percent of common stock		$450,000
Book value of common stock of Sonco	485,000	
	90%	436,500
Purchase discrepancy		13,500
Allocated: franchise agreement		13,500
Balance		$ –0–
Noncontrolling interest, January 1, Year 2		
Preferred shares (115,000 × 100%)		$115,000
Common shares (485,000 × 10%)		48,500
		$163,500

The preparation of the consolidated balance sheet on January 1, Year 2, will not be illustrated, but it should be obvious that the only difference from previous examples lies in how the noncontrolling interest is calculated on this date.

The financial statements of Parco and Sonco on December 31, Year 2, are shown in Exhibit 9.1.

In order to prepare the Year 2 consolidated financial statements, it is again necessary to split the shareholders' equity of Sonco into its preferred and common components. Because there has been no change in total contributed capital, the allocation of this component is identical to the one made as at January 1 (see page 371). But retained earnings *has* changed, and so we will allocate the retained earnings statement in the following manner:

	Total	Preferred	Common
Balance, January 1, Year 2	$140,000	$10,000	$130,000
Net income (see point #2)	60,000	10,000	50,000
	200,000	20,000	180,000
Dividends (see point #1)	50,000	20,000	30,000
Balance, December 31, Year 2	$150,000	–0–	$150,000

Exhibit 9.1

YEAR 2 INCOME STATEMENTS

	Parco	Sonco
Revenues — miscellaneous	$750,000	$420,000
Dividends from Sonco	27,000	—
	777,000	420,000
Expenses — miscellaneous	688,000	360,000
Net income	$ 89,000	$ 60,000

YEAR 2 RETAINED EARNINGS STATEMENTS

	Parco	Sonco
Balance, January 1	$381,000	$140,000
Net income	89,000	60,000
	470,000	200,000
Dividends	90,000	50,000
Balance, December 31	$380,000	$150,000

BALANCE SHEETS — December 31, Year 2

	Parco	Sonco
Assets — miscellaneous	$510,000	$810,000
Investment in Sonco — at cost	450,000	—
	$960,000	$810,000
Liabilities	$180,000	$200,000
Preferred shares	—	100,000
Common shares	400,000	360,000
Retained earnings	380,000	150,000
	$960,000	$810,000

It is important to note the following regarding the allocation process:

1. All dividends in arrears plus the current year's dividends must be paid to preferred shareholders before any dividends are paid to common shareholders. In this situation the dividends paid by Sonco were:

Preferred	$20,000
Common	30,000
	$50,000

2. When preferred shares are cumulative, the preferred shareholders are entitled to the yearly dividend even when the company has no income or has suffered a loss for the year. This means that the net income (or loss) for a particular year must be allocated to its preferred and common components. In the situation we are examining, the Year 2 net income is allocated this way:

To preferred equity	$10,000
To common equity	50,000
Total net income	$60,000

The allocation of total shareholders' equity as at December 31, Year 2, can now be prepared as shown below:

	Total	Preferred	Common
Contributed capital	$460,000	$105,000	$355,000
Retained earnings	150,000	–0–	150,000
	$610,000	$105,000	$505,000

Because Parco has used the cost method to account for its investment, we must make the following two calculations before preparing the Year 2 consolidated financial statements:

CALCULATION OF CONSOLIDATED NET INCOME, YEAR 2

Net income, Parco		$ 89,000
Less common dividends from Sonco (90% × 30,000)	27,000	
Purchase discrepancy amortization (13,500 ÷ 10)	1,350	28,350
		60,650
Net income, Sonco	60,000	
Less allocated to preferred shares	10,000	
Net income, common shares	50,000	
	90%	45,000
Consolidated net income		$105,650
Noncontrolling interest in net income		
Preferred net income (100% × 10,000)		$ 10,000
Common net income (10% × 50,000)		5,000
		$ 15,000

CALCULATION OF NONCONTROLLING INTEREST
December 31, Year 2

Preferred equity	105,000 × 100%	$105,000
Common equity	505,000 × 10%	50,500
		$155,500

The Year 2 consolidated financial statements are shown in Exhibit 9.2.

Exhibit 9.2

Year 2 Consolidated Statements
(when subsidiary has preferred shares)

PARCO LTD.
CONSOLIDATED INCOME STATEMENT
for the Year Ended December 31, Year 2

Revenues (750,000 + 420,000)	$1,170,000
Expenses (688,000 + 360,000 + 1,350*)	1,049,350
Net income — entity	$ 120,650
Less noncontrolling interest	15,000
Net income	$ 105,650

* Purchase discrepancy amortization

PARCO LTD.
CONSOLIDATED RETAINED EARNINGS STATEMENT
for the Year Ended December 31, Year 2

Balance, January 1	$ 381,000
Net income	105,650
	486,650
Dividends	90,000
Balance, December 31	$ 396,650

PARCO LTD.
CONSOLIDATED BALANCE SHEET
December 31, Year 2

Assets — miscellaneous (510,000 + 810,000)		$1,320,000
Franchise agreements (13,500 – 1,350)		12,150
		$1,332,150
Liabilities (180,000 + 200,000)		$ 380,000
Noncontrolling interest		155,500
Shareholders equity		
Common stock	400,000	
Retained earnings	396,650	796,650
		$1,332,150

Other Types of Preferred Shares

In the example above, the preferred shares are cumulative. If the shares were non-cumulative, net income would be allocated to the preferred shares only if preferred dividends were declared during the year, and of course dividends are never in arrears with this type of preferred share. If the preferred shares are participating, the allocation of net income will follow the participation provisions.

Subsidiary Preferred Shares Owned by Parent

A parent company may own all or a portion of its subsidiary's preferred shares in addition to its common share investment. When the cost of the investment in preferred shares is different from the book value of the stock acquired, a problem arises as to how to treat the preferred stock purchase discrepancy in the consolidated financial statements. Since preferred shares do not share in the value changes that take place in the subsidiary (the exception would be fully participating shares), market price changes in preferreds result from changes in interest rates. Because of this, the purchase discrepancy should not be used to revalue the subsidiary's identifiable net assets or goodwill. Instead it should be treated as a capital transaction and adjusted to consolidated contributed surplus or retained earnings. For example, assume that in addition to its common share investment in its subsidiary, a parent owns 30 percent of the subsidiary's noncumulative preferred shares. The parent uses the equity method to account for both investments, and on December 31, Year 9, had retained earnings amounting to $136,500 and no contributed surplus. On this date the purchase discrepancy from the 30 percent interest in preferred shares amounted to $11,865. Instead of presenting this amount among the assets on the consolidated balance sheet, we should deduct it from retained earnings so that consolidated retained earnings on December 31, Year 9, will be reported at $124,635 (136,500 − 11,865 = 124,635).

Indirect Shareholdings

When one company has control over another company, financial reporting by means of consolidated financial statements is required. The *Handbook* describes the concept of control as follows:

> An enterprise is presumed to control another enterprise when it owns, directly or indirectly, an equity interest that carries the right to elect the majority of the members of the other enterprise's board of directors, and is presumed not to control the other enterprise without such ownership. In a particular situation, these presumptions may be overcome by other factors that clearly demonstrate that control exists or does not exist.[4]

In all examples that we have used up to this point, the parent has had a direct ownership of over 50 percent of the common shares of the subsidiary. We continue to assume that over 50 percent ownership of the voting shares is necessary for control, but we now modify the assumption to allow this percentage to be achieved by both direct and indirect ownership. The following diagrams illustrate both direct and indirect holdings. In the first diagram, B and C are subsidiaries of A through direct control:

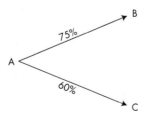

---

[4] *CICA Handbook*, paragraph 1590.08.

The second example, below, illustrates indirect control. G is a subsidiary of F, but F in turn is a subsidiary of E. Because E can control the voting shares of G through its control of F, G is also a subsidiary of E.

In the third example, K is a subsidiary of J through direct control. L is also a subsidiary of J through indirect control, because 55 percent of its voting shares are controlled directly or indirectly by J, even though only 43 percent [25% + (60% × 30%)] of L's net income will flow to J under the equity method of accounting.

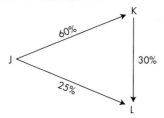

While many Canadian companies have intercorporate structures that are far more complex than those illustrated, the consolidation procedures for indirect holdings are not as complicated as the diagrams might indicate. Remember that if a parent company has 50 subsidiaries, the amount of cash appearing on the consolidated balance sheet is the sum of the cash from 51 separate balance sheets. This basic concept applies to most items appearing in the consolidated statements. In addition, we emphasized in past chapters the following statements that describe the fundamental relationships resulting from the parent's use of the equity method to account for its investment:

1. Parent's net income equals consolidated net income.

2. Parent's retained earnings equal consolidated retained earnings.

3. The elimination of the parent's share of the shareholders' equity of the subsidiary against the investment account leaves a balance consisting of the unamortized purchase discrepancy. This balance is used to revalue the net assets of the subsidiary when the consolidated balance sheet is prepared.

4. The portion of the shareholders' equity of the subsidiary that is not eliminated appears on the consolidated balance sheet as noncontrolling interest.

Since these fundamental relationships also apply when we have indirect holdings, the key to the preparation of consolidated statements when control is achieved by a mixture of direct and indirect investments is the use of the equity method of accounting for each investment. (If the cost method has been used, adjustments to the equity method must be made.) The following example will illustrate these concepts.

Parent Inc. owns 80 percent of the common shares of Subone Ltd. (which is sufficient for control) and 45 percent of the common shares of Subtwo Ltd. (which we assume is not sufficient for control). However, Subone owns 25 percent of the common shares of Subtwo. This investment combined with the parent's 45 percent investment gives the parent control of 70 percent of the voting shares; therefore, Subtwo is considered to be a subsidiary of Parent.

Each investment is accounted for using the equity method. In order to simplify the illustration, we assume that on acquisition date the fair values of the identifiable net assets of the investee corporations were equal to their book values, with the purchase discrepancies from each investment being allocated to unrecorded computer databases.

We will illustrate the preparation of consolidated financial statements for Year 6 in Exhibit 9.3, during which Parent had a net income from its own operations amounting to $135,000. Subone had a net income from its own operations amounting to $75,000, while the net income of Subtwo was $40,000. The following schedule, showing the calculation of the Year 6 consolidated net income, is useful because it illustrates the use of the equity method of accounting by both Subone and Parent.

Regarding the preparation and interpretation of the schedule, the following should be noted:

1. Purchase discrepancy amortizations are recorded by each company that has an investment in another company in the group. This is the first adjustment shown. The amounts have been assumed. Any adjustments required for intercompany gains and losses would also be made here (as would the deduction for intercompany dividends if the cost method had been used by Parent and Subone).

2. Because Parent cannot record its 80 percent share of Subone's net income until Subone has recorded its 25 percent share of Subtwo's net income, Subtwo's net income is allocated first.

3. Subone's net income using the equity method can now be determined.

4. After Subone's net income has been allocated, Parent's net income using the equity method is determined. This amount, of course, equals consolidated net income.

Exhibit 9.3

CALCULATION OF CONSOLIDATED NET INCOME — Year 6

	Parent	Subone	Subtwo	Total
Net income before investment income	$135,000	$75,000	$40,000	$250,000
Less database amortization				
Subone	(125)			(125)
Subtwo	(250)	(25)		(275)
	134,625	74,975	40,000	249,600
Allocate Subtwo				
25% to Subone		10,000	(10,000)	
45% to Parent	18,000		(18,000)	
Subone net income — equity method		84,975		
Allocate Subone				
80% to Parent	67,980	(67,980)		
Unallocated		$16,995	$12,000	28,995
Parent net income — equity method	$220,605			
Consolidated net income				$220,605

5. The portion of the net income of Subtwo and Subone that was not allocated is the noncontrolling interest in that net income.

6. The "Total" column shows amounts that appear in the consolidated income statement. Net income for the entity is $249,600, while noncontrolling interest is $28,995.

Exhibit 9.4 shows the Year 6 financial statements of the three companies.

In preparing the Year 6 consolidated income statement, we eliminate the three investment income accounts and replace them with the revenues and expenses of the two subsidiaries, the database amortization expense, and the noncontrolling interest in the net incomes of the subsidiaries. The consolidated retained earnings statement is identical to that of Parent and requires no preparation.

Exhibit 9.4

INCOME STATEMENTS — Year 6

	Parent	Subone	Subtwo
Miscellaneous revenues	$475,000	$285,000	$ 90,000
Investment income — Subone	67,855	—	—
Investment income — Subtwo	17,750	9,975	—
	560,605	294,975	90,000
Miscellaneous expenses	340,000	210,000	50,000
Net income	$220,605	$ 84,975	$ 40,000

RETAINED EARNINGS STATEMENTS — Year 6

	Parent	Subone	Subtwo
Balance, January 1	$279,120	$116,400	$ 80,000
Net income	220,605	84,975	40,000
	499,725	201,375	120,000
Dividends	45,000	30,000	10,000
Balance, December 31	$454,725	$171,375	$110,000

BALANCE SHEETS — December 31, Year 6

	Parent	Subone	Subtwo
Other assets	$608,500	$402,925	$460,000
Investment in Subone	281,975	—	—
Investment in Subtwo	104,250	53,450	—
	$994,725	$456,375	$460,000
Liabilities	$300,000	$110,000	$250,000
Common stock	240,000	175,000	100,000
Retained earnings	454,725	171,375	110,000
	$994,725	$456,375	$460,000

In preparing the consolidated balance sheet, we eliminate the investors' portion of the shareholders' equity of the investee companies against the investment accounts; this leaves a balance consisting of the unamortized purchase discrepancies. The amount of shareholders' equity not eliminated represents noncontrolling interest. The following calculations illustrate this:

Parent:

Investment in Subone		$281,975
Shareholders' equity, Subone		
Common stock	175,000	
Retained earnings	171,375	
	346,375	
Parent ownership	80%	277,100
Balance — unamortized databases		$ 4,875
Investment in Subtwo		$104,250
Shareholders' equity, Subtwo		
Common stock	100,000	
Retained earnings	110,000	
	210,000	
Parent's ownership	45%	94,500
Balance — unamortized databases		$ 9,750

Subone:

Investment in Subtwo		$ 53,450
Shareholders' equity, Subtwo (above)	210,000	
Subone ownership	25%	52,500
Balance — unamortized databases		$ 950

CALCULATION OF NONCONTROLLING INTEREST
December 31, Year 6

Shareholders' equity, Subone	346,375	
	20%	$ 69,275
Shareholders' equity, Subtwo	210,000	
	30%	63,000
		$132,275

Exhibit 9.5 shows the preparation of the Year 6 consolidated financial statements using the direct approach.

Exhibit 9.5

PARENT INC.
CONSOLIDATED FINANCIAL STATEMENTS
December 31, Year 6

CONSOLIDATED INCOME STATEMENT

Revenues (475,000 + 285,000 + 90,000)	$850,000
Miscellaneous expense (340,000 + 210,000 + 50,000)	$600,000
Database amortization (125 + 250 + 25)	400
	$600,400
Net income — entity	$249,600
Less noncontrolling interest	28,995
Net income	$220,605

CONSOLIDATED RETAINED EARNINGS STATEMENT

Balance, January 1	$279,120
Net income	220,605
	499,725
Dividends	45,000
Balance, December 31	$454,725

CONSOLIDATED BALANCE SHEET

Other assets (608,500 + 402,925 + 460,000)		$1,471,425
Databases (4,875 + 9,750 + 950)		15,575
		$1,487,000
Liabilities (300,000 + 110,000 + 250,000)		$ 660,000
Noncontrolling interest		132,275
Shareholders' equity		
Common stock	240,000	
Retained earnings	454,725	694,725
		$1,487,000

SUMMARY

In this chapter we examined four topics that present special problems in consolidated financial statement preparation. While the consolidated balance sheet and income statement are prepared by combining the statements of the parent and its subsidiaries, the consolidated statement of cash flows is best prepared by analyzing the changes in successive consolidated balance sheets.

The next topic was concerned with changes in the parent's percentage ownership and the effect that such changes have on the noncontrolling interest and particularly on unamortized purchase discrepancies. These ownership changes also require special attention when the consolidated cash flow statement is prepared.

Preferred shares in the capital structure of subsidiary companies present unique problems in calculating noncontrolling interest if the parent's ownership of the preferred shares is not the same as its ownership of the common shares.

The problem is solved by allocating shareholders' equity and any changes therein to preferred and common share components.

Control by a parent company can be achieved through direct ownership of the subsidiary's voting shares or through indirect ownership by other subsidiaries or investees. If the equity method is used for all of the investment accounts, the consolidation process is fairly easy, because the major problem involved with indirect holdings is how to determine the amount for noncontrolling interest. If the cost method is used to account for the investments, we would apply the basic procedure of adjusting from cost to equity, and then continue preparing the consolidated statements in the normal manner. This adjustment from cost to equity can be very involved when the affiliation structure is complex.

REVIEW QUESTIONS

1. Is the consolidated cash flow statement prepared in the same manner as the consolidated balance sheet and income statement? Explain.

2. A parent company acquired a 75% interest in a subsidiary company in Year 4. The acquisition price was $1,000,000, made up of cash of $700,000 and the parent's common shares with a current market value of $300,000. Explain how this acquisition should be reflected in the Year 4 consolidated cash flow statement.

3. Why is income assigned to the noncontrolling interest added back to consolidated net income to compute net cash flow from operating activities in the consolidated statement of cash flows?

4. Why are dividend payments to noncontrolling shareholders treated as an outflow of cash in the consolidated cash flow statement but not included as dividends paid in the consolidated retained earnings statement?

5. A parent company will realize a loss or gain when its subsidiary issues common stock at a price per share that differs from the carrying amount per share of the parent's investment, and the parent's ownership percentage declines. Explain why this is so.

6. Is a gain or loss realized by a parent company as a result of the sale of a portion of the investment in a subsidiary eliminated in the preparation of the consolidated income statement? Explain.

7. The shareholders' equity of a subsidiary company contains preferred and common shares. The parent company owns 100% of the subsidiary's common shares. Will the consolidated financial statements show noncontrolling interest? Explain.

8. A company's net income for the year was $7,000. During the year the company paid preferred dividends amounting to $12,000. Calculate the amount of the year's net income that "belongs to" the common shares.

9. Explain how a purchase discrepancy from an investment in preferred shares should be reflected in the consolidated financial statements.

10. Explain how the noncontrolling interest in the net assets and net income of a subsidiary is reported when the parent owns 90% of the subsidiary's common shares and 30% of the subsidiary's cumulative preferred shares.

11. What is the major consolidation problem associated with indirect shareholdings?

MULTIPLE CHOICE

The abbreviated consolidated financial statements of Print Inc. and its subsidiary, Set Inc., for the two years ended December 31, 2002 and 2003, were as follows:

BALANCE SHEETS

	2003	2002	Increase (decrease)
Cash	$ 150,000	$ 290,000	$(140,000)
Accounts receivable	1,515,000	1,350,000	165,000
Inventory	380,000	400,000	(20,000)
Investment in Run Inc.	185,000	160,000	25,000
Plant and equipment (net)	1,170,000	900,000	270,000
	$3,400,000	$3,100,000	$ 300,000
Current liabilities	$ 510,000	$ 750,000	$(240,000)
10% debentures	800,000	600,000	200,000
Noncontrolling interest	190,000	150,000	40,000
Common stock	1,000,000	900,000	100,000
Retained earnings	900,000	700,000	200,000
	$3,400,000	$3,100,000	$ 300,000

COMBINED INCOME AND RETAINED EARNINGS STATEMENT
for the Year Ended December 31, 2003

Sales	$2,500,000
Cost of goods sold	$1,140,000
Depreciation expense	440,000
Administration expenses	375,000
	$1,955,000
Net operating income	$ 545,000
Investment income from Run	35,000
Total net income	580,000
Less: noncontrolling interest	80,000
Consolidated net income	500,000
Retained earnings at January 1, 2003	700,000
	1,200,000
Dividends declared and paid	300,000
Retained earnings at December 31, 2003	$ 900,000

Additional Information

- Set is a 75% owned subsidiary of Print.
- Print owns a 25% interest in Run that is accounted for using the equity method.
- During 2003, Set declared and paid $160,000 in dividends and Run declared and paid $40,000 in dividends.

Use the above data to answer Questions 1 to 8.

The questions are based on Print's consolidated cash flow statement for the year ended December 31, 2003.

1. The first figure in the operations section of Print's consolidated cash flow statement for the year ended December 31, 2003, would be consolidated net income of $500,000. Which of the following would be shown as an adjustment to this figure for depreciation on plant and equipment?
    a. +$440,000
    b. +$270,000
    c. −$270,000
    d. −$440,000

2. Which of the following would be shown as an adjustment to Print's consolidated net income for investment income from Run?
    a. $0
    b. +$25,000
    c. +$35,000
    d. −$35,000

3. Which of the following would be shown as an adjustment to Print's consolidated net income for noncontrolling interest on the consolidated income statement?
    a. −$80,000
    b. +$40,000
    c. +$80,000
    d. −$40,000

4. Which of the following is the correct disclosure for the change in property, plant, and equipment in the investing section of Print's consolidated cash flow statement for the year ended December 31, 2003?
    a. Purchase of property, plant, and equipment, −$710,000.
    b. Proceeds from sale of property, plant, and equipment, +$270,000.
    c. Purchase of property, plant, and equipment, −$270,000.
    d. Proceeds from sale of property, plant, and equipment, +710,000.

5. Print classifies all dividend payments to and received from affiliated corporations as financing activities, along with its own dividend payments. Which of the following is the correct amount that must be disclosed for dividends paid to noncontrolling interests on Print's consolidated cash flow statement for the year ended December 31, 2003?
    a. −$40,000
    b. −$50,000
    c. +$40,000
    d. +$50,000

6. Which of the following is the correct amount that must be disclosed for dividends received from Run on Print's consolidated cash flow statement for the year ended December 31, 2003?
    a. $0
    b. +$10,000
    c. +$30,000
    d. +$40,000

7. Which of the following is the correct disclosure for the increase in the 10% debentures on Print's consolidated cash flow statement for the year ended December 31, 2003?
    a. Under "Operations" as a source of cash, $200,000.
    b. Under "Investing" as a source of cash, $200,000.
    c. Under "Financing" as a source of cash, $200,000.
    d. Under "Financing" as a source of cash, $600,000.

8. Which of the following best describes the disclosure required on the cash flow statement in the year a parent corporation acquires a controlling interest in a subsidiary corporation?
   a. The net investment should be disclosed as an operating activity.
   b. The net assets acquired, other than cash and cash equivalents, should be disclosed as an investing activity, and the method of financing the acquisition should be disclosed separately.
   c. The working capital assets acquired, other than cash and cash equivalents, should be disclosed as an operating activity, the long-term assets acquired should be disclosed as an investing activity, and the financing acquired should be disclosed as a financing activity.
   d. The net increase in the investment account should be disclosed as an investing activity, and no other disclosure is required.

Pot Inc. acquired a 75% interest in Shot Inc. on July 1, 2002, for $265,000. The equity sections of Pot and Shot at December 31, 2001, were as follows:

	Pot	Shot
Common shares	$400,000	$200,000
Preferred shares (10,000 8% shares redeemable at $12 each)	—	100,000
Retained earnings	70,000	60,000
	$470,000	$360,000

Additional Information

- The after-tax net income of Shot for 2002 amounted to $80,000 earned evenly throughout the year.
- The preferred shares are cumulative and nonvoting.
- Dividends on the preferred shares are payable on June 30 and December 31 each year. Dividends were 2 years in arrears at December 31, 2001, and were not paid on June 30, 2002.

Use the above data to answer Questions 9 to 14.

For Questions 9 to 12, assume Pot did not purchase any of Shot's preferred shares at July 1, 2002.

9. When Pot Inc. calculates goodwill arising from its purchase of Shot Inc., which of the following represents the claim of the preferred shareholders on Shot's net asset position for dividends in arrears?
   a. $0
   b. $4,000
   c. $16,000
   d. $20,000

10. When Pot Inc. calculates goodwill arising from its purchase of Shot Inc., which of the following represents the claim of the preferred shareholders at redemption (other than dividends in arrears) on Shot's net asset position?
   a. $120,000
   b. $108,000
   c. $100,000
   d. $0

11. When Pot Inc. consolidates Shot Inc. immediately after acquisition, what amount will be disclosed as noncontrolling interest related to common shares?
   a. $55,000
   b. $65,000
   c. $70,000
   d. $100,000

12. When Pot Inc. consolidates Shot Inc. immediately after acquisition, what amount will be disclosed as noncontrolling interest related to preferred shares?
    a. $100,000
    b. $120,000
    c. $128,000
    d. $140,000

For questions 13 and 14, assume that at July 1, 2002, Pot purchases 40% of Shot's preferred shares in addition to the 75% of common shares. Pot pays an additional $40,000 for these shares.

13. Which method will be used to record the investment in preferred shares on Pot's separate entity books?
    a. Cost.
    b. Equity.
    c. Modified equity.
    d. Consolidation.

14. At December 31, 2002, Shot pays $24,000 in dividends to preferred shareholders. What amount will Pot disclose as dividend revenue from preferred shares on its consolidated financial statements at December 31, 2002?
    a. $0
    b. $1,600
    c. $4,000
    d. $9,600

Use the following information to answer Questions 15 to 19.
On August 31, 2003, Plow Inc. purchased 75% of the outstanding common stock of Share Inc. for $750,000. At January 1, 2003, Share had common stock of $500,000 and retained earnings of $240,000. At the date of acquisition, plant and equipment on Share's books was undervalued by $40,000. This plant had a remaining useful life of 5 years. The balance of the purchase discrepancy, amounting to $120,000, was allocated to unrecorded trademarks of Share to be amortized over a 10-year period. Net income for 2003 was $90,000, earned evenly throughout the year. On December 15, 2003, Share declared and paid dividends of $10,000.
On December 31, 2003, Plow sold 20% of its 75% interest in Share for $160,000.

15. What is the amount of the gain or loss that will arise from Plow's disposition of Share at December 31, 2003?
    a. $46,150
    b. $10,000
    c. $8,700
    d. $8,200

16. Which one of the following is the correct amount of trademarks that should appear on Plow's consolidated statements at December 31, 2003 (assuming Share is Plow's only subsidiary)?
    a. $102,000
    b. $96,000
    c. $92,800
    d. $86,400

17. What percentage of Share does Plow own after the disposition?
    a. 55%
    b. 60%
    c. 67.5%
    d. 85%

18. What will Plow disclose as "Noncontrolling interest" on its balance sheet at December 31, 2003?
    a. $246,000
    b. $280,000
    c. $328,000
    d. $332,000

19. How will the gain or loss from partial disposition of ownership in Share be disclosed on Plow's consolidated financial statements at December 31, 2003?
    a. It will not appear on the consolidated financial statements.
    b. It will appear in the notes only.
    c. It will appear in the retained earnings section of the consolidated balance sheet.
    d. It will appear on the consolidated income statement.

PROBLEMS

Problem 1   The following 2002 consolidated statement was prepared for Standard Manufacturing Corp. and its 60% owned subsidiary, Pritchard Windows Inc.:

STANDARD MANUFACTURING CORP.
CONSOLIDATED STATEMENT OF CASH FLOWS
for the Year Ended December 31, 2002

Cash flows from operations:		
Consolidated net income	120,000	
Noncash items included in income		
Depreciation	45,000	
Goodwill impairment loss	1,000	
Bond premium amortization	(2,000)	
Noncontrolling interest	10,000	
Loss on sale of equipment	23,000	
Decrease in inventory	20,000	
Increase in accounts receivable	(12,000)	
Net cash provided by operations		$205,000
Cash flow from investing		
Purchase of buildings	(150,000)	
Sale of equipment	60,000	
Net cash used from investing		(90,000)
Cash flow from financing		
Dividends paid		
To Standard shareholders	$ (50,000)	
To noncontrolling shareholders	(6,000)	
Bond issue	100,000	
Preferred share redemption	(120,000)	
Net cash used in financing		(76,000)
Net increase in cash		39,000
Cash balance, January 1		50,000
Cash balance, December 31		$ 89,000

Required:

(a) Did the loss on the sale of equipment shown above result from a sale to an affiliate or a nonaffiliate? Explain.

(b) Explain why the amortization of bond premium is treated as a deduction from net income in arriving at net cash flow from operations.

(c) Determine the net income of Pritchard Windows for 2002 (assume no intercompany transactions or unrealized profits).

(d) Explain why dividends to noncontrolling shareholders are not shown as a dividend in the consolidated retained earnings statement but are shown as a distribution of cash in the consolidated cash flow statement.

(e) Determine the amount of dividends paid by Pritchard Windows in 2002.

Problem 2   Company A owns 80% of Company X and 70% of Company Y.
Company X owns 90% of Company B and 10% of Company Y.
Company Y owns 15% of Company Z.
Company B owns 75% of Company Z.

All investments have been accounted for using the cost method. During the current year, net incomes were reported as follows:

Company A	$50,000
Company X	30,000
Company Y	20,000
Company B	15,000
Company Z	10,000

No dividends were declared or paid during the current year, and any purchase discrepancies have been fully amortized for consolidated purposes prior to the current year.

Required:

Calculate:

(a) Noncontrolling interest in net income.

(b) Consolidated net income.

Show your calculations.

Problem 3   On January 1, Year 5, Alyson Inc. owned 90% of the outstanding common shares of Victor Corp. Alyson accounts for its investment using the equity method. The balance in the investment account on January 1, Year 5, amounted to $226,800. The unamortized purchase discrepancy on this date was allocated entirely to vacant land held by Victor.

The shareholders' equity of Victor on January 1, Year 5, was as follows:

Common stock (7,200 shares outstanding)	$ 28,000
Retained earnings	134,000
	$162,000

The following events occurred in Year 5:

- The net income of Victor for Year 5 amounted to $36,000, earned equally throughout the year.
- On April 1, Year 5, Victor issued 1,800 shares at a price of $25 per share. Alyson did not acquire any of these shares.
- On June 30, Year 5, Victor paid dividends amounting to $12,000.
- On September 15, Year 5, Victor sold 25% of its vacant land.
- On December 31, Year 5, Alyson sold 648 shares from its investment in Victor for $22,000.

Required:

Calculate the following as at December 31, Year 5:

(a) The purchase discrepancy allocated to vacant land.

(b) The balance in the investment account using the equity method.

(c) The amount of noncontrolling interest.

Problem 4

The comparative consolidated balance sheets at December 31, Year 2, and the consolidated income statement for Year 2, of Parent Ltd. and its 70% owned subsidiary are shown below.

	Year 2	Year 1
Cash	$ 810,000	$ 335,000
Accounts receivable	600,000	710,000
Inventory	990,000	490,000
Plant and equipment	5,350,000	5,100,000
Accumulated depreciation	(2,350,000)	(1,980,000)
Goodwill	360,000	$ 565,000
	$5,760,000	$5,220,000
Current liabilities	$ 598,400	$1,300,000
Long-term liabilities	3,100,000	2,600,000
Noncontrolling interest	345,600	—
Capital stock	800,000	800,000
Retained earnings	916,000	520,000
	$5,760,000	$5,220,000
Revenues	8,500,000	
Gain on sale of investment in Sub	123,500	
	$8,623,500	
Cost of sales and expenses	$7,679,600	
Depreciation	370,000	
Goodwill impairment loss	35,500	
	$8,085,100	
Net income—entity	$ 538,400	
Noncontrolling interest	38,400	
Net income	$ 500,000	

Additional Information

- On December 31, Year 1, Parent owned 100% of Sub. On this date the shareholders' equity of Sub amounted to $1,120,000 and the parent's unamortized purchase discrepancy of $565,000 was allocated entirely to the goodwill of Sub.
- On January 1, Year 2, Parent sold 30% of its shares of Sub for $629,000 cash and recorded a gain of $123,500 on the transaction. Parent uses the equity method to account for its investment.
- Parent paid $104,000 in dividends during Year 2.

Required:

Prepare in good form a consolidated cash flow statement for Year 2 in accordance with the requirements of the *CICA Handbook*.

Problem 5 On December 31, Year 5, the accountant of Regent Corporation prepared a reconciliation (see below), which was used in the preparation of the consolidated financial statements on that date.

Investment in Argyle Ltd. — equity method balance		$315,000
Shareholders' equity of Argyle		
8,000 common shares	50,000	
Retained earnings	175,000	
	225,000	
Regent's ownership	90%	202,500
Purchase discrepancy — unamortized		$112,500
Allocated: Land		25,500
Equipment — remaining life 8 years		40,000
Trademarks — remaining life 10 years		47,000
		$112,500

Other Information

- On December 31, Year 6, Argyle reported a net income of $50,000 (earned evenly throughout the year) and declared dividends of $20,000.
- On April 1, Year 6, Argyle issued an additional 2,000 common shares at a price of $75 each. Regent did not acquire any of these shares.
- On October 1, Year 6, because the market price of Argyle's common stock had fallen, Regent purchased 1,300 shares of Argyle on the open market at $50 per share. Any purchase discrepancy was allocated to land.

Required:

(a) Calculate the equity method balance in the account investment in Argyle on December 31, Year 6.
(b) Calculate the balance of the unamortized purchase discrepancy, and its allocation, as at December 31, Year 6.

Problem 6 Below are condensed consolidated comparative balance sheets of Prill Company and its 70% owned subsidiary:

	Year 6	Year 5
Cash	$ 790,000	$ 840,000
Accounts receivable	620,000	710,000
Inventory	990,000	490,000
Plant and equipment	4,800,000	5,100,000
Accumulated depreciation	(1,800,000)	(1,980,000)
Goodwill	360,000	396,000
Total assets	$ 5,760,000	$ 5,556,000
Accounts payable	$ 1,250,000	$ 1,680,000
Accrued liabilities	288,400	120,000
Long-term liabilities	2,160,000	2,100,000
Noncontrolling interest	345,600	336,000
Shareholders' equity	1,716,000	1,320,000
Total liabilities and shareholders' equity	$ 5,760,000	$ 5,556,000

Additional Information

- During Year 6 the subsidiary company paid dividends totalling $96,000.
- Net income for Year 6 was $480,000.
- Equipment that was worn out and obsolete was retired during the year. The equipment originally cost $600,000 and had a net book value of $65,000 on the date it was retired.
- Prill paid $84,000 in dividends during the year.
- There were no changes in Prill's 70% interest during the year.

Required:

Prepare a consolidated cash flow statement for the year.

Problem 7 Intercompany shareholdings of an affiliated group during the year ended December 31, Year 2, were as follows:

B Ltd.:	G Company:	D Company:
90% of G Company	70% of C Ltd.	60% of E Ltd.
80% of D Company	10% of D Company	

The equity method is being used for intercompany investments, but no entries have been made in Year 2. The net incomes before equity method earnings for Year 2 were as follows:

	Net income
B Ltd.	$54,000
G Company	32,000
D Company	26,700
C Ltd.	15,400
E Ltd.	11,600

Intercompany profits in the December 31, Year 2, inventories and the affiliated companies involved were:

Selling corporation	Profit made by selling corporation
B Ltd.	$5,000
D Company	1,000
C Ltd.	2,400

Use income tax allocation at a 40% rate.

Required:

(a) Calculate consolidated net income for Year 2.
(b) Calculate the amount of noncontrolling interest in subsidiary net income that would appear on the Year 2 consolidated income statement.

Problem 8 On January 1, Year 1, X Company acquired 800 shares of Y Company's common stock for $24,000 and 180 shares of its $5 cumulative, nonparticipating preferred stock for $19,800. On this date the shareholders' equity accounts of Y Company were:

Common stock (no par value)	$10,000
Preferred stock (200 no par value shares issued)	20,000
Retained earnings (note 1)	12,000

Note 1 — Preferred dividends were two years in arrears on January 1, Year 1.

The following income statements are for the two companies for the year ended December 31, Year 5:

	X Company	Y Company
Sales	$600,000	$400,000
Dividend and management fee revenues	27,300	—
Rental revenue	—	11,200
	$627,300	$411,200
Cost of sales	$343,900	$234,700
Depreciation expense	20,000	70,000
Rental expense	5,000	—
Selling and administration expense	207,000	74,000
Interest expense	1,700	6,000
Income tax expense	20,000	9,000
	$597,600	$393,700
Net income	$ 29,700	$ 17,500

Additional Information

- In Year 5, Y paid dividends totalling $9,000. There were no preferred dividends in arrears on December 31, Year 4.
- X uses the cost method to account for its investment in Y.
- Y purchases merchandise for resale from X. In Year 5, Y purchased $33,000 in merchandise from X and had items in inventory on December 31, Year 5, on which X had made a profit of $2,500. The January 1, Year 5, inventory contained an intercompany profit of $1,400.
- X rents equipment from Y and in Year 5 paid a rental charge of $3,000 and recorded an account payable to Y of $2,000 for the balance of the rentals.
- On July 1, Year 3, Y sold a building to X at a profit of $13,000. X is depreciating this building on a straight-line basis over a 10-year life.
- Y paid $20,000 to X for management fees in Year 5.
- Assume a corporate tax rate of 40%.
- Any purchase discrepancy is allocated to brand names, to be amortized over 40 years.

Required:

Prepare a consolidated income statement for Year 5.

Problem 9   BP Inc. owns 80% of WLC Corp. The consolidated financial statements of BP Inc. are shown below:

BP INC.
CONSOLIDATED BALANCE SHEET
December 31, Year 4

	Year 4	Year 3
Cash	$108,600	$ 49,800
Accounts receivable	105,000	126,000
Inventory	222,000	192,000
Land	96,000	114,000
Buildings and equipment	588,000	510,000
Accumulated depreciation	(195,000)	(168,000)
Goodwill	16,800	19,200
	$941,400	$843,000
Accounts payable	$ 44,400	$ 31,200
Accrued liabilities	18,000	27,000
Bonds payable	300,000	240,000
Bond premium	9,600	10,800
Noncontrolling interest	26,400	24,000
Common stock	180,000	180,000
Retained earnings	363,000	330,000
	$941,400	$843,000

BP INC.
CONSOLIDATED INCOME STATEMENT
for the Year Ended December 31, Year 4

Sales		$360,000
Cost of sales	225,000	
Depreciation	27,000	
Interest expense	41,400	
Loss on land sale	12,000	
Database amortization	2,400	307,800
Net income — entity		52,200
Noncontrolling interest		4,200
Net income		$ 48,000

BP Inc. purchased its 80% interest in WLC Corp. on January 1, Year 2, for $114,000 when WLC had net assets of $90,000. The purchase discrepancy was allocated $24,000 to databases (10-year life), with the balance allocated to equipment (20-year life).

BP issued $60,000 in bonds on December 31, Year 4. WLC reported a net income of $21,000 for Year 4 and paid dividends of $9,000.

BP reported a Year 4 equity method income of $48,000 and paid dividends of $15,000.

Required:

Prepare a consolidated statement of cash flows for Year 4.

Problem 10 The accountant of Consolidated Enterprises has just finished preparing the consolidated balance sheet, income statement, and retained earnings statement for 2002, and has asked you for assistance in preparing the consolidated cash flow statement. Consolidated has only one subsidiary, which is 80% owned, and in addition has a long-term investment in 45% of the outstanding shares of Pacific Finance Co.

The following items have been prepared from the analysis of the 2002 consolidated statements:

Decrease in accounts receivable	$ 23,000
Increase in accounts payable	5,000
Increase in inventory	15,000
Equity earnings from Pacific Finance	90,000
Increase in bonds payable	120,000
Building purchased for cash	580,000
Depreciation reported for current period	73,000
Gain recorded on sale of equipment	8,000
Carrying value of equipment sold	37,000
Goodwill impairment loss	3,000
Dividends received from Pacific Finance	25,000
Consolidated net income for the year	450,000
Entity net income allocated to noncontrolling interest	14,000
Dividends paid by parent company	60,000
Dividends paid by subsidiary company	30,000
Cash balance, January 1, 2002	42,000

Required:

Prepare the consolidated cash flow statement.

Problem 11 Parent Co. owns 9,500 shares of Sub Co. and accounts for its investment by the equity method. On December 31, Year 5, the shareholders' equity of Sub was as follows:

Common shares (10,000 shares issued)	$100,000
Retained earnings	170,000

On January 1, Year 6, Parent sold 1,900 shares from its holdings in Sub for $66,500. On this date the balance in the investment in Sub account was $320,000, and the amortized purchase discrepancy was allocated in the following manner:

35% to land
40% to equipment (remaining life 4 years)
25% to patents (remaining life 10 years)

During Year 6, Sub reported a net income of $150,000 and paid dividends totalling $70,000.

Required:

PART A

(a) Prepare the journal entry that Parent would make on January 1, Year 6, to record the sale of the 1,900 shares.

(b) Calculate the amount of the unamortized purchase discrepancy that would be allocated to land, equipment, and patents on December 31, Year 6.

(c) Prepare an independent proof of the unamortized purchase discrepancy on December 31, Year 6.

PART B

The accountant of Parent is going to prepare a consolidated cash flow statement for Year 6 by analyzing the changes in the consolidated balance sheets from December 31, Year 5, to December 31, Year 6. She needs some assistance in determining what effect Parent's sale of 1,900 shares had on the consolidated financial statements.

Prepare a journal entry to record the effect that the January 1, Year 6, sale of shares had on the consolidated entity.

Problem 12   On April 1, Year 7, Potter Corp. purchased 70% of the common shares of Sorel Ltd. for $900,000. On this same date, Sorel purchased 60% of the common shares of Salto Inc. for $600,000. On April 1, Year 7, the purchase discrepancies from the two investments were allocated entirely to broadcast rights to be amortized over 10 years. The cost method is being used to account for both investments.

During Year 7, the three companies sold merchandise to each other. On December 31, Year 7, the inventory of Potter contained merchandise on which Sorel recorded a profit of $32,000. On the same date, the inventory of Salto contained merchandise on which Potter recorded a profit of $18,000. (Assume a 40% tax rate.)

The following information is available:

	Potter	Sorel	Salto
Common stock	$600,000	$550,000	$300,000
Retained earnings — Jan. 1, Year 7	650,000	400,000	300,000
Net income — Year 7*	100,000	200,000	150,000
Dividends declared — Dec. 31	25,000	30,000	70,000

* Earned evenly throughout the year.

Required:

Calculate the following:

(a) Consolidated net income — Year 7.
(b) Noncontrolling interest as at December 31, Year 7.
(c) Consolidated broadcast rights as at December 31, Year 7.

Problem 13   Craft Ltd. held 80% of the outstanding common shares of Delta Corp. as at December 30, 2002. Balance sheets for the two companies on that date were as follows:

CRAFT LTD.
BALANCE SHEET
December 30, 2002

Cash	$ 50,000	Accounts payable	$ 70,000
Accounts receivable	90,000	Mortgage payable	250,000
Inventory	180,000	Common stock	480,000
Buildings and equipment (net)	600,000	Retained earnings	610,000
Investment in Delta	490,000		—
	$1,410,000		$1,410,000

DELTA CORP.
BALANCE SHEET
December 30, 2002

Cash	$ 65,000	Accounts payable	$100,000
Accounts receivable	120,000	Accrued liabilities	85,000
Inventory	200,000	Common stock [note]	250,000
Buildings and equipment (net)	400,000	Retained earnings	350,000
	$785,000		$785,000

Note: 24,500 common shares outstanding on December 30, 2002.

In order to establish a closer relationship with Nonaffiliated Corporation, a major supplier to both Craft and Delta, all three companies agreed that Nonaffiliated would take an equity position in Delta. Accordingly, for a cash payment of $30 per share, Delta issued 6,125 additional common shares to Nonaffiliated on December 31, 2002. This was the only transaction that occurred on this date.

Other Information
- Craft has used the equity method of accounting for its investment in Delta since it acquired Delta in 1990. At that time the purchase discrepancy was entirely allocated to inventory and computer software.
- There were no unrealized intercompany asset profits as at December 30, 2002.

Required:

Prepare a consolidated balance sheet as at December 31, 2002 (show calculation details for all items on the balance sheet).

Problem 14   A Company owns 75% of B Company and 40% of C Company. B Company owns 40% of C Company. The following balance sheets were prepared at December 31, Year 7.

	A Company	B Company	C Company
Cash	$ 117,800	$ 49,300	$ 20,000
Accounts receivable	200,000	100,000	44,000
Inventory	277,000	206,000	58,000
Investment in C	85,000	92,000	—
Investment in B	409,250	—	—
Property, plant, and equipment	2,800,000	1,500,000	220,000
Accumulated depreciation	(1,120,000)	(593,000)	(90,000)
	$2,769,050	$1,354,300	$252,000
Accounts payable	$ 206,000	$ 88,000	$ 2,000
Bonds payable	1,000,000	700,000	—
Preferred stock	—	50,000	—
Common stock	1,200,000	400,000	200,000
Retained earnings, January 1	314,250	61,000	30,000
Net income	118,800	55,300	20,000
Dividends	(70,000)	—	—
	$2,769,050	$1,354,300	$252,000

Other Information

- A Company purchased its 40% interest in C Company on January 1, Year 4. On that date the negative purchase discrepancy of $10,000 was allocated to equipment with an estimated life of 10 years.
- A Company purchased its 75% of B Company's common shares on January 1, Year 6. On that date the purchase discrepancy was allocated $30,000 to buildings with an estimated life of 20 years, and $40,000 to patents to be amortized over 8 years. The preferred shares of B Company are noncumulative.
- On January 1, Year 7, B Company purchased its 40% interest in C Company for $92,000. The book value of C Company's net assets approximated fair market value on this date.
- The inventory of B Company contains a profit of $2,400 on merchandise purchased from A Company. The inventory of A Company contains a profit of $3,000 on merchandise purchased from C Company.
- On December 31, Year 7, A Company owes $20,000 to C Company and B Company owes $2,000 to A Company.
- Both A Company and B Company use the equity method to account for their investments but have made no equity method adjustments in Year 7.
- An income tax rate of 40% is used for consolidation purposes.

Required:

(a) Calculate noncontrolling interest in net income for Year 7.
(b) Prepare a statement of consolidated retained earnings for Year 7.
(c) Prepare a consolidated balance sheet on December 31, Year 7.
Show all calculations.

Problem 15   On January 1, Year 8, S Company's shareholders' equity was as follows:

Common stock	$20,000
Retained earnings	70,000
	$90,000

Company P held 90% of the 4,000 outstanding shares of S on January 1, Year 8, and its investment in S Company account had a balance of $126,000 on that date. P accounts for its investment by the equity method. Any purchase difference was allocated to unrecorded trademarks with a remaining life on January 1, Year 8, of 10 years.

The following events took place subsequent to January 1, Year 8:

- On July 1, Year 8, P sold 600 of the S Company shares it held at a price of $30 per share.
- During Year 8, S reported a net income of $20,000 (earned equally throughout the year) and declared dividends of $5,000 on December 31.
- During Year 9, S reported a net income of $38,000 and paid dividends of $8,000 on November 15.
- On December 29, Year 9, S issued an additional 1,000 shares to third parties at a price of $46 per share.

Required:

(a) Calculate the gain or loss in Year 8 and Year 9 as a result of the ownership change that took place each year.
(b) Would the gain or loss appear on the consolidated income statement each year? Explain.
(c)   Calculate the consolidated trademarks as at December 31, Year 9.

Problem 16   Financial statements of Polar Corp. and its subsidiary Sable Inc. on December 31, 2002, are shown below:

BALANCE SHEETS
as at December 31, 2002

	Polar	Sable
Cash	$ 40,000	$ 1,000
Accounts receivable	90,000	85,000
Inventories	55,000	48,000
Land 20,000	70,000	
Plant and equipment	400,000	700,000
Accumulated depreciation	(180,000)	(300,000)
Investment in Sable common shares	300,000	—
	$725,000	$604,000
Accounts payable	$ 92,000	$180,000
Accrued liabilities	8,000	10,000
Preferred stock	—	50,000
Common stock	450,000	200,000
Retained earnings	175,000	164,000
	$725,000	$604,000

RETAINED EARNINGS STATEMENTS
for Year Ended December 31, 2002

	Polar	Sable
Balance, January 1	$180,000	$208,000
Net income (loss)	30,000	(24,000)
	210,000	184,000
Dividends	35,000	20,000
Balance, December 31	$175,000	$164,000

Other Information

- On January 1, 1995, the balance sheet of Sable showed the following shareholders' equity:

$8 cumulative preferred stock, 500 shares issued	$ 50,000
Common stock, 2,000 shares issued	200,000
Deficit [note 1]	(80,000)
	$170,000

Note 1: Dividends on preferred shares are two years in arrears.

On this date Polar acquired 1,400 common shares of Sable for a cash payment of $300,000.

The fair market values of Sable's identifiable net assets differed from carrying values only with respect to the following:

	Carrying amount	Fair value
Accounts receivable	$ 42,000	$ 40,000
Inventory	65,000	72,000
Plant	600,000	650,000
Long-term liabilities	400,000	420,000

INCOME STATEMENT

	Panet	Saffer
Sales	$15,000,000	$9,000,000
Dividend revenue	120,000	—
	$15,120,000	$9,000,000
Cost of goods sold	$ 9,500,000	$6,200,000
Depreciation expense	2,500,000	530,000
Income tax	1,032,000	730,000
Other expense	468,000	440,000
	$13,500,000	$7,900,000
Net Income	$ 1,620,000	$1,100,000

Additional Information

- Dividends declared and paid during 2002:

Panet	$500,000
Saffer	200,000

- On January 1, 2002, the inventory of Panet contained an $85,000 intercompany profit, and the inventory of Saffer contained an intercompany profit amounting to $190,000.
- During 2002, Saffer sold inventory to Panet for $2,600,000 at a gross profit margin of 35%. Sales of $400,000 remained in Panet's inventory at December 31, 2002.
- During 2002, Panet sold inventory to Saffer for $3,900,000 at a gross profit margin of 45%. Sales of $250,000 remained in Saffer's inventory at December 31, 2002.
- Saffer sold a piece of equipment to Panet on July 1, 2002, for $450,000. At that time the carrying value of the equipment in Saffer's books was $240,000, and it had a remaining life of 10.5 years. Panet still owes Saffer for 30% of the purchase price of the equipment. The gain on sale has been netted against other expenses in Saffer's 2002 income statement.
- Both companies follow the straight-line method for depreciating fixed assets.
- A goodwill impairment loss of $41,200 was recorded in 2001, and a further loss of $25,875 occurred in 2002.
- Assume a 40% tax rate.

Required:

Prepare the following 2002 consolidated financial statements:
(a) Income statement.
(b) Balance sheet.

Problem 18   On December 31, 2001, Ultra Software Limited purchased 70,000 common shares (70%) of a major competitor, Personal Program Corporation (PPC), at $30.00 per share. The remaining common and the preferred shares were owned by several shareholders who were unwilling to sell at that time.

   The preferred shares, which are noncumulative, are entitled to a $12 dividend. Each is convertible into 2 shares of common stock. Immediate conversion of these preferred shares has been, and will continue to be, highly unlikely due to the current market conditions for the shares. Management is concerned, however, about the effect that any future conversion would have.

At December 31, 2001, PPC's net assets had a book value of $1,525,000. The identifiable assets and liabilities had book values equal to fair values, with the following exceptions:

- Land, with a book value of $200,000, had a fair value of $295,000.
- Software patents and copyrights had a total market value estimated as $300,000 above book value. These were expected to have a 5-year life.
- Inventories of packaged software had a cost to PPC of $20,000 and an estimated selling price of $140,000. Estimated future selling expenses for these items were $15,000, and a gross margin of 40% would be considered normal.
- An unrecorded brand name had an estimated fair value of $2,375,000. This will be amortized over 40 years.

The trial balances at December 31, 2003, for these two companies are provided as Exhibit 9.6, which follows.

In 2002, PPC sold packaged software costing $30,000 to Ultra at a price of $45,000. Of this software, 60% was still in Ultra's inventory at December 31, 2002. During 2003, packaged software costing $42,000 was sold by PPC to Ultra for $60,000. Ultra's inventory at December 31, 2003, included $22,000 of goods purchased in this sale. Neither of these packaged software inventories sold to Ultra had a fair value difference at acquisition.

Included in the 2003 income of PPC was a gain of $50,000 on the sale of patents to another company. This sale took place on June 30, 2003. These patents had a fair value difference of $20,000 at acquisition.

On September 30, 2003, Ultra sold surplus computer hardware to PPC. This equipment had a cost of $6,000,000, was one-half depreciated, and was sold for its fair value of $2,000,000. Disassembly and shipping costs of $80,000 were paid by Ultra. There was estimated to be a 9-year remaining life in its new use.

Preferred dividends were paid in all years, and no new shares have been issued since the acquisition date.

Assume a 40% tax rate.

Required:

PART A

In accordance with GAAP, prepare the following (assume a 40% tax rate):
(a) A consolidated income statement for the period ended December 31, 2003.
(b) A consolidated statement of retained earnings for the period ended December 31, 2003.
(c) A schedule showing the values of the following balance sheet accounts as at December 31, 2003:
   (i) Software patents and copyrights.
   (ii) Packaged software inventory.
   (iii) Noncontrolling interest.

PART B

Write a brief note to the management of Ultra in which you outline the financial reporting implications in the event that the preferred shareholders of PPC exercise their conversion privilege.

(Prepared by Peter Secord, St. Mary's University)

Exhibit 9.6

TRIAL BALANCES
December 31, 2003 ($000s)

	Ultra Software		Personal Program	
Cash	$ 320		$ 150	
Accounts receivable	300		280	
Inventory	350		380	
Patents and copyrights	350		450	
Furniture and equipment (net)	540		675	
Building (net)	800		925	
Land	450		200	
Investment in PPC	2,100		—	
Accounts payable		340		138
Mortgage payable		350		
Bank loan payable				320
Preferred shares (12,500 outstanding)				1,400
Common shares (300,000 outstanding)		3,000		
Common shares (100,000 outstanding)				100
Retained earnings		1,300		117
Sales		6,200		4,530
Other income		120		7
Gain on sale of patent				50
Loss on sale of computer	1,080			
Cost of sales	4,050		2,600	
Other expenses (incl. tax)	850		675	
Depreciation	75		142	
Interest	45		35	
Dividends			150	
	$11,310	$11,310	$6,662	$6,662

Problem 19 The summarized trial balances of Phase Limited and Step Limited as of December 31, 2002, are as follows (amounts in thousands):

	Phase	Step
Current assets	$ 176	$ 89
Investment in Step	254	—
Plant and equipment	540	298
Dividends declared	80	40
Cost of goods sold	610	260
Other expenses	190	55
	$1,850	$742
Liabilities	$ 88	$ 32
Capital stock	400	200
Retained earnings	360	110
Sales, gains, and other revenue	1,002	400
	$1,850	$742

Phase had acquired the investment in Step in three stages:

Date	Shares	Cost	Step retained earnings
Jan 1/99	4,000	$ 50,000	$ 28,000
Jan 1/01	6,000	98,000	69,000
Jan 1/02	6,000	106,000	110,000

The January 1, 1999, acquisition enabled Phase to elect 3 members to the 10-member board of directors of Step. Any difference between cost and the underlying book value for each acquisition is attributable equally to land and to patents, which are to be amortized over 10 years. Step had issued 20,000 shares of stock on July 1, 1997, the date of incorporation, and has neither issued nor retired shares since that date. Other information follows:

- Sale of depreciable assets (6-year remaining life), from Phase to Step, on June 30, 2002, at a gain of $60,000.
- Intercompany sales:

2001	Phase to Step	$50,000
	Step to Phase	20,000
2002	Phase to Step	80,000
	Step to Phase	10,000

- Opening inventory of Phase contained merchandise purchased from Step for $10,000. Company policy was for a 20% gross margin on intercompany sales. Ending inventory of Phase contained merchandise purchased from Step for $5,000. One-half of the goods sold intercompany during 2002 had not been paid for by year-end.
- Assume a 40% tax rate.

Required:

Compute the following consolidated amounts as of December 31, 2002:
(a) Patents.
(b) Plant and equipment.
(c) Inventory.
(d) Retained earnings.
(e) Cost of goods sold.
(f) Net income (statement not required).

(Prepared by Peter Secord, St. Mary's University)

CHAPTER 10

Other Consolidation Reporting Issues

CHAPTER OUTLINE

LEARNING OBJECTIVES

After studying this chapter, you should be able to do the following:

- Describe and apply the current accounting standards that govern the reporting of interests in joint ventures.
- Understand the future income tax implications to the accounting for a business combination.
- Describe the *Handbook*'s requirements for segment disclosures and apply the quantitative thresholds to determine reportable segments.

In this chapter we discuss some additional consolidation issues that were not previously covered. In Chapter 2 we described four types of long-term investments. So far we have discussed the accounting for the first three. We now examine the fourth, an investment in a joint venture. After that, we look at how a new *Handbook* section on future income taxes affects the accounting for a business combination. This chapter concludes with the disclosure requirements associated with a company's business segments.

Interests in Joint Ventures

A joint venture is a business arrangement whereby several venturers agree to contribute resources for a specific undertaking. A common example: one venturer provides the technical expertise, and the other provides marketing and/or financial expertise. Joint venture organizations are often formed for expensive and risky projects. They are fairly common in the oil-and-gas exploration sector and in large real-estate developments. Also, a Canadian company will often form a joint venture with a foreign company or the government of a foreign country as a means of expanding into international markets.

Item of Interest   In February 2001, Coca-Cola Co. and Procter & Gamble Co. announced the formation of a 50–50 joint venture that will develop and market juices, juice-based drinks, and snacks. The idea behind the creation of this new company is for P&G to benefit from Coke's international distribution system and for Coke to benefit from P&G's scientific research in nutrition-enhanced juice drinks and snacks. Coke will contribute its Minute Maid juice unit while P&G will contribute Pringles chips and Sunny Delight juice drinks.

Item of Interest   Shoppers from three neighbouring countries — the Czech Republic, Austria, and Hungary — have been flocking to shop at the Polus City Center located in Bratislava, Slovakia. This North American–style mall, which cost $105 million to build, contains numerous shops and restaurants, office space, a bowling alley and an eight-screen multiplex. The mall is a joint venture owned 50 percent each by Polus Investment Co. of Hungary and Canadian based TrizecHahn Corp.

A joint venture need not be a separate entity. Under a situation of jointly controlled operations, each venturer contributes the use of assets or resources to the joint venture activity but maintains individual title to and control of these assets and resources. An example would be a case in which one venturer manufactures part of a product, a second venturer completes the manufacturing process, and a third venturer handles the marketing of the product. Revenue and expenses are shared in accordance with the joint venture agreement. Some joint ventures involve only the joint control of assets used in the joint venture. An oil pipeline is an example of this: each oil-producing venturer uses the pipeline to transfer its oil and shares the cost in accordance with an agreement. If the separate-entity form is used, the joint venture may be created as a partnership; or it may be incorporated, with the venturers being shareholders.

Of the 200 companies that made up the sample used in the 2000 edition of *Financial Reporting in Canada*, 68 reported investments in joint ventures. Our discussions will focus on situations where a venturer has an investment in a separate-entity joint venture. The basic concepts discussed for this situation would apply with slight modifications to the nonseparate-entity examples discussed earlier.

The accounting principles involved for reporting an investment in a joint venture are contained in Section 3055 of the *Handbook*. This section, which was extensively revised in 1994, is complementary to sections 3050, "Long-term Investments," and 1590, "Subsidiaries." Section 3055 presents the following descriptions relevant to our discussions:[1]

> **Joint control** of an economic activity is the contractually agreed sharing of the continuing power to determine its strategic operating, investing and financing policies.

> A **joint venture** is an economic activity resulting from a contractual arrangement whereby two or more venturers jointly control the economic activity.

> A **venturer** is a party to a joint venture, has joint control over that joint venture, has the right and ability to obtain future economic benefits from the resources of the joint venture and is exposed to the related risks.

A distinctive feature of these descriptions is the concept of *joint control*, which must be present for a joint venture to exist. Joint control is established by an agreement between the venturers (usually in writing), whereby no one venturer can unilaterally control the joint venture regardless of the amount of assets it contributes. For example, a single venturer (Company L) could own more than 50 percent of the voting shares of Company M. This would normally indicate that Company M is a subsidiary; however, if there was an agreement establishing joint control, Company M would be a joint venture and not a subsidiary, and Company L would be a venturer and not a parent. To change the percentages, Company L could also own 32 percent of Company M. Without a further examination of the facts, this percentage would initially indicate that Company L has a significant influence investment, to be reported using the equity method. However, because of the joint control agreement, it must report its joint venture investment using proportionate consolidation.

Accounting for an Investment in a Joint Venture

Section 3055 is concerned only with the financial reporting for an interest in a joint venture by a venturer; it does not cover the accounting for the joint venture itself.[2] This section requires the venturer to report an investment in a joint venture by the *proportionate consolidation method*, which is an application of the proprietary theory of consolidation, which was discussed in chapters 4 and 7. You will recall that under this concept, no amount for noncontrolling interest is shown in the consolidated financial statements. Applying this concept to an investment in a joint venture, consolidated statements using the proportionate consolidation method would be prepared by combining, on a line-by-line basis, the financial statement items of the venturer with the venturer's share of the financial statement items of the joint venture. By definition there must be at least two venturers; thus, we have a situation where a

---

[1] *CICA Handbook*, paragraph 3055.03.

[2] In July 1992, the Emerging Issues Committee issued EIC-38, "Accounting by Newly Formed Joint Ventures," which examines the accounting by the joint venture of assets contributed to it by the venturers.

joint venture's assets, liabilities, revenues, and expenses are apportioned among the financial statements of each of the venturers.

Intercompany Transactions

You will recall from our discussions in past chapters that intercompany profits in assets are fully eliminated from the consolidated statements of a parent and its subsidiaries. If the subsidiary was the selling company, 100 percent of the profit, net of income tax, is eliminated and allocated to both noncontrolling interest and consolidated retained earnings in the consolidated balance sheet. If the parent was the selling company, the entire net-of-tax profit is eliminated and allocated to consolidated retained earnings. This is not the case when we proportionately consolidate a venturer and a joint venture.

If the joint venture sells assets at a profit to the venturer, and these assets have not been resold by the venturer to independent third parties, only the venturer's share of this after-tax profit is eliminated because there is no noncontrolling interest to allocate the remaining percentage to. Paragraph 3055.40 of the *Handbook* presents an alternative explanation, suggesting that the venturer cannot recognize a profit on a transaction with itself.

If the venturer sells assets at a profit to the joint venture, which the joint venture has not resold to independent third parties, it would be possible to eliminate 100 percent of the profit from consolidated retained earnings (i.e., the venturer's) because these retained earnings contain all of this profit. However, Section 3055 suggests that because the joint venture agreement does not allow a particular venturer to exercise control, a venturer selling to the venture is considered to be dealing at arm's length with the other venturers, and therefore a portion of the profit equal to the other venturers' ownership interest can be considered realized. However, if any of the other venturers are affiliated with the selling venturer, only the portion of the profit equal to the nonaffiliated venturers' interest should be considered realized.

The same treatment is prescribed for the sale of assets at a loss, except in situations where the transaction provides evidence of a reduction in the net realizable value of the asset, in which case the full amount of the loss is immediately recognized.

Intercompany revenues and expenses are not specifically mentioned in Section 3055, nor are *intercompany receivables and payables*. To be consistent with the general concept of consolidations, it would seem logical that they should be eliminated. However, due to the nature of the proportionate consolidation process, only the venturer's ownership percentage can be eliminated. To eliminate 100 percent of these items, as is done under full consolidation, would result in negative amounts because only the venturer's proportion of a joint venture's receivables or payables, revenues or expenses, is available for elimination under the proportionate method.

Purchase Discrepancies

The formation of a joint venture by its venturers cannot result in purchase discrepancies in the investment accounts of the venturers. However, if one of the founding venturers sells its ownership interest, the new venturer could pay an amount different from its interest in the carrying value of the joint venture's net assets, resulting in a purchase discrepancy. This purchase discrepancy would be allocated and amortized in the same manner illustrated previously for parent–subsidiary affiliations.

Illustration of the Consolidation of a Venturer and a Joint Venture

Explor Ltd. is a joint venture in which A Company has a 45 percent ownership interest. A Company, an original founder of Explor, uses the equity method to account for its investment but has made no entries to its investment account for Year 4. The following are the financial statements of the two companies on December 31, Year 4:

INCOME STATEMENT — Year 4

	A Company	Explor
Sales	$900,000	$300,000
Cost of sales	$630,000	$180,000
Miscellaneous expenses	100,000	40,000
	$730,000	$220,000
Net income	$170,000	$ 80,000

BALANCE SHEETS — December 31, Year 4

	A Company	Explor
Miscellaneous assets	$654,500	$277,000
Inventory	110,000	90,000
Investment in Explor	85,500	—
	$850,000	$367,000
Miscellaneous liabilities	$130,000	$ 97,000
Capital stock	300,000	100,000
Retained earnings, January 1	250,000	90,000
Net income — Year 4	170,000	80,000
	$850,000	$367,000

During Year 4, A Company sold merchandise totalling $110,000 to Explor and recorded a gross profit of 30 percent on these sales. On December 31, Year 4, the inventory of Explor contained items purchased from A Company for $22,000, and Explor had a payable of $5,000 to A Company on this date. A Company will use the proportionate consolidation method when it reports its investment in Explor for Year 4.

The following are the calculations of the amounts that are used in the elimination of intercompany transactions in the preparation of the consolidated financial statements:

Intercompany sales and purchases:	
Total for the year	$110,000
A Company's ownership interest	45%
Amount eliminated	$ 49,500
Intercompany receivables and payables:	
Total at end of year	$ 5,000
A Company's ownership interest	45%
Amount eliminated	$ 2,250

Intercompany profits in inventory:		
Total at end of year (22,000 × 30%)		$ 6,600
Profit considered realized — 55%		3,630
Unrealized — 45 percent		$ 2,970

The following explanations will clarify the calculations made:

1. Because the proportionate consolidation method will use 45 percent of Explor's financial statement items, we eliminate only 45 percent of the intercompany revenues, expenses, receivables, and payables. If we eliminated 100 percent of these items, we would be eliminating more than we are using in the consolidation process.

2. The inventory of Explor contains an intercompany profit of $6,600 recorded by A Company. Because there is joint control, A Company has realized $3,630 of this profit by selling to the other unaffiliated venturers, and therefore only A Company's 45 percent ownership interest is considered unrealized.

3. Income tax allocation is required when timing differences occur. Assuming that A Company pays income tax at a rate of 40 percent, the income tax effects of the inventory profit elimination can be calculated as follows:

	Before tax	40% tax	After tax
Inventory — A selling	$2,970	$1,188	$1,782

Because A Company has not recorded this year's equity method journal entries, we must calculate consolidated net income for Year 4 as follows:

Income of A Company		$170,000
Less unrealized inventory profit		1,782
Adjusted net income		168,218
Income of Explor	$80,000	
A's ownership interest	45%	36,000
Consolidated net income		$204,218

A Company has used the equity method prior to this year, and therefore its retained earnings at the beginning of the year are equal to consolidated retained earnings. We can prepare the consolidated retained earnings statement for Year 4 as follows:

A COMPANY
CONSOLIDATED STATEMENT OF RETAINED EARNINGS
for the Year Ended December 31, Year 4

Balance, January 1	$250,000
Net income	204,218
Balance, December 31	$454,218

The preparation of the remaining Year 4 consolidated statements without the use of a working paper is illustrated as follows:

A COMPANY
CONSOLIDATED INCOME STATEMENT
for the Year Ended December 31, Year 4

Sales (900,000 + [45% × 300,000] – 49,500(a))	$985,500
Cost of sales	
(630,000 + [45% × 180,000] – 49,500(a) + 2,970(c))	$664,470
Miscellaneous expenses	
(100,000 + [45% × 40,000] – 1,188(d))	116,812
	$781,282
Net income	$204,218

A COMPANY
CONSOLIDATED BALANCE SHEET
December 31, Year 4

Miscellaneous assets		
(654,500 + [45% × 277,000] – 2,250(b))		$776,900
Inventory (110,000 + [45% × 90,000] – 2,970(c))		147,530
Future income taxes	(d)	1,188
Total assets		$925,618
Miscellaneous liabilities		
(130,000 + [45% × 97,000] – 2,250(b))		$171,400
Shareholders' equity		
Capital stock	300,000	
Retained earnings	454,218	754,218
Total liabilities and shareholders' equity		$925,618

The amounts used in the preparation are explained as follows:

1. With the exception of shareholders' equity and future income tax, the first two amounts used come from the individual financial statements and consist of 100 percent of A Company plus 45 percent of Explor.

2. The adjustment labelled (a) is the elimination of intercompany revenues and expenses.

3. The adjustment labelled (b) is the elimination of intercompany receivables and payables.

4. The adjustment labelled (c) is the elimination of the before-tax unrealized inventory profit.

5. The adjustment labelled (d) is the elimination of the income tax on the unrealized inventory profit. It is assumed that miscellaneous expenses include income tax expense.

6. The investment account and shareholders' equity of Explor were eliminated in the following manner:

Investment in Explor		$85,500
Shareholders' equity of Explor		
Capital stock	$100,000	
Retained earnings, January 1	90,000	
	$190,000	
A Company's ownership interest	45%	85,500
Purchase discrepancy		–0–

7. Consolidated shareholders' equity consists of the capital stock of A Company plus consolidated retained earnings.

The calculation of consolidated net income (page 409) yields the amounts that A Company uses when it prepares the following Year 4 equity method journal entry:

Investment in Explor	34,218	
Equity earnings from Explor		34,218

To record 45% of the net income of Explor less the holdback of after-tax unrealized profit in inventory (36,000 − 1,782 = 34,218)

Assets Contributed as an Investment in a Joint Venture

Suppose that on the date of formation of a joint venture, instead of contributing cash, a venturer contributes nonmonetary assets and receives an interest in the joint venture, and that the assets contributed have a fair value that is greater than their carrying value in the records of the venturer. Would it be appropriate for the venturer to record a gain from investing in the joint venture? And if so, how much gain should be realized, and when should it be recognized? The requirements set out in Section 3055 of the *Handbook* regarding this matter are as follows:

1. The investment should be recorded at the fair value of the nonmonetary assets transferred to the joint venture.

2. Only the gain represented by interests of the other nonrelated venturers should be realized in the financial statements. This gain should be recognized in a systematic manner over the life of the contributed assets, or if nondepreciable, on a basis appropriate to the expected services provided or revenues earned.

3. The portion of the gain represented by the venturer's own interest should be deferred until the asset has been sold to unrelated outsiders by the joint venture. This deferred gain will be deducted from the venturer's share of the related joint venture asset, so that the asset appears on the consolidated balance sheet at an amount equal to the venturer's share of the cost of the asset transferred.

4. If a loss results from the recording of the investment, the portion of the loss represented by the interest of the other unrelated venturers is recognized immediately into income. An exception: when it is evident that the loss is permanent, the entire loss is immediately recognized.

5. When the venturer transfers assets to the joint venture and receives cash in addition to an interest in the joint venture, the cash received can be considered the proceeds from the partial sale of the assets to the other unrelated venturers, provided that the cash came from the investment of the other venturers or from the other venturers' share of joint venture borrowings.

The following examples will illustrate these concepts.

Example 1   A Co. and B Inc. formed JV Ltd. on January 1, Year 1. A Co. invested land with a book value of $200,000 and a fair value of $700,000 for a 40 percent interest in JV Ltd., while B Inc. contributed assets with a total fair value of $1,050,000, for a 60 percent interest in JV Ltd. Cash of $130,000 was included in the assets invested by B Inc. We will concern ourselves only with the recording by A Co. of its

40 percent interest in JV Ltd., and we will assume that the land contributed will provide services for an estimated 10-year period. On December 31, Year 1, JV Ltd. reported a net income of $204,000. The deferred gains are calculated as follows:

Fair value of land transferred to JV Ltd.	$700,000
Carrying value of land on A Co.'s books	200,000
Gain on transfer to JV Ltd.	500,000
A Co.'s portion to be netted against land (40%)	200,000
B Inc.'s portion to be deferred and amortized (60%)	$300,000

A Co.'s journal entry to record the initial investment on January 1, Year 1, is as follows:

Investment in JV Ltd.	700,000	
Land		200,000
Deferred gain, A Co.		200,000
Deferred gain, B Inc.		300,000

Using the equity method of accounting, A Co. will record its 40 percent share of the yearly net incomes or losses reported by JV Ltd.; in addition, it will recognize a portion of the $300,000 gain it realized by selling to the unrelated venturer, B Inc. The portion recognized will be based on an estimate that the land will provide equal services each year for 10 years.

The December 31, Year 1, entries are as follows:

Investment in JV Ltd.	81,600	
Equity earnings from JV Ltd. (40% × 204,000)		81,600
Deferred gain, B Inc.	30,000	
Gain on transfer of land to JV Ltd. (300,000 ÷ 10 years)		30,000

Equity earnings of $81,600 will be eliminated in the preparation of the Year 1 consolidated income statement; they will be replaced with 40 percent of the revenues and expenses of JV Ltd. The $30,000 gain on transfer of land to JV Ltd. will appear in the consolidated income statement, and the unamortized balance of the deferred gain to B Inc. of $270,000 will appear in the consolidated balance sheet. The $200,000 deferred gain to A Co. will be deducted from land in the preparation of the consolidated balance sheet. Note that if the land transferred to JV Ltd. had been recorded at the carrying value of A Co., it would appear in the balance sheet of JV Ltd. at $200,000. On A Co.'s consolidated balance sheet it would appear at $80,000 (40% × 200,000). The land appears on JV's balance sheet at $700,000 and will appear on the consolidated balance sheet as follows:

40% × 700,000	$280,000
Less deferred gain, A Co.	200,000
Consolidated land	$ 80,000

This method of recognizing the gain from investing will be repeated over the next nine years, unless JV Ltd. sells this land before that period expires. If it does, A Co. will immediately take the balances in the two deferred gains accounts into income.

Example 2   The facts from this example are identical in all respects to those from the previous example except that we assume that A Co. receives a 40 percent interest in JV Ltd. plus $130,000 in cash in return for investing land with a fair value of $700,000.

The original gain on the transfer ($500,000) and the allocation to A Co. ($200,000) and B Inc. ($300,000) is the same as in Example 1. However, because the $130,000 in cash received by A Co. came entirely from the cash invested by B Inc., it is considered to be the sale proceeds of the portion of the land deemed to have been sold. In other words, A Co. is considered to have sold a portion of the land to B Inc. (through the joint venture) and will immediately record a gain from selling, computed as follows:

Sale proceeds	$130,000
Carrying value of land sold (130 ÷ 700 × 200,000)	37,143
Immediate gain from selling land to B Inc.	$ 92,857

A Co.'s January 1, Year 1, journal entry to record the investment of land and the receipt of cash would be as follows:

Cash	130,000	
Investment in JV Ltd.	570,000	
Land		200,000
Deferred gain, A Co.		200,000
Gain on transfer of land to JV Ltd.		92,857
Deferred gain, B Inc.		207,143

The December 31, Year 1, entries are as follows:

Investment in JV Ltd.	81,600	
Equity earnings from JV Ltd. (40% × 204,000)		81,600
Deferred gain, B Inc.	20,714	
Gain on transfer of land to JV Ltd. (207,143 ÷ 10 years)		20,714

Assuming a December 31 year-end, the $113,571 gain on transfer of land to JV Ltd. will appear in the Year 1 consolidated income statement. The unamortized balance of the deferred gain to B Inc. of $186,429 will appear on the consolidated balance sheet. The $200,000 deferred gain to A Co. will be deducted from land in the consolidated balance sheet in the same manner as was illustrated in Example 1.

Example 3   In this last example, we will increase the amount of cash that A Co. received when it invested land for a 40 percent interest in JV Ltd. Let us assume that the cash received was $150,000 instead of the $130,000 that we used in Example 2. Because B Ltd. only invested $130,000 cash in the joint venture, the additional $20,000 was borrowed by JV Ltd. In this situation, the $150,000 cash received is considered to be partly sale proceeds and partly a return of equity to A Co. The allocation of the cash between sale proceeds and return of equity is made as follows:

Sale proceeds:

From B Inc. investment in JV Ltd.			$130,000
From borrowings of JV Ltd.	20,000		
B Inc.'s proportion	60%		12,000
			142,000
Return of equity to A Co.:			
A Co.'s proportion of JV borrowings	40%		8,000
Total cash received			$150,000

The gain from selling is computed as follows:

Sale proceeds	$142,000
Carrying value of assets sold (142/700 × 200,000)	40,571
Immediate gain from selling to B Inc.	$101,429

A Co.'s January 1, Year 1, journal entry would be as follows:

Cash	150,000	
Investment in JV Ltd.	550,000	
Land		200,000
Deferred gain, A Co.		200,000
Gain from transfer of land to JV Ltd.		101,429
Deferred gain, B Inc.		198,571

On December 31, Year 1, A Co.'s journal entries would be:

Investment in JV Ltd.	81,600	
Equity earnings from JV Ltd. (40% × 204,000)		81,600
Deferred gain, B Inc.	19,857	
Gain from transfer of land to JV Ltd. (198,571 ÷ 10 years)		19,857

The $121,286 gain on transfer of land to JV Ltd. will appear on the Year 1 consolidated income statement, while the unamortized balance of the deferred gain to B Inc. of $178,714 will appear on the consolidated balance sheet. The $200,000 deferred gain to A Co. will be deducted from land in the preparation of the consolidated balance sheet in exactly the same manner as was previously illustrated, as follows:

40% × 700,000	$280,000
Less deferred gain, A Co.	200,000
Consolidated land	$ 80,000

Future Income Taxes and Business Combinations

Up to this point, we have ignored the income tax implications associated with business combinations. Corporate tax law in this area is quite complex and can be fully understood only by readers who have been exposed to the topic through in-depth tax courses. There is always the danger that essential accounting concepts associated with business combinations and consolidated financial statements could be overshadowed if an attempt is made to combine basic accounting issues with the complex tax allocation procedures. Attentive readers will now have achieved a reasonable understanding of the broad accounting concepts behind consolidated statements. To complete our coverage of this financial reporting process, we now turn our attention to the additional effects that income tax allocation can have on the accounting for a business combination. But before we do this, we provide the following useful background material.

Future Income Tax Concepts

In December 1997, *Handbook* Section 3465, "Income Taxes," was introduced, and the method of accounting for interperiod tax allocation was thereby changed. The income statement (or deferral) approach, used in the former Section 3470, was abandoned in favour of the balance sheet (or liability) approach. Under the income statement approach, differences between accounting income and taxable income were reconciled using approaches that focused on timing differences and permanent differences. *Timing* differences arise when revenues and expenses are reflected in the income statement in different periods than their appearance on a company's tax return. *Permanent* differences involve revenues that are not taxable and expenses that are not deductible for tax purposes. Under the income statement approach, permanent differences were not accounted for and therefore interperiod tax allocation was required only for timing differences. A switch to the balance sheet approach will produce the same results for items that formerly were considered timing differences (except when tax rates change); but in addition, some of the former permanent differences under the income statement approach are now subject to income tax allocation procedures.

The new, balance sheet approach requires that the differences between the carrying value of an asset or liability and its tax basis be accounted for. These differences are called *temporary differences*. The tax basis of an asset is described as the amount that could be deducted in determining taxable income if the asset was recovered for its carrying value. The tax basis of a liability is its carrying amount *less* the amount that will be deductible for tax purposes with respect to that liability in future periods.

Under the new section, there are two basic types of temporary differences: deductible and taxable. A *deductible temporary difference* is one that can be deducted in determining taxable income in the future when the asset or liability is recovered or settled for its carrying amount. These differences exist when (a) the carrying amount of an asset is less than its tax basis, or (b) an amount related to a liability can be deducted for tax purposes. Accounting for these differences results in *future income tax assets*.

A *taxable temporary difference* is one that will result in future taxable amounts when the carrying amount of the asset or liability is recovered or settled. Such differences, which result in *future income tax liabilities*, occur mainly when the carrying amount of an asset is greater than its tax basis.

A few examples will illustrate some of these concepts. We assume a 40 percent tax rate in each case.

Example 1   A company has an account payable of $3,000 on its balance sheet at the end of Year 1, for unpaid expenses that were deducted for tax purposes during Year 1. The carrying amount is $3,000. The tax basis of the liability is:

Carrying amount	$3,000
Less: amount deductible for tax in future periods	–0–
Tax basis	$3,000

Because the carrying amount and the tax basis are equal, a temporary difference does not exist.

Example 2   At the end of Year 1, a company has an account receivable of $1,000 from sales made during the year. This receivable is expected to be collected through a series of instalments during Years 2 and 3. For tax purposes, the revenue is taxable in the year of collection. The carrying amount at the end of Year 1 is $1,000, while the tax basis is zero. This creates a taxable temporary difference of $1,000, requiring a future tax liability of $400.

Example 3   At the end of Year 1, a company has a warranty liability of $1,500. Warranty costs are only deductible for tax purposes when they have been paid. The carrying value is $1,500, while the tax basis is zero, We have a deductible temporary difference of $1,500, requiring a future tax asset of $600.

Example 4   An asset is purchased at a cost of $2,000. For financial statement purposes, it will be depreciated using the straight-line method over a five-year life, with no estimated salvage value. For tax purposes, capital cost allowance will be taken at a 30 percent rate, subject to the half-year rule in the first year. The following illustrates the yearly depreciation and capital cost allowance over the first three years:

	Carrying value	Tax basis
Year 1 cost	$2,000	$2,000
Year 1: Depreciation	400	—
CCA	—	300
Balance, end of Year 1	1,600	1,700
Year 2: Depreciation	400	—
CCA	—	510
Balance, end of Year 2	1,200	1,190
Year 3: Depreciation	400	—
CCA	—	357
Balance, end of Year 3	$ 800	$ 833

Note that at the end of Year 1 there is a deductible temporary difference of $100, requiring a future tax asset of $40. At the end of Year 2 we have a taxable temporary difference of $10, requiring a future tax liability of $4. By the end of Year 3 we are back to a deductible temporary difference of $33, requiring a future tax asset of approximately $13. Note also that while the carrying value of this asset becomes zero at the end of Year 5, it will have a positive tax basis for an infinite number of future years. In other words, the reversing that inevitably must occur is often a very long time happening.

These examples have focused on some of the basics behind the balance sheet approach, and will be useful in understanding some of the business combination illustrations that follow. However, before we examine the future income tax effects associated with a business combination, there is one other interesting provision of Section 3465 that needs to be examined.

The Acquisition of an Asset at a Price Different than the Tax Basis (other than in a business combination)   Because the balance sheet approach requires the recording of a future tax asset or liability whenever the carrying value of an asset or liability differs from its tax basis, a unique situation exists when a single asset is purchased and its tax

basis is different from its cost on the date that it was acquired. The required accounting is outlined in the *Handbook* as follows:

> When an asset is acquired other than in a business combination and the tax basis of the asset is less than its cost, the cost of future income taxes recognized at the time of the acquisition should be added to the cost of the asset. When an asset is acquired other than in a business combination and the tax basis of that asset is greater than its cost, the benefit related to future income taxes recognized at the time of acquisition should be deducted from the cost of the asset [3465.43]
>
> In some circumstances, an asset acquired, other than an asset acquired in a business combination, has a tax basis which is less than its cost. This gives rise to a taxable temporary difference that results in the recognition of a future income tax liability. Adding the cost of future income taxes to the cost of the asset reflects the following:
>
> (a) the carrying amount of the asset would include the cost to acquire the asset and the unavoidable income tax consequences of utilizing the asset; and
>
> (b) the carrying amount will represent the minimum future cash flows necessary to recover the investment in the asset including any tax consequences associated with the asset [3465.44].

An example of the application of this section follows.

Example   A company purchases a piece of equipment for $1,000. Because of the special nature of the asset, only 25 percent of its cost is deductible for tax purposes. Therefore, the tax basis of this equipment is $250. The initial carrying value of the asset is determined by the following formula:

$$\text{Cost of the asset} \quad + \quad \frac{[(\text{Cost} - \text{Tax basis}) \times \text{tax rate}]}{(1 - \text{tax rate})}$$

In this example, if we assume a 40% tax rate, the calculation to determine the initial carrying value of this equipment is:

$$1,000 \quad + \quad \frac{[(1,000 - 250) \times .40]}{(1 - .40)} \quad = \quad \$1,500$$

The journal entry required to record the acquisition of this equipment is as follows:

Equipment	1,500	
Future income taxes		500
Cash		1,000

If we compare the carrying value of the equipment with its tax basis and calculate the tax liability, we can see that the amount recorded for the asset satisfies the requirements of this section as follows:

Carrying amount of equipment	$1,500
Tax basis	250
Taxable temporary difference	1,250
Tax rate	40%
Future income tax liability	$ 500

It should be noted that this gross-up of cost applies only to the purchase of a single asset and does not apply to the acquisition of assets in a business combination. Particularly, it does not apply to goodwill that normally results from such a combination.

Business Combination Illustrations

Section 3465 not only requires a shift to the balance sheet approach, but also requires that future income taxes associated with the purchase discrepancy be accounted for.

We use the following simple illustrations to convey the basic concepts involved and the reasoning behind them.

Illustration 1   Sub Co. has a single productive asset. The balance sheet of this company is shown below:

SUB CO. — BALANCE SHEET
December 31, Year 3

Asset	$800
Future income taxes	12
	$812
Liabilities	$300
Shareholders' equity	512
	$812

The tax basis of the single asset and the liabilities is:

Asset	$830
Liabilities	300
Net	$530

Using a 40 percent tax rate, Sub Co. has correctly applied the provisions of Section 3465 by setting up in its separate entity statements a future tax asset of $12 for the deductible temporary difference of $30.

On January 1, Year 4, Parent Inc. purchased 100 percent of Sub Co. for $1,000 cash. Parent determines that the fair value of Sub's single asset is $950 and that the fair value of its liabilities is $300. The calculation of the purchase discrepancy is made in the following manner:

Cost of 100% of Sub Co.		$1,000
Shareholders' equity of Sub Co.	512	
Less: future income tax asset	12	
	500	
Parent's ownership	100%	500
Purchase discrepancy		500
Allocated:		
Asset (950 – 800)	150	
Future income tax liability (see calculation on page 419)	48	102
Balance, goodwill		$ 398

There are two new components to this calculation, which require elaboration. The first relates to the deduction of Sub Co.'s future income tax asset from its shareholders' equity. This concept was first introduced in Chapter 3. Paragraph 1581.45 states that an acquired company's future income tax assets or liabilities are not to be carried forward to the consolidated financial statements.

The second point is that paragraph 1581.47 requires that the provisions of Section 3465 be followed with respect to the differences between the fair values assigned to the assets and liabilities of the acquired company and their tax basis. These differences, multiplied by the tax rate of the subsidiary, produce future income tax assets and liabilities, which are to be included as part of the allocation of the purchase cost. Paragraph 1581.46 also requires that the fair values be determined without reference to their values for tax purposes.

Returning to this particular example, the calculation of the future tax liability to be used for consolidation purposes is as follows:

Asset fair value used in consolidation	$950
Tax basis of the asset	830
Taxable temporary difference	120
Tax rate of Sub Co.	40%
Future income tax liability	$ 48

Because the fair value and the tax basis of Sub's liabilities are both $300, no future income tax implications are associated with these liabilities. Note that in applying these concepts, we are replacing a $12 future income tax asset on the balance sheet of Sub Co. with a future income tax liability of $48 on the consolidated balance sheet with respect to the same asset. Note also that no future income taxes are recorded in relation to the goodwill of $398. The following paragraph from Section 3465 explains why:

> Any difference between the carrying amount of goodwill and its tax basis is a taxable temporary difference that would usually result in a future income tax liability. This section does not permit such a future income tax liability because goodwill itself is a residual and recognition of the future income tax liability would merely increase the carrying amount of that residual. [3465.23]

Note that because this paragraph does not allow the recording of a future tax liability for the taxable temporary difference that is associated with goodwill, the provisions of paragraph 3465.43 (discussed previously) do not apply. If those provisions did apply, goodwill would have to be grossed up in a manner similar to the case where a single asset is purchased and the cost and tax basis are different.

Let us assume that Parent Inc. was formed on December 31, Year 3, by the issuance of common stock for $1,000 in cash. The nonconsolidated balance sheet of Parent is shown below, followed by the consolidated balance sheet (with bracketed amounts indicating its preparation using the direct approach):

PARENT INC. — BALANCE SHEET
January 1, Year 4

Investment in Sub Co.	$1,000
Common stock	$1,000

PARENT INC. — CONSOLIDATED BALANCE SHEET
January 1, Year 4

Assets (800 + 150)	$ 950
Goodwill	398
	$1,348
Liabilities	$ 300
Future income taxes	48
Common stock	1,000
	$1,348

The future income tax liability that appears on the consolidated balance sheet can be verified as follows:

Carrying value of assets above (excluding goodwill)	$950
Tax basis of assets	830
Taxable temporary difference	120
Tax rate	40%
Future income tax liability	$ 48

Illustration 2   We will use the same facts about the two companies as in Illustration 1, except that we assume that Parent Inc. purchased 90 percent of Sub Co. for $900 cash. Parent's nonconsolidated balance sheet is presented below:

PARENT INC. — BALANCE SHEET
January 1, Year 4

Cash	$ 100
Investment in Sub Co.	900
	$1,000
Common stock	$1,000

The balance sheet of Sub Co. is unchanged (see page 418). The purchase discrepancy is calculated as follows:

Cost of 90% of Sub Co.		$900
Shareholders' equity of Sub Co.	512	
Less: future income tax asset	12	
	500	
Parent's ownership	90%	450
Purchase discrepancy		450
Allocated:		
Asset (950 – 800) × 90%	135	
Future income tax liability	42	93
Balance, goodwill		$357

The future tax liability associated with this single asset of Sub Co. used in the allocation is calculated as follows:

Value used for consolidation (800 + 135)	$935
Tax basis	830
Taxable temporary difference	105
Tax rate	40%
Future tax liability for consolidation	$ 42

The consolidated balance sheet of Parent is prepared as follows:

PARENT INC. — CONSOLIDATED BALANCE SHEET
January 1, Year 4

Cash	$ 100
Assets (800 + 135)	935
Goodwill	357
	$1,392
Liabilities	$ 300
Future income taxes	42
Noncontrolling interest (10% × 500)	50
Common stock	1,000
	$1,392

Note that the amount for noncontrolling interest is based on the carrying value of the net assets of the subsidiary used in the consolidation process. Section 1581 does not allow the cost of the acquisition to be allocated to future income taxes "recognized by an acquired enterprise before its acquisition," nor does it allow such future income taxes to be recognized in the consolidated statements of the acquirer.

Assessment of the Balance Sheet Approach

Under the previous income statement approach of recording income taxes, deferred income tax balances on a subsidiary's balance sheet were carried forward to the consolidated balance sheet. In addition, it was suggested that the acquirer, when establishing the amounts for the acquiree's assets, should take into account that the value of an asset that is not fully claimable for tax purposes is less than the value of an identical asset that is. It has not been established how these guiding principles were actually put into practice when the acquisition costs of purchase business combinations were allocated; but it seems obvious that the standard setters felt that the principles were not being applied correctly.

The new provisions make it more complicated to allocate the purchase cost, and will probably result in larger amounts being reflected in goodwill than was the case previously. It will also be more complicated to prepare consolidated financial statements in periods subsequent to the date of acquisition. Under the old system, the purchase discrepancy allocations were amortized on a systematic basis. This will not work well under the new method, because the balance sheet approach requires that we compare the carrying value of an asset or liability to its tax basis on each date that a balance sheet is prepared, and make an adjustment to previously recorded future income tax balances. When we prepare a consolidated balance sheet subsequent to acquisition, we will have to compare the values used in the consolidation for a subsidiary's net assets with the tax basis of these assets in the records of the subsidiary. In addition, any future taxes that have been reflected in the subsidiary's statements will probably have to be reversed, because different future tax balances are used for consolidated purposes. The use of push-down accounting (discussed in the next chapter) will probably remove much of this complexity.

Operating Loss Carry-forwards

Under Section 3465, accounting recognition can be given to the carry-forward of unused tax losses if it is "more likely than not that a future income tax asset will be realized." This makes it easier to recognize such a future tax asset than under the "old" Section 3470, which required "virtual certainty." If the acquired company has already recognized a future tax asset due to the potential carry-forward of unused tax losses, this future tax asset will be allowed to stand on the date of the business combination. The combining of the two companies does not ordinarily change this status. However, if the acquired company was not able to recognize unused tax losses, the fact that it is combining with the acquiring company may provide the additional impetus to satisfy the "more likely than not" criterion. This could result because the two companies combined will do business with each other or will be able to reduce future costs, all of which could result in greater possibilities of having future taxable incomes than was the case before the combination. The acquirer could also benefit in the future, in that its previously unrecognized tax losses could be recognized at the time of the combination. In both situations, the future income tax asset would be included when the cost of the purchase is allocated. Note that recognizing such a future tax asset as part of the allocation of the acquisition cost reduces the amount that otherwise would have been allocated to goodwill. This concept must also be taken into account in situations where a future tax asset was *not* recognized as an allocation of the acquisition cost, but subsequently becomes recognizable. In this situation the future tax asset would be set up in the consolidated statements; the amount so recognized would be used first to reduce the amount of goodwill from the combination, then to reduce any unamortized intangible properties from the combination; any amount left would then be used to reduce (consolidated) income tax expense.

Segment Disclosures

For simplicity, most of the examples used in previous chapters were unrealistic, in that they consisted of a parent company and a single subsidiary. When you consider all companies that trade on the Toronto Stock Exchange, very few are made up of only two companies, and many of the larger ones consist of the parent and a substantial number of subsidiaries. The consolidation process treats these separate legal entities as a single economic entity by aggregating the components of their financial statements. In past years, all companies comprising a given consolidated group were often in a single line of business and were located in Canada, so this aggregation of statements provided useful information to the users of the consolidated statements. However, the tremendous corporate expansion that started in the 1970s created companies engaged in diversified activities in many parts of the world, and it became obvious that the basic consolidated financial statements were not providing adequate information. Financial statement users needed information about a company that would allow them to assess all of its different components, which have different growth potentials, profitability characteristics, and inherent risks, which vary with the products and services being provided and the markets being entered. Consolidated financial statements do not provide this information.

In 1979, *Handbook* Section 1700, "Segmented Information," was issued as a response to this user need. This section required footnote disclosures that disaggregated the consolidated financial statements into industry segments and geographic segments. It also required that information be provided about the company's export sales. This section remained unchanged until September 1997, when a new Section 1701 was issued to replace it. This new section was the result of the joint efforts of the Accounting Standards Board of the CICA and the Financial Accounting Standards Board in the United States, and is identical to FASB #131, issued at approximately the same time. Before we examine the requirements of this new section, it may be useful to assess the shortcomings of the previous reporting requirements.

Shortcomings of the Old Section 1700

This section required a company to report information about the industries in which it operated and, if it had operations outside of Canada, further information about the geographic areas in which it had revenue-producing assets. Although the information required included amounts for revenues, operating profits, and assets, management was given only very broad guidelines to use in identifying the *operating* and *geographic* segments for which it should supply such information. Reporting on this basis was supposed to enhance the usefulness of a company's financial statements. One important attribute of useful information is comparability. Not only should the financial statements of a single company be comparable from year to year, but also, the company's statements should be comparable with those of other companies. Unfortunately, this was not achieved under Section 1700 because the standard left the composition of both industry and geographic segments almost entirely to the discretion of management. Hence two very similar companies would not appear similar if their two managements identified their respective segments differently. Take, for example, a company producing baseball bats and hockey sticks in two separate plants. Under the old guidelines, this could be viewed as a single segment — sporting goods — or alternatively as two separate segments — baseball bats and hockey sticks. (Unfortunately the requirements of the new standard have not solved this problem.)

In addition to the lack of comparability between companies, the reporting requirements were criticized by financial analysts for not requiring sufficient disaggregation. The new Section 1701 appears to have alleviated this particular problem, as the following two items of interest indicate.

Item of Interest In 1997, Agra Inc., an international engineering, construction, and technology company, had over 5,000 employees and operated in 22 countries. In the nonfinancial section of its 1997 annual report it provided descriptions (with no financial data) about 9 different categories of its business. Yet footnote 19 of its 1997 audited financial statements reported only 2 industry segments, described as "Engineering, Construction & Technology" and "Asset Development & Investments," and 2 geographic segments, described as "Canadian" and "Foreign."

In the 1999 financial statements, information provided under the new Section 1701 showed financial information for 4 industry segments as well the geographic areas of Canada, United States, Grand Cayman Island, and "Other." (In April 2000, Agra merged with AMEC, a British company, and as a result no longer issues financial statements to the public.)

Item of Interest Magna International Inc. is a well-known Canadian company employing over 36,000 people at 128 manufacturing facilities located in Canada, the United States, Europe, and Asia. In the body of its 1997 annual report, it described itself as the developer and manufacturer of body and chassis systems; interior systems; mirror systems; closure and electronic systems; and powertrain, fuelling, and cooling systems; but did not provide any quantitative information regarding these areas of business. In footnote 16 of its 1997 audited financial statements, entitled "Segmented Information," it showed no industry segments, with the explanation that management considered it to have a single segment — automotive parts. It did provide information about the following three geographic segments: "Canada," "Europe," and "United States and Other."

In its December 31, 2000, financial statements it continued to provide geographic area information under the same headings, and improved its industry segment offerings by showing headings for three segments, each of which was broken down between North America and Europe.

If these two examples are representative, it appears that the new requirements of Section 1701 have improved the reporting in this vital area.

Section 1701, "Segment Disclosures"

Section 1701 was introduced in January 1998 as a replacement for the old Section 1700. It requires a public company to disclose information about its operating segments and, in addition, information about its products and services, the countries in which it operates, and its major customers. As the Items of Interest illustrate, it is expected that such information will provide users with a better understanding of a company's performance and its prospects for future cash flows.

The term used in the previous section, *industry segment*, has been replaced by a new term, *operating segment*. This is more than a cosmetic change; it also signals a change in approach. This new *management approach* is based on the way that a company's management organizes its components internally for assessing performance and making strategic decisions. It focuses on the financial information that the company's decision makers use for that purpose. Each component is called an operating segment and is defined as one:

(a) that engages in business activities from which it may earn revenues and incur expenses (including revenues and expenses relating to transactions with other components of the same enterprise),

(b) whose operating results are regularly reviewed by the enterprise's chief operating decision maker to make decisions about resources to be allocated to the segment and assess its performance, and

(c) for which discrete financial information is available. [1701.10]

The presentation of management's operating breakdown, and of related information generated for internal assessment purposes, should provide more useful information to external users than was provided under the old section. However, it should also be noted that full comparability between two companies is still not likely, because definitions of operating segments will still vary. Even so, additional comparability will be achieved through the requirement for disclosures about products and their associated revenues, and about countries in which the company earns revenues and holds assets.

Identification of Reportable Operating Segments

Section 1701 requires information to be disclosed about all operating segments that meet certain *quantitative thresholds*. This requirement is described as follows:

An enterprise should disclose separately information about an operating segment that meets *any* of the following quantitative thresholds:

(a) Its reported revenue, including both sales to external customers and intersegment sales or transfers, is 10 percent or more of the combined revenue, internal and external, of all reported operating segments.

(b) The absolute amount of its reported profit or loss is 10 percent or more of the greater, in absolute amount, of:

(i) the combined reported profit of all operating segments that did not report a loss, or

(ii) the combined reported loss of all operating segments that did report a loss.

(c) Its assets are 10 percent or more of the combined assets of all operating segments. [1701.19]

These quantitative thresholds (which are essentially the same as those of the old Section 1700) establish which reportable operating segments require separate disclosures. Any segments falling outside these guidelines may be combined under the category "Other," provided that at least 75 percent of a company's total external revenue is included in reportable segments. If it is not, additional operating segments must be disclosed. The section also suggests that from a practical point of view, the total number of operating segments reported will probably not exceed 10 or 11 segments.

Illustration   The following illustrates an application of quantitative thresholds. For internal evaluation purposes, JK Enterprises Inc. generates information from its six divisions. In terms of Section 1701, these divisions are operating segments. The following amounts (stated in millions) have been assembled to determine which of these operating segments are reportable in accordance with the section's quantitative thresholds.

Operating segments	Revenues	Operating profit (loss)	Assets
Autoparts	$53.9	$18.1	$10.9
Office furnishings	8.6	1.3	1.2
Publishing	6.5	(2.1)	1.4
Retail	5.0	(2.8)	3.2
Finance	11.8	3.7	14.0
Software	7.9	3.9	0.9
	$93.7	$22.1	$31.6

Revenue Test

10% × $93.7 = $9.37

From this test, Autoparts and Finance are identified.

Operating Profit (loss) Test

To apply this test, first compute separate totals for all profits and all losses. Then choose the largest of the absolute amount of the two totals, as follows:

Total of all operating profits	$27.0*
Total of all operating losses	4.9

10% × $27.0 = $2.7

Autoparts, Retail, Finance, and Software are identified.

Asset Test

10% × $31.6 = $3.16

Autoparts, Retail, and Finance are identified.

Following is a summary of all three quantitative tests for JK Enterprises:

Operating segments	Revenues	Operating profit (loss)	Assets
Autoparts	X	X	X
Office furnishings			
Publishing			
Retail		X	X
Finance	X	X	X
Software		X	

Thus, separate disclosures are required for Autoparts, Retail, Finance, and Software, as each satisfies at least one of the tests. Office furnishings and Publishing can be combined and reported under the heading "Other."

Information To Be Disclosed

The following disclosures are required for *each reportable segment* that has been identified by the quantitative thresholds:

1. Factors used by management to identify segments.
2. The types of products and services that generate revenues.
3. A measure of profit (loss).
4. Total assets.
5. Each of the following *if* the specific amounts are included in the measure of profit (loss) above:
    (a) Revenues from external customers.
    (b) Intersegment revenues.
    (c) Interest revenue and expense. (This may be netted for a particular segment only if that segment receives a majority of its revenues from interest *and* if the chief operating decision maker uses the net number to assess performance.)
    (d) Amortization of capital assets and goodwill.
    (e) Unusual revenues, expenses, and gains (losses).
    (f) Equity income from significant influence investments.
    (g) Income taxes.
    (h) Extraordinary items.
    (i) Significant noncash items other than the amortizations above.
6. The amount of significant influence investments, if such investments are included in segment assets.
7. Total expenditures for additions to capital assets and goodwill.
8. An explanation of how a segment's profit (loss) and assets have been measured, and how common costs and jointly used assets have been allocated, and of the accounting policies that have been used.
9. Reconciliations of the following:
    (a) Total segment revenue to consolidated revenues.
    (b) Total segment profit (loss) to consolidated net income (loss).
    (c) Total segment assets to consolidated assets.

Enterprise-wide Disclosures

The following information must also be disclosed, unless such information has already been clearly provided as part of the segment disclosures. This additional information is also required in situations where the company has only a single reportable segment.

1. The revenue from external customers for each product or service, or for each group of similar products and services, whenever practical.

2. The revenue from external customers broken down between those from the company's country of domicile (i.e., Canada) and those from all foreign countries. Where revenue from an individual country is material, it must be separately disclosed.

3. Goodwill and capital assets broken down between those located in Canada and those located in foreign countries. Where assets located in an individual country are material, they must be separately disclosed.

4. When a company's sales to a single external customer are 10 percent or more of total revenues, the company must disclose this fact, as well as the total amount of revenues from each customer and which operating segment reported such revenues. The identity of the customer does not have to be disclosed.

As with all financial reporting, comparative amounts for at least the last fiscal year must also be presented.

The disclosures required by the new Section 1701 are a radical departure from those of the old Section 1700. This new approach seems to be a better one because it provides external users with the information that top management uses to assess performance.

Exhibit 10.1 (see page 428) shows the segment disclosures by Domco Tarkett Inc., a Canadian company that manufactures floor coverings in plants located in the United States and Canada.

An International Perspective

Canada, Australia, and New Zealand seem to be the only countries in the world requiring or allowing proportionate consolidation for an investment in a joint venture. Many countries require accounting for long-term investments in accordance with rigid quantitative guidelines, and as a result joint ventures are reported using the equity method because this type of investment is considered to be significant influence.

In the United States, some companies are allowed to follow industry practice and proportionately consolidate; but aside from these exceptions, most companies with joint venture investments are required to use the equity method. However, if a venturer owns greater than 50 percent of a joint venture, it is considered to be a control investment requiring full consolidation. This whole area is being re-examined by the FASB, and so it is quite possible that there may be some changes to accounting standards in the future. The IASB standard for joint ventures allows an investment to be accounted for using either proportionate consolidation or the equity method.

It should be noted that there has been some criticism of the proportionate consolidation method because assets are presented in consolidated statements that are neither owned nor controlled. It is quite possible that Canada and the IASB, along with the other countries mentioned, may reconsider the allowing of this method in the future.

The concept of interperiod income tax allocation has always been a controversial one, not just in Canada but in many other countries as well. First, there is the

Exhibit 10.1

DOMCO TARKETT INC.
NOTES TO CONSOLIDATED FINANCIAL STATEMENTS
Years Ended December 31, 2000 and 1999 ($000s, except shares)

Segment Disclosures:

The Corporation operates in three reportable segments: two manufacturing segments (resilient floor covering products and hardwood floor covering products) with sales to Canadian and US distributors, and a Canadian distribution segment engaged in the distribution of floor covering products, mainly manufactured by the manufacturing segments. The accounting policies of the segments are the same as those described in note 1. Intersegment revenues are based on terms similar to those with third parties.

	Manufacturing — Resilient floor covering products		Manufacturing — Hardwood floor covering products		Canadian distribution		Total	
	2000	1999	**2000**	1999	**2000**	1999	**2000**	1999
External revenues	**$420,666**	$354,365	**$159,116**	$62,437	**$77,515**	$74,650	**$657,297**	$491,452
Intersegment revenues	**33,133**	35,783	**975**	—	**—**	—	**34,108**	35,783
Revenues	**453,799**	390,148	**160,091**	62,437	**77,515**	74,650	**691,405**	527,235
Depreciation	**15,839**	12,145	**7,643**	3,265	**80**	71	**23,562**	15,481
Segment income (loss) from operations	**12,810**	29,205	**18,025**	8,214	**1,524**	(1,252)	**32,359**	36,167
Non-segment expenses:								
Interest on long-term debt							**(13,912)**	(8,350)
Amortization of goodwill							**(7,250)**	(6,552)
Other							**(2,584)**	(430)
Income before provision for income taxes							**8,613**	20,835
Identifiable assets	**267,835**	264,144	**124,425**	112,134	**26,191**	28,373	**418,451**	404,651
Elimination							**(1,361)**	(1,709)
Non-segment assets:								
Goodwill							**132,964**	135,448
Other							**44,746**	35,926
Total assets							**$594,800**	$574,316

Geographic information:

	Revenues		Property, plant and equipment and goodwill	
	2000	1999	**2000**	1999
Canada	**$ 95,853**	$ 89,804	**$ 44,708**	$ 39,527
United States	**557,637**	398,739	**251,658**	263,835
Other	**3,807**	2,909	**—**	—
	$657,297	$491,452	**$296,366**	$303,362

issue as to whether it should be used at all. Next is the "partial" versus "full" allocation debate about accounting only for differences that will reverse in the near future. Finally, there are the two approaches to accounting for these differences: the deferral (income statement) approach and the liability (balance sheet) approach. With all these potential differences, it should not be surprising that practices vary around the world. Countries whose accounting principles closely follow, or are identical to, income tax rules do not have a need for income tax allocation. Japan does not use it at all; and it is largely unnecessary in Germany, Sweden, and Brazil, even though the accounting standards in these countries permit the use of it. The flow-through method (no tax allocation) is used by both China and South Korea.

The United Kingdom uses partial allocation, while most industrialized countries use comprehensive tax allocation. The United States, the United Kingdom, Australia, New Zealand, Hong Kong, and Mexico require the liability method, while France requires the deferral method. Switzerland, Denmark, and the Netherlands permit either method, while India recommends the liability method but does not require the use of income tax allocation.

The IASB used to allow both methods in addition to allowing either partial or comprehensive allocation; but on January 1, 1988, it began requiring the liability method for "nearly all temporary differences." It is interesting that of all of the countries that use the liability method, Canada seems to be the only one to use the terminology "future income tax assets" and "future income tax liabilities." The rest of the countries that switched to the liability method have retained the term "deferred income taxes."

Canada's new tax accounting requirements relating to business combinations are very similar to FASB #109, which was adopted in 1992. The IASB's requirements are also similar in that they do not require the setting up of the tax effects of nondeductible goodwill. Whether these concepts are adopted or not by countries that use the liability method depends on the income tax regulations of each particular country.

The requirement that business and geographic segments be disclosed is also not uniform. South Korea, Chile, Brazil, Japan, and Germany do not require any disclosure of segment information. Mexico's standards do not specifically address the issue, but companies there are encouraged to follow the IASB standards. The United Kingdom requires disclosure of information about both geographic areas and lines of business, while Sweden requires only lines-of-business disclosure. The segment reporting standards in the United States are identical to those in Canada. The standards of the IASB are similar to Canada's in that a management approach has been adopted, but overall they are not identical. Even when some form of segment reporting is required, the quality of the information reported depends greatly on how segments are defined by a particular standard.

SUMMARY

In this chapter we have examined three different topics, which almost wind up our study of business combinations and the preparation of consolidated financial statements. The proportionate, line-by-line consolidation of a joint venture has some unique features associated with it, particularly in the areas of the elimination of intercompany profits and of the accounting for assets contributed as equity investments in the venture.

The consolidated expenses resulting from the allocation of the purchase discrepancy are not deductible for tax purposes, but under the balance sheet approach the reflection of future tax assets and liabilities is required for the differences between the carrying values and the tax bases of subsidiary company net assets shown on consolidated balance sheets.

Consolidation hides information about the lines of business conducted by multinational conglomerates. Required segment disclosures are designed to provide financial statement users with relevant information that will aid them in assessing company results.

REVIEW QUESTIONS

1. In what way is the proportionate consolidation method different from the full consolidation method?

2. Y Company has a 62 percent interest in Z Company. Are there circumstances where this would not result in Z Company being a subsidiary of Y Company? Explain.

3. The consolidating treatment of an unrealized intercompany inventory profit differs between a parent–subsidiary affiliation and a venturer–joint venture affiliation. Explain where the differences lie.

4. A venturer invested nonmonetary assets in the formation of a new joint venture. The fair value of the assets invested was greater than the book value in the accounting records of the venturer. Explain how the venturer should account for the investment.

5. X Company recently acquired control over Y Company. On the date of acquisition the fair values of Y Company's assets exceeded their tax bases. How does this difference affect the consolidated balance sheet?

6. A parent company has recently acquired a subsidiary. On the date of acquisition, both the parent and the subsidiary had unused income tax losses that were unrecognized in their financial statements. How would this affect the consolidation figures on date of acquisition?

7. Switching from an income statement approach to a balance sheet approach often produces the same results. But other times the results are different. Explain why.

8. What is the difference between a *deductible* temporary difference and a *taxable* temporary difference?

9. Explain how it is possible to have a future tax liability with regard to the presentation of a subsidiary's assets in a consolidated balance sheet, whereas on the subsidiary's balance sheet the same assets produce a future tax asset.

10. What was a major shortcoming with the segmented disclosures required in the old Section 1700?

11. Describe the three tests for identifying reportable operating segments.

12. The new Section 1701 is expected to satisfy the criticisms that were voiced about the segmented disclosures of the old section. Explain how.

13. For each of its operating segments that require separate disclosure, what information must an enterprise report?

14. In accordance with Section 1701, "Segment Disclosures":
    (a) What information must be disclosed about business carried out in other countries?
    (b) What information must be disclosed about a company's products or services?
    (c) What information must be provided about a company's customers?

15. What are the basic concepts behind the "management approach" to segmented reporting? How is it expected to be an improvement over the previous method of segment reporting?

16. What sort of reconciliations are required for segmented reporting?

MULTIPLE CHOICE

Use the following data for Questions 1 to 3.

The balance sheets for Darcy Co. and its 40% owned investment Stacey Ltd., as at December 31, Year 1, are as follows:

	Darcy	Stacey
Assets		
Cash	$ 32,000	$ 8,000
Current receivables	350,000	290,000
Inventories	1,560,000	580,000
Equipment (net)	6,040,000	2,900,000
Investment in Stacey (at cost)	600,000	—
Total assets	$8,582,000	$3,778,000
Liabilities and shareholders' equity		
Current liabilities	$ 500,000	$ 175,000
Long-term liabilities	4,000,000	386,000
Common stock	2,500,000	1,500,000
Retained earnings	1,582,000	1,717,000
Total liabilities and shareholders' equity	$8,582,000	$3,778,000

Additional Information

On January 1, Year 1, Darcy, Bailey, and Abraham formed Stacey as a joint venture. Darcy invested $600,000 cash on that date for a 40% interest. During Year 1, Darcy sold inventory to Stacey for a profit of $80,000. Stacey sold 50% of that inventory during the year. Both Darcy and Stacey are taxed at 30%.

1. Under the equity method, which of the following is the amount that Darcy would report as its investment in Stacey?
   a. $1,258,800
   b. $1,270,800
   c. $1,275,600
   d. $1,286,800

2. Which of the following is the amount that would be reported for inventory on Darcy's consolidated balance sheet?
   a. $1,776,000
   b. $1,792,000
   c. $2,100,000
   d. $2,124,000

3. Which of the following is the amount that would be reported for noncontrolling interest on Darcy's consolidated balance sheet?
   a. $0
   b. $1,913,400
   c. $1,919,000
   d. $1,930,200

Use the following data for Questions 4 and 5.

Golden Company has assembled the following data regarding its operating segments (000s omitted):

Segment	Revenues	Operating profit	Assets
A – Prepackaged food	$ 77,000	$ 4,500	$ 180,000
B – Canned food	465,000	(39,000)	235,000
C – Frozen food	156,000	12,400	900,000
D – Frozen beverages	820,000	35,000	750,000
E – Canned beverages	1,200,000	305,000	350,000
	$2,718,000	$317,900	$2,415,000

4. Using only the operating profit test, which of the operating segments would be reportable?
   a. B, E.
   b. D, E.
   c. E.
   d. B, D, E.

5. Using all of the tests for operating segments in Section 1701, which of the above would be reportable?
   a. A, B, C, D, E.
   b. B, C, D, E.
   c. B, D, E.
   d. D, E.

6. Which one of the following conditions is *not* required for an investment to be classified as a joint venture by an investor?
   a. Equity interest equal to that of other venturers.
   b. Exposure to related risks.
   c. Involvement in decision making.
   d. Right and ability to obtain future economic benefits from the resources of the joint venture.

(*CICA adapted*)

Use the following data for Questions 7 and 8.
   A Canadian company presents the following segment disclosure information in its audited financial statements (in millions of Canadian dollars):

	Canada	US	Europe	Other	Elimination	Total
2000						
Total revenue	29,878	17,874	8,104	3,082	(9,690)	49,248
Intersegment transfers	(6,522)	(1,774)	(1,044)	(350)	9,690	—
Revenue from external customers	23,356	16,100	7,060	2,732		49,248
Segment profit	5,768	3,762	1,196	130		10,856
Segment assets	52,902	11,526	12,258	4,106		80,792
1999						
Total revenue	28,380	16,116	4,502	1,596	(7,254)	43,340
Intersegment transfers	(5,476)	(1,190)	(270)	(318)	7,254	—
Revenue from external customers	22,904	14,926	4,232	1,278		43,340
Segment profit	6,044	3,488	708	(24)		10,216
Segment assets	52,392	12,196	12,524	2,500		79,612

7. In which segment in 2000 are the assets most profitable?
   a. Canada.
   b. Europe.
   c. U.S.
   d. Other.

8. Management has decided to invest in the segment with the highest sales margin on outside sales. In which segment will the parent company make a further investment?
   a. Canada.
   b. Europe.
   c. U.S.
   d. Other.

   (*CICA adapted*)

9. On January 1, 1999, Gaspe Ltd. purchased an asset for $250,000. The company amortizes the capital asset on a straight-line basis over its useful life of 5 years. The residual value is expected to be $75,000. The capital cost allowance rate is 30% and the tax rate for 1999 is 30%. Which one of the following statements best describes the items and amounts that would be shown on the balance sheet of Gaspe Ltd. as at December 31, 1999, if the asset acquired was the company's only capital asset?
   a. A capital asset with a net carrying amount of $140,000 and a future income tax asset of $2,500.
   b. A capital asset with a net carrying amount of $175,000 and a future income tax liability of $2,500.
   c. A capital asset with a net carrying amount of $215,000 and a future income tax asset of $750.
   d. A capital asset with a net carrying amount of $215,000 and a future income tax liability of $750.

   (*CICA adapted*)

10. Which of the following would be criteria for identifying a reportable operating segment for segmented reporting purposes?
    a. Discrete financial information is available for the segment, which is reviewed by the company's chief operating decision maker.
    b. The activities of the segment fall into a different Statistics Canada industry classification than other company operations.
    c. The segment incurs both revenues and expenses.
    d. Revenue of the segment is 10% or more of the total of revenue from all segments.
    e. (a) and (b).
    f. (a) and (d).
    g. (a), (c), and (d).

Use the following data for Questions 11 and 12.

On January 1, 2000, a joint venture named JV Corporation was formed. At this time A Ltd. contributed cash of $75,000 and took back a 20% interest in JV Corporation. During 2000, A Ltd. sold merchandise to JV Corporation at a profit of $15,000 before taxes. Half of this remained in JV Corporation's inventory at December 31, 2000. With respect to these sales, JV Corporation owed A Ltd. $10,000 at December 31, 2000. Both companies are subject to 40% tax rates. Year-end balance sheets of both companies follow:

BALANCE SHEETS — December 31, 2000

	A Ltd.	JV Corporation
Cash and accounts receivable	$ 80,000	$ 60,000
Inventory	240,000	110,000
Fixed assets (net)	500,000	350,000
Investment in JV Corp.	75,000	—
	$895,000	$520,000
Liabilities	$495,000	$ 95,000
Common shares	100,000	375,000
Retained earnings	300,000	50,000
	$895,000	$520,000

11. What would be the inventory reported on A Ltd.'s consolidated balance sheet at December 31, 2000?
    a. $257,500
    b. $260,500
    c. $261,100
    d. $345,500

12. What would be the liabilities reported on A Ltd.'s consolidated balance sheet at December 31, 2000?
    a. $580,000
    b. $514,000
    c. $512,000
    d. $504,000

13. On January 1, 2000, Holiday Corporation purchased a 100% interest in the common shares of Card Ltd. for $270,000. At this date, Card Ltd.'s balance sheet included the following:

	Book Value	Fair Value	Tax Basis
Assets	$560,000	$600,000	$375,000
Current liabilities	360,000	360,000	360,000
Future income tax liability	74,000		
Common shares	50,000		
Retained earnings	72,000		

Assume that Holiday has a future income tax liability of $98,000 on its January 1, 2000, balance sheet. Both companies are subject to 40% income tax rates. If a consolidated balance sheet was prepared for Holiday immediately following the acquisition of Card Ltd., what would be reported for a future income tax liability?
    a. $90,000
    b. $172,000
    c. $176,000
    d. $188,000
    e. None of the above.

14. Robertson Inc. purchased all of Gaddy Corp for $420,000. On that date Gaddy had net assets with a $400,000 fair market value and a carrying value of $300,000. The tax basis of the net assets was also $300,000. Assuming a 30% tax rate, what amount of goodwill should be recognized for this acquisition?
    a. $20,000
    b. $36,000
    c. $50,000
    d. $120,000

CASES

Case 1* In December 1997 the Ladbroke Group, a prominent British hotel and gaming company, bought the 827-location betting shop chain Coral from brewing and leisure group Bass for £376 million. These shops were quickly integrated into the Ladbroke chain, the largest operator in the off-course betting industry in Britain.

The deal collapsed in September 1998, when Trade and Industry Secretary Peter Mandelson blocked it on competition grounds and ordered the company to sell Coral within six months. Several potential suitors rapidly appeared.

In December 1998 the Ladbroke Group announced that it had agreed to sell the Coral chain to a company backed by Morgan Grenfell Private Equity for £390 million cash. Under the plan, Coral would retain its 50 betting shops in Ireland and 8 in Jersey in the Channel Islands, which would be rebranded as Ladbrokes. Coral would also retain a 5% stake in horse racing's Satellite Information Services, which Ladbroke had acquired from Bass as part of the initial purchase. This aspect is the subject of further discussions with the Office of Fair Trading of the Trade and Industry Secretariat.

(Adapted from a Reuters press release, December 22, 1998)

Required:

Assume that the provisions of the *CICA Handbook* apply to this series of real events. Outline the appropriate accounting policies to be followed by the Ladbroke Group for the investment in Coral for the years 1997 and 1998. Remember to consider the implications of the various components of the transactions.

Case 2* The Coca-Cola Company (see www.cocacola.com) is a world leader in the beverage industry; an estimated 1 billion servings of Coca-Cola products are consumed every day. Coca-Cola manufactures syrups, concentrates, and beverage bases; bottling is carried out under contract by authorized local businesses, which have rights to particular territories. With some exceptions, these bottling and distribution operations are locally owned and operated by independent businesspeople who are native to the nations in which they are located, and who often also bottle other local or international brands of soft drinks. The Coca-Cola Company has an equity position in a significant proportion of these bottlers, especially 10 strategically aligned business partners, referred to as the "anchor bottlers." These anchor bottlers are also distinguished by:

- A pursuit of the same strategic aims as the Coca-Cola Company in developing the nonalcoholic beverage business.
- A commitment to long-term growth.
- Commitment to the Coca-Cola system.
- Service to a large, geographically diverse area.
- Sufficient financial resources to make long-term investments.
- Managerial expertise and depth.

Among these anchor bottlers, Coca-Cola Enterprises (see www.cokecce.com) is the largest soft drink bottler in the world; 44% of the common shares of Coca-Cola Enterprises are owned by the Coca-Cola Company, the only significant shareholder. Sales of US$2.5 billion (13% of revenue) were made in 1997 by the Coca-Cola Company to Coca-Cola Enterprises. The Company provides certain administrative and other services to Coca-Cola Enterprises under negotiated fee arrangements; it also provides direct support for certain marketing activities of Coca-Cola Enterprises and participates in co-operative advertising and other marketing programs (amounting to $604 million in 1997). In

---

* Case prepared by Peter Secord, St. Mary's University.

addition, during 1997 and 1996 the Company committed approximately $190 million to Coca-Cola Enterprises under a company program that encourages bottlers to invest in building and supporting beverage infrastructure.

Coca-Cola Enterprises, with 56,000 employees and operations in 46 American states, in Canada, and in several European Union countries, is publicly traded on the New York Stock Exchange. Revenues in 1997 totalled $11.2 billion, of which over 90% arose from the sale of Coca-Cola Company products. The Coca-Cola Company uses the equity method to account for its investment in Coca-Cola Enterprises. If valued at the December 31, 1997, quoted closing price for Coca-Cola Enterprises shares, the calculated value of this investment in Coca-Cola Enterprises would have exceeded the 1997 carrying value of US$184 million, by approximately $5.8 billion.

Technical Note:

It is clear that certain assumptions as to the nature of significant influence and control are being employed in the accounting policy choices of the Coca-Cola Company, which follows U.S. rules. Since 1988, U.S. GAAP has required consolidation of all majority-owned subsidiaries unless control is temporary or does not rest with the majority owner. FASB Statement #94 requires consolidation of a majority-owned subsidiary even if it has "nonhomogeneous" operations, a large minority interest, or a foreign location.

However, accounting standards in North America (and indeed globally) are evolving so that the "old" standard of legal (*de jure*) control is being superseded by a standard based on "*de facto*" control (control as determined by the facts and circumstances of the relationship). Canadian standards have already moved significantly in this direction. U.S. GAAP (consult the FASB website, www.fasb.org, for current details) is also moving in this direction. North American harmonization of consolidation principles is the ultimate goal, so standards and practices in this and other areas should have a high degree of congruity throughout the NAFTA countries.

Required:

(a) Review the above facts, drawn from 1997 annual reports, carefully. Considering both the current and likely future state of accounting standards governing consolidation, analyze the financial reporting practices of the Coca-Cola Company with respect to its significant investments in the anchor bottlers.

(b) Consult the website of the Coca-Cola Company (www.cocacola.com) for information. The notes to the financial statements included at this site will contain information as to the current accounting practices for these investments. Determine how these financial reporting practices have evolved (if at all) and evaluate the results of your analysis in part (a) relative to current practices of the Company.

PROBLEMS

Problem 1   The accountant of Exacto Ltd. has approached you for advice. Exacto and two other companies have just formed Bayle Resources Inc. Although the three companies have signed an agreement establishing joint control over Bayle, Exacto has been issued 60% of that company's outstanding common shares. The accountant is not sure how Exacto will be required to report this investment in accordance with the *CICA Handbook*. She mentions to you that she has heard of both the purchase and the pooling of interests methods and is wondering if either of these methods would be appropriate in this particular situation.

Required:

Outline the advice that you will give to the accountant.

Problem 2   On January 1, Year 1, Able Ltd., Baker Ltd., and Drexal Ltd. entered into a joint venture agreement to form the Frontier Exploration Company. Able contributed 30% of the assets to the venture and agreed that its share of the venture would be the same percentage. Presented below are the financial statements of Able and Frontier as at December 31, Year 6:

BALANCE SHEETS

	Able	Frontier
Current assets	$247,000	$ 40,000
Investment in Frontier	27,000	—
Other assets	530,000	70,000
	$804,000	$110,000
Current liabilities	$ 94,000	$ 20,000
Long-term debt	400,000	—
Capital stock	200,000	10,000
Retained earnings	110,000	80,000
	$804,000	$110,000

INCOME STATEMENTS

	Able	Frontier
Revenues	$900,000	$100,000
Income from Frontier	9,000	—
Total revenues	909,000	100,000
Cost of sales and expenses	812,000	70,000
Net income	$ 97,000	$ 30,000

Able's investment has been accounted for by the partial equity method (no adjustments have been made for intercompany transactions).

Able acts as the sole supplier for certain materials used by Frontier in its exploration activities. The December 31, Year 6, inventory of Frontier contains items purchased from Able on which Able recorded a gross profit of $10,000. At December 31, Year 6, Frontier owed Able $12,000 representing invoices not yet paid. Frontier's Year 6 intercompany purchases amounted to $70,000.

Required:

Prepare the necessary financial statements for Able on a proportionate consolidated basis in accordance with Section 3055 of the *CICA Handbook*. (Use a rate of 40% for income tax effects.)

Problem 3   The following are the 2002 income statements of Ignace Corp. and Jasper Ltd.

INCOME STATEMENTS
for the Year Ended December 31, 2002

	Ignace	Jasper
Sales	$3,000,000	$1,200,000
Other income	200,000	70,000
Gain on sale of land	—	100,000
	$3,200,000	$1,370,000
Cost of sales	$1,400,000	$ 560,000
Operating expenses	500,000	300,000
Depreciation expense	100,000	130,000
Income tax	400,000	150,000
	$2,400,000	$1,140,000
Net income	$ 800,000	$ 230,000

Other Information

- Ignace acquired its 40% interest in the common shares of Jasper in 1996 at a cost of $825,000 and uses the cost method to account for its investment.
- The purchase discrepancy amortization schedule showed the following write-off for 2002:

Buildings	$ 9,000
Goodwill impairment loss	13,000
	22,000
Long-term liabilities	12,500
Purchase discrepancy amortization — 2002	$ 9,500

- In 2002, rent amounting to $125,000 was paid by Jasper to Ignace. Ignace has recorded this as other income.
- In 1999, Ignace sold land to Jasper and recorded a profit of $75,000 on the transaction. During 2002, Jasper sold one-half of the land to an unrelated land development company.
- During 2002, Jasper paid dividends totalling $80,000.
- It has been established that Ignace's 40% interest would *not* be considered control in accordance with the *CICA Handbook*.
- Assume a 40% tax rate.

Required:

(a) Assume that Jasper is a joint venture that is owned by Ignace and two other unrelated venturers. Also assume that Ignace acquired its interest after Jasper's initial formation, and that the purchase discrepancies are therefore valid. Prepare the income statement of Ignace for 2002 in accordance with GAAP (show all calculations).

(b) Assume that Jasper is *not* a joint venture, and furthermore, that Ignace's long-term investment in Jasper is *not* a portfolio investment. Prepare the income statement of Ignace for 2002 in accordance with GAAP (show all calculations).

Problem 4 Leighton Corp. has just acquired 100% of the voting shares of Knightbridge Inc. and is now preparing the financial data needed to consolidate this new subsidiary. Leighton paid $700,000 for its investment. Details of all of Knightbridge's assets and liabilities on acquisition date were as follows:

	Fair market value	Tax basis
Instalment accounts receivable	$120,000	$ –0–
Inventory	150,000	150,000
Land	100,000	100,000
Buildings	180,000	110,000
Equipment	200,000	130,000
Trade liabilities	240,000	240,000

Required:

Determine the amounts that will be used to prepare a consolidated balance sheet on the date of acquisition, assuming that Knightbridge's tax rate is 45%. Knightbridge has not set up future tax amounts for any of its assets or liabilities.

Problem 5 A Company and B Company formed Venture Ltd. on January 1, Year 3. Venture is a joint venture according to Section 3055 of the *CICA Handbook*. Both venturers contributed 50% of the capital, and profits and losses are shared on a 50–50 basis.

The following financial statements were prepared on December 31, Year 3:

BALANCE SHEETS

	A Company	Venture
Current assets	$ 75,000	$ 6,000
Investment in Venture Ltd. — cost	10,000	—
Fixed assets	190,000	72,000
Accumulated depreciation	(60,000)	(5,000)
Other assets	18,000	8,000
	$233,000	$81,000
Current liabilities	$ 33,000	$18,500
Long-term debt	45,000	40,000
Capital stock	85,000	20,000
Retained earnings, January 1	30,000	—
Net income for the year	40,000	2,500
	$233,000	$81,000

INCOME STATEMENTS

	A Company	Venture
Sales	$150,000	$20,000
Cost of sales	$ 90,000	$11,000
Expenses	20,000	6,500
	$110,000	$17,500
Net income	$ 40,000	$ 2,500

Additional Information

- During Year 3, Venture made purchases totalling $4,000 from A Company. A Company recorded a gross profit of $1,200 on its sales to Venture.
- On December 31, Year 3, the inventories of Venture contain 25% of the items purchased from A Company.
- A Company has used the cost method to account for its investment in Venture.
- A Company wishes to prepare consolidated statements in accordance with Section 3055 of the *Handbook*.
- Use income tax allocation at a rate of 40%.

Required:

Prepare the consolidated financial statements for A Company as at December 31, Year 3.

Problem 6 While the consolidated statements of a multinational or diversified enterprise are useful for assessing performance as a whole, the aggregation that is the product of the consolidation process has been found to have some serious shortcomings. In response to this, a section of the *CICA Handbook* has been devoted to addressing this problem.

Required:

Discuss this statement and describe how this particular section alleviates the shortcomings.

Problem 7 Investor Company has an investment in the voting shares of Investee Ltd. On December 31, 2002, Investee reported a net income of $860,000 and declared dividends of $200,000.

During 2002, Investor had sales to Investee of $915,000, and Investee had sales to Investor of $500,000. On December 31, 2002, the inventory of Investor contained an after-tax intercompany profit of $40,000, and the inventory of Investee contained an after-tax intercompany profit of $72,000.

On January 1, 2001, Investor sold equipment to Investee and recorded an after-tax profit of $120,000 on the transaction. The equipment had a remaining life of 5 years on this date. Investor uses the equity method to account for its investment in Investee.

Required:

Prepare Investor's 2002 equity method journal entries under each of the following two assumptions:

(a) Investor owns 64% of Investee.

(b) Investor owns 30% of Investee and Investee is a joint venture.

Problem 8 On January 1, Year 1, Green Inc. purchased 100% of the common shares of Mansford Corp. for $335,000. Green's balance sheet data on this date just prior to this acquisition are as follows:

	Book value	Tax basis
Cash	$ 340,000	$ 340,000
Accounts receivable	167,200	–0–
Inventory	274,120	274,120
Land	325,000	325,000
Buildings (net)	250,000	150,000
Equipment (net)	79,000	46,200
	$1,435,320	$1,135,320
Current liabilities	$ 133,000	133,000
Future income tax	120,000	—
Noncurrent liabilities	—	
Common stock	380,000	
Retained earnings	802,320	
	$1,435,320	

The balance sheet and other related data for Mansford are as follows:

MANSFORD CORP. — BALANCE SHEET
January 1, Year 1

	Book value	Fair value	Tax basis
Cash	$ 52,500	$ 52,500	$ 52,500
Accounts receivable	61,450	61,450	61,450
Inventory	110,000	134,000	110,000
Land75,000	210,000	75,000	
Buildings (net)	21,000	24,000	15,000
Equipment (net)	17,000	16,000	12,000
	$336,950		$325,950
Current liabilities	$ 41,115	41,115	41,115
Noncurrent liabilities	150,000	155,000	150,000
Future income taxes	4,400		—
Common stock	100,000		
Retained earnings	41,435		
	$336,950		

For both companies, the income tax rate is 40%.

Required:

Prepare a consolidated balance sheet.

Problem 9   Assume that all of the facts in Problem 8 remain unchanged except that Green paid $268,000 for 80% of the voting shares of Mansford.

Required:

Prepare a consolidated balance sheet.

Problem 10   The following information has been assembled about Casbar Corp. as at December 31, 2002 (amounts are in thousands):

Operating segment	Revenues	Profit	Assets
A	$12,000	$2,100	$24,000
B	9,600	1,680	21,000
C	7,200	1,440	15,000
D	3,600	660	9,000
E	5,100	810	8,400
F	1,800	270	3,600

Required:

Determine which operating segments require separate disclosures.

Problem 11   The following are the December 31, 2002, balance sheets of three related companies:

	Pro Ltd.	Forma Corp.	Apex Inc.
Cash	$ 70,000	$ 1,500	$200,000
Accounts receivable	210,000	90,000	110,000
Inventory	100,000	62,500	70,000
Investment in Forma Corp. — at cost	326,000	—	—
Investment in Apex Inc. — at cost	150,000	—	—
Land	100,000	110,000	60,000
Plant and equipment	726,000	550,000	290,000
Accumulated depreciation	(185,000)	(329,000)	(60,000)
	$1,497,000	$485,000	$670,000
Accounts payable	$ 175,000	$ 90,000	$130,000
Bonds payable	312,000	—	—
Common shares	800,000	100,000	500,000
$12 preferred shares	—	200,000	—
Retained earnings	210,000	95,000	40,000
	$1,497,000	$485,000	$670,000

Other Information

- On January 1, 1998, Pro purchased 40% of Forma for $116,000. On that date, Forma's shareholders' equity was as follows:

Common shares	$100,000
Retained earnings	80,000
	$180,000

All of the identifiable net assets of Forma had fair values equal to carrying values except for the following, for which fair values exceeded carrying values by:

Inventory	$20,000
Land	40,000
Plant and equipment	50,000

- On September 30, 2000, Pro purchased the remaining 60% of Forma for $210,000. On that date, Forma's shareholders' equity was as follows:

Common shares	$100,000
Retained earnings	110,000
	$210,000

On this date the following net assets of Forma were undervalued by the amounts shown:

Inventory	$10,000
Plant and equipment	70,000

- For consolidation purposes, any purchase discrepancy allocated to plant and equipment is amortized over 20 years. A goodwill impairment loss amounting to $2,025 was recorded in 2001.
- During 2001, Forma issued 2,000 cumulative, $12, no-par-value preferred shares. Pro did not acquire any of these shares.
- The inventories of Pro contained intercompany profits from items purchased from Forma in the following amounts:

December 31, 2001	$40,000
December 31, 2002	45,000

- During 2002, Pro and two other unrelated companies formed Apex, which is a joint venture. Pro invested $150,000 cash for its 30% interest in the venture.
- The year-end inventories of Apex contained a $12,000 intercompany profit from items purchased from Pro since its formation in 2002.
- Forma paid dividends in all years prior to 2002. The company's directors, in assessing the effect of the 2002 operating loss on the company's liquidity position, did not declare dividends in 2002.
- On December 31, 2002, the accounts receivable of Pro contained the following:

Receivable from Forma	$13,000
Receivable from Apex	$40,000

Required:

Prepare the 2002 consolidated balance sheet. (Use income tax allocation at a 40% rate as it applies to unrealized profits only).

Problem 12 On January 1, 2002, Amco Ltd. and Newstar Inc. formed Bearcat Resources, a joint venture. Newstar contributed miscellaneous assets with a fair value of $900,000 for a 60% interest in the venture. Amco contributed plant and equipment with a book value of $300,000 and a fair value of $1,000,000 for a 40% interest in the venture and $500,000 in cash. On December 31, 2002, Bearcat reported a net income of $180,000 and declared a dividend of $75,000. Amco has a December 31 year-end and will account for its 40% interest using the equity method. (Assume a 20-year life for the plant and equipment.)

Required:

PART A

Assume that the miscellaneous assets contributed by Newstar included cash of $500,000.
(a) Prepare Amco's 2002 journal entries.

PART B

Assume that there was no cash in the assets contributed by Newstar.

(a) Prepare Amco's 2002 journal entries.

(b) For all accounts (except cash) that you used to answer Part B(a), provide a brief description as to where each would appear in Amco's 2002 consolidated financial statements.

Problem 13   Since 1979, segmented reporting has been a requirement of the *CICA Handbook*. Due to user dissatisfaction with the old section, a new Section 1701 was issued in 1998. It is expected that the provisions of this new section will improve this type of reporting.

Required:

(a) What is the purpose of segmented reporting?

(b) What was the problem with the information that was provided in accordance with the old section?

(c) Why is it expected that the new Section 1701 will improve the situation?

(d) Section 1701 has certain quantitative thresholds. What are these thresholds and how are they used?

Problem 14   Jager Ltd., a joint venture, was formed on January 1, Year 3. Cliffcord Corp., one of the three founding venturers, invested land for a 40% interest in the joint venture. The other two venturers invested equipment and cash for their 60% equity in Jager. All of the venturers agreed that the land had a fair market value of $2,000,000, and would provide services to the venture for approximately 8 years. This land had been acquired by Cliffcord over 20 years ago, and as a result the carrying value on Cliffcord's records on January 1 was only $600,000. Cliffcord recorded its investment in the joint venture at $2,000,000. On December 31, Year 3, Jager recorded a net loss of $100,000.

Cliffcord uses the equity method to record its investment.

Required:

(a) Prepare Cliffcord's Year 3 journal entries.

(b) Describe how the accounts you created in (a) would be presented in Cliffcord's Year 3 consolidated financial statements.

(c) If Cliffcord had received a 40% interest and $1,000,000 in cash in return for investing this land in the venture, briefly explain how the entries that you made in (a) would be different. You may assume that the other venturers contributed cash in excess of $1,000,000 for their ownership interests.

Problem 15   The following balance sheets have been prepared as at December 31, Year 5, for Kay Corp. and Adams Co. Ltd.:

	Kay	Adams
Cash	$ 68,000	$ 30,000
Accounts receivable	80,000	170,000
Inventory	600,000	400,000
Property and plant	1,400,000	900,000
Investment in Adams	352,000	—
	$2,500,000	$1,500,000
Current liabilities	$ 400,000	$ 150,000
Bonds payable	500,000	600,000
Capital stock	900,000	450,000
Retained earnings	700,000	300,000
	$2,500,000	$1,500,000

Additional Information

- Kay acquired its 40% interest in Adams for $352,000 in Year 1, when Adams's retained earnings amounted to $170,000. The purchase discrepancy on that date was fully amortized by the end of Year 5.
- In Year 4, Kay sold land to Adams and recorded a gain of $60,000 on the transaction. This land is still being used by Adams.
- The December 31, Year 5, inventory of Kay contained a profit recorded by Adams amounting to $35,000.
- On December 31, Year 5, Adams owes Kay $29,000.
- Kay has used the cost method to account for its investment in Adams.
- Use income tax allocation at a rate of 40%.

Required:

Prepare *three* separate balance sheets for Kay as at December 31, Year 5, in accordance with GAAP, assuming that the investment in Adams:

(a) is a control investment.
(b) is a joint venture investment.
(c) is a significant influence investment.

CHAPTER 11

(A) Comprehensive Revaluation of Assets and Liabilities
(B) Bankruptcy and Receivership

CHAPTER OUTLINE

LEARNING OBJECTIVES

After studying this chapter, you should be able to do the following:

- Describe the conditions necessary for a comprehensive revaluation of the assets and liabilities of an enterprise.
- Describe and apply the concepts of push-down accounting.
- Apply the concepts of comprehensive revaluation when a financial reorganization has taken place.
- Distinguish between bankruptcy and receivership.

- Be familiar with the terminology and basic concepts associated with bankruptcy and receivership.
- Prepare calculations showing the estimated amounts that would be distributed to the various classes of creditors in a business insolvency situation.

This chapter is divided into two parts. Part A examines comprehensive revaluation of assets and liabilities, while Part B looks at bankruptcy and receivership. At first glance, the two parts may seem divergent and unrelated; however, as we develop these topics, it should become obvious that the type of comprehensive revaluation that results from a corporate reorganization has a direct relationship to the topic of bankruptcy and receivership. This is because such a reorganization occurs only when a business is in dire financial straits.

A second type of comprehensive revaluation that we examine involves push-down accounting, which has a direct relationship to some of the material on consolidation that we discussed in earlier chapters.

(A) Comprehensive Revaluation of Assets and Liabilities

In December 1992, Section 1625 of the *Handbook*, "Comprehensive Revaluation of Assets and Liabilities," was issued by the Accounting Standards Board of the CICA. Under this new section, an enterprise may depart from the historical cost model and comprehensively revalue its assets and liabilities, provided that certain conditions have been satisfied. Before this section was issued, fixed asset appraisals were allowed in certain limited instances; the resulting revaluation increments can still be seen in the financial statements of a small number of companies.

At the time when the "old" Canadian standards allowed the limited use of fixed asset appraisals, appraisal accounting was not sanctioned at all by the FASB in the United States. However, in the early 1980s the concept of push-down accounting (which uses appraised values) gained some acceptance in that country. The Securities and Exchange Commission required push-down accounting by companies that had become substantially wholly owned as a result of a business combination. This requirement applied only to the filings with the commission and did not apply to the general purpose statements issued to the public. Subsequently, debate began as to whether or not push-down accounting should become part of GAAP. A similar debate began in Canada, and in 1987 the CICA issued an Accounting Guideline on the subject, which stated:

> the use of push-down accounting by a reporting enterprise is acceptable only when:
> (a) virtually all of its voting shares have been acquired; and
> (b) no significant outstanding public interest remains in its debt securities, preferred shares, non-voting common shares or other securities.

The Accounting Guideline quoted above was withdrawn when the new Section 1625 was issued in 1992. This section deals with recognition, measurement, and disclosure standards involved in establishing a new cost basis as a result of the comprehensive revaluation of all of the assets and liabilities of a profit-oriented enterprise. This is basically a one-time revaluation, and any subsequent revaluations of the individual assets and liabilities of the enterprise would have to be made in accordance with other relevant *Handbook* sections.[1] This is not a shift to a current-value model, since such a model would provide for the continuous yearly recognition of changing values.

Under this section, a comprehensive revaluation of an enterprise can take place only if:

(a) all or virtually all of the equity interests (at least 90 percent) have been acquired by an acquirer who controls the enterprise after the transaction; or

(b) the enterprise has been subject to a financial reorganization (i.e., as provided for under the Bankruptcy Act, or the Companies Creditors Arrangements Act), and there has been a change in control as a result of a substantial realignment of nonequity and equity interests; and

(c) new costs can reasonably be determined in either situation.

The section also states that the transaction resulting in the acquisition of virtually all of the equity interests of the enterprise must be between nonrelated parties. Furthermore, even when an acquirer has obtained virtually all of the equity interests of a company, the existence of control must still be established in accordance with the guidelines provided in Section 1590, "Subsidiaries."

The revaluation when condition (a) has been met is the application of push-down accounting and is *optional* under Section 1625. This concept will be illustrated first. Revaluations as a result of financial reorganizations are *required* and will be illustrated later (see page 461).

Push-down Accounting

The basic point of push-down accounting is to record in the accounts of a subsidiary the fair value increments used by the parent in the preparation of the consolidated statements. The acquirer's costs of the business combination are "pushed down" and recorded in the accounting records of the acquiree company. An example follows.

On January 1, Year 1, P Company acquired all of the outstanding common shares of S Company at a cost of $162,000. On this date the asset and liability values on the balance sheet of S Company were reflective of fair market values except for the following assets, whose fair values were:

	Fair value
Inventory	$60,000
Land	36,000
Plant and equipment	56,000

The plant and equipment have a remaining life of 10 years. Goodwill will be evaluated yearly for impairment.

Exhibit 11.1 shows the separate balance sheets of P Company and S Company on January 1, Year 1, and the consolidated balance sheet prepared on that date. S Company

---

[1] For example, lower of cost or market applications.

has *not* used push-down accounting in this illustration. The calculation and allocation of the purchase discrepancy is also shown.

The consolidated balance sheet was prepared by eliminating the shareholders' equity accounts of S Company ($150,000) against the investment account of P Company ($162,000). The resulting purchase discrepancy ($12,000) was allocated to revalue the inventory, land, and plant and equipment, with the balance reflected as goodwill.

Application of Push-down Accounting

With push-down accounting, the following journal entries are made by S Company as at January 1, Year 1:

Retained earnings	80,000	
Common stock		80,000
To reclassify retained earnings as share capital on acquisition date		

Exhibit 11.1

BALANCE SHEET — January 1, Year 1

	P Company	S Company without push-down	P Company consolidated
Cash	$ 32,000	$ 35,000	$ 67,000
Accounts receivable	90,000	63,000	153,000
Inventory	120,000	59,000	180,000
Land	100,000	30,000	136,000
Plant and equipment	300,000	54,000	356,000
Investment in S	162,000	—	—
Goodwill	—	—	3,000
	$804,000	$241,000	$895,000
Liabilities	$120,000	$ 91,000	$211,000
Common stock	400,000	70,000	400,000
Retained earnings	284,000	80,000	284,000
	$804,000	$241,000	$895,000

PURCHASE DISCREPANCY

Cost of 100% of S			$162,000
Book value of S			
Common stock		70,000	
Retained earnings		80,000	150,000
Purchase discrepancy			12,000
Allocated			
Inventory		1,000	
Land		6,000	
Plant and equipment		2,000	9,000
Goodwill			$ 3,000

Any retained earnings on acquisition date are to be reclassified as either share capital, contributed surplus, or a separately identified component of shareholders' equity.[2] This reclassification produces a retained earnings amount comparable to that which would exist if P Company had purchased the net assets of S Company instead of its shares.

The next journal entry records the comprehensive revaluation of all of the assets and liabilities of S Company.

Inventory	1,000	
Land	6,000	
Plant and equipment	2,000	
Goodwill	3,000	
Common stock		12,000
To comprehensively revalue the net assets based on the price paid by P Company for 100% of its common shares		

Section 1625 states that the net-asset increases or decreases resulting from a comprehensive revaluation must not be reflected in the income statement of the enterprise (i.e., it is a capital transaction); rather, they should be recorded as either share capital, contributed surplus, or some other component of shareholders' equity that is readily identified.[3]

Exhibit 11.2 contains the January 1, Year 1, balance sheet of P Company, the balance sheet of S Company after the recording of the push-down journal entries, and the consolidated balance sheet of P Company.

Exhibit 11.2

BALANCE SHEET — January 1, Year 1

	P Company	S Company push-down	P Company consolidated
Cash	$ 32,000	$ 35,000	$ 67,000
Accounts receivable	90,000	63,000	153,000
Inventory	120,000	60,000	180,000
Land	100,000	36,000	136,000
Plant and equipment	300,000	56,000	356,000
Goodwill	—	3,000	3,000
Investment in S	162,000	—	—
	$804,000	$253,000	$895,000
Liabilities	$120,000	$ 91,000	$211,000
Common stock	400,000	162,000	400,000
Retained earnings	284,000	—	284,000
	$804,000	$253,000	$895,000

ELIMINATION

Investment in S	$162,000
Shareholders' equity — S	
Common stock	162,000
Difference	–0–

---

[2] *CICA Handbook*, paragraph 1625.29.
[3] *CICA Handbook*, paragraph 1625.30.

When push-down accounting has been used, the preparation of the consolidated balance sheet is considerably simplified, requiring only the elimination of the shareholders' equity accounts of S Company against the investment account of P Company. A comparison of Exhibit 11.2 with Exhibit 11.1 shows that the consolidated amounts are identical.

The preparation of S Company's consolidated financial statements one year after acquisition will be examined next: first *without* push-down accounting applied, and then *with* push-down accounting applied.

Subsequent Consolidation Without Push-down Accounting   Exhibit 11.3 contains the financial statements of P Company and S Company, and the consolidated financial statements of P Company, prepared as at December 31, Year 1. A goodwill impairment test conducted on this date yielded a loss of $600. S Company did not pay dividends during Year 1, and P Company has used the equity method to account for its investment.

Exhibit 11.3

Financial Statements

INCOME STATEMENT — December 31, Year 1

	P Company	S Company without push-down	P Company consolidated
Sales	$310,000	$115,000	$425,000
Income from S	28,200	—	—
	$338,200	$115,000	$425,000
Cost of sales	$120,000	$ 59,000	$180,000
Miscellaneous expenses	70,000	20,600	90,600
Amortization — plant and equipment	40,000	5,400	45,600
Goodwill impairment loss	—	—	600
	$230,000	$ 85,000	$316,800
Net Income	$108,200	$ 30,000	$108,200

BALANCE SHEET

	P Company	S Company without push-down	P Company consolidated
Cash	$ 54,000	$ 28,400	$ 82,400
Accounts receivable	150,000	100,000	250,000
Inventory	138,000	71,000	209,000
Land	100,000	30,000	136,000
Plant and equipment	260,000	48,600	310,400
Investment in S	190,200	—	—
Goodwill	—	—	$ 2,400
	$892,200	$278,000	$990,200
Liabilities	$100,000	$ 98,000	$198,000
Common stock	400,000	70,000	400,000
Retained earnings, Jan. 1	284,000	80,000	284,000
Net income	108,200	30,000	108,200
	$892,200	$278,000	$990,200

The purchase discrepancy amortization schedule (shown below) was prepared by the accountant of P Company, to be used for the equity method journal entries and for the preparation of the consolidated financial statements.

	Balance Jan. 1	Amortization Year 1	Balance Dec. 31
Inventory	$ 1,000	$1,000	—
Land	6,000	—	6,000
Plant and equipment	2,000	200	1,800
Goodwill	3,000	600	2,400
	$12,000	$1,800	$10,200

The use of the equity method resulted in the changes in the investment account of P Company shown below. (The equity method accounts used in P Company's financial statements are shown in boldface.)

Investment in S, January 1, Year 1		$162,000
S net income, Year 1	30,000	
Less purchase discrepancy amortization	1,800	
Income from S (equity method)		28,200
Investment in S, December 31, Year 1		$190,200

When the consolidated income statement is prepared, the item "Income from S" on P Company's income statement is replaced by the revenues and expenses from S Company's income statement and the purchase discrepancy amortization, as follows:

Replace —

Income from S	$28,200

With —

	S Co.	Purchase discrep.	
Sales	$115,000		$115,000
Cost of sales	$ 59,000	$1,000	$ 60,000
Miscellaneous expenses	20,600	—	20,600
Amortization			
Plant and equipment	5,400	200	5,600
Goodwill impairment loss	—	600	600
	$ 85,000	$1,800	$ 86,800
Adjusted net income, S Company			$ 28,200

In a similar manner, the consolidated balance sheet is prepared by replacing the asset "Investment in S" on the balance sheet of P Company with the assets and liabilities from S Company's balance sheet revalued by the unamortized purchase discrepancy. The following illustrates this concept:

Replace —

Investment in S Company	$190,200

With —

	S Co.	Purchase discrep.	
Cash	$ 28,400		$ 28,400
Accounts receivable	100,000		100,000
Inventory	71,000		71,000
Land	30,000	6,000	36,000
Plant and equipment	48,600	1,800	50,400
Goodwill	—	2,400	2,400
	$278,000	$10,200	$288,200
Liabilities	$ 98,000		$ 98,000
Revalued net assets, S Company			$190,200

Subsequent Consolidation with Push-down Accounting Exhibit 11.4 shows the December 31, Year 1, financial statements of P Company and S Company, as well as P Company's consolidated statements. Push-down accounting has been used in the preparation of S Company's statements, and P Company has used the equity method to account for the investment.

The Year 1 financial statements of S Company *without* push-down and *with* push-down are presented below for comparative purposes:

	Exhibit 11.3 (without push-down)	Exhibit 11.4 (with push-down)	Difference
Sales	$115,000	$115,000	—
Cost of sales	$ 59,000	$ 60,000	$ 1,000
Miscellaneous expense	20,600	20,600	—
Amortization — plant and equipment	5,400	5,600	200
Goodwill impairment loss	—	600	600
	$ 85,000	$ 86,800	$ 1,800
Net income	$ 30,000	$ 28,200	($ 1,800)
Cash	$ 28,400	$ 28,400	—
Accounts receivable	100,000	100,000	—
Inventory	71,000	71,000	—
Land	30,000	36,000	6,000
Plant and equipment	48,600	50,400	1,800
Goodwill	—	2,400	2,400
	$278,000	$288,200	$10,200
Liabilities	$ 98,000	$ 98,000	—
Common stock	70,000	162,000	92,000
Retained earnings, Jan. 1	80,000	—	(80,000)
Net income	30,000	28,200	(1,800)
	$278,000	$288,200	$10,200

The differences in push-down expenses result from the write-off and amortization of the acquisition-date fair-value increments that were "pushed down" to S Company. The differences in push-down assets are the result of the unamortized fair-value increments. These same differences were shown above, where they were used to prepare the consolidated financial statements when S Company had not used push-down accounting.

Exhibit 11.4

FINANCIAL STATEMENTS — December 31, Year 1
INCOME STATEMENT

	P Company	S Company push-down	P Company consolidated
Sales	$310,000	$115,000	$425,000
Income from S	28,200	—	—
	$338,200	$115,000	$425,000
Cost of sales	$120,000	$ 60,000	$180,000
Misc. expenses	70,000	20,600	90,600
Amortization — plant and equipment	40,000	5,600	45,600
Goodwill impairment loss	—	600	600
	$230,000	$ 86,800	$316,800
Net income	$108,200	$ 28,200	$108,200

BALANCE SHEET

	P Company	S Company push-down	P Company consolidated
Cash	$ 54,000	$ 28,400	$ 82,400
Accounts receivable	150,000	100,000	250,000
Inventory	138,000	71,000	209,000
Land	100,000	36,000	136,000
Plant and equipment	260,000	50,400	310,400
Investment in S	190,200	—	—
Goodwill	—	2,400	2,400
	$892,200	$288,200	$990,200
Liabilities	$100,000	$ 98,000	$198,000
Common stock	400,000	162,000	400,000
Retained earnings, Jan. 1	284,000	—	284,000
Net income	108,200	28,200	108,200
	$892,200	$288,200	$990,200

The differences in shareholders' equity require further elaboration. Push-down common stock ($162,000) is the sum of the original capital stock, the reclassified acquisition-date retained earnings, and the increase from the comprehensive revaluation of the net assets (70,000 + 80,000 + 12,000). As a result, push-down retained earnings as at January 1, Year 1, has a zero balance.

CICA Handbook, paragraph 1625.33, states: "The revaluation adjustment is accounted for as capital of the acquired enterprise." This implies that a transfer from this recorded increase to retained earnings, based on a realization through sale or depreciation, should *not* take place.

P Company's equity method adjustments to the investment account are simplified, as the following shows:

Investment in S, January 1, Year 1		$162,000
S net income, Year 1	28,200	
	100%	
Income from S (equity method)		28,200
Investment in S December 31, Year 1		$190,200

The preparation of the consolidated income statement (Exhibit 11.4) should be obvious and requires no further explanation. When the consolidated balance sheet is prepared, the parent's share of the shareholders' equity of S Company is eliminated against the parent's investment account as follows:

Investment in S		$190,200
S Company		
Common stock	$162,000	
Retained earnings	28,200	190,200
		–0–

Reasons for Push-down Accounting

The following reasons have been advanced for the use of push-down accounting:

Creditor Requirements   If the parent company financed the acquisition of the subsidiary with borrowed funds, and the amount of the loan was based on (or even secured by) the fair value of the subsidiary's assets, the lender may insist that the fair values be reflected in the audited financial statements of the subsidiary. The lender may also insist that the loan itself be shown in these statements, but Section 1625 does not allow this:

> When an acquisition is financed by debt, in whole or in part, it is not considered appropriate for the acquired enterprise to record the debt, unless it is a liability of the acquired enterprise. [1625.28]

Based on this paragraph, the loan could not appear on the subsidiary's balance sheet because it is a liability of the parent. However, it is possible to structure the acquisition so that the loan *does* appear on the balance sheet, as the lender wishes. This could be achieved in the following manner:

1. P Company forms a wholly owned subsidiary, "A Company."
2. A Company obtains a bank loan, and with the loan proceeds and the money from P Company's investment acquires all of the outstanding shares of S Company. The loan is secured by the assets of S Company, and P Company guarantees the loan.
3. S Company applies push-down accounting based on the price paid by A Company.
4. A Company and S Company amalgamate into a single surviving company. The balance sheet of this surviving company, a subsidiary of P Company, contains both the net assets of S Company and the related bank loan used to finance their acquisition.

Assessing Returns on the Acquisition   With push-down accounting, the net income of the subsidiary is measured using fair-value amortizations. Return-on-investment calculations thus show the situation more accurately than would old historical costs, especially in the years immediately preceding the revaluation. Of course, in later years, the return-on-investment measurements exhibit the usual historical-cost handicaps.

Simplicity of Consolidation   When push-down accounting has been used, the preparation of the consolidated statements is simplified because no consolidation adjustments are needed for the fair-value increments and amortizations. Exhibits 11.2 and 11.4 have illustrated this.

Arguments Against Push-down Accounting

Even though a case can be made for the use of push-down accounting in certain circumstances, the following points can be made against it.[4]

- Since the subsidiary itself did not participate in the transaction (the purchase of all of its net assets), the recording of the transaction is a violation of the historical cost concept. Accounting has not adopted a current value model, and a departure from historical costs to appraised values is not acceptable.

- Some readers of the financial statements (e.g., creditors) may be frustrated by the lack of comparability in the statements. Also, the lack of consistency over time in applying accounting principles may make the numbers less useful.

- The concept could be extended to situations where a company makes a large treasury acquisition of its shares and revalues its assets on the basis of the price paid. It is doubtful that this variation would receive widespread acceptance.

In general, however, there is probably some justification for the optional use of push-down accounting, as provided in Section 1625.

Push-down Accounting with a Noncontrolling Interest

Push-down accounting simplifies the consolidation process *only* when the subsidiary is 100 percent owned by the parent company. If the subsidiary is less than 100 percent owned, the consolidation becomes much more complex because the amount for the noncontrolling interest is based on the carrying value of the subsidiary's net assets before push-down accounting was applied.

In the previous illustration, P Company acquired 100 percent of S Company for $162,000. Assume instead that P Company purchased 95 percent of S Company on January 1, Year 1, for $153,900. The following calculation would be made by P Company:

PURCHASE DISCREPANCY

Cost of 95% of S		$153,900
Book value of S		
Common stock	70,000	
Retained earnings	80,000	
	150,000	
	95%	142,500
Purchase discrepancy		11,400
Allocated		
Inventory (1,000 × .95)	950	
Land (6,000 × .95)	5,700	
Plant and equipment (2,000 × .95)	1,900	8,550
Goodwill		$ 2,850

---

[4] For a further discussion, see Michael E. Cunningham, "Push-down Accounting: Pros and Cons," *Journal of Accountancy*, June 1984, p. 72.

The noncontrolling interest is based on the carrying value of S Company's identifiable net assets and would appear on the consolidated balance sheet in the amount $7,500 (150,000 × .05).

Conditions for the use of push-down accounting from Section 1625 have been met because P Company has acquired at least 90 percent of S Company.[5] Also assumed is that control has been established in accordance with Section 1590, "Subsidiaries."

It should be noted again that Section 1625 does not require the use of push-down accounting by S Company. If P Company directs that push-down accounting be used, S Company would make the following journal entries as at January 1, Year 1:

Retained earnings	76,000	
Contributed surplus		76,000
To reclassify 95% of the retained earnings on the date of acquisition		

Paragraph 1625.29 of the *Handbook* requires the reclassification of "that portion of retained earnings which has not been included in the consolidated retained earnings of the acquirer, or is not related to any continuing non-controlling interests in the enterprise ..."

Inventory	950	
Land	5,700	
Plant and equipment	1,900	
Goodwill	2,850	
Contributed surplus		11,400
To comprehensively revalue the net assets on the basis of the price paid by P Company for 95% of the common shares		

Only the parent's share of the fair value differences is "pushed down" to the subsidiary (see paragraphs 1625.25–26).

The reclassified retained earnings and the revaluation adjustment have been recorded as contributed surplus in order to simplify the noncontrolling interest calculation that is needed to prepare the consolidated statements.

After the push-down accounting has been applied, the balance sheet of S Company as at January 1, Year 1, would appear as shown below:

Cash	$ 35,000
Accounts receivable	63,000
Inventory	59,950
Land	35,700
Plant and equipment	55,900
Goodwill	2,850
	$252,400
Liabilities	$ 91,000
Common stock	70,000
Contributed surplus	87,400
Retained earnings	4,000
	$252,400

---

[5] This 90 percent interest is also consistent with the level of ownership required by many of the corporation acts in Canada when they allow a parent company to apply for an order to force the minority shareholders to sell their ownership interest in a subsidiary to the parent.

In comparing this push-down balance sheet with the previous one for a 100 percent interest (see Exhibit 11.2), we should note that only 95 percent of the fair value increments have been "pushed down"; the goodwill is 95 percent of the previous goodwill; the parent company's share of the acquisition retained earnings and the revaluation adjustment have been recorded as contributed surplus; and the noncontrolling interest in acquisition retained earnings is carried forward. If at a later date P Company acquires the remaining 5 percent of the shares from the minority shareholders, a further revaluation of the identifiable net assets of S Company will have to be made based on the additional cost incurred with the second purchase. This would require additional push-down entries, including an entry to reclassify the retained earnings that previously belonged to the noncontrolling interest.

Section 1625 requires the following financial statement disclosures by S Company in the first year of application of push-down accounting and during the next three years (see paragraphs 1625.34–35):

- The date that push-down accounting was applied.
- The date of acquisition by P Company, and the reason that push-down accounting was used.
- The amount of the changes recorded in the major classes of assets, liabilities, and shareholders' equity.
- The amount and description of the revaluation adjustment.
- The amount and description of the retained earnings reclassified.

Exhibit 11.5 shows the preparation of P Company's January 1, Year 1, consolidated balance sheet. Because there is a noncontrolling interest, the eliminations shown at the bottom of the exhibit are more complex than those required when there is 100 percent ownership.

Subsequent Consolidation with Push-down Accounting

Consolidation in subsequent years is also more complex because the noncontrolling interest shown in the consolidated statements cannot be based on the amounts shown in the subsidiary's financial statements. When a subsidiary has not used push-down accounting, the noncontrolling interest on the consolidated balance sheet is based on the carrying values of the subsidiary's net assets, and the noncontrolling interest on the consolidated income statement is based on the subsidiary's net income. Consolidated statements prepared when the subsidiary has used push-down accounting must produce identical results.

S Company's December 31, Year 1, financial statements using push-down accounting are shown in boldface in Exhibit 11.6. A goodwill impairment test conducted on this date yielded a loss of $570.

The statements without the use of push-down accounting, which have been reproduced from Exhibit 11.3, are also presented for comparison. The differences between the two statements are easily understood by examining how the fair value increments were amortized in the push-down statements.

Exhibit 11.5

BALANCE SHEET — January 1, Year 1

	P Company	S Company push-down	P Company consolidated
Cash	$ 40,100	$ 35,000	$ 75,100
Accounts receivable	90,000	63,000	153,000
Inventory	120,000	59,950	179,950
Land	100,000	35,700	135,700
Plant and equipment	300,000	55,900	355,900
Goodwill	—	2,850	2,850
Investment in S	153,900	—	—
	$804,000	$252,400	$902,500
Liabilities	$120,000	$ 91,000	$211,000
Noncontrolling interest	—	—	7,500
Common stock	400,000	70,000	400,000
Contributed surplus	—	87,400	—
Retained earnings	284,000	4,000	284,000
	$804,000	$252,400	$902,500

ELIMINATION

Investment in S		$153,900
Shareholders' equity — S		
Capital stock	70,000	
Parents ownership	95%	
	66,500	
Contributed surplus	87,400	153,900
Difference		–0–
Noncontrolling interest calculation:		
Shareholders' equity — S		
Capital stock		$ 70,000
Noncontrolling ownership		5%
		3,500
Acquisition retained earnings — not reclassified		4,000
Noncontrolling interest		$ 7,500

Exhibit 11.7, on page 460, shows the December 31, Year 1, financial statements of P Company and S Company, and P Company's consolidated statements.

The use of the equity method resulted in changes in the investment account of P Company (see next page). (Note that the equity method accounts used in P Company's financial statements are shown in boldface.)

Exhibit 11.6

S COMPANY
FINANCIAL STATEMENTS
December 31, Year 1
("without push-down" compared to "with push-down")

	Without push-down	With push-down	Difference
Sales	$115,000	$115,000	—
Cost of sales	$ 59,000	$ 59,950	$ 950
Miscellaneous expense	20,600	20,600	—
Amortization – plant and equipment	5,400	5,590	190
Goodwill impairment loss	—	570	570
	$ 85,000	$ 86,710	$ 1,710
Net income	$ 30,000	$ 28,290	$ (1,710)
Cash	$ 28,400	$ 28,400	—
Accounts receivable	100,000	100,000	—
Inventory	71,000	71,000	—
Land	30,000	35,700	5,700
Plant and equipment	48,600	50,310	1,710
Goodwill	—	2,280	2,280
	$278,000	$287,690	$ 9,690
Liabilities	$ 98,000	$ 98,000	—
Common stock	70,000	70,000	—
Contributed surplus	—	87,400	87,400
Retained earnings, Jan. 1	80,000	4,000	(76,000)
Net income	30,000	28,290	(1,710)
	$278,000	$287,690	$ 9,690

The fair value increments that were "pushed down" to S Company were amortized and reflected in the financial statements shown above as follows:

	Balance Jan. 1	Amortization Year 1	Balance Dec. 31
Inventory	$ 950	$ 950	—
Land	5,700	—	5,700
Plant and equipment	1,900	190	1,710
Goodwill	2,850	570	2,280
	$11,400	$1,710	$9,690

Investment in S, January 1, Year 1		$153,900
S Company's push-down net income, Year 1	28,290	
Add amortization of fair value increments	1,710	
Net income without push-down	30,000	
P Company's ownership	.95	
	28,500	
Less amortization of fair value increments	1,710	
Income from S, (equity method)		26,790
Investment in S, December 31, Year 1		$180,690

Exhibit 11.7

FINANCIAL STATEMENTS — December 31, Year 1
INCOME STATEMENT

	P Company	S Company push-down	P Company consolidated
Sales	$310,000	$115,000	$425,000
Income from S	26,790	—	—
	$336,790	$115,000	$425,000
Cost of sales	$120,000	$ 59,950	$179,950
Miscellaneous expenses	70,000	20,600	90,600
Amortization – plant and equipment	40,000	5,590	45,590
Goodwill impairment loss	—	570	570
	$230,000	$ 86,710	$316,710
Net incomes	$106,790	$ 28,290	
Net income — entity			$108,290
Less noncontrolling interest			1,500
Net income			$106,790

BALANCE SHEET

	P Company	S Company push-down	P Company consolidated
Cash	$ 62,100	$ 28,400	$ 90,500
Accounts receivable	150,000	100,000	250,000
Inventory	138,000	71,000	209,000
Land	100,000	35,700	135,700
Plant and equipment	260,000	50,310	310,310
Investment in S	180,690	—	—
Goodwill	—	2,280	2,280
	$890,790	$287,690	$997,790
Liabilities	$100,000	$ 98,000	$198,000
Noncontrolling interest	—	—	9,000
Common stock	400,000	70,000	400,000
Contributed surplus	—	87,400	—
Retained earnings, Jan. 1	284,000	4,000	284,000
Net income	106,790	28,290	106,790
	$890,790	$287,690	$997,790

The following points should be noted regarding the consolidated income statement:

- Noncontrolling interest is based on S Company's net income without push-down (30,000 × .05 = 1,500).

- S Company's push-down net income $28,290
  Less noncontrolling interest   1,500
      P Company's "Income from S" $26,790

- "Net income — entity" is equal to consolidated revenues less expenses.

The eliminations used to prepare the consolidated balance sheet follow.

Investment in S Company			$180,690
S Company			
Common stock		70,000	
Post-acquisition retained earnings without			
push-down, December 31:			
Net income	28,290		
Add fair value amortizations	1,710		
Retained earnings without push-down		30,000	
		100,000	
Parent company's ownership		95%	
		95,000	
Less fair-value amortizations		1,710	
		93,290	
Contributed surplus		87,400	180,690
Difference			–0–

Noncontrolling interest as at December 31, Year 1, is calculated as follows:

S Company capital stock	$ 70,000
Post-acquisition retained earnings without push-down (see above)	30,000
	100,000
Noncontrolling ownership	5%
	5,000
Acquisition retained earnings — not reclassified	4,000
Noncontrolling interest	$ 9,000

To summarize, the concepts of push-down accounting can be applied only if virtually all of the equity interests (at least 90 percent) have been acquired and the new costs to be used in the revaluation can be determined. Its use is not mandatory and will depend on whether it is required by a creditor involved in the financing of the acquisition, or whether the acquirer feels that it will provide a better measurement of return on investment. Its use can simplify the preparation of the consolidated statements if all of the equity interests were acquired. If there is a noncontrolling interest, the consolidation is more complex.

Comprehensive Revaluation Under a Financial Reorganization

The previous discussion focused on push-down accounting. Under the provisions of Section 1625, a comprehensive revaluation can also take place as a result of a financial reorganization.

In a business sense, the term "reorganization" often reflects a situation where major changes in the management, policies, or financial structure of a company have occurred. In the past, the term reorganization had a more specific meaning for accountants. It was used to depict the accounting involved when, due to serious cash flow problems and/or a history of successive losses, the shareholders and creditors of a corporation agreed to reduce their rights and claims. Usually, asset amounts were adjusted to reflect more realistic values, share capital and creditor claims were reduced, and accumulated deficits were removed. The term "quasi-reorganization" has had a similar meaning, except that creditors are not involved in this particular type of reorganization.

Section 1625 is even more specific in its definition. It describes a "financial reorganization" as:

> a substantial realignment of the equity and non-equity interests of an enterprise such that the holders of one or more of the significant classes of non-equity interest and the holders of all of the significant classes of equity interests give up some (or all) of their rights and claims upon the enterprise. [1625.03]

In accordance with this section, the comprehensive revaluation of an enterprise's assets and liabilities *must* take place if:

(a) there has been a financial reorganization, and

(b) the original shareholders have lost control, and

(c) new costs can reasonably be determined.

A substantial realignment of equity and nonequity interests is assumed not to have taken place if the same party that had control before the reorganization has control after the reorganization. Using Section 1590, "Subsidiaries," the number of shares held before and after a reorganization would be persuasive evidence regarding a change in control. However, it must be remembered that "control" as described in this section involves the continuing power to determine strategic operating, financing, and investing policies without the co-operation of others.

A financial reorganization often takes place when a corporation seeks protection from the actions of its creditors by making a "proposal" under a statute such as the Bankruptcy and Insolvency Act or the Companies' Creditors Arrangement Act. (The legal provisions concerning proposals are discussed later in this chapter in the section on bankruptcy and receivership.) Proposals can also be made outside of statutes such as these. The form of the reorganization is not important; if the substance does not result in a loss of control, the provisions of Section 1625 do not apply, and a revaluation of net assets cannot take place.

Item of Interest In September 2001, Loewen Group Inc. announced that it was emerging from the court protection from creditors in the United States and Canada that had existed since 1999. The company, headquartered in Canada, has 11,000 employees and operates more than 900 funeral homes and over 300 cemeteries in Canada, the U.S.A., and the United Kingdom. The plan allows Loewen to cut its debt load by about $1.5 billion by issuing up to 100 million shares of new common stock.

Accounting for a Comprehensive Revaluation

A financial reorganization involves self-interest bargaining between creditors and shareholders; both sides negotiate the realignment of their rights and claims, recognizing that the company has financial and operating problems. They also recognize that the end result may provide greater benefits to both groups than would have been received if the company had been liquidated. The rights and claims being negotiated are those associated with the assets and future cash flows of the company. The historical cost asset values presented on the most recent balance sheet of the company are not the values being considered by the two sides in the negotiations.

Rather, they are examining the current fair values of individual assets and the value of the company as a whole (perhaps by discounting expected future cash flows). It is these negotiated values that are recorded in a comprehensive revaluation and establish the new costs for the company on a fresh-start basis.

Measurement of New Costs If the negotiations do not establish the fair values for individual net assets, the fair values to be used for accounting purposes are estimated in accordance with the provisions of Section 1581, "Business Combinations." If a fair value has been established for the company as a whole, and the sum of the fair values of the identifiable net assets exceeds this total value, the excess is used to reduce the values assigned to noncurrent assets. If the value established for the company as a whole exceeds the sum of the fair values of the identifiable net assets, the excess is *not* recorded as goodwill, as would be the case in a business combination. On reflection, it does not make sense to record goodwill for a company that has just experienced severe financial difficulty. To summarize, if a fair value has been established for the company as a whole, this fair value will be used only when it is less than the fair values of the individual net assets.

The increase or decrease in equity resulting from the revaluation is treated as a capital transaction and is not reflected in the income statement. However, losses due to the write-downs of assets that relate to circumstances existing prior to the reorganization would appear in the income statement for the period prior to the fresh start. An example of this might be the recognition that the allowance for bad debts or the liability for warranties was inadequate at the time of the financial reorganization. Any retained earnings balance that existed prior to the reorganization is reclassified to reflect a fresh start.

Illustration of a Comprehensive Revaluation Fabricore Corporation is in financial difficulty due to its inability to discharge its liabilities and meet the interest payments on its debentures. On December 31, Year 1, it filed for protection from creditor actions under statutory provisions. The balance sheet of the company on this date is shown in Exhibit 11.8. After extensive negotiations, nonequity and equity interests have agreed upon a plan of reorganization. The essence of the plan is as follows:

- Management has agreed that prior to the comprehensive revaluation of assets and liabilities, the allowance for bad debts should be increased by $3,000, and the goodwill should be written off.

- Fabricore's trade creditors have agreed to accept the payment of 80 percent of their claims, with payment to be made at such time as cash becomes available.

- The bank loan that is now payable on demand will be changed to a two-year loan, payable in quarterly instalments.

- The holders of 14 percent debentures agree to forgive the amount of interest owing and to exchange their debentures for $100,000, 9 percent, first-mortgage bonds and 250,000 newly issued no-par-value common shares.

Exhibit 11.8

FABRICORE CORPORATION
BALANCE SHEET
December 31, Year 1
(before financial reorganization)

Cash	$ 5,000
Accounts receivable (net)	40,000
Inventory	45,000
Land	20,000
Buildings and equipment (net)	100,000
Goodwill	15,000
	$225,000
Accounts payable	$ 40,000
Note payable — bank	30,000
Accrued interest — 14% debentures	20,000
14% debentures	150,000
Common stock (100,000 NPV shares)	140,000
Retained earnings (deficit)	(155,000)
	$225,000

- The parties have determined the following fair values for the company's assets:

	Fair value
Cash	$ 5,000
Accounts receivable (net)	37,000
Inventory	45,000
Land	32,000
Buildings and equipment (net)	109,000
	$228,000

They also agree that the fair value of the company is the sum of the individual fair values of its assets.

Because there has been a substantial realignment of the equity and nonequity interests, and because new costs have been established, the Section 1625 conditions for comprehensive revaluation have been satisfied.

Fabricore's entries to record the revaluation as at January 1, Year 2, are as follows:

Retained earnings	18,000	
Accounts receivable		3,000
Goodwill		15,000

To increase the allowance for bad debts and to write off the goodwill

This write-down will be reflected in the Year 1 income statement because it is considered to be related to circumstances that existed prior to the reorganization.

CICA Handbook, paragraph 1625.43, requires any retained earnings (in this case a deficit) existing prior to reorganization to be reclassified to either share capital, or contributed surplus, or some other shareholders' equity account. In this case, the journal entry is:

Common stock	173,000	
Retained earnings		173,000
To reclassify the deficit on December 31, Year 1		

Paragraph 1625.44 states that the revaluation adjustment resulting from the comprehensive revaluation of assets and liabilities should be accounted for as a capital transaction and may be recorded as either share capital, or contributed surplus, or some other shareholders' equity account. In this case, share capital will be used. Fabricore will record this adjustment in a reorganization account to reflect the loss or gain on the revaluation, then transfer the balance to common stock.

Accounts payable	8,000	
Accrued interest on debentures	20,000	
Reorganization account		28,000
To record the forgiveness of 20% of the accounts payable and the accrued debenture interest		
14% debentures	150,000	
9% first-mortgage bonds		100,000
Reorganization account		50,000
To record the exchange of the debentures for first-mortgage bonds and 250,000 common shares		
Land	12,000	
Buildings and equipment (net)	9,000	
Reorganization account		21,000
To revalue land, buildings, and equipment to fair values as per the agreement		
Reorganization account	99,000	
Common stock		99,000
To reclassify the reorganization account to share capital		

Exhibit 11.9 shows the balance sheet of Fabricore as at January 1, Year 2, reflecting a "fresh start" for the company. Consistent with this view, retained earnings accumulate from the date of the reorganization.

Exhibit 11.9

FABRICORE CORPORATION
BALANCE SHEET
January 1, Year 2
(after financial reorganization)

Cash	$ 5,000
Accounts receivable (net)	37,000
Inventory	45,000
Land	32,000
Buildings and equipment (net)	109,000
	$228,000
Accounts payable	$ 32,000
Notes payable — bank	30,000
9% first-mortgage bonds	100,000
Common stock (350,000 NPV shares)	66,000
	$228,000

Disclosure The footnotes to Fabricore's financial statements should disclose the following in the year of the financial reorganization and the next three years (see paragraphs 1625.50–.52).

- The date of the financial reorganization and a description thereof.
- The amount of the changes recorded in the major classes of assets, liabilities, and shareholders' equity.
- The amount and description of the revaluation adjustment.
- The amount and description of the retained earnings reclassified.
- The measurement basis of the affected assets and liabilities.

Comprehensive Revaluation and Future Income Taxes In Chapter 10 we discussed the effects that Section 3465, "Income Taxes," will have on the allocation of the acquisition cost of a business combination. Future income tax assets and liabilities arising from new temporary differences will have to form part of the allocation of the purchase discrepancy. This is also the case for the future tax assets arising from the availability of the carry-forward of unused tax losses. Because push-down accounting results in the subsidiary recording its parent's purchase discrepancy allocations, these future income tax assets and liabilities will be recorded by the subsidiary. Each year, the subsidiary will compare carrying values with tax basis, and make the required adjustments to the future income tax balances. This will obviously simplify the parent's consolidation procedures.

The new income tax section will also require the accounting recognition of temporary differences created by the comprehensive revaluations required as a result of a financial reorganization. The following paragraph outlines the treatment required:

> Revaluation adjustments to specific classes of identifiable assets and liabilities are made without reference to their values for tax purposes, or tax bases. The tax effects of differences between the revalued amounts of the identifiable assets and liabilities and their tax bases would be recorded as future income tax liabilities and assets in accordance with INCOME TAXES, Section 3465. In addition, the benefit of any unused tax losses or income tax reductions that meet the recognition criteria set out in INCOME TAXES, Section 3465, would be recognized as future income tax assets. The future income tax liabilities and assets recognized at the time of the financial reorganization would be included with the new costs of the other identifiable assets and liabilities in determining the amount of the total revaluation adjustment. [1625.42]

Assessment of Section 1625 The comprehensive revaluation of assets and liabilities from historical costs to fair market values can take place only under very restrictive conditions. Because of this, it seems fairly clear it will not be a recurring event for most Canadian companies. Since the concept was first introduced as a Canadian accounting standard in 1992, it has been difficult to assess how widely it has been used. The 2000 edition of *Financial Reporting in Canada* stated the following with regard to its survey of the 1996 to 1999 financial statements of 200 Canadian companies:

> From the point of view of the acquiring or parent company, the use of push down accounting is simply a procedural convenience. The use of this approach

would make absolutely no difference in the financial statements that emerge from the consolidation process. This means that, from the point of view of the parent company, there is no need for any disclosure related to push down accounting. This is not the case for the subsidiary.... As none of our survey companies are subsidiaries for which push down accounting would be applicable, it is not surprising that we found no reference to the use of push down accounting in any of the annual reports surveyed.

Because push-down accounting can only be used if the ownership is 90 percent or greater, then at least 90 percent of a company's shares must be owned by a parent. All companies making up the survey sample trade on Canada's major stock exchanges. Because of the 90 percent or greater restriction, the amount that is available for trading must be the very small percentage not owned by the parent — an amount that is probably not large enough to warrant a stock exchange listing.

Interestingly, although the concept of push-down accounting originated in the United States, it has not yet been the subject of a FASB pronouncement. Its use is required by the SEC for any subsidiary that must file with the commission. A company need only file in situations where it is planning to issue debt or equity securities to the public. In both Canada and the United States, the main advantage of push-down accounting from the standpoint of companies is that it simplifies the consolidation process. Thus, one might question the need for a standard in this area.

Financial Reporting in Canada also reported that none of the companies surveyed was subject to a financial reorganization during the periods covered. However, that publication also reported that a few prominent Canadian companies, including Canadian Airlines International, Dylex Limited, Silcorp Limited, and Trizec Corporation, reported financial reorganizations between 1993 and 1995.

(B) Bankruptcy and Receivership
Business Failure

Because of the many risks involved with business ventures, there is always the possibility of failure. Even in good economic times, some businesses fail, and when the country enters prolonged periods of economic decline the number of failures increases dramatically. This was the case during the economic recession of the 1980s, and particularly during the longer recession of the early 1990s. During this latter severe recession, size did not seem to have a bearing on which companies were affected, and we saw many very large companies such as Cadillac Fairview and Trizec Corporation making radical changes to avoid going under. In this section we discuss the various legal and accounting issues involved with business failures, as well as the common terms associated with such failure — namely, receivership and bankruptcy. Because business failure often results from creditor actions, it is useful to start by looking at the various classes of creditors.

Secured and Unsecured Creditors

A secured creditor is one that holds a mortgage, charge, or lien against the property of a debtor as security for a debt due from that debtor. Secured creditors can be either fully secured or partially secured depending on the amount of the debt relative to the value of the property that is pledged.

An unsecured creditor is one that holds a debt due from a debtor against which no property has been pledged. The Bankruptcy and Insolvency Act, which exists primarily to provide remedies for unsecured creditors, further classifies this unsecured category of creditors by describing certain types of claims as having a first priority for full payment before any payment is made to the remaining unsecured creditors.

In conjunction with the going concern concept, accountants classify the liabilities of a business as *current* and *long-term*. When it is questionable that a company is a going concern, such as when a business is in financial difficulty, it is often more informative to view (and sometimes account for) liabilities as fully secured, partially secured, unsecured with priority, and unsecured. These classifications will be discussed in more detail in a later section.

Receivership vs. Bankruptcy

Receivership and *bankruptcy* both describe a state of financial difficulty of a particular business. The two terms are not interchangeable; in fact, they refer to two quite different conditions. A condition of receivership exists when, due to the violation of a debt covenant, a secured creditor has appointed an agent to seize the debtor's property pledged against the debt. The agent is often called the receiver, or the receiver-manager. While the result of this action is often the complete liquidation of the business, the business itself is not legally bankrupt. The Bankruptcy Act contains terms such as "official receiver," "receiving order," and "interim receiving order," and this has probably added to the confusion that exists between the terms receivership and bankruptcy.

Bankruptcy is a legal state under which the assets of a debtor have been seized by a licensed trustee in bankruptcy for the protection and benefit of the unsecured creditors. This legal state may be the result of actions taken by unsecured creditors (involuntary bankruptcy) or by the debtor (voluntary bankruptcy). The eventual result, in nearly all bankruptcy cases, is the complete liquidation of the business.

Receivership

Many bank loans are secured by a general assignment of accounts receivable and/or inventory under Section 178 of the Bank Act, and land, buildings, and equipment are often pledged as security to the mortgage and debenture liabilities of a business. Sometimes assets are pledged more than once (first mortgage, second mortgage, etc.). As a remedy to a loan default, a secured creditor will often appoint a receiver-manager to seize the pledged assets. It is the duty of the receiver to sell these assets at the highest possible price on behalf of the client, the secured creditor. If the proceeds from the sale are greater than the debt, the amount of the excess reverts to the debtor. If the proceeds are not sufficient to discharge the debt, the deficiency becomes an unsecured liability. Any payment of this unsecured claim may only be possible if the business is forced into bankruptcy.

The person appointed as the receiver-manager is often a licensed trustee in bankruptcy. In some instances this receiver-manager operates the business for a period of time in order to maximize the total proceeds from the sale of the pledged assets. For example, inventory that is in the process of manufacture does not have much value. It makes good economic sense for the receiver-manager to operate a factory for a time in order to transform raw materials and work in process into finished products.

The receiver-manager may also attempt to sell a business as a going concern, rather than sell the individual assets piecemeal, especially if the business itself appears to be viable and an infusion of capital and new management is all that is necessary to turn the operation around. In all of the situations described, the owners will probably lose most if not all of their equity in the business.

Bankruptcy

The Bankruptcy Act is a federal statute. It was first passed in 1919 and has been amended from time to time, with the last significant amendment occurring in 1992. At that time the name was changed to the Bankruptcy and Insolvency Act. While all creditors come under the jurisdiction of the act, most of the remedies that are available to secured creditors because of their loan agreements are not affected. For this reason, it is safe to say that the act's provisions and remedies exist primarily for the benefit of the unsecured creditors of a business.

Administration   The Bankruptcy and Insolvency Act falls within the portfolio of the Minister of Consumer and Corporate Affairs. The senior civil servant responsible for the act's administration is called the Superintendent of Bankruptcy. This person, located in Ottawa, is also responsible for the licensing of bankruptcy trustees.

Each province in Canada is designated as a bankruptcy district; some provinces are further divided into two or more divisions. Each division comes under the administration of a person called the Official Receiver. The Official Receiver becomes involved when bankruptcy proceedings are first initiated; among other things, he or she examines the bankrupt under oath and chairs the first meeting of creditors.

The act provides the senior court of each province with jurisdiction over bankruptcy proceedings. All bankruptcy matters are heard by either the bankruptcy judge or, if judicial interpretation is not required, by the registrar of the court. The actual administration of the estate of the bankrupt is handled by a licensed trustee in bankruptcy. Upon receiving his or her appointment by the court, the trustee:

(a) takes possession of all of the assets as well as the accounting records of the bankrupt,

(b) prepares an inventory of the assets,

(c) takes all necessary precautions to protect the assets, including insuring all insurable assets,

(d) notifies all creditors as to the date of the first meeting of creditors, and

(e) verifies the bankrupt's statement of affairs.[6]

The first meeting of creditors is held to examine the bankrupt's statement of affairs, to confirm the appointment of the trustee, and to elect inspectors to oversee the trustee in the administration of the estate. Creditors must file a proof of claim with the trustee if they wish to share in the proceeds from the sale of assets and to participate at meetings. The trustee sells the unpledged assets in the estate and

---

[6] The reference here is to a legal document required by the act, in which the debtor provides details of all liabilities and assets. An *accounting statement of affairs* is a report that departs from the historical cost principle and presents assets at their estimated liquidation values while at the same time providing an estimate of the amount that the various classes of creditors would receive under a bankruptcy liquidation.

distributes the proceeds to the unsecured creditors in accordance with the provisions of the act. Pledged assets are not normally realized by the trustee, although the secured creditors may ask the trustee to sell the assets on their behalf.

It is not uncommon to have a business go into receivership upon the action of a secured creditor and later be declared bankrupt upon actions of unsecured creditors. Complications may arise if the receiver-manager and the bankruptcy trustee are different persons. Such a situation requires cooperation between the two trustees and may involve court intervention to resolve conflicts.

Insolvency and Bankruptcy   The act provides descriptions of insolvent persons and bankrupt persons.[7] Insolvent persons are ones:

(a) who are not bankrupt but carry on business in Canada and have liabilities exceeding $1,000 *and*

(b) who are unable to meet, or have ceased paying, their obligations as they come due, *or*

(c) whose assets, measured at fair market value, are less than the amount of their debts.

Bankrupt persons are ones who, in accordance with provisions of the act:

(a) have made an assignment of their assets for the benefit of their creditors, or

(b) against whom a receiving order has been made.

Bankruptcy is a legal state, while insolvency is not. A person can be insolvent without being bankrupt, but cannot be bankrupt without being insolvent.

Voluntary and Involuntary Bankruptcy   Persons may declare bankruptcy voluntarily (as a result of their own actions), or they may be declared bankrupt involuntarily (as a result of the actions of their creditors). Voluntary bankruptcy occurs when persons make an assignment of their assets for the benefit of their creditors. The assignment is made to the Official Receiver and is accompanied by a statement of affairs and a listing of creditors. A trustee is appointed and the administration of the bankrupt's estate commences. There is one other voluntary action that a person may enter into that might possibly result in bankruptcy. This action, called a proposal, will be discussed later in this chapter.

Persons may be declared bankrupt involuntarily as a result of an action taken by their creditors. The act provides that one or more creditors with claims totalling at least $1,000 may file a petition with the court to have a receiving order granted against a debtor. The petitioning creditor(s) must show that the debtor has committed an "act of bankruptcy" within the preceding six months. The following is a partial listing of "acts of bankruptcy":

- Debtors give notice to any of their creditors that they have suspended or are about to suspend payments of their debts.

---

[7]   Persons include individuals, partnerships, unincorporated associations, corporations, and cooperative societies. Not included are banks, insurance companies, trust and loan companies, and railway companies. Bankruptcy provisions for these companies are covered under their own incorporation statutes. The main focus of our discussion will be on the bankruptcy provisions that apply to incorporated businesses, although most of the items would also apply to individuals.

- Debtors exhibit to any meetings of their creditors a statement of assets and liabilities that shows that they are insolvent.
- Debtors make a fraudulent conveyance, gift, or transfer of their property or any part thereof.
- Debtors cease to meet their liabilities as they become due.

If the court agrees with the petition and grants a receiving order, a debtor is bankrupt.

It might appear from this discussion that it is fairly easy for a creditor to have a debtor declared bankrupt. However, it is not quite as easy as it seems. The petition for the receiving order must include the name of a licensed trustee who is willing to act. The trustee's fees come only from the proceeds from the sale of the nonpledged (or free) assets of the debtor. If a large percentage of the debtor's assets is pledged, the trustee may not be able to collect his or her fee from this source; that trustee will therefore be unwilling to act unless the petitioning creditors guarantee the fees. In some involved and complex cases, a trustee's fees can be very large, and this guarantee may be considered too great a risk for the creditor to assume.

Proposals and Reorganizations In general, the word "proposal" describes a situation where a debtor corporation calls a meeting of its creditors, outlines its financial difficulties, and suggests remedies to alleviate the situation, such as all or some of the following:

- Postponement of interest and principal payments.
- Reduction of the interest rate.
- Debt forgiveness.
- Acceptance of the payment of a percentage of the claims as full payment.
- Conversion of debt to equity.

The idea is to convince the creditors that the business is viable and worth saving, and that a larger payment will eventually be forthcoming as a result of the suggested remedies than would be the case under a forced bankruptcy liquidation.

Proposals can be made either outside of or within the provisions of the Bankruptcy and Insolvency Act.[8] There are dangers involved when proposals are made outside of the acts. The creditors are now aware of the extent of the debtor's financial difficulties, and any one creditor armed with this knowledge could commence receivership or bankruptcy proceedings.

Under the Bankruptcy and Insolvency Act, a bankrupt or an insolvent debtor may file a notice of intent to file a plan of reorganization with the Official Receiver. Accompanying the notice is a listing of creditors and the name of a trustee who is willing to act. This act of filing the notice of intent results in all creditor actions being stayed for 30 days. This 30-day period can be extended by the court for an additional 5 months in certain circumstances. During this period the trustee monitors the debtor's financial position and reports on it periodically to the court. If a proposal (reorganization plan) is not filed before the allotted time expires, the debtor is deemed to have filed an assignment in bankruptcy.

---

[8] A proposal can also be made under the provisions of the Companies' Creditors Arrangement Act.

Once the proposal is filed, a further stay is imposed on all creditors to whom the proposal is directed (secured and unsecured). The Official Receiver chairs the first meeting of creditors. A vote is taken by the various classes of creditors, and if the proposal is accepted it proceeds to the court for approval. If the proposal is rejected by either the creditors or the court, the debtor is deemed to have made an assignment in bankruptcy.

Item of Interest   In June 2001, Laidlaw Inc. announced that it intended to seek bankruptcy protection in order to restructure its US$3.5 billion debt. It would appear that this was a classic case of over-ambitious expansion into unfamiliar areas of business. Once regarded as a premier waste management company with headquarters in Canada, it acquired 38 ambulance companies in 1997 alone for a total cost of $1.3 billion. These acquisitions made it the largest ambulance operator in the United States. Shortly thereafter, it acquired both Safety-Kleen Corp. and Greyhound Lines Inc. In 1999, Safety-Kleen filed for bankruptcy protection, and in 2000, Laidlaw wrote off its $2.2 billion investment in Safety-Kleen.

Interim Receivership   During the period between the presentation of a proposal made under the act and its consideration by the creditors, the debtor's assets are not held under the jurisdiction of the court. This is also the case during the period between the application for and the granting of a receiving order. In order to protect the interests of the creditors during this time, the act allows the court to appoint an interim receiver upon the application of one or more creditors. If the application is granted, a trustee is appointed. The trustee does not take title to the debtor's assets, as is the case in bankruptcy, but rather is given the power to control the debtor's cash flows during the period. The interim receivership ends with the acceptance or rejection of the proposal or with the granting of the receiving order. Note that the term "receivership" as used here is a bankruptcy term; more often, it describes the seizing of pledged assets by a secured creditor.

Item of Interest   When Dylex Ltd. sought protection from its creditors under the Bankruptcy and Insolvency Act, Richter & Partners of Toronto were appointed interim receiver by the courts and subsequently proceeded to arrange the sale of Dylex's 71-store Fairweather chain and to unload leases for its BiWay discount stores, which had all been closed.

Unsecured Liabilities with Priority   During the liquidation of the bankrupt's estate, the nonpledged (free) assets are sold and the proceeds therefrom — together with the excess of the proceeds from the sale of pledged assets over the amount of their related secured claims — become available for payment to the unsecured creditors. However, Section 136 of the act describes certain unsecured claims as having priority for payment in full before any payment is made to the remaining unsecured creditors. This is much like saying that all unsecured creditors are equal but some are more equal than others. The priorities listed in Section 136 can be summarized as follows:

1. Funeral expenses of a deceased bankrupt. (Obviously, this does not apply to incorporated businesses.)
2. Costs of administering the bankrupt estate, including the trustee's fees and any legal costs associated with such administration.

3. The levy of the Superintendent of Bankruptcy. The act provides for a levy to be deducted from funds distributed to unsecured creditors to help defray the costs of administering the act. The levy is 5 percent on the first $1,000,000, with a decreasing percentage on amounts in excess of this.

4. Wages owed to employees for a period not exceeding six months prior to bankruptcy, provided that the maximum owing to each employee does not exceed $2,000. Any amount owing that exceeds $2,000, but is within the six-month period, or any amount owing for a period exceeding six months, is unsecured without priority.

5. Municipal taxes, not including property taxes, but only to a maximum of the bankrupt's interest in the property.

6. A maximum of three months' rental arrears owing, with the proviso that the total owing to the landlord cannot exceed the value of the bankrupt's property contained in the rented premises.

After these unsecured claims listed in Section 136 have been paid in full, the remaining cash is paid ratably to the remaining unsecured creditors, subject of course to the deduction for the superintendent's levy.

Funds Held in Trust   The act allows the trustee to seize all of the property of the bankrupt, but specifies that property held in trust is not part of the bankrupt's property. This simply clarifies the notion that property held in trust belongs to someone else, and therefore the bankruptcy trustee would have to return this property to the rightful owner(s). The Income Tax Act, the Unemployment Insurance Act, and the Canada Pension Plan Act all require employers to make deductions from their employees' pay and to remit these to the government; furthermore, each act specifies that these deductions are held in trust by the employer. Under the provisions of the Bankruptcy and Insolvency Act, unremitted deductions do not constitute property of a bankrupt. Before the act was amended in 1992, items such as these were included in the unsecured claims with priority.

Unpaid Suppliers   This feature, provided in the 1992 amendment, gives unpaid suppliers the right to repossess goods within 30 days after delivery, if the debtor is in a state of bankruptcy or receivership at the time that the demand is made. This applies only to unsold goods in possession of the debtor, or the trustee, or the receiver, and to goods that are identifiable and are in exactly the same state as when they were delivered. Obviously, this would not apply to the work-in-process inventories of the debtor, or to services purchased but unpaid. This new provision will probably result in inventory being less attractive as security for bank loans.

Creditor Preferences and Customer Deposits   Bankruptcy law attempts to ensure that an insolvent person's creditors within a particular class receive equal treatment. There are provisions within the act that require the trustee to examine all transactions entered into by the bankrupt for varying time periods prior to the date of bankruptcy. For example, if unsecured creditor X of a bankrupt had received preferential treatment by being paid in full, whereas unsecured creditors Y and Z received no payment, the trustee could apply to the court to have the transaction set aside, and require X to return the amount of the payment to the trustee. Transactions under which assets were sold for less than fair value could also be set aside. The transfer of assets to a spouse by an insolvent individual would be viewed as a transaction entered into to avoid payment to creditors; as such, it could also be annulled by the court.

How to treat deposits made by customers of a business that subsequently goes bankrupt has long been a contentious issue. Too often, innocent people have made large deposits with furniture stores or automobile dealers, only to learn the next afternoon that the store or dealership went bankrupt that morning. They are understandably dismayed when they learn that they rank as ordinary unsecured creditors without priority, and will probably receive very little (if any) of their deposit back. It is small consolation that the bankrupt might be charged under the act for accepting deposits while in a state of insolvency.

The Accounting Statement of Affairs

As previously mentioned, the act requires an insolvent company to file a statement of affairs with the court. Another statement that is not officially filed under bankruptcy, but could provide useful information for creditors, is the accounting statement of affairs. This financial statement is prepared under a quitting concern concept and shows the estimated amounts that the various classes of creditors might receive under a bankruptcy liquidation. In this statement, assets are measured at estimated current values and classified as to their availability to settle fully secured, partially secured, and unsecured claims, as well as unsecured liabilities with priority under the act. The book values of the assets are often included as a tie-in to the most recent historical cost, going concern balance sheet.

Illustration: Statement of Affairs   Jurassic Corporation was declared bankrupt on May 14, Year 3. The company's balance sheet is shown in Exhibit 11.10.

The trustee has gathered the following information about the company's assets and liabilities:

- The notes receivable, which are considered to be fully collectible, are pledged as security to the note payable to the Bank of Commerce.
- The inventory will probably be sold for $50,000, and only 60 percent of the accounts receivable are expected to be collected. The supplies and prepaid expenses have no value.
- The land and buildings have an estimated market value of $110,000 and are pledged against the first-mortgage bonds.
- The equipment has been pledged against the note payable to trade suppliers. The trustee believes that $45,000 is the maximum amount that the equipment can be sold for.
- The wages and salaries fall within the requirements of Section 136 of the Bankruptcy and Insolvency Act. Trustee's fees are estimated to be $4,300.

The statement of affairs of Jurassic as at May 14, Year 3, is presented in Exhibit 11.11.

It should be noted that current and noncurrent classifications are no longer relevant for this company. Instead, assets and liabilities are presented in order of priority for liquidation by the trustee. The estimated proceeds represent the trustee's best estimate as of this date. Actual proceeds from the sale of the assets will probably be different.

Exhibit 11.10

JURASSIC CORPORATION
BALANCE SHEET
May 14, Year 3

Current assets		
Cash		$ 3,100
Notes receivable		15,200
Accounts receivable		18,500
Merchandise inventories		76,700
Supplies		7,500
Prepaid expenses		1,100
		122,100
Property and plant at cost (less accumulated depreciation)		
Land and buildings	70,500	
Equipment	73,000	143,500
		$265,600
Current liabilities		
Notes payable (including accrued interest)		
Bank of Commerce		$ 17,600
Trade suppliers		59,000
Accounts payable		60,000
Wages and salaries payable		10,200
Accrued interest on first-mortgage bonds		2,000
Legal and audit fees		3,300
UIC and income taxes withheld		1,700
		153,800
Long-term liabilities		
First-mortgage bonds		104,000
Total liabilities		257,800
Shareholders' equity		
Common stock	87,000	
Retained earnings (deficit)	(79,200)	7,800
		$265,600

Fully secured creditors are expected to be paid in full from the proceeds from the sale of pledged assets. In this example, an additional $4,000 from the sale of the land and buildings becomes a free asset available for unsecured creditors.

Partially secured creditors will not have their claims fully paid because the proceeds from the sale of pledged assets will be less than the amount of the claim. In this example the amounts still owing — $2,400 on the Bank of Commerce note and $14,000 on the notes to trade creditors — become unsecured claims without priority.

Free assets are available for unsecured creditors, and in this case monies held in statutory trust are deducted first because this money is not the property of the company. Liabilities having priority under Section 136 of the act are deducted next because they are entitled to full payment before any payment is made to the remaining unsecured creditors. Regarding the remaining $79,700 in unsecured liabilities: There is an estimated $52,000 in cash available to satisfy these claims. This represents a payment of 65 cents on the dollar before the levy for the Superintendent of Bankruptcy. In this particular case, after the levy of 5 percent, the unsecured creditors would receive a payment estimated to be 61.98 cents on the dollar.

Exhibit 11.11

JURASSIC CORPORATION
STATEMENT OF AFFAIRS
May 14, Year 3

Book values	Assets	Estimated current values	Estimated amount available, unsecured claims
	Assets pledged with fully secured creditors:		
$ 70,500	Land and buildings	110,000	
	Less first-mortgage bonds	106,000	$ 4,000
	Assets pledged with partially secured claims:		
15,200	Notes receivable (deducted contra)	15,200	
73,000	Equipment (deducted contra)	45,000	
	Free assets:		
3,100	Cash	3,100	
18,500	Accounts receivable	11,100	
76,700	Merchandise inventory	50,000	
7,500	Supplies	–0–	
1,100	Prepaid expenses	–0–	64,200
			68,200
	Less liability for funds held in trust		1,700
	Estimated amount available		66,500
	Less unsecured claims with priority		14,500
	Net estimated amount available to unsecured		
	creditors (65 cents on the dollar)		52,000
	Estimated deficiency to unsecured creditors		27,700
$265,600			
	Total unsecured claims		$79,700

Book values	Liabilities and shareholders' equity		Amount unsecured
	Fully secured creditors:		
$104,000	First-mortgage bonds	104,000	
2,000	Accrued interest	2,000	
	Total (deducted contra)	106,000	
	Partially secured creditors:		
17,600	Notes payable, Bank of Commerce	17,600	
	Less notes receivable pledged as collateral	15,200	$ 2,400
59,000	Notes payable, trade creditors	59,000	
	Less equipment pledged as collateral	45,000	14,000
	Liability for funds held in trust:		
	UIC and income tax withholdings		
1,700	(deducted contra)	1,700	

continued

Exhibit 11.11 *continued*

	Creditors with priority under Section 136:	
10,200	Wages and salaries payable	10,200
	Trustee's fees	4,300
	Total (deducted contra)	14,500
	Unsecured creditors:	
60,000	Accounts payable	60,000
3,300	Legal and audit fees payable	3,300
	Shareholders' equity:	
87,000	Common stock	
(79,200)	Retained earnings (deficit)	
$265,600		$79,700

SUMMARY

Push-down accounting is one application of the comprehensive revaluation of all of the assets and liabilities of a company. It can be applied only if the company was party to a business combination in which at least 90 percent of its voting shares were acquired by another company, and its use is not mandatory in this situation.

Another application arises when, due to severe financial difficulties, a company undertakes a financial reorganization and as a result its previous shareholders lose their control in the company. The proposal to reorganize is often made when the company is in a situation of insolvency and receivership or bankruptcy appears imminent. If control changes, comprehensive revaluation must take place.

REVIEW QUESTIONS

1. What is the purpose of push-down accounting?

2. "The use of push-down accounting greatly simplifies the consolidation process." Discuss and evaluate this statement.

3. Not all accountants favour the use of push-down accounting. What are some of the arguments against it?

4. Accountants have historically recognized corporate reorganizations in the accounting records. Section 1625 provides a new key condition that must be present before a revaluation of assets and liabilities can occur. What is this key condition?

5. In a business combination situation, goodwill is recorded when the fair value of the firm is greater than the fair values of its individual assets and liabilities. Would this be the case if a financial reorganization has occurred under Section 1625? Explain.

6. Identify the various classes of creditors whose claims are dealt with in bankruptcy liquidations.

7.   What is the difference between voluntary and involuntary bankruptcy?

8.   What is an accounting statement of affairs?

9.   Explain the difference between secured and unsecured creditors.

10. Describe three ways in which a business organization could be declared bankrupt.

11. Is there any difference between an insolvent person and a bankrupt person? Explain.

12. A business that has fallen under the jurisdiction of a licensed trustee in bankruptcy shows a future tax liability on its balance sheet caused by undepreciated capital cost allowance/book value differences. How will this liability be reported on the statement of affairs? Explain.

13. Explain the following terms: official receiver, receivership, receiving order, interim receiver, and receiver-manager.

14. What potential future problem may exist when an individual makes a deposit with a retailer to hold merchandise for a future purchase?

MULTIPLE CHOICE

Use the following data for Questions 1 to 3.
The balance sheet for Prairie Co. as at December 31, Year 4, is as follows:

Assets

Cash	$ (5,000)
Current receivables	635,000
Inventories	900,000
Equipment (net)	670,000
Intangibles	160,000
	$2,360,000

Liabilities and shareholders' equity

Current liabilities	$ 900,000
Note payable	1,330,000
Long-term liabilities	300,000
Common stock	100,000
Retained earnings	(270,000)
	$2,360,000

The creditors and shareholders have accepted the following financial reorganization agreement, whereby the assets will be revalued to fair value as follows:

Accounts receivable	$160,000 write-down
Inventory	$340,000 write-down
Intangibles	$160,000 write-off
Equipment	$200,000 write-up

The holders of the current liabilities will accept 50% of the amount they are owed in a 3-year note, forgive 30%, and retain a current claim on 20%. The current common shares will be surrendered and cancelled, and the holder of the note payable will receive 10,000 newly issued shares in satisfaction of the amount due. The other balance sheet items will remain unchanged.

1. Which of the following is the amount that will be reported as common shares after the financial reorganization?
   a. $680,000
   b. $880,000
   c. $970,000
   d. $1,330,000

2. Which of the following is the amount that will be reported as current liabilities after the financial reorganization?
   a. $0
   b. $180,000
   c. $270,000
   d. $630,000

3. Which of the following is the amount that will be reported as retained earnings after the financial reorganization?
   a. ($360,000)
   b. ($270,000)
   c. $0
   d. $360,000

4. Which of the following is the best description of "push-down accounting"?
   a. The subsidiary is required to adopt the accounting policies of the parent.
   b. The parent requires the subsidiary to revalue its assets and liabilities on its books based on the purchase transaction.
   c. The subsidiary records its assets at lower values to reduce its attractiveness for takeover bids.
   d. The parent allocates any negative goodwill that arose on the purchase transaction to the subsidiary's nonmonetary assets and liabilities.

5. Which of the following is the best description of involuntary bankruptcy?
   a. Upon default of payment, a secured creditor appoints an agent to seize the debtor's property that has been pledged against the debt.
   b. A company liquidates its assets and uses the proceeds to settle debt, with any remaining amount being distributed to preferred, then common shareholders.
   c. Upon default of payment, unsecured creditors appoint a trustee to seize all of a debtor's property and protect them until further actions can be taken.
   d. A person is unable to meet his or her obligations and holds assets that have fair values less than the amount of these obligations.

CASES

Case 1   Southern Ltd. is negotiating the takeover of Northern Corp. and intends to finance the acquisition in part with a loan provided by a large Canadian pension fund. To date it has been agreed that the assets of Northern will be pledged as partial security to the loan.

   The president of Southern has just completed further talks with the pension fund managers and has called you into his office. He explains what has transpired and then exclaims, "These guys not only want the fair values of Northern's assets to appear on its balance sheet, but they also want their loan to appear there as well. I wasn't aware that this was possible under GAAP. Draft up a memo for me so I can report on this to the executive committee tomorrow morning."

Required:

Prepare your memo to the president.

Case 2 Reed Corporation is under creditor protection in accordance with the provisions in the Companies' Creditors Arrangement Act. The last two years have not been profitable and the company has a sizable deficit. Cash flows have been substantially reduced, and as a result the company has been having trouble paying suppliers on time and paying interest when it is due. Concerned that its creditors might take legal action against it, Reed was granted court permission to make a proposal to its creditors. After extensive negotiations, the creditor groups have accepted the following proposal:

- Trade creditors have agreed to accept 90% of the amounts owing to them as payment in full.
- Holders of unsecured notes have agreed to an extension of maturity date and a reduction of interest.
- Existing shareholders will subscribe to a new share issue on the basis of two new shares for each share currently held.
- Debenture holders have agreed to an exchange of five newly issued cumulative redeemable preferred shares for each $1,000 bond held. If dividends fall into arrears, the preferred shareholders have the option of converting the preferred shares into common shares of the company. Such a conversion would allow the election of 2 members on the 12-member board of directors.

The president of Reed has asked you to provide advice regarding the proper accounting for this reorganization. He feels that for some of the company's assets, the fair values are greater than carrying values, while for others, the opposite is the case. He would like to reflect these fair values in the financial statements and at the same time write off the accumulated deficit to reflect the fresh start.

Required:

Prepare a report for the president.

Case 3 Late last evening, your favourite uncle Harry phoned you because he knows that you are nearly ready to write your professional accounting entrance examinations. He is excited, and also quite upset because as he was perusing the business section of the local newspaper he came across a notice that involves one of his major customers. He is quite worried about the potential consequences. After he reads the notice to you, you tell him that you will call him tomorrow and explain the situation. After the call, you locate the following notice that he was referring to in the paper:

IN THE MATTER OF THE BANKRUPTCY OF SUMMERSET ENTERPRISES INC., A COMPANY DULY INCORPORATED UNDER THE LAWS OF THE PROVINCE OF ONTARIO, WITH A HEAD OFFICE IN THE CITY OF DUNDAS.
NOTICE IS HEREBY GIVEN THAT A RECEIVING ORDER WAS MADE AGAINST SUMMERSET INDUSTRIES LIMITED ON MONDAY THE 6th DAY OF MARCH 2003, AND THAT THE FIRST MEETING OF CREDITORS WILL BE HELD ON THE 10th DAY OF APRIL 2003 AT THE HOUR OF 1:00 O'CLOCK IN THE AFTERNOON AT 55 ST. CLAIR AVENUE, ROOM 308, TORONTO ONTARIO. TO BE ELIGIBLE TO VOTE, CREDITORS MUST FILE WITH ME PROOFS OF CLAIM PRIOR TO THE MEETING.

YARRUM NOTLIH
Trustee.

Required:

Outline what you will say tomorrow.

Case 4 The following article appeared a few years ago in *The Globe and Mail*:

Bramalea Ltd. creditors have given their blessing to a plan that calls for the once high-flying developer to shrink by more than a third, a decision that almost assures the company's smooth exit from bankruptcy court.

The final two of Bramalea's six creditor classes cast their votes in favour of the plan yesterday, concluding protracted negotiations that started last spring with lenders to restructure $4.9 billion of debt.

"It's very, very satisfying to see a positive outcome," said Bramalea president Marvin Marshall. "Now the challenge is to keep our commitments and to be able to follow through on all the things we've agreed to."

The vote marks a personal victory for Mr. Marshall, installed in the president's chair by Bramalea parent Trizec Corp. Ltd. in 1990 after a costly and ill-fated string of land acquisitions. Mr. Marshall, hired away from a Houston-based Trizec affiliate, had a reputation as a skilled performer of real estate turnarounds.

On the stock exchange, Bramalea shares reversed Thursday's sharp climb, dropping 11 cents to 69 cents on volume of 1.5 million shares. The stock changed hands 557 times, with no block of shares trading larger than 25,000. Although ownership of Bramalea's common shareholders will be substantially diluted under the plan, the stock appeared buoyed by creditors' strong endorsement of the plan.

In the end, the developer profited from the high-profile demise of Olympia & York Developments Ltd., which fell apart only months before Bramalea was confronting its own liquidity crisis. Relative to O&Y, Bramalea endeared itself to the banks by throwing open its books and confessing the magnitude of its financial problems.

When Bramalea filed for protection under the Companies' Creditors Arrangement Act last December, it had in hand a plan that already had been negotiated with lenders. So the official approval won yesterday came as little surprise.

The next step will be a request next Wednesday for a court order making the plan binding on the company and its creditors, including the small minority that rejected the plan.

The plan, to go into effect March 18, calls for the ambitious sale of $2.2-billion of properties, the deferral of principal repayments and the exchange of unsecured debt for shares. Because 775 million new shares will be issued under the plan, Trizec's 72-per-cent stake will be diluted to about 20 percent.

Required:

Based on this article (which is skimpy on detail) and any reasonable assumptions you wish to make, discuss the financial accounting implications resulting from the "plan."

PROBLEMS

Problem 1 The balance sheets of Peach Corp. and Sabourin Ltd. on December 31, Year 1, are shown below:

	Peach	Sabourin
Cash	$100,000	$ 2,000
Accounts receivable	25,000	7,000
Inventory	30,000	21,000
Plant	175,000	51,000
Trademarks	—	7,000
	$330,000	$88,000
Current liabilities	$ 50,000	$10,000
Long-term debt	80,000	20,000
Common stock	110,000	30,000
Retained earnings	90,000	28,000
	$330,000	$88,000

The fair values of the identifiable net assets of Sabourin on December 31, Year 1, are as follows:

Cash		$ 2,000
Accounts receivable		7,000
Inventory		26,000
Plant		60,000
Trademarks		14,000
		109,000
Current liabilities	10,000	
Long-term debt	19,000	29,000
Net assets		$ 80,000

On January 1, Year 2, Peach paid $95,000 in cash to acquire all of the common shares of Sabourin, and instructed the management of Sabourin to apply push-down accounting as an aid in the preparation of future consolidated financial statements.

Required:

(a) Prepare Sabourin's push-down journal entries.

(b) Prepare the consolidated balance sheet on January 1, Year 2.

Problem 2 An agreement has been reached whereby Pace Company will issue 6,000 common shares on January 1, Year 2, for all of the outstanding shares of Stetlar Company in a purchase-method business combination. Push-down accounting will be applied. Pace's shares are currently trading at $4.90. The following information has been assembled as at December 31, Year 1:

| | **Pace** | | **Stetlar** | |
	Book value	Fair value	Book value	Fair value
Cash	$ 10,000	$10,000	$ 2,000	$ 2,000
Accounts receivable	12,000	12,000	—	
Inventory	18,000	22,500	8,000	5,200
Plant assets	60,000	70,000	20,000	25,000
	$100,000		$30,000	
Current liabilities	$ 20,000	20,000	$ 5,000	$ 5,000
Long-term debt	15,000	19,000	2,500	3,200
Common stock	30,000		10,000	
Retained earnings	35,000		12,500	
	$100,000		$30,000	

Required:

(a) Prepare the required push-down journal entries on January 1, Year 2.
(b) Prepare a consolidated balance sheet on January 1, Year 2.

Problem 3 The balance sheets of Peko Corp. and Scott Ltd. on December 31, Year 4, are as follows:

	Peko book value	Scott book value
Cash	$ 10,000	$ 5,000
Accounts receivable	100,000	35,000
Inventory	90,000	160,000
Land	70,000	40,000
Plant and equipment	360,000	290,000
Investment in Scott	261,000	—
Goodwill	90,000	30,000
	$981,000	$560,000
Current liabilities	$120,000	$ 80,000
Long-term debt	320,000	220,000
Common stock	400,000	300,000
Retained earnings	141,000	(40,000)
	$981,000	$560,000

On December 30, Year 4, Peko purchased all of the common shares of Scott for $261,000. On this date the inventory of Scott had a fair value of $165,000, its land had a fair value of $70,000, and its plant and equipment had a fair value of $280,000. Scott has been directed to apply push-down accounting.

Required:

Prepare the necessary push-down journal entries and the consolidated balance sheet as at December 31, Year 4.

Problem 4   On January 1, Year 2, Pic Ltd. gained control over Bic Inc. through an acquisition of the common shares of that company.

Balance sheet data of Bic on December 31, Year 1, are presented next.

	Book value	Fair value
Cash	$ 2,000	$ 2,000
Accounts receivable	7,000	7,000
Inventory	21,000	26,000
Plant	51,000	60,000
Trademarks	7,000	14,000
	$88,000	
Current liabilities	$10,000	$10,000
Long-term debt	20,000	19,000
Common stock	30,000	
Retained earnings	28,000	
	$88,000	

Required:

PART A

Assume that Pic paid $97,000 for 100% of the outstanding common shares of Bic.

Prepare Bic's journal entries to apply push-down accounting.

PART B

Assume that Pic paid $63,000 for 90% of Bic's shares.

Prepare Bic's journal entries to apply push-down accounting.

Problem 5   On July 1, 2002, Peaks Corp. purchased 100% of the voting shares of Valleys Inc. for $679,800. The balance sheet of Valleys on that date was as follows:

VALLEYS INC.
BALANCE SHEET
as at July 1, 2002

	Net book value	Fair market value
Cash	$ 96,000	$ 96,000
Accounts receivable	120,000	144,000
Inventory	180,000	228,000
Fixed assets (net)	540,000	450,000
	$936,000	
Current liabilities	$107,200	$107,200
Bonds payable	200,000	190,000
Common shares	120,000	
Retained earnings	508,800	
	$936,000	

The accounts receivable of Valleys were collected in October 2002, and the inventory was completely sold by May 2003. The fixed assets had a remaining life of 15 years on July 1, 2002, and the bonds payable mature on June 30, 2006. A goodwill impairment loss of $14,750 was recorded in 2003.

The financial statements for Peaks and Valleys as at December 31, 2004, are presented below. Peaks has used the equity method to account for its investment; Valleys applied push-down accounting effective with the acquisition date.

BALANCE SHEETS

	Peaks	Valleys
Cash	$ 120,000	$ 84,000
Accounts receivable	180,000	114,000
Inventory	300,000	276,000
Fixed assets (net)	720,000	465,000
Investment in Valleys	651,200	—
Goodwill	—	44,250
Other investments	250,666	—
	$2,221,866	$983,250
Current liabilities	$ 180,200	$115,000
Bonds payable	315,000	217,050
Common shares	300,600	679,800
Retained earnings	1,348,066	(29,600)
Net income	128,000	6,000
Dividends	(50,000)	(5,000)
	$2,221,866	$983,250

INCOME STATEMENTS

	Peaks	Valleys
Sales	$1,261,000	$1,200,000
Investment income (equity method)	6,000	—
Income from other investments	25,000	—
	$1,292,000	$1,200,000
Cost of goods sold	$ 840,000	$1,020,000
Depreciation	60,000	48,000
Interest	37,000	28,900
Other	227,000	97,100
	$1,164,000	$1,194,000
Net income	$ 128,000	$ 6,000

Required:

Prepare the consolidated financial statements for the year ended December 31, 2004.

Problem 6   The following financial statements were prepared on December 31, Year 6.

BALANCE SHEET

	Pearl	Strand
Cash	$ 300,000	$ 100,000
Accounts receivable	200,000	600,000
Inventory	2,000,000	420,000
Plant and equipment	3,000,000	2,340,000
Accumulated depreciation	(750,000)	(450,625)
Goodwill	—	55,000
Investment in Strand — equity method	2,764,375	—
	$7,514,375	$3,064,375
Accounts payable	$ 900,000	$ 300,000
Capital stock	3,850,000	2,500,000
Retained earnings	2,764,375	264,375
	$7,514,375	$3,064,375

INCOME STATEMENT

	Pearl	Strand
Sales	$4,000,000	$1,000,000
Investment income	358,750	—
	$4,358,750	$1,000,000
Cost of sales	$2,500,000	$ 400,000
Miscellaneous expenses	370,000	70,000
Depreciation expense	80,000	41,250
Goodwill impairment loss	—	10,000
Income tax expense	250,000	120,000
	$3,200,000	$ 641,250
Net income	$1,158,750	$ 358,750

RETAINED EARNINGS STATEMENT

	Pearl	Strand
Balance, January 1	$2,105,625	$ 105,625
Net income	1,158,750	358,750
	3,264,375	464,375
Dividends	500,000	200,000
Balance, December 31	$2,764,375	$ 264,375

Other Information

Pearl purchased 100% of the outstanding voting stock of Strand for $2,500,000 on July 1, Year 2, at which time Strand's retained earnings were $400,000 and common stock amounted to $1,600,000. The purchase discrepancy on this date was allocated as follows: 30% to undervalued inventory; 50% to equipment (remaining life: 8 years); and balance to goodwill.

Strand applied push-down accounting on acquisition date, and Pearl has used the equity method to account for its investment since that date.

Strand owes Pearl $75,000 on December 31, Year 6.

Required:

Prepare consolidated financial statements on December 31, Year 6.

Problem 7   Even though Tizoc Development Corp. has a history as a very successful property developer, its fortunes have waned in recent years, and it has been unable to service its debt due to cash flow difficulties. Rather than force the liquidation of the company, the creditors have accepted a proposal from management as a last-ditch effort to salvage the operation. The corporation's balance sheet as at May 31 of the current year is presented below:

TIZOC DEVELOPMENT CORP.
BALANCE SHEET — May 31

Cash	$ 34,730
Investments	252,890
Land	550,000
Buildings	908,731
Accumulated depreciation	(512,481)
Goodwill	50,000
	$1,283,870
Current liabilities	$ 136,860
12% first-mortgage bonds	600,000
14% debenture bonds	200,000
Common stock (10,000 shares)	170,940
Retained earnings	176,070
	$1,283,870

The following is a summary of the reorganization plan.
- The investments are portfolio and significant interest investments in other land development companies. These companies have also experienced high vacancy rates and declining property values. These investments are to be written down to $100,000.
- All concerned agree that the land is overvalued by $120,000 and the net book value of the buildings by $90,000. The goodwill has no value.
- The 12% first-mortgage bonds are to be exchanged for $400,000, 7.5% first-mortgage bonds and 25,000 new common shares.
- The current liabilities will be paid as cash becomes available.
- Each 14% debenture is to be exchanged for a 5% debenture. This interest rate is far below current interest rates. The present value of the future cash payments discounted at today's market interest rates amounts to $185,000.

Required:
(a) Prepare the journal entries to record the reorganization.
(b) Prepare a balance sheet after the reorganization.

Problem 8   The trial balance of Sussex Inc. as at December 31, Year 6, is as follows:

	Debit	Credit
Cash	$ 45,000	
Accounts receivable	95,000	
Allowance for doubtful accounts		18,000
Inventory	150,000	
Property, plant, and equipment	540,000	
Accumulated depreciation		210,000
Patents	120,000	
Accounts payable		110,000
Notes payable (10% interest)		150,000
Accrued interest on notes		40,000
12% bonds payable		400,000
Common stock (9,000 shares)		200,000
Retained earnings (deficit)	178,000	
	$1,128,000	$1,128,000

The following reorganization plan has been approved by the shareholders and the creditors:

- The holders of the notes payable agree to cancel the accrued interest owing, to extend the due date, and to reduce the interest rate. In return they will receive a pledge of inventory and receivables as security throughout the life of the notes.
- Trade creditors agree to accept a payment of $95,000 as full settlement of their claims.
- The bondholders agree to exchange their bonds for $250,000 in 8% first-mortgage bonds and 15,000 common shares.
- The deficit is to be eliminated.
- All parties have agreed that the following reflect the fair values of the individual assets:

Accounts receivable	$ 72,000
Allowance for doubtful accounts	2,000
Inventory	130,000
Property, plant, and equipment	250,000
Patents	190,000

Required:

(a) Prepare the journal entries to record the reorganization.
(b) Prepare a balance sheet after the reorganization.

Problem 9   The following information was taken from the accounting records of Pembina Manufacturing Limited, which has recently come under the jurisdiction of a licensed trustee in bankruptcy:

	Carrying amount
Cash	$ 4,000
Accounts receivable (100% estimated collectible)	46,000
Inventories: estimated fair value, $18,000; pledged on $21,000 of notes payable	39,000
Equipment: Est. fair value, $67,400; pledged on mortgage note payable	107,000
Manufacturing supplies: Est. fair value, $1,500	2,000
Wages payable: current month	5,800
Income tax and CPP source deductions	1,200
Trade accounts payable	60,000
Notes payable, $21,000 secured by inventory	40,000
Mortgage note payable	50,000
Accrued interest on mortgage note	400
Common stock	100,000
Deficit	59,400

Required:

Prepare a statement of affairs.

CHAPTER 12
Foreign Currency Transactions

CHAPTER OUTLINE

Currency Exchange Rates

Accounting for Foreign Currency Transactions

    Import/Export Transactions Denominated in Foreign Currency

    Transaction Gains and Losses from Noncurrent Monetary Items

Accounting for Hedges

    Forward Exchange Contracts

    Hedging a Future Revenue Stream

Summary

Self-study Problem 1

Self-study Problem 2

Review and Multiple-choice Questions, Case, and Problems

LEARNING OBJECTIVES

After studying this chapter, you should be able to do the following:

- Distinguish between the one- and two-transaction approaches to recording a foreign currency transaction.
- Describe the concept of hedging, and prepare a list of items that could be used as a hedge.
- Prepare journal entries and subsequent financial statement presentation for forward exchange contracts that hedge existing or expected monetary positions, or are entered into for speculative purposes.
- Apply the concept of hedge accounting to long-term debt acting as a hedge to a future revenue stream.

Many Canadian companies conduct business in foreign countries as well as in Canada. For some companies, foreign business simply means purchasing products and services from foreign suppliers, or selling products and services to foreign customers. Other companies go far beyond importing and exporting and conduct business in foreign countries through sales offices, branches, subsidiaries, and joint ventures. Of 200 Canadian public companies recently sampled, 139 made disclosures about geographic areas.[1] These companies are generating revenues, incurring costs, and employing assets in countries other than Canada.

No specific accounting issues arise when the parties involved in an import or export transaction agree that the settlement will be in Canadian dollars. Because it is a *Canadian dollar denominated transaction*, the company will record the foreign purchase or sale in exactly the same manner as any domestic purchase or sale. In many situations, however, the agreement calls for the transaction to be settled in a foreign currency. This means one of two things: (a) the Canadian company will have to acquire foreign currency in order to discharge the obligations resulting from its imports; or (b) the Canadian company will receive foreign currency as a result of its exports, and will have to sell the foreign currency in order to receive Canadian dollars. Transactions such as these are called *foreign currency denominated transactions.* Accounting issues arise when the value of the Canadian dollar has changed relative to the value of the foreign currency at the time financial statements need to be prepared or on the date of the subsequent settlement of the receivable or payable.

In similar manner, when Canadian companies borrow money in foreign markets, they often receive the loan proceeds in a foreign currency and are required to make interest and principal payments in that currency. Also, some Canadian companies lend money in foreign markets with terms that require payment in a foreign currency. The changing value of the Canadian dollar over the term of the loan poses the same type of accounting problems as those just mentioned. When business is conducted outside Canada through foreign branches, subsidiaries, or joint ventures, additional accounting problems arise because the financial statements are often prepared using a foreign currency as the unit of measure. In such cases, the statements need to be translated so that the Canadian dollar becomes the unit of measure. In addition, accounting principles used in other countries are often different from those used in Canada, and adjustments need to be made to the financial statements so that they reflect Canadian standards.

Before we examine the accounting required for foreign currency denominated transactions and statements in this chapter and the next, we will take a brief look at exchange rates.

Currency Exchange Rates

Both the recording of foreign currency denominated transactions and the translation of foreign currency financial statements require the use of currency exchange rates. An exchange rate is simply the price of one currency in terms of another currency. Exchange rates fluctuate on a daily basis. Historically, governments have tried to stabilize rates between their currencies. Shortly after World War II, a group of the world's major trading nations agreed to "peg" the rates at which their currencies

---

[1] *Financial Reporting in Canada 2000*, 25th edition. Toronto: CICA, p. 202.

would be exchanged in terms of U.S. dollars. Since these pegged rates stayed reasonably steady, the accounting for foreign transactions was fairly simple. Differences in inflation rates and major changes in the balance of payments among the participating nations were contributing factors in the eventual demise of this agreement in the early 1970s.

The end of pegged rates led to the present system, in which long-term rates are determined by market forces. This system of floating exchange rates is not totally market driven in the short term, because governments often intervene in the marketplace to lessen the swings in the value of their currencies. It is not uncommon to hear that the Canadian dollar has weakened in relation to the U.S. dollar, and that the Bank of Canada has made massive purchases of Canadian dollars in order to soften the decline; or that the U.S. Federal Reserve Bank and the central banks of other countries intervened in the foreign currency markets by purchasing U.S. dollars because the U.S. dollar was declining in relation to other major currencies. Sometimes interventions of this nature are fruitless, as was the case in 1994, when Mexico's central bank abandoned its attempt to prop up the peso and allowed a substantial devaluation to take place.

The European Union   As outlined in Chapter 1, 11 of the 15 countries that make up the membership of the European Union agreed to adopt a common currency called the euro effective January 1, 2002. Euro coins and notes became the sole currency on that date, with the proviso that all local currencies be removed from circulation by July 1, 2002. (Prior to 2002 the euro circulated and traded on the world's currency exchanges, but at the same time member countries were allowed to continue using their own currencies). Three EU members (Denmark, Great Britain, and Sweden) chose not to adopt the common currency at this time, while a fourth member, Greece, could not meet the required economic conditions for adoption. Most of the countries in Western Europe are part of the EU, with the notable exception of Switzerland.

Reasons for Fluctuating Exchange Rates   Currencies trade in markets in such major cities as New York, London, Paris, and Tokyo; and transfers of enormous amounts of currency between countries can take place in a matter of seconds. The price of a currency will fluctuate in much the same manner as the price of any other commodity. There are many reasons why a country's currency price changes, of which the major ones are the following:

- *Inflation rates.* As a general rule, if country A has a higher rate of inflation than country B, the price of A's currency will weaken relative to B's. In a period of inflation, the purchasing power of a country's currency declines. If this currency will not buy as much in goods as it did before, then neither will it buy as much currency of another country as it did before.

- *Interest rates.* Higher interest rates attract foreign investment to a country and in so doing drive up the price of its currency.

- *Trade surpluses and deficits.* As a country exports more than it imports, its currency strengthens and becomes worth more.

Exchange Rate Quotations   Exchange rates showing the value of the Canadian dollar in terms of other foreign currencies are quoted daily in many Canadian business newspapers. The amounts that usually appear are called *direct quotations*, which means that the amount represents the cost in Canadian dollars to purchase one unit of foreign currency. For example, a quotation of 1 pound = CDN$2.2972 means that it costs 2.2972 Canadian dollars to purchase 1 British pound. An *indirect quotation* would state the cost in a foreign currency to purchase one Canadian dollar. For example, a quotation of 1 dollar = .4353 pounds indicates that it costs .4353 British pounds to purchase 1 Canadian dollar. An indirect quotation can be obtained by computing the reciprocal of the *direct* quotation. Conversely, a direct quotation can be obtained by computing the reciprocal of the *indirect* quotation (1 ÷ 2.2972 = .4353, and 1 ÷ .4353 = 2.2972).

Direct quotations are the most useful ones for recording transactions denominated in foreign currencies. Using the exchange rates quoted above, a Canadian company would record the purchase of £10,000 of inventory from a British supplier as $22,972.

Examples of foreign exchange quotations on a particular day for four countries' currencies are shown in Exhibit 12.1. These rates represent the amount in Canadian dollars that a commercial bank would charge if it sold one unit of foreign currency to a major customer. The first rate quoted is called the *spot rate*. In subsequent discussions we will also refer to this rate as the "current rate," because it represents the rate at which a unit of foreign currency could be purchased on that particular date. If a customer wanted to purchase 5,000 euros on the date that these rates were quoted, the cost would be $7,248 (5,000 × 1.4496). Note that if the bank were to purchase euros from the customer, the amount that it would pay the customer would be slightly less than the amount quoted per euro. The bank's selling rate has to be greater than its purchasing rate if it is to make a profit dealing in foreign currencies. The forward rates quoted (1 month forward, 2 months forward, etc.) are the rates for forward exchange contracts. A *forward exchange contract* is an agreement between a bank and a customer to exchange currencies on a specified future date at a specified rate. For example, when a bank enters into a forward exchange contract with a customer to purchase 5,000 euros 6 months forward, the bank is committing itself to take delivery of this quantity of euros six months from this date, and to pay the customer $7,233 (5,000 × 1.4466) at that time. Of course, there is also a commitment on the part of the customer to sell 5,000 euros to the bank in six months' time. The use of forward exchange contracts in hedging transactions will be illustrated later in this chapter.

Accounting for Foreign Currency Transactions

We will now focus on the issues associated with import/export transactions and foreign currency denominated debt. Accounting problems arise when there are exchange rate changes between the date of a transaction and the eventual settlement in foreign currency. During this period the company holds foreign currency denominated monetary assets and liabilities, and questions arise as to how to measure these items if financial statements need to be prepared in the intervening period, and what to do with any gains or losses that may result from such measurements. A monetary asset or liability is one that is fixed by contract or otherwise in terms of a monetary unit. Accounts receivable and investments in bonds are examples of monetary assets; accounts payable and bond liabilities are monetary liabilities. In much the same

Exhibit 12.1

FOREIGN EXCHANGE QUOTATIONS

Country	Currency	CDN$ per unit
Britain	Pound	2.2972
1 month forward		2.2947
2 months forward		2.2931
3 months forward		2.2906
6 months forward		2.2821
12 months forward		2.2686
European Union	Euro	1.4496
1 month forward		1.4497
3 months forward		1.4487
6 months forward		1.4466
12 months forward		1.4450
Japan	Yen	0.013380
1 month forward		0.013423
3 months forward		0.013489
6 months forward		0.013596
12 months forward		0.013814
United States	Dollar	1.5708
1 month forward		1.5717
2 months forward		1.5727
3 months forward		1.5734
6 months forward		1.5745
12 months forward		1.5766

way, a foreign currency denominated monetary position is a net asset position if monetary assets exceed monetary liabilities, or the opposite if monetary liabilities exceed monetary assets.

Import/Export Transactions Denominated in Foreign Currency

Until Section 1650 of the *Handbook* was issued, accountants had two alternatives for recording foreign currency denominated import and export transactions. The "one-transaction approach" will be illustrated first, for an import transaction. The "two-transaction approach" was chosen by the Accounting Standards Committee[2] as the preferred approach for use in Canada. This method will be illustrated later and will form the basis of all subsequent illustrations.

The One-transaction Approach Under the one-transaction approach, a foreign currency denominated purchase or sale and the eventual settlement of the resulting payable or receivable constitute a single transaction, the amount of which will not be finally determined until such settlement has occurred. The following example will illustrate this approach.

---

[2] Since 1991, called the Accounting Standards Board.

Let us assume that on June 1, Year 1, Maritime Importers Inc. purchased merchandise from a supplier in Switzerland at a cost of 10,000 Swiss francs, with payment in full to be made in 60 days. The exchange rate on the date of purchase was SF1 = $0.941. Maritime paid its supplier on July 30, Year 1, when the exchange rate was SF1 = $0.953. The following journal entries, recorded in Canadian dollars, illustrate the company's purchase of merchandise and subsequent payment using the one-transaction approach.

June 1, Year 1

Inventory	9,410	
Accounts payable (10,000 × 0.941)		9,410

July 30, Year 1

Inventory	120	
Accounts payable	9,410	
Cash (10,000 × 0.953)		9,530

The first entry records the purchase of inventory and the resulting account payable at the spot (or current) rate on June 1, Year 1. By July 30, Year 1, the Canadian dollar has weakened in relation to the Swiss franc and Maritime has to pay $9,530 to purchase the 10,000 Swiss francs needed to settle the liability. The difference of $120 is charged to inventory under the one-transaction approach, because the amount used initially to record the purchase on June 1 is considered to be an estimate of the final amount, which is established on the date of settlement. There are a number of practical and theoretical problems associated with this approach. If a portion of the inventory has been sold by the settlement date, the $120 will have to be apportioned between the inventory still on hand and cost of goods sold. An even greater problem exists if the company's year-end occurs before the settlement date. The account payable (a current monetary position) would not reflect the dollar equivalent of the liability on that date. Section 1650 makes it clear that the end-of-year spot rate must be used:

> At each balance sheet date, monetary items denominated in a foreign currency should be adjusted to reflect the exchange rate in effect at the balance sheet date. [1650.16]

If the year-end of Maritime was June 30, Year 1, and the exchange rate was SF1 = $0.949 on that date, the accounts payable would have to be increased by $80 to reflect a balance of $9,490 (10,000 × 0.949). The allocation of the $80 to inventory still on hand and to cost of goods sold would not be a particularly difficult task. But on the July 30 settlement date, when the cost of 10,000 Swiss francs turns out to be $9,530, the allocation of the additional $40 difference creates a more difficult problem. The records were closed at June 30, Year 1, and the amount used to record cost of goods sold was incorrect in retrospect. Of course, in this particular example it is probable that the year-end financial statements would not have been released by the settlement date. The $40 could be allocated to increase cost of goods sold and inventory. But even so, where would the balancing credit entry go? Should the year-end account payable also be increased by $40? If this was done, the payable would not represent the Canadian dollar equivalent of the liability on that date as required by Section 1650.

It is not hard to see that the one-transaction approach creates a number of accounting problems, especially when the settlement date occurs many months after a balance sheet date. Under the one-transaction approach, the amount recorded for a purchase (or a sale) depends on how the transaction is financed. This approach was rejected by the Accounting Standards Committee.

The Two-transaction Approach   In adopting the two-transaction approach, the committee recognized that a credit transaction comprises a purchase or sale and the financing associated with the transaction, *and* that each component must be accounted for separately. Maritime could have purchased 10,000 Swiss francs on June 1, Year 1, or it could have hedged its liability on this date. (Hedging will be discussed in a subsequent section.) When it chose not to do either, it left itself exposed to foreign currency fluctuations. The effect of this exposure must be recorded and disclosed separately in the financial statements. Section 1650 chose the two-transaction approach with the following paragraphs:

> When the reporting enterprise purchases or sells goods or services on credit with settlement to be in a foreign currency, this will give rise to a payable or receivable in foreign currency. Any subsequent change in exchange rate between the Canadian dollar and the foreign currency will affect the Canadian dollar equivalent of that payable or receivable. [1650.11]
>
> Once foreign currency purchases and sales, or inventories, fixed assets and other non-monetary items obtained through foreign currency transactions, have been translated and recorded, any subsequent changes in the exchange rate will not affect those recorded amounts. [1650.13]
>
> At the transaction date, each asset, liability, revenue or expense arising from a foreign currency transaction of the reporting enterprise should be translated into Canadian dollars by use of the exchange rate in effect at that date, except when the transaction is hedged, in which case the rate established by the terms of the hedge should be used (see paragraph 1650.52). [1650.14]

We will now return to the Maritime Importers example to illustrate the two-transaction approach. These are the significant dates:

Transaction date — June 1, Year 1
    Inventory purchased for SF10,000
    Exchange rate SF1 = $0.941
Year end — June 30, Year 1
    Exchange rate SF1 = $0.949
Settlement date — July 30, Year 1
    Exchange rate SF1 = $0.953

Maritime's journal entries are as follows:

June 1, Year 1
Inventory   9,410
    Accounts payable   9,410

The purchase of the inventory at a cost of 10,000 Swiss francs and the related liability are translated at the spot rate on the date of purchase. Maritime now has a monetary position (the liability) that is exposed to exchange fluctuations. The price of the inventory has been fixed and is not exposed to exchange fluctuations, except in the situation where the market price in Swiss francs declines and the lower of cost or market rule is applied.[3] In such a case, the lower of cost or market rule would be applied by comparing the Canadian dollar historical cost of the inventory with the market price in Swiss francs translated at the current exchange rate.[4]

On the company's year-end, the account payable of 10,000 Swiss francs must be translated at the spot rate. The previously recorded amount ($9,410) is increased by $80 to reflect a translated liability of $9,490 (10,000 × 0.949).

June 30, Year 1

Exchange loss	80	
Accounts payable		80
To adjust the account payable to the spot rate		

The resulting foreign exchange loss would appear on the income statement for the year ended June 30.

On the settlement date, the exchange rate has increased from $0.949 to $0.953. The SF10,000 account payable is increased by $40 to reflect its translation at the spot rate at this date (10,000 × 0.953 = 9,530). The company purchases 10,000 Swiss francs from its bank at a cost of $9,530 and remits the francs to its Swiss supplier. The foreign exchange loss of $40 will appear on the income statement for the year ended June 30, Year 2. The following journal entries record the transactions:

July 30, Year 1

Exchange loss	40	
Accounts payable		40
To adjust the account payable to the spot rate		
Accounts payable	9,530	
Cash		9,530
Payment to supplier		

An Export Example   We will continue the illustration of the two-transaction approach by using an example of the export of goods by a Canadian company.

On November 15, Year 1, Regina Malt Producers Ltd. shipped a carload of malt to a brewery in the United States, with full payment to be received on January 31, Year 2. The selling price of the malt was US$26,000. Regina Malt has a December 31 year-end. The following exchange rates existed on the dates significant for accounting purposes:

Transaction date — Nov. 15, Year 1
    Selling price US$26,000
    Exchange rate US$1 = CDN$1.325
Year end — Dec. 31, Year 1
    Exchange rate US$1 = CDN$1.329
Settlement date — Jan. 31, Year 2
    Exchange rate US$1 = CDN$1.319

---

[3] See *CICA Handbook*, paragraph 1650.18.

[4] For example, if the market price of the inventory purchased had declined to SF9,950 on June 30 (assuming that none of the inventory purchased had been sold by year-end), the market price in Canadian dollars would be $9,443 (SF9,950 × 0.949). Because the translated market price is greater than the previous translated historical cost of $9,410, the lower of cost or market rule would not apply.

The journal entries required on the dates noted above are as follows:

Nov. 15, Year 1

Accounts receivable	34,450	
Sales		34,450

The accounts receivable and the sales are recorded at the November 15 spot rate (US26,000 × 1.325 = CDN$34,450). The sales amount has been established and is unaffected by future exchange rate fluctuations. The accounts receivable (a monetary item) is at risk to exchange rate fluctuations. Note that while accounts receivable has been recorded at CDN$34,450, it is in fact a receivable of US$26,000.

At the company's year-end, the exchange rate has changed to US$1 = CDN$1.329, and the receivable must appear in the financial statements at $34,554 (US$26,000 × 1.329 = CDN$34,554). The following journal entry adjusts the accounts receivable to the year-end spot rate:

Dec. 31, Year 1

Accounts receivable	104	
Exchange gain		104

This exchange gain will appear in the company's Year 1 income statement.

By January 31, Year 2, which is the settlement date, the value of the U.S. dollar has declined relative to the Canadian dollar. When Regina Malt collects US$26,000 from its customer and delivers the U.S. dollars to its bank, it only receives CDN$34,294 (26,000 × 1.319). The journal entry to record the receipt of US$26,000, and its conversion to Canadian dollars and the resultant loss, is as follows:

Jan. 31, Year 2

Cash	34,294	
Exchange loss	260	
Accounts receivable		34,554
Payment from U.S. customer		

The exchange loss of $260 will appear in the Year 2 income statement. Note that the actual exchange loss between the transaction date and the settlement date was $156 (34,450 – 34,294). Because the company's year-end occurred between these two dates, the exchange loss will appear in two income statements in the following manner:

Year 1 income statement	
Exchange gain	$104
Year 2 income statement	
Exchange loss	260
Total exchange loss on the transaction	$156

The previous examples have illustrated the concept that exchange gains and losses resulting from the translation of a *current monetary position* (i.e., a receivable or payable that is due within one year from the date of a balance sheet) are reflected in income in the year in which they occur. Note that these exchange gains and losses are actually unrealized in the sense that they result from the translation of a liability or a receivable. The actual exchange gain or loss results from the settlement of the position, as was illustrated above. In the United Kingdom and the United States, the same concept has been applied to *noncurrent monetary positions*. In Canada, any exchange gains or losses resulting from the translation of noncurrent monetary positions have been treated differently. This is discussed in the next section.

Transaction Gains and Losses from Noncurrent Monetary Items

Many Canadian companies borrow money in foreign markets, mainly because the capital markets in Canada are relatively small. Before Section 1650 was issued in 1983, Canadian companies often translated their foreign debt at a historical rate throughout the term of the loan. The rate used was usually the spot rate in effect on the date of the original borrowing. This resulted in no exchange gains or losses being reported during the life of the loan. Of course, an exchange gain or loss had to be reported in the period when the loan came due for payment, if the exchange rate had changed since the date of the original borrowing.

The Defer-and-Amortize Approach This approach was removed from the *Handbook* effective January 1, 2002, but because it was in use for so many years in Canada, and had a pronounced effect on financial reporting, it deserves some mention at this time. When Section 1650 was first introduced into the *Handbook*, it required that monetary items denominated in foreign currencies be adjusted to reflect the current rate on each balance sheet date. Gains and losses from translating current monetary items were immediately reflected in income in the same manner as our previous examples have illustrated. However, gains and losses from the translation of monetary items due beyond one year from the date of a balance sheet were *not* reflected in income immediately, but rather were deferred and amortized.

Take for example a Canadian company issuing bonds denominated in foreign currency due in 10 years. If, at the end of the first year, the translation of the liability at the current rate resulted in an exchange loss of $10,000, only $1,000 would be reflected in the Year 1 income statement, while the balance sheet would show the balance as a deferred exchange loss of $9,000 among the assets. Each year until maturity a loss of $1,000 would be charged against income and the amount of the deferred loss on the balance sheet would be reduced by this amount. At the end of the second year, a translation gain of $18,000 would be deferred and amortized over nine years. Thus $2,000 would be immediately reflected in income, offset by a $1,000 amortization of the previous year's translation loss, while a $16,000 deferred gain appeared on the liability side of the balance sheet. This approach was adopted to soften the impact that foreign currency changes would have on the reported incomes of Canadian companies.

The defer-and-amortize approach, while popular with many corporate managers, was nonetheless subject to criticism. Because the IASB, the G4+1 countries of Australia, New Zealand, Great Britain, and the United States, and the other European Union countries plus Japan did not allow this method, Canada stood out as being out of step with the rest of the industrialized world. In addition, it was argued that the accounting and economic effects resulting from foreign exchange volatility could be avoided if management employed sound hedging practices, and that the defer-and-amortize smoothing simply hides the real impact of being in an unhedged position. Finally, it was hard to conceptualize the fact that a loss that had been granted deferral status is really an asset.

Canadian companies that have registered their securities with the SEC in the United States are required to reconcile their reported Canadian GAAP income to the income number that would have resulted if U.S. GAAP had been used. The differences that resulted from the defer-and-amortize policy accounted for a substantial portion of the total differences in many cases.

A Practical Problem with Defer-and-Amortize   An interesting example of the *Handbook*'s requirements apparently being circumvented can be seen in the 2000 financial statements of Air Canada. The company has four subordinated perpetual bond issues outstanding. One is for ¥49 billion, another is for DM200 million, and two are for a total of SF500 million. When these bonds were issued, the amount received totalled CDN$840 million. If the company had translated the liability at the current rate on December 31, 2000, the balance sheet amount would have been reported as CDN$1.25 billion. But Air Canada valued the bonds in its balance sheet at $840 million and disclosed the difference in the footnotes. In other words, it translated the bonds at the historical rate on the date of issuance and made no provision for the foreign exchange fluctuations that occurred after that date. The reasons given for this treatment were that these are perpetual callable bonds, and the company's management consided it highly improbable that the bonds would ever be called.

Because there is no maturity date, the Canadian standard of defer-and-amortize could not be applied. But as indicated previously, paragraph 1650.16 of the *Handbook* required an adjustment of monetary items denominated in foreign currency on each balance sheet date. The following paragraphs clearly describe the treatment of the resulting exchange gains and losses that existed at that time.

> An exchange gain or loss of the reporting enterprise that arises on translation or settlement of a foreign currency denominated monetary item or a non-monetary item carried at market should be included in the determination of net income for the current period, except for:
>
> (a) any portion that has been included in income of previous accounting periods; and
>
> (b) any exchange gain or loss related to a foreign currency denominated monetary item with a fixed or ascertainable life extending beyond the end of the following fiscal year (see paragraph 1650.23). [1650.20]
>
> If the monetary item does not have a fixed or ascertainable life, the exchange gain or loss would be included in the determination of net income for the current period. [1650.22]

While it is difficult to reconcile Air Canada's accounting policy regarding this foreign debt with the *Handbook*'s requirements at the time its 2000 financial statements were issued, we must not forget that there were at that time two major components to Canadian GAAP. One was the reflection of a monetary item at the current rate in the balance sheet, and the other was the deferral and amortization of certain of the exchange gains and losses that resulted. In a situation of perpetual debt the satisfaction of both components would have been impossible. It seems that Air Canada and its auditors (it received a clear audit opinion) felt that the method chosen was an acceptable approach.

Now that defer-and-amortize has been eliminated as an acceptable practice, Air Canada will be forced to report these bonds at current rates and take the resultant loss into income. To avoid such a loss, Air Canada may take steps to effectively hedge these liabilities.

The Immediate Recognition Approach In order to bring Canada's standard into the mainstream, the Accounting Standards Board amended Section 1650 effective January 1, 2002, and removed the defer-and-amortize provisions. As a result, accounting for foreign currency denominated debt has been substantially simplified, as the following example will illustrate.

Example Sable Company has a calendar year-end. On January 1, Year 1, the company borrowed 2,000,000 Swiss francs from a Swiss bank. The loan is to be repaid on January 1, Year 5, and requires interest at 8 percent to be paid each December 31. Both the annual interest payments and the loan repayment are to be made in Swiss francs.

During the term of the loan, the following exchange rates necessary for our analysis were in effect:

Jan. 1, Year 1	SF1 = $0.945
Average, Year 1	SF1 = $0.942
Dec. 31, Year 1	SF1 = $0.939
Average, Year 2	SF1 = $0.940
Dec. 31, Year 2	SF1 = $0.942
Dec. 31, Year 3	SF1 = $0.941
Dec. 31, Year 4	SF1 = $0.946

Sable Company would record the transactions as follows:

Jan. 1, Year 1

Cash	1,890,000	
Loan payable (2,000,000 × 0.945)		1,890,000

This entry records the incurrence of a four-year loan of SF2,000,000 translated at the current exchange rate. On December 31, the company purchases 160,000 Swiss francs (2,000,000 × 8 percent) from its bank to make the interest payment, at a cost of $150,240 (160,000 × 0.939). A question arises as to whether the amount paid should be reflected as the interest expense for the past year. Remember that interest expense was SF160,000, which accrued throughout the year. It seems logical, therefore, to translate the interest expense using the average of the Year 1 exchange rates, or better still to translate the monthly interest at the average for each month. In either case, when the interest is actually paid at the end of the year an exchange gain or loss will have to be recorded. Using the average exchange rate for Year 1, the journal entries to record the interest expense and payment are as follows:

Dec. 31, Year 1

Interest expense	150,720	
Exchange gain		480
Cash		150,240

To record interest expense at the average Year 1 rate of SF1 = $0.942, and the payment of interest at the year-end rate of SF1 = $0.939

On December 31, the loan is translated for financial statement purposes at $1,878,000 (2,000,000 × 0.939). The next entry adjusts the loan payable to the amount required on that date:

Dec. 31, Year 1
Loan payable   12,000
    Exchange gain   12,000

The $12,480 total exchange gain resulting from the interest payment and the translation of the loan will appear in the Year 1 income statement.

The Year 2 journal entries to record the interest expense of SF160,000 at an average rate of $0.940, and the payment of interest when the year-end rate is $0.942, will be as follows:

Dec. 31, Year 2
Interest expense   150,400
Exchange loss   320
    Cash   150,720

On December 31, Year 2, the loan is translated for financial statement purposes at $1,884,000 (2,000,000 × 0.942). The loan account still contains the December 31, Year 1, balance of $1,878,000. Therefore, the account balance must be increased by $6,000 with the following entry:

Dec. 31, Year 2
Exchange loss   6,000
    Loan payable   6,000

A $6,320 exchange loss, made up of the loss from translating the loan liability and the exchange loss resulting from the payment of the interest for the year, will appear in the Year 2 income statement.

Journal entries for years 3 and 4 will not be illustrated; however, the following summarizes the yearly exchange gains and losses from translating this loan liability.

	Total	*Year 1*	*Year 2*	*Year 3*	*Year 4*
Exchange gain (loss)	$(2,000)	$12,000	$(6,000)	$2,000	$(10,000)

Accounting for Hedges

The previous examples illustrated the accounting for the foreign exchange gains and losses that result from holding a foreign currency denominated monetary position during a period of exchange rate changes. If an enterprise wishes to protect itself from the economic (and accounting) effects that result from such a position, there are many possible ways. This type of protection is generally referred to as "hedging," which can be defined as a means of transferring risk arising from foreign exchange (or interest rate, or price) fluctuations from those who wish to avoid it to those who are willing to assume it.[5] In order to hedge the risk of exchange rate fluctuations, a company takes a foreign currency position opposite to the position that it wishes to protect. Section 1650 suggests that the following items could act as a hedge:[6]

---

[5] See John E. Stewart. "The Challenges of Hedge Accounting." *Journal of Accountancy* (November 1989), pp. 48–56.
[6] *CICA Handbook*, paragraph 1650.47.

- *A foreign exchange contract.* Examples include:
  - forward exchange contracts
  - foreign currency futures contracts
  - foreign currency option contracts.
- *A foreign currency denominated monetary item.* An item such as this can act as a hedge if it is opposite in position to the item being hedged. Examples include:
  - holding foreign currency denominated marketable securities as a hedge of a liability in the same currency
  - having foreign currency denominated debt act as a hedge of the net investment in a self-sustaining foreign subsidiary.[7]
- *A nonmonetary foreign currency denominated asset.* For example, land situated in a foreign country could act as a hedge of foreign currency denominated debt if it appears reasonable that it could be sold at the maturity date of the debt.
- *A future revenue stream denominated in a foreign currency.* For example, a contract for future services that will generate the receipt of foreign currency could be designated as a hedge of a liability denominated in the same foreign currency.

The *Handbook*'s guidelines for accepting items as hedges for accounting purposes are as follows:

> If a foreign exchange contract, asset, liability or future revenue stream is to be regarded as a hedge of a specific foreign currency exposure:
> (a) it should be identified as a hedge of the item(s) to which it relates; and
> (b) there should be reasonable assurance that it is and will continue to be effective as a hedge. [1650.50]

As indicated, a company can obtain a hedge in many ways. It is beyond the scope of this book to present accounting examples for all of the items mentioned; however, forward exchange contracts provide an excellent illustration of the basic concepts involved.

Forward Exchange Contracts

A forward exchange contract is one in which a bank and its customer agree to exchange currencies at a set price on a future date. Forward contracts can be either fixed dated or option dated. A fixed dated contract specifies a fixed date such as June 18. An option dated contract specifies a certain period such as the month of June. There are two major reasons for entering into a forward exchange contract: to hedge an existing monetary position, and to hedge an expected monetary position.

Below we illustrate the recording of the forward exchange contract in the accounting records. Some accountants object to this procedure because forward exchange contracts are "executory" in nature. An executory contract is one in which neither party has performed its obligation to the other. Most contracts trigger accounting recognition only when one of the parties fulfils the obligation as agreed.

---

[7] Self-sustaining subsidiaries are discussed in Chapter 13.

For example, when a company places an order with a manufacturer for the purchase of machinery, neither party makes an accounting entry. The delivery of the machinery, or a down payment prior to delivery, results in accounting recognition by both parties because of the performance by one.

While forward exchange contracts are certainly executory, they are also firm commitments, and once entered cannot be cancelled. For this reason we feel that it is preferable to record the contract, provided that the resulting "assets and liabilities" are *not* reflected as such in the company's financial statements. Furthermore, the Accounting Standards Committee seemed to envision the recording of hedges with the statement "both the hedge and the item that is hedged would be translated at the current exchange rate" (*Handbook*, paragraph 1650.53).

The actual accounting entries involve recording the forward contract at the spot rate on the date of entering the contract, and recording a receivable or payable at the contract's forward rate, with the difference reflected as a premium or discount. If the forward rate is greater than the spot rate, the difference is called a premium. If the forward rate is less than the spot rate, the difference is a discount. The eventual disposition of the premium/discount depends on whether the contract is hedging an existing monetary position or an expected monetary position.

If the contract hedges an existing monetary position, the premium/discount is accounted for as a period expense and is amortized on a rational basis over the life of the contract. For a contract to purchase foreign currency from a bank, a premium results in hedge expense and a discount in hedge revenue (negative expense). For a contract to sell (deliver) foreign currency, a premium results in hedge revenue and a discount in hedge expense.

If the forward contract hedges an expected monetary position, the accounting for the premium/discount is different:

> When a purchase or sale of goods or services in a foreign currency is hedged before the transaction, the Canadian dollar price of such goods or services is established by the terms of the hedge. [1650.52]

This means that the contract's forward rate establishes the cost of items to be purchased or the selling price of items to be sold. Any premiums/discounts recorded at the inception of the forward contract are subsequently adjusted to determine the price of items purchased or sold.

We will illustrate the hedge of an *existing* monetary position and then the hedge of an *expected* monetary position. We will then illustrate the speculative use of forward contracts.

Hedging an Existing Monetary Position   Vulcan Corporation of Toronto, Ontario, has a December 31 year-end. On November 1, Year 1, when the Swiss franc was worth $0.87, Vulcan sold merchandise to a Swiss customer for SF200,000. The terms of the sale required payment in full on February 15, Year 2. On November 15, Year 1, the spot rate was SF1 = $0.865 and the three-month forward rate was SF1 = $0.842. In order to protect the account receivable from further exchange losses, Vulcan entered into a contract with its bank on this date, to deliver SF200,000 in three months' time. The spot rate at year-end was SF1 = $0.869. On February 15, Year 2, Vulcan received SF200,000 from the customer and settled the forward contract with the bank. The significant dates are as follows:

Transaction date — Nov. 1, Year 1
  Sale of merchandise
  Selling price SF200,000
  Spot rate SF1 = $0.87

Hedge date — Nov. 15, Year 1
  Forward contract to deliver SF200,000
  Spot rate SF1 = $0.865
  Three-month forward rate SF1 = $0.842

Year-end — Dec. 31, Year 1
  Spot rate SF1 = $0.869

Settlement date — Feb. 15, Year 2
  Spot rate SF1 = $0.86

Vulcan will record the sale and the receivable at the spot rate on the transaction date with the following journal entry:

Nov. 1, Year 1

Accounts receivable	174,000	
Sales		174,000
SF200,000 × 0.87 = 174,000		

On November 15, the receivable is hedged when the spot rate is SF1 = $0.865. The exchange loss that occurred during the period when the account receivable was *not* hedged is recorded next, followed by the entry to record the forward contract.

Nov. 15, Year 1

Exchange gains and losses	1,000	
Accounts receivable		1,000
Exchange loss prior to the date of hedge, SF200,000 × (0.87 − 0.865)		
Receivable from bank	168,400	
Discount on contract	4,600	
Forward contract — SF		173,000
To record forward contract		

The receivable from the bank is recorded at the forward rate and represents the amount of Canadian dollars that Vulcan will receive when it delivers SF200,000 to the bank in three months (200,000 × 0.842). As this is denominated in Canadian dollars, it will not be affected by subsequent changes in the spot rate. The forward contract represents an obligation of Vulcan to deliver SF200,000 to the bank in three months' time and is denominated in Swiss francs. It was translated at the spot rate on this date (200,000 × 0.865). The accounting records now contain the account receivable and the hedge (the forward contract), both of which are denominated in Swiss francs. If exchange rates change later on, gains or losses on one will be offset by equal losses or gains on the other. The discount on the contract represents the total expense for the three-month hedge.

At year-end, both the account receivable from the Swiss customer and the forward contract are adjusted to the December 31 spot rate; also, the hedge expense for one-and-a-half months of the contract period is recorded.

Dec. 31, Year 1

Accounts receivable	800	
Exchange gains and losses		800

To adjust the account receivable to the December 31 spot rate
— SF200,000 × (0.869 – 0.865)

Exchange gains and losses	800	
Forward contract — SF		800

To adjust the forward contract to the December 31 spot rate
— SF200,000 × (0.869 – 0.865)

Hedge expense	2,300	
Discount on contract		2,300

To amortize the discount — $(4{,}600 \div 3 \times 1^1/2)$

Financial statements are prepared as at December 31. The following partial trial balance is presented to show only the accounts used to record these particular transactions.

PARTIAL TRIAL BALANCE
December 31, Year 1

	Dr.	Cr.
Accounts receivable	$173,800	
Exchange gains and losses	1,000	
Hedge expense	2,300	
Sales		174,000
Receivable from bank	168,400	
Discount on contract	2,300	
Forward contract — SF		173,800
	$347,800	$347,800

The accounts associated with the hedge have been segregated in the trial balance to emphasize their nature. These executory contract items should be shown at their net amount in the balance sheet because they do not represent actual assets and liabilities of the company. The presentation of the items shown on the trial balance in the year-end financial statements is shown next.

VULCAN CORP.
PARTIAL BALANCE SHEET
December 31, Year 1

Assets

Accounts receivable	$173,800
Other items	XXX
	$ XXX

Liabilities and shareholders' equity

Deferred foreign exchange	$ 3,100
Other items	XXX
	$ XXX

VULCAN CORP.
PARTIAL INCOME STATEMENT
for the Year Ended December 31, Year 1

Sales		$174,000
Expenses:		
Foreign exchange loss	1,000	
Hedge expense	2,300	
Other	XXX	XXX
Net income		$ XXX

The amount of the deferred foreign exchange credit shown in the balance sheet is obtained by netting the following hedge accounts:

Forward contract — SF		$173,800 Cr.
Receivable from bank	168,400 Dr.	
Discount on contract	2,300 Dr.	170,700 Dr.
		$ 3,100 Cr.

On the February 15 settlement date, the receivable from the Swiss customer and the forward contract are adjusted to the spot rate of SF1 = $0.86, and the remaining discount on the contract is amortized with the following entries:

Feb. 15, Year 2

Exchange gains and losses	1,800	
Accounts receivable		1,800

To adjust the account receivable to the spot rate —
SF200,000 × (0.869 – 0.86)

Forward contract — SF	1,800	
Exchange gains and losses		1,800

To adjust the forward contract to the spot rate —
SF200,000 × (0.869 – 0.86)

Hedge expense	2,300	
Discount on contract		2,300

To amortize remainder of discount

The Swiss customer sends SF200,000 to Vulcan, which is recorded in a Swiss franc cash account. Vulcan delivers the SF200,000 to the bank to discharge its forward contract obligation and receives C$168,400 as agreed. The following journal entries record these events:

Feb. 15, Year 2

Cash — SF	172,000	
Accounts receivable		172,000

Collection from Swiss customer

Forward contract — SF	172,000	
Cash — SF		172,000

Delivery of francs to bank

Cash	168,400	
Receivable from bank		168,400

Receipt of Canadian dollars from bank

Hedging an Expected Monetary Position   The next example illustrates the recording of the hedge of an *expected* monetary position. Note that in the previous example, the contract discount was treated as an expense of hedging. In this example, the discount or premium is accounted for as an adjustment to the cost of the transaction because the Canadian dollar price has been established by the forward contract.

Example   On May 14, Year 2, when the spot rate was US$1 = CDN$1.26, Manning Inc. of Vancouver, British Columbia, ordered merchandise from an American supplier for US$350,000. Delivery was scheduled for the month of June, with payment in full to be made before August 31, Year 2.

Upon placing the order, Manning immediately entered into a forward contract with its bank to purchase US$350,000 in August at the forward rate of US$1 = CDN$1.28.

The merchandise was received on June 3, Year 2, when the spot rate was US$1 = CDN$1.268. On June 30, Year 2, the company's year-end, the spot rate was US$1 = CDN$1.272. On August 15, Year 2, when the spot rate was US$1 = CDN$1.285, Manning purchased the U.S. dollars and paid its supplier.

The significant dates for accounting purposes are shown in the following recap of events:

Commitment date — May 14, Year 2.
    Merchandise ordered — cost US$350,000.

Hedge date — May 14, Year 2.
    Forward contract to purchase US$350,000 in August.
    Spot rate US$1 = CDN$1.260
    Aug. forward rate US$1 = CDN$1.280

Delivery date — June 3, Year 2
    Received merchandise ordered.
    Spot rate US$1 = CDN$1.268

June year-end — June 30, Year 2
    Spot rate US$1 = CDN$1.272

Settlement date — Aug. 15, Year 2
    Purchased U.S. funds and paid supplier.
    Spot rate US$1 = CDN$1.285

Manning would not make a journal entry to record the merchandise ordered. However, the hedging of the commitment by entering into a forward contract to purchase U.S. dollars would be recorded with the following entry:

May 14, Year 2		
Forward contract	441,000	
Premium on contract	7,000	
Payable to bank		448,000
To record forward contract		

"Payable to bank" is recorded at the forward rate and represents the amount of Canadian dollars that Manning will pay the bank in August when it purchases US$350,000. The amount recorded will not be affected by future exchange rate fluctuations. The forward contract is the hedge of the expected future liability. It is denominated in U.S. dollars and represents Manning's right to receive U.S. dollars from the bank in August. It was translated at the spot rate on this date (350,000 × 1.260). Note that the net balance of these executory contract accounts is zero, and if a balance sheet were prepared at this time the accounts would not be shown.

The receipt of the merchandise from the American supplier is recorded as follows:

June 3, Year 2

Inventory	443,800	
Account payable		443,800

To record the inventory purchase and the account payable at the June 3 spot rate (350,000 × 1.268)

The next two entries adjust the forward contract to the spot rate on June 3, and close the resulting deferred exchange gain and the premium on the forward contract to the cost of the inventory purchased.

Forward contract	2,800	
Deferred exchange gain		2,800

To adjust forward contract to the June 3 spot rate — 350,000 × (1.268 – 1.260)

Inventory	4,200	
Deferred exchange gain	2,800	
Premium on contract		7,000

To close exchange gain and premium on forward contract to inventory

The total inventory cost is now $448,000, and is equal to the forward rate of the contract. This cost will not change unless the lower of cost or market rule needs to be applied. The forward contract and the account payable to the supplier are now equal in amount, and any future exchange gains and losses will offset each other.

At the company's year-end, the contract and the account payable are adjusted to reflect the spot rate on that date. To this end, the following entries are made:

June 30, Year 2

Forward contract	1,400	
Exchange gains and losses		1,400

To adjust forward contract to June 30 spot rate — 350,000 × (1.272 – 1.268)

Exchange gains and losses	1,400	
Accounts payable		1,400

To adjust account payable to June 30 spot rate — 350,000 × (1.272 – 1.268)

Financial statements can now be prepared. The following partial trial balance shows only the accounts used to record the inventory purchase and the hedge.

PARTIAL TRIAL BALANCE
June 30, Year 2

	Dr.	Cr.
Inventory	$448,000	
Accounts payable		445,200
Forward contract	445,200	
Payable to bank		448,000
	$893,200	$893,200

The balances in the hedge accounts are netted and presented on the balance sheet as a deferred credit:

Payable to bank	$448,000	Cr.
Forward contract	445,200	Dr.
Net	$ 2,800	Cr.

Because the income statement has not been affected by the transactions to date, the following partial balance sheet shows the disposition of the accounts in the trial balance:

MANNING INC.
PARTIAL BALANCE SHEET
June 30, Year 2

Assets	
Inventory	$448,000
Other items	XXX
	$ XXX
Liabilities and shareholders' equity	
Accounts payable	$445,200
Deferred foreign exchange	2,800
Other items	XXX
	$ XXX

The following entries are made on the date of settlement:

Aug. 15, Year 2		
Exchange gains and losses	4,550	
Accounts payable		4,550
To adjust account payable to the August 15 spot rate — 350,000 × (1.285 – 1.272)		
Forward contract	4,550	
Exchange gains and losses		4,550
To adjust forward contract to the August 15 spot rate — 350,000 × (1.285 – 1.272)		
Payable to bank	448,000	
Cash		448,000
Payment to bank		

Cash — US$	449,750	
Forward contract		449,750
Receipt of US$350,000 from bank, translated at the		
August 15 spot rate		
Accounts payable	449,750	
Cash — US$		449,750
Cash sent to U.S. supplier		

Speculative Forward Exchange Contracts   Section 1650 does not cover the accounting for speculative forward contracts. If such contracts were entered into by Canadian companies, accountants would probably seek guidance from the U.S. standard on foreign currency transactions.[8] This standard requires that the contract be valued at forward rates throughout its life, with any gains or losses reflected in income as they occur. A company may enter into a forward exchange contract purely to speculate on future exchange movements. For example, a company might enter into a contract to purchase foreign currency at a 60-day forward rate in anticipation that the spot rate in 60 days' time will be greater than the original forward rate. If its projection turns out to be accurate, it would purchase the foreign currency from the bank at the contracted price, and immediately sell the currency to the bank at the higher spot rate.

Alternatively, a company might find itself holding a speculative forward contract when this was not its original intention. In the previous example, Manning Inc. ordered merchandise at a cost of US$350,000 on May 14, Year 2, and immediately hedged the price with a forward contact. Let us assume that on May 30, Year 2, it cancelled its purchase commitment with its American supplier. The forward contract that previously hedged an expected monetary position has now become a speculative forward contract. The events are as follows:

Commitment date — May 14, Year 2
    Merchandise ordered — cost US$350,000
    Entered forward contract to purchase US$350,000 in August
    Spot rate — US$1 = CDN$1.260
    Aug. forward rate — US$1 = CDN$1.280

Cancellation date — May 30, Year 2
    Merchandise order cancelled.
    Aug. forward rate — US$1 = CDN$1.281

Year end — June 30, Year 2
    Aug. forward rate — US$1 = CDN$1.283

Contract settlement date — Aug. 15, Year 2
    Spot rate — US$1 = CDN$1.285

We will now illustrate the journal entries that Manning would have to make.

May 14, Year 2		
Forward contract	441,000	
Premium on contract	7,000	
Payable to bank		448,000
To record forward contract		

---

[8]   Statement of Financial Accounting Standards #52, "Foreign Currency Translation." Financial Accounting Standards Board, 1981.

"Forward contract" was recorded at the spot rate, "Payable to bank" at the August forward rate. The forward contract account is the hedge of the expected monetary position. When the commitment to purchase merchandise is cancelled on May 30, Year 2, this hedge becomes a speculative forward contract. "Payable to bank" remains unchanged because it is denominated in Canadian dollars. However, the forward contract account is denominated in U.S. dollars, and FASB's Statement #52 requires that it be adjusted to the forward rate for financial statement purposes throughout the life of the contract. The premium account is no longer useful. The following entry closes this account and adjusts "Forward contract" to the August forward rate of US$1 = CDN$1.281.

May 30, Year 2

Forward contract	7,350	
Premium on contract		7,000
Exchange gain		350

To close the premium account and adjust the contract to the August forward
rate on this date

The company's year end is June 30, and the August forward rate is now US$1 = CDN$1.283. The forward contract is adjusted to reflect this forward rate.

June 30, Year 2

Forward contract	700	
Exchange gain		700

To adjust contract to the August forward rate

A partial trial balance showing only the hedge accounts is as follows:

PARTIAL TRIAL BALANCE
June 30, Year 2

	Dr.	Cr.
Forward contract	$449,050	—
Exchange gain	—	1,050
Payable to bank	—	448,000
	$449,050	$449,050

The exchange gain would appear in the Year 2 income statement. "Forward contract" and "Payable to bank" are both accounts of an executory contract and should be netted and presented on the balance sheet as a deferred foreign exchange charge of $1,050.

On August 15, Year 2, Manning pays the bank CDN$448,000 and takes delivery of US$350,000, which it immediately sells back at the current spot rate. It receives CDN$449,750 (350,000 × 1.285). The following entries record these events:

Aug. 15, Year 2

Payable to bank	448,000	
Cash		448,000

Pay bank as per contract

Cash — U.S.	449,750	
Forward contract		449,050
Exchange gain		700

Receive US$350,000 from bank as per contract translated at the August 15 spot rate

Cash	449,750	
Cash — U.S.		449,750

Sell US$350,000 to bank at spot rate.

Hedging a Future Revenue Stream

As mentioned earlier, *Handbook* Section 1650 was amended on January 1, 2002, and as a result the defer-and-amortize provisions were removed. Previous exposure drafts issued to accomplish the same thing also presented illustrations of the use of hedge accounting; because while the *Handbook* discusses the concept of hedge accounting, it leaves the practical implementation to the imagination and judgment of the accountant. Though the expanded discussion on hedge accounting from the exposure drafts was not carried forward with the new amendments, it nonetheless presented some interesting illustrations as to how hedge accounting might be applied. The discussion that follows is based on the material contained in the exposure drafts.

The current Section 1650 suggests that a future foreign currency revenue stream could serve as a hedge for long-term debt denominated in a foreign currency, while one of the previous exposure drafts took the opposite view and suggested that long-term debt could act as a hedge against a future revenue stream. Both of these would be accomplished by applying the concepts of hedge accounting, the purpose of which is to ensure that the gains or losses from a hedged position are offset in the same accounting period by the losses and gains from the hedging instrument. Following the concept of hedge accounting, if gains or losses from one of the items must be recognized before the losses or gains from the other item, the gains and losses that are required to be recognized are deferred. For example, in the case of long-term debt acting as a hedge for a future revenue stream, the use of hedge accounting would require that any exchange gains and losses that occur from the translation of the debt at current rates be deferred, and recognized in income only when the foreign currency revenues occur. The hedging instrument is monetary (the long-term debt) and the item hedged is an anticipated foreign currency exposure (the future revenue stream) — a necessary condition for the use of hedge accounting. The discussion in the exposure drafts also provided a reminder of the obvious when it suggested that hedge accounting as described is not required when the item hedged and the hedging instrument are both monetary items, because recorded gains from one are automatically offset by recorded losses from the other.

In order for long-term debt to be considered as a hedge of a future revenue stream in accordance with the provisions contained in the exposure drafts, (a) management must designate both items as a hedge, (b) there must be a high degree of correlation between changes in exchange rates in both items,[9] and (c) it must be highly probable that the future revenue stream will occur. The following example illustrates the accounting when long-term debt is used as a hedge of a future revenue stream.

---

[9] This correlation between changes in exchange rates is of importance when the hedging instrument and the item to be hedged are denominated in different currencies.

Example   Alana Enterprises, a Canadian company that has carried out business activities in Switzerland for a number of years, has decided to protect itself against foreign currency fluctuations over the next three years, during which it expects a revenue stream of SF200,000 per year. On January 1, Year 1, the company borrows SF600,000, payable in full at the end of three years, and designates the loan as a hedge against the future three-year revenue stream. In order to simplify the illustration, we are going to omit the payment of yearly interest and assume that there is no difference between the exchange rate at the end of each year and the average exchange rate for that year.

Relevant exchange rates for the Swiss franc are as follows:

Jan. 1, Year 1	$0.852
Dec. 31, Year 1	$0.849
Dec. 31, Year 2	$0.835
Dec. 31, Year 3	$0.840

Applying the concepts of hedge accounting, Alana will make the following journal entries:

Jan. 1, Year 1

Cash	511,200	
Loan payable		511,200
(600,000 × 0.852)		

During Year 1 the revenue stream is recorded at the average exchange rate for the year. Thus, the following entry is recorded:

Cash	169,800	
Revenue		169,800
(200,000 × 0.849)		

On December 31, Year 1, the loan payable has to be reflected in the financial statements at the current rate. The entry to record the exchange gain on the loan payable resulting from a decrease in the exchange rate from $0.852 to $0.849 is as follows:

Dec. 31, Year 1

Loan payable	1,800	
Deferred exchange gain, Year 1		1,800
(600,000 × 0.003)		

One-third of the hedged revenue stream has been received, and so the following adjusting entry is made to match one-third of the gain from the hedge against the revenue received:

Dec. 31, Year 1

Deferred exchange gain, Year 1	600	
Exchange gain		600
(200/600 × 1,800)		

Two-thirds of the exchange gain is deferred to be matched against the foreign currency revenues when they are received in the following two years. The company has *lost* because it has received less revenue in Canadian dollars than would be the case if the exchange rate had not changed, but it has also *gained* due to the fact that its liability (measured in Canadian dollars) has decreased. The liability hedges the revenue stream; consequently, the gain in one offsets the loss in the other. The total revenue for the year is $170,400, which is made up of the translated revenue of $169,800 *plus* the recognized exchange gain on the hedge of $600. Note that this is the same amount as would have been received in translated revenue if the exchange rates had not changed since January 1, Year 1 (200,000 × 0.852). If the exchange rates do not change over the next two years, the total translated revenue *plus* the recognized revenue from the hedge will be $170,400 each year.

Note also that while the loan is still SF600,000, one-third of the foreign revenue stream has been received; therefore, one-third of this loan balance no longer qualifies as a hedge and is exposed to foreign currency risk. Because of this, any future exchange gains and losses on this portion must be reflected immediately in income.

During Year 2, revenue in Swiss francs is received and translated at the average rate. This results in the following entry:

Cash	167,000	
Revenue		167,000
(200,000 × 0.835)		

On December 31, the loan payable is reduced by $8,400 (600,000 × 0.014) to reflect its translation at the current rate; also, the gain on the one-third portion that no longer qualifies as a hedge is immediately reflected in income, and the balance of the gain from the hedge portion is initially deferred with the following entry:

Dec. 31, Year 2

Loan payable	8,400	
Exchange gain ($1/3 × 8,400$)		2,800
Deferred exchange gain, Year 2		5,600

The Year 2 deferred exchange gain hedges the foreign currency revenues of years 2 and 3. Year 2 revenue has been received and translated at the average exchange rate for the year. Therefore, the Year 2 portion (one-half) of the deferred gain is matched against this revenue with the following entry:

Dec. 31, Year 2

Deferred exchange gain, Year 2	2,800	
Exchange gain ($1/2 × 5,600$)		2,800

In addition, the portion of the Year 1 exchange gain must be matched against Year 2 revenues with the following entry:

Dec. 31, Year 2

Deferred exchange gain, Year 1	600	
Exchange gain		600

Remember that the purpose of the hedge was to ensure that the foreign currency revenue in Year 2 was at least $170,400 (200,000 × 0.852). The actual foreign revenue adjusted for the hedge gains was equal to this amount, as the following calculation indicates:

Foreign currency revenue (200,000 × 0.835)	$167,000
Exchange gain on Year 1 hedge	600
Exchange gain on Year 2 hedge	2,800
	$170,400

In addition, the Year 2 income statement will reflect the additional exchange gain ($2,800) that came from the portion of the loan that no longer qualifies as a hedge.

The balance of the deferred hedge gains that will appear on the December 31, Year 2, balance sheet is:

Deferred gain, Year 1		1,800	
Less reflected in income:			
Year 1	600		
Year 2	600	1,200	600
Deferred gain, Year 2		5,600	
Less reflected in income Year 2		2,800	2,800
Deferred hedge gains,			
December 31, Year 2			$3,400

Because SF400,000 from the total revenue of SF600,000 has been received at the end of Year 2, the loan balance that still qualifies as a hedge is only SF200,000.

The Year 3 entries to record the foreign currency revenues and to adjust the loan to the current rate are as follows:

Cash	168,000	
Revenue		168,000
(200,000 × 0.840)		

Dec. 31, Year 3		
Exchange loss	3,000	
Loan payable		3,000
(600,000 × 0.005)		

The foreign currency revenue has all been received, so none of the Year 3 hedge loss of $1,000 needs to be deferred. The remaining loss from the portion of the loan that is not a hedge ($2,000) is also expensed in the year.

A final entry is made to match the balance of the deferred hedge gains from prior years against the Year 3 foreign currency revenue:

Deferred exchange gain, Year 1	600	
Deferred exchange gain, Year 2	2,800	
Exchange gain		3,400

An entry would also be made to pay off the loan that is due on this date. The following calculation summarizes the amount reflected in net income in Year 3 from the foreign currency revenue, the hedge gains and losses, and the exchange loss from the non-hedge portion of the loan:

Foreign currency revenue (200,000 × 0.840)		$168,000
Year 1 and 2 exchange gains on hedge	3,400	
Year 3 exchange loss on hedge	1,000	2,400
Hedged foreign currency revenue		170,400
Remainder of Year 3 loan exchange loss		2,000
Effect on Year 3 net income		$168,400

This simplified example has illustrated the possible use of hedge accounting. In a more realistic situation, differences would occur because the average rates used to translate the revenue stream are different from the year-end rates used to translate the foreign currency loan, and the actual revenues would probably turn out to be different from those expected when the hedge was designated. However, the broad concepts illustrated would still apply, and because an increasing portion of the foreign currency denominated debt ceases to be eligible for a hedge each year, the resultant income recognition pattern is similar to the defer-and-amortize pattern that used to occur for foreign currency debt.

A Cautionary Note   A new financial instrument standard has been in the works for a number of years. It is being developed jointly by CICA and nine other international accounting bodies. When it is finally issued it may require all financial instruments to be recorded at fair market values, thereby clarifying the accounting standards for all hedging instruments, whether foreign currency or not. Because of this, it should be noted that this example may not be representative of hedge accounting in the future. Previous exposure drafts have not resulted in a new standard because CICA is reluctant to make changes to hedge accounting that might result in standards for foreign currency hedging instruments being inconsistent with similar items in the upcoming financial instruments standard.

SUMMARY

Transactions denominated in foreign currency are recorded in Canadian dollars at the spot rate in effect on the date of the transaction. A gain or loss is reflected in income if the exchange rate has changed at the date of settlement. If settlement has not occurred by the date of a balance sheet, the monetary balances are adjusted to the spot rate on that date. Gains or losses from the adjustment of all monetary items are taken into income.

The use of hedging instruments, such as forward exchange contracts, removes the risks associated with exchange rate changes. If all risks are removed, the hedge is "perfect." It also is possible to have a situation in which only a portion of a position is hedged and the balance is at risk, or in which, as was illustrated, a portion of the hedging instrument ceases to act as a hedge and becomes exposed to foreign currency risk.

SELF-STUDY PROBLEM 1

Hedging an Existing Monetary Position

On November 15, 2002, Domco Ltd. of Montreal sold merchandise to a customer located in Switzerland for SF100,000. The Swiss franc was trading at $.81 on that date, and the terms of the sale required the customer to pay the account on January 30, 2003. On December 1, when the spot rate was SF1 = $.805, Domco entered into a forward contract with its bank to deliver SF100,000 at the 60-day forward rate of SF1 = $.82.

On December 31, 2002, the company's year-end, the spot rate was SF1 = $.795. The Swiss customer paid Domco SF100,000 on January 30, 2003, and Domco settled the forward contract with its bank. The spot rate on that date was SF1 = .825.

Required:

(a) Prepare the journal entries required in 2002 and 2003.

(b) Prepare a partial balance sheet as at December 31, 2002, which shows the accounts receivable and the presentation of the hedge accounts.

Solution to Self-study Problem 1

(a) *Nov. 15, 2002*

Accounts receivable	81,000	
Sales		81,000
(SF100,000 × .81)		

Dec. 1, 2002

Exchange loss	500	
Accounts receivable		500
To adjust the receivable to the Dec. 1 spot rate of SF1 = $.805		

Receivable from bank (SF100,000 × .81)	82,000	
Premium on forward contract		1,500
Forward contract (SF100,000 × .805)		80,500
To record the hedge		

Dec. 31, 2002

Exchange gains/losses	1,000	
Accounts receivable		1,000
To adjust the receivable to the Dec. 31 spot rate of SF1 = $.795		

Forward contract	1,000	
Exchange gains and losses		1,000
To adjust the forward contract to the Dec. 31 spot rate		

Premium on forward contract	750	
Hedge revenue		750
To amortize the premium over the life of the contract ($1,500 × 30/60)		

Jan. 30, 2003

Accounts receivable	3,000	
Exchange gains/losses		3,000
To adjust the receivable to the spot rate of SF1 = $.825		

Exchange gains/losses	3,000	
Forward contract		3,000
To adjust the forward contract to the spot rate		

Cash — SF100,000	82,500	
Accounts receivable		82,500
Collect SF100,000 from customer		

Forward contract	82,500	
Cash — SF100,000		82,500
Deliver SF100,000 to bank		

Cash	82,000	
Receivable from bank		82,000
Receive $82,000 from bank as per forward contract		
Premium on contract	750	
Hedge revenue		750
To amortize remainder of premium		

(b)

DOMCO LTD
BALANCE SHEET
December 31, 2002

Assets			
Accounts receivable			$79,500
Deferred foreign exchange*			1,750
* *Receivable from bank*			82,000
Premium on forward contract		750	
Forward contract		79,500	80,250
Deferred foreign exchange			1,750

SELF-STUDY PROBLEM 2

Hedging an Expected Monetary Position

On October 15, 2002, Buycompany Ltd., located in Canada, signed a contract to purchase equipment from Sellcompany, which is located in a country whose currency is the foreign currency unit (FCU). The cost of the equipment was FCU200,000, and the terms of this purchase order called for delivery to be made within the first 15 days in December and payment in full no later than January 31, 2003.

Having signed the purchase order, Buycompany immediately entered into a forward contract with its bank to purchase FCU200,000 on January 31, 2003, at the forward rate of 1FCU = $1.22. The spot rate on October 15 was 1FCU = $1.20. The equipment was delivered on December 9 when the spot rate was 1FCU = $1.18. On December 31, the year-end of Buycompany, the spot rate was 1FCU = $1.19.

Buycompany paid the invoice for this equipment on January 31, 2003, at which time the spot rate was 1FCU = $1.24.

Required:

(a) Prepare all of Buycompany's journal entries related to the machinery purchase and the hedge.
(b) Prepare a partial balance sheet as at December 31, 2002, showing the equipment, the account payable, and the disposition of the hedge accounts.

Solution to Self-study Problem 2

(a)   *Oct. 15, 2002*

Forward contract (FCU 200,000 × 1.20)	240,000	
Premium on forward contract	4,000	
Payable to bank (FCU 200,000 × 1.22)		244,000
To record the forward contract		

Dec. 9, 2002

Equipment	236,000	
Accounts payable		236,000

To record the equipment acquisition at the spot rate of $1.18

Deferred exchange loss	4,000	
Forward contract		4,000

To adjust the forward contract to the spot rate on Dec. 9

Equipment	8,000	
Premium on forward contract		4,000
Deferred exchange loss		4,000

To close the exchange loss and premium accounts

Dec. 31, 2002

Exchange gains/losses	2,000	
Accounts payable		2,000

To adjust the account payable to the year-end spot rate of $1.19

Forward contract	2,000	
Exchange gains/losses		2,000

To adjust the forward contract to the year-end spot rate

Jan. 31, 2003

Exchange gains/losses	10,000	
Accounts payable		10,000

To adjust the payable to the spot rate of $1.24

Forward contract	10,000	
Exchange gains/losses		10,000

To adjust the forward contract to the spot rate

Payable to bank	244,000	
Cash		244,000

Pay bank as per contract

Cash — FCU 200,000	248,000	
Forward contract		248,000

Receive FCU 200,000 from bank

Accounts payable	248,000	
Cash – FCU 200,000		248,000

Deliver FCU 200,000 to Sellcompany

(b)

BUY COMPANY
BALANCE SHEET
December 31, 2002

Assets

Equipment	$244,000

Liabilities

Accounts payable	$238,000
Deferred foreign exchange*	6,000

* Payable to bank	244,000	
Forward contract	238,000	
Deferred foreign exchange	6,000	

REVIEW QUESTIONS

1. Briefly summarize the accounting issues arising from foreign currency denominated transactions.

2. What is the difference between pegged and floating exchange rates?

3. You read in the newspaper: "One U.S. dollar can be exchanged for 1.57 Canadian dollars." Is this a direct or an indirect quotation? If your answer is "indirect," what is the direct quotation? If your answer is "direct," what is the indirect quotation?

4. Differentiate between a "spot" rate and a "forward" rate.

5. Distinguish between the one-transaction and the two-transaction approaches.

6. How are foreign currency denominated assets and liabilities measured on the transaction date? How are they measured on a subsequent balance sheet date?

7. "The deferral of exchange gains and losses was adopted as a smoothing device." Explain.

8. List some ways that a Canadian company could hedge against foreign currency exchange rate fluctuations.

9. What are the reasons for acquiring a forward exchange contract?

10. If a foreign currency denominated payable has been hedged, why is it necessary to adjust the liability for balance sheet purposes?

11. How is the accounting for a speculative forward exchange contract different from that for hedging a monetary position?

12. Explain the application of lower of cost or market to inventory that was purchased from a foreign supplier.

13. How does the accounting for a forward exchange contract that hedges an *existing* monetary position differ from the accounting for one that hedges an *expected* monetary position?

14. What is the suggested financial statement treatment of recorded hedge accounts? Why?

15. What is meant by "hedge accounting"?

16. Would hedge accounting be used in a situation where the hedged item and the hedging instrument were both monetary items on a company's balance sheet? Explain.

17. When long-term debt hedges a revenue stream, a portion of the hedge becomes exposed to the risk of changes in exchange rates. Why is this?

MULTIPLE CHOICE

Use the following data for Questions 1 to 4.

On April 15, 2002, Bailey Inc. negotiated a large sale of their premium maple syrup to Sweet Co. for US$3,000,000. The contract was for a three-year term from the date of delivery of he goods. Bailey delivered the goods on July 15, 2002. The company has a December 31 year-end.

The exchange rates at various dates are given below.

April 15, 2002	US$1 = CDN$1.28
July 15, 2002	US$1 = CDN$1.30
December 31, 2002	US$1 = CDN$1.42
December 31, 2003	US$1 = CDN$1.28
December 31, 2004	US$1 = CDN$1.25
July 15, 2005	US$1 = CDN$1.15

In addition, the forward exchange contract rate for a July 15, 2005, contract was US$1 = CDN$1.22 on April 15, 2002, and US$1 = CDN$1.20 on July 15, 2002.

1. Assuming the transaction is *not* hedged, which of the following is the amount that will be used to record the receivable in Bailey's books at July 15, 2002?
    a. $3,000,000
    b. $3,840,000
    c. $3,900,000
    d. $4,260,000

2. Assuming the transaction is *not* hedged, which of the following is the amount that will be reported on Bailey's December 31, 2002, income statement as an exchange gain from this transaction?
    a. $0
    b. $300,000
    c. $360,000
    d. $420,000

3. Assuming the transaction *is* hedged on July 15, 2002, which of the following is the amount that will be used to record the receivable on Bailey's December 31, 2003, balance sheet?
    a. $3,600,000
    b. $3,660,000
    c. $3,840,000
    d. $3,900,000

4. Assuming the transaction *is* hedged on April 15, 2002, which of the following is the amount that will be used to report the receivable on Bailey's December 31, 2002, balance sheet?
    a. $3,600,000
    b. $3,660,000
    c. $3,840,000
    d. $4,260,000

    (*CGA adapted*)

5. During the current year, Roy Incorporated purchased marketable securities, which it intended to hold for 3 months for US$100,000 when the exchange rate was US$1 = CDN$1.25. At year-end the securities had a market value of US$95,000 and the exchange rate was $1.30. What will be the foreign exchange gain (loss) on translation at year-end?
    a. $1,500 loss.
    b. $4,750 gain.
    c. $5,000 gain.
    d. $6,500 loss.

    (*CICA adapted*)

6. A company purchases a piece of equipment from a Swiss supplier for SF100,000, payable 1 month later. The company enters into a foreign-exchange forward contract whereby it agrees to purchase francs on the payment date of the equipment. Considering the following exchange rates, what will the carrying value of the equipment be after the transaction has taken place?

When the order was placed: SF1 = CDN$0.83
When the equipment was received: SF1 = CDN$0.84
When the payment was made: SF1 = CDN$0.86
Foreign exchange contract rate: SF1 = CDN$0.85

    a. $83,000
    b. $84,000
    c. $85,000
    d. $86,000

(CICA adapted)

7. On October 12, 2002, Jiambalvo International, a clothing manufacturer, ordered bolts of fabric from an Asian supplier. The agreed upon price for the goods was FCU800,000. The fabric was received by Jiambalvo on December 1, 2002. The invoice was paid on December 28, 2002. All fabric from this order was in the company's inventory at their December 31 year-end. Exchanges rates during the period were as follows:

October 12   FCU1 = $.36
December 1   FCU1 = $.32
December 28   FCU1 = $.33
December 31   FCU1 = $.34

For inventory valuation purposes, what would be the cost the purchased fabric?
    a. $256,000
    b. $264,000
    c. $272,000
    d. $288,000

8. If a company hedges an *expected* foreign currency denominated payable position that will arise due to a capital asset purchase, how will the premium on the forward contract be treated?
    a. It will be amortized over the useful life of the related capital asset.
    b. It will be closed directly to retained earnings.
    c. It will be added to the balance of cumulative translation adjustment.
    d. It will be closed to the related capital asset account.

Use the following data for Questions 9 to 11.

PL Corporation has a December 31, 2002, year-end. It submitted a purchase order for US$30,000 of equipment on July 1, 2002, when the exchange rate was CDN$1 = US$0.6500. It received the equipment on September 30, 2002, when the exchange rate was US$0.6667; it paid US$20,000 to the supplier on December 1, 2002, when the exchange rate was US$0.6900. On December 31, 2002, the exchange rate was US$0.7000. The company uses straight-line amortization commencing in the month following acquisition. The equipment is expected to last 5 years and has no residual value.

9. What would be the net book value of PL's equipment on its December 31, 2002, balance sheet?
    a. $40,715
    b. $42,748
    c. $43,850
    d. $45,000

10. On PL's December 31, 2002, financial statements, what amount would the accounts payable relating to the equipment purchase be recorded at?
   a. $6,500
   b. $7,000
   c. $14,286
   d. $15,385

11. Assume PL entered into a forward contract with the bank for the remaining $10,000 accounts payable on December 1, 2002, to provide US$10,000 on January 31, 2003 — the expected date of payment to the equipment manufacturer. Assume the forward rate on December 1, 2002, was CDN$1 = US$0.6750. How much hedge expense would PL record for the year ended December 31, 2002?
   a. CDN$0
   b. CDN$161
   c. CDN$265
   d. CDN$322

(*CGA adapted*)

Use the following data for Questions 12 and 13.

On November 2, 2002, a company purchased a machine for 100,000 Swiss francs with payment required on March 1, 2003. To eliminate the risk of foreign exchange losses on this payable, the company entered into a forward exchange contract on December 1, 2002, to receive SF100,000 at a forward rate of SF1 = $2 on March 1, 2003. The spot rate was SF1 = $1.95 on November 2, 2002, and SF1 = $1.97 on December 1, 2002.

12. What is the amount of the premium or discount on the forward exchange contract?
   a. A premium of $3,000.
   b. A premium of $5,000.
   c. A discount of $3,000.
   d. A discount of $5,000.

(*CICA adapted*)

13. How should the premium or discount on the forward exchange contract be accounted for?
   a. It should be expensed on the inception date of the forward exchange contract.
   b. It should be expensed on the maturity date of the forward exchange contract.
   c. It should be expensed over the 3-month term of the forward exchange contract.
   d. It should be added to the cost of the machine.

(*CGA adapted*)

CASE

Case*   Long Life Enterprises was a long-established, Toronto-based company engaged in the importation and wholesale marketing of specialty grocery items originating in various countries of the western Pacific rim. They had recently also entered the high-risk business of exportation, to several of these same countries, of fresh Atlantic lobster and crab.

Although Canada has extensive trading relationships with several countries in the Pacific rim, these transactions were not normally priced or settled in terms of the Canadian dollar. Both the U.S. dollar and the Japanese yen were somewhat more

---

* Case prepared by Peter Secord, St. Mary's University.

common in these transactions. Further, various local currencies were involved, especially for small transactions involving specialty items, and a wide variety of credit terms were in use for both imports and exports. The entire situation was complicated by the perishable nature of some of the imports and the high mortality risk for both lobster and crab. Both situations led to uncertainty as to the face amount of the associated receivable or payable, and hindered the ability of the firm to adopt the policy of specific hedging of each of the receivable or payable contracts.

Most recently, the Canadian dollar had risen against other major currencies, leading to major losses on the large receivables outstanding because of the seasonal lobster harvest. More generally, management was concerned about losses that might arise from both export and import transactions. For the most recent fiscal year, foreign currency losses had exceeded gains by some $40,000 — an amount more than the company could afford during the present stage of rapid growth.

Required:

What steps would you propose to the management of Long Life Enterprises to reduce the costs associated with their receivables and payables? As a part of this process, suggest a way of structuring transactions or affairs that would reduce the impact of fluctuations in the relative values of currencies.

PROBLEMS

Note: Some problems use direct exchange rate quotations, others use indirect quotations.

Problem 1   Manitoba Exporters Inc. (MEI) sells Inuit carvings to countries throughout the world. On December 1, 2002, MEI sold 10,000 carvings to a wholesaler in a foreign country at a total cost of 600,000 foreign currency units (FCUs) when the spot rate was FCU1 = $0.741. The invoice required the foreign wholesaler to remit by April 1, 2003. On December 3, 2002, MEI entered into a hedge with the Royal Bank at the 120-day forward rate of FCU1 = $0.781.

The fiscal year-end of MEI is December 31, and on this date the spot rate was FCU1 = $0.757. The payment from the foreign customer was received on April 1, 2003, when the spot rate was FCU1 = $0.802.

Required:

(a) Prepare the journal entries to record:
   (i)   the sale and the hedge.
   (ii) any adjustments required on December 31.
   (iii) the cash received in 2003.
(b) Prepare a partial balance sheet of MEI on December 31, 2002, that shows the presentation of the receivable and the accounts associated with the hedge.

Problem 2   Almer Manufacturing Corp. (AMC), a Canadian company, manufactures instruments used to measure the moisture content of barley and wheat. The company sells primarily to the domestic market, but in 2000 it developed a small market in France. In 2001, AMC began purchasing semifinished components from a supplier in Mexico. The management of AMC is concerned about the possible adverse effects of foreign exchange fluctuations. To deal with this matter, all of AMC's foreign currency denominated receivables and payables are hedged with contracts with the company's bank. The year-end of AMC is December 31.

The following transactions occurred late in 2001:

to translate the related assets. Revenues and all other expenses are translated at the average of the rates that existed during the period covered by the income statement.[2] The rate that should be used is the actual rate in effect when the revenue was recognized and the expense incurred; but because of practical difficulties, the average rate is used as a surrogate for the actual rates. Share capital is translated at the historical rates when the shares were issued. This preserves the historical cost relationship of the share capital with the parent's investment account. Under this method, the working capital of the foreign entity is exposed to foreign exchange fluctuations, because only the current assets and liabilities are translated at current rates. Historically, managers found favour with this method because it enabled them to manage the amount at risk to foreign currency fluctuations by managing the size of the working capital. A working capital amount that is close to zero will not produce sizable exchange losses or gains.

Although the current/noncurrent method was popular, it has some serious shortcomings. While accounts receivable and current liabilities are translated at the current exchange rate and thus reflect the Canadian dollar equivalent of realizing or discharging these items on the date of the financial statements, noncurrent liabilities and noncurrent receivables are not translated in this manner. This difference in treatment is difficult to defend. The balance sheet valuation of inventories presents another problem. If the exchange rate changed between the date of purchasing inventory and the date of presenting it on the balance sheet, one would not be showing the inventory at its historical cost in Canadian dollars by translating it using the current rate.

The Monetary/Nonmonetary Method

This method translates monetary items on the balance sheet at current exchange rates; nonmonetary items are translated at historical rates. Thus cash, receivables, investments in bonds, and most liabilities are translated at the current rate, while inventories, investments in shares, and capital assets are translated at historical rates. Because monetary items represent money and claims to money that are fixed by contract, translating these items at current exchange rates results in a representation in today's dollars of amounts to be received or paid in the future. This is particularly true for current items, because the associated cash flows will occur fairly soon after the date of the balance sheet. However, it may not be true for noncurrent monetary items such as bond liabilities that mature many years in the future. In the latter case, the amount to be paid in dollars at some future maturity date may be vastly different from the translated amount for the liability today. Income statement items are translated using a mix of historical rates (for depreciation and amortization) and average rates for the period (for all other expenses and for revenues). Share capital is translated using historical rates. Under this method the firm's net monetary position (monetary assets less monetary liabilities) is exposed to fluctuating exchange rates.

A shortcoming of this method relates to the treatment of nonmonetary items carried at market values. Current price is the measurement base for cash and receivables. Translating these items at the current rate preserves the measurement base. But

---

[2] Cost of sales requires a separate calculation because its components are translated at historical and average rates.

certain nonmonetary items are also measured at current prices. Inventories and investments in shares measured at the lower of cost or market are examples. Translating items such as these at historical rates does not preserve this measurement base. The temporal method addresses this shortcoming.

The Temporal Method

The temporal method is identical to the monetary/nonmonetary method except in its treatment of nonmonetary items carried at current market values. Assets measured at current market values in foreign currency are translated at current rates, thus preserving the measurement base. If a foreign company's nonmonetary assets were all measured using historical cost, there would be no difference between the two methods. As we shall see in later discussions, the temporal method is one of the methods currently required under Canadian accounting principles. While it is called the temporal method, in most cases it is equivalent to the monetary/nonmonetary method.

When Section 1650 was first issued in 1978, it required that the temporal method of translation be used for all foreign entities. The reaction from the business community was highly critical. It was alleged that companies that had previously used the current/noncurrent method (the most popular method), or the current rate method, would now show unduly large swings in net income. It was also suggested that for certain companies the accounting exposure was quite different from the economic exposure, and that management would concentrate on taking steps to alleviate the accounting exposure with hedging devices, when the concentration should really be on the economic exposure.

The following example illustrates the difference between accounting and economic exposure; it also illustrates a situation where potential economic gains would be reflected as accounting losses under the temporal method of translation.

Example A Canadian company has an investment in a foreign subsidiary. During the year, the Canadian dollar weakens in relation to the foreign currency. Because of this, when dividends are received from the foreign subsidiary, the parent will receive more Canadian dollars than it would have had the exchange rate not changed. However, the monetary liabilities of the foreign subsidiary are larger than its assets carried at current values, and the translation of its financial statements using the temporal method produces an exchange loss. An accounting loss is shown when from an economic view there is a gain.

Because of the strong objections to the standard, the CICA suspended Section 1650 in 1979 in order to rethink the issues raised.

The Current Rate Method

Under the current rate method, all of the assets and liabilities of a foreign entity are translated at the current rate on the date of the balance sheet; this preserves the relationship in dollars between all balance sheet items that formerly existed in the foreign currency. Share capital is translated at historical rates. All revenues and expenses are translated using the average exchange rate for the period. Under the current rate method, the net assets of the foreign entity (and therefore the Canadian parent's investment) are exposed to foreign exchange fluctuations. A peculiarity resulting from this method is that a capital asset carried at historical cost in the foreign entity's statements will be translated into differing Canadian dollar values if exchange rates fluctuate over some time frame. This effect is particularly obvious with a capital asset not subject to amortization. The following example will illustrate this.

Example   A German entity has land in its balance sheet with a historical cost of 100,000 euros. On five successive balance sheets, denominated in euros, the land appears as €100,000. If the value of the euro changes with respect to the Canadian dollar each year during the five-year period, and the current rate method of translation is used, the translated amount will be different each year. A reader of the German financial statements would observe the same amount reflected each year. A reader of the translated financial statements would see a different amount each year and may improperly conclude that land sales or purchases have taken place. Despite this particular shortcoming, this method is one of the two methods currently sanctioned under Canadian GAAP.

Each of the three main translation methods that have been discussed (current/noncurrent, temporal, current) will produce different amounts for balance sheet and income statement items and different amounts for the translation gain or loss[3] because the total amount of the balance sheet items at risk to exchange rate changes is different under each. Historically, Canadian companies were not consistent in the translation methods used, or in the circumstances under which they were used; they were also inconsistent in the financial statement treatment given to the translation gains and losses that these various methods produced. Before the current Section 1650 was issued in 1983, the following alternatives for the treatment of exchange gains and losses in financial statements found some acceptance:[4]

- Reflect all losses in income, but defer any gains.
- Reflect all gains and losses in income.
- Defer recognition of gains and losses until realization by the remittance of funds to the parent company.
- Reflect all gains and losses in income if it is unlikely that the movement in exchange rates will reverse.
- Defer all gains and losses if it is likely that the exchange rate movement will reverse. Gains and losses deferred could be amortized over some future period.

With such a diversity of practice in the translation methods used and the treatment of gains and losses, it is not surprising that the Accounting Standards Committee decided to tighten the standards when it issued Section 1650.

---

[3] It is not inconceivable to have an exchange gain from the use of one method and an exchange loss from the use of a different method.

[4] See R. MacDonald Parkinson, *Translation of Foreign Currencies: A Research Study.* Toronto: CICA, 1972.

Foreign Currency Risk

The focus of the translation methods just discussed was on the accounting measurement, in foreign currency denominated financial statements, of the risks associated with fluctuations in foreign currencies. This *foreign currency risk* has been defined as "the net potential gain or loss which can arise from exchange rate changes to the foreign currency exposure of the enterprise."[5] In this context foreign currency risk can be viewed as having three components: translation exposure (accounting exposure), transaction exposure, and economic exposure.[6] Readers must keep these in mind as they interpret financial statements that contain foreign currency gains and losses.

Translation (Accounting) Exposure This exposure results from the translation of foreign currency denominated financial statements into dollars. The amount of the exposure depends on the translation method chosen. The gains and losses that result are unrealized in the sense that they do not represent actual cash flows. Because these accounting gains and losses are reflected in the financial statements, they may have an impact on the enterprise's dividend policies, share prices, and so on. It is important to assess the extent to which they represent transaction and/or economic exposure.

Transaction Exposure This exposure exists between the time of entering a transaction and the time of settling it. It affects the current cash flows of the enterprise. The resulting cash gains and losses are realized and affect the enterprise's working capital and earnings. The concept of transaction exposure was discussed in Chapter 12.

Economic Exposure Economic exposure takes a longer-term view of the situation than either of the others. It arises because of "the possible reduction, in terms of the domestic reporting currency, of the discounted future cash flows generated from foreign investments or operations due to real changes (inflation adjusted) in exchange rates."[7] It represents a long-term potential threat or benefit to a company carrying out business in foreign countries.

For example, a Canadian assembly plant that purchases components from a company in Japan will suffer economically if the dollar weakens in relation to the Japanese yen and the Canadian competition is such that the cost increase cannot be passed on to the company's customers. The situation is no different if the Japanese supplier is related to, or is a subsidiary of, the Canadian assembler, because it measures its results in yen and expects to be paid in that currency. Economically, there is a potential loss in this particular situation when the Canadian dollar weakens in relation to the yen. However, assume now that the Canadian parent does *not* purchase the output of its Japanese subsidiary. If this was a standalone foreign operation with no intercompany transactions, the Canadian parent would benefit by receiving more dollars from its subsidiary's dividends. Section 1650, in its 1983 form, tried to capture the economic effects

---

[5] See "Foreign Currency Risk Management." Management Accounting Guideline #6. Hamilton: Society of Management Accountants of Canada, 1987.

[6] Ibid.

[7] Ibid.

by establishing a situational approach to determining the translation method to be used for certain foreign operations.

Translation Under Section 1650

Section 1650 establishes accounting standards for the translation of the financial statements of a foreign operation (a subsidiary, joint venture, significant influence investee, etc.) for use by a reporting enterprise (a Canadian investor). A foreign operation is viewed as either *integrated* or *self-sustaining* for translation purposes. The division of foreign operations into two categories was made in order to achieve a major objective of translation, which is "to express financial statements of the foreign operation in Canadian dollars in a manner which best reflects the reporting enterprise's exposure to exchange rate changes as determined by the economic facts and circumstances" (*CICA Handbook*, paragraph 1650.06).

Conformity with Canadian GAAP Section 1650 also requires that the financial statements of foreign operations reflect Canadian accounting principles. In situations where the principles used are different from Canada's, the foreign operation financial statements must be adjusted to conform with Canadian GAAP and then translated into Canadian dollars.

Integrated Foreign Operations

An integrated foreign operation is one "which is financially or operationally interdependent with the reporting enterprise such that the exposure to exchange rate changes is similar to the exposure which would exist had the transactions and activities of the foreign operation been undertaken by the reporting enterprise" (*CICA Handbook*, paragraph 1650.03).

The *temporal method* of translation was chosen for this type of operation because it produces essentially the same results that would have occurred had the reporting enterprise itself undertaken all of the transactions that were incurred by the foreign operation.

If a foreign operation is considered to be integrated, the relationship between the two entities is such that the activities of the reporting enterprise are or will be directly affected by the cash flows of the foreign operation.

Self-sustaining Foreign Operations

A self-sustaining foreign operation is one "which is financially and operationally independent of the reporting enterprise such that the exposure to exchange rate changes is limited to the reporting enterprise's net investment in the foreign operation." (*CICA Handbook*, paragraph 1650.03)

Because the foreign operation is assumed to be independent in all respects, exchange rate changes should not have a direct impact on the immediate or short-term future cash flows of the reporting enterprise. The current rate method was chosen to translate the foreign currency financial statements of a self-sustaining operation, with *one* exception, discussed next.

Highly Inflationary Economies While Canada has had fairly low rates of inflation in the past 20 years, this has not been the case in other parts of the world. Argentina,

Brazil, Chile, Mexico, Turkey, and Israel have all had inflation rates higher than Canada's during this period. Between 1985 and 1993, Brazil experienced yearly rates of between 200 percent and 1,400 percent.

If the self-sustaining foreign operation operates in a highly inflationary environment relative to that of the reporting enterprise, translation using the current rate method could produce distorted and meaningless results. The CICA Accounting Standards Board has concluded that the temporal method should be used in such a situation. A definition of highly inflationary is not given, but both IASB and FASB standards suggest that a cumulative inflation rate of 100 percent over a three-year period would fit the description. The following example illustrates the kind of distortion that can occur when the current rate method is used during a period of very high inflation.

Example   In Year 1, a Canadian company purchases a self-sustaining foreign susidiary located in Chile. The exchange rate at this time is 1 peso = $1.00, and it remains constant during the year. The subsidiary has land carried at a historical cost of Ps1,000,000. On December 31, Year 1, the land is translated into dollars for consolidation purposes as follows:

$$Ps1,000,000 \quad \times \quad 1.00 \quad = \quad \$1,000,000$$

During Year 2, Chile experiences an inflation rate of 500 percent. Because the inflation rate in Canada is minuscule during this period, this large inflation differential is fully reflected in the foreign exchange market. The result is a weakening of the peso relative to the Canadian dollar.

On December 31, Year 2, the exchange rate is Ps1 = $0.20. If the land were translated at the current rate on this date, the result would be as follows:

$$Ps1,000,000 \quad \times \quad 0.20 \quad = \quad \$200,000$$

While it is easy to see in this example that the $800,000 difference is due to the exchange rate change, large differences such as this are difficult to interpret without all the facts. When this self-sustaining operation is translated by the temporal method, the value of the land appears as $1,000,000 (which reflects the historical rate).

In passing, it should be noted that if the Chilean subsidiary prepared price level–adjusted historical cost statements, the land would appear on the subsidiary's balance sheet at Ps5,000,000.

Translation using the current rate method on December 31, Year 2, would *not* produce distorted results, as the following illustrates:

$$Ps5,000,000 \quad \times \quad 0.20 \quad = \quad \$1,000,000$$

But price-level accounting is not GAAP in Canada, and therefore the subsidiary's financial statements must be adjusted back to nominal pesos before being translated using the temporal method.

Determining the Classification of Foreign Operations   Section 1650 acknowledges that in the evaluation of the exchange rate exposure, the classification of a foreign operation as either integrated or self-sustaining requires professional judgment. It suggests that six factors should be considered in making the required evaluation. These are summarized in Exhibit 13.1.

Exhibit 13.1

FACTORS IN EVALUATING A FOREIGN OPERATION

Factor	Integrated	Self-sustaining
1. Cash flows of the enterprise.	Directly affected by day-to-day activities of the foreign operation.	Insulated from day-to-day activities of the foreign operation.
2. Sales prices of the foreign operation.	Determined more by world-wide competition and international prices.	Determined more by local competition and local government regulation.
	Responsive on a short-term basis to changes in exchange rates.	Immune on a short-term basis to changes in exchange rates.
3. Sales market of the foreign operation.	Primarily within the country of the reporting enterprise.	Primarily outside the country of the reporting enterprise.
4. Products and service costs of the foreign operation.	Obtained primarily from the country of reporting enterprise.	Obtained primarily from the foreign country.
5. Financing of day-to-day activities of the foreign operation.	Primarily from the reporting enterprise or borrowing from the country of the reporting enterprise.	Primarily from its own operations and local borrowings.
6. Day-to-day activity between the foreign operation and the reporting enterprise.	Strong interrelationship because of a high volume of intercompany transactions.	Weak interrelationship because of a low volume of intercompany transactions.

Accounting for Translation Gains and Losses

CICA came to the following conclusions regarding the presentation of the resulting exchange gains and losses from the two types of foreign operations.

Because of the interdependent relationship that exists between the reporting enterprise and the integrated foreign operation, the translation should reflect the same results "as if the underlying transactions had been undertaken by the reporting enterprise" (*CICA Handbook*, paragraph 1650.30). If the Canadian parent had undertaken the year's transactions of the foreign operation denominated in foreign currency, any exchange gains and losses from the translation of monetary items would be taken into income. (Prior to January 1, 2002, exchange gains and losses from the translation of noncurrent monetary items with a fixed life had to be deferred and amortized. This requirement was eliminated with *Handbook* changes that occurred on this date.)

Because of the independent relationship that exists between the reporting enterprise and the self-sustaining foreign operation, the exposure of the reporting enterprise is limited to its net investment in the foreign operation. Since the resulting translation gain or loss has no direct effect on the activities of the reporting enterprise, the committee concluded that such gains and losses should not be reflected in the reporting enterprise's income statement. Instead, they should be reported as a separate component of the shareholders' equity of the reporting enterprise.[8] A term commonly used to describe this amount is "cumulative translation adjustment." A transfer from this account to the income statement should be made during a period in which there has been a reduction in the parent's investment.

Unit of Measure

Section 1650 indicates that the two methods of translation actually use different currencies as the unit of measure. The temporal method uses the Canadian dollar as the measuring unit, while the current rate method uses the foreign currency.

Because it produces results that are identical to those that would have been produced had the Canadian parent itself entered into all of the transactions incurred by the foreign operation, the temporal method of translation essentially takes all of the transactions that have been measured in a foreign currency and remeasures them in Canadian dollars using the exchange rate in effect on the date of the transaction. Financial statement ratios computed using the foreign currency as the original measuring unit will change when the statements are remeasured using the Canadian dollar.

Under the current rate method, the unit of measure is the foreign currency. Each transaction of the foreign operation is measured in foreign currency. In order that the consolidation can take place by adding dollars to dollars, the foreign currency financial statements are translated at the *current* rate for balance sheet items and at the *average* rate for income statement items. Balance sheet ratios (e.g., the current ratio) and income statement ratios (e.g., net income to sales) remain unchanged. Ratios of income statement items to balance sheet items (e.g., return on investment) will be different after the translation because the rates used to translate the balance sheet are different from the rates used for the income statement.

Illustration of Translation and Consolidation

The translation and preparation of consolidated financial statements will now be illustrated under the two translation methods required by Section 1650.

Example   On December 31, Year 1, Starmont Inc., a Canadian company, acquired 100 percent of the common shares of Controlada S.A., located in Venezuela, at a cost of 2,000,000 bolivars. The exchange rate was B1 = $0.128 on this date. Starmont's journal entry (in Canadian dollars) to record the share acquisition is:

Dec. 31, Year 1

Investment in Controlada	256,000	
Cash		256,000
(B2,000,000 × 0.128)		

This example assumes that the carrying values of the subsidiary's net assets were equal to fair values and that there is no goodwill on consolidation. Because this is a "purchase" business combination, the exchange rate on the date of acquisition is

---

[8]   After the translation process, this amount appears as part of the shareholders' equity of the foreign operation. In the consolidation process, it becomes part of the shareholders' equity of the reporting enterprise.

used to translate all accounts of the subsidiary on acquisition date and becomes the historical rate to be used in subsequent years, where appropriate.

The balance sheet of Controlada in bolivars and translated into Canadian dollars is shown in Exhibit 13.2.

The subsidiary's bonds payable mature in 10 years and require interest payments each December 31. Note that the translation of a subsidiary on the date of acquisition is the same regardless of whether the entity is integrated or self-sustaining.

The preparation of the acquisition date consolidated balance sheet appears in Exhibit 13.3. Note that the translated shareholders' equity of the subsidiary is equal to the parent's investment account, so the consolidating procedure is simply to eliminate one against the other.

Exhibit 13.2

CONTROLADA S.A.
TRANSLATION OF BALANCE SHEET TO CANADIAN DOLLARS
December 31, Year 1

	Venezuelan bolivars	Exchange rate	Canadian dollars
Cash	B 40,000	0.128	$ 5,120
Accounts receivable	360,000	0.128	46,080
Inventories	1,200,000	0.128	153,600
Plant and equipment (net)	900,000	0.128	115,200
	B2,500,000		$320,000
Current liabilities	B 50,000	0.128	$ 6,400
Bonds payable	450,000	0.128	57,600
Common stock	1,500,000	0.128	192,000
Retained earnings	500,000	0.128	64,000
	B2,500,000		$320,000

Exhibit 13.3

PREPARATION OF CONSOLIDATED BALANCE SHEET
December 31, Year 1

	Starmont	Controlada	Starmont Consolidated
Cash	$ 70,000	$ 5,120	$ 75,120
Accounts receivable	90,000	46,080	136,080
Inventories	200,000	153,600	353,600
Plant and equipment	300,000	115,200	415,200
Investment in Controlada	256,000	—	—
	$916,000	$320,000	$980,000
Current liabilities	$ 80,000	$ 6,400	$ 86,400
Bonds payable	300,000	57,600	357,600
Common stock	200,000	192,000	200,000
Retained earnings	336,000	64,000	336,000
	$916,000	$320,000	$980,000

Translation and Consolidation Subsequent to Acquisition

On December 31, Year 2, Controlada forwarded the financial statements shown in Exhibit 13.4 to the Canadian parent.

The translation process will now be illustrated under these two assumptions: (a) the subsidiary is self-sustaining, and (b) the subsidiary is integrated.

The exchange rates for the year were as follows:[9]

December 31, Year 1	B1 = $0.128
December 31, Year 2	B1 = $0.104
Average for year 2	B1 = $0.115
Date of purchase of inventory on hand	B1 = $0.110
Date dividends declared	B1 = $0.104

Exhibit 13.5 illustrates the rates to be used for self-sustaining operations (the current rate method) and integrated operations (the temporal method).

Self-sustaining Foreign Operation   If the subsidiary is considered self-sustaining, the translation of its Year 2 financial statements will be as shown in Exhibit 13.6 on page 544.

The procedure used in Exhibit 13.6 was to translate the income statement first, then the retained earnings statement, then the balance sheet. The following features of the current rate translation process are emphasized:

- All assets and liabilities are translated at the current rate.

- Common stock and beginning retained earnings are translated at the acquisition date historical rate, thus establishing the translated amount on that date. In future periods the amount for the translated beginning retained earnings will have to be calculated. In practice, the accountant will look at last year's translated financial statements for this amount. Dividends are translated at the historical rate on the date of declaration. In situations where the dividends were not paid by year-end, the dividends payable will be translated at the current rate, and a hidden exchange gain or loss will result from the translation of these items. (In this example, the dividends were declared and paid on December 31.)

- The average rate for Year 2 is used for all revenues and expenses in the income statement.

- The balancing amount labelled as cumulative translation adjustment is used to balance total assets with total liabilities and shareholders' equity. This amount, shown as a separate component of shareholders' equity, represents the Year 2 exchange loss from the translation of the subsidiary's financial statements using the current rate method.

In this illustration, the financial statements were translated sequentially, with the foreign exchange loss being the "plug" needed to complete the balance sheet. In reality, the gain or loss can be calculated before attempting the translation process. Exhibit 13.7 illustrates this process. In a self-sustaining operation such as

---

[9] It is assumed here that the subsidiary's dividends were declared and paid on December 31, Year 2.

Exhibit 13.4

CONTROLADA S.A.
FINANCIAL STATEMENTS
December 31, Year 2
(in bolivars)
INCOME STATEMENT

Sales	B9,000,000
Cost of goods sold	B7,000,000
Depreciation expense	100,000
Bond interest expense	45,000
Other expense	1,555,000
	B8,700,000
Net income	B 300,000

STATEMENT OF RETAINED EARNINGS

Balance, beginning of year	B 500,000
Net income	300,000
	800,000
Dividends	100,000
Balance, end of year	B 700,000

BALANCE SHEET

Cash	B 100,000
Accounts receivable	400,000
Inventory	1,600,000
Plant and equipment (net)	800,000
	B2,900,000
Current liabilities	B 250,000
Bonds payable	450,000
Common stock	1,500,000
Retained earnings	700,000
	B2,900,000

Exhibit 13.5

	Exchange Rates	
Financial statement items	*Self-sustaining*	*Integrated*
Monetary	current	current
Nonmonetary — at cost	current	historical
Nonmonetary — at current values	current	current
Capital stock	historical	historical
Dividends	historical	historical
Revenues	average	average
Depreciation and amortization	average	historical
Cost of sales	average	—
Opening inventory	—	historical
Purchases	—	average
Ending inventory	—	historical

Exhibit 13.6

CONTROLADA S.A.
TRANSLATION OF FINANCIAL STATEMENTS TO CANADIAN DOLLARS
December 31, Year 2
(self-sustaining foreign operation)

INCOME STATEMENT

	Bolivars	Exchange rate	Dollars
Sales	B9,000,000	0.115	$1,035,000
Cost of goods sold	7,000,000	0.115	805,000
Depreciation expense	100,000	0.115	11,500
Bond interest expense	45,000	0.115	5,175
Other expense	1,555,000		178,825
	B8,700,000		$1,000,500
Net income	B 300,000	0.115	$ 34,500

STATEMENT OF RETAINED EARNINGS

	Bolivars	Exchange rate	Dollars
Balance, beginning of year	B 500,000	0.128	$ 64,000
Net income	300,000	0.115	34,500
	800,000		98,500
Dividends	100,000	0.104	10,400
Balance, end of year	B 700,000		$ 88,100

BALANCE SHEET

	Bolivars	Exchange rate	Dollars
Cash	B 100,000	0.104	$ 10,400
Accounts receivable	400,000	0.104	41,600
Inventory	1,600,000	0.104	166,400
Plant and equipment (net)	800,000	0.104	83,200
	B2,900,000		$ 301,600
Current liabilities	B 250,000	0.104	$ 26,000
Bonds payable	450,000	0.104	46,800
Common stock	1,500,000	0.128	192,000
Retained earnings	700,000		88,100
Cumulative translation adjustment	—		(51,300)
	B2,900,000		$ 301,600

this one, it is the net assets (assets less liabilities) that are at risk and are exposed to currency fluctuations. Net assets equal shareholders' equity, and if the capital stock remains unchanged, the only changes that usually occur are the net income and dividend changes to retained earnings. The process involves translating the opening position, using the historical rates at that time, and translating the changes at the rates at which they occurred. The result is a calculated position. The actual end of year net asset position is translated at current rates, with the difference between

Exhibit 13.7

INDEPENDENT CALCULATION OF YEAR 2
TRANSLATION LOSS
(self-sustaining foreign operation)

	Bolivars	Exchange rate	Dollars
Net assets, December 31, Year 1	B2,000,000 ×	$0.128	$256,000
Changes in net assets, Year 2			
Net income	300,000 ×	0.115	34,500
Dividends	(100,000) ×	0.104	(10,400)
Calculated net assets			280,100
Actual net assets	B2,200,000 ×	0.104	228,800
Exchange loss from translation			$ 51,300

the two numbers representing the exchange gain or loss from translation. Notice that if the exchange rate had remained constant throughout Year 2, all items in Exhibit 13.7 would have been translated at $0.128 with no exchange gain or loss occurring.

Using the equity method of accounting, Starmont would make the following journal entries on December 31, Year 2:

Investment in Controlada	34,500	
Equity earnings		34,500
100% of translated net income		

Cash	10,400	
Investment in Controlada		10,400
Dividend received		

Cumulative translation adjustment	51,300	
Investment in Controlada		51,300

To record 100% of the change in the cumulative translation adjustment for Year 2

Exhibit 13.8 illustrates the preparation of the consolidated financial statements. Notice that equity earnings are equal to the subsidiary's net income ($34,500), and are therefore eliminated and replaced with the subsidiary's revenue and expenses. The parent's investment account is eliminated against the shareholders' equity of the subsidiary in the following manner:

Investment in Controlada		$228,800
Shareholders equity — Controlada		
Common stock	192,000	
Retained earnings	88,100	
Cumulative translation adjustment	(51,300)	228,800
Purchase discrepancy		–0–

With no purchase discrepancy or noncontrolling interest, the investment account is replaced with the assets and liabilities of the subsidiary. Notice that the parent's share (in this case 100 percent) of the subsidiary's cumulative translation adjustment appears as a separate component of consolidated shareholders' equity. The parent's equity method journal entry to record this made the consolidation process straightforward.

Exhibit 13.8

PREPARATION OF CONSOLIDATED FINANCIAL STATEMENTS
YEAR 2
(self-sustaining foreign operation)
INCOME STATEMENT

	Starmont	Controlada	Starmont Consolidated
Sales	$3,000,000	$1,035,000	$4,035,000
Equity earnings	34,500	—	—
	$3,034,500	$1,035,000	$4,035,000
Cost of goods sold	$2,500,000	$ 805,000	$3,305,000
Depreciation	20,000	11,500	31,500
Bond interest	30,000	5,175	35,175
Other	200,000	178,825	378,825
	$2,750,000	$1,000,500	$3,750,500
Net income	$ 284,500	$ 34,500	$ 284,500

RETAINED EARNINGS

	Starmont	Controlada	Starmont Consolidated
Balance — beginning	$ 336,000	$ 64,000	$ 336,000
Net income	284,500	34,500	284,500
	620,500	98,500	620,500
Dividends	50,000	10,400	50,000
Balance — end	$ 570,500	$ 88,100	$ 570,500

BALANCE SHEETS

	Starmont	Controlada	Starmont Consolidated
Cash	$ 100,000	$ 10,400	$ 110,400
Accounts receivable	290,400	41,600	332,000
Inventories	220,000	166,400	386,400
Plant and equipment (net)	280,000	83,200	363,200
Investment in Controlada (equity method)	228,800	—	—
	$1,119,200	$ 301,600	$1,192,000
Current liabilities	$ 100,000	$ 26,000	$ 126,000
Bonds payable	300,000	46,800	346,800
Common stock	200,000	192,000	200,000
Retained earnings	570,500	88,100	570,500
Cumulative translation adjustment	(51,300)	(51,300)	(51,300)
	$1,119,200	$ 301,600	$1,192,000

Integrated Foreign Operation Assuming that Controlada is an integrated foreign operation, the statements would be translated using the temporal method. Exhibit 13.9 illustrates this process. The following discussion regarding the exchange rates used and the disposition of the translation gain should be noted:

- Monetary items are translated at the current rate, nonmonetary items at appropriate historical rates.

Exhibit 13.9	

CONTROLADA S.A.
TRANSLATION OF FINANCIAL STATEMENTS TO CANADIAN DOLLARS
Year Ended December 31, Year 2
(integrated foreign operation)

INCOME STATEMENT

	Bolivars	Exchange rate	Dollars
Sales	B9,000,000	0.115	$1,035,000
Cost of goods sold	B7,000,000	calculated	$ 828,600
Depreciation expense	100,000	0.128	12,800
Bond interest expense	45,000	0.115	5,175
Other expense	1,555,000	0.115	178,825
Total expense	B8,700,000		$1,025,400
Net income (before translation loss — note 1)	B 300,000		$ 9,600

RETAINED EARNINGS

	Bolivars	Exchange rate	Dollars
Balance — beginning	B 500,000	0.128	$ 64,000
Net income (note 1)	300,000		9,600
	800,000		73,600
Dividends	100,000	0.104	10,400
Balance — end	B 700,000		$ 63,200

BALANCE SHEET

	Bolivars	Exchange rate	Dollars
Cash	B 100,000	0.104	$ 10,400
Accounts receivable	400,000	0.104	41,600
Inventory	1,600,000	0.110	176,000
Plant and equipment (net)	800,000	0.128	102,400
	B2,900,000		$ 330,400
Current liabilities	B 250,000	0.104	$ 26,000
Bonds payable	450,000	0.104	46,800
Common stock	1,500,000	0.128	192,000
Retained earnings (note 1)	700,000		63,200
			$ 328,000
Balancing translation adjustment (note 1)	—		2,400
	B2,900,000		$ 330,400

Note 1: Because this translation adjustment is a preliminary balancing amount, the net income and retained earnings are not the final translated amounts.

- Common stock and beginning-of-year retained earnings are translated at the historical rate on the date of acquisition. In future years the translated amount for retained earnings will have to be calculated.

- Revenue and expenses, with the exception of depreciation and cost of goods sold, are translated at the average rate for the year. Depreciation is translated at the historical rates used to translate the related assets.

- Because the components of cost of goods sold are translated using different rates, the translated amount for this item is calculated as follows:

Beginning inventory	B1,200,000	×	0.128	=	$	153,600
Purchases	7,400,000	×	0.115	=		851,000
	8,600,000					1,004,600
Ending inventory	1,600,000	×	0.110	=		176,000
Cost of goods sold	B7,000,000				$	828,600

Purchases in bolivars were calculated as a balancing amount, and are translated at the average rate for the year. Inventories are translated at historical rates.

- The balance sheet item "Balancing translation adjustment" is the "plug" needed to balance the statements after translation. It represents the foreign exchange gain due to changes in the monetary position during the year. The *Handbook* requires that this amount be reflected in the Year 2 income statement. In Exhibit 13.11 on page 550, the financial statements of Controlada have been adjusted accordingly. The sequential translation illustrated in Exhibit 13.9 is cumbersome, because the translated net income does not contain the year's exchange gain or loss. A better method would be to first calculate the exchange gain or loss resulting from the monetary position, and then translate the financial statements and include the gain or loss in the income statement. Exhibit 13.10 shows how the gain or loss can be calculated before the actual financial statement translation takes place.

After the translation adjustment is reflected in Controlada's income statement (see Exhibit 13.11), the translated statements are ready for the consolidation process. They become the basis for the following equity method journal entries by Starmont on December 31, Year 2:

Investment in Controlada	12,000	
Equity earnings		12,000
To record 100% of the Year 2 net income of Controlada Company		

Cash	10,400	
Investment in Controlada		10,400
Dividend received from Controlada Company		

Exhibit 13.10

CALCULATION OF YEAR 2 TRANSLATION ADJUSTMENT

	Bolivars		Exchange rates	Dollars
Net monetary position				
Dec. 31, Year 1*	B (100,000)	×	0.128	$ (12,800)
Changes during Year 2				
Sales	B 9,000,000	×	0.115	$1,035,000
Purchases	(7,400,000)	×	0.115	(851,000)
Bond interest expense	(45,000)	×	0.115	(5,175)
Other expense	(1,555,000)	×	0.115	(178,825)
Dividends	(100,000)	×	0.104	(10,400)
Net changes	B (100,000)			$ (10,400)
Calculated net monetary position				
Dec. 31, Year 2				$ (23,200)
Actual net monetary position				
Dec. 31, Year 2*	B (200,000)	×	0.104	$ (20,800)
Exchange gain, Year 2				$ 2,400

*NET MONETARY POSITION, BOLIVARS

	December 31	
	Year 2	Year 1
Cash	B 100,000	B 40,000
Accounts receivable	400,000	360,000
Current liabilities	(150,000)	(50,000)
Bonds payable	(450,000)	(450,000)
Net monetary position	B(200,000)	B(100,000)

Exhibit 13.11 shows the Year 2 financial statements of Starmont, the translated statements of Controlada using the temporal method, and the consolidated financial statements. Note that the investment account equals the shareholders' equity of the subsidiary, and that there is no noncontrolling interest or purchase discrepancy. The investment account is replaced with the assets and liabilities of Controlada, and equity earnings are replaced with revenues and expenses.

In both illustrations (self-sustaining and integrated), the financial statements were translated first with the foreign exchange gain or loss determined as a plug to balance. Then, as a proof, the foreign exchange gain or loss was verified by translating the changes that had occurred in either the net asset position or the net monetary position. It should be obvious that in both situations the exchange gains and losses can be determined prior to the translation of the financial statements.

Exhibit 13.11

PREPARATION OF CONSOLIDATED FINANCIAL STATEMENTS
YEAR 2
(integrated)

INCOME STATEMENT

	Starmont	Controlada	Starmont Consolidated
Sales	$3,000,000	$1,035,000	$4,035,000
Equity earnings	12,000	—	—
	$3,012,000	$1,035,000	$4,035,000
Cost of goods sold	$2,500,000	$ 828,600	$3,328,600
Depreciation	20,000	12,800	32,800
Bond interest	30,000	5,175	35,175
Other	200,000	178,825	378,825
Foreign exchange gain	—	(2,400)	(2,400)
	$2,750,000	$1,023,000	$3,773,000
Net income	$ 262,000	$ 12,000	$ 262,000

RETAINED EARNINGS

	Starmont	Controlada	Starmont Consolidated
Balance — beginning	$ 336,000	$ 64,000	$ 336,000
Net income	262,000	12,000	262,000
	598,000	76,000	598,000
Dividends	50,000	10,400	50,000
Balance — end	$ 548,000	$ 65,600	$ 548,000

BALANCE SHEETS

	Starmont	Controlada	Starmont Consolidated
Cash	$ 100,000	$ 10,400	$ 110,400
Accounts receivable	290,400	41,600	332,000
Inventories	220,000	176,000	396,000
Plant and equipment (net)	280,000	102,400	382,400
Investment in Controlada (equity)	257,600	—	—
	$1,148,000	$ 330,400	$1,220,800
Current liabilities	$ 100,000	$ 26,000	$ 126,000
Bonds payable	300,000	46,800	346,800
Common stock	200,000	192,000	200,000
Retained earnings	548,000	65,600	548,000
	$1,148,000	$ 330,400	$1,220,800

Comparative Observations of the Two Translation Methods

Under the current rate method, the net assets position of the foreign entity is at risk from currency fluctuations, while under the temporal method it is the monetary position that is at risk. For most companies, monetary liabilities are greater than monetary assets, so they are usually in a net monetary liability position. This is the case with Controlada S.A. If the foreign currency weakens with respect to the Canadian dollar, a self-sustaining operation will show a foreign exchange loss while an integrated foreign operation will show a foreign exchange gain. This can be seen in Exhibit 13.7, where a self-sustaining operation produced a loss of $51,300, and Exhibit 13.10, where an integrated operation produced a gain of $2,400. If the Canadian dollar weakens with respect to the foreign currency (i.e., the foreign currency strengthens) a self-sustaining operation will reflect an exchange gain and an integrated operation will reflect an exchange loss. These observations are only true when monetary liabilities are greater than monetary assets.

Complications with a Purchase Discrepancy

The previous example assumed a 100 percent controlled subsidiary and no purchase discrepancy. The existence of a purchase discrepancy presents complications in the consolidation process when the current rate method is used and the subsidiary is less than 100 percent owned. We will change some of the facts from the previous example in order to illustrate this.

Example   Assume that Starmont purchased 90 percent of Controlada on December 31, Year 1, at a cost of B2,250,000. The carrying values of Controlada's net assets were equal to fair values on this date, resulting in goodwill of B450,000. The same exchange rates are assumed; thus, the financial statements of Controlada and their translation will not change from the previous example. However, the change in the acquisition cost and the percentage purchased creates a purchase discrepancy and a noncontrolling interest. Starmont's journal entry to record the acquisition on December 31, Year 1, is as follows:

Investment in Controlada	288,000	
Cash		288,000

To record the acquisition of 90% of Controlada for $288,000
(2,250,000 × 0.128)

The following calculation of the purchase discrepancy in bolivars and dollars on December 31, Year 1, is made to prepare the acquisition date consolidated balance sheet:

Investment cost	B2,250,000	×	.128	=	$288,000
Book value of subsidiary					
Common stock	1,500,000	×	.128	=	192,000
Retained earnings	500,000	×	.128	=	64,000
Shareholders' equity	2,000,000				256,000
Parent's percentage	90%				90%
	B1,800,000				$230,400
Purchase discrepancy	B 450,000	×	.128	=	$ 57,600
Fair value differences × 90 percent	–0–				–0–
Balance — goodwill	B 450,000	×	.128	=	$ 57,600

Exhibit 13.12 shows the December 31, Year 1, balance sheets of the parent and subsidiary and the consolidated balance sheet.

Exhibit 13.12

PREPARATION OF CONSOLIDATED BALANCE SHEET
December 31, Year 1

	Starmont	Controlada	Starmont Consolidated
Cash	$ 38,000	$ 5,120	$ 43,120
Accounts receivable	90,000	46,080	136,080
Inventories	200,000	153,600	353,600
Plant and equipment	300,000	115,200	415,200
Investment in Controlada	288,000	—	—
Goodwill	—	—	57,600
	$916,000	$320,000	$1,005,600
Current liabilities	$ 80,000	$ 6,400	$ 86,400
Bonds payable	300,000	57,600	357,600
Noncontrolling interest*	—	—	25,600
Common stock	200,000	192,000	200,000
Retained earnings	336,000	64,000	336,000
	$916,000	$320,000	$1,005,600

* 10% × $256,000 = $25,600

Consolidation — Self-sustaining   Assuming that Controlada is a self-sustaining operation, we will now illustrate the preparation of the Year 2 consolidated financial statements. The translated financial statements are the same as were shown in the previous example, and are reproduced again as part of Exhibit 13.13. Included in the subsidiary's shareholders' equity is the cumulative translation adjustment of $51,300. The noncontrolling interest in the consolidated balance sheet represents 10 percent of the subsidiary's shareholders' equity and therefore includes 10 percent of this cumulative translation adjustment. Consolidated shareholders' equity will show 90 percent of this translation adjustment. A further exchange loss arises in the consolidation process because of the manner in which the purchase discrepancy amortization schedule is translated. Assume that after a goodwill impairment test was conducted at the end of Year 2, it was determined that a loss of B45,000 should be reflected. The changes between the opening and closing amounts must be calculated in the foreign currency and then translated into dollars. This process, which is followed only if the foreign operation is self-sustaining, is as follows:

TRANSLATION OF PURCHASE DISCREPANCY AMORTIZATION SCHEDULE

Goodwill — December 31/1	B450,000	×	.128	=	$57,600
Impairment loss — Year 2	B 45,000	×	.115	=	5,175
Calculated goodwill — December 31/2					$52,425
Actual goodwill — December 31/2	B405,000	×	.104	=	42,120
Exchange loss — (cumulative translation adjustment)					$10,305

The following points should be noted:

- The purchase discrepancy (in this case goodwill) on December 31, Year 1, is translated at the historical rate on that date.

- The Year 2 impairment loss is translated at the average rate for Year 2. In this case the entire purchase discrepancy amortization was due to a goodwill impairment loss. A question arises as to which exchange rate to use to translate this loss. The logical answer is the average rate, because this is the rate used to translate all of the items on the income statement of a self-sustaining foreign subsidiary. If this subsidiary had used push-down accounting, the goodwill impairment loss would appear on its income statement and would be translated at the average rate. The fact that push-down accounting was not used should not result in a different translated amount for this loss.

- The unamortized balance on December 31, Year 2, is translated at the current rate.

When different exchange rates are used to translate the schedule, an exchange gain or loss will always result. In this case there is a loss of $10,305, which appears as part of the cumulative translation adjustment in the shareholders' equity of the parent company. The allocation of the two exchange losses resulting from the translation of the financial statements and the purchase discrepancy to controlling and noncontrolling interests is illustrated next.

DISPOSITION OF CUMULATIVE TRANSLATION ADJUSTMENTS

	Total	90% control	10% noncontrol
Cumulative translation adjustment — subsidiary statements	$51,300	$46,170	$5,130
Cumulative translation adjustment — purchase discrepancy	10,305	10,305	—
	$61,605	$56,475	$5,130

Using the translated financial statements of Controlada (see Exhibit 13.13) and the translated purchase discrepancy amortization schedule, Starmont would make the following equity method journal entries on December 31, Year 2:

Cash (90% × 10,400)	9,360	
Cumulative translation adjustment (90% × 51,300)	46,170	
Equity earnings (90% × 34,500)		31,050
Investment in Controlada		24,480
To record the parent's share of dividends, net income, and loss on translation of statements		
Equity earnings	5,175	
Cumulative translation adjustment	10,305	
Investment in Controlada		15,480
To record the amortization and translation of the purchase discrepancy		

The preparation of the Year 2 consolidated financial statements is illustrated in Exhibit 13.13.

Exhibit 13.13

PREPARATION OF CONSOLIDATED FINANCIAL STATEMENTS — YEAR 2
(self-sustaining)

INCOME STATEMENT

	Starmont	Controlada	Starmont Consolidated
Sales	$3,000,000	$1,035,000	$4,035,000
Equity earnings	25,875	—	—
	$3,025,875	$1,035,000	$4,035,000
Cost of goods sold	$2,500,000	$ 805,000	$3,305,000
Depreciation	20,000	11,500	31,500
Bond interest	30,000	5,175	35,175
Other	200,000	178,825	378,825
Goodwill impairment loss	—	—	5,175
	$2,750,000	$1,000,500	$3,755,675
Individual net incomes	$ 275,875	$ 34,500	
Net income — entity			$ 279,325
Noncontrolling interest			3,450
Net income			$ 275,875

RETAINED EARNINGS

	Starmont	Controlada	Starmont Consolidated
Balance — beginning	$ 336,000	$ 64,000	$ 336,000
Net income	275,875	34,500	275,875
	$ 611,875	$ 98,500	$ 611,875
Dividends	50,000	10,400	50,000
Balance — end	$ 561,875	$ 88,100	$ 561,875

BALANCE SHEETS

	Starmont	Controlada	Starmont Consolidated
Cash	$ 66,960	$ 10,400	$ 77,360
Accounts receivable	290,400	41,600	332,000
Inventories	220,000	166,400	386,400
Plant and equipment	280,000	83,200	363,200
Investment in Controlada (equity)	248,040	—	—
Goodwill	—	—	42,120
	$1,105,400	$ 301,600	$1,201,080
Current liabilities	$ 100,000	$ 26,000	$ 126,000
Bonds payable	300,000	46,800	346,800
Noncontrolling interest	—	—	22,880
Common stock	200,000	192,000	200,000
Retained earnings	561,875	88,100	561,875
Cumulative translation adjustment	(56,475)	(51,300)	(56,475)
	$1,105,400	$ 301,600	$1,201,080

The following explanations regarding the preparation of the consolidated statements should be noted:

1. Consolidated income statement —

    (a) Equity earnings are eliminated and replaced with the revenues and expenses of the subsidiary, the goodwill impairment loss, and the noncontrolling interest.

    (b) Noncontrolling interest is 10 percent of subsidiary net income.

2. Consolidated retained earnings —

    Because the parent has used the equity method, all items are identical to the parent's retained earnings.

3. Consolidated balance sheet —

    (a) The investment account is eliminated and replaced with the assets and liabilities of the subsidiary, the unamortized purchase discrepancy, and the noncontrolling interest.

    (b) The noncontrolling interest is calculated as follows:

Common stock	$192,000
Retained earnings	88,100
Cumulative translation adjustment	(51,300)
	228,800
	10%
	$ 22,880

The unamortized purchase discrepancy can be verified by the following calculation:

Investment in Controlada		$248,040
Shareholders' equity of Controlada (as above)	228,800	
	90%	205,920
Unamortized purchase discrepancy (goodwill)		$ 42,120

Consolidation — Integrated We will conclude this example by assuming that 90 percent owned Controlada is an integrated foreign operation. In this case the existence of a purchase discrepancy and a noncontrolling interest poses no particular consolidation problems. The purchase discrepancy amortization schedule for Year 2 is shown below:

PURCHASE DISCREPANCY AMORTIZATION SCHEDULE

Goodwill — December 31/1	B450,000	×	.128	=	$57,600
Impairment loss — Year 2	B 45,000	×	.128	=	5,760
Goodwill — December 31/2	B405,000	×	.128	=	$51,840

The schedule is presented in bolivars and dollars only to be consistent with the previous illustration. However, because all items are translated at historical rates, it is probably easier to make the calculation in dollars.

Using the Year 2 purchase discrepancy amortization schedule and Controlada's translated financial statements (see Exhibit 13.14), Starmont would make the following equity-method journal entries on December 31, Year 2:

Exhibit 13.14

PREPARATION OF CONSOLIDATED FINANCIAL STATEMENTS — YEAR 2
(integrated)

INCOME STATEMENT

	Starmont	Controlada	Starmont Consolidated
Sales	$3,000,000	$1,035,000	$4,035,000
Equity earnings	5,040	—	—
	$3,005,040	$1,035,000	$4,035,000
Cost of goods sold	$2,500,000	$ 828,600	$3,328,600
Depreciation	20,000	12,800	32,800
Bond interest	30,000	5,175	35,175
Other	200,000	178,825	378,825
Goodwill impairment loss	—	—	5,760
Foreign exchange gain	—	(2,400)	(2,400)
	$2,750,000	$1,023,000	$3,778,760
Individual net incomes	$ 255,040	$ 12,000	
Net income — entity			$ 256,240
Less noncontrolling interest			1,200
Net income			$ 255,040

RETAINED EARNINGS

	Starmont	Controlada	Starmont Consolidated
Balance — beginning	$ 336,000	$ 64,000	$ 336,000
Net income	255,040	12,000	255,040
	591,040	76,000	591,040
Dividends	50,000	10,400	50,000
Balance — end	$ 541,040	$ 65,600	$ 541,040

BALANCE SHEETS

	Starmont	Controlada	Starmont Consolidated
Cash	$ 66,960	$ 10,400	$ 77,360
Accounts receivable	290,400	41,600	332,000
Inventories	220,000	176,000	396,000
Plant and equipment (net)	280,000	102,400	382,400
Investment in Controlada (equity)	283,680	—	—
Goodwill	—	—	51,840
	$1,141,040	$ 330,400	$1,239,600
Current liabilities	$ 100,000	$ 26,000	$ 126,000
Bonds payable	300,000	46,800	346,800
Noncontrolling interest	—	—	25,760
Common stock	200,000	192,000	200,000
Retained earnings	541,040	65,600	541,040
	$1,141,040	$ 330,400	$1,239,600

Cash (90% × 10,400)	9,360	
Investment in Controlada	1,440	
Equity earnings (90% × 12,000)		10,800
To record parent's share of dividends and net income		
Equity earnings	5,760	
Investment in Controlada		5,760
Amortization of purchase discrepancy		

Note that Year 2 equity earnings are $5,040 in this example (integrated); in the previous example (self-sustaining), equity earnings were $25,875. The difference is due to (a) the use of different exchange rates in the translation, and (b) the fact that there is no exchange loss on the translation of the purchase discrepancy amortization schedule.

Exhibit 13.14 shows the preparation of the Year 2 consolidated financial statements.

The following points are worth noting in regard to the preparation of the consolidated statements:

1. Consolidated income statement —

   (a) Equity earnings are eliminated, and replaced with the revenues and expenses of the subsidiary, the goodwill impairment loss, and the noncontrolling interest, as follows:

Net income, Controlada (revenues less expenses)	$12,000
Goodwill impairment loss	(5,760)
Noncontrolling interest	(1,200)
Equity earnings	$(5,040)

   (b) Noncontrolling interest is 10 percent of subsidiary net income.

2. Consolidated retained earnings —

   Because the parent has used the equity method, all items are identical to the parent's retained earnings.

3. Consolidated balance sheet —

   (a) The investment account is eliminated and replaced with the assets and liabilities of the subsidiary, the unamortized purchase discrepancy, and the noncontrolling interest.

   (b) The noncontrolling interest is calculated as follows:

Common stock	$192,000
Retained earnings	65,600
	$257,600
	10%
	$ 25,760

The unamortized purchase discrepancy can be verified by the following calculation:

Investment in Controlada		$283,680
Shareholders' equity of Controlada (as above)	257,600	
	90%	231,840
Unamortized purchase discrepancy (goodwill)		$ 51,840

Other Considerations

The previous examples have illustrated the translation of a foreign operation's financial statements and the consolidation of these statements with those of the reporting enterprise. We will now look at some other items that must be considered when a foreign subsidiary is being consolidated.

Lower of Cost or Market   If the foreign operation applies Canadian accounting principles when preparing its financial statements, it will value certain items, such as inventory, at the lower of cost or market. If the subsidiary is self-sustaining, the method of valuation used is of no consequence in the translation because all of the assets are translated at the current rate regardless of whether they are carried at past prices (cost) or current prices (market).

If the foreign operation is integrated, assets carried at cost are translated at historical rates while assets carried at market are translated at the current rate. Remember that the temporal method remeasures, in Canadian dollars, transactions that have been incurred by the foreign operation. Therefore, the translated financial statements should reflect the lower of cost or market in Canadian dollars as if the parent itself had carried out the inventory acquisitions of its foreign subsidiary.

Section 1650 describes the proper treatment for assets of an integrated operation as follows:

> When assets are valued at the lower of cost and market, a write-down to market may be required in the translated financial statements even though no write-down is required in the foreign currency financial statements. [1650.65]

For example, if the market price (denominated in foreign currency) is greater than historical cost (denominated in foreign currency), no write-down will have occurred in the foreign operation's statements. But if the foreign currency weakens, it is quite possible that the market price translated at the current rate will be less than historical cost translated at the historical rate. In this situation, translated market price will be used in the translated financial statements.

> On the other hand, it may be necessary to reverse a write-down in the foreign currency financial statements prior to translation if the market amount translated at the current rate exceeds historical cost translated at the historical rates. [1650.66]

For example, if the market price (denominated in foreign currency) is less than historical cost (denominated in foreign currency), a write-down would have taken place in the foreign operation's statements. If the foreign currency has strengthened so that the market price translated at the current rate is greater than historical cost translated at the historical rate, this write-down will have to be reversed prior to translation. The inventory (now carried at cost) will be translated at the historical rate.

Intercompany Profits   In the preparation of consolidated financial statements, intercompany profits in assets are eliminated. If the profits are contained in the assets of the Canadian parent, there is no particular problem eliminating them. The asset acquired was recorded by the parent at the foreign currency denominated price translated at the exchange rate on the date of the transaction. The profit rate can be applied for the items still on hand to determine the amount of profit to be eliminated. If the profits are contained in the assets of an integrated subsidiary, the amount of unrealized profit can still be determined in foreign currency. Because the asset itself is translated at the historical rate, using the historical rate to translate and eliminate the profit will result in a translated asset at historical cost to the consolidated entity.

When the profit is contained in the assets of a translated self-sustaining subsidiary, the asset has been translated at the current rate. The question becomes this: What rate should be used to translate the profit before eliminating it in the consolidation process? The committee concluded that the historical exchange rate should be used to calculate the amount of the profit. This will *not* result in a translated asset recorded at historical cost to the entity.[10]

An International Perspective

The foreign currency accounting standards of the United States and the IASB are very similar to those of Canada. Terminology differs, but a close examination concludes that all three standards yield the same results. This harmonization that appears to have been achieved between these three bodies has not been reflected in the accounting standards used in other countries.

Some countries follow conservative accounting practices whereby unrealized gains resulting from foreign currency transactions are not reflected in the income statement. The foreign currency gain from the translation of an account receivable or payable would be a violation of the rule of nonrecognition of unrealized gains; so these receivables are translated, using historical rates, to avoid this. Any loss resulting from the translation is allowed to stand and is reflected in income. Germany and Austria follow these practices. Chile's accounting rules recommend against recording the unrealized gains resulting from translating long-term monetary items denominated in foreign currency.

A variation in practices is observed when the translation of foreign currency financial statements is examined. Companies in the United Kingdom tend to use the current rate method, with the translation adjustment reflected in an equity reserve. Either the current rate or an average rate can be used to translate the income statement. Subsidiaries in highly inflationary economies can be adjusted first for inflation and then translated using the current method. The temporal method is used for those subsidiaries whose activities are closely related to the parent. Mexico's rules do not address this topic, and companies are urged to follow IASB standards.

The accounting rules in France and Germany are also silent in this regard. Many companies in both countries use the current rate method; but in Germany, companies following conservative practice would reflect translation losses in income and take translation gains directly to equity.

Japan's translation rules tend to follow the current/noncurrent approach, except that translation losses show up as assets and gains are reflected in liabilities.

Chile uses the current rate method with translation adjustments shown in equity, while Brazil uses the same method but reflects the exchange gains and losses in income.

---

[10] For a more detailed discussion of this, see Dr. Pierre Vezina, "Foreign Currency Translation," Toronto: CICA, 1985.

SUMMARY

Before the equity method or consolidation accounting can be used, the financial statements of foreign investees must be translated into Canadian dollars. If the investee is considered to be an integrated foreign operation, the temporal method of translation is used. Exchange gains or losses resulting from the translation of the current monetary position are included in income.

The current rate method is used when the foreign operation is self-sustaining. Exchange gains and losses from the translation are not reflected in income, but rather are shown in a separate component of shareholders' equity. The consolidation of the translated financial statements of a self-sustaining subsidiary creates additional exchange gains and losses from the translation of the purchase discrepancy.

REVIEW QUESTIONS

1. "The current/noncurrent, monetary/nonmonetary, and current rate methods each produced different amounts for translation gains and losses due to the items at risk." Explain.

2. How is the temporal method different from the monetary/nonmonetary method?

3. What is the major objective to be achieved in the translation of foreign currency denominated financial statements?

4. What should happen if a foreign subsidiary's financial statements have been prepared using accounting principles different from those used in Canada?

5. What is the difference between a self-sustaining foreign operation and an integrated operation? What method of translation should be used for each?

6. What translation method should be used for a self-sustaining subsidiary that operates in a highly inflationary environment? Why?

7. How are translation exchange gains and losses reflected in financial statements if the foreign operation is integrated? Would the treatment be different if the foreign operation were self-sustaining? Explain.

8. Does the temporal method use the same unit of measure as the current rate method? Explain.

9. The amount of the cumulative translation adjustment appearing in the translated financial statements of a subsidiary could be different from the amount appearing in the consolidated financial statements. Explain how.

10. The application of the lower of cost or market rule to the translated financial statements requires different treatment with regard to the two classifications of foreign operations described in the *CICA Handbook*. Explain fully.

11. If the translation of an integrated foreign operation produced a gain, the translation of the same company could produce a loss if the operation was instead considered to be self-sustaining. Do you agree with this statement? Explain.

MULTIPLE CHOICE

1. What happens when the temporal method of foreign currency translation is used?
   a. Monetary assets and liabilities are translated at the current rate.
   b. The lower of cost and market rule to determine the need for a write-down of inventory is applied after translation.
   c. Translation gains and losses are shown in shareholders' equity.
   d. a and b.
   e. a and c.

2. The temporal and current rate methods are being compared. Which of the following statements is true?
   a. The amount reported for inventory is normally the same under both methods.
   b. The amount reported for equipment is normally the same under both methods.
   c. The amount reported for sales is normally the same under both methods.
   d. The amount reported for depreciation expense is normally the same under both methods.

3. What rates should be used to translate the following balance sheet accounts of a self-sustaining foreign operation?

Equipment	Accumulated amortization – equipment
a. current	current
b. historical	historical
c. average for the year	current
d. current	historical

4. An integrated subsidiary of a Canadian parent is located in Australia, whose currency is the dollar (A$). The subsidiary acquires inventory on October 31, 2002, for A$150,000 which is sold on January 15, 2003, for A$200,000. Collection of the money takes place on February 10, 2003. Applicable exchange rates are as follows:

October 31, 2002	A$1 = CDN$0.5075
December 31, 2002	A$1 = CDN$0.5050
January 15, 2003	A$1 = CDN$0.5000

   After translation, what amount should reported for this inventory on December 31, 2002?
   a. $76,125
   b. $75,750
   c. $75,000
   d. $100,000

5. At what point in the process should a Canadian parent company adjust its foreign subsidiary's accounts to bring them in accordance with GAAP?
   a. Prior to the beginning of the translation process.
   b. After translation, but prior to consolidation.
   c. After consolidation, but prior to reporting.
   d. No adjustments are necessary, since most foreign countries already use GAAP.

6. What rates should be used to translate the following balance sheet accounts of an integrated foreign operation?

Equipment	*Accumulated amortization – equipment*
a. current	current
b. current	average for the year
c. current	historical
d. historical	historical

Use the following data for Questions 7 and 8.

The following balance sheet accounts of a foreign entity have been translated into Canadian dollars using the following rates:

	Historical	*Current*
Accounts receivable	$264,000	$240,000
Investment in bonds	132,000	120,000
Land	66,000	60,000
Patents	102,000	96,000

7. The foreign entity is considered to be integrated. What total should appear on the balance sheet of this entity's Canadian parent for these items?
    a. $516,000
    b. $522,000
    c. $528,000
    d. $540,000

8. The foreign entity is considered to be self-sustaining. What total should appear on the balance sheet of its Canadian parent for these items?
    a. $516,000
    b. $522,000
    c. $528,000
    d. $540,000

9. A Canadian company owns a self-sustaining subsidiary in Argentina, where the currency is the peso (Ps). On January 1, 2002, the subsidiary had Ps500,000 in cash and no other assets or liabilities. On February 15, the subsidiary used Ps100,000 to purchase equipment. On April 1, the subsidiary used cash to purchase merchandise inventory costing Ps80,000. This merchandise was sold on May 29 for Ps120,000 in cash. On November 29, the subsidiary paid cash dividends in the amount of Ps60,000, and on December 31 it recorded depreciation on the equipment for the year of Ps50,000. The appropriate exchange rates were as follows:

January 1, 2002	Ps1 = $1.48
February 15, 2002	Ps1 = $1.50
April 1, 2002	Ps1 = $1.52
May 29, 2002	Ps1 = $1.55
November 29, 2002	Ps1 = $1.53
December 31, 2002	Ps1 = $1.56
Average for 2002	Ps1 = $1.50

    What is the amount of the cumulative translation adjustment to be reported in the stockholders' equity section of the translated balance sheet?
    a. $31,000 debit.
    b. $31,000 credit.
    c. $37,600 debit.
    d. $37,600 credit.

Use the following data for Questions 10 and 11.

A subsidiary of a Canadian company purchased government bonds and inventory on March 1, 2002, for 80,000 pesos each. Both of these items were paid for on May 1, 2002, and were still on hand at year-end. Inventory is carried at cost under the lower of cost or market rule. Currency exchange rates are as follows:

March 1, 2002	Ps1 = $0.20
May 1, 2002	Ps1 = $0.22
December 31, 2002	Ps1 = $0.24

10. Assuming that the subsidiary is integrated, what balances are reported on the December 31, 2002, consolidated balance sheet?
    a. Government bonds = $16,000, inventory = $16,000.
    b. Government bonds = $17,600, inventory = $17,600.
    c. Government bonds = $19,200, inventory = $16,000.
    d. Government bonds = $19,200, inventory = $19,200.
    e. Government bonds = $17,600, inventory = $16,000.

11. Assuming the subsidiary is self-sustaining, what balances are reported on the December 31, 2001, consolidated balance sheet?
    a. Government bonds = $16,000, inventory = $16,000.
    b. Government bonds = $17,600, inventory = $17,600.
    c. Government bonds = $19,200, inventory = $16,000.
    d. Government bonds = $19,200, inventory = $19,200.
    e. Government bonds = $17,600, inventory = $16,000.

Use the following data for Questions 12 to 16.

On January 1, 2001, Pizza purchased 100% of the outstanding common shares of Saza for 50,000 foreign currency units (FCUs). Saza is located in Zania, and on January 1, 2001, had common shares of FCU30,000 and retained earnings of FCU10,000. At the date of acquisition, the purchase discrepancy was allocated entirely to buildings, with a remaining life of 20 years.

Saza's financial statements at December 31, 2002, are shown below in the FCUs of its native country:

STATEMENT OF INCOME AND RETAINED EARNINGS
for the Year Ended December 31, 2002

Sales	FCU130,000
Beginning inventory	12,000
Purchases	72,000
Ending inventory	(15,000)
Cost of goods sold	69,000
Gross profit	61,000
Operating expenses	32,000
Amortization expense	11,000
Net income	18,000
Retained earnings, Jan. 1, 2002	12,000
	30,000
Dividends declared and paid	(15,000)
Retained earnings, Dec. 31, 2002	FCU 15,000

BALANCE SHEETS

Current monetary assets	FCU 43,000
Inventory	15,000
Plant and equipment (net)	34,000
	FCU 92,000
Current monetary liabilities	FCU 27,000
10% bonds payable	20,000
Common stock	30,000
Retained earnings	15,000
	FCU 92,000

Sales, purchases, and operating expenses were made evenly throughout the year. Year-end inventory was purchased at the year-end rate. Equipment additions of FCU5,000 with a useful life of 5 years were purchased on January 1, 2002. In 2001, Saza earned FCU20,000 and paid dividends of FCU18,000. Dividends were declared and paid on December 31 of each year. The bonds payable were issued on January 1, 2001, and mature on January 1, 2006.

Saza's net current monetary position at December 31, 2001, was FCU10,000. Exchange rates at various dates are given below.

January 1, 2001	FCU1 = $2.10
Average, 2001	FCU1 = $2.15
January 1, 2002	FCU1 = $2.20
Average, 2002	FCU1 = $2.25
December 31, 2002	FCU1 = $2.30

12. Which of the following is the amount that would be reported as cost of goods sold on Saza's translated financial statements at December 31, 2002, assuming it is an integrated subsidiary?
    a. $153,900
    b. $154,500
    c. $155,250
    d. $158,700

13. Which of the following is the amount that would be reported as a deferred exchange loss on Saza's translated financial statements at December 31, 2002, assuming it is an integrated subsidiary?
    a. 0
    b. $1,500
    c. $2,700
    d. $2,800

14. Which of the following is the amount that would be reported as the foreign currency gain or loss on Saza's translated income statement for the year ended December 31, 2002, assuming it is a self-sustaining subsidiary?
    a. There would be no amount reported on the income statement; however, a cumulative translation adjustment would be disclosed in Saza's equity section.
    b. $900 gain.
    c. $900 loss.
    d. $1,800 gain.

15. Which of the following is the amount that would be reported as the cumulative translation gain on Saza's translated financial statements at December 31, 2002, assuming it is a self-sustaining subsidiary?

    a. $5,000
    b. $5,100
    c. $6,000
    d. $10,100

16. Which of the following is the translation gain that would arise from the translation of the purchase discrepancy on Pizza's consolidated financial statements at December 31, 2001, assuming a self-sustaining operation?

    a. $0
    b. $900
    c. $950
    d. $975

(CGA adapted)

CASES

Case 1 Summarized below are the balances in the cumulative translation adjustment accounts in the consolidated balance sheets of four companies at the end of two successive years. Each company reported in footnote disclosures that its foreign subsidiaries were self-sustaining, and that the financial statements of the subsidiaries had been translated into Canadian dollars using the current rate method. Assume that the balance sheets of each of the companies' foreign subsidiaries have not changed significantly during Year 6.

	Cumulative translation adjustment (millions of dollars)	
	Year 6	Year 5
A Company	201	30
B Company	52	(75)
C Company	(170)	(100)
D Company	(18)	(164)

Required:

For each company, give a logical explanation for the change that has occurred in the cumulative translation adjustment account during the year. For each company, indicate whether the Canadian dollar is stronger or weaker in Year 6, compared with Year 5.

Case 2* The items shown as Exhibit 13.15 below are extracted from the summary of significant accounting policies of Altos Hornos de México (AHMSA), a steel producer. Your firm, a major Canadian steel producer, is contemplating a major equity investment in AHMSA; there is the potential for an eventual business combination between the firms.

Required:

In your capacity as financial analyst with the acquisitions department, prepare a briefing note for your chief financial officer on the financial reporting implications of the items outlined below.

What problems do you foresee in (a) the analytical process, and (b) the interface of the accounting systems of your firm and those of the proposed acquisition? (Note that you are primarily interested in raising questions at this stage, not in providing answers.)

---

*Case prepared by Peter Secord, St. Mary's Universtiy.

Exhibit 13.15

SUMMARY OF SIGNIFICANT ACCOUNTING POLICIES [EXCERPTS]

The significant accounting policies followed by the Company, which are in accordance with generally accepted accounting principles (GAAP) in Mexico, are as follows:

a) *Application of new accounting principles*

Beginning January 1, 1997, the Fifth Amendment to Bulletin B-10 issued by the Mexican Institute of Public Accountants became effective. This amendment states that the only method to be used for the restatement of nonmonetary assets is the adjustment from changes in the NCPI (National Consumer Price Index). However it permits the use of replacement costs for the recognition of the effects of inflation in the case of inventories and costs of sales and imported machinery and equipment, which is restated using the inflation rate of the country of origin and period-end exchange rate.

The Company, following the provisions of Bulletin A-8 issued by the Mexican Institute of Public Accountants ("Supplementary Application of International Accounting Standards") recorded the amortization of the excess of book value over the cost of certain shares ("negative goodwill") in other sales in the consolidated income statement.

b) *Recognition of the effects of inflation in the financial statements*

The Company restates its financial statements to reflect the purchasing power of the Mexican peso as of the most recent reporting date, thereby comprehensively recognizing the effects of inflation. The financial statements of prior periods have also been restated in terms of the purchasing power of the Mexican peso as of the most recent reporting date. Accordingly, prior period amounts differ from those previously reported. As a result, the amounts reported for the most current period are comparable with those of prior periods, being expressed in terms of the same purchasing power.

To recognize the effects of inflation in terms of Mexican pesos with purchasing power as of the most recent reporting date, the procedures used are as follows:

Balance Sheets

Inventories are restated to their most recent production or purchase cost, up to a maximum of their realizable value.

The laminating rollers are amortized based on units of production determined by the Company's technicians.

Inventory of scrap is valued at its recovery cost, in accordance with its market value, less the contribution margin and the cost incurred to process. Scrap is a by-product of AHMSA's production of molten pig iron that can be reused as a secondary raw material.

Property, plant, and equipment are initially recorded at cost of acquisition and/or construction and through 1996 were adjusted annually, to reflect their net replacement cost reported by independent appraisers. Beginning in 1997, domestic property, plant, and equipment are restated using NCPI factors, based on the restated value as of December 31, 1996, and imported equipment is restated using the inflation rate of the country of origin and the period-end exchange rate.

Depreciation of fixed assets is computed using the straight-line method, based on the estimated useful lives and appraisers' value of the assets and is restated to constant Mexican pesos using the NCPI.

Shareholders' equity and nonmonetary items other than inventory and property, plant and equipment are restated using factors derived from the NCPI, cumulative from the date of contribution or generation.

Statements of Income
Revenues and expenses that are associated with a monetary item (trade receivables, cash, liabilities, etc.) are restated from the month in which they arise through the most recent reporting date, based on the NCPI.

Cost of sales is restated to estimated replacement cost at the time of the sale, through the use of standard costs that are periodically updated. Other costs and expenses associated with nonmonetary items are restated from the time incurred through period end, as a function of the restatement of the nonmonetary assets that are being consumed or sold.

The gain from monetary position in the income statement represents the effect of inflation on monetary items. This amount is computed on the net monetary position at the beginning of each month, adjusted by changes in the NCPI, and the monthly result is restated in terms of the purchasing power of the Mexican peso at period end.

Other Statements
The statement of changes in financial position presents the changes in financial resources measured in constant Mexican pesos, based on the financial position at the prior period end, restated to Mexican pesos as of the end of the most recent reporting period.

The cumulative restatement effect in shareholders' equity consists principally of the gain or loss from holding nonmonetary assets, which represents the change in the specific price level of those assets in relation to general inflation, as measured by the NCPI.

c) *Cash and cash equivalents*
Cash equivalents include short-term highly liquid investments with an original maturity of three months or less (including Mexican treasury bills) and bank deposits valued at market (cost plus accrued interest).

At December 31, 2002, there are Ps87,500 of security investments that guarantee the timely payment of the unsecured obligations of MINOSA, a subsidiary. For financial statements purposes this concept is recorded net of the related liability.

d) *Income tax and employee profit sharing*
The provisions for income tax and employee profit sharing are calculated based upon taxable income, which differs from income for financial reporting purposes due to certain permanent and timing differences which are expected to be replaced by items of a similar nature and amount.

e) *Financing and related costs*
Financing and related costs include interest income and expense, foreign exchange gains and losses, and gains or losses from monetary position.

Transactions denominated in foreign currencies are recorded at the exchange rate at the date on which they occur. The assets and liabilities denominated in foreign currencies are valued at the exchange rate in effect at the balance sheet date.

f) *Negative goodwill*

Negative goodwill represents the excess of the book value of shares acquired over the purchase price. Amortization is calculated on a straight-line basis during the period in which the new subsidiary will be integrated, the three-year period beginning January 1, 2001.

g) *Restatement of shareholders' equity*

Capital stock and accumulated earnings are restated by applying the NCPI from the date contributed or accrued. The restatement represents the amount necessary to maintain shareholders' equity in terms of purchasing power at year-end.

h) *Minority interest*

The minority interest principally represents the minority shareholders' proportionate share of the earnings and equity of 5% of Hullera Mexicana, S.A. de C.V.

Case 3* Nova Mine Engineering is a junior Canadian company with a variety of operating subsidiaries and other undertakings that provide mine engineering and management services in Canada and in several less developed countries. One of these subsidiaries is active in Zimbabwe, which is rich in mineral resources and has an active mining industry. This company, Zimbabwe Platinum Management (ZPM), is under review prior to year-end translation and consolidation. The staff of ZPM consists primarily of junior and intermediate Nova staff who have been seconded to the operation on one- to three-year terms. Between the companies there is information flow but no product movement. Capital investment in Zimbabwe is restricted to movable equipment and working capital with a value of about CDN$3,000,000.

Management of Nova has long been concerned about its inability to hedge against fluctuations in the Zimbabwean dollar. All payments to ZPM from the state Mineral Marketing Corporation have recently been made in this currency, rather than in U.S. dollars as specified in earlier contracts. It is this inability to hedge that has increased Nova's concern about the long-run fit of ZPM within the portfolio of Nova companies, and about current financial statement presentation. The currency has declined in value by 65 percent during the year. Other concerns include Zimbabwe's persistent high inflation, recently about 35 percent, which is expected to increase even further. Political uncertainty is also a concern, as a result of recent nationalizations in the agricultural sector and growing unrest among the poor.

Required:

In a briefing note, advise senior management of Nova how the investment in the subsidiary ZPM should be measured and reported, and what disclosures should be made with respect to this investment in the annual report of the parent company.

---

*Case prepared by Peter Secord, St. Mary's University.

PROBLEMS

Note: Some problems use direct exchange rate quotations, while others use indirect quotations. For direct quotations, the foreign currency is multiplied by the exchange rate to arrive at Canadian dollars; for indirect quotations, division is used.

Problem 1   On December 31, 2001, Precision Manufacturing Inc. (PMI) of Edmonton purchased 100% of the outstanding common shares of Sandora Corp. of Flint, Michigan. Sandora's comparative balance sheets and 2002 income statement are as follows:

BALANCE SHEET
December 31

	2002	2001
Cash	US$ 780,000	US$ 900,000
Accounts receivable	6,100,000	4,800,000
Inventory	5,700,000	6,300,000
Plant and equipment (net)	6,600,000	7,200,000
	US$19,180,000	US$19,200,000
Current liabilities	US$ 1,900,000	US$ 2,400,000
Bonds payable —		
due Dec. 31, 2006	4,800,000	4,800,000
Common stock	5,000,000	5,000,000
Retained earnings	7,480,000	7,000,000
	US$19,180,000	US$19,200,000

INCOME STATEMENT
Year Ended December 31, 2002

Sales	US$ 6,000,000
Cost of sales	4,440,000
Depreciation expense	600,000
Other expense	360,000
	5,400,000
Net income	US$ 600,000

Other Information
- Exchange rates (US$ to CDN$)

December 31, 2001	US$ 1 = CDN$0.86
September 30, 2002	US$ 1 = CDN$0.82
December 31, 2002	US$ 1 = CDN$0.80
Average for 2002	US$ 1 = CDN$0.83

- Sandora declared and paid dividends on September 30, 2002.
- The inventories on hand on December 31, 2002, were purchased when the exchange rate was US$1 = CDN$0.81.

Required:

PART A
Assume that Sandora is an integrated foreign subsidiary.
(a) Calculate the 2002 exchange gain (loss) that would result from the translation of Sandora's financial statements.
(b) Translate the financial statements into Canadian dollars.

PART B

Assume that Sandora is a self-sustaining foreign subsidiary.

(a) Calculate the 2002 exchange gain (loss) that would result from the translation of Sandora's financial statements.

(b) Translate the financial statements into Canadian dollars.

(c) Clearly explain how the exchange gain or loss would be reflected in the 2002 consolidated financial statements of PMI.

Problem 2   On December 31, Year 1, Kelly Corporation of Toronto paid DM13 million for 100% of the outstanding common shares of Krugor Company of Germany. On this date the fair values of Krugor's identifiable assets and liabilities were equal to their carrying values. Krugor's comparative balance sheets and Year 2 income statement are as follows:

BALANCE SHEET
December 31

	Year 2	Year 1
Current monetary assets	DM10,780,000	DM 9,600,000
Inventory	1,800,000	2,400,000
Plant and equipment (net)	6,600,000	7,200,000
	DM19,180,000	DM19,200,000
Current liabilities	DM 1,900,000	DM 2,400,000
Bonds payable, due Dec. 31, Year 6	4,800,000	4,800,000
Common stock	5,000,000	5,000,000
Retained earnings	7,480,000	7,000,000
	DM19,180,000	DM19,200,000

INCOME STATEMENT
Year Ended December 31, Year 2

Sales	DM 6,000,000
Inventory, January 1	DM 2,400,000
Purchases	3,840,000
Inventory, December 31	(1,800,000)
Depreciation expense	600,000
Other expense	360,000
	DM 5,400,000
Net income	DM 600,000

Other Information

- Exchange rates

December 31, Year 1	DM1 = $0.52
September 30, Year 2	DM1 = $0.62
December 31, Year 2	DM1 = $0.65
Average for Year 2	DM1 = $0.58

- Krugor Company declared and paid dividends totalling DM120,000 on September 30, Year 2.

- The inventories on hand on December 31, Year 2, were purchased when the exchange rate was DM1 = $0.63.

Required:

PART A

Krugor is an integrated foreign subsidiary.
(a) Calculate the Year 2 exchange gain or loss that would result from the translation of Krugor's financial statements.
(b) Prepare translated financial statements.

PART B

Krugor is a self-sustaining foreign subsidiary.
(a) Calculate the Year 2 exchange gain or loss that would result from the translation of Krugor's financial statements.
(b) Prepare translated financial statements.
(c) Calculate the amount of goodwill that would appear on the December 31, Year 2, consolidated balance sheet, if there was an impairment loss of DM50,000 during the year.
(d) Calculate the amount, description, and location of the exchange gain or loss that would appear in Kelly's Year 2 consolidated financial statements.

Problem 3 The following are the financial statements of Werner, Inc., of Germany, as at December 31, Year 1.

FINANCIAL STATEMENTS
December 31, Year 1

BALANCE SHEET

Cash		DM 105,000
Accounts receivable		168,000
Inventories — at cost		357,000
Land		420,000
Buildings	1,470,000	
Accumulated depreciation	420,000	1,050,000
Equipment	483,000	
Accumulated depreciation	168,000	315,000
		DM2,415,000
Accounts payable		DM 210,000
Miscellaneous current payables		105,000
Bonds payable		600,000
Capital stock		850,000
Retained earnings		650,000
		DM2,415,000

RETAINED EARNINGS STATEMENT

Balance, January 1	DM 420,000
Net income	630,000
	1,050,000
Dividends	400,000
Balance, December 31	DM 650,000

INCOME STATEMENT

Sales	DM3,150,000
Cost of sales	DM1,680,000
Depreciation — building	105,000
Depreciation — equipment	63,000
Other expense	672,000
	DM2,520,000
Net Income	DM 630,000

Other Information

- On January 1, Year 1, Elgin Corporation of Toronto acquired a controlling interest in Werner.
- Relevant exchange rates for the mark were:

January 1, Year 1	$0.45
December 31, Year 1	$0.50
Average for Year 1	$0.48

- The land and buildings were held on the date the subsidiary was acquired, and there have been no additions or disposals since that date.
- During the year, equipment costing DM126,000 was purchased for cash. Depreciation totalling DM21,000 has been recorded on this equipment. The exchange rate on the date of the equipment purchase was $0.46.

  The remaining equipment was held on the date the subsidiary was acquired, and no other changes have taken place since that date.
- The December 31, Year 1, inventory was acquired during the last quarter of the year, when the average exchange rate was $0.49.
- On January 1, Year 1, the inventory was DM525,000, and was acquired when the average exchange rate was $0.44.
- The bonds mature on December 31, Year 6.
- Other operating expenses were incurred equally throughout the year.
- Dividends were declared and paid on December 31, Year 1.
- On January 1, Year 1, liabilities were greater than monetary assets by the amount of DM1,082,000.

Required:

PART A

Assume that Werner is an integrated foreign operation. Translate the financial statements into Canadian dollars.

PART B

Assume that Werner is a self-sustaining foreign operation. Translate the balance sheet only into Canadian dollars.

Problem 4   On January 1, Year 1, P Company (a Canadian company) purchased 90% of S Company (located in a foreign country) at a cost of 14,000 foreign currency units (FCUs).

The book values of S Company's net assets were equal to fair market values on this date except for plant and equipment, which had a fair market value of FCU22,000, with a remaining life of 10 years. A goodwill impairment loss of FCU100 occurred in Year 1.

The balance sheet of S Company on January 1, Year 1, is shown below:

	S Company (FCUs)
Monetary assets (current)	10,000
Inventory	8,000
Plant and equipment	20,000
	38,000
Current liabilities	9,000
Bonds payable (mature in 8 years)	16,000
Capital stock	10,000
Retained earnings	3,000
	38,000

The following exchange rates were in effect during Year 1:

January 1/1	1FCU = $1.10
Average for year	1FCU = $1.16
When inventory purchased	1FCU = $1.19
December 31/1	1FCU = $1.22

The financial statements of P Company (in $) and S Company (in FCUs) as at December 31, Year 1, are shown below.

Required:

Prepare the December 31, Year 1, consolidated financial statements, assuming that S Company is:
(a) an integrated foreign subsidiary.
(b) a self-sustaining foreign subsidiary.

BALANCE SHEETS

	P Company $	S Company FCUs
Monetary assets (current)	31,992	17,000
Inventory	30,000	11,000
Plant and equipment	60,000	18,000
Investment in S Company (at cost)	15,400	—
	137,392	46,000
Current liabilities	26,000	12,000
Bonds payable	40,000	16,000
Capital stock	30,000	10,000
Retained earnings, Jan.1	22,000	3,000
Net income	29,392	9,000
Dividends (declared on Dec. 31)	(10,000)	(4,000)
	137,392	46,000

INCOME STATEMENTS

	P Company $	S Company FCUs
Sales	160,000	40,000
Dividend income	4,392	—
Cost of sales	(80,000)	(19,000)
Depreciation	(11,000)	(2,000)
Other expense	(44,000)	(10,000)
Net income	29,392	9,000

Problem 5 Mex Ltd. is an integrated foreign subsidiary. At the end of the current year the inventory of the company was:

Cost	14,862,000 pesos
Market	12,100,000 pesos

Applying the lower of cost or market, the company wrote the inventory down by Ps2,762,000 for presentation in its financial statements. When these financial statements were received by the parent company in Canada for translation, it was determined that the year-end spot rate was $1 = Ps392. The closing inventory at cost is composed of the following:

Purchase	Amount in pesos	Historical exchange rate
1	3,200,000	$1 = Ps341
2	6,132,000	$1 = Ps360
3	5,530,000	$1 = Ps375

Required:

(a) At what amount would the inventory be shown on the translated balance sheet of Mex? And what is the amount of the loss from write-down that would appear on the translated income statement?

(b) If the year-end spot rate was $1 = Ps281, at what amount would the inventory be shown on the translated balance sheet? And what is the amount of the loss from write-down that would appear on the translated income statement?

(CGA *adapted*)

Problem 6 Hague Corp., located in the Netherlands, is a 90% owned subsidiary of a Canadian parent. The company was incorporated on January 1, Year 1, and issued its no-par common shares for 5.0 million guilders. The Canadian parent acquired 90% of these shares at this time for $2.25 million when the exchange rate was G1 = $0.50. The financial statements for Hague on December 31, Year 2, are shown below.

BALANCE SHEET
December 31, Year 2

	Year 2	Year 1
Cash	G1,000,000	G 500,000
Accounts receivable	2,710,000	2,550,000
Inventory	1,050,000	1,155,000
Plant assets	6,000,000	6,000,000
Accumulated depreciation	(1,000,000)	(500,000)
	G9,760,000	G9,705,000
Accounts payable	G 50,000	G 850,000
Accrued liabilities	50,000	350,000
Bonds payable — due Jan. 3, Year 11	2,500,000	2,500,000
Common shares	5,000,000	5,000,000
Retained earnings	2,160,000	1,005,000
	G9,760,000	G9,705,000

INCOME STATEMENT
for the Year Ended December 31, Year 2

Sales	G35,000,000
Cost of sales	G28,150,000
Depreciation	500,000
Interest	200,000
Selling	1,940,000
Miscellaneous	800,000
Income tax	1,045,000
	G32,635,000
Net income	G 2,365,000

STATEMENT OF RETAINED EARNINGS
for the Year Ended December 31, Year 2

Balance, January 1	G1,005,000
Net income	2,365,000
	3,370,000
Dividends	1,210,000
Balance, December 31	G2,160,000

Other Information

- On January 3, Year 1, Hague issued bonds for G2.5 million.
- Hague acquired the plant assets on February 1, Year 1, for G6.0 million. The plant assets are being depreciated on a straight-line basis over a 12-year life.
- Hague uses the FIFO basis to value inventory. The December 31, Year 1, inventory was acquired on October 1, Year 1. The inventory on hand on December 31, Year 2, was acquired on November 15.
- Hague did not pay dividends in Year 1, and the Year 2 dividends were declared on December 31, Year 2.
- Under the temporal method, Hague's December 31, Year 1, retained earnings were translated as $637,750.
- Exchange rate information:

January 3, Year 1	G1 = $0.51
February 1, Year 1	G1 = $0.52
October 1, Year 1	G1 = $0.55
Average, Year 1	G1 = $0.54
December 31, Year 1	G1 = $0.55
November 15, Year 2	G1 = $0.60
Average, Year 2	G1 = $0.62
December 31, Year 2	G1 = $0.65

Required:

(a) Translate Hague's Year 2 financial statements into dollars, assuming that it is an integrated foreign operation.

(b) Assume that Hague is a self-sustaining operation:
  (i) Translate the Year 2 financial statements.
  (ii) Prepare the Year 2 equity method journal entries that would be made by the Canadian parent.

Problem 7   In preparation for translating the financial statements of a foreign subsidiary that is inte-grated, you have the following information:

	French francs
Inventory (FIFO cost, net realizable value, 1,300,000 French francs)	1,150,000

An examination of the working papers of the foreign subsidiary's auditors shows the following information:

Opening inventory	FF 350,000
Purchases	
February 15, 2001	205,000
April 15, 2001	588,000
August 1, 2001	410,000
October 12, 2001	362,000
November 15, 2001	547,000
Cost of goods sold for the year	1,312,000

Exchange rates:

January 1, 2001 (opening inventory)	$1 = FF2.5
February 15, 2001	$1 = FF3.1
April 15, 2001	$1 = FF3.4
August 1, 2001	$1 = FF4.3
October 12, 2001	$1 = FF4.8
November 15, 2001	$1 = FF5.5
December 31, 2001	$1 = FF6.1
2001 average	$1 = FF4.0

Note: This is not considered excessive or high inflation in terms of the temporal method.

Required:

(a) Calculate the Canadian dollar amount of the inventory at the fiscal year-end (December 31), and the Canadian dollar amount of any item(s) that would appear on the income statement.

(b) If the foreign subsidiary were self-sustaining, what would your answer to part (a) be?

(CGA adapted)

Problem 8   On January 1, 2001, Parent Ltd., a Winnipeg-based company, purchased 80% of the shares of Francesub Inc. for FF1,900,000 — an amount which, at that date, translated to $655,172.

The financial statements for Francesub at the end of the fiscal year 1999 are:

BALANCE SHEET
December 31, 2001

Cash	FF 820,000
Accounts receivable	317,500
Inventory	730,000
Fixed assets, net	1,722,500
	FF3,590,000
Current liabilities	FF 380,000
Notes payable	700,000
Common shares	900,000
Retained earnings	1,350,000
Dividends	(200,000)
Net income	460,000
	FF3,590,000

INCOME STATEMENT
for the Year Ended December 31, 2001

Sales	FF1,350,000
Cost of sales	(640,000)
	710,000
Depreciation	(122,500)
Other	(127,500)
Net income	FF 460,000

Additional Information

- The FIFO inventory method is used. The opening inventory, which was purchased before December 31, 2000, cost FF600,000. The exchange rate at the time of inventory purchase was $1 = FF2.71.
  The purchases during the year were:

	FF	Exchange Rate
Purchase Number 1	200,000	$1 = FF3.0
Purchase Number 2	570,000	$1 = FF3.12

- The fixed assets were purchased when the company was formed (January 1, 1993). The common shares were issued at the same time. The exchange rate at that date was $1 = FF1.5. The cost of the fixed assets is FF2,450,000, and the accumulated depreciation is FF727,500 at December 31, 2001.
- The notes payable are due on January 1, 2005, and were issued on December 31, 2000. There is no interest on these notes.
- The "sales" and "other" on the income statement were incurred evenly throughout the year. Also, the "other" represents a monetary outflow.
- The dividends were paid on December 31, 2001.
- The balances in francs at December 31, 2000:

Cash	FF 350,000
Account receivable	FF 405,000
Current liabilities	FF(250,000)
Notes payable*	FF(700,000)

  * The notes were issued on December 31, 2000.

- Exchange rates:

December 31, 2000	$1 = FF2.9
January 1, 2001	$1 = FF2.9
2001 average	$1 = FF3.25
December 31, 2001	$1 = FF3.6

Required:

(a) There will be a foreign exchange gain or loss on the translated income statement prepared in part (b). Prepare a schedule to explain the calculation of the foreign exchange gain or loss.

(b) Prepare the Canadian dollar income statement for Francesub for 2001, using the temporal method and assuming that the income statement will be used to consolidate with Parent.

(CGA adapted)

Problem 9 Dom Ltd. has a subsidiary, Tarzan Inc., in the country of Tarzania, which uses the tar (Tz) as its currency. Before this 100% owned subsidiary can be consolidated, the financial statements must be translated from tars to Canadian dollars. However, the person responsible for the translation has quit suddenly and left you with a half-finished job. Certain information is available but the rest you must determine.

TARZAN INC.
FINANCIAL STATEMENTS (IN TZ)
for the Year Ended December 31, 2002

Cash	Tz 100,000
Accounts receivable	200,000
Inventory (1)	400,000
Land	500,000
Buildings (2)	800,000
Accumulated depreciation	(300,000)
	Tz1,700,000
Accounts payable	Tz 250,000
Note payable (3)	400,000
Common shares	300,000
Retained earnings, January 1, 2002	600,000
Net income, 2002	150,000
	Tz1,700,000
Sales	Tz1,000,000
Cost of goods sold	(600,000)
	400,000
Depreciation	(80,000)
Other expenses (4)	(170,000)
Net income	Tz 150,000

Other Information

- The opening inventory was Tz500,000, and the purchases during the period were Tz500,000. Tarzan uses a periodic LIFO inventory system. The opening inventory had an exchange rate of $1 = Tz3.1, and the purchases were made 30% from the parent and 70% from the local area. The local area purchases were made evenly throughout the year; the purchases from the parent were recorded by the parent at $35,714.
- There were two buildings and one piece of land. The land and building #1 (Tz300,000) were acquired when Tarzan was formed by Dom. The exchange rate at that time was $1 = Tz2. Building #2 was acquired when the exchange rate was $1 = Tz3.2. The depreciation expense is proportional to the purchase prices. The accumulated depreciation relating to Building #2 is Tz200,000.
- The note payable, which is due on January 1, 2006, was created on July 1, 2002.
- The other expenses were incurred evenly throughout the year.
  The opening retained earnings translated into $181,818.
- Exchange rates:

January 1, 2002	$1 = Tz3.7
2002 average, July 1, 2002	$1 = Tz3.9
December 31, 2002	$1 = Tz4.1

Required:

(a) Assume that Tarzan is integrated. Prepare the financial statements of Tarzan in Canadian dollars. Show your calculations *in good form*.

(b) If the fair market value of the inventory was Tz350,000, and the year-end exchange rate was $1 = Tz2.4, what would the Canadian dollar value of the inventory be? Assume all the other information given in the question remains constant.

(*CGA adapted*)

Problem 10   In 1999, Victoria Textiles Limited decided that its European operations had expanded such that a European office should be established. The office would be involved in selling Victoria's current product lines; it was also expected to establish supplier contacts. In the European market there were a number of small manufacturers of top-quality fabrics, particularly wool and lace, but from Victoria's home office in Ontario it was difficult to find and maintain these suppliers. To assist in doing so, a wholly owned company, Victoria Textiles (Luxembourg) Limited, was created, and a facility was established in Luxembourg in January 2000. The new company, VTLL, was given the mandate from head office to buy and sell with other Victoria divisions and offices across Canada, as if it were an autonomous, independent unit. To establish the company, an investment of 10,000,000 Luxembourg francs (LF) was made on January 1, 2000.

VTLL proved to be quite successful, as shown in the financial statements at December 31, 2002. After one year of operations, VTLL had borrowed funds and expanded facilities substantially, as the initial market estimates had turned out to be quite conservative. However, during this time the Luxembourg franc had fallen in value relative to the Canadian dollar. As a result, Victoria's management was somewhat confused about how to evaluate VTLL's success, given the changing currency values.

Required:

(a) Prepare a Canadian-dollar balance sheet at December 31, 2002, and an income statement for the year then ended, assuming that VTLL is:
 (i) an integrated foreign subsidiary.
 (ii) a self-sustaining foreign subsidiary.
(b) Discuss the factors involved in making a choice between these methods, as they apply to the case of VTLL. What is the underlying rationale?
(c) Which method should Victoria Textiles Limited apply to its investment in this subsidiary?

FINANCIAL STATEMENTS
(000s, Luxembourg francs)

BALANCE SHEET

	2002	2001
Cash	4,100	3,900
Accounts receivable	2,900	2,100
Inventories	4,800	3,500
Prepaid expenses	1,900	1,700
Fixed assets (net)	7,900	8,900
	21,600	20,100
Current liabilities	2,400	900
Unearned revenue	800	500
Long-term debt	6,000	6,000
	9,200	7,400
Common stock	10,000	10,000
Retained earnings	2,400	2,700
	21,600	20,100

INCOME AND RETAINED EARNINGS STATEMENTS

	2002	2001
Sales	20,200	12,000
Cost of sales	11,300	6,300
Gross profit	8,900	5,700
Operating expenses	3,400	2,100
Depreciation	1,000	700
Interest	700	400
Taxes	600	400
Net income	3,200	2,100
Opening retained earnings	2,700	1,100
	5,900	3,200
Dividends	3,500	500
Closing retained earnings	2,400	2,700

Additional Information

1. The exchange rate at January 1, 2000, when VTLL was originally established, was $0.075 per Luxembourg franc.
2. Of the original investment of LF10 million, LF4 million was used to acquire plant and equipment, which is being depreciated on a straight-line basis over 10 years.
3. At June 30, 2001, an expansion was completed at a cost of LF6 million, which was financed entirely by a 6-year note obtained from a Luxembourg bank. Interest is to be paid semiannually. The exchange rate at July 1, 2001, was $0.062 per Luxembourg franc. The new expansion is also to be depreciated on a straight-line basis over 10 years. (A half-year's depreciation was recorded in 2001.)
4. Inventory is accounted for on the FIFO basis. The exchange rate at the end of 2001 and 2002 for the inventory was $0.045 and $0.027 per Luxembourg franc respectively.
5. Sales, purchases, and operating expenses were incurred evenly throughout the year, and the exchange rate average for the year was $0.031.
6. The exchange rates for the prepaid expenses and unearned revenue at December 31, 2002, were $0.03 and $0.028 per Luxembourg franc respectively.
7. Income taxes were paid in equal monthly instalments throughout the year.
8. Dividends are declared and paid each year on December 31.
9. The foreign exchange rates per Luxembourg franc at each of the following dates were as follows:

December 31, 2001	LF$0.041
June 30, 2002	LF$0.036
December 31, 2002	LF$0.025

(Prepared by Peter Secord, St. Mary's University)

CHAPTER 14

Accounting for Not-for-Profit Organizations

LEARNING OBJECTIVES

After studying this chapter, you should be able to do the following:

- Describe the not-for-profit accounting practices currently mandated in the *CICA Handbook* and compare them to the practices in use prior to the issuance of these sections.
- Explain the purpose behind fund reporting.
- Explain the use and the workings of a budgetary control system that uses encumbrances.
- Prepare journal entries and financial statements using the deferred contribution method of recording contributions.

- Prepare journal entries and financial statements using the restricted fund method of recording contributions.

Introduction

A substantial portion of Canada's economic activity is conducted by organizations whose purpose is to provide services (or products) on a nonprofit basis. The size of the portion becomes clear when one considers that included in this *nonbusiness area* is the *government sector* encompassing the federal, provincial, and local governments, as well as the *not-for-profit sector*. This latter sector encompasses a wide variety of organizations such as charities, hospitals, universities, professional and fraternal organizations, and community clubs. Our concern in this chapter is with the accounting and financial reporting for Canadian not-for-profit organizations (NFPOs). Even with governments excluded, this is still a very large sector in our economy, consisting of over 75,000 registered charities and an additional 100,000 voluntary organizations. It has been estimated that the charity sector alone receives over $70 billion a year from governments, private individuals, and corporations.

Not-for-profit organizations are defined in the *CICA Handbook* as:

> ... entities, normally without transferable ownership interests, organized and operated exclusively for social, educational, professional, religious, health, charitable or any other not-for-profit purpose. A not-for-profit organization's members, contributors and other resource providers do not, in such capacity, receive any financial return directly from the organization. [4400.02]

NFPOs differ from profit-oriented organizations in the following ways:

- They typically provide services or goods to identifiable segments of society without the expectation of profit. They accomplish this by raising resources and subsequently spending or distributing these resources in a manner that fulfils the organization's objectives.
- The resources are provided by contributors without the expectation of gain or repayment. Most of these resources consist of donations from the general public and grants from governments and other NFPOs. Often a portion of the resources received have restrictions attached that govern the manner in which they can be spent.
- As the definition cited above indicates, there is no readily defined ownership interest that can be sold, transferred, or redeemed in any way by the organization.
- While many NFPOs have paid employees, they are governed by volunteers who receive no remuneration or gain for the time and effort they provide. In some small organizations there are no paid employees and all effort is provided entirely by volunteers.

While financial reporting for NFPOs in Canada is well defined today, this has only been the case since April 1997, when seven very detailed *Handbook* sections became operational. Prior to this date, accounting in this area was in a state of flux, moving from a situation where there were no real authoritative pronouncements at all, to one where there was only a single *Handbook* section that gave only broad guidance for some issues and left many other important ones unresolved. A few large organizations, such as hospitals and universities, published detailed manuals in an attempt to establish consistent reporting practices for all members of a given association. Unfortunately, the practices set out for hospitals were different from those recommended for universities, and in both situations members did not have to follow their organization's recommendations. Smaller NFPOs followed a wide range of diverse practices such as using the cash basis only, or a mixture of cash and accrual accounting. Many did not capitalize capital asset acquisitions, and of the few that did capitalize, many did not provide for subsequent periodic amortization. A wide range of practices was also followed for donated materials, services, and capital assets, ranging from no recording to a full recording of all items. A large number of NFPOs used fund accounting in their end-of-year financial statement presentations. Later in this chapter we fully explore the concepts involved in fund accounting and fund presentations in accordance with current *Handbook* requirements. First, though, it is useful to examine the basic idea behind fund accounting and to give a brief illustration as to how various funds were presented in an organization's financial statements.

The Basics of Fund Accounting

The resources that an NFPO receives can be broadly categorized as *unrestricted* or *restricted*. *Unrestricted resources* can be used for any purposes that are consistent with the goals and objectives of the organization. *Restricted resources* can be used only in accordance with the wishes of the contributor. For example, a donation may be received with the proviso that it be spent in some specified manner. In some situations the original donation must be maintained intact, and only the interest earned on the funds invested can be spent by the organization. A donation of this type is called an *endowment*.

There are many examples of endowments. University scholarships are often funded by the interest earned on endowment contributions made by donors in prior years. Some famous private universities, such as Harvard and Stanford, have hundreds of millions of dollars in endowment funds, and use the earnings as their major source of revenue, since they do not receive government funding. The Toronto Symphony Orchestra has established an endowment fund as a device to help fund its daily operations. And finally, the Winnipeg Foundation, whose financial statements are reproduced in an appendix to this chapter, operates with substantial endowment funds.

Quite often, restrictions are also placed on how the endowment interest can be spent. In other words, interest revenue can be restricted or unrestricted. NFPOs sometimes conduct special campaigns to raise money for major acquisitions of buildings and equipment, and any moneys raised are restricted to this particular purpose. In some cases, the board of directors of a NFPO may pass a resolution designating a portion of unrestricted resources as restricted for a certain purpose, or to be held indefinitely, with only the interest earned to be spent. While such designations require disclosure, these resources are not technically considered as restricted, because future boards could reverse the designation. In accordance with the *Handbook*'s definition, true restricted resources are those that may only be spent in accordance with the wishes of the donor (or, in the case of endowments, may never be spent).

Fund accounting has been used very successfully to keep track of restricted resources and to convey information through the financial statements about the restrictions placed on the organization's resources. The concepts involved can be summarized as follows:

> Fund accounting comprises the collective accounting procedures resulting in a self-balancing set of accounts for each fund established by legal, contractual or voluntary actions of an organization. Elements of a fund can include assets, liabilities, net assets, revenues and expenses (and gains and losses where appropriate). Fund accounting involves an accounting segregation, although not necessarily a physical segregation, of resources. [4400.02]

Historically, it was typical to present a balance sheet and a statement of revenue and expenditure for each fund. Combined with the general practice of noncapitalization of land, buildings, and equipment, the results were a form of stewardship reporting, showing the resources received and spent during a period and the resources on hand at the end of the period that were available for future spending. The following simple example illustrates the use of fund accounting as a means of reporting this form of stewardship.

Example   The financial statements of the Helpful Society (HS) at the end of the current year are presented in Exhibit 14.1.

HS presents two funds in its year-end financial statements. The resources in the *general* fund can be used to carry out the normal activities of the organization, while the resources in the *building* fund, which was established during the current year, are restricted. Each year the organization raises money through donations and spends the funds raised on programs A, B, and C. During the current year, the general fund's revenues were $7,100 greater than its expenditures; as a result, its equity (described as fund balance) increased by this amount. Note that revenues and expenditures are measured under the accrual method, so the statement does not show cash inflows and outflows. During the year, the general fund acquired equipment at a cost of $25,000. Because this organization follows a policy of noncapitalization, the acquisition appears in the Program A expenditures on the revenue and expenditure statement. As a result, the assets on hand at the end of the year can be viewed as resources that are spendable. The liabilities at this date are a claim against these resources; therefore, the fund balance at the end of the current year represents net resources amounting to $32,200 that are available for spending next year.

During the current year a special fundraising campaign was initiated to raise the money necessary to purchase and furnish a building. The building fund's resources on hand at the end of the year, amounting to $94,635, were the result of $102,000 that was collected during the year less the fundraising costs and miscellaneous expenses incurred, which amounted to $7,365. The campaign will continue until its goal is reached. At that time the purchase of the building and furnishings will be recorded as an expenditure of this fund. Once the liabilities have been settled, the building fund will cease to exist. Of course, if the organization raises more than the cost of the building, the fund will be continued until the surplus cash is spent in accordance with the conditions imposed.

Exhibit 14.1

HELPFUL SOCIETY
BALANCE SHEET
December 31, Current Year

	General Fund	Building Fund	Total
Assets			
Cash	$17,500	$ 6,000	$ 23,500
Pledges receivable	50,000		50,000
Investments	25,000	88,635	113,635
Total	$92,500	$94,635	$187,135
Liabilities and fund balance			
Accounts payable and accrued liabilities	$60,300		$ 60,300
Fund balance	32,200	$94,635	126,835
Total	$92,500	$94,635	$187,135

STATEMENT OF REVENUE AND EXPENDITURE
AND CHANGES IN FUND BALANCE
for the Year Ended December 31, Current Year

	General Fund	Building Fund	Total
Revenues			
Contributions	$923,000	$102,000	$1,025,000
Interest	2,700		2,700
Total	925,700	102,000	1,027,700
Expenditures			
Program A	$625,000		$ 625,000
Program B	190,000		190,000
Program C	100,000		100,000
Fundraising	3,600	6,410	10,010
Miscellaneous		955	955
Total	918,600	7365	925,965
Excess of revenue over expenditure	7,100	94,635	101,735
Fund balance, January 1	25,100	0	25,100
Fund balance, December 31	$ 32,200	$ 94,635	$ 126,835

This example was presented to illustrate the basic idea behind financial reporting on a fund basis. When capital asset purchases are shown as expenditures, the result is a reporting of resources received and spent and resources on hand that can be spent in the future. On April 1, 1997, the new *Handbook* sections became effective, and as a result many NFPOs must now capitalize and depreciate their long-lived assets. This changes the reporting to one of cost of services provided, rather than one of reporting resources spent to provide services, which was the previous case. It should be noted that the columnar approach was used to present the two funds. An alternative that gained some prior acceptance was the layered approach, which presented funds one after another, so that the first page would show the operating fund statements, the second page would show the building fund, and so on. Under the provisions of the new *Handbook* sections, this approach is cumbersome because of a requirement to show totals for each financial statement item for all funds presented.

Not-for-Profit Reporting Today

The first response by the Accounting Standards Board of the CICA to deal with the problems involved with NFPO reporting was made in 1989. The introduction to the *Handbook* was amended to make it applicable to both profit-oriented and not-for-profit organizations. As a result, all sections of the *Handbook* were viewed as possibly being applicable to the financial reporting of NFPOs. The definition and concept sections of Section 1000 were subtly amended to include features unique to NFPOs, and a relatively small Section 4230 was introduced to deal with matters specific to not-for-profit organizations that were not covered by other *Handbook* sections. The coverage in this section was broad and brief and was considered to be a temporary solution until some controversial reporting issues could be resolved.

Finally, the standards board tackled the controversial areas, and two separate exposure drafts were released that made significant changes to NFPO financial reporting. The two most controversial areas related to the capitalization and amortization of long-lived assets and the consolidation of controlled entities. After considering the large volume of comments received, compromises were made and seven new *Handbook* sections were released. Because it was no longer applicable, Section 4230 was withdrawn. The introduction to the not-for-profit area contains a table that sets out the applicability of the various *Handbook* sections to NFPOs. Each section is characterized as generally applicable (9 sections), applicable to a NFPO with relevant transactions (21 sections), or having limited or no applicability (26 sections). Exhibit 14.2 lists the sections that have limited or no applicability. Note that while Section 4100, "Pension Plans," is not applicable, Section 3461, "Employee Future Benefits," would be applicable for those organizations that provide pension benefits to their employees.

The new *Handbook* sections are as follows:

- Section 4400, "Financial Statement Presentation By Not-for-Profit Organizations"
- Section 4410, "Contributions — Revenue Recognition"
- Section 4420, "Contributions Receivable"
- Section 4430, "Capital Assets Held by Not-for-Profit Organizations"
- Section 4440, "Collections Held by Not-for-Profit Organizations"
- Section 4450, "Reporting Controlled and Related Entities by Not-for-Profit Organizations"
- Section 4460, "Disclosure of Related Party Transactions by Not-for-Profit Organizations"

These sections deal with accounting issues that either are unique to not-for-profit organizations or are dealt with in the existing *Handbook* sections in a manner that is not appropriate for not-for-profit organizations. For example, Section 3061, "Property, Plant and Equipment," would apply to both not-for-profit and profit organizations if it were not for the existence of Section 4430, "Capital Assets Held by Not-for-Profit Organizations."

In the material that follows, the pronouncements of each section will be discussed and in some instances illustrated. Sections 4400 and 4410 will be discussed and illustrated last because they are closely related and involve fund reporting.

Section 4420, "Contributions Receivable"
A contribution is a type of revenue that is unique to not-for-profit organizations. It is defined as "a non-reciprocal transfer to a not-for-profit organization of cash or other assets or a non-reciprocal settlement or

Exhibit 14.2

CICA HANDBOOK SECTIONS
WITH LIMITED OR NO APPLICABILITY TO NFPOs

Section 1300, Differential Reporting
Section 1501, International Accounting Standards
Section 1520, Income Statement
Section 1540, Cash Flow Statements
Section 1581, Business Combinations*
Section 1590, Subsidiaries*
Section 1625, Comprehensive Revaluation of Assets & Liabilities
Section 1701, Segment Disclosures
Section 1751, Interim Financial Statements
Section 1800, Unincorporated Businesses
Section 3055, Interests in Joint Ventures*
Section 3061, Property, Plant and Equipment
Section 3062, Goodwill and Other Intangible Assets
Section 3240, Share Capital
Section 3250, Surplus
Section 3260, Reserves
Section 3465, Income Taxes
Section 3500, Earnings Per Share
Section 3610, Capital Transactions
Section 3800, Accounting for Government Assistance
Section 3805, Investment Tax Credits
Section 3840, Related Party Transactions
Section 3841, Economic Dependence
Section 3870, Stock-based Compensation and Other Stock-based Payments
Section 4100, Pension Plans
Section 4210, Life Insurance Enterprises

*These sections contain guidance that may be relevent to NFPOs

cancellation of its liabilities" (paragraph 4410.02). Nonreciprocal means that the contributor does not directly receive anything for the contribution. Included here are donations of cash, property or services, government grants, pledges, and bequests. Besides receiving contribution revenue, not-for-profit organizations may also receive other types of revenue such as those from investments or from the sale of goods and services. These other types of revenue are accounted for in accordance with the regular *Handbook* Section 3400, "Revenue." Section 4420 provides guidance on how to apply accrual accounting concepts to contributions. It states the following:

A contribution receivable should be recognized as an asset when it meets the following criteria:

(a) the amount to be received can be reasonably estimated; and

(b) ultimate collection is reasonably assured. [4420.03]

Normally a contribution receivable represents a future inflow of cash, but it could also represent the future receipt of other assets or services valued at fair value. The credit side of the journal entry could be to revenue, using the restricted fund method, or if the deferral method of recording is being used, to deferred revenue for a restricted contribution, or to increase net assets of endowments for an endowment contribution. (The restricted fund and deferral methods are discussed later in this chapter). The section provides additional guidelines for the recording of receivables associated with pledges and bequests.

Because pledges cannot be legally enforced, collectibility is out of the control of the organization. If the organization has the ability to estimate the collectibility based on historical results, it should recognize the pledged amounts as a receivable offset with an allowance for estimated uncollectible amounts. Otherwise, pledges should only be recorded at the time cash is received. It should be noted that when an allowance is established, the debit is typically made to contribution revenue rather than to bad debt expense.

Bequests also pose a problem of uncertainty relating both to the timing of receipt and to the amount to be collected. Wills must be probated and at times are subject to legal challenges. Because of this extreme uncertainty, bequests generally are not accrued until probation has been completed and the time for appeal has passed.

Section 4450, "Reporting Controlled and Related Entities by Not-for-Profit Organizations"

This section outlines the financial statement presentation and disclosures required when an NFPO has a control, significant influence, joint venture, or economic interest type of relationship with both profit-oriented and not-for-profit organizations. The breakdown used is quite similar to that for profit-oriented organizations, but the required financial reporting has some differences.

Control Investments An NFPO can have an investment or relationship that gives it the continuing power to determine the strategic operating, investing, and financing policies of another entity without the co-operation of others. The other entity can be profit-oriented or a not-for-profit organization. Control of a profit-oriented organization would normally be evidenced by the right to appoint the majority of the board of directors because of ownership of voting shares. Because a not-for-profit entity does not issue shares, control of such an entity is normally evidenced by the right to appoint the majority of the board of directors as allowed by that entity's by-laws.

Control over Not-for-Profit Organizations An example of a not-for-profit control situation is a national organization with local chapters. A large portion of funds raised by the local chapters goes to the national body, and any projects carried out by the local bodies must be approved (and perhaps funded) by the national organization.

The *Handbook*'s reporting requirements are as follows:

An organization should report each controlled not-for-profit organization in one of the following ways:
(a) by consolidating the controlled organization in its financial statements;
(b) by providing the disclosure set out in Paragraph 4450.22; or
(c) if the controlled organization is one of a large number of individually immaterial organizations, by providing the disclosure set out in Paragraph 4450.26 [4450.14].

Because there is no investment account in one balance sheet and no shareholders' equity in the others, consolidation is achieved by simply combining the financial statements on a line-by-line basis and at the same time eliminating any transactions that occurred between the organizations.

Since three alternatives are allowed, the management of the organization has to determine the accounting policy to be used. Note that the alternatives are for each controlled entity. This means that if an organization has control over three not-for-profit organizations, all of which are material, it could choose to consolidate only one, and provide the required disclosure for the other two, provided that it reports consistently on a year-to-year basis.

Paragraph 22 requires the disclosure of the totals of all of the assets, liabilities, net assets, revenues, expenses, and cash flows of any controlled not-for-profit entities that are not consolidated.

Consolidation was a controversial topic when it was proposed in the earlier exposure drafts. The following arguments were presented in its favour:

- The statements present the economic substance of the situation.

- All controlled economic resources are reflected in a single set of financial statements.

- Users of the financial statements get a much better picture than would be the case if unconsolidated statements were presented.

Some arguments presented against consolidation were:

- Consolidation of entities that have different activities may be confusing to users.

- The consolidation of a research centre (with substantial endowments) with a hospital that struggles to break even on a yearly basis may present a misleading financial picture.

- The yearly cost of financial reporting will increase.

Control over Profit-Oriented Companies   The *Handbook* states the following:

> An organization should report each controlled profit-oriented enterprise in either of the following ways:
> (a) by consolidating the controlled enterprise in its financial statements; or
> (b) by accounting for its investment in the controlled enterprise using the equity method and providing the disclosure set out in paragraph 4450.32 [4450.30].

Control in this situation is defined in Section 1590 (discussed in Chapter 3). It should be noted that the requirements here are also applicable to each controlled entity, which could result in some subsidiaries being reported under the equity method and others being consolidated. Consolidation of profit-oriented enterprises was also controversial, with similar arguments for and against as those presented above. The final result was also a compromise.

Joint Control   This is the contractual right to jointly control an organization with at least one other entity. An interest in a joint venture would be reported either by:

- proportionately consolidating the joint venture, or
- reporting the interest using the equity method.

Consistent with the requirements for controlled entities, the alternatives here apply to each joint venture, so that some may be proportionately consolidated and others may not, depending on the accounting policy determined by management. The arguments for and against using the proportionate consolidation method are basically the same as those presented previously for controlled investments. The section also states that if the NFPO's proportionate interest in the joint venture cannot be determined, it should not be considered to be a joint venture in accordance with this section, but might be either a significant influence or control type of relationship. This would seem to indicate that the joint venture would have to be one that issued shares, and thus probably a profit-oriented organization. However, if two or three NFPOs created another NFPO as a joint venture to carry out certain activities, and agreed to the percentage owned by each of the non-profit venturers, then the reporting alternatives outlined here would apply.

Significant Influence   When control is not present, the NFPO may still be able to exercise significant influence over the strategic operating, investing, and financing activities of the other entity. Factors suggesting the presence of significant influence include the ability to place members on the board of directors, the ability to participate in policymaking, substantial transactions between the entities, and the sharing of senior personnel. If the significant influence investment is in a profit-oriented enterprise, it must be accounted for using the equity method. If the significant influence relationship is with another NFPO, the equity method is not used; instead, full disclosure of the relationship is required.

Economic Interest   An economic interest in another NFPO exists if that organization holds resources for the reporting organization or if the reporting organization is responsible for the other organization's debts. There are varying degrees of economic interest, ranging from control or significant influence to neither of the two. The reporting requirement is stated in following manner: "When an organization has an economic interest in another not-for-profit organization over which it does not have control or significant influence, the nature and extent of this interest should be disclosed" (paragraph 4450.45).

An investment in a profit-oriented organization that is neither control, nor significant influence, nor joint control, must be a portfolio investment, to be accounted for using the cost method.

This concludes the discussion of Section 4450. A summary of the various types of investment that a NFPO can have and the reporting requirements for each follows:

Investment	Required reporting
Control of NFPO	Consolidate or disclose
Control of profit entity	Consolidate or equity method
Joint venture	Proportionately consolidate or equity method
Significant Influence	
NFPO	Full disclosure
Profit entity	Equity method
Economic interest	Full disclosure
Portfolio	
Profit entity	Cost method

Section 4460, "Disclosure of Related Party Transactions by Not-for-Profit Organizations"

Related parties exist where one party is able to exercise control, joint control, or significant influence over another party. The other party may be either another NFPO or a profit-oriented enterprise. If one NFPO has an economic interest in another NFPO, the two parties are related. A related party transaction has occurred when there has been a transfer of economic resources or obligations or services between the parties. Unlike *Handbook* Section 3840, which prescribes both measurements and disclosures, this not-for-profit section prescribes only disclosures for related party transactions. The disclosures required here are virtually identical to those of Section 3840.

Section 4430, "Capital Assets Held by Not-for-Profit Organizations" Prior to the introduction of this section into the *Handbook*, NFPOs followed a variety of practices with regard to the financial reporting of their capital assets. Some organizations capitalized all acquisitions and amortized them over their estimated useful lives in the operating statement. Others capitalized them, but did not provide amortization. A fairly large number wrote them off in their operating statements in the year of acquisition in a manner similar to the equipment purchase illustrated in Exhibit 14.1, page 585. In this latter situation, the operating statement showed revenues and expenditures measured under the accrual method, and from a user perspective reflected the inflow and outflow of spendable resources.

When the Accounting Standards Board proposed the requirement of capitalization and amortization of all acquisitions, respondents to the exposure drafts voiced strong opposition. The arguments against capitalization were that:

- It would change the nature of the operating statement from one that reflects resources spent to one that reflects the cost of resources used.

- Users would not understand the new accounting, having become used to seeing capital asset acquisitions as expenditures.

- As most other assets appearing in a balance sheet represent spendable resources, the addition of non-spendable resources such as unamortized capital assets would confuse readers.

- Capitalization and amortization would be costly to apply, especially on a retroactive basis.

- Small NFPO financial statement users are only interested in seeing what money has been spent and what money is left over.

The counter-arguments in favour of capitalization were that:

- Readers of the financial statements of profit-oriented entities are quite used to seeing capital assets in the balance sheet and amortization in the operating statement. They are confused when they do not see it in the financial statements of a NFPO.

- The cash flow statement adequately shows resources spent. The operating statement should reflect resources used.

Section 4430 requires a NFPO to capitalize all capital assets in the balance sheet and to amortize them as appropriate in the statement of operations. The cost of a purchased capital asset includes all costs incurred to make the asset ready for use. When a capital asset is donated, it is recorded at fair value (if known), and the resultant credit is to restricted contribution revenue. (The concept of restricted contributions is discussed later.) Capital assets of limited useful life are to be amortized on a rational basis over their estimated useful lives. No maximum period of amortization is specified. When an NFPO enters into a lease agreement that would be treated as a capital lease in accordance with *Handbook* Section 3065, the asset will be capitalized in accordance with the provisions of that section. When an asset no longer contributes to the organization's ability to provide services, it should be written down to estimated residual value, with the resulting loss reported as an expense in the statement of operations. Note that this section does not provide a quantitative impairment test in the same manner as prescribed by *Handbook* Section 3061.

Provisions must be made for future removal and site restoration costs. This requires determining the estimated cost and recording a yearly expense so that the resulting liability builds up to the date that the costs will be incurred. An example where this would apply to an NFPO is where the removal of leasehold improvements is required at the end of a lease.

Small NFPOs Section 4430 contains a compromise applicable to NFPOs whose provision two-year average annual revenues are less than $500,000. Organizations such as these are encouraged to follow the section's recommendations, but are exempted from doing so if they disclose:

- their accounting policy for capital assets,
- information about capital assets not shown in the balance sheet, and
- the amount expensed in the current period if their policy is to expense capital assets when acquired.

This leaves a small NFPO the choice of:

- expensing when acquired,
- capitalizing but not amortizing, or
- capitalizing and amortizing.

If an NFPO has revenues above $500,000, it is required to capitalize and amortize. If its revenues subsequently fall below $500,000, it is not allowed to change its policy.

If an NFPO has revenues below $500,000, chooses not to capitalize and amortize and subsequently has revenues above $500,000, then it ceases to be a small NFPO, and must capitalize and amortize retroactively. This requirement should be recognized by all small NFPOs that decide to exempt themselves from the section's recommendations, because retroactive restatement can be costly.

Capitalization of capital assets was a contentious issue when the not-for-profit exposure drafts were being discussed. The small-organization exemption and the special provisions for collections were introduced to satisfy some of the objections that were raised.

Section 4440, "Collections Held by Not-for-Profit Organizations" Collections are works of art and historical treasures that have been excluded from the definition of capital assets because they meet all of the following criteria:

- They are held for public exhibition, education, and research.
- They are protected, cared for, and preserved.
- They are subject to organizational policies that require any proceeds from their sale to be used to acquire other items for the collection, or for the direct care of the existing collection.

The requirements of Section 4440 allow an NFPO to choose an accounting policy from the following:

- Expense when acquired.
- Capitalize but do not amortize.
- Capitalize and amortize.

NFPOs that have collections are required to include in their disclosures a description of the accounting policies followed with regard to collections; a description of the collection; any significant changes made to the collection during the period; the amount spent on the collection during the period; and the proceeds from any sales of collection items, and a statement of how the proceeds were used.

Sections 4400 and 4410   Section 4400, "Financial Statement Presentation By Not-for-Profit Organizations," and Section 4410, "Contributions — Revenue Recognition," are so directly related to each other that we will discuss their requirements as a single topic. There are two very key points embodied in these two sections:

- Restrictions on an organization's resources should be clearly stated in the financial statements.
- The matching concept as it applies to NFPOs must be applied in the measurement of yearly results.

For an NFPO that has restricted revenues, the concept of revenue and expense matching is the exact opposite to that for a profit-oriented enterprise. With the latter, revenues are recognized and then expenses are matched with those revenues. With an NFPO, restricted revenues are matched to expenses. This means that if contributions have been collected to fund certain expenses, and those expenses have yet to be incurred, the contributions are deferred until a later period, when they can be matched with the expenses. When the restricted fund method of accounting is used to account for restricted resources, this matching is not necessary; when this method is not used, this form of matching for restricted resources is imperative.

As outlined earlier, an NFPO can have two basic types of revenues:

- Contributions.
- Other types (from investments, or from the sale of goods and services).

Contributions are a type of revenue unique to NFPOs. They are specifically described in order to apply recognition and presentation principles. The *Handbook* defines three different types of contributions:

- Restricted contributions.
- Endowment contributions.
- Unrestricted contributions.

Restricted contributions are subject to *externally imposed* stipulations as to how the funds are to be spent or used. The organization must use the resources in the manner specified by the donor. There may be times when the directors of an organization decide to use certain contributions for certain purposes, but these are considered to be *internally imposed* restrictions, and do not fall within the definition of restricted contributions.

Endowment contributions are a special type of restricted contribution. The donor has specified that the contribution cannot be spent, but must be maintained permanently. Endowment contributions are often invested in high-grade securities.

Unrestricted contributions are those which are not restricted or endowment contributions.

As we shall see in the next section, financial statement presentations for NFPOs are based in part on these three types of contributions.

Financial Statements

An NFPO must present the following financial statements for external reporting purposes:

- A statement of financial position.
- A statement of operations.
- A statement of changes in net assets.
- A statement of cash flows.

The names provided here are for descriptive purposes only; an organization can choose the titles it wishes to use. The statement of operations can be combined with the statement of changes in net assets.

A fund basis can be used, but it is not necessary to prepare all statements using this method. For example, the operating statement could be presented on a fund basis while the rest of the statements could be presented on a nonfund basis.

The statement of financial position should show classifications for current assets, noncurrent assets, current liabilities, and noncurrent liabilities. Net assets (total assets less total liabilities) must be broken down into the following categories (if applicable):

- Net assets invested in capital assets.
- Net assets maintained permanently in endowments.
- Other restricted net assets.
- Unrestricted net assets.

The statement of operations will show the revenues and expenses for the period.

The statement of changes in net assets must show changes in each of the four categories required to be shown on the balance sheet. The statement of cash flows must report changes in cash under two classifications:

- Cash flows from operations.
- Cash flows from financing and investing activities.

Cash flows from operations can be presented using either the direct method or the indirect method.

Accounting for Contributions

To capture the matching concept that is unique to NFPOs, the *Handbook* has defined two methods of accounting for contributions: the *deferral* method and the *restricted fund* method.

An NFPO has to determine which method it is going to use. If it does not wish to report on a fund accounting basis, it will use the deferral method. If it does wish to report on a fund accounting basis, it will normally choose the restricted fund method, keeping in mind that some parts of the deferral method may also have to be used. This particular concept will be discussed later. However, it should be noted that an NFPO may chose to report on a fund basis without using the restricted fund method of accounting for contributions. For example, it may choose to draw attention to its programs by reporting each as a fund in its financial statements. If the program funds receive both restricted and unrestricted resources, the deferred contribution method of accounting for contributions must be used even though financial reporting is carried out on a fund basis.

The Deferral Method

The deferral method matches revenues with related expenses. Unrestricted contributions are reported as revenue in the period received because there are no particular related expenses associated with them.

Endowment contributions are not shown in the operating statement; rather, they are reflected in the statement of changes in net assets. This is because endowment contributions, by definition, will never have related expenses.

Restricted contributions have to be matched against related expenses. This matching principle has different implications for different kinds of restricted contributions, as follows:

- Restricted contributions for expenses of future periods are deferred and recognized as revenue in the same periods as the related expenses are incurred.

- The handling of restricted contributions for the acquisition of capital assets depends on whether related expenses are associated with them. If the capital asset is subject to amortization, the related expense is the yearly amortization. The restricted contribution is deferred and recognized as revenue on the same basis as the asset is being amortized. If the capital asset is not subject to amortization (e.g., land), there will be no expenses to match against. In the same manner as for endowment contributions, the restricted capital asset contributions of this type are reflected in the statement of changes in net assets.

- Restricted contributions for expenses of the current period are recognized as revenue in the current period. Matching is achieved, and there is no need for deferral.

Investment income can be either unrestricted or restricted. Unrestricted investment income is recognized as revenue when it is earned. Restricted investment income has to be recognized in the same manner as restricted contributions. For example, if an endowment contribution states that the purchasing power of the contribution must be preserved, some portion of the interest earned must be used to increase the endowment. This portion would be treated in exactly the same manner as an endowment contribution, and would be reflected in the statement of changes in net assets. Other types of restricted investment income must be deferred and matched against expense in the manner previously discussed. If all investment income is restricted, it is quite possible that all investment income earned in a period will be deferred.

The Restricted Fund Method

This method requires an NFPO to report a general fund, at least one restricted fund, and, if it has endowments or receives endowment contributions, an endowment fund. The restricted funds will be used to record externally restricted revenue. Specific requirements are outlined as follows:

- Endowment contributions will be reported as revenue in the endowment fund, and because there are no related expenses associated with endowment contributions, no expenses will appear in the statement of operations of the endowment fund.

- The general fund records all unrestricted contributions and investment income, including unrestricted income from endowment fund investments.

- If some of the endowment fund income is restricted, it is reflected as revenue in the particular restricted fund involved.

- If some of the endowment fund income is permanently restricted, because the purchasing power of the endowment is required to be maintained, it is recorded as revenue of the endowment fund.

- If an externally restricted contribution or externally restricted investment income is received, for which there is no corresponding restricted fund, the amounts are recorded in the general fund in accordance with the deferral method. In other words they are recorded as deferred revenue in the general fund and matched with the related expenses in that fund when these expenses are incurred.

- If management decides to impose internal restrictions on general fund unrestricted contributions, these amounts are transferred to the relevant restricted or endowment fund, and such transfers are reported in the statement of operations and changes in net assets below the line "excess of revenue over expenses." Note disclosure should clearly indicate the amount of resources shown in restricted funds that have been designated as such by management, because these amounts do not satisfy the *Handbook*'s definition of a restricted resource.

The excess of revenues over expenses in the general fund represents the increase in unrestricted resources during the period. The fund balance in the general fund shows the unrestricted net assets at the end of the period.

A restricted fund shows no deferred revenue. The fund balance of a restricted fund represents the amount of net assets that are restricted for that particular fund's purpose.

The fund balance in the endowment fund represents the net assets that have permanent restrictions on them.

Under the restricted fund method, instead of presenting a statement of changes in net assets (as is required under the deferral method of recording contributions), a statement of changes in fund balances is prepared. Because of the requirement to capitalize long-lived assets, capital assets must appear on the balance sheet of either the general fund or one of the restricted funds (excluding the endowment fund). The fund balance section of that particular fund's balance sheet will have to show a corresponding investment in capital assets.

This has been a summary of the two methods of accounting for contributions. Before we illustrate these concepts in an extensive illustration, there are some additional topics that must be addressed.

Net Assets Invested in Capital Assets

The *Handbook* requires that the net asset (or fund balance) section of the balance sheet show a category called "net assets invested in capital assets." This amount represents resources spent on capital assets and therefore not available for future spending. The amount shown depends on the method used to account for contributions. If the restricted fund method is used, the amount represents the unamortized portion of *all* capital assets, regardless of whether they were purchased from restricted or unrestricted resources. If the deferral method is used, the amount presented represents the unamortized portion of capital assets that were purchased with *unrestricted* resources. The following example will illustrate the differences.

At the beginning of the current period, NFPO purchases equipment costing $5,000 with a useful life of two years. We will assume first that the equipment is acquired from restricted resources, and then from unrestricted resources. We will focus on the equipment transaction only and the effect of the transaction on the financial statements of NFPO. In order to do this, we also assume that the organization was formed at the beginning of the period and that the equipment acquisition is the only transaction that has occurred.

The Restricted Fund Method

Purchase from Restricted Resources   Assume that the equipment is purchased from a restricted fund contribution of $5,100. The capital fund records contributions of this nature, as well as the acquisition of capital assets and their subsequent amortization. The journal entries would be as follows:

Capital fund

Cash	5,100	
Contribution revenue		5,100
Equipment	5,000	
Cash		5,000
Amortization expense	2,500	
Accumulated amortization		2,500

Because the capital fund did not exist before the start of the period, the financial statements at the end of the period would appear as follows:

CAPITAL FUND
OPERATING STATEMENT AND CHANGES IN FUND BALANCE

Contribution revenue	$5,100
Amortization expense	2,500
Excess of revenue over expense	2,600
Fund balance — start of period	0
Fund balance — end of period	$2,600

BALANCE SHEET

Cash		$ 100
Equipment	$5,000	
Accumulated amortization	2,500	2,500
Total assets		$2,600
Fund balance		
Invested in capital assets		$2,500
Externally restricted funds		100
Total fund balance		$2,600

Note that the fund balance section shows two classifications:

- The $2,500 invested in capital assets represents the unamortized balance of spent resources that have not yet been reflected in the statement of operations as an expense.

- Externally restricted funds of $100 represent resources that can only be spent to acquire capital assets.

As the equipment is amortized on the operating statement, the fund balance itself is reduced, and it is the balance sheet category "invested in capital assets" that reflects the reduction.

Purchase from Unrestricted Resources   Now assume that the equipment is purchased from unrestricted resources. The general fund receives an unrestricted contribution of $5,000 and uses it to acquire equipment.

The journal entries in the general fund and the capital fund would be as follows:

General fund

Cash	5,000	
Contribution revenue		5,000
Transfer to capital fund	5,000	
Cash		5,000

The general fund's operating statement after the transaction would show the following:

GENERAL FUND
STATEMENT OF OPERATIONS AND CHANGES IN FUND BALANCE

Revenues	$5,000
Expenses	0
Excess of revenue over expense	5,000
Transfer to capital fund	(5,000)
Fund balance — start of period	0
Fund balance — end of period	$ 0

It should be obvious that the general fund's balance sheet at the end of the period contains no elements.

The capital fund would record the acquisition of the equipment and its amortization with the following entries:

Capital fund

Equipment	5,000	
Transfer from general fund		5,000
Amortization expense	2,500	
Accumulated amortization		2,500

The end-of-period financial statements would show the following:

CAPITAL FUND
STATEMENT OF OPERATIONS AND CHANGES IN FUND BALANCE

Amortization expense	$2,500
Excess of revenue over expense	(2,500)
Transfer from general fund	5,000
	2,500
Fund balance — start of period	0
Fund balance — end of period	$2,500

BALANCE SHEET

Equipment	$5,000
Accumulated amortization	2,500
Total assets	$2,500
Fund balance	
Invested in capital assets	$2,500
Total fund balance	$2,500

Note that regardless of the source of resources used to acquire the equipment (restricted or unrestricted), the unamortized balance appears as an asset on the balance sheet of the capital fund, and the fund balance shows a classification "invested in capital assets" in an amount equal to the asset balance. This is not the case when the deferred contribution method is used.

The Deferred Contribution Method

Purchase from Restricted Resources   Assume that the equipment is purchased from a restricted fund contribution of $5,100. The journal entries to record the contribution, the acquisition, and the first year's amortization are as follows:

Cash	5,100	
Deferred contributions — equipment purchases		5,100
Equipment	5,000	
Cash		5,000
Deferred contribution — equipment purchases	5,000	
Deferred contributions — capital assets		5,000
Amortization expense	2,500	
Accumulated amortization		2,500
Deferred contributions — capital assets	2,500	
Contribution revenue		2,500

Financial statements that reflect these transactions are as follows:

STATEMENT OF OPERATIONS AND CHANGES IN FUND BALANCE

Contribution revenue	$2,500
Amortization expense	2,500
Excess of revenue over expenses	0
Net assets start of period	0
Net assets end of period	$ 0

BALANCE SHEET

Cash		$ 100
Equipment	$5,000	
Accumulated amortization	2,500	2,500
Total assets		$2,600
Deferred contributions		
Equipment purchases		$ 100
Capital assets		2,500
Total deferred contribution		2,600
Net Assets		
Unrestricted		0
Total		$2,600

You will notice that two deferred contribution accounts have been used. "Deferred contributions — equipment purchases" represents unspent resources restricted to future spending on capital assets. "Deferred contributions — capital assets" represents restricted resources that have been spent acquiring capital assets, but have not yet been reflected as revenue on the operating statement because there has yet to be an expense to match it against. When amortization occurs, an equal amount is recognized as revenue. Because there is no effect on the "excess of revenue over expense" amount, there is no effect on the equity section "net assets." As the equipment decreases on the asset side due to amortization, the amount "deferred contributions — capital assets" decreases by the same amount on the liability side. Because this equipment was purchased from restricted resources, there can be no amount shown under "invested in capital assets" in the equity section "net assets."

Purchase from Unrestricted Resources   Assume now that the equipment was purchased from an unrestricted contribution of $5,000. The journal entries to record the events are as follows:

Cash	5,000	
Contribution revenue		5,000
Equipment	5,000	
Cash		5,000
Amortization expense	2,500	
Accumulated amortization		2,500

The financial statements that reflect these transactions are as follows:

STATEMENT OF OPERATIONS

Contribution revenue	$5,000
Amortization expense	2,500
Excess of revenue over expenses	$2,500

BALANCE SHEET

Equipment	$5,000
Accumulated amortization	2,500
Total assets	$2,500
Net Assets	
Invested in capital assets	2,500
Unrestricted	0
Total	$2,500

Note that the statement of operations does not include a reconciliation of open-ing and ending net assets. A separate statement is usually presented. Because "net assets" represents total equity, the changes in the classifications of this equity must be shown in a statement as follows:

STATEMENT OF CHANGES IN NET ASSETS

	Invested in capital assets	Unrestricted	Total
Balance start of period	$ 0	$ 0	$ 0
Excess of revenue over expenses	(2,500)	5,000	2,500
Investment in capital assets	5,000	(5,000)	0
Balance end of period	$2,500	$ 0	$2,500

The "unrestricted" column represents resources that can be spent for any pur-pose. The organization received an unrestricted contribution of $5,000 and spent it on equipment. At the end of the period it has no resources left to spend. The trans-fer of $5,000 to the category "invested in capital assets" depicts the acquisition of capital assets from unrestricted resources. The operating statement shows an excess of revenue over expenses of $2,500. A $2,500 deduction for the amortization of assets purchased with unrestricted resources was used to arrive at these operating results. Note that this does not represent resources spent, but rather the cost of serv-ices provided by the equipment. By transferring this deduction to "invested in capi-tal assets," the amount of the operating results allocated to unrestricted resources becomes $5,000, which represents the actual inflow of spendable resources, and the amount shown for "invested in capital assets" is equal to the unamortized balance of the equipment purchased from unrestricted resources.

Donated Capital Assets, Materials, and Services

An NFPO is required to record the donation of capital assets at fair value. If fair value cannot be determined, a nominal value will be used. A nominal value could be in the range of $1 to $100 for small NFPOs, and $1,000 and higher for large NFPOs. If an organization receives an unsolicited donation of a capital asset that it has no intention of using, it should be reflected in its financial statements as "other assets" instead of "capital assets," and a loss or gain should be reflected in the statement of operations when disposal of the asset occurs. The following illustrates the recording of donated capital assets.

Example   A capital asset with a fair value of $10,000 is donated to an NFPO. The initial treatment depends on which of the two methods of recording contributions is being used.

If the deferral method is being used, and the capital asset is subject to amortization (e.g., equipment), the journal entry is:

Equipment	10,000	
Deferred contributions — capital assets		10,000

Assuming a five-year life, in each succeeding year the following entry will be made as the equipment is amortized:

Amortization expense	2,000	
Accumulated amortization		2,000
Deferred contributions — capital assets	2,000	
Contribution revenue		2,000

If the deferral method is being used and the asset is not subject to amortization (e.g., land), the following entry is made:

Land	10,000	
Net assets invested in capital assets		10,000

Because no future expense will be associated with the asset, deferral is not required and the donation of land is reflected in the statement of net assets.

If the restricted fund method is being used, the fair value of the donated capital asset is recorded as revenue in the capital fund as follows:

Capital fund		
Equipment	10,000	
Contributions — donated equipment		10,000

Donated land will be treated in the same manner, except that the debit will be to land instead of equipment. Small NFPOs that have adopted a policy of non-capitalization of acquisitions of capital assets will still be required to record donated capital assets at fair value. For example, the donation of equipment with a fair value of $10,000 would be recorded in the following manner:

Equipment expense	10,000	
Contributions — donated equipment		10,000

Regardless of whether the organization uses the deferred contribution method or the restricted fund method, the entry is the same because the required matching automatically occurs with the entry.

The requirements for the reporting of donated materials and services are different from those for donated capital assets. An NFPO has the option of reporting or not reporting donated material and services; however, it should only do so if fair value can be determined, and if the materials and services would normally be used in the organization's operations and would have been purchased if they had not been donated.

The *Handbook* section also makes it clear that the fair value of the services of volunteers are normally not recognized due to the difficulty in determining such values. Furthermore, an organization would probably not record donated materials if it acts as an intermediary for immediate distribution. For example, due to the difficulty of determining fair values and the large number of transactions, a food bank would not normally record the donation of food that it distributes to its clients.

Example   A radio station donated free air time to help a charity publicize its fundraising campaign. The fair value of the air time is $5,200, and the policy of the organization is to record the value of donated materials and services. The journal entry is:

Advertising expense	5,200	
Revenue — donated air time		5,200

If the restricted fund method was being used, this entry would be made in the general fund.

If the donation consisted of office supplies rather than air time, the entry to record the donation under be the deferred contribution method would be:

Office supplies (asset)	5,200	
Deferred contribution		5,200

If half of the supplies were used, the entries would be:

Supplies expense	2,600	
Office supplies		2,600
Deferred contribution	2,600	
Contribution revenue		2,600

In order to achieve proper matching, the same entries would be used under the restricted fund method. Due to the nature of the items donated, the transaction would normally be recorded in the general fund.

Budgetary Control and Encumbrances

Governments and many NFPOs often use a *formal budget recording system* together with an *encumbrance system* as a device to help control spending. Prior to the commencement of a fiscal year, a formal budget is drawn up that shows the budgeted revenues and expenses for the coming year. The usual starting point in the process is a preliminary expense budget based on how the managers of the organization would like to see spending take place. Then a revenue budget is prepared based on the expected results from the revenue-raising activities of the coming year. If this revenue budget is realistic, the next step is to scale down the controllable expenses so that the organization does not plan to have expenses greater than its expected revenues. NFPOs and local governments do not (and in the case of many local governments, are not allowed to) budget for a deficit in any one year unless they have a surplus from prior years. Because both types of organizations raise money each year and then spend it, any deficit spending in a particular year eventually must be offset by surplus spending in later years. Once the budget has been formally passed by the board of directors (or the local government legislative body), the spending for applicable budgeted expenses commences. Often an NFPO's actual expenses turn out to be equal to the amount budgeted, and problems arise when actual revenues are less than budget. Government grants are sometimes reduced, or do not increase as much as was budgeted for, or some fundraising activity is not as successful as was forecast. If this happens over a series of years, the accumulated deficit problem will have to be addressed and the NFPO will have to organize special deficit-reduction fundraising activities in addition to the normal, annual fundraising for operations.

Budgetary Control   If deficits are to be avoided, the managers of NFPOs must have timely information regarding actual results compared with amounts budgeted. This can be accomplished by formally recording the budget into the accounting system.

Example   The following is the summarized budget that was approved by the board of directors of an NFPO:

Budgeted revenues (in detail)	$900,000
Budgeted expenses (in detail)	890,000
Budgeted surplus	$ 10,000

If the organization records the budget in its accounting records, the following journal entry is made at the start of the fiscal year:

Estimated revenues (control account)	900,000	
Appropriations (control account)		890,000
Budgetary fund balance		10,000

While it may appear strange to debit an account for budgeted revenues, and to credit an account for budgeted expenses, the logic becomes clearer when one considers that budgeted revenues represent *expected* resource inflows and that budgeted expenses (with the exception of amortization) represent *expected* resource outflows. The general ledger accounts used are control accounts to the very detailed subsidiary ledger accounts needed to keep track of actual versus budgeted amounts, particularly in relation to expenses. Spending is often a continuous process, while revenues are received at various times throughout the year. If during the year it appears that actual revenues will be less than budget, it is a difficult task to make reductions to the budgeted expenses remaining in order to avoid a deficit. It is, however, possible with a system such as this to ensure that actual expenses do not exceed budget. The overall concept of "spending" in this context is based on an accrual system of measurement, not on a cash basis. At the end of the fiscal year the budget accounts are reversed as part of the closing journal entries, and these amounts are not reflected in the organization's external financial statements.

Encumbrance Accounting   This involves making entries in the accounting records to record the issue of purchase orders for the acquisition of goods and services from outside suppliers. The amounts recorded are estimates of the actual costs. It is not the normal practice to use encumbrance accounting for employee wage costs because this particular type of expenditure can be controlled by other means; nor is it normal to use encumbrances for amortization. When the goods and services ordered are actually received, the original encumbrance entry is reversed and the invoiced cost of the goods or services acquired is recorded.

Example Purchase order #3056A is issued for the acquisition of office supplies expected to cost $950. The journal entry to record the purchase order is:

Encumbrances	950	
Estimated commitments[1]		950

When the supplies ordered under purchase order #3056A are received at an invoiced cost of $954, the journal entries required are:

Estimated commitments	950	
Encumbrances		950
Supplies expense	954	
Accounts payable		954

Control over expenditures is achieved by mandating that the spending of a budgeted amount has occurred when the purchase order is issued, not when the goods are received or paid for. In this example, if the budgeted amount for supplies is $3,000, there is an unspent budget amount of $2,050 after the purchase order is issued, and an unspent amount of $2,046 after the receipt of the actual supplies. The use of encumbrance accounting along with a system of budgetary control prevents the issuing of purchase orders when there are no uncommitted budgeted amounts.

The only accounting problem involved is the financial statement presentation of outstanding purchase orders at the end of a fiscal period. Should the encumbrances be reflected in the operations statement as similar to expenses, and the estimated commitments appear in the balance sheet as liabilities? In the past, NFPOs have presented these accounts in this manner. The *Handbook* sections do not mention the concept of encumbrances; however, a purchase order is an executory contract under which neither party has performed. It follows that outstanding encumbrances should not be reflected as elements of financial statements, but rather should be disclosed in the footnotes to the statements if the amounts are material.[2]

Illustration of the Restricted Fund Method

The following example will be used to illustrate the journal entries made for various funds, and the annual general-purpose financial statements prepared using the restricted fund method of accounting for contributions.

The Blue Shield Agency is a charitable organization located in a mid-sized Canadian city. The major goal of the organization is to provide food and shelter for the homeless. It operates out of its own premises, and while it has some permanent employees, it also relies heavily on volunteers.

---

[1] An alternative term often used is "reserve for encumbrances."

[2] A similar conclusion was made in a CICA research study. See "Financial Reporting for Non-profit organizations, p. 52 (Toronto: CICA, 1980).

The agency's funds have four sources:

- Government grants are received annually to fund the regular food and shelter operating activities. When the need arises, special government grants are solicited to fund capital asset additions and major renovations.
- Donations are received as a result of public campaigns held each March to raise funds for the current year's operating costs.
- A United Way grant is received each November to help fund the next year's operations.
- Interest is received from an endowment fund and other investments.

The agency maintains its records in accordance with the restricted fund method of accounting for contributions, and prepares its annual financial statements on this basis. The three funds being used are described below.

General Fund This fund is used to record the agency's operating activities. Revenues consist of government operating grants, the proceeds from the annual fundraising campaign, the United Way grant, interest from the endowment fund, and term deposit interest. Each year the grant from the United Way is recorded as deferred revenue to be matched against the operating expenses of the year following. Expenses are for the food and shelter programs and for administration costs. An encumbrance system is used to ensure that costs do not exceed budgeted amounts, but the budget itself is not formally recorded in the accounting records. While some donated materials and services are received each year, no record of these donations is made in the ledger accounts. Small-equipment purchases made from this fund are capitalized in the capital fund.

Capital Fund This fund is used to account for restricted funds raised for building and equipment acquisitions. The capital fund also records the capitalization of buildings and equipment and the amortization taken. Equipment acquisitions made from the general fund are also capitalized in this fund.

Approximately 20 years ago the city donated a building to the agency. While the city retained title to the land on which the building is situated, the agency will not be required to move, and the building will not be torn down, as long as the agency continues with its programs. The value of the donated building was *not* recorded at the time of the donation because it was the organization's policy not to capitalize buildings and equipment. When the current *Handbook* sections became operative several years ago, the organization spent considerable time and money searching past records to determine the cost of capital assets purchased from both restricted and nonrestricted contributions and the fair values of capital assets donated. The new *Handbook* sections had to be applied retroactively, and the following journal entry was made at that time to accomplish this (000s omitted):

Equipment and furniture	1,100	
Buildings	2,000	
Accumulated amortization		1,200
Net assets (capital fund balance)		1,900

Endowment Fund The $500,000 in this fund was bequeathed to the agency by its founder five years ago. Interest earned is to be used for operating purposes and is recorded in the general fund.

The balance sheets of the funds of Blue Shield as at January 1, Year 6 (the start of the next fiscal year), are presented in Exhibit 14.3.

This form of presentation of fund financial statements is called the *multicolumn approach* because each of the fund's financial statements is presented in its own separate column. If fund accounting is used, the *Handbook* requires that totals be shown for each item presented, so that the "big picture" for the entire organization can be seen. This approach can become very cumbersome if an organization has a large number of funds that need to be presented separately because of all of the restrictions involved. An alternative is to combine the funds into a single set of statements (the deferral method of accounting for contributions), with extensive footnote disclosure of resource restrictions.

Exhibit 14.3

BLUE SHIELD AGENCY
BALANCE SHEET
January 1, Year 6
(in thousands of dollars)

	General fund	Capital fund	Endowment fund	Total
Current assets				
Cash and term deposits	$417	$ 62		$ 479
Pledges receivable	490			490
	907	62		969
Investments			$500	500
Capital assets				
Equipment and furniture		1,482		1,482
Buildings		2,095		2,095
Accumulated amortization		(1,517)		(1,517)
		2,060		2,060
Total assets	$907	$2,122	$500	$3,529
Current liabilities				
Accounts payable	$613	$ 50		$ 663
Wages payable	70			70
Accrued liabilities	82			82
	765	50		815
Deferred revenue	40			40
Fund balances				
Investment in capital assets		2,060		2,060
Externally restricted		12	500	512
Unrestricted	102			102
	102	2,072	500	2,674
Total liabilities and fund balances	$907	$2,122	$500	$3,529

Year 6 Events The year's events are summarized as follows (all dollar amounts are in thousands unless stated otherwise):

(a) The accounts and wages payable and the accrued liabilities at the beginning of the year were paid.

(b) The deferred revenue from Year 5 consisted of the grant from the United Way. An entry was made to recognize this as revenue in Year 6.

(c) The pledges receivable at the beginning of the year were collected in full.

(d) The Year 6 fundraising campaign was held in March. Cash of $1,187 was collected, and pledges expected to realize $800 were received. Total fundraising costs were $516, of which $453 was paid in cash, $50 is owed to suppliers, and $13 has been accrued.

(e) During Year 6 the agency announced a plan to construct an addition to its building at an estimated cost of $1.5 million. The budget includes equipment acquisitions. The addition will be built in two phases, with final completion expected in Year 8. At the end of Year 6 the first phase was out for tender, with construction to commence early in Year 7.

   The government announced a grant of $600 in Year 6 to cover the first phase and has remitted $450 of this, with the balance promised in Year 7. The agency spent $103 on equipment near the end of Year 6, of which $91 has been paid and $12 is still owing. At the beginning of the year the agency had $62 on hand from a previous building campaign and an unpaid liability of $50 for capital asset purchases. A public campaign will be conducted next year to raise the balance of the funds needed to complete the project.

(f) Government grants for operating purposes totalled $1,200 in Year 6, of which $910 was received during the year, with the balance expected in January, Year 7.

(g) The agency uses an encumbrance system as a means of controlling expenditures. (Note: Wages of agency employees are not subject to encumbrance because purchase orders are not issued for this type of expenditure.) During the year, orders estimated to total $1,964 were issued for the purchase of goods and services.

(h) Invoices totalling $1,866 were received on purchase orders originally recorded at an estimated cost of $1,870. Suppliers were paid $1,446 on account for these invoices, and the balance owing is still outstanding. The costs were allocated as follows:

Shelter program	$650
Food program	960
Administration	256

(i) The total wage costs were:

Shelter program	$ 90
Food program	150
Administration	300

of which $357 was paid and $183 is payable at year-end.

(j) The United Way grant amounting to $65 was received in December.

(k) Late in the year a prominent supporter donated $50 to be held in endowment, with the interest earned to be unrestricted.

(l) The investments in the endowment fund earned interest of \$40; a further \$14 in interest was received from the term deposits held in the general fund.

(m) Refrigeration equipment costing \$3 was purchased with general fund cash.

(n) The Year 6 amortization charges amounted to \$150.

(o) At the end of the year the balances in the encumbrance accounts were closed.

The journal entries required to record these events in each of the three funds are presented next in the order listed:

(a) *General fund*

Accounts payable	613	
Wages payable	70	
Accrued liabilities	82	
Cash		765

Capital fund

Accounts payable	50	
Cash		50

(b) *General fund*

Deferred revenue	40	
Revenue — United Way grant		40

(c) *General fund*

Cash	490	
Pledges receivable		490

(d) *General fund*

Cash	1,187	
Pledges receivable	800	
Revenue — donations		1,987
Expenses — fundraising	516	
Cash		453
Accounts payable		50
Accrued liabilities		13

(e) *Capital fund*

Cash	450	
Government grant receivable	150	
Revenue — government grant		600
Equipment	103	
Cash		91
Accounts payable		12

(f) *General fund*

Cash	910	
Government grant receivable	290	
Revenue — government grant		1,200

(g) *General fund*

Encumbrances	1,964	
Estimated commitments		1,964

(h) *General fund*

Estimated commitments	1,870	
Encumbrances		1,870
Expenses — shelter program	650	
Expenses — food program	960	
Expenses — administration	256	
Cash		1,446
Accounts payable		420

(i) *General fund*

Expenses — shelter program	90	
Expenses — food program	150	
Expenses — administration	300	
Cash		357
Wages payable		183

(j) *General fund*

Cash	65	
Deferred revenue — United Way		65

(k) *Endowment fund*

Cash	50	
Revenue — contribution		50

(l) *General fund*

Cash	54	
Revenue — investment income		54

(m) *General fund*

Transfer to capital fund	3	
Cash		3
Capital fund		
Equipment	3	
Transfer from general fund		3

(n) *Capital fund*

Expenses — amortization	150	
Accumulated amortization		150

(o) *General fund*

Estimated commitments	94	
Encumbrances		94

After these journal entries are posted, financial statements as at December 31, Year 6, can be prepared as shown in Exhibit 14.4.

Note that while a fund type of cash flow statement could be prepared, the one in this illustration has been prepared on a nonfund basis, which is in accordance with the *Handbook*'s pronouncements. Letters shown in parentheses represent the journal entries affecting the cash account.

Exhibit 14.4

BLUE SHIELD AGENCY
BALANCE SHEET
December 31, Year 6
(in thousands of dollars)

	General fund	Capital fund	Endowment fund	Total
Current assets				
Cash and term deposits	$ 99	$ 371	$ 50	$ 520
Pledges receivable	800			800
Government grants receivable	290	150		440
	1,189	521	50	1,760
Investments			500	500
Capital assets				
Equipment and furniture		1,588		1,588
Buildings		2,095		2,095
Accumulated depreciation		(1,667)		(1,667)
		2,016		2,016
Total assets	$1,189	$2,537	$550	$4,276
Current liabilities				
Accounts payable	$ 470	$ 12		$ 482
Wages payable	183			183
Accrued liabilities	13			13
	666	12		678
Deferred revenue	65			65
Fund balances				
Investment in capital assets		2,016		2,016
Externally restricted funds		509	550	1,059
Unrestricted funds	458			458
	458	2,525	550	3,533
Total liabilities and fund balances	$1,189	$2,537	$550	$4,276

continued

Exhibit 14.4   *continued*

BLUE SHIELD AGENCY
STATEMENT OF REVENUES, EXPENSES, AND
CHANGES IN FUND BALANCES
for the Year Ended December 31, Year 6
(in thousands of dollars)

	General fund	Capital fund	Endowment fund	Total
Revenues				
Government grants	$1,200	$ 600		$1,800
United Way grant	40			40
Contributions	1,987		$ 50	2,037
Investment income	54			54
	3,281	600	50	3,931
Expenses				
Shelter program	740			740
Food program	1,110			1,110
Administration	556			556
Fund raising	516			516
Amortization		150		150
	2,922	150		3,072
Excess of revenue over expenses	$ 359	$ 450	$ 50	$ 859
Interfund transfers	(3)	3		
Fund balances, January 1	102	2,072	500	2,674
Fund balances, December 31	$ 458	$2,525	$550	$3,533

BLUE SHIELD AGENCY
STATEMENT OF CASH FLOWS
for the Year Ended December 31, Year 6
(in thousands of dollars)

Cash flows from operating activities
Cash received from government operating grants (f)	$ 910
Cash received from United Way grant (j)	65
Cash received from general contributions (c), (d)	1,677
Cash received from investment income (l)	54
Cash paid to suppliers (a), (h)	(2,141)
Cash paid to employees (a), (i)	(427)
Cash paid for fund raising (d)	(453)
Net cash used in operating activities	(315)

Cash flows from financing and investing activities
Contributions of cash for endowment (k)	50
Cash received from government grant (e)	450
Cash paid for capital asset acquisitions (a), (e), (m)	(144)
Net cash generated through financing and investing activities	356
Net increase in cash and term deposits	41
Cash and term deposits — January 1	479
Cash and term deposits — December 31	$ 520

Closing entries as at December 31, Year 6, are presented next.

Revenue — government grant	1,200	
Revenue — United Way grant	40	
Revenue — contributions	1,987	
Revenue — investment income	54	
Expenses — shelter program		740
Expenses — food program		1,110
Expenses — administration		556
Expenses — fund raising		516
Unrestricted net assets		359
To close the unrestricted revenues and expenses		
Unrestricted net assets	3	
Net assets invested in capital assets		3
To transfer the amount of capital assets acquired from unrestricted resources		
Net assets invested in capital assets	60	
Amortization of deferred contributions	90	
Expenses — amortization		150
To close restricted revenues and the expenses related to capital assets		

SUMMARY

The seven detailed sections that were introduced into the *Handbook* in 1997 have dramatically changed financial reporting in the not-for-profit area. We have moved from a situation where few standards existed, to one where full and proportionate consolidation of the financial statements of other entities is a possibility, and capitalization and amortization of capital assets is mandatory for all but "small" organizations. The deferred contribution and restricted fund methods result in two quite different presentations of financial statement elements. While all of these changes have moved not-for-profit reporting much closer to that used by profit-oriented enterprises, not-for-profit reporting is still distinct and complex.

APPENDIX

Sample Financial Statements

This appendix contains the 2000 balance sheet, statement of operations, and statement of changes in net assets of the Winnipeg Foundation. The Foundation was established in 1921 by a prominent Winnipeg citizen who made an initial contribution of $100,000. Since that date, endowment assets have grown to $161 million and encompass over 1,200 separate endowment funds. The board of directors has established an occupancy reserve fund to cover the costs of physical premises and an administration fund to fund the Foundation's day-to-day administration costs. The deferral method of accounting has been used for contributions, and expenses have been recorded using the accrual basis. The category "other assets" contains donated works of art, cash surrender value of life insurance, and capital assets with a net book value of $236,452.

THE WINNIPEG FOUNDATION
BALANCE SHEET
October 31, 2000

	2000	*1999*
Assets		
Cash and short-term investments	$ 25,070,673	$ 19,630,359
Investment income receivable	1,769,374	1,618,179
Bonds and debentures		
Government of Canada	33,125,250	25,490,529
Provincial Government	10,402,646	12,351,928
Corporate	42,771,170	31,420,496
Preferred and common shares	60,954,823	52,043,329
Other	1,187,121	1,101,126
(Market value $210,591,293; 1998 — $173,171,495)	$175,281,057	$143,655,946
Liabilities		
Accounts payable	$ 175,723	$ 51,912
Grant commitments	6,547,918	5,636,121
	6,723,641	5,688,033
Capital held for investments		
Managed funds	6,246,919	4,399,492
Net Assets		
Endowment funds	161,142,716	133,187,745
Invested in capital assets	236,452	158,710
Occupancy reserve fund	40,497	24,647
Administration fund	240,110	72,410
Unrestricted	650,722	124,909
	$175,281,057	$143,655,946

Approved by the Board

Helen Hayles .... Director

.... Director

STATEMENT OF OPERATIONS
Year Ended October 31, 2000

	2000	1999
Income		
Investment income	$8,006,436	$6,025,072
Net realized capital gains apportioned to income	1,249,619	2,296,000
Gifts received for immediate granting	1,347,780	120,000
Grants returned	8,487	39,467
	10,612,322	8,480,539
Less: Investment manager and trust company custodian fees	635,756	524,805
	9,976,566	7,955,734
Grants approved		
Seniors	509,511	318,086
Children and youth	948,047	568,248
Family and community	1,753,856	1,330,612
Medical research	377,958	506,903
Health	593,179	321,506
Education	2,101,836	2,105,888
Arts and culture	1,567,994	1,515,451
Recreation	284,249	228,715
Designated religious organizations	133,789	142,892
	8,270,419	7,038,301
Less: Grants paid from endowment funds	—	53,380
	8,270,419	6,984,921
Administration and other expenses	952,788	840,462
Total expenditures	9,223,207	7,825,383
Increase in unrestricted net assets for the year	$ 753,359	$ 130,351

STATEMENT OF CHANGES IN NET ASSETS
Year Ended October 31, 2000

	2000						1999
	Administration fund	Occupancy reserve fund	Endowment fund	Invested in capital assets	Unrestricted	Total	Total
Balance beginning of year	$ 72,410	$24,647	$133,187,745	$158,710	$124,909	$133,568,421	$121,914,049
Add							
New gifts	2,810	—	8,261,828	—	—	8,264,638	7,215,699
Additions to prior gifts	—	—	2,873,819	—	—	2,873,819	957,087
Increase in cash surrender value	—	—	8,253	—	—	8,253	48,024
Net realized capital gains apportioned to funds	22,775	2,676	16,815,845	—	—	16,841,296	3,270,427
Investment income	9,103	986	(10,089)	—	—	—	99,372
Income capitalized	—	—	17,748	—	—	17,748	—
Deduct							
Grants paid from endowment funds	—	—	—	—	—	—	(53,380)
Endowment funds returned	—	—	(17,037)	—	—	(17,037)	(13,208)
Increase in unrestricted Net assets for the year	—	—	—	—	753,359	753,359	130,351
Transfers							
Acquisitions of capital assets	—	—	—	147,933	(147,933)	—	—
Depreciation charge for the year	—	—	—	(70,191)	70,191	—	—
Other	133,012	12,188	4,604	—	(149,804)	—	—
Balance, end of year	$240,110	$40,497	$161,142,716	$236,452	$650,722	$162,310,497	$133,568,421

REVIEW QUESTIONS

1. Briefly outline how NFPOs differ from profit-oriented organizations.

2. The *Handbook* describes revenue that is unique to not-for-profit organizations. What is this revenue called, and what characteristic does it have that makes it unique?

3. Distinguish between unrestricted and restricted resources of a charitable organization.

4. Briefly explain the concept of fund accounting.

5. Fund accounting is often used for external reporting purposes. Explain why.

6. It is common for an NFPO to receive donated supplies, equipment, and services. Do current accounting standards require the recording of donations of this kind? Explain.

7. Outline the *Handbook*'s requirements with regard to accounting for capital assets.

8. What revenue recognition guidelines does the *Handbook* provide for pledges received by an NFPO?

9. The equity section of an NFPO's balance sheet should be divided into four main sections. List the sections, and explain the reasons for each.

10. How should transfers of resources between funds be presented in fund financial statements? How should they be presented in a single set of nonfund financial statements?

11. Is the layered approach to presenting fund financial statements allowed under current GAAP? Explain.

12. What is the major difference between the capital asset impairment tests used by profit-oriented and not-for-profit organizations?

13. Contrast the revenue recognition and matching concepts that apply to profit-oriented organizations with those that apply to NFPOs.

14. Outline the financial reporting requirements for an NFPO's investments in other organizations.

15. Explain the use of budgetary accounting and encumbrances by NFPOs.

16. Name the two methods of accounting for contributions, and explain how the methods differ from each other.

17. Is it possible that an organization would be required to use certain aspects of the deferral method even though it reports using the restricted fund method? Explain.

18. An organization raises funds for purchasing capital assets. Briefly outline how the accounting for such funds raised would differ under the two methods envisioned by the *Handbook*.

19. Distinguish between the ways in which the two methods of accounting for contributions report the amount "invested in capital assets."

MULTIPLE CHOICE

1. Which of the following are acceptable methods of accounting for NFPOs under GAAP?
   a. Cash only.
   b. Cash and accrual.
   c. Cash, modified cash, and accrual.
   d. Accrual only.

   (CGA adapted)

2. NH is an NFPO which owns several nursing homes. NH received donated materials with a fair value of $7,000 for use in one of its nursing homes. Although the donated material was appreciated, it would not have been purchased otherwise due to cash flow constraints. Which of the following best reflects proper accounting for the donated materials under the *CICA Handbook*?
   a. The $7,000 of donated materials should not be recorded in the financial statements of NH.
   b. The $7,000 of donated materials should only be recorded in the financial statements of NH if the organization is using the deferral method of accounting.

c. NH has the option of either recording or not recording the $7,000 of donated materials in its financial statements.

d. The $7,000 of donated materials should only be recorded in the financial statements of NH if the organization is using the restricted fund method of accounting.

(CGA adapted)

3. PJ is an NFPO and has a relationship with QK, another NFPO. This relationship gives PJ the continuing power to determine the strategic operating, investing, and financing policies of QK without the cooperation of others. This control of PJ over QK is evidenced in part by PJ's ability to appoint 8 of the 12 members of QK's board of directors. Which of the following is true?
   a. PJ must consolidate the accounts of QK in its financial statements.
   b. PJ may either consolidate the accounts of QK or use the equity method with footnote disclosures about QK.
   c. PJ must use the equity method of accounting for QK with footnote disclosures about QK.
   d. PJ may either consolidate the accounts of QK in its financial statements or provide footnote disclosures about QK.

(CGA adapted)

4. An NFPO completed its annual fundraising drive in June 2003. It received $50,000 in cash donations and an additional $20,000 in pledges, up slightly from 2002, when it had collected all but $2,800 of its pledges. In preparing its June 30, 2003, financial statements, the controller noted that $18,000 of pledges remained uncollected as of June 30, 2003. Which of the following would be the recommended accounting treatment for contributions receivable?
   a. Contributions receivable of $20,000 should be recorded.
   b. Contributions receivable should not be recorded. The pledges of $18,000 should be recorded as revenue as the cash is received.
   c. Contributions receivable of $70,000 should be recorded.
   d. Contributions receivable of $18,000 should be recorded, partially offset by an allowance for estimated uncollectable amounts.

(CGA adapted)

5. Under the deferral method, how should endowment contributions be recognized?
   a. As revenue in the year they are received.
   b. As revenue in a systematic and rational manner over time.
   c. According to the terms of the endowment agreement.
   d. As direct increases in net assets in the period they are received.

(CGA adapted)

6. George Rogers takes a 6-month leave of absence from his job to work voluntarily, full-time, for an NFPO. Rogers fills the position of finance director because the incumbent is on paid sick leave during this period. This position normally pays $38,000 per year. How should the NFPO record Rogers's contribution?
   a. As revenue of $19,000 and expense of $19,000.
   b. As revenue of $19,000.
   c. As deferred revenue of $19,000.
   d. No entry should be recorded.

7. In 2002, Mercy Clinic, a not-for-profit health care facility, received an unrestricted bequest of common stock with a fair market value of $50,000 in accordance with the will of a deceased benefactor. The testator had paid $20,000 for the stock in 1999. How should the clinic record the bequest?
    a. As unrestricted revenue of $20,000.
    b. As unrestricted revenue of $50,000.
    c. As endowment revenue of $50,000.
    d. As deferred revenue of $50,000.

8. The Smythe family lost its possessions in a fire. On December 23, 2002, an anonymous benefactor sent money to the Aylmer Benevolent Society, an NFPO, to purchase furniture for the Smythe family. During January 2003, Aylmer purchased this furniture for the Smythe family. How should Aylmer report the receipt of this money in its 2002 financial statements?
    a. As an unrestricted contribution.
    b. As a restricted contribution.
    c. As a deferred contribution.
    d. As a liability.

The following scenario applies to Questions 9 and 10, although each question should be considered independently.

First Harvest (FH) collects food for distribution to people in need. During November 2002, its first month of operations, the organization collected a substantial amount of food and also $26,000 in cash from a very wealthy donor. The donor specified that the money was to be used to pay down a loan that the organization had with the local bank. The loan had been taken out to buy land, on which the organization plans to build a warehouse facility. A warehouse is needed since, although the organization does not plan to keep a lot of food in stock, sorting and distribution facilities are crucial. FH has also received $100,000, which according to the donor is to be deposited, with any income earned to be used as FH sees fit.

9. In which of the following ways should the food donation and the $26,000 be reflected in the financial statements? Assume that fair market values are available and that FH uses the deferral method and does not maintain separate funds.

Food donations	$26,000 cash donation
a. Not recorded	Deferred revenues
b. Deferred revenues	Increase in net assets
c. Revenues	Increase in net assets
d. Revenues	Deferred revenues

(CICA adapted)

10. In which of the following ways should the $100,000 contribution be accounted for under the following revenue recognition methods?

Deferral method	Restricted fund method
a. Direct increase in net assets	Revenue of the endowment fund
b. Direct increase in net assets	Revenue of the general fund
c. Revenue	Revenue of the endowment fund
d. Revenue	Revenue of the general fund

(CICA adapted)

11. Home Care Services Inc. (HCS), an NFPO, has a roster of volunteers who visit sick and elderly people to provide companionship. These volunteers do not provide any other services. HCS staff estimate that these services have a fair value of $8.00 per hour. If these services were not contributed on a volunteer basis, HCS would not pay for them.

    How should HCS account for these contributed services?
    a. Do not recognize these donated services in the financial statements.
    b. Recognize contributed services as revenue, and record salaries expense for only the number of hours for which time sheets were kept.
    c. Recognize these donated services as contributed services revenue and as salaries expense.
    d. Recognize these donated services as salaries expense and as increase in the unrestricted fund balance.

    (*CICA adapted*)

12. Eagle uses an encumbrance system of accounting for its commitments as an NFPO. When a purchase order is issued for $1,000 of office supplies, which of the following should be part of the entry to record it?
    a. A debit to an encumbrance account.
    b. A credit to an encumbrance account.
    c. A debit to an estimated commitment account.
    d. A memo entry to serve as a reminder that the purchase order was issued, but neither a debit nor credit to any specific account.

    (*CGA adapted*)

13. TK is an NFPO which received a donated capital asset with a fair value of $20,000 on July 1, 2003. The capital asset has an expected life of 5 years, with no residual value. TK uses the straight-line method of amortization (and uses the half-year rule for amortization in the year of acquisition). Which of the following is true regarding this donated capital asset, assuming TK uses the deferral method of accounting? (TK has a December 31 year-end.)
    a. Contribution revenue will exceed amortization expense in 2003, and thereafter.
    b. Contribution revenue will exceed amortization expense in 2003, but not thereafter.
    c. Amortization expense will exceed contribution revenue in 2003.
    d. Amortization expense will equal contribution revenue each year.

    (*CGA adapted*)

14. For the 2002 fiscal year, ZU Care, an NFPO, received $300,000 of unrestricted donations and $175,000 of donations designated specifically for cancer research. Unrestricted donations of $200,000 and restricted donations of $100,000 were expended in 2002 for current operations and cancer research, respectively. ZU did not set up a separate fund for the restricted donations. How much of the donations should be reported as revenue in the statement of operations for the 2002 fiscal year?
    a. $300,000
    b. $375,000
    c. $400,000
    d. $475,000

    (*CGA adapted*)

15. Which of the following is consistent with GAAP for large-scale not-for-profit organizations?
    a. Expenditures for equipment are recognized on the statement of operations when the equipment is acquired by the organization, regardless of when it is used.
    b. Expenditures for equipment are recognized on the statement of operations when the equipment is used by the organization, regardless of when it was acquired.
    c. Expenditures for equipment are capitalized on the balance sheet and are not amortized.
    d. Expenditures for equipment are recognized on the statement of operations when the equipment is paid for.

    (CGA adapted)

16. The statement of changes in net assets for an NFPO is most similar to which of the following financial statements for a profit-oriented organization?
    a. Balance sheet.
    b. Income statement.
    c. Cash flow statement.
    d. Statement of retained earnings.

    (CGA adapted)

17. The following related entries were recorded in sequence in the general fund of a not-for-profit organization:

Encumbrances	12,000	
Estimated commitments		12,000
Estimated commitments	12,000	
Encumbrances		12,000
Expenditures	12,350	
Accounts payable		12,350

    What do these three entries indicate?
    a. An adverse event was foreseen and a reserve of $12,000 was created; later, the reserve was cancelled and a liability for the item was acknowledged.
    b. An order was placed for goods or services estimated to cost $12,000; the actual cost was $12,350, for which a liability was acknowledged upon receipt.
    c. Encumbrances were anticipated but later failed to materialize and were reversed. A liability of $12,350 was incurred.
    d. The first entry was erroneous and was reversed; a liability of $12,350 was acknowledged.

    (CGA adapted)

18. A medium-sized NFPO has annual revenues of $375,000. In fiscal 2003, it received a $35,000 donation in the form of a new truck from a local businessperson. How should the NFPO account for this donated truck?
    a. It must capitalize and subsequently amortize the new truck.
    b. It must write off the new truck as an expense.
    c. It should either capitalize and subsequently amortize the new truck, or expense it.
    d. It should capitalize the new truck and should only amortize the truck if it intends to dispose of it in the future.

    (CGA adapted)

19. AV Home Care is an NFPO with revenues of approximately $700,000. Which of the following contributions should be reported as a direct increase in net assets?
    a. Endowment contributions for which an endowment fund is presented.
    b. Restricted contributions for which a corresponding restricted fund is presented.
    c. Restricted contributions for the purchase of land, for which a corresponding restricted fund is not presented.
    d. Unrestricted contributions.

    (CGA adapted)

20. Mr. Able donated $100,000 to AWE University and specified that the principal amount not be spent but be maintained permanently. Interest on the invested funds can be used to award scholarships to third-year accounting students. How should the $100,000 contribution be reported by AWE University under the restricted fund method?
    a. As revenue of the endowment fund.
    b. As revenue of the operating fund.
    c. As a direct increase in net assets of the endowment fund.
    d. As deferred revenue of the operating fund.

    (CGA adapted)

21. GK is an NFPO that received a $50,000 donation on January 1, 2002, from a retired geography teacher. The donation was to be used to finance purchases to enhance GK's 18th-century map collection. GK invested the donation in a 1-year treasury bill and plans to spend the funds in 2003. GK uses the deferral method for reporting contributions, and therefore should account for the donation using which of the following approaches?
    a. The $50,000 and related interest are recognized as revenue during 2002.
    b. The $50,000 is recorded as a deferred contribution, and the related interest is recorded as investment income for 2002.
    c. The $50,000 and related interest are both recorded in a deferred contribution account.
    d. The donation and related interest should not be recorded on GK's balance sheet or income statement, but the relevant details should be disclosed in GK's notes to its financial statements.

    (CGA adapted)

22. Which of the following statements about accounting for capital assets for large-scale NFPOs is false?
    a. Capital assets should be amortized over their useful lives, with amortization being recognized as a direct charge to net assets.
    b. Capital assets should be capitalized at fair value if they were contributed to the organization.
    c. The net carrying value of capital assets not being amortized should be disclosed.
    d. Contributions for the purchase in a future period of amortizable capital assets should be recorded as deferred revenue.

    (CGA adapted)

23. BD Home Care is an NFPO. It uses the deferral method of accounting for contributions. Which of the following contributions should be reported as direct increases in net assets?
    a. Restricted contributions for expenses of one or more future periods.
    b. Restricted contributions for the purchase of capital assets that will be amortized.
    c. Restricted contributions for the purchase of a capital asset that will not be amortized.
    d. Unrestricted contributions.

(CGA adapted)

CASES

Case 1 You have just completed an interview with the newly formed audit committee of the Andrews Street Youth Centre (ASYC). This organization was created to keep neighbourhood youth off the streets by providing recreational facilities where they can meet, exercise, play indoor sports, and hold dances. Since its inception, the organization has managed to survive on the basis of user fees charged to parents whose children use the program. This year the centre received support from a new provincial government program, in the form of an operating grant along with subsidy fees for those parents whose income is considered insufficient to pay the user fee. A local foundation, with a long history in the community and a reputation for honouring its commitments, has also come to the aid of the centre. This outside financial support came with the provision that the centre must now present audited financial statements annually.

Your firm is attempting to obtain the audit, as it is a November year-end, and the audit would be completed at a traditionally slow time of year. Many questions were posed during the interview and the ASYC audit committee has requested a written response to the issues raised. Excerpts from the interview follow:

- "We are looking for financial statements that are understandable to the Board. For example, we have heard that we might have to capitalize and depreciate leasehold improvements. We have just completed $20,000 in expenditures to set up a weight room. We don't understand this amortization idea. Will it make us look like we exceeded our operating budget since this budget is based on all expenditures, capital and operating? The government might consider reducing our next operating grant because of this accounting. If you were selected as our auditor would you have any problem if we simply expensed fixed assets as incurred?"

- "The Parent Advisory Group has organized several fundraising events and the net receipts have been deposited in a separate 'Computer Fund' bank account to allow for the purchase of some PCs. Last year, our financial statements did not reflect this fund. Is that okay with you?"

- "The manager of Sports Supplies Ltd. is a good friend of the Centre. This year his company gave us a variety of items such as exercise and body-building apparatus and some basketball equipment. This is pretty neat stuff and must be worth at least $12,000 to $15,000. The audit committee does not want to record this because they are concerned that if it ends up in revenue our operating grants might be reduced."

- "Certain of the parents have donated goods or their time, and would like to receive a tax receipt for the value of these donations. We are not certain whether we will have to reflect these in our financial statements this year. For example:

    1. Jane Barnes provided valuable advice on improved management efficiency. She is a professional consultant and although these consulting fees were not

> budgeted for, the centre made several changes that resulted in a reduction of administrative costs. Ms. Barnes estimates that her full-rate fee would have been $7,500.
>
> 2. Rick James, who is a qualified Phys. Ed. instructor, has been substituting one day a week at no charge, which reduced our budgeted expenditures by $4,500 this year.
>
> 3. Parents have donated an awful lot of their time to operate fundraising activities (in addition to those involved with the Computer Fund). This time must be worth thousands of dollars."

- "Some of the staff have not been able to take their vacation this year, due to scheduling problems. As a result, we will have to pay them vacation pay. These funds will be paid out after the year-end, and will likely be covered by next year's operating grant. To keep revenues and expenses matched, we want to record the vacation pay on a cash basis. Would that be okay? Otherwise, we'll record a portion of next year's grant as receivable, this year."

- "The local foundation has provided the Centre with a $30,000 grant to cover the expenses of a volunteer coordinator for two years. We received an instalment of $12,000, but we haven't hired a coordinator yet. The coordinator will be paid on an hourly basis, and the number of hours each month will fluctuate over the next two years depending on the monthly activities."

Required:

Prepare a draft of the response that will be sent to the audit committee.

Case 2   Affordable Housing For All (AHFA) was organized several years ago to assist people with low incomes to obtain decent housing. In order to accomplish this objective, AHFA is involved in a variety of activities that promote and make available affordable and subsidized housing, including the administering of rental assistance programs and subsidies from the provincial government. AHFA's revenues are derived mainly from private contributions, grants from funding agencies, and contracts.

Janice Ober, the CEO of AHFA, is concerned about the long-term viability of the organization. She believes that future government grants and private contributions will be significantly reduced, and contract awards will become much more competitive. Should this occur, Janice feels that donors, especially large corporate ones, will be reluctant to support a scaled down version of AHFA. Thus, she concludes that it is extremely important for the agency to report increasing revenues and, at the same time, not report any deficits.

For the first time, AHFA has a contract with a provincial agency to administer a government rent subsidy program. Under the terms of the contract, AHFA will receive about $30 million annually, including a fee of about $5 million for the organization's overhead to administer the program. The remaining funds will be paid out as rental assistance payments to qualified program participants. Contract advances not paid to program participants must be returned at the termination of the program.

As this is the first time the organization has become involved with this particular rent subsidy program, AHFA must determine its accounting policy for the program. Ms. Ober plans to recognize housing assistance receipts and administrative fees as revenues, and to recognize expenses for administrative costs and housing assistance payments when incurred. Under this policy the total receipts for rental assistance will be reported as both a revenue and an expense.

During the year, a new program was established and directed at the organization's faithful supporters. The brochure outlining the program stated the following:

> A gift of life insurance can be made to AHFA at a very modest cost to you. When you make the AHFA the owner and beneficiary of a new $20,000 policy, this entitles you to a donation receipt for the cash value of the policy and further receipts for every premium you subsequently pay. AHFA will receive the proceeds when the policy is paid out. When you name your estate as the beneficiary and leave a bequest of equal value to AHFA, you do not receive a donation receipt but your estate will receive a tax receipt for the face value of the policy. The policy can be purchased from Star Life Insurance Ltd. They have structured it in such a way that the policy can be purchased with a single premium, or by installment payments over a five-year period.

During the year, 50 policies were delivered by Star Life to AHFA, of which 15 were fully paid up policies. Janice Ober was delighted with the results, because they would result in $1 million in revenue this year.

During the year AHFA entered into a first-time 3-year union contract, covering the terms of employment of its nonmanagement personnel. Because the organization was new to labour negotiations, they hired a law firm that specialized in this area to handle the bargaining for them. Legal costs of $95,000 were incurred, which Ms. Ober feels will specifically benefit the agency over the life of the contract. She intends to defer this amount and write it off over 3 years.

You are in charge of the audit of AHFA this year. Ms. Ober has asked you to send her a memo indicating your agreement (or lack of agreement) with her accounting policy proposals. Your memo should include the reasons for any recommendations that you make.

Required:

Prepare the memo to Janice Ober.

Case 3 The Sassawinni First Nation is located adjacent to a town in northern Saskatchewan. The Nation is under the jurisdiction of the federal government's Department of Indian Affairs, and for years has received substantial funding from that department. The money has been used mainly to fund housing construction on the reserve and to provide maintenance payments to families that do not have a source of income. The houses are the property of the Sassawinni First Nation, and the band council allocates them to families on the basis of need. In addition to the housing, the band has been able to build a recreational centre, which also contains the band's council chamber and administrative offices.

A few years ago some council members with an entrepreneurial flair persuaded the Nation's members to build a shopping centre containing a large grocery store and several small specialty stores. The shopping centre is located on reserve land, and the band provided approximately 20% of the financing with the balance coming from a provincially guaranteed bank loan. The shopping centre operates under the name Great Northern Centre, Inc., and the Sassawinni First Nation owns 100% of its outstanding common shares. The centre has been a financial success, drawing a large proportion of its business from the adjoining town and surrounding agricultural area. Not only has it been a source of employment for First Nation families, but it has also generated enough cash to keep its loan payments current, and recently has been able to declare and pay a dividend.

Flushed with its success, the Sassawinni First Nation has submitted to the provincial government a business plan to construct a gambling casino on band property. It will be an incorporated entity, and will be under the complete control of the Nation, subject only to provincial government gambling regulations.

Up to the present time, the band has provided stewardship reports to the Department of Indian Affairs which outline the funds received from the federal government and the manner in which they has been spent. Government auditors have verified these statements but no formal audit reports have been considered necessary. Now, with all of this new business activity taking place, proper audited financial statements will be required for the next fiscal year. You are employed by Fox, Fox, and Jameson, the public accounting firm that is the auditor of Great Northern Centre, Inc. Your firm has just been appointed auditor of Sassawinni First Nation and this will be the firm's first audit of an organization of this nature. Jane Fox, the managing partner in charge of this audit, has asked you to provide her with a written report outlining the specific accounting principles that will be applicable in this case. "I am going to have to catch up quickly," she said. "I am aware that there have been some changes in GAAP recently, but because our firm has not been involved with audits of this nature I have not paid much attention to what has been going on. One of the benefits of hiring new university grads like yourself is that you provide us with up-to-date technical knowledge."

You have just returned from interviewing the band chief, Joe Sullivan. "I am absolutely certain that we are going to get this casino," he said. "The announcement will be made by the premier within two weeks, and I have received information from a knowledgeable insider that we will be on the list of First Nations to be granted casino licenses. It will be a financial godsend to our people, employing well over 100 band members and providing us with substantial profits, a portion of which will have to be devoted entirely to accommodations in accordance with the licensing agreement. This will allow us to build more housing for our members, but with all the jobs that we now have, we will probably start charging rent for housing provided to those with jobs. Not only that, but we have three permanent employees who have been with us for a while, and council has instructed me to investigate the possibility of providing a pension plan for them as well as for the permanent employees in our business enterprises."

When asked about the band's accounting records, Sullivan responded, "We have a very good bookkeeper, and the government auditor has always complimented her on the accuracy of her records. She provides timely statements showing us how much we have to spend. Our records are all here and go back at least 20 years. I would just as soon carry on the way we have been doing things, but with this new casino we'll have to provide audited financial statements to the two governments — and, of course, to our members."

Required:

Prepare the report requested by you firm's managing partner.

Case 4   TreesMeanAir Incorporated (TMA) is an NFPO that has been helping preserve Brazilian rainforests since 1989. Prior to the year ended June 30, 2002, its funding came exclusively from annual Government of Canada grants of approximately $300,000 per year. Due to recent changes to the government's funding structure, TMA will no longer be receiving annual grants but, during the 2002–2003 fiscal year, it will be given a one-time $2,000,000 endowment to help support future projects.

Additional funds must be raised from the general public, and the board of directors is confident that if they focus their efforts, fundraising should approximate $100,000 in

2002–2003, $400,000 in 2003–2004, and $600,000 per year thereafter. In addition, TMA has always expensed its capital assets such as furniture, fixtures, and computer equipment. It has made no mention of capital assets in its financial statements other than to include a line on the income statement entitled "Capital asset expenses."

You have recently been appointed to the board of TMA. Under the terms of the endowment agreement, TMA will be required to provide audited financial statements that comply with the *CICA Handbook* for the year ended June 30, 2003, and subsequent years.

Required:

(a) Describe the key differences in accounting for unrestricted, endowment, and restricted contributions under the deferral method of accounting for contributions.

(b) Describe how TMA should account for its $2,000,000 endowment if it uses the restricted fund method of accounting for contributions. Include the journal entry that TMA should make upon receipt of the $2,000,000 endowment.

(c) Explain how TMA should account for any pledges outstanding at June 30, 2003.

(d) Was TMA's accounting treatment of capital assets for the years up to June 30, 2002, acceptable according to *CICA Handbook* requirements? Explain why or why not.

(e) Explain what changes (if any) you would recommend regarding TMA's accounting for capital assets, to ensure that TMA is in compliance with the terms of the endowment agreement in 2002–2003 and for the foreseeable future.

(CGA adapted)

Case 5   Zak Organization is an NFPO set up for famine relief. It uses the restricted fund method of accounting and has three funds: a general fund, a capital fund (through which it is raising cash to support the purchase of a new administrative building), and an endowment fund. Zak has been operating for 25 years and has a December 31 year-end. Zak's policy with respect to capital assets is to capitalize and amortize the capital assets over their expected useful lives.

On June 30, 2002, Zak received three donations from a former director:

- $30,000 cash for general famine relief efforts.
- $50,000 to be used solely for construction of the new administrative building. Of the $50,000, 70% was received in cash, with the remainder promised in February 2003. (Construction is expected to commence in October 2003.)
- $600,000 cash, which was invested on July 1, 2002, in long-term Government of Canada bonds, with 10% interest to be paid semi-annually on December 31 and June 30. The $600,000 donation was given with the stipulation that it be invested in interest-bearing securities with the principal to be maintained by Zak, although interest earned on the securities is not restricted.

Required:

(a) Briefly explain how each of the three donations should be accounted for using the restricted fund method of accounting. In particular, should each of the donations be recognized as revenue for the year ended December 31, 2002? If yes, in which fund(s) would the revenue be recognized (including interest earned in fiscal 2002 on the bonds purchased with the $600,000 donation)? Note: Do not prepare journal entries.

(b) If Zak used the deferral method of accounting instead of the restricted fund method, how would this change the requirements for accounting for the $50,000 and $600,000 donations?

(c) Despite the recent donations from its former director, Zak is increasingly faced with severe budgetary constraints. Zak is considering implementing encumbrance accounting in the coming year.

i) Briefly describe the process of encumbrance accounting.

ii) Briefly describe how encumbrance accounting might serve as a device to help control spending when it is used in conjunction with a formal budgeting system.

(*CGA adapted*)

Case 6 The TGF Care Facility (TGF) is an NFPO dedicated to providing services in the care and rehabilitation of seniors suffering from physical or mental disabilities. The principal programs are the seniors' residence program and the home care program. TGF also sponsors research activities and conducts educational activities for its clients, their relatives, and the general public.

TGF has an 8-person board of directors that sets policy and approves plans, but the day-to-day operations are left to Joe, the full-time, salaried executive director. At a recent meeting, Joe told you that he is not satisfied with the information provided in the annual financial statements. He does not see how he and the board can make useful decisions on the basis of the information presented in the financial statements. He wants the financial statements to be audited as this may help improve financial reporting and may provide credibility to the financial statements, which may, in turn, increase donor confidence and donations. The financial statements have never been audited in the past.

Revenues for TGF's activities exceeded $600,000 per year in 2001 and 2002. Revenues are obtained from a variety of sources. About 50% of the total revenue is obtained from the residents in the form of a user fee; about 30% is obtained from the Ministry of Social Services; and most of the remainder is obtained from bequests and from donations by foundations, corporations, and individuals.

The Ministry of Social Services provides funds on the basis of annual budgets prepared for each program. Many of the public donations are also designated for specific programs or purposes such as research. The bequests are usually given under the condition that the principal amount cannot be spent. The income from investing the bequests can only be used for designated purposes. The board at its discretion can allocate unrestricted donations.

TGF has constructed several buildings over the years to house the various programs. All the buildings were paid for by a combination of specific capital grants from the municipal and provincial governments and funds raised for capital projects by public campaigns. The repair and maintenance of the furniture and equipment, as well as general maintenance of the buildings, are paid for out of operating funds as needed.

You have been asked by Joe to prepare a memo to the board of directors. The memo should describe the changes in accounting practices necessary to ensure a clean audit opinion in accordance with GAAP for NFPOs, for the December 31, 2002, year-end. The memo should also explain how these accounting practices will better serve the needs of the users of TGF's financial statements. Current accounting practices for TGF are as follows:

- The annual financial statements consist of a balance sheet, a statement of cash receipts and disbursements, and a statement of changes in net assets. The statement of cash receipts and disbursements compares the actual results for the year against the original budget for the year.
- The budget is prepared annually by the treasurer of the board in cooperation with the executive director. A monthly comparison of the year-to-date expenditure with the total budgeted amounts, on a line-by-line basis, is prepared by the bookkeeper and forwarded to the executive director and treasurer.

- Grants from governments, foundations, and corporations are recorded as revenue when pledges are made or grants are announced. Donations from individuals are recorded as revenue when the cash, cheque, or credit card voucher is received, regardless of whether the cheque or voucher is current-dated or post-dated.
- Expenditures are charged to accounts as paid, on the basis of the type of expenditure; for example, all salaries are charged to a single account, all furniture replacements and repairs are charged to a single account, and so forth.
- The historical cost of the buildings and the land is carried on the balance sheet. Amortization is not taken. The cost of furniture and equipment is charged to operations when the expenditure is made.

Required:

Prepare the memo to the board of directors. Revenue recognition policies should follow the deferral method.

(CGA adapted)

Case 7   Senior Transitions Ltd. (STL) is an NFPO that has been set up to assist senior citizens who wish to move into nursing homes. STL provides counselling services and owns several moving trucks and related equipment. Two full-time paid counsellors are on staff to help seniors cope emotionally with the transition to nursing homes.

STL's accountant had been implementing changes to its reporting system and financial statements in order to ensure that the organization is in compliance with *CICA Handbook* requirements. However, the accountant recently quit to take a new position at another NFPO.

You have just been hired. Your first task is to complete the implementation of the *Handbook* requirements. In particular, you have been asked to provide advice to the board of directors regarding the following matters relating to the December 31, 2002, year-end financial statements.

1. *Accounting for contributions:* STL has received a government grant of $500,000 for each of the last 5 years to cover its operating costs. It also runs an annual campaign in which it telephones potential donors and asks for cash contributions and/or pledges to cover special needs, such as the acquisition of new trucks. Over the past 3 years, STL has run 3 successful campaigns and raised a total of $150,000, $40,000 of which was restricted for the purchase of a truck. STL used $40,000 to acquire a new truck and the remainder for general operating purposes. During the 2002 campaign, $30,000 in cash was raised and pledges were received for an additional $21,500. The pledges are expected to be paid to STL by March 31, 2003.

2. *Accounting for capital assets:* STL has always accounted for its capital assets on a cash basis (that is, the expenditures were expensed in the year of purchase).

Required:

Prepare a memorandum to the board of directors explaining how the following matters/items should be accounted for under *CICA Handbook* requirements, in order to ensure that STL can get an unqualified audit opinion from its auditors. Write a single memorandum that covers both (a) and (b).

(a) How should STL account for contributions and contributions receivable to ensure that it is in compliance with *CICA Handbook* requirements?

(b) How should STL account for capital assets to ensure that it is in compliance with *CICA Handbook* requirements?

(CGA adapted)

Case 8 You have been hired to prepare a report for the board of directors of a large art gallery. The board has been advised that effective this year, the seven new sections recently added to the *CICA Handbook* become operative. They wish to know how these new not-for-profit reporting requirements will affect the gallery. You have been provided with the following information:

- The principal activity of the art gallery is the acquisition and exhibition of modern and contemporary works of art. The gallery is open to the general public on a daily basis and schedules special exhibits for specific interest groups. Each year the gallery holds a number of fundraising activities to help support operating costs and the acquisition of art. These activities are organized by the support staff, but volunteers are required to staff the various functions. The major fundraising activity is an Annual Rennaise Telethon (ART), which solicits pledges from corporations and individuals and has been very successful.

- Capital assets (which do not include works of art) include a building, maintenance equipment, office furniture, and fixtures. The gallery is housed in a Victorian mansion that was donated by a prominent local family several years ago. Because the building has been designated a heritage property, utilities are provided by the local utility companies for a nominal fee of one dollar per year. As well, the municipal government has exempted the gallery from property taxes. Funding for capital asset acquisitions comes from various granting agencies and from the fundraising activities of the gallery.

- The gallery also operates a gift shop on a break-even basis, with the objective of attracting visitors to the gallery. The gift shop has a small staff of salaried employees, augmented by a number of volunteers. The gift shop has an annual inventory of $175,000 on annual sales of approximately $1 million.

- The gallery has a support staff of 17 employees, a curator, and a director who is responsible for the general operations of the gallery. The total annual budget for the gallery is $4.2 million.

Required:

(a) Prepare a report addressing the concerns of the board of directors of the art gallery.
(b) Your report should include a brief description of the purpose and objectives of a fund accounting system. As well, you have been asked to recommend the different types of funds that would be most appropriate for the gallery. A discussion of relevant accounting policies is also required.

(CGA adapted)

PROBLEMS

Problem 1 Gold Development (GD), a newly incorporated NFPO with a December 31 year-end, will offer low-rent housing services for families of the working poor.

GD reports to Logimex, a government agency that requires audited financial statements to be filed. Mr. Bilodeau, the project originator and administrator of GD, is not familiar with the preparation of financial statements.

In February 2002, GD received a nonrepayable grant from Logimex for the construction of an eight-storey apartment building. Construction began in April 2002. Residents will start moving into the apartment building between October and December 2002, although it will not be entirely completed until the end of December 2002. By December 2002 all apartments should be rented.

GD receives donations from companies and individuals in the region. It has received pledges from large, well-known companies for the next five years, and pledges from individuals for this year and next. Pledge amounts have been set out in writing on forms signed by the donors.

For a nominal salary, Mr. Bilodeau manages the organization with the help of his wife and the local priest, both of whom are volunteers.

Required:

PART A

Explain to Mr. Bilodeau what is meant by "reporting on a restricted fund accounting basis" in accordance with the *CICA Handbook*.

PART B

Advise Mr. Bilodeau on how the *Handbook*'s recommendations will apply to the above facts if GD decides to report on a restricted fund-accounting basis.

(*CICA adapted*)

Problem 2   A 35-year-old member of the board of directors of an NFPO recently sent a letter to the organization's president in which he stated the following: "I wish to notify you that I have purchased a $100,000 life insurance policy and have paid the first year's premium. I have named our organization as the beneficiary of this policy."

The president of the organization is ecstatic because a donation of this size will reflect well on this year's fundraising activities and will make a substantial difference to the financial statements. He sends you a copy of the letter and requests that, as an accounting advisor to the organization, you advise him how this will be treated.

Required:

Advise the president, giving reasons.

Problem 3   Camp Faraway is a charitable organization that provides summer vacations for underprivileged children. You have volunteered your services to this organization. The director of the camp is happy to have you aboard and is especially delighted to hear that you are knowledgeable in the area of not-for-profit accounting.

The organization has just received a sizable donation of capital assets. The director is preparing for a board meeting tomorrow and has asked you to brief her as to how the organization will be required to reflect such a donation in this year's financial statements.

Required:

Outline what you will say to the director.

Problem 4   The bookkeeper of Sesame Co-operative Nursery School Inc., a small NFPO, has approached you for some advice regarding the preparation of the nursery school's 2002 year-end financial statements. According to the school's bylaws, the financial statements must be prepared according to GAAP and presented to, and accepted by, the school-children's parents at the next general meeting.

The financial statements include a balance sheet, a statement of operations, and applicable notes. The parents are especially interested in knowing how funds are being spent. Since the bookkeeper is a volunteer parent with limited experience in preparing financial statements, she is unsure how to record the $2,000 of outdoor play equipment purchased during the current year and would like your advice. The purchase of the equipment represents 10% of the total expenditures for the year, excluding teacher salaries.

Required:

Provide advice to the bookkeeper, including a supported recommendation regarding the accounting for the outdoor play equipment.

(*SMA adapted*)

Problem 5   The NFP Society is a charitable organization located in New Brunswick that uses the restricted fund basis. It uses the following three funds for its financial record keeping and reporting:

Operating fund. This fund accounts for the normal operating activities of the society. Its revenue consists of government grants, proceeds from fundraising campaigns, and interest earned on investments. Control is achieved by formally recording the annual budget and by the use of an encumbrance system. Donated materials and services are recorded in this fund.

Capital fund. This fund records the capitalization of all fixed assets donated to or purchased by the society and the yearly depreciation taken thereon.

Endowment fund. This fund records the society's endowments, the interest from which is unrestricted.

The following selected events took place in 2002.

- The board of directors passed the budget for the coming year, which included revenues of $750,000 and expenses of $739,000.
- An endowment contribution of $125,000 was received from a long-time supporter of the society. Interest earned is to be unrestricted.
- Purchase orders were issued for operating goods and services estimated to cost $435,000.
- The government announced grants to the society of $360,000 to fund its regular operating activities. All but $40,000 was received during the year.
- A campaign to raise funds for 2003 operations was held late in the year. Cash of $240,000 was collected, and pledges amounting to $75,000 were received. It is estimated that 10% of the pledges will not be collected. Fundraising expenses were $46,000, of which $19,000 had not been paid at year-end.
- Air time publicizing the society's annual fundraising campaign was donated by a local radio station. The fair value of this donated air time was $1,175.
- Invoices for good and services totalling $130,000 were received on purchase orders that were originally issued for $131,200.
- A computer was purchased from operating fund cash for $3,200.
- The 2002 depreciation on capital assets amounted to $26,250.
- Interest earned on endowment investments amounted to $92,300.

Required:

Prepare the journal entries required to record the 10 events described. For each entry made, clearly indicate which fund will be used.

Problem 6   The following are selected transactions of the Eastern Kidney Association, which uses the restricted fund method and has an operating fund, a capital fund, and an endowment fund:

- Pledges totalling $325,000 were received, of which $65,000 applies to the operations of the following year. It is estimated that 3% of pledges will be uncollectible.
- The association purchased office equipment at a cost of $5,100.

- Pledges of $285,000 were collected, and pledges totalling $3,750 were written off as uncollectible.
- Air time with a value of $7,200 was donated by a local radio station.
- Interest and dividends received were $13,700 on endowment fund investments. Endowment fund earnings are unrestricted.
- Depreciation for the year amounted to $35,600.

Required:

Prepare journal entries for the transactions, indicating which fund will be used for each transaction.

Problem 7 The Rossbrook Services Agency, a charitable health and welfare organization, conducts a dental services program and a neighbourhood oral health program. The restricted fund method is used, and financial reporting is carried out through operating, capital, and endowment funds. The agency had the following transactions during the current year:

- Received the following contributions:

Pledges for general operations	$ 350,000
Building fund pledges	200,000
Cash donations to the endowment fund	4,800

- Received cash as follows:

Building fund pledges	195,000
Fundraising dinner (net of direct costs)	52,000
Bequests (unrestricted)	15,000
Membership dues	9,100
Investment income (unrestricted)	3,900

- Processed vouchers for the following:

Dental services	92,000
Neighbourhood oral health	75,000
Administration	110,000
Fundraising	102,000

- Fixed assets purchases for cash   32,000

- Depreciation of buildings and equipment   19,000

- Paid vouchers payable   270,000

Required:

Prepare journal entries for these transactions. For each entry, indicate the fund that will be used.

Problem 8 The Red City Humane Society received the following donations during the current year:
- A local television station donated a series of 20-second spots advertising the society's forthcoming fundraising campaign. If this advertising had been purchased, cost to the organization would have been $14,200.
- An anonymous benefactor donated land with a fair value of $168,000 (to be used when new premises are built) and computer and office equipment valued at $20,000.

- During the fundraising campaign, volunteers spent approximately 300,000 hours soliciting campaign donations. The minimum hourly wage in this city was $7.00 during the year.

Required:

Prepare the journal entries necessary to record these transactions if the organization uses:
(a) The deferral method of accounting for contributions.
(b) The restricted fund method of accounting for contributions.

Problem 9 The Far North Centre is an antipoverty organization funded by contributions from governments and the general public. For a number of years it has been run by a small group of permanent employees with the help of part-timers and dedicated volunteers. It owns its premises, which are in the process of being renovated. The funds for this were obtained through a special capital-fund campaign carried out last year. Its main program is the daily provision of meals to the needy. It also distributes clothing, most of which is donated. Operating funds come from government grants, interest earned from endowment investments, and a public campaign held in the latter part of each year to raise funds for the needs of the next fiscal year. The organization maintains its records in accordance with the restricted fund method of accounting for contributions, and prepares its financial statements using an operating fund, a capital fund, and an endowment fund.

The following are the fund trial balances as at January 1, 2002:

	Debit	Credit
Operating fund		
Cash	$ 570,500	
Pledges receivable	705,000	
Allowance for uncollectible pledges		30,000
Grants receivable	217,500	
Accounts payable		427,500
Wages payable		137,250
Accrued liabilities		9,750
Deferred revenue		800,000
Fund balance		88,500
	$1,493,000	$1,493,000
Capital fund		
Cash	$ 287,500	
Grants receivable	112,500	
Furniture and equipment	491,000	
Land and building	810,250	
Accumulated amortization		648,200
Accounts payable		9,000
Investment in capital assets		653,050
Fund balance		391,000
	$1,701,250	$1,701,250
Endowment Fund		
Cash	$ 37,500	
Investments	375,000	
Fund balance		412,500
	$ 412,500	$ 412,500

The following transactions took place in 2002.

1. The 2002 budget, the totals of which are summarized below, was recorded.

Budgeted revenues	$2,200,000
Budgeted expenses	2,150,000
Budgeted deficit	$ 50,000

2. The agency uses an encumbrance system in the operating fund as a means of controlling expenditures. During the year, purchase orders for goods and services at an estimated amount of $1,450,000 were issued.
3. $35,000 from endowment fund cash was invested in marketable securities.
4. Office equipment costing $2,500 was purchased with operating fund cash.
5. Invoices totalling $1,375,000 were received on purchase orders originally recorded at an estimated cost of $1,392,000. These invoices were recorded as accounts payable and were allocated 55% to food program, 20% to clothing program, and 25% to administration.
6. The capital fund grants receivable were collected in full, and the $9,000 in accounts payable was paid. During 2002, building renovations costing $300,000 and equipment purchases of $85,000 were made. Of this cost, 90% was paid, with the balance held back and still owing at year-end.
7. Operating fund accounts payable amounting to $1,560,000, and the wages payable and accrued liabilities at the beginning of the year, were all paid.
8. All of the operating fund pledges and grants receivable at the beginning of the year were collected in full.
9. The deferred revenue from the 2001 fundraising campaign was made up of:

Contributions	$1,200,000
Less: campaign expense	400,000
	$ 800,000

An entry was made to recognize these items as 2002 revenues and expenses.
10. Government grants for operating purposes totalled $900,000, of which $850,000 was received during the year, with the balance expected early in 2003.
11. The total wage costs for the year amounted to $400,000, of which $325,000 was paid and $75,000 is payable at year-end. These costs are to be allocated 40% each to the food and clothing programs, with the balance to administration.
12. The campaign to raise funds for next year's operations was held in December. Cash of $500,000 was collected and pledges of $700,000 were received. It is expected that 5% of these pledges will be uncollectible. Total fundraising costs were $322,000, of which $75,000 is still owed to suppliers.
13. An endowment contribution of $8,000 cash was received. In addition, the investments in the endowment fund earned $31,200 in interest.
14. The annual depreciation on the buildings and equipment amounted to $92,000.
15. At the end of the year, the balances in the encumbrance accounts and the budget accounts were closed.

Required:

(a) Prepare the journal entries necessary to reflect the 2002 events.
(b) For each fund, prepare a 2002 balance sheet and statement of revenues and expenses and changes in fund balance.
(c) Prepare a statement of cash flows on a non–fund basis.
(d) Prepare closing entries.

Problem 10   All facts about this NFPO are identical to those described in Problem 9, except that the deferred contribution approach to recording contributions is used for accounting and for external financial reporting. Fund accounting is not used. The 2002 transactions are also identical to those described in Problem 9.

The organization's balance sheet on January 1, 2002, is shown below:

FAR EAST CENTRE
BALANCE SHEET
January 1, 2002

Current assets	
Cash	$ 895,500
Pledges receivable	705,000
Allowance for uncollectible pledges	(30,000)
Grants receivable	330,000
	$1,900,500
Investments	$ 375,000
Capital assets	
Furniture and equipment	$ 491,000
Land and buildings	810,250
Accumulated depreciation	(648,200)
	653,050
	$2,928,550
Current liabilities	
Accounts payable	$ 436,500
Wages payable	137,250
Accrued liabilities	9,750
	$ 583,500
Deferred revenue	
Deferred contributions	$ 800,000
Deferred building campaign contributions	391,000
Deferred contributions related to capital assets	240,500
	$1,431,500
Net assets	
Net assets invested in capital assets	$ 412,550
Net assets restricted for endowment purposes	412,500
Unrestricted net assets	88,500
	$ 913,550
	$2,928,550

Required:

(a) Prepare the journal entries necessary to reflect the 2002 events.

(b) Prepare a 2002 balance sheet, a statement of revenues and expenses, and a statement of changes in net assets for the year.

(c) Prepare a statement of cash flows for the year.

(d) Prepare closing entries.

Problem 11   NP Inc. is an NFPO that was formed at the beginning of 2002 when its founder made a substantial contribution under the condition that only the interest earned from the money that she donated could be spent on operations. The remainder of the necessary funds were to come from government grants and donations from the general public. A board of directors was appointed and immediately launched two fundraising campaigns: one for daily operations, and the other to raise funds to acquire a small building. The directors propose to report externally using the deferred contribution method and to set up an accounting system on that basis. An encumbrance system is to be used as a means of controlling expenditures.

The following summarizes some of the transactions that were made in 2002.

- The 2002 operating budget, the totals of which are summarized below, was recorded:

Budgeted revenues	$900,000
Budgeted expenses	885,000

- The founder's original contribution (discussed above) amounted to $700,000. This money was immediately invested in marketable securities.
- During the year, purchase orders for goods and services necessary for daily operations were issued at an estimated amount of $580,000.
- Office equipment costing $8,500 was purchased with operating fund cash.
- A public campaign to raise funds for daily operations was held at the beginning of the year. Cash of $200,000 was collected, and pledges of $150,000 were received. It is estimated that approximately 10% of these pledges will be uncollectible.
- Total fundraising costs for the operating campaign were $89,000, of which $22,750 is still owing.
- Government grants were announced as follows:

For 2002 operations	$290,000
For building acquisition	95,000

All of the building grant was received, as was 95% of the operating grant, with the balance promised very early in 2003.

- Invoices totalling $415,000 were received on purchase orders originally recorded at an estimated cost of $414,100. These invoices were allocated 55% to Program A, 20% to Program B, and 25% to administration. None have been paid by year-end.
- The marketable securities earned revenues amounting to $63,000 during the year. 70% of this had not been received by year-end.
- Total wages paid during the year amounted to $82,500. This cost was allocated 40% each to Programs A and B, with the balance to administration.
- The first year's depreciation on the office equipment amounted to $850.
- During the fundraising campaign, a local radio station donated air time to advertise the campaign. The market value of this air time amounted to $3,900.

Required:

In accordance with the *CICA Handbook*, prepare the journal entries necessary to reflect the 2002 events described above, using the deferral method of accounting for contributions.

Problem 12   The following are *selected transactions* for Rossbrook Care Centre, an NFPO.

- Pledges totalling $365,000 were received, of which $105,000 applies to the operations of the following year. It is estimated that 3% of pledges will be uncollectible.
- The association purchased office equipment at a cost of $45,100 and paid for this equipment using cash from unrestricted contributions.
- Pledges of $325,000 were collected, and pledges totalling $9,750 were written off as uncollectible.
- Air time with a value of $13,900 was donated by a local radio station.
- Interest and dividends received were $33,700 on endowment fund investments. This revenue can only be used to purchase specialized equipment.
- Depreciation for the year amounted to $72,100.

Required:

Prepare the journal entries for these transactions, using the deferred contribution method.

Problem 13   The William Robertson Society is a charitable organization funded by government grants and private donations. It prepares its annual financial statements using the restricted fund method in accordance with the *CICA Handbook*, and uses both an operating fund and a capital fund.

The operating fund records the regular operating activities of the society. An encumbrance system is used within the fund to ensure that expenditures made in any one year do not exceed the amounts budgeted. It is the policy of the society to record donated materials and services received during the year, if such items would have been purchased had they not been received as donations.

The capital fund accounts for moneys received from special fundraising campaigns conducted when there is a need for major fixed assets acquisitions.

The following are *some* selected events that took place during the current year:

- Pledges amounting to $125,000 were received, of which $90,000 was collected in cash.
- Purchase orders were issued during the year as follows:

For office equipment	$ 15,000
For goods and services	100,000

- A grant of $70,000 for this year's operations was announced by the government, of which $55,000 had been received by the society at year-end.
- Employee wages totalled $60,000 for the year. Wages amounting to $2,000 were unpaid at year-end.
- Invoices for all of the goods and services ordered during the year were received. Of the invoiced amounts, 80% was paid. The invoiced amounts were equal to those on the purchase orders.
- The office equipment that was ordered arrived. The invoiced amount of $15,030 was paid in cash, using operating funds.
- A local radio station donated free air time to the society. The station would normally bill a customer $3,000 for this air time.

- A prominent citizen made a pledge of $35,000 to help fund the operating expenditures of the next fiscal year.

Required:

Prepare the journal entries required to record these events, and indicate which fund each journal entry will be recorded in.

Credits

Page	Description	Source
53	Multiple Choice 6, 7	CGA adapted
54	Multiple Choice 10	CGA adapted
56	Multiple Choice 18, 19, 20	CGA adapted
61	Problem 9	CGA adapted
133	Multiple Choice 8	CICA adapted
134	Multiple Choice 9, 10	CICA adapted
141	Problem 8	CICA adapted
180	Multiple Choice 9, 10	CGA adapted
222	Multiple Choice 12	CGA adapted
343	Problem 8	SMA adapted
345	Problem 9	SMA adapted
431	Multiple Choice 6	CICA adapted
433	Multiple Choice 8, 9	CICA adapted
521	Multiple Choice 4	CGA adapted
521	Multiple Choice 5	CICA adapted
522	Multiple Choice 6	CICA adapted
523	Multiple Choice 11, 13	CGA adapted
523	Multiple Choice 12	CICA adapted
527	Problem 7, 8, 9	CGA adapted
528	Problem 10, 11	CGA adapted
530	Problem 15	CGA adapted
565	Multiple Choice 16	CGA adapted
574	Problem 5	CGA adapted
576	Problem 7, 8	CGA adapted
578	Problem 9	CGA adapted
625	Multiple Choice 1, 2	CGA adapted
626	Multiple Choice 3, 4, 5	CGA adapted
627	Multiple Choice 9, 10	CICA adapted
628	Multiple Choice 11	CICA adapted
628	Multiple Choice 12, 13, 14	CGA adapted
629	Multiple Choice 15, 16, 17, 18	CGA adapted
630	Multiple Choice 19, 20, 21, 22	CGA adapted
631	Multiple Choice 23	CGA adapted
634	Case 4	CGA adapted
635	Case 5	CGA adapted
636	Case 6	CGA adapted
637	Case 7	CGA adapted
638	Case 8	CGA adapted
638	Problem 1	CICA adapted
639	Problem 4	SMA adapted

Index